THE
SPECTATOR

EUSTACE BUDGELL
From the engraving by Knight after the portrait by D. Firmin.
(British Museum Add. MS. 37232)

THE
SPECTATOR

EDITED
WITH AN INTRODUCTION
AND NOTES BY
DONALD F. BOND

VOLUME III

OXFORD
AT THE CLARENDON PRESS
1965

Oxford University Press, Amen House, London E.C.4

GLASGOW NEW YORK TORONTO MELBOURNE WELLINGTON
BOMBAY CALCUTTA MADRAS KARACHI LAHORE DACCA
CAPE TOWN SALISBURY NAIROBI IBADAN
KUALA LUMPUR HONG KONG

© *Oxford University Press 1965*

PRINTED IN GREAT BRITAIN
AT THE UNIVERSITY PRESS, OXFORD
BY VIVIAN RIDLER
PRINTER TO THE UNIVERSITY

CONTENTS

VOLUME I

VOLUME II

CONTENTS

VOLUME III

VOLUME IV

VOLUME V

> Magister artis & largitor ingeni
> Venter . . .
>
> Pers.

*L*UCIAN rallies the Philosophers in his Time, who could not agree whether they should admit *Riches* into the number of *real Goods*; the Professors of the Severer Sects threw them quite out, while others as resolutely inserted them.[2]

I am apt to believe, that as the World grew more Polite, the rigid Doctrines of the first were wholly discarded; and I do not find any one so hardy at present, as to deny that there are very great Advantages in the Enjoyment of a plentiful Fortune. Indeed the best and wisest of Men, tho' they may possibly despise a good Part of those things which the World calls Pleasures, can, I think, hardly be insensible of that Weight and Dignity which a moderate share of Wealth adds to their Characters, Councils and Actions.

We find it a general Complaint in Professions and Trades, that the Richest Members of them are chiefly encouraged, and this is falsely imputed to the Ill-nature of Mankind, who are ever bestowing their Favours on such as least want them. Whereas, if we fairly consider their Proceedings in this Case, we shall find them founded on undoubted Reason: Since supposing both equal in their natural Integrity, I ought, in common Prudence, to fear foul Play from an Indigent Person, rather than from one whose Circumstances seem to have placed him above the bare Temptation of Money.

This Reason also makes the Common-wealth regard her richest Subjects, as those who are most concerned for her Quiet and Interest, and consequently fittest to be entrusted with her highest Imployments. On the contrary, *Catiline*'s Saying to those Men of desperate Fortunes, who applied themselves to him, and of whom he afterwards composed his Army, that *They had nothing to hope for but a Civil War*,[3] was too true not to make the Impressions he desired.

---

[1] *Motto.* Persius, *Satires*, Prologue 10–11 (altered):

'Twas witty Want, fierce Hunger to appease:
Want taught their Masters, and their Masters these. DRYDEN.

[2] See 'The Eunuch, or Pamphilus', in Lucian's *Works* (1711), iii. 3–4.

[3] Sallust, *Bellum Catilinae*, 20. 13–15.

I believe I need not fear but that what I have said in Praise of Money, will be more than sufficient with most of my Readers to excuse the Subject of my present Paper, which I intend, as an Essay on *The Ways to raise a Man's Fortune*, or *The Art of growing Rich*.

The first and most infallible Method towards the attaining of this End, is *Thrift*: All Men are not equally qualified for getting Mony, but it is in the Power of every one alike to practise this Virtue, and I believe there are very few Persons, who, if they please to reflect on their past Lives, will not find that had they saved all those little Sums, which they have spent unnecessarily, they might at present have been Masters[a] of a competent Fortune. *Diligence* justly claims the next Place to *Thrift*: I[b] find both these[c] excellently well recommended to common use in the three following *Italian* Proverbs.[1]

> *Never do that by Proxy which you can do your self.*
> *Never defer that 'till to Morrow which you can do to Day.*
> *Never neglect small Matters and Expences.*

A third Instrument of growing Rich, is *Method in Business*, which, as well as the two former, is also attainable by Persons of the meanest Capacities.

The famous *De Wit*, one of the greatest Statesmen of the Age in which he lived, being asked by a Friend, How he was able to dispatch that Multitude of Affairs in which he was engaged? replyed That his whole Art consisted in *doing one thing at once*.[d] If, says he, I have any necessary Dispatches to make, I think of nothing else 'till those are finished; If any Domestick Affairs require my Attention, I give my self up wholly to them 'till they are set in Order.[2]

In short, we often see Men of dull and phlegmatick Tempers, arriving to great Estates, by making a regular and orderly Disposition of their Business, and that without it the greatest Parts and most lively Imaginations rather puzzle their Affairs, than bring them to an happy issue.

---

[a] been Masters] been the Masters *Fol.*   [b] *Thrift*: I] *Thrift*: and I *Fol.*
[c] both these] these two *Fol.*   [d] *Italics added in 8vo and 12mo*

---

[1] For the first of these see Tilley (D401), who gives examples in English from 1541. The second is in both Tilley (T378) and Apperson. The third does not seem to be a proverb.

[2] I do not find this actual saying recorded of Jan De Wit. In his *True Interest and Political Maxims of the Republick of Holland and West-Friesland* (1702), p. 252, there is a somewhat similar observation: '*Do well, and look not backward*, is the greatest Polity *Holland* can use.'

From what has been said, I think I may lay it down as a Maxim, that every Man of good Common Sense may, if he pleases, in his particular station of Life, most certainly be Rich. The Reason why we sometimes see that Men of the greatest Capacities are not so, is either because they despise Wealth in Comparison of something else; or at least are not content to be getting an Estate, unless they may do it their own way, and at the same time enjoy all the Pleasures and Gratifications of Life.

But besides these ordinary forms of growing Rich, it must be allowed that there is room for Genius, as well in this as in all other Circumstances of Life.

Tho' the ways of getting Money were long since very numerous; and tho' so many new ones have been found out of late Years, there is certainly still remaining so large a Field for Invention, that a Man of an indifferent Head might easily sit down and draw up such a Plan for the Conduct and Support of his Life, as was never yet once thought of.

We daily see Methods put in Practice by Hungry and Ingenious Men, which demonstrate the Power of Invention in this Particular.

It is reported of *Scaramouch*,[1] the first famous *Italian* Comedian, that being at *Paris*, and in great Want, he bethought himself of constantly plying near the Door of a noted Perfumer in that City, and when any one came out who had been buying Snuff, never failed to desire a Taste of them; when he had by this means got together a quantity made up of several different sorts, he sold it again at a lower rate to the same Perfumer, who finding out the Trick, called it *Tabac de mille fleures*, or *Snuff of a thousand Flowers*. The Story farther tells us, that by this means he got a very comfortable Subsistance, 'till making too much haste to grow Rich, he one Day took such an unreasonable Pinch out of the Box of a *Swiss* Officer, as engaged him in a Quarrel, and obliged him to quit this Ingenious way of Life.

Nor can I in this place omit doing Justice to a Youth of my own Country, who, tho' he is scarce yet twelve Years old, has with great Industry and Application attained to the Art of beating the Grenadiers March on his Chin. I am credibly informed, that by this means

---

[1] Originally a character in Italian farce ridiculing the Spanish don. The reference here is to the actor, Tiberio Fiurelli (or Fiorilli), who impersonated the part and who brought his company of Italian players to London in 1673. The anecdote is told in Angelo Constantini's *Vie de Scaramouche* (Paris, 1698), pp. 5–9, although there the incident is said to have occurred in Rome and not Paris.

he does not only maintain himself and his Mother, but that he is laying up Money every Day, with a design, if the War continues, to purchase a Drum at least, if not a Colours.

I shall conclude these Instances with the Device of the famous *Rabelais*, when he was at a great distance from *Paris*, and without Money to bear his Expences thither.[1] This Ingenious Author being thus sharp set,[a] got together a convenient quantity of Brick-Dust, and having disposed of it into several Papers, writ upon one *Poyson for Monsieur*, upon a second *Poyson for the Dauphin*, and on a third *Poyson for the King*. Having made this Provision for the Royal Family of *France*, he laid his Papers so that his Landlord, who was an inquisitive Man, and a good Subject, might get a sight of them.

The Plot succeeded as he desired: The Host gave immediate[b] Intelligence to the Secretary of State. The Secretary presently sent down a Special Messenger, who brought up the Traitor to Court, and provided him at the King's Expence with proper Accommodations on the Road. As soon as he appeared he was known to be the Celebrated *Rabelais*, and his Powder upon Examination being found very Innocent, the Jest was only laught at; for which a less eminent *Drole* would have been sent to the Gallies.

Trade and Commerce might doubtless be still varied a thousand ways, out of which would arise such Branches as have not yet been touched. The famous *Doily* is still fresh in every ones Memory, who raised a Fortune by finding out Materials for such Stuffs as might at once be cheap and genteel.[2] I have heard it affirmed, that had not he discovered this frugal Method of gratifying our Pride, we should hardly have been able to carry[c] on the last War.

I regard Trade not only as highly advantageous to the Commonwealth in general; but as the most natural and likely Method of making a Man's Fortune; having observed, since my being a Spectator in the World, greater Estates got about *Change*, than at

---

[a] being thus sharp set,] being sharp set, *Fol.*   [b] immediate] immediately *Fol.*   [c] able to carry] able so well to carry *Fol.*

[1] See the biography prefixed to *The Whole Works of F. Rabelais, M.D. . . . Done out of French, by Sir Thomas Urchard, Knight, Mr. Motteux, and Others* (1708), pp. ix–xi, where the story is told. This seems to be the basis for the absurd attribution of all the numbers signed X to Motteux, in the *General Index to the Spectators, Tatlers and Guardians* (1760), sig. A6. Cf. Robert N. Cunningham, *Peter Anthony Motteux* (Oxford, 1933), pp. 51–55.
[2] Thomas Doyly 'at the Nun in Henrietta street Convent Garden, Linnen Draper' advertises in the *Post-Man* (13 Jan. 1705) that he is selling off his goods and that his shop is to be let at Lady Day. In the *Journal to Stella* (23 Apr. 1711) Swift speaks of 'coarse *Doiley* napkins, fringed at each end, upon the table'.

Whitehall or *St. James's*. I believe I may also add, that the first Acquisitions are generally attended with more Satisfaction, and as good a Conscience.

I must not however close this Essay, without observing, that what has been said is only intended for Persons in the common ways of Thriving, and is not designed for those Men who from low Beginnings push themselves up to the Top of States, and the most considerable Figures in Life. My Maxim of *Saving* is not designed for such as these, since nothing is more usual than for *Thrift* to disappoint the Ends of *Ambition*, it being almost impossible that the Mind should be intent[a] upon Trifles, while it is at the same time forming some great Design.

I may therefore compare these Men to a great Poet, who, as *Longinus* says, while he is full of the most magnificent Ideas, is not always at leisure to mind the little Beauties and Niceties of his Art.[1]

I would however have all my Readers take great care how they mistake themselves for uncommon *Genius's*, and Men above Rule, since it is very easie for them to be deceived in this Particular.

X

[a] should be intent] should descend to, and be intent *Fol.*

---

[1] *On the Sublime*, 33 (chap. 27 in Boileau's version): 'In the *Sublime*, where the Riches of Discourse are Immense, every thing cannot be so Carefully look'd after, as it ought to be; and something, let the Orator or Poet be never so Exact, will be Neglected' (Boileau, *Works*, 1711–12, ii. 68).

The British Museum contains a copy of a pamphlet entitled, *Supplement to the Spectator's Essay on the Ways of Raising a Man's Fortune, or the Art of Growing Rich: With the Essay it self Prefix'd* (Edinburgh, Printed in the Year MDCCXXXV), and dedicated 'to Mr. Samuel Clark, Edenburgh'. 'What the *Spectator* here means by *Thrift*', says the anonymous writer, 'is only *Savingness* and *Sparingness* . . .; and indeed it is certain, that in the ordinary Ways of Life, there is hardly a Possibility of growing *rich* without a *thrifty Œconomy*' (p. 15). The rest of the pamphlet is chiefly taken up with advice on temperance and saving, with many illustrations from other essays in the *Spectator*.

No. 284
[STEELE]

Friday, January 25, 1712[1]

Posthabui tamen illorum mea seria Ludo.

Virg.

AN unaffected Behaviour is without Question a very great Charm; but under the Notion of being unconstrained and disengaged, People take upon them to be unconcerned in any Duty of Life. A general Negligence is what they assume upon all Occasions, and set up for an Aversion to all manner of Business and Attention. *I am the carelessest Creature in the World, I have certainly the worst Memory of any Man living*, are frequent Expressions in the Mouth of a Pretender of this sort. It is a professed Maxim with these People never to *think*; there is something so solemn in Reflexion, they, forsooth, can never give themselves Time for such a way of employing themselves. It happens often that this sort of Man is heavy enough in his Nature to be a good Proficient in such Matters as are attainable by Industry; but alas! he has such an ardent Desire to be what he is not, to be too volatile, to have the Faults of a Person of Spirit, that he professes himself the most unfit Man living for any manner of Application. When this Humour enters into the Head of a Female, she generally professes Sickness upon all Occasions, and acts all things with an indisposed Air: She is offended, but her Mind is too lazy to raise her to Anger; therefore she lives only as actuated by a violent Spleen and gentle Scorn. She has hardly Curiosity to listen to Scandal of her Acquaintance, and has never Attention enough to hear them commended. This Affectation in both Sexes makes them vain of being useless, and take a certain Pride in their Insignificancy.

Opposite to this Folly is another no less unreasonable, and that is the Impertinence of being always in a Hurry. There are those who visit Ladies, and beg Pardon, afore they are well seated in their Chairs, that they just called in, but are obliged to attend Business of Importance elsewhere the very next Moment: Thus they run from Place to Place, professing that they are obliged to be still in another Company than that which they are in. These Persons who are just

---

[1] *Motto.* Virgil, *Eclogues*, 7. 17:

And I preferr'd my Pleasure to my Gains. DRYDEN.

The motto in the original folio sheets was Horace, *Epistles*, I. 11. 28, which had been used for No. 54 (vol. i).

a going some where else should never be detained; but all the World allow that Business is to be minded, and their Affairs will be at an end. Their Vanity is to be importuned, and Compliance with their Multiplicity of Affairs would effectually dispatch 'em. The Travelling Ladies who have half the Town to see in an Afternoon, may be pardoned for being in constant Hurry; but it is inexcusable in Men to come where they have no Business, to profess they absent themselves where they have. It has been remarked by some nice Observers and Criticks, That there is nothing discovers the true Temper of a Person so much as his Letters. I have by me two Epistles, which are written by two People of the different Humours above-mentioned. It is wonderful that a Man cannot observe upon himself when he sits down to write, but that he will gravely commit himself to Paper the same Man that he is in the Freedom of Conversation. I have hardly seen a Line from any of these Gentlemen, but spoke them as absent[1] from what they were doing, as they profess they are when they come into Company: For the Folly is, that they have perswaded themselves they really are busy. Thus their whole Time is spent in suspence[2] of the present Moment to the next, and then from the next to the succeeding, which to the end of Life is to pass away with Pretence to many things, and Execution of nothing.

SIR,

'THE Post is just going out, and I have many other Letters of very great Importance to write this Evening, but I could not omit making my Compliments to you for your Civilities to me when I was last in Town. It is my Misfortune to be so full of Business, that I cannot tell you a Thousand Things which I have to say to you. I must desire you to communicate the Contents of this to no one living; but believe me to be, with the greatest Fidelity,

SIR,

Your most Obedient,

Humble Servant,

Stephen Courier.'

Madam,

'I Hate Writing of all things in the World; however, tho' I have drank the Waters, and am told I ought not to use my Eyes so much, I cannot forbear writing to you, to tell you I have been to

---

[1] See No. 30 (vol. i).
[2] Used in the now obsolete sense of 'deferment' or 'delay' (cf. OED).

the last Degree hipp'd[1] since I saw you. How could you entertain such a Thought, as that I should hear of that silly Fellow with Patience? Take my Word for it, there is nothing in it; and you may believe it when so lazy a Creature as I am undergo the Pains to assure you of it by taking Pen, Ink, and Paper in my Hand. Forgive this, you know I shall not often offend in this Kind. I am very much

Your Servant,
Bridget Eitherdown.'

The Fellow is of your Country, prithee send me Word however whether he has so great an Estate.

Mr. SPECTATOR,   *Jan.* 24. 1712.

'I AM Clerk of the Parish from whence Mrs. *Simper* sends her Complaint, in your Yesterday *Spectator*.[2] I must beg of you to publish this as a publick Admonition to the aforesaid Mrs. *Simper*, otherwise all my honest Care in the Disposition of the Greens in the Church will have no Effect: I shall therefore with your Leave lay before you the whole Matter. I was formerly, as she charges me, for several Years a Gardener in the County of *Kent*: But I must absolutely deny that 'tis out of any Affection I retain for my old Employment, that I have placed my Greens so liberally about the Church, but out of a particular Spleen[3] I conceived against Mrs. *Simper* (and others of the same Sisterhood) some time ago. As to herself, I had one Day set[4] the Hundredth *Psalm*, and was singing the first Line in order to put the Congregation into the Tune, she was all the while curtsying to Sir *Anthony* in so affected and indecent a Manner, that the Indignation I conceived at it made me forget my self so far, as from the Tune of that *Psalm* to wander into *Southwell* Tune, and from thence into *Windsor* Tune, still unable to recover my self till I had with the utmost Confusion set a new one. Nay, I have often seen her rise up and smile and courtsy to one at the lower End of the Church in the Midst of a *Gloria Patri*; and when I have spoke the Ascent to a Prayer with a long *Amen* uttered with decent Gravity, she has been rolling her Eyes round about in such a Manner, as plainly shewed however she was moved, it was not towards an heavenly Object. In fine, she extended her Conquests so

---

[1] i.e. affected with hypochondria; morbidly depressed or low-spirited. OED gives one quotation (*c.* 1710) earlier than this.
[2] No. 282 (vol. ii).
[3] A grudge. OED gives quotations from 1616 to 1722.
[4] To set, i.e. to start the psalm for others to take up.

far over the Males, and raised such Envy in the Females, that what between Love of those and the Jealousy of these, I was almost the only Person that looked in a Prayer-Book all Church-time. I had several Projects in my Head to put a Stop to this growing Mischief; but as I have long lived in *Kent*, and there often heard how the Kentish Men evaded the Conqueror, by carrying green Boughs over their Heads, it put me in Mind of practising this Device against Mrs. *Simper*. I find I have preserved many a young Man from her Eye-shot by this Means; therefore humbly pray the Boughs may be fixed, till she shall give Security for her peaceable Intentions.

Your humble Servant,
Francis Sternhold.'

T

No. 285
[ADDISON]

Saturday, January 26, 1712[1]

Ne quicunque Deus, quicunque adhibebitur heros,
Regali conspectus in auro nuper & ostro,
Migret in Obscuras humili sermone tabernas:
Aut dum vitat humum, nubes & inania captet.

Hor.

HAVING already treated of the Fable, the Characters, and Sentiments in the *Paradise Lost*, we are in the last place to consider the *Language*; and as the learned World is very much divided upon *Milton* as to this Point, I hope they will excuse me if I appear particular in any of my Opinions, and encline to those who judge the most advantagiously of the Author.[2]

---

[1] *Motto.* Horace, *Ars poetica*, 227-30:
> But then they did not wrong themselves so much
> To make a God, a Hero, or a King,
> (Stript of his golden Crown and purple Robe)
> Descend to a Mechanick Dialect,
> Nor (to avoid such Meanness) soaring high
> With empty Sound, and airy Notions fly. ROSCOMMON

[2] For Dryden's views see Ker, i. 268; ii. 29, 109. The letter 'to Mr. T. S.' in vindication of Milton, printed in Gildon's *Miscellaneous Letters and Essays* of 1694 (Spingarn, iii. 198-200), defends Milton's '*Antient* and consequently *less Intelligible* Words, Phrases, and Similies'. On the whole subject see R. D. Havens, *The Influence of Milton on English Poetry* (Cambridge, Mass., 1922), pp. 64-68.

It is requisite that the Language of an Heroic Poem should be both Perspicuous and Sublime.[1] In proportion as either of these two Qualities are wanting, the Language is imperfect. Perspicuity is the first and most necessary Qualification; insomuch, that a good-natured Reader sometimes overlooks a little Slip even in the Grammar or Syntax, where it is impossible for him to mistake the Poet's Sense. Of this kind is that Passage in *Milton*, wherein he speaks of *Satan*.

> . . . *God and his Son except,*
> *Created thing nought valu'd he nor shunn'd.*[2]

And that in which he describes *Adam* and *Eve*.

> Adam *the goodliest Man of Men since born*
> *His Sons, the fairest of her Daughters* Eve.[3]

It is plain, that in the former of these Passages, according to the natural Syntax, the Divine Persons mentioned in the first Line are represented as created Beings; and that in the other, *Adam* and *Eve* are confounded with their Sons and Daughters. Such little Blemishes as these, when the Thought is great and natural, we should, with *Horace*,[4] impute to a pardonable Inadvertency, or to the Weakness of Human Nature, which cannot attend to each minute Particular, and give the last finishing to every Circumstance in so long a Work. The Ancient Criticks therefore, who were acted by a Spirit of Candour, rather than that of Cavilling, invented certain figures of Speech, on purpose to palliate little Errors of this nature in the Writings of those Authors, who had so many greater Beauties to attone for them.

If Clearness and Perspicuity were only to be consulted, the Poet would have nothing else to do but to cloath his Thoughts in the most plain and natural Expressions. But, since it often happens, that the most obvious Phrases, and those which are used in ordinary Conversation, become too familiar to the Ear, and contract a kind of Meanness by passing through the Mouths of the Vulgar, a Poet should take particular care to guard himself against Idiomatick[5] ways of speaking. *Ovid* and *Lucan* have many Poornesses of Expression upon this account, as taking up with the first Phrases that

---

[1] Addison here follows Aristotle's *Poetics*, 22. 1.
[2] *PL*, ii. 678–9. [3] *PL*, iv. 323–4.
[4] *Ars poetica*, 351–3.
[5] This is the first quotation in *OED* to illustrate this sense of the word, i.e. vernacular, colloquial.

offered, without putting themselves to the trouble of looking after such as would not only be[a] natural, but also elevated and sublime. *Milton* has but a few[b] Failings in this kind, of which, however, you may meet with some Instances, as in the following Passages.[c]

> *Embrio's and Idiots, Eremites and Fryars*
> White, Black and Grey, *with all their* Trumpery,
> *Here Pilgrims roam . . .*[1]
> *. . . A while Discourse they hold,*
> No fear lest Dinner cool; *when thus began*
> *Our Author . . .*[2]
> *Who of all Ages to succeed, but feeling*
> *The Evil on him brought by me, will curse*
> *My Head, ill fare our Ancestor impure,*
> For this we may thank *Adam . . .*[3]

[d]The great Masters in Composition know very well that many an elegant Phrase becomes improper for a Poet or an Orator,[e] when it has been debased by common use. For this reason the Works of Ancient Authors, which are written in dead Languages, have a great Advantage over those which are written in Languages that are now spoken. Were there any mean Phrases or Idioms in *Virgil* and *Homer*, they would not shock the Ear of the most delicate Modern Reader, so much as they would have done that of an old *Greek* or *Roman*, because we never hear them pronounced in our Streets, or in ordinary Conversation.

It is not therefore sufficient, that the Language of an Epic Poem be Perspicuous, unless it be also Sublime. To this end it ought to deviate from the common Forms and ordinary Phrases of Speech. The Judgment of a Poet very much discovers it self in shunning the common Roads of Expression, without falling into such ways of Speech as may seem stiff and unnatural; he must not swell into a false Sublime, by endeavouring to avoid the other Extream. Among the *Greeks*, *Eschylus*, and sometimes *Sophocles*, were guilty of this Fault; among the *Latins*, *Claudian* and *Statius*; and among our own Countrymen, *Shakespear* and *Lee*. In these Authors the Affecta-

---

[a] be] *19*; have been *Fol., 8vo, 12mo*   [b] but a few] *19*; but few *Fol., 8vo, 12mo*
[c] you may . . . Passages.] you may see an Instance or two in the following Passages. *Fol.*   [d] *No paragraph in 19*; new paragraph in *Fol., 8vo, 12mo*   [e] or an Orator,] or Orator, *Fol.*

---

[1] *PL*, iii. 474–6.   [2] *PL*, v. 395–7.   [3] *PL*, x. 733–6.

tion of Greatness often hurts the Perspicuity of the Stile, as in many others the Endeavour after Perspicuity prejudices its Greatness.

Aristotle has observed, that the Idiomatick Stile may be avoided, and the Sublime formed, by the following Methods.[1] First, by the use of Metaphors: such are those[a] in *Milton*.

> Imparadis'd *in one anothers Arms*,[2]
> ... *And in his Hand a Reed*
> *Stood waving* tipt *with Fire*; ...[3]
> *The grassie Clods now* calv'd. ...[4]
> Spangled *with Eyes* ...[b][5]

In these and innumerable[c] other Instances, the Metaphors are very bold but just;[d] I must however observe, that the Metaphors are not thick sown in *Milton*, which always savours too much of Wit; that they never clash with one another, which as *Aristotle* observes, turns a Sentence into a kind of an Enigma or Riddle;[6] and that he seldom has Recourse to[e] them where the proper and natural Words will do as well.

Another way of raising the Language, and giving it a Poetical Turn, is to make use of the Idioms of other Tongues.[7] *Virgil* is full of the *Greek* Forms of Speech, which the Criticks call *Hellenisms*, as *Horace* in his Odes abounds with them much more than *Virgil*. I need not mention the several Dialects which *Homer* has made use of for this end. *Milton*, in conformity with the Practice of the Ancient Poets, and with *Aristotle*'s Rule has infused a great many *Latinisms*, as well as *Græcisms*, and sometimes *Hebraisms*,[f] into the Language of his Poem, as towards the Beginning of it.

> *Nor did they not perceive the evil plight*
> *In which they were, or the fierce Pains not feel.*
> *Yet to their Gen'ral's Voice they soon obey'd.*[g][8]
> ... *Who shall tempt with wandring Feet*
> *The dark unbottom'd Infinite Abyss,*
> *And through the* palpable Obscure *find out*[h]
> *His uncouth way, or spread his airy Flight*

---

[a] Metaphors: such are those] 19; Metaphors, like those *Fol.*, *8vo*, *12mo*   [b] *Added in 19*   [c] innumerable] several *Fol.*   [d] just;] 19; beautiful; *Fol.*, *12mo*; beautiful: *8vo.*   [e] has Recourse to] 19; makes use of *Fol.*, *8vo*, *12mo*   [f] and sometimes *Hebraisms*,] om. *Fol.*   [g] om. *Fol.*   [h] find out] 19; find out his way, *Fol.*, *8vo*, *12mo*

---

[1] *Poetics*, 22. 1.   [2] *PL*, iv. 506.   [3] *PL*, vi. 579–80.
[4] *PL*, vii. 463.   [5] *PL*, xi. 130.   [6] Aristotle, *Poetics*, 22. 2.
[7] Aristotle, *Poetics*, 22. 2–3.   [8] *PL*, i. 335–7.

> Upborn with indefatigable Wings
> Over the vast Abrupt![1]
>
> [a]. . . So both ascend
> In the Visions of God . . .[a][2] B. II.

Under this Head may be reckoned the placing the Adjective after the Substantive, the transposition of Words, the turning the Adjective into a Substantive, with several other Foreign Modes of Speech, which this Poet has naturalized to give his Verse the greater Sound, and throw it out of Prose.

The third Method mentioned by *Aristotle*,[3] is what[b] agrees with the Genius of the *Greek* Language more than with that of any other Tongue, and is therefore more used by *Homer* than by any other Poet. I mean the lengthning of a Phrase by the Addition of Words, which may either be inserted or omitted, as also by the extending or contracting of particular Words by the Insertion or Omission of certain Syllables. *Milton* has put in practice this Method of raising his Language, as far as the nature of our Tongue will permit, as in the Passage above-mentioned, *Eremite*, for what[c] is Hermit, in common Discourse. If you observe the Measure of his Verse, he has with great Judgment suppressed a Syllable in several Words, and shortned those of two Syllables into one, by which Method, besides the abovementioned Advantage, he has given a greater Variety to his Numbers. But this Practice is more particularly remarkable in the Names of Persons and of Countries, as *Beëlzebub*,[4] *Hessebon*, and in many other Particulars, wherein he has either changed the Name, or made use of that which is not the most commonly known, that he might the better depart from[d] the Language of the Vulgar.

The same Reason recommended to him several old Words, which also makes his Poem appear the more venerable, and gives it a greater Air of Antiquity.[5]

I must likewise take notice, that there are in *Milton* several Words of his own Coining, as *Cerberean, miscreated, Hell-doom'd, Embryon*

[a-a] *om. Fol.*   [b] what] that which *Fol.*   [c] for what] what *Fol.*
[d] depart from] *19*; deviate from *Fol., 8vo, 12mo*

---

[1] *PL*, ii. 404-9.   [2] *PL*, xi. 376-7.
[3] *Poetics*, 22. 4.
[4] The Latin Vulgate form of the Hebrew *Baal-zebub.* Hesebon (*PL*, i. 408), the Greek form of the Hebrew *Heshbon.*
[5] For Dryden's criticism of Milton's revival of 'antiquated words' (in the Discourse on Satire) see Ker, ii. 29.

Atoms, and many others.[1] If the Reader is offended at this Liberty in our *English* Poet, I would recommend him to a Discourse in *Plutarch*, which shews us how frequently *Homer* has made use of the same Liberty.[2]

Milton, by the above-mentioned Helps, and by the choice of the noblest Words and Phrases which our Tongue wou'd afford him, has carried our Language to a greater height than any of the *English* Poets have ever done before or after him, and made the Sublimity of his Stile equal to that of his Sentiments.

I have been the more particular in these Observations on[a] *Milton's* Stile, because it is that part of him in which he appears the most singular. The Remarks I have here made upon the Practice of other Poets, with my Observations out of *Aristotle*, will perhaps alleviate the Prejudice which some have taken to his Poem upon this Account; tho' after all, I must confess, that I think his Stile, tho' admirable in general, is in some places too much stiffened and obscured by the frequent use of those Methods, which *Aristotle* has prescribed for the raising of it.

This Redundancy of those several ways of Speech which *Aristotle* calls *foreign Language*,[3] and with which *Milton* has so very much enriched, and in some places darkned the Language of his Poem, was[b] the more proper for his use, because his Poem is written in Blank Verse. Rhyme, without any other Assistance, throws the Language off from Prose, and very often makes an indifferent Phrase pass unregarded; but where the Verse is not built upon Rhymes, there Pomp of Sound, and Energy of Expression, are indispensably necessary to support the Stile, and keep it from falling into the Flatness of Prose.

Those who have not a Taste for this Elevation of Stile, and are apt to ridicule a Poet when he goes out of[c] the common Forms of Expression, would do well to see how *Aristotle* has treated an Ancient Author, called *Euclid*,[4] for his insipid Mirth upon this

---

[a] on] *19*; of *Fol.*, *8vo*, *12mo*   [b] was] *8vo*, *19*; is *Fol.*, *12mo*   [c] goes out of] *19*; departs from *Fol.*, *8vo*, *12mo*

---

[1] *PL*, ii. 655, 683, 697, 900. J. D. (*Gentleman's Magazine*, April 1780, p. 175) pointed out that 'miscreated' was not coined by Milton, having been used by Spenser in *The Faerie Queene* [I. ii. 3. 1; II. vii. 42. 9].
[2] *The Life and Poetry of Homer* (1. 16), formerly attributed to Plutarch.
[3] *Poetics*, 22. 1.
[4] *Poetics*, 22. 5.

Occasion. Mr. *Dryden* used to call this sort of Men his Prose-Criticks.[1]

I should, under this Head of the Language, consider *Milton*'s Numbers, in which he has made use of several Elisions, that are not customary among other *English* Poets, as may be particularly observed in his cutting off the Letter *Y.* when it precedes a Vowel. This, and some other Innovations in the Measure of his Verse, has varied his Numbers in such a manner, as makes them incapable of satiating the Ear and cloying the Reader, which the same uniform Measure would certainly have done, and which the perpetual Returns of Rhime never fail to do in long Narrative Poems. I shall close these Reflections upon the Language of *Paradise Lost*, with observing that *Milton* has copied after *Homer*, rather than *Virgil*, in the length of his Periods, the Copiousness of his Phrases, and the running of his Verses into one another.   L

No. 286   *Monday, January 28, 1712*[2]

Nomina Honesta prætenduntur vitiis.
Tacit.

Mr. SPECTATOR,   *York, Jan.* 18. 1712.

'I PRETEND not to inform a Gentleman[3] of so just a Taste whenever he pleases to use it; but it may not be amiss to inform your Reader that there is a false Delicacy as well as a true one. True Delicacy, as I take it, consists in Exactness of Judgment and Dignity of Sentiment, or if you will, Purity of Affection, as this is opposed to Corruption and Grossness. There are Pedants in Breeding as well as in Learning. The Eye that cannot bear the Light is not delicate but sore. A good Constitution appears in the Soundness and Vigour of the Parts, not in the Squeamishness of the Stomach: And a false Delicacy is Affectation, not Politeness. What then can be the Standard of Delicacy but Truth and Virtue? Virtue, which, as the

---

[1] I have not found this reference in Dryden. He uses the combination *prose-wits* in *An Evening's Love* (III. i).

[2] *Motto.* Adapted from Tacitus, *Annals*, 14. 21: Vice often lies cloaked under an honest name. No. 286 is of unknown authorship. See Introduction, p. xlix.

[3] Francis Courtly in No. 276 (vol. ii).

Satyrist long since observed, is real Honour;[1] whereas the other Distinctions among Mankind are meerly titular. Judging by that Rule, in my Opinion, and in that of many of your virtuous Female Readers, you are so far from deserving Mr. *Courtly's* Accusation, that you seem too gentle, and to allow too many Excuses for an enormous Crime, which is the Reproach of the Age, and is in all its Branches and Degrees expresly forbidden by that Religion we pretend to profess; and whose Laws, in a Nation that calls it self Christian, one would think should take Place of those Rules which Men of corrupt Minds, and those of weak Understandings follow. I know not any thing more pernicious to good Manners, than the giving fair Names to foul Actions; for this confounds Vice and Virtue, and takes off that natural Horrour we have to Evil. An innocent Creature, who would start at the Name of Strumpet, may think it pretty to be called a Mistress, especially if her Seducer has taken care to inform her, that a Union of Hearts is the principal Matter in the Sight of Heaven, and that the Business at Church is a meer idle Ceremony. Who knows not that the Difference between obscene and modest Words expressing the same Action, consists only in the accessary Idea, for there is nothing immodest in Letters and Syllables. Fornication and Adultery are modest Words, because they express an evil Action as criminal, and so as to excite Horrour and Aversion: Whereas Words representing the Pleasure rather than the Sin, are for this Reason indecent and dishonest. Your Papers would be chargeable with something worse than Indelicacy, they would be immoral, did you treat the detestable Sins of Uncleanness in the same Manner as you rally an impertinent Self-love and an artful Glance; As those Laws wou'd be very unjust, that shou'd chastise Murder and Petty Larceny with the same Punishment. Even Delicacy requires that the Pity shewn to distressed indigent Wickedness, first betray'd into, and then expell'd the Harbours of the Brothel, shou'd be chang'd to Detestation, when we consider pamper'd Vice in the Habitations of the Wealthy.[2] The most free Person of Quality, in Mr. *Courtly's* Phrase, that is to speak properly, a Woman of Figure who has forgot her Birth and Breeding, dishonour'd her Relations and her self, abandon'd her Virtue and Reputation, together with the natural Modesty of her Sex, and

---

[1] Professor Benedict Einarson kindly refers me to Juvenal, *Satires*, 8. 20: *Nobilitas sola est atque unica virtus* (the one and only nobility is virtue).

[2] This phrase occurs in the last sentence of No. 266 (vol. ii).

risqued her very Soul, is so far from deserving to be treated with
no worse Character than that of a kind Woman, (which is doubtless
Mr. *Courtly*'s Meaning if he has any) that one can scarce be too
severe on her, in as much as she sins against greater Restraints,
is less expos'd, and liable to fewer Temptations, than Beauty in
Poverty and Distress. It is hop'd therefore Sir, that you will not lay
aside your generous Design of exposing that monstrous Wickedness
of the Town, whereby a Multitude of Innocents are sacrificed in
a more barbarous Manner than those who were offer'd to *Moloch*.
The Unchaste are provoked to see their Vice expos'd, and the
Chaste cannot rake into such Filth without Danger of Defilement;
but a meer SPECTATOR, may look into the bottom, and come off
without partaking in the Guilt. The doing so will convince us you
pursue publick Good, and not meerly your own Advantage: But if
your Zeal slackens, how can one help thinking that Mr. *Courtly*'s
Letter is but a Feint to get off from a Subject, in which either your
own, or the private and base Ends of others to whom you are partial,
or those of whom[a] you are afraid, wou'd not endure a Reformation?

> *I am, Sir, your humble Servant and Admirer, so*
> *long as you tread in the Paths of Truth,*
> *Virtue, and Honour.*'

Mr. SPECTATOR,   *Trin. Col. Cantab. Jan.* 12, 1711–12.
'IT is my Fortune to have a Chamber-Fellow, with whom, tho'
I agree very well in many Sentiments, yet there is one in which
we are as contrary as Light and Darkness. We are both in Love; his
Mistress is a lovely Fair, and mine a lovely Brown. Now as the
Praise of our Mistress's Beauty employs much of our Time, we have
frequent Quarrels in entering upon that Subject, while each says all
he can to defend his Choice. For my own Part, I have rack'd my
Fancy to the utmost; and sometimes, with the greatest Warmth of
Imagination, have told him, That Night was made before Day, and
many more fine things, tho' without any Effect: Nay, last Night
I could not forbear saying, with more Heat than Judgment, that the
Devil ought to be painted white. Now my Desire is, Sir, That you
would be pleas'd to give us in Black and White your Opinion in the
Matter of Dispute between us; which will either furnish me with
fresh and prevailing Arguments to maintain my own Taste, or make
me with less Repining allow that of my Chamber-Fellow. I know

---

[a] or those of whom] *12mo*; or of those whom *Fol*., *8vo*

very well that I have *Jack Cleveland*,[1] and *Bond's Horace*[2] on my Side; but then he has such a Band of Rhymers and Romance-Writers, with which he opposes me, and is so continualy chiming to the Tune of golden Tresses, yellow Locks, Milk, Marble, Ivory, Silver, Swans, Snow, Dazies, Doves, and the Lord knows what; which he is always sounding with so much Vehemence in my Ears, that he often puts me into a brown Study how to answer him; and I find that I'm in a fair Way to be quite confounded, without your timely Assistance afforded to,

> SIR,
> *Your humble Servant*,
> Philobrune.'

Z

No. 287
[ADDISON]

Tuesday, January 29, 1712[3]

Ὦ φιλτάτη γῆ μῆτερ, ὡς σεμνὸν σφόδρ' εἶ
Τοῖς νοῦν ἔχουσι κτῆμα; . . .

Menand.

I LOOK upon it as a peculiar Happiness, that were I to chuse or what Religion I would be, and under what Government I would live, I should most certainly give the Preference to that form of Religion and Government which is established in my own Country. In this point I think I am determined by Reason and Conviction; but if I shall be told that I am acted by Prejudice, I am sure it is an honest Prejudice, it is a Prejudice that arises from the Love of my Country, and therefore such an one as I will always indulge. I have in several Papers endeavoured to express my Duty and Esteem for the Church of *England*, and design this as an Essay upon the Civil

---

[1] John Cleveland, in his poem 'To the State of Love, or, The Sences Festivall' (*Poems*, 1651), praises the brown complexion of his mistress.

[2] John Bond's notes on Horace (1606) were often reprinted during the seventeenth and eighteenth centuries. In his notes on *Odes* I. 32. 11–12 and *Ars poetica* 37 he comments on the praise of dark eyes and dark hair among the ancients. See *Q. Horatius Flaccus cum commentariis selectissimis variorum & scholiis integris Johannis Bond* (Leyden, 1663), pp. 77, 775.

[3] *Motto*. Menander, *Naucleros*, 349 (Meineke, *Fragmenta*, iv. 175):

> Dear *Native* Land, how do the good and wise
> Thy happy clime and countless blessings prize!

part of our Constitution, having often entertained my self with Reflections on this Subject, which I have not met with in other Writers.

That form of Government appears to me the most reasonable, which is most conformable to the Equality that we find in Human Nature, provided it be consistent with Publick[a] Peace and Tranquillity. This is what may properly be called Liberty, which exempts one Man from Subjection to another, so far as the Order and Oeconomy of Government will permit.

Liberty should reach every Individual of a People, as they all share one common Nature; if it only spreads among particular Branches, there had better be none at all, since such a Liberty only aggravates the Misfortune of those who are deprived of it, by setting before them a disagreeable subject of Comparison.

This Liberty is best preserved, where the Legislative Power is lodged in several Persons, especially if those Persons are of different Ranks and Interests; for where they are of the same Rank, and consequently have an Interest to manage peculiar to that Rank, it differs but little from a Despotical Government in a single Person.[b] But the greatest Security a People can have for their Liberty, is when the Legislative Power is in the Hands of Persons so happily distinguished, that by providing for the particular Interest of their several Ranks, they are providing for the whole Body of the People; or in other Words, when there is no part of the People that has not a common Interest with at least one part of the Legislators.

If there be but one Body of Legislators, it is no better than a Tyranny; if there are only two, there will want a casting Voice, and one of them must at length be swallowed up by Disputes and Contentions that will necessarily arise between them. Four would have the same Inconvenience as two, and a greater number would cause too much Confusion. I could never read a Passage in *Polybius*,[1] and another in *Cicero*,[2] to this purpose, without a secret Pleasure in applying it to the *English* Constitution, which it suits much better than the *Roman*. Both these great Authors give the Pre-eminence to a mixt Government, consisting of three Branches, the Regal, the

---

[a] with Publick] with the Publick *Fol.*   [b] Person.] Person: *Fol.*

[1] *History*, 6. 3–18.
[2] *De re publica*, 2. 23. 41. In *Freeholder* 51 Addison remarks that Aristotle, Polybius, and Cicero all 'give the pre-eminence to a mixed government, consisting of three branches, the regal, the noble, and the popular'.

Noble, and the Popular. They had doubtless in their Thoughts the Constitution of the *Roman* Common-wealth, in which the Consul represented the King, the Senate the Nobles, and the Tribunes the People. This Division of the three Powers in the *Roman* Constitution was by no means so distinct and natural, as it is in the *English* form of Government. Among several Objections that might be made to it, I think the chief are those that affect the Consular Power, which had only the Ornaments without the Force of the Regal Authority. Their Number had not a casting Voice in it; for which reason, if one did not chance to be employed Abroad, while the other sat at Home, the Publick Business was sometimes at a stand, while the Consuls pulled two different ways in it. Besides, I do not find that the Consuls had ever a Negative Voice in the passing of a Law, or Decree of Senate, so that indeed they were rather the chief Body of the Nobility, or the first Ministers of State, than a distinct Branch of the Sovereignty, in which none can be looked upon as a part, who are not a part of the Legislature. Had the Consuls been invested with the Regal Authority to as great a Degree as our Monarchs, there would never have been any Occasions for a Dictatorship, which had in it the Power of all the three Orders, and ended in the Subversion of the whole Constitution.

Such an History as that of *Suetonius*,[1] which gives us a Succession of absolute Princes, is to me an unanswerable Argument against Despotick Power. Where the Prince is a Man of Wisdom and Virtue, it is indeed happy for his People that he is Absolute; but since in the common run[2] of Mankind, for one that is Wise and Good you find ten of a contrary Character, it is very dangerous for a Nation to stand to its Chance, or to have its Publick Happiness or Misery depend[a] on the Virtues or Vices of a single Person. Look into the Historian I have mentioned, or into any Series of Absolute Princes, how many Tyrants must you read through, before you come at an Emperor that is supportable. But this is not all, an Honest private Man often grows cruel and abandoned, when converted into an Absolute Prince. Give a Man Power of doing what he pleases with Impunity, you extinguish his Fear, and consequently

---

[a] depend] *8vo*; to depend *Fol.*, *12mo*

---

[1] The *History of the Twelve Caesars*, translated 'by several hands', appeared in 1672 and ran through several editions.
[2] See *OED*, 'Run', *sb.* II. 8, where this is cited as the earliest example of the word in this sense.

overturn in him one of the great Pillars of Morality. This too we find confirmed by matter of Fact. How many hopeful Heirs apparent to great Empires, when in the Possession of them have become such Monsters of Lust and Cruelty as are a Reproach to Human Nature?

Some tell us we ought to make our Governments on Earth like that in Heaven, which, say they, is altogether Monarchical and Unlimited.[1] Was Man like his Creator in Goodness and Justice, I should be for following this great Model; but where Goodness and Justice are not essential to the Ruler, I would by no means put my self into his Hands to be disposed of according to his particular Will and Pleasure.

It is odd to consider the Connection between Despotic Government and Barbarity, and how the making of one Person more than Man, makes the rest less. Above nine parts of the World in ten are in the lowest State of Slavery, and consequently sunk into the most gross and brutal Ignorance. *European* Slavery is indeed a State of Liberty, if compared with that which prevails in the other three divisions of the World; and therefore it is no wonder that those who grovel under it have many tracks of Light among them, of which the others are wholly destitute.

Riches and Plenty are the natural Fruits of Liberty, and where these abound, Learning and all the Liberal Arts will immediately lift up their Heads and flourish. As a Man must have no slavish Fears and Apprehensions hanging upon his Mind, who[a] will indulge the Flights of Fancy or Speculation, and push his Researches into all the abstruse Corners of Truth, so it is necessary for him to have about him a Competency of all the Conveniencies of Life.[2]

The first thing every one looks after, is to provide himself with Necessaries. This Point will engross our Thoughts till it be satisfied: If[b] this is taken Care of to our Hands, we look out for Pleasures and Amusements; and among a great number of idle People, there will be many whose Pleasures will lie in Reading and Contemplation. These are the two great Sources of Knowledge, and as Men grow

---

^a who] that *Fol.*   ^b satisfied: If] *8vo*; satisfied; if *Fol.*; satisfied. If *12mo*

---

[1] Evelyn's *Diary* (29 May 1678, 30 Jan. 1694) reports sermons stressing the monarchical form of government in Heaven (ed. De Beer, iv. 135; v. 165). It was probably not without design that Addison brought out the present paper just before 30 Jan., the anniversary of Charles I's death, a day on which Tory divines were likely to rhapsodize over the 'divinely' monarchical form of government.

[2] Cf. Cowley, Preface to *Poems* (1656): 'A warlike, various, and a tragical age is best to *write of*, but worst to *write in*' (Spingarn, ii. 80).

Wise they naturally love to communicate their Discoveries; and others seeing the Happiness of such a Learned Life, and improving by their Conversation, emulate, imitate and surpass one another, till a Nation is filled with Races of Wise and Understanding Persons. Ease and Plenty are therefore the great Cherishers of Knowledge; and as most of the Despotic Governments of the World have neither of them, they are naturally over-run with Ignorance and Barbarity. In *Europe*, indeed, notwithstanding several of its Princes are absolute, there are Men famous for Knowledge and Learning, but the Reason is because the Subjects are many of them rich and wealthy, the Prince not thinking fit to exert himself in his full Tyranny like the Princes of the Eastern Nations, least his Subjects should be invited to new-mould their Constitution, having so many Prospects of Liberty within their View. But[a] in all Despotic Governments, tho' a particular Prince may favour Arts and Letters, there is a natural Degeneracy of Mankind, as you may observe from *Augustus*'s Reign, how the *Romans* lost themselves by Degrees, till they fell to an Equality with the most barbarous Nations that surrounded them. Look upon *Greece* under its free States, and you would think its Inhabitants lived in different Climates, and under different Heavens, from those at present; so different are the Genius's which are formed under *Turkish* Slavery, and *Grecian* Liberty.

Besides Poverty and Want, there are other Reasons that debase the Minds of Men, who live under Slavery, though I look on this as the Principal. This natural Tendency of Despotic Power to Ignorance and Barbarity, tho' not insisted upon by others, is, I think, an unanswerable Argument against that Form of Government, as it shows how repugnant it is to the Good of Mankind and the Perfection of human Nature, which ought to be the great Ends of all Civil Institutions.   L

---

[a] View. But] View; but *Fol.*

> . . . *Pavor est utrique molestus.*
>
> Hor.

Mr. SPECTATOR,

'WHEN you spoke of the Jilts and Coquets, you then promised
to be very impartial, and not to spare even your own Sex,[2]
should any of their secret or open Faults come under your Cognizance; which has given me Encouragement to describe a certain
Species of Mankind under the Denomination of *Male Jilts.* They are
Gentlemen who do not design to marry, yet, that they may appear
to have some Sense of Gallantry, think they must pay their *Devoirs*
to one particular Fair; in order to which they single out from
amongst the Herd of Females her to whom they design to make
their fruitless Addresses. This done, they first take every Opportunity of being in her Company, and then never fail upon all
Occasions to be particular to her, laying themselves at her Feet,
protesting the Reality of their Passion with a thousand Oaths,
solliciting a Return, and saying as many fine things as their Stock
of Wit will allow; and if they are not deficient that way, generally
speak so as to admit of a double Interpretation; which the credulous
Fair is too apt to turn to her own Advantage, since it frequently
happens to be a raw, innocent, young Creature, who thinks all the
World as sincere as her self; and so her unwary Heart becomes an
easy Prey to those deceitful Monsters, who no sooner perceive it,
but immediately they grow cool, and shun her whom they before
seem'd so much to admire, and proceed to act the same commonplace Villany towards another. A Coxcomb flushed with many of
these infamous Victories shall say he is sorry for the poor Fools,
protest and vow he never thought of Matrimony, and wonder
talking civilly can be so strangely misinterpreted. Now, Mr.
SPECTATOR, you that are a professed Friend to Love, will, I hope,
observe upon those who abuse that noble Passion, and raise it in

---

[1] *Motto.* Horace, *Epistles,* 1. 6. 10 (altered): Both sides feel uneasy fears.

[2] The chief discussion of jilts occurs in the letter from Charles Yellow in No. 187
(vol. ii), but the specific promise of impartial criticism of both sexes which
'Melainia' mentions does not appear. It is, however, consistent with the general
point of view of Mr. Spectator; in No. 4 he had announced his endeavour 'to make
both Sexes appear in their Conduct what they are in their Hearts'. One concludes
that this is a letter invented by Steele in order to introduce the discussion which
follows.

innocent Minds by a deceitful Affectation of it, after which they desert the Enamoured. Pray bestow a little of your Counsel to those fond believing Females who already have or are in Danger of broken Hearts; in which you will oblige a great Part of this Town, but in a particular Manner,

SIR,

Your (yet Heart-whole) Admirer,
and devoted humble Servant,
Melainia.'

Melainia's Complaint is occasioned by so general a Folly, that it is wonderful one could so long overlook it. But this false Gallantry proceeds from an Impotence of Mind, which makes those who are guilty of it incapable of pursuing what they themselves approve. Many a Man wishes a Woman his Wife whom he dare not take for such. Tho' no one has Power over his Inclinations or Fortunes, he is a Slave to common Fame. For this Reason I think *Melainia* gives them too soft a Name in that of Male Coquets. I know not why Irresolution of Mind should not be more contemptible than Impotence of Body; and these frivolous Admirers would be but tenderly used, in being only included in the same Term with the Insufficient another Way. They whom my Correspondent calls Male Coquets, shall hereafter be called *Friblers.*[1] A Fribler is one who professes Rapture and Admiration for the Woman to whom he addresses, and dreads nothing so much as her Consent. His Heart can flutter by the Force of Imagination, but cannot fix from the Force of Judgment.

[1] The verb *to frible* had been in use since the early seventeenth century, first with the meaning 'to falter, stammer; totter in walking' (used in this sense by Steele in *Tatler* 49), and later 'to act aimlessly or feebly, to busy oneself to no purpose' (*OED*). One of the characters (Faschinetti) in Charles Johnson's farce, *Love in a Chest* (1710), is called an 'Impotent Fribler' (I. i). A letter signed Will. Grible (*sic*) and dated 30 Jan. 1712 (Lillie, ii. 192) testifies to the effect of this essay on Fribblers.

Your paper of this day has ruined all my designs towards one, whom I had free toleration to visit at my own pleasure; but calling to day, and being seated in the parlour next the old gentleman (who you must know I never designed should be my father-in-law) I very briskly asked him, what was the best news? he very gravely told me he had a great piece of news to tell me, which was this, That if I designed to make his daughter my wife, I should be welcome to his house as formerly, if not, he desired I would never come over the threshold of his door. I give you (says he) till Sunday to consider of it. I said little to the purpose, finding my self disappointed in my design. At my parting, my mistress softly told me, I might thank Mr. Spectator for what had happened; so that I find your paper of this day will be as remarkable to some people as the m—— of K—— C—— is to

Your disappointed servant,
WILL. GRIBLE.

It is not uncommon for the Parents of young Women of moderate Fortune to wink at the Addresses of Friblers, and expose their Children to the ambiguous Behaviour which *Melainia* complains of, till by the Fondness to one they are to lose, they become incapable of Love towards others, and by Consequence in their future Marriage lead a joyless or a miserable Life. As therefore I shall in the Speculations which regard Love be as severe as I ought on Jilts and libertine Women, so will I be as little merciful to insignificant and mischievous Men. In order to this all Visitants who frequent Families wherein there are young Females, are forthwith required to declare themselves, or absent[1] from Places where their Presence banishes such as would pass their Time more to the Advantage of those whom they visit. It is a Matter of too great Moment to be dallied with; and I shall expect from all my young People a satisfactory Account of Appearances. *Strephon* has from the Publication hereof seven Days to explain the Riddle he presented to *Eudamia*; and *Chloris* an Hour after this comes to her Hand, to declare whether she will have *Philotas*, whom a Woman of no less Merit than her self, and of superiour Fortune, languishes to call her own.

To the SPECTATOR.

SIR,

'SINCE so many Dealers turn Authors, and write quaint Advertisements in Praise of their Wares, one, who from an Author turned Dealer, may be allowed for the Advancement of Trade to turn Author again.[2] I will not however set up, like some of 'em, for selling cheaper than the most able honest Tradesmen can; nor do I send this to be better known for Choice and Cheapness of China and Japan-Wares, Tea, Fans, Muslins, Pictures, Arrack, and other *Indian* Goods. Placed as I am in *Leaden-hall-street* near the *India-Company*, and the Centre of that Trade, Thanks to my fair Customers,

---

[1] Used here in the intransitive obsolete sense, 'to be or stay away'. Cf. *OED*.

[2] Peter Anthony Motteux (1663–1718) came to England from France in 1685, conducted the *Gentleman's Journal*, translated Rabelais and *Don Quixote*, and wrote several plays and opera librettos before opening his shop in Leadenhall Street. He was a friend of Steele, and in 1705 had been associated with Clayton, Dieupart, and Haym in the composition of *Arsinoe* (cf. No. 18, vol. i). He is probably the gentleman of *Tatler* 106 who, after 'some Years devoted . . . wholly to the Muses', announces his intention of applying himself to business. In the *Daily Courant* of 2 Apr. 1711 he offers a reward of two guineas for cloths, &c., taken 'from a Counter in a China-Shop in Leaden-hall-street'. In *Guardian* 114 Addison speaks of 'my ingenious friend Mr. Motteux's' as a place 'frequented by the wits and beauties of the sex'. There are no advertisements by Motteux in the *Spectator*. See further the study of Motteux by R. N. Cunningham (Oxford, 1933).

my Ware-house is graced as well as the Benefit Days of my Plays and Operas; and the foreign Goods I sell seem no less acceptable than the foreign Books I translated, *Rabelais* and Don *Quixote*: This the Criticks allow me, and while they like my Wares they may dispraise my Writing. But as 'tis not so well known yet that I frequently cross the Seas of late, and speaking *Dutch* and *French*, besides other Languages, I have the Conveniency of buying and importing rich Brocades, *Dutch* Atlasses,[1] with Gold and Silver or without, and other foreign Silks of the newest Modes and best Fabricks, fine *Flanders* Lace, Linnens, and Pictures at the best Hand.[2] This my new way of Trade I have fallen into I cannot better publish than by an Application to you. My Wares are fit only for such as your Readers; and I would beg of you to print this Address in your Paper, that those whose Minds you adorn may take the Ornaments for their Persons and Houses from me. This, Sir, if I may presume to beg it, will be the greater Favour, as I have lately receiv'd rich Silks and fine Lace to a considerable Value, which will be sold cheap for a quick Return, and as I have also a large Stock of other Goods. *Indian* Silks were formerly a great Branch of our Trade; and since we must not sell 'em, we must seek Amends by dealing in others. This I hope will plead for one who would lessen the Number of Teazers of the Muses, and who, suiting his Spirit to his Circumstances, humbles the Poet to exalt the Citizen. Like a true Tradesman I hardly ever look into any Books but those of Accompts. To say the Truth, I cannot, I think, give you a better Idea of my being a downright Man of Traffick, than by acknowledging I oftner read the Advertisements, than the Matter of even your Paper. I am under a very great Temptation to take this Opportunity of admonishing other Writers to follow my Example, and trouble the Town no more; but as it is my present Business to encrease the Number of Buyers rather than Sellers, I hasten to tell you that I am,

SIR,

Your most humble,
and most obedient Servant,

Peter Motteux.'

T

---

[1] A silk-satin manufactured in the East. In Shadwell's *Bury Fair* (II. ii) the Indian-Gownman advertises 'Fine Morning Gowns, very rich *Indian* Stuffs; choice of fine Atlasses . . .'.

[2] At the best hand, i.e. most profitably or cheaply. The last quotation in *OED* is dated 1811.

Vitæ summa brevis spem nos vetat incohare longam.

Hor.

UPON taking my Seat in a Coffee-house I often draw the Eyes of the whole Room upon me, when in the hottest Seasons of News, and at a time that perhaps the *Dutch* Mail is just come in, they hear me ask the Coffee-man for his last Week's Bill of Mortality:[2] I find that I have been sometimes taken on this occasion for a Parish Sexton, sometimes for an Undertaker, and sometimes for a Doctor of Physick. In this, however, I am guided by the Spirit of a Philosopher, as I take occasion from hence to reflect upon the regular Encrease and Diminution of Mankind,[3] and consider the several various ways through which we pass from Life to Eternity. I am very well pleased with these Weekly Admonitions, that bring into my Mind such Thoughts as ought to be the daily Entertainment of every reasonable Creature;[a] and can consider with Pleasure to my self, by which of those Deliverances, or, as we commonly call them, Distempers, I may possibly make my Escape out of this World of Sorrows, into that Condition of Existence, wherein I hope to be happier than it is possible for me at present to conceive.

But this is not all the use I make of the above-mentioned Weekly Paper. A Bill of Mortality is in my Opinion an unanswerable Argument for a Providence; how can we, without supposing our selves under the constant Care of a Supreme Being, give any possible Account for that nice proportion which we find in every great City, between the Deaths and Births of its Inhabitants, and between the number of Males, and that of Females, who are brought into the World? What else cou'd adjust in so exact a manner the Recruits of

[a] Creature;] Creature, *Fol.*

---

[1] *Motto.* Horace, *Odes,* I. 4. 15:
   Life's span forbids Thee to extend thy Cares,
   And stretch thy Hopes beyond thy Years. CREECH.

[2] Bills of mortality, issued every Wednesday by the London Company of Parish Clerks, gave the weekly number of christenings and deaths. See Miege, p. 137.

[3] It was only in the mid-eighteenth century, with advances in medical knowledge, that the population of England began to rise with startling rapidity. Cf. Trevelyan, i. 74.

every Nation to its Losses,[1] and divide these new Supplies of People into such equal Bodies of both Sexes? Chance could never hold the Balance with so steady a hand. Were we not counted out by an intelligent Supervisor, we should sometimes be over-charg'd with Multitudes, and at others waste away into a Desart: We should be sometimes a *populus virorum*, as *Florus* elegantly expresses it[2], *a Generation of Males*, and at others a Species of Women. We may extend this Consideration to every Species of living Creatures, and consider the whole Animal World as an huge Army made up of an innumerable *Corps*,[a][3] if I may use that term, whose Quota's have been kept entire near five thousand Years, in so wonderful a manner, that there is not probably a single Species lost during this long tract of Time. Could we have general Bills of Mortality of every kind of Animal, or particular ones of every Species in each Continent and Island, I could almost say in every Wood, Marsh or Mountain, what astonishing Instances would they be of that Providence which watches over all its Works?

I have heard of a great Man in the *Romish* Church, who upon reading those Words in the fifth Chapter of *Genesis*, *And all the days that* Adam *lived were nine hundred and thirty Years, and he died; and all the days of* Seth *were nine hundred and twelve Years, and he died; and all the days of* Methusalah *were nine hundred and sixty nine Years, and he died;* immediately shut himself up in a Convent, and retired from the World, as not thinking any thing in this Life worth pursuing, which had not regard to another.[4]

The truth of it is, there is nothing in History which is so improving to the Reader as those Accounts which we meet with of the

---

[a] of an innumerable *Corps*,] *12mo*; of innumerable Corps, *Fol.*, *8vo*

---

[1] Bossuet in his sermon *Sur la mort* had used the same figure, with a different application: 'Cette recrue continuelle du genre humain, je veux dire les enfants qui naissent, à mesure qu'ils croissent et qu'ils s'avancent, semblent nous pousser de l'épaule, et nous dire: Retirez-vous, c'est maintenant notre tour' (*Sermons choisis*, Paris, 1901, p. 293).

[2] Lucius Annaeus Florus, *Epitome*, I. I. 10. The phrase is quoted by Bayle, art. Abelard, Remark F.

[3] A new term in English. See No. 165 (vol. ii).

[4] The story is No. 174 in L'Estrange's *Fables and Stories Moralized* (1699), p. 163:

'Tis written in the *Fifth* of *Genesis*, that all the Days that *Adam* liv'd, were *Nine Hundred and Thirty Years*, and he DY'D: and *all the Days of* Seth *were Nine Hundred and Twelve Years*, and he DY'D: the Days of *Enos* were *Nine Hundred and Five Years*, and he DY'D. The Days of *Methusalem* were *Nine Hundred and Sixty Nine Years*, and HE DY'D. One *Guericus*, upon the bare hearing of This Chapter read; quitted the World, and Retir'd.

Deaths of eminent Persons, and of their Behaviour in that dreadful Season. I may also add, that there are no parts in History which affect and please the Reader in so sensible a manner. The Reason I take to be this, because there is no other single Circumstance in the Story of any Person which can possibly be the case of every one who reads it. A Battel or a Triumph are Conjunctures in which not one Man in a Million is likely to be engaged; but when we see a Person at the point of Death, we cannot forbear being attentive to every thing he says or does, because we are sure, that some time or other we shall our selves be in the same melancholy Circumstances. The General, the Statesman, or the Philosopher, are perhaps Characters which we may never act in; but the dying Man is one whom, sooner or later, we shall certainly resemble.

It is, perhaps, for the same kind of Reason that few Books, written[a] in *English*, have been so much perused as Doctor *Sherlock*'s Discourse upon Death; though at the same time I must own, that he, who has not perused this Excellent Piece, has not perhaps read one of the strongest Persuasives to a Religious Life that was ever written in any Language.[1]

The Consideration, with which I shall close this Essay upon Death, is[b] one of the most ancient and most beaten Morals that has been recommended to Mankind. But its being so very common, and so universally received, though it takes away from it the Grace of Novelty, adds very much to the Weight of it, as it shews that it falls in with the general Sense of Mankind. In short, I would have every one consider, that he is in this Life nothing more than a Passenger, and that he is not to set up his Rest here, but to keep an attentive Eye upon that State of Being to which he approaches every Moment, and which will be for ever fixed and permanent. This single Consideration would be sufficient to extinguish the Bitterness of Hatred, the Thirst of Avarice, and the Cruelty of Ambition.

I am very much pleased with the Passage of *Antiphanes*, a very ancient Poet, who lived near an hundred Years before *Socrates*, which represents the Life of Man under this View, as I have here translated it Word for Word. *Be not grieved*, says he, *above measure*,

---

[a] written] which have been written *Fol.*   [b] is] is, *Fol.*

---

[1] *A Practical Discourse concerning Death* (1689), by William Sherlock, Master of the Temple, went through many editions in the early eighteenth century.

for thy deceased Friends. They[a] *are not dead, but have only finished that Journey which it is necessary for every one of us to take: We our selves must go to that great Place of Reception in which they are all of them assembled, and, in this general Rendezvous of Mankind, live together in another State of Being.*[1]

I think I have, in a former Paper,[2] taken notice of those beautiful Metaphors in Scripture,[3] where Life is termed a Pilgrimage, and those who pass through it are called Strangers, and Sojourners upon Earth. I shall conclude this with a Story, which I have some where read in the Travels of Sir *John Chardin;*[4] that Gentleman, after having told us, that the Inns which receive the Caravans in *Persia,* and the Eastern Countries, are called by the Name of *Caravansaries,* gives us a Relation to the following Purpose.

A *Dervise,* travelling through *Tartary,* being arrived at the Town of *Balk,* went into the King's Palace by a Mistake, as thinking it to be a publick Inn or Caravansary. Having looked about him for some time, he entered into a long Gallery, where he laid down his Wallet, and spread his Carpet, in order to repose himself upon it after the manner of the Eastern Nations. He had not been long in this Posture before he was discovered by some of the Guards, who asked him what was his Business in that place? The *Dervise* told them, he intended to take up his Night's Lodging in that Caravansary. The Guards let him know, in a very angry manner, that the House he was in, was not a Caravansary, but the King's Palace. It happened that the King himself passed through the Gallery during this Debate, and smiling at the Mistake of the *Dervise,* asked him how he could possibly be so dull as not to distinguish a Palace from a Caravansary? Sir, says the *Dervise,* give me leave to ask your

[a] *Friends. They*] *Friends; for they* Fol.

---

[1] See Meineke, *Fragmenta Comicorum Graecorum,* iii. 29. The passage is No. vi in the quotations from Antiphanes in Winterton, *Poetae Minores Graeci* (ed. Cambridge, 1677), p. 483. As editors have noted, Antiphanes lived a hundred years later than Socrates, rather than a hundred years earlier. The error probably derives from Winterton, who places Antiphanes at the time of Thespis, i.e. sixth century B.C.

[2] No. 219 (vol. ii).

[3] Gen. xlvii. 9; Ps. xxxix. 12.

[4] The first and only volume of the translation (*The Travels of Sir John Chardin into Persia and the East Indies,* 1686) does not contain the anecdote. It is to be found, however, in the French edition of Chardin's travels (*Voyages en Perse, et autres lieux de l'Orient*) published at Amsterdam in 1711 (10 vols., 12mo), at vol. ii, pp. 209–10. Addison follows the French text closely, so that his statement of having 'some where read' this in Chardin is perhaps a little disingenuous. He may possibly have read it in a review of the first three volumes of Chardin in the *Bibliothèque Choisie,* xxiii (1711), 369–70.

Majesty a Question or two. Who were the Persons that lodged in this House when it was first Built? the King replied, *His Ancestors*. And who, says the *Dervise*, was the last Person that lodged here? The King replied, *His Father*. And who is it, says the *Dervise*, that lodges here at present? the King told him *that it was he himself*. And who, says the *Dervise*, will be here after you? The King answer'd, *The young Prince his Son*. 'Ah Sir, said the *Dervise*, a House that changes its Inhabitants so often, and receives such a perpetual Succession of Guests, is not a Palace but a *Caravansary*.'

L

No. 290   *Friday, February* 1, 1712[1]

[STEELE]

Projicit ampullas & sesquipedalia verba.
            Hor.

THE Players, who know I am very much their Friend, take all Opportunities to express a Gratitude to me for being so. They could not have a better Occasion of obliging me, than one which they lately took Hold of. They desired my Friend WILL. HONEYCOMB to bring me to the Reading of a new Tragedy, it is called *The distressed Mother*.[2] I must confess, tho' some Days are passed since I enjoyed that Entertainment, the Passions of the several Characters dwell strongly upon my Imagination; and I congratulate to the Age, that they are at last to see Truth and humane Life represented in the Incidents which concern Heroes and Heroines.

[1] *Motto*. Horace, *Ars poetica*, 97:
         Forget their swelling and gigantick Words. ROSCOMMON.
The motto in the original Folio sheets was Horace, *Epistles*, 2. 1. 166 (used for *Tatler* 99): Spirat Tragicum satis, & feliciter Audet (He has some tragic inspiration, and is happy in his ventures).
[2] *The Distressed Mother*, a version of Racine's *Andromaque* by Ambrose Philips, was first acted on 17 Mar. 1712 at Drury Lane and had an initial run of eight performances (17, 18, 20, 22, 24, 25, 27, and 29 Mar.). It was published on 28 Mar. (advertised in No. 338) by Buckley and Tonson, with a dedication to the Duchess of Montague, in which her illustrious father the Duke of Marlborough is compared to Hector. The part of Pyrrhus was taken by Booth and that of Andromache by Mrs. Oldfield. The Prologue was written by Steele and the Epilogue by Budgell, possibly with the help of Addison. Philips had already been praised in Nos. 223 and 229 (vol. ii), and *The Distressed Mother* is again discussed in No. 335.

The Stile of the Play is such as becomes those of the first Education, and the Sentiments worthy those of the highest Figure. It was a most exquisite Pleasure to me, to observe real Tears drop from the Eyes of those who had long made it their Profession to dissemble Affliction; and the Player who read, frequently throw down the Book, till he had given Vent to the Humanity which rose in him at some irresistible Touches of the imagined Sorrow. We have seldom had any Female Distress on the Stage, which did not, upon cool Examination, appear to flow from the Weakness rather than the Misfortune of the Person represented: But in this Tragedy you are not entertained with the ungoverned Passions of such as are enamoured of each other meerly as they are Men and Women, but their Regards are founded upon high Conceptions of each other's Virtue and Merit; and the Character which gives Name to the Play, is one who has behaved her self with heroick Virtue in the most important Circumstances of a female Life, those of a Wife, a Widow, and a Mother.[1] If there be those whose Minds have been too attentive upon the Affairs of Life, to have any Notion of the Passion of Love in such Extremes as are known only to particular Tempers, yet in the above-mentioned Considerations, the Sorrow of the Heroine will move even the Generality of Mankind. Domestick Virtues concern all the World, and there is no one living who is not interested that *Andromache* should be an imitable Character. The generous Affection to the Memory of her deceased Husband, that tender Care for her Son, which is ever heightned with the Consideration of his Father, and these Regards preserved in spite of being tempted with the Possession of the highest Greatness, are what cannot but be venerable even to such an Audience as at present frequents the *English* Theatre. My Friend WILL. HONEYCOMB commended several tender things that were said, and told me they were very genteel; but whispered me, that he feared the Piece was not busy enough for the present Taste. To supply this, he recommended to the Players to be very careful in their Scenes, and above all things, that every Part should be perfectly new dress'd. I was very glad to find they did not neglect my Friend's Admonition, because there are a great many in his Class of Criticism who may be gained by it; but indeed the Truth is, that as to the

---

[1] The Preface notes that the life of Astyanax is a little prolonged in the play in order 'to heighten in *Andromache* the Character of a tender Mother, an affectionate Wife, and a Widow full of Veneration for the Memory of her deceased Husband'.

Work it self, it is every where Nature. The Persons are of the highest Quality in Life, even that of Princes; but their Quality is not represented by the Poet with Direction that Guards and Waiters[1] should follow them in every Scene, but their Grandeur appears in Greatness of Sentiment, flowing from Minds worthy their Condition.[2] To make a Character truly Great, this Author understands that it should have its Foundation in superiour Thoughts and Maxims of Conduct. It is very certain, that many an honest Woman would make no Difficulty, tho' she had been the Wife of *Hector*, for the Sake of a Kingdom, to marry the Enemy of her Husband's Family and Country; and indeed who can deny but she might be still an honest Woman, but no Heroine? That may be defensible, nay laudable, in one Character, which would be in the highest Degree exceptionable in another. When *Cato Uticensis* killed himself, *Cottius*, a *Roman* of ordinary Quality and Character, did the same thing; upon which one said, smiling, '*Cottius* might have lived tho' *Cæsar* has siezed the *Roman* Liberty.' *Cottius*'s Condition might have been the same, let things at the upper End of the World pass as they would. What is further very extraordinary in this Work, is, that the Persons are all of them laudable, and their Misfortunes arise rather from unguarded Virtue than Propensity to Vice. The Town has an Opportunity of doing it self Justice in supporting the Representations of Passion, Sorrow, Indignation, even Despair it self, within the Rules of Decency, Honour, and good Breeding; and since there is no one can flatter himself his Life will be always fortunate, they may here see Sorrow as they would wish to bear it whenever it arrives.

---

[1] In the Prologue Steele says of Pyrrhus

> His Sentiments confess a Royal Mind,
> Nor is he known a King from Guards behind.

The last quotation for *waiter* in this sense in *OED* is dated 1714.

[2] Cf. the opening lines of Philips's Preface:

In all the Works of Genius and Invention, whether in Verse or Prose, there are in general but two Manners of Style; the one simple, natural and easie; the other swelling, forced, and unnatural. An injudicious Affectation of Sublimity is what has betrayed a great many Authors into the latter; not considering that real Greatness in Writing, as well as in Manners, consists in an unaffected Simplicity. The true Sublime does not lie in strained Metaphors and the Pomp of Words; but rises out of noble Sentiments and strong Images of Nature; which will always appear the more conspicuous, when the Language does not swell to hide and overshadow them. These are the Considerations, that have induced me to write this Tragedy in a Style very different from what has been usually practised amongst us in Poems of this Nature.

Mr. SPECTATOR,

'I AM appointed to act a Part in the new Tragedy, called *The distressed Mother*: It is the celebrated Grief of *Orestes* which I am to personate; but I shall not act as I ought, for I shall feel it too intimately to be able to utter it. I was last night repeating a Paragraph to my self, which I took to be an Expression of Rage, and in the Middle of the Sentence there was a Stroke of Self-pity which quite unmanned me.[1] Be pleased, Sir, to print this Letter, that when I am oppressed in this Manner at such an Interval, a certain Part of the Audience may not think I am out; and I hope with this Allowance to do it to Satisfaction.

I am,

SIR,

Your most humble Servant,

George Powell.'[2]

Mr. SPECTATOR,

'AS I was walking t'other Day in the *Park*, I saw a Gentleman with a very short Face; I desire to know whether it was you. Pray inform me assoon as you can, lest I become the most heroick *Hecatissa*'s[3] Rival.

Your humble Servant to Command,

Sophia.'

Dear Madam,

'IT is not me you are in love with, for I was very ill, and kept my Chamber all that Day.

Your most humble Servant,

The SPECTATOR.'

T

---

[1] Powell, who took the part of Orestes, is probably referring here to III. i, the scene between Orestes and his friend Pylades (played by Mills).

[2] *A Modest Survey of that Celebrated Tragedy The Distrest Mother, So often and so highly Applauded by the Ingenious Spectator* (Printed and Sold by William Redmayne in Jewenstreet, and John Morphew near Stationers-hall, 1712) criticizes Philips's play for thinness of thought and style, unnaturalness of characterization, and clumsiness of plot—all the more surprising, says the author, after 'so profuse a Recommendation given it, so long before its publick Appearance, by the most Ingenious *Spectator*' (p. 3). The anonymous critic pays tribute to the far-reaching effect of Mr. Spectator's judgment on plays; even this *Modest Survey*, he says, 'shall appear not so much an Affront to his *Judgment*, as a Congratulation of his POWER, when a Stroke of his Ingenious Pen could carry so Universal a Sway o'er the Town in Favour to that Play' (p. 7). The *Modest Survey* was published on 22 May 1712 (advertisement in *Post Boy*).

[3] See Nos. 48 and 79 (vol. i).

[ADDISON]

> . . . *Ubi plura nitent in carmine, non ego paucis*
> *Offendar maculis, quas aut Incuria fudit,*
> *Aut Humana parum cavit Natura* . . .
>
> Hor.

I HAVE now consider'd *Milton's Paradise Lost* under those four great Heads of the Fable, the Characters, the Sentiments, and the Language; and have shewn that he excels, in general, under each of these Heads. I hope that I have made several Discoveries which[a] may appear new, even to those who are versed in Critical Learning. Were I indeed to chuse my Readers, by whose Judgment I would stand or fall, they should not be such as are acquainted only with the *French* and *Italian* Criticks, but also with the Ancient and Modern[b] who have written in either of the learned Languages. Above all, I would have them well versed in the *Greek* and *Latin* Poets, without which a Man very often fancies that he understands a Critick, when in reality he does not comprehend his Meaning.

It is in Criticism, as in all other Sciences and Speculations; one who brings with him any implicit Notions and Observations which he has made in his reading of the Poets, will find his own Reflections methodized and explained, and perhaps several little Hints that had passed in his Mind, perfected and improved in the Works of a good Critick; whereas one who has not these previous Lights, is very often an utter Stranger to what he reads, and apt to put a wrong Interpretation upon it.

Nor is it sufficient, that a Man who sets up for a Judge in Criticism, should have perused the Authors above-mentioned, unless he has also a clear and Logical Head. Without this Talent he is perpetually puzzled and perplexed amidst his own Blunders, mistakes the Sense of those he would confute, or if he chances to think right, does not know how to convey his Thoughts to another with Clearness and Perspicuity. *Aristotle*, who was the best Critick, was also one of the best Logicians that ever appeared in the World.

---

^a which] that *Fol.*   ^b Modern] *19*; Moderns *Fol., 8vo, 12mo*

---

1 *Motto.* Horace, *Ars poetica,* 351–3:
>   If *numerous Graces* shine in what he writes,
>   I'le not condemn tho some few Faults appear,
>   Which common frailty leaves, or want of Care. CREECH.

Mr. *Lock*'s Essay on Human Understanding would be thought a very odd Book for a Man to make himself Master of, who would get a Reputation by Critical Writings; though at the same time it is very certain, that an Author who has not learn'd the Art of distinguishing between Words and Things, and of ranging his Thoughts, and setting them in proper Lights, whatever Notions he may have, will lose himself in Confusion and Obscurity. I might further observe, that there is not a *Greek* or *Latin* Critick who has not shewn, even in the stile of his Criticisms, that he was a Master of all the Elegance and Delicacy of his Native Tongue.

The truth of it is, there is nothing more absurd, than for a Man to set up for a Critick, without a good Insight into all the Parts of Learning; whereas many of those who have endeavoured to signalize themselves by Works of this Nature among our *English* Writers, are not only defective in the above-mentioned Particulars, but plainly discover by the Phrases which they make use of, and by their confused way of thinking, that they are not acquainted with the most common and ordinary Systems of Arts and Sciences. A few general Rules extracted out of the *French* Authors, with a certain Cant of Words, has sometimes set up an Illiterate heavy Writer for a most judicious and formidable Critick.

One great Mark, by which you may discover a Critick who has neither Taste nor Learning, is this, that he seldom ventures to praise any Passage in an Author which has not been before received and applauded by the Publick,[1] and that his Criticism turns wholly upon little Faults and Errors. This part of a Critick is so very easie to succeed in, that we find every ordinary Reader, upon the publishing of a new Poem, has Wit and Ill-nature enough to turn several Passages of it into Ridicule, and very often in the right Place. This Mr. *Dryden* has very agreeably remarked in those two celebrated Lines,

> *Errors, like Straws, upon the Surface flow;*
> *He who would search for Pearls must dive below.*[2]

A true Critick ought to dwell rather upon Excellencies than Imperfections, to discover the concealed Beauties of a Writer, and

---

[1] Cf. Pope, *Essay on Criticism*, 408–9:

> Some ne'er advance a judgment of their own,
> But catch the spreading notion of the town.

[2] Dryden, *All for Love, Prologue*, 25–26.

communicate to the World such things as are worth their Observation.[1] The most exquisite Words and finest Strokes of an Author are those which very often appear the most doubtful and exceptionable, to a Man who wants a Relish for polite Learning; and they are these, which a sower undistinguishing Critick[2] generally attacks with the greatest Violence. *Tully* observes, that it is very easie to brand or fix a Mark upon what he calls *Verbum ardens*, or, as it may be rendered into *English, a glowing bold Expression*, and to turn it into Ridicule by a cold ill-natured Criticism.[3] A little Wit is equally capable of exposing a Beauty, and of aggravating a Fault; and though such a Treatment of an Author naturally produces Indignation in the Mind of an understanding Reader, it has however its effect among the generality of those whose Hands it falls into, the Rabble of Mankind being very apt to think that every thing which is laughed at with any mixture of Wit, is ridiculous in it self.

Such a Mirth as this, is always unseasonable in a Critick, as it rather prejudices the Reader than convinces him, and is capable of making a Beauty, as well as a Blemish, the Subject of Derision. A Man, who cannot write with Wit on a proper Subject, is dull and stupid, but one who shews it in an improper place, is as impertinent and absurd. Besides, a Man who has the Gift of Ridicule is apt[a] to find Fault with any thing that gives him an Opportunity of exerting his beloved Talent, and very often censures a Passage, not because there is any Fault in it, but because he can be merry upon it. Such kinds of Pleasantry are very unfair and disingenuous in Works of Criticism, in which the greatest Masters, both Ancient and Modern, have always appeared with a serious and instructive Air.

As I intend in my next Paper to shew the Defects in *Milton's Paradise Lost*, I thought fit to premise these few Particulars, to the End that the Reader may know I enter upon it, as on a very ungrateful Work, and that I shall just point at the Imperfections, without

---

[a] apt] very apt *Fol.*

[1] Addison's position is close to that of Dryden, who wrote in the Preface to *The State of Innocence* (1677): 'They wholly mistake the nature of criticism who think its business is principally to find fault. Criticism, as it was first instituted by Aristotle, was meant a standard of judging well; the chiefest part of which is, to observe those excellencies which should delight a reasonable reader' (Ker, i. 179).

[2] Contemporary readers doubtless saw in this a reference to John Dennis, the 'Critick of the Woful Countenance' of the *Critical Specimen* (1711), probably by Pope, and the butt of much contemporary sarcasm (see Hooker, ii, pp. lvii–lviii). Hooker quotes from the *Examiner* of 10 Jan. 1712 a reference to Dennis as 'an old sowr dry Critick'. [3] Cicero, *Ad Marcum Brutum Orator*, 8. 27.

endeavouring to enflame them with Ridicule. I must also observe with *Longinus*, that the Productions of a great Genius, with many Lapses and Inadvertencies, are infinitely preferable to the Works of an inferior kind of Author, which are scrupulously exact and conformable to all the Rules of correct Writing.[1]

I shall conclude my Paper with a Story out of *Boccalini*,[2] which sufficiently shews us the Opinion that Judicious Author entertained of the sort of Criticks I have been here mentioning. A famous Critick, says he, having gathered together all the Faults of an Eminent Poet, made a Present of them to *Apollo*, who received them very graciously, and resolved to make the Author a suitable Return for the Trouble he had been at in collecting them. In order to this, he set before him a Sack of Wheat, as it had been just threshed out of the Sheaf. He then bid him pick out the Chaff from among the Corn, and lay it aside by it self. The Critick applied himself to the Task with great Industry and Pleasure, and after having made the due Separation, was presented by *Apollo* with the Chaff for his Pains. L

No. 292   *Monday, February 4, 1712*[3]

Illam, quicquid agit, quoquo Vestigia flectit,
Componit furtim, subsequiturque decor.
                                        Tibull. L. 4.

AS no one can be said to enjoy Health, who is only not sick, without he feel within himself a lightsome and invigorating Principle, which will not suffer him to remain idle, but still spurs him on to Action; so in the Practice of every Virtue, there is some additional Grace required, to give a Claim of excelling in this or that

[1] *On the Sublime*, 33 (chap. 27 in Boileau's translation). Dryden in the passage from the Preface to *The State of Innocence* cited above had also referred to Longinus, who 'has judiciously preferred the sublime genius that sometimes errs, to the middling or indifferent one, which makes few faults, but seldom or never rises to any excellence' (Ker, i. 180).

[2] *Advices from Parnassus in Two Centuries ... translated from the Italian by several hands: Revis'd and Corrected by Mr. Hughes* (1706), pp. 184–5. The anecdote here summarized is the last article in the first 'century'.

[3] *Motto.* Tibullus, *Elegies*, 4. 2. 7–8 (altered):

> Whate'er she does, where'er her steps she bends,
> **Grace on each action silently attends.**

particular Action. A Diamond may want polishing, though the Value be still intrinsically the same; and the same Good may be done with different Degrees of Lustre. No Man should be contented with himself that he barely does well, but he should perform every thing in the best and most becoming Manner that he is able.

Tully tells us, he wrote his Book of *Offices*, because there was no Time of Life in which some correspondent Duty might not be practis'd;[1] nor is there a Duty without a certain Decency accompanying it, by which every Virtue 'tis joined to will seem to be doubled. Another may do the same thing, and yet the Action want that Air and Beauty which distinguish it from others; like that inimitable Sun-shine *Titian* is said to have diffus'd over his Landschapes; which denotes them his, and has been always unequall'd by any other Person.

There is no one Action in which this Quality I am speaking of will be more sensibly perceived, than in granting a Request, or doing an Office of Kindness. *Mummius*, by his Way of consenting to a Benefaction, shall make it lose its Name; while *Carus* doubles the Kindness and the Obligation: From the first the desir'd Request drops indeed at last, but from so doubtful a Brow, that the obliged has almost as much reason to resent the Manner of bestowing it, as to be thankful for the Favour it self. *Carus* invites with a pleasing Air, to give him an Opportunity of doing an Act of Humanity, meets the Petition half Way, and consents to a Request with a Countenance which proclaims the Satisfaction of his Mind in assisting the Distressed.

The Decency then that is to be observed in Liberality, seems to consist in its being performed with such Cheerfulness, as may express the godlike Pleasure is to be met with in obliging one's Fellow-Creatures; that may shew good Nature and Benevolence overflow'd, and do not, as in some Men, run upon the Tilt,[2] and Taste of the Sediments of a grutching[3] uncommunicative Disposition.

Since I have intimated that the greatest Decorum is to be preserved in the bestowing our good Offices, I will illustrate it a little by an Example drawn from private Life, which carries with it such a Profusion of Liberality, that it can be exceeded by nothing but the Humanity and good Nature which accompanies it. It is a Letter

[1] *De Officiis*, 1. 2. 4.
[2] The figure is of a cask or wine-vessel raised on one side when nearly empty.
[3] Grumbling, complaining; reluctant. This is the last quotation to illustrate this meaning in *OED*.

of *Pliny's*, which I shall here translate, because the Action will best appear in its first Dress of Thought, without any foreign or ambitious Ornaments.

PLINY to QUINTILIAN.

'THO' I am fully acquainted with the Contentment and just Moderation of your Mind, and the Conformity the Education you have given your Daughter bears to your own Character; yet since she is suddenly to be married to a Person of Distinction, whose Figure in the World makes it necessary for her to be at a more than ordinary Expence in Cloaths and Equipage suitable to her Husband's Quality; by which, tho' her intrinsick Worth be not augmented, yet will it receive both Ornament and Lustre: And knowing your Estate to be as moderate as the Riches of your Mind are abundant, I must challenge to my self some Part of the Burthen; and as a Parent of your Child, I present her with Twelve hundred and fifty Crowns towards these Expences; which Sum had been much larger, had I not feared the Smallness of it would be the greatest Inducement with you to accept of it. Farewell.'[1]

Thus should a Benefaction be done with a good Grace, and shine in the strongest Point of Light; it should not only answer all the Hopes and Exigences of the Receiver, but even out-run his Wishes: 'Tis this happy manner of Behaviour which adds new Charms to it, and softens those Gifts of Art and Nature, which otherwise would be rather distasteful than agreeable. Without it Valour would degenerate into Brutality, Learning into Pedantry, and the genteelest Demeanour into Affectation. Even Religion its self, unless Decency be the Handmaid which waits upon her, is apt to make People appear guilty of Sourness and ill Humour: But this shews Virtue in her first original Form, adds a Comeliness to Religion, and gives its Professors the justest Title to the Beauty of Holiness. A Man fully instructed in this Art, may assume a thousand Shapes, and please in all: He may do a thousand Actions shall become none other but himself; not that the things themselves are different, but the manner of doing them.

If you examine each Feature by its self, *Aglaura*[2] and *Calliclea* are equally handsome; but take them in the Whole, and you cannot

---

[1] Pliny, *Letters*, book 6, letter 32.
[2] In Ovid's *Metamorphoses* (2. 737–832) Aglauros, the daughter of Cecrops, is turned into stone because of her overwhelming envy of her sister's happiness. Cf. *Tatler* 54.

suffer the Comparison: The one is full of numberless nameless Graces, the other of as many nameless Faults.

The Comeliness of Person and Decency of Behaviour, add infinite Weight to what is pronounc'd by any one. 'Tis the want of this that often makes the Rebukes and Advice of old rigid Persons of no Effect, and leave a Displeasure in the Minds of those they are directed to: But Youth and Beauty, if accompanied with a graceful and becoming Severity, is of mighty Force to raise, even in the most Profligate, a Sense of Shame. In *Milton* the Devil is never describ'd asham'd but once, and that at the Rebuke of a beauteous Angel.

> *So spake the Cherub, and his grave Rebuke*
> *Severe in youthful Beauty, added Grace*
> *Invincible: Abash'd the Devil stood,*
> *And felt how awful Goodness is, and saw*
> *Virtue in her own Shape how lovely! saw, and pin'd*
> *His Loss.*[1]

The Care of doing nothing unbecoming has accompanied the greatest Minds to their last Moments: They avoided even an indecent Posture in the very Article of Death. Thus *Cæsar* gather'd his Robe about him, that he might not fall in a Manner unbecoming of himself;[2] and the greatest Concern that appeared in the Behaviour of *Lucretia*, when she stabb'd her self, was, that her Body should lie in an Attitude worthy the Mind which had inhabited it.

> *. . . Ne non procumbat honestè*
> *Extrema hæc etiam cura, cadentis erat.*[3]

> *'Twas her last Thought, How decently to fall.*

Mr. SPECTATOR,

I AM a young Woman without a Fortune; but of a very high Mind: That is, Good Sir, I am to the last Degree proud and Vain. I am ever railing at the Rich, for doing things which, upon Search into my Heart, I find I am only angry because I cannot do the same my self. I wear the Hoop'd Petticoat, and am all in

---

[1] *Paradise Lost*, iv. 844-9 ('Vertue in her shape').
[2] Suetonius, *Lives of the Twelve Caesars* (1692), p. 60:

And now seeing the Ruffians ready to assail him on every side, with naked Daggers in their Hands, he muffled up his Head in his Gown, and at the same time, with his left hand, threw his Robes about his Legs, that being covered all over, he might die with the greater decency.

In *Tatler* 86 the same incident is mentioned apropos of modesty.
[3] Ovid, *Fasti*, 2. 833-4.

Callicoes what the finest are in Silks. It is a dreadfull thing to be poor and proud; therefore, if you please, a Lecture on that Subject for the Satisfaction of

Your Uneasy,
Humble Servant,
Jezebell.'

Z

No. 293   *Tuesday, February 5, 1712*[1]
[ADDISON]

Πᾶσιν γὰρ εὖ φρονοῦσι συμμαχεῖ τύχη.
Frag. Vet. Po.

THE Famous *Gratian*,[2] in his little Book wherein he lays down Maxims for a Man's advancing himself at Court, advises his Reader to associate himself with the Fortunate, and to shun the Company of the Unfortunate; which, notwithstanding the Baseness of the Precept to an honest Mind, may have something useful in it for those who push their Interest in the World. It is certain a great part of what we call good or ill Fortune, rises out of right or wrong Measures, and Schemes of Life. When I hear a Man complain of his being unfortunate in all his Undertakings, I shrewdly suspect him for a very weak Man in his Affairs. In conformity with this way of thinking, Cardinal *Richelieu* used to say, that unfortunate and imprudent, were but two words for the same thing.[3] As the Cardinal

---

[1] *Motto.* Winterton, *Poetae Minores Graeci* (ed. Cambridge, 1677), p. 527 (one of the 'Sententiae singulis versibus contentae, e diversis Poetis'): The prudent still have fortune on their side.

[2] Baltasar Gracián (1601–58), the Spanish Jesuit, author of *El Oráculo manual y arte de prudencia* (1647). It was translated in 1694 as *The Courtier's Oracle; or the Art of Prudence,* and in 1702 as *The Art of Prudence, or a Companion for a Man of Sense* (2nd ed., 1705). The reference is to Maxim XXXI: 'To know happy People, that one may make use of them; and the unhappy, that one may avoid them' (ed. 1702, pp. 28–29).

[3] Here and elsewhere in this paper Addison has drawn on Bayle, art. Timoleon. In Remark L Bayle discusses Cardinal Richelieu and the disgrace of the Duke of Olivarez. 'The Motive or Pretext of his Disgrace, was the ill Success which accompanied all his Enterprises. This was in effect to accuse him of Imprudence. In Cardinal *Richelieu*'s Opinion, Imprudent and Unfortunate are but two words to express the same thing.' (Gaspar de Guzman, Count of Olivares, who died in 1645, was minister and favourite of Philip IV of Spain.)

himself had a great share both of Prudence and Good-Fortune, his famous Antagonist, the Count *d'Olivarez*, was disgraced at the Court of *Madrid*, because it was alledged against him that he had never any Success in his Undertakings. This, says an Eminent Author, was *indirectly* accusing him of Imprudence.

Cicero recommended *Pompey* to the *Romans* for their General upon three Accounts, as he was a Man of Courage, Conduct and Good-Fortune.[1] It was, perhaps, for the Reason abovementioned, namely, that a Series of Good-Fortune supposes a prudent Management in the Person whom it befalls, that not only *Sylla*[2] the Dictator, but several of the *Roman* Emperors, as is still to be seen upon their Medals, among their other Titles, gave themselves that of *Felix*, or Fortunate. The Heathens, indeed, seem to have valued a Man more for his Good-Fortune than for any other Quality, which I think is very natural for those who have not a strong Belief of another World. For how can I conceive a Man crowned with many distinguishing Blessings, that has not some extraordinary Fund of Merit and Perfection in him, which lies open to the Supream Eye, tho' perhaps it is not discovered by my Observation? What is the Reason *Homer*'s and *Virgil*'s Heroes do not form a Resolution, or strike a Blow, without the Conduct and Direction of some Deity? Doubtless, because the Poets esteemed it the greatest Honour to be favoured by the Gods, and thought the best way of praising a Man was to recount those Favours which naturally implied an extraordinary Merit in the Person on whom they descended.

Those who believe a future State of Rewards and Punishments act very absurdly, if they form their Opinions of a Man's Merit from his Successes. But certainly, if I thought the whole Circle of our Being was concluded between our Births and Deaths, I should think a Man's Good-Fortune the Measure and Standard of his real Merit, since Providence would have no Opportunity of rewarding his Vertue and Perfections, but in the present Life. A Vertuous Unbeliever, who lies under the Pressure of Misfortunes, has reason to cry out, as they say *Brutus* did a little before his Death, *O Vertue*,

---

[1] Cicero, *De Imperio Cn. Pompei Oratio*, 10. 28, mentions four qualities: *scientiam rei militaris, virtutem, auctoritatem, felicitatem*. Addison cites this also in *Freeholder* No. 2.

[2] Lucius Cornelius Sulla (138–78 B.C.). Several of the medals illustrated in Addison's *Dialogues on Ancient Medals* contain the word *Felix*, but Addison does not comment on Sulla. For Sulla's giving the honour of his achievements to Fortune see Plutarch, *Life of Sulla*, 6. 3–4; for his asking to receive the surname of Felix or Fortunate, ibid., 34. 2.

I have worshiped thee as a Substantial Good, but I find thou art an empty Name.[1]

But to return to our first Point. Tho' Prudence does undoubtedly in a great measure produce our good or ill Fortune in the World, it is certain there are many unforeseen Accidents and Occurrences, which very often pervert the finest Schemes that can be laid by Human Wisdom.[2] The Race is not always to the Swift, nor the Battel to the Strong.[3] Nothing less than infinite Wisdom can have an absolute Command over Fortune; the highest degree of it which Man can possess, is by no means equal to fortuituous Events, and to such Contingencies as may rise in the Prosecution of our Affairs. Nay, it very often happens, that Prudence, which has always in it a great mixture of Caution, hinders a Man from being so fortunate, as he might possibly have been without it. A Person who only aims at what is likely to succeed, and follows closely the Dictates of Human Prudence, never meets with those great and unforeseen Successes, which are often the effect of a Sanguine Temper, or a more happy Rashness; and this perhaps may be the Reason, that according to the common Observation, Fortune, like other Females, delights rather in favouring the young than the old.[4]

Upon the whole, since Man is so short-sighted a Creature, and the Accidents which may happen to him so various, I cannot but be of Dr. *Tillotson*'s Opinion in another Case, that were there any doubt of a Providence, yet it certainly would be very desirable there[a] should be such a Being of infinite Wisdom and Goodness, on whose Direction we might rely in the Conduct of Human Life.[5]

[a] desirable there] desirable that there *Fol.*

[1] L. Annaeus Florus, 2. 17. 11.

[2] Cf. Bayle, art. Timoleon, Remark K: 'There is then a good or ill *Fortune* in Humane life, independent on Prudence or Imprudence. . . .'   [3] Eccles. ix. 11.

[4] Cf. Bayle, art. Charles V, Remark I: 'I perceive very well, said he, that Fortune is like Women, she prefers young Persons to the old.'

[5] Tillotson more than once expresses this opinion: 'So that if a man had arguments sufficient to persuade him that there is no God . . . yet the belief of a God is so necessary to the comfort and happiness of our lives, that a wise man could not but be heartily troubled to quit so pleasant an error, and to part with a delusion which is apt to yield such unspeakable satisfaction to the mind of man' (Sermon I, 'The Wisdom of Being Religious', *Works*, ed. 1728, i. 19). 'Religion is the strongest Band of Humane Society, and so necessary to the welfare and happiness of Mankind, as it could not have been more, if we could suppose the Being of God himself to have been purposely designed and contrived for the Benefit and Advantage of Men' (Sermon XXVII, 'The Protestant Religion Vindicated from the Charge of Singularity and Novelty', *Works*, i. 247). 'The *goodness* of God gives us a lovely character of him, makes him so good a father, so gracious a governour of men, that if there were no such being in the world, it were infinitely desirable to mankind, that there should be; he is such an one, *qualem omnes cuperent, si deesset, as if he were wanting, all men ought*

It is a great Presumption to ascribe our Successes to our own Management, and not to esteem our selves upon any Blessing, rather as it is the Bounty of Heaven, than the Acquisition of our own Prudence. I am very well pleased with a Medal which was struck by Queen *Elizabeth* a little after the Defeat of the Invincible Armada, to perpetuate the Memory of that extraordinary Event.[1] It is well known how the King of *Spain*, and others who were the Enemies of that great Princess, to derogate from her Glory, ascribed the Ruin of their Fleet rather to the Violence of Storms and Tempests, than to the Bravery of the *English*. Queen *Elizabeth*, instead of looking upon this as a Diminution of her Honour, valued her self upon such a signal Favour of Providence; and accordingly in the Reverse of the Medal above-mentioned, has represented a Fleet[a] beaten by a Tempest, and falling foul upon one another, with that Religious Inscription, *Afflavit Deus & dissipantur. He blew with his Wind, and they were scattered.*

It is remarked of a famous *Græcian* General,[2] whose Name I cannot at present recollect, and who had been a particular Favourite of Fortune, that upon recounting his Victories among his Friends, he added at the end of several great Actions, *And in this Fortune had no share.* After which it is observed in History, that he never prospered in any thing he undertook.

As Arrogance, and a Conceitedness of our own Abilities, are very shocking and offensive to Men of Sense and Vertue, we may be sure

---

[a] accordingly . . . Fleet] accordingly in the Reverse of the Medal above-mentioned, a Fleet *Fol. Corrected in Errata No. 295:* '*after* accordingly, *r.* you see.'

---

to wish for. The being of God is so comfortable, so convenient, so necessary to the felicity of mankind, that (as *Tully* admirably says) *Dii immortales ad usum hominum fabricati penè videantur, If God were not a necessary being of himself, he might almost seem to be made on purpose for the use and benefit of men;* so that atheism is not only an instance of the most horrible impiety, but of the greatest stupidity . . .' (Sermon, 2nd ser., XCIII, 'The Goodness of God', *Works*, ii. 620).

[1] The medal was actually struck in the Netherlands in 1588, when the Dutch and English were making common cause against the Spaniards. The inscription on the obverse reads 'Flavit Jehovah et dissipati sunt'. See *British and Foreign Medals relating to Naval and Maritime Affairs*, arranged and indexed by the Earl of Sandwich (Greenwich, 1937), No. A5, pp. 8-9.

[2] Timotheus the Athenian. The anecdote is related in Plutarch's *Life of Sulla* and quoted in Bayle, art. Timoleon, Remark I:

Timotheus an *Athenian* the Son of *Conon* . . . on his return from a successful War after having given an account to the People, and publickly recited the particulars of his Expedition, he added, *Athenian* Lords, I can assure you that Fortune has no Hand in what I have related. The Gods were so enraged at this ridiculous ambition, that after this he never was successful. . . .

It is also quoted in Bacon's essay 'Of Fortune', which draws on Plutarch for the anecdote about Sulla quoted earlier in this essay.

they are highly displeasing to that Being who delights in an humble Mind, and by several of his Dispensations seems purposely to shew us, that our own Schemes or Prudence have no share in our Advancement.

Since on this Subject I have already admitted several Quotations which have occurred to my Memory upon writing this Paper, I will conclude it with a little *Persian* Fable.[1] A Drop of Water fell out of a Cloud into the Sea, and finding it self lost in such an Immensity of fluid Matter, broke out into the following Reflection: 'Alas! What an inconsiderable[a] Creature am I in this prodigious Ocean of Waters; my Existence is of no Concern[b] to the Universe, I am reduced to a kind of nothing, and am less than the least of the Works of God.' It so happened, that an Oyster, which lay in the neighbourhood of this Drop, chanced to gape and swallow it up in the midst of this his humble Soliloquy. The Drop, says the Fable, lay a great while hardning in the Shell, 'till by degrees it was ripen'd into a Pearl, which falling into the Hands of a Diver, after a long Series of Adventures, is at present that famous Pearl which is fixed on the Top of the *Persian* Diadem.

L

[a] inconsiderable] *12mo*; insignificant *Fol.* (*corrected in Errata, No. 295*), *8vo*
[b] Concern] significancy *Fol.*

---

[1] From the *Bustan*, or Garden, of the Persian poet Sadi. It is quoted in the *Voyages de Chardin* (Amsterdam, 1711), viii. 19 (cf. No. 289):

Une goûte d'eau tomba de la nüe dans la mer,
Elle demeura toute étourdie en considerant l'immensité de la mer.
Helas! dit-elle, en comparaison de la mer, que suis je?
Sûrement où la mer est, je ne suis qu'un vrai rien.
Pendant qu'elle se consideroit ainsi en son neant,
Une huitre la reçût dans son sein, & l'y éleva.
Le Ciel avança la chose, & la porta à ce point,
Qu'elle devint la Perle fameuse de la Couronne du Roi.

Difficile est plurimum virtutem revereri qui semper secunda fortuna sit usus.

Tull. ad Herennium.

INSOLENCE is the Crime of all others which every Man is most apt to rail at; and yet is there one Respect in which almost all Men living are guilty of it, and that is in the Case of laying a greater Value upon the Gifts of Fortune than we ought. It is here in *England* come into our very Language, as a Propriety of Distinction, to say, when we would speak of Persons to their Advantage, they are People of Condition. There is no Doubt but the proper Use of Riches implies that a Man should exert all the good Qualities imaginable; and if we mean by a Man of Condition or Quality one who, according to the Wealth he is Master of, shews himself just, beneficent, and charitable, that Term ought very deservedly to be had in the highest Veneration; but when Wealth is used only as it is the Support of Pomp and Luxury, to be rich is very far from being a Recommendation to Honour and Respect. It is indeed the greatest Insolence imaginable, in a Creature who would feel the Extremes of Thirst and Hunger if he did not prevent his Appetites before they call upon him, to be so forgetful of the common Necessity of humane Nature as never to cast an Eye upon the Poor and Needy. The Fellow who escaped from a Ship which struck upon a Rock in the West, and joined with the Country-People to destroy his Brother-Sailors and make her a Wreck, was thought a most execrable Creature; but does not every Man who enjoys the Possession of what he naturally wants, and is unmindful of the unsupplied Distress of other Men, betray the same Temper of Mind? When a Man looks about him, and with Regard to Riches and Poverty beholds some drawn in Pomp and Equipage, and they and their very Servants with an Air of Scorn and Triumph overlooking the Multitude that pass by them: and in the same Street a Creature of the same Make crying out in the Name of all that is good and sacred to behold his Misery, and give him some Supply against Hunger and

[1] *Motto. Ad Herennium de arte rhetorica* (formerly attributed to Cicero), 4. 17. 24 (altered): It is a hard matter to pay much regard to that virtue which is dependent entirely on good fortune.

Nakedness, who would believe these two Beings were of the same Species? But so it is, that the Consideration of Fortune has taken up all our Minds, and, as I have often complained,[1] Poverty and Riches stand in our Imaginations in the Places of Guilt and Innocence. But in all Seasons there will be some Instances of Persons who have Souls too large to be taken with popular Prejudices, and while the rest of Mankind are contending for Superiority in Power and Wealth, have their Thoughts bent upon the Necessities of those below them. The Charity-Schools which have been erected of late Years, are the greatest Instances of publick Spirit the Age has produced: But indeed when we consider how long this sort of Beneficence has been on Foot, it is rather from the good Management of those Institutions, than from the Number or Value of the Benefactions to them, that they make so great a Figure.[2] One would think it impossible, that in the Space of fourteen Years there should not have been five thousand Pounds bestowed in Gifts this Way, nor sixteen hundred Children, including Males and Females, put out into Methods of Industry. It is not allowed me to speak of Luxury and Folly with the severe Spirit they deserve; I shall only therefore say, I shall very readily compound with any Lady in a Hoop-Petticoat, if she gives the Price of one half Yard of the Silk towards cloathing, feeding, and instructing an innocent helpless Creature of her own Sex in one of these Schools. The Consciousness of such an Action will give her Features a nobler Life on this illustrious Day,[3] than all the Jewels that can hang in her Hair, or can be clustered at her Bosom. It would be uncourtly to speak in harsher Words to the Fair, but to Men one may take a little more Freedom. It is monstrous how a Man can live with so little Reflection, as to fancy he is not in a Condition

[1] Nos. 167, 219, 268 (vol. ii).

[2] In *Guardian* 105 Addison praises the institution of charity-schools as 'the glory of the age we live in, and the most proper means that can be made use of to recover it out of its present degeneracy and depravation of manners'. Hatton (p. 580) gives a list of churches which have sermons and collections for maintaining these schools and adds: 'Charity Schools within the Bills of Mortality there are 60; wherein are taught 2248 Children, of which there are clothed 1874, set to work 861; Apprenticed 862; for maintaining of whom, the Annual Subscriptions are 536; Collections at Sermons 1434 *l*. Gifts 5861 *l*.' In *An Account of Charity-Schools in Great Britain and Ireland* (11th ed. with large additions, 1712) the number of schools 'in and about London and Westminster, and within Ten Miles thereof'is given as 119, with a total of 4,687 children taught (pp. 11–14). It describes the chief design of the schools as 'the Education of Poor Children in the Knowledge and Practice of the Christian Religion, as Profess'd and Taught in the Church of England' (p. 5). See also Mary G. Jones, *The Charity School Movement: a study of eighteenth-century Puritanism in action* (Cambridge, 1938).

[3] The birthday of Queen Anne.

very unjust, and disproportioned to the rest of Mankind, while he enjoys Wealth, and exerts no Benevolence or Bounty to others. As for this particular Occasion of these Schools, there cannot any offer more worthy a generous Mind. Would you do an handsome thing without Return? do it for an Infant that is not sensible of the Obligation: Would you do it for publick Good? do it for one who will be an honest Artificer: Would you do it for the Sake of Heaven? give it to one who shall be instructed in the Worship of him for whose Sake you gave it. It is methinks a most laudable Institution; this, if it were of no other Expectation than that of producing a Race of good and useful Servants, who will have more than a liberal, a religious Education. What would not a Man do, in common Prudence, to lay out in Purchase of one about him, who would add to all his Orders he gave the Weight of the Commandments to inforce an Obedience to them? for one who would consider his Master as his Father, his Friend, and Benefactor upon the easy Terms, and in Expectation of no other Return but moderate Wages and gentle Usage? It is the common Vice of Children to run too much among the Servants; from such as are educated in these Places they would see nothing but Lowliness in the Servant, which would not be disingenuous in the Child. All the ill Offices and defamatory Whispers, which take their Birth from Domesticks, would be prevented if this Charity could be made universal; and a good Man might have a Knowledge of the whole Life of the Persons he designs to take into his House for his own Service, or that of his Family or Children, long before they were admitted. This would create endearing Dependencies; and the Obligation would have a paternal Air in the Master, who would be relieved from much Care and Anxiety from the Gratitude and Diligence of an humble Friend attending him as his Servant. I fall into this Discourse from a Letter sent to me, to give me Notice that Fifty Boys would be cloathed and take their Seats (at the Charge of some generous Benefactors) in St. *Bride*'s Church[1] on *Sunday* next. I wish I could promise to my self any thing which my Correspondent seems to expect from a Publication of it in this Paper; for there can be nothing added to what so many excellent and learned Men have said on this Occasion: But that there may be something here which would move a generous

---

[1] St. Bride's Church, on the south side of Fleet Street, had been rebuilt in 1680. In the parish of St. Bride's there was a charity school for fifty boys, and later for fifty girls also (cf. No. 380).

Mind, like that of him who writ to me, I shall transcribe an handsome Paragraph of Dr. *Snape's*[1] Sermon on these Charities, which my Correspondent enclosed with his Letter.

The wise Providence has amply compensated the Disadvantages of the Poor and Indigent, in wanting many of the Conveniencies of this Life, by a more abundant Provision for their Happiness in the next. Had they been higher born, or more richly endowed, they would have wanted this Manner of Education, of which those only enjoy the Benefit, who are low enough to submit to it; where they have such Advantages without Money, and without Price, as the Rich cannot purchase with it. The Learning which is giv'n, is generally more edifying to them, than that which is sold to others: Thus do they become more exalted in Goodness, by being depressed in Fortune, and their Poverty is, in Reality, their Preferment.   T

No. 295   *Thursday, February 7, 1712*[2]
[ADDISON]

Prodiga non sentit pereuntem fœmina censum:
At velut exhaustâ redivivus pullulet arcâ
Nummus, & è pleno semper tollatur acervo,
Non unquam reputant quanti sibi gaudia constent.
                       Juv.

Mr. SPECTATOR,

'I AM turned of my great Climacteric,[3] and am naturally a Man of a meek Temper. About a dozen Years ago I was married, for

---

[1] Andrew Snape, D.D. (1675–1742), was Rector of St. Mary-at-Hill. He had preached at St. Sepulchre's Church on Thursday, 24 May 1711 (on Matt. xi. 25), before the trustees of the several charity schools in and about London, 'with about 4000 poor Children, mostly new Cloath'd' (*Post-Man*, 26 May). The sermon was published on 13 July 1711 (*Daily Courant*); the passage quoted here occurs near the end (p. 26) and begins: 'Thus amply has the wise Providence of God, compensated the Disadvantages of the Poor and Indigent . . . .'

[2] *Motto.* Juvenal, *Satires*, 6. 362–5.

> But Womankind, that never knows a mean,
> Down to the Dregs their sinking Fortune drain;
> Hourly they give, and spend, and waste, and wear;
> And think no Pleasure can be bought too dear. DRYDEN.

[3] The 63rd year. In the Dedication to Vol. VIII of the original reprint Will Honeycomb is said to have stepped into his grand Climacterick.

my Sins, to a young Woman of a good Family, and of an high Spirit; but could not bring her to close with me, before I had entred into a Treaty with her longer than that of the Grand Alliance.[1] Among other Articles it was therein stipulated, that she should have 400 *l.* a Year for *Pin-money*,[2] which I obliged my self to pay Quarterly into the hands of one who acted as her Plenipotentiary in that Affair. I have ever since religiously observed my part in this solemn Agreement. Now, Sir, so it is, that the Lady has had several Children since I married her; to which, if I should credit our malicious Neighbours, her *Pin-money* has not a little contributed. The Education of these my Children, who, contrary to my Expectation, are born to me every Year, streightens me so much, that I have begged their Mother to free me from the Obligation of the above-mentioned *Pin-money*, that it may go towards making a Provision for her Family. This Proposal makes her noble Blood swell in her Veins, insomuch that finding me a little tardy in her last Quarter's Payment, she threatens me every Day to arrest me; and proceeds so far as to tell me, that if I do not do her Justice, I shall die in a Jayl. To this she adds, when her Passion will let her argue calmly, that she has several Play-Debts on her Hand, which must be discharged very suddenly, and that she cannot lose her Money as becomes a Woman of her Fashion, if she makes me any Abatements in this Article. I hope, Sir, you will take an occasion from hence to give your Opinion upon a Subject which you have not yet touched, and inform us if there are any Precedents for this Usage among our Ancestors; or whether you find any mention of *Pin-money* in *Grotius*, *Puffendorf*, or any other of the Civilians.[3]

I am ever
the humblest of your Admirers,
Josiah Fribble, *Esq;*'

---

[1] The Grand Alliance was concluded at The Hague in 1701 between England, Holland, and the Emperor, against France.

[2] According to Steele (*Tatler* 199): 'When the Theatre in some late Reigns owed its chief Support to those Scenes which were written to put Matrimony out of Countenance, and render that State terrible; then was it, that Pin-Money first prevailed, and all the other Articles inserted which create a Diffidence; and intimate to the young People, that they are very soon to be in a State of War with each other....' In *The Tender Husband* (I. ii) Steele represents two fathers disputing over marriage-settlements.

[3] Hugo Grotius and Samuel Pufendorf were perhaps the two best-known 'civilians' or political scientists, both of whom stated the case for natural or unwritten law as contrasted with positive or man-made laws. The *De jure belli et pacis* of Grotius was published in 1625, Pufendorf's *De jure naturae et gentium* in 1672.

As there is no Man Living, who is a more professed Advocate for the Fair Sex than my self, so there is none that wou'd be more unwilling to invade any of their ancient Rights and Privileges; but as the Doctrine of *Pin-money* is of a very late Date,[1] unknown to our Great Grand-mothers, and not yet received by many of our Modern Ladies, I think it is for the Interest of both Sexes to keep it from spreading.

Mr. *Fribble* may not, perhaps, be much mistaken, where he intimates, that the supplying a Man's Wife with *Pin-money*, is furnishing her with Arms against himself, and in a manner becoming accessary to his own Dishonour. We may, indeed, generally observe, that in proportion as a Woman is more or less beautiful, and her Husband advanced in Years, she stands in need of a greater or less number of *Pins*, and upon a Treaty of Marriage, rises or falls in her Demands accordingly. It must likewise be owned, that high Quality in a Mistress does very much inflame this Article in the Marriage reckoning.

But where the Age and Circumstances of both Parties are pretty much upon a level, I cannot but think the insisting upon *Pin-money* is very extraordinary;[2] and yet we find several Matches broken off upon this very Head. What would a Foreigner, or one who is a Stranger to this Practice, think of a Lover that forsakes his Mistress, because he is not willing to keep her in *Pins*; but what would he think of the Mistress, shou'd he be inform'd that she asks five or six hundred Pounds a Year for this use? Should a Man unacquainted with our Customs be told the Sums which are allowed in *Great Britain*, under the Title of *Pin-money*, what a prodigious Consumption of *Pins* would he think there was in this Island? *A Pin a Day*, says our frugal Proverb, *is a Groat a Year*,[3] so that according to this Calculation, my Friend *Fribble*'s Wife must every Year make use of Eight Millions six hundred and forty thousand *new Pins*.

I am not ignorant that our *British* Ladies alledge they comprehend under this general Term several other Conveniencies of Life; I cou'd therefore wish, for the Honour of my Country-women, that they

---

[1] The earliest date for the word in *OED* is 1697. Cf. Steele's statement in *Tatler* 199 quoted above.

[2] Addison may have in mind the negotiations between his friend Edward Wortley Montagu and Lady Mary Pierrepont which finally resulted in their elopement in the summer of 1712. Cf. *Tatlers* 199 and 223; *Letters of Lady Mary Wortley Montagu*, ed. Moy Thomas, i. 5, 10, 62; and her *Life* by Robert Halsband (Oxford, 1956), pp. 23–28.

[3] This is the earliest recorded quotation of this proverb in Apperson and the *Oxford Dictionary of English Proverbs*. It is not in Tilley.

had rather call'd it *Needle-money*, which might have implied something of Good-housewifry, and not have given the malicious World occasion to think, that Dress and Trifles have always the uppermost Place in a Woman's Thoughts.

I know several of my fair Reasoners urge, in defence of this Practice, that it is but a necessary Provision they make for themselves, in case their Husband proves a Churl or a Miser; so that they consider this Allowance as a kind of Alimony, which they may lay their Claim to, without actually separating from their Husbands. But with Submission, I think a Woman who will give up her self to a Man in Marriage, where there is the least room for such an Apprehension, and trust her Person to one whom she will not rely on for the common Necessaries of Life, may very properly be accused (in the Phrase of an homely Proverb) of being *Penny wise and Pound foolish*.[1]

It is observed of over-cautious Generals, that they never engage in a Battel without securing a Retreat, in case the Event should not answer their Expectations; on the other hand, your greatest Conquerors have burnt their Ships, or broke down the Bridges behind them, as being determined either to succeed or die in the Engagement. In the same manner I should very much suspect a Woman who takes such Precautions for her Retreat, and contrives Methods how she may live happily, without the Affection of one to whom she joins herself for Life. Separate Purses, between Man and Wife, are, in my Opinion, as unnatural as separate Beds. A Marriage cannot be happy, where the Pleasures, Inclinations and Interests of both Parties are not the same. There is no greater Incitement to Love in the Mind of Man, than the Sense of a Person's depending upon him for her Ease and Happiness; as a Woman uses all her Endeavours to please the Person whom she looks upon as her Honour, her Comfort, and her Support.

For this Reason I am not very much surprised at the Behaviour of a rough Country 'Squire, who, being not a little shocked at the Proceeding of a young Widow that would not recede from her Demands of *Pin-money*, was so enraged at her mercenary Temper, that he told her in great wrath, 'as much as she thought him her Slave he would shew all the World he did not care a Pin for her'. Upon which he flew out of the Room, and never saw her more.

Socrates,[2] in *Plato's Alcibiades*, says, he was informed by one, who

---

[1] See Tilley (P218).　　　　　　[2] Plato, *Alcibiades*, i. 123B.

had travelled through *Persia*, that as he passed over a great Tract of Lands, and enquired what the Name of the Place was, they told him it was the *Queen's Girdle*; to which he adds, that another wide Field, which lay by it, was called the *Queen's Veil*, and that in the same manner there was a large Portion of Ground set aside for every part of Her Majesty's Dress. These Lands might not be improperly called the Queen of *Persia's Pin-Money*.

I remember my Friend, Sir ROGER, who I dare say never read this Passage in *Plato*, told me some time since, that upon his courting the Perverse Widow (of whom I have given an Account in former Papers) he had disposed of an hundred Acres in a Diamond-Ring, which he would have presented her with, had she thought fit to accept it; and that upon her Wedding-Day she should have carried on her Head fifty of the tallest Oaks upon his Estate. He further informed me, that he would have given her a Colepit to keep her in clean Linnen, that he would have allowed her the Profits of a Windmill for her Fans, and have presented her, once in three Years, with the Sheering of his Sheep for her[a] Under-Petti-coats. To which the Knight always adds, that though he did not care for fine Cloaths himself, there should not have been a Woman in the County better dressed than my Lady *Coverly*. Sir ROGER, perhaps, may in this, as well as in many other of his Devices, appear something odd and singular; but if the Humour of *Pin-money* prevails, I think it would be very proper for every Gentleman of an Estate, to marke out so many Acres of it under the Title of *The Pins*.

L

No. 296   *Friday, February 8, 1712*[1]
[STEELE]

         . . . *Nugis addere pondus.*
                       Hor.

Dear SPEC.

'HAVING lately conversed much with the fair Sex on the Subject of your Speculations, (which, since their Appearance in

    [a] for her] to keep her in *Fol.*

---

[1] *Motto.* Horace, *Epistles* 1. 19. 42: To add weight to trifles. Addison had used this as motto for *Tatler* 216.

Publick, have been the chief Exercise of the female loquacious Faculty) I found the fair Ones possess'd with a Dissatisfaction at your prefixing *Greek* Mottos to the Frontispiece of your late Papers;[1] and, as a Man of Gallantry, I thought it a Duty incumbent on me to impart it to you, in Hopes of a Reformation, which is only to be effected by a Restoration of the *Latin* to the usual Dignity in your Papers, which of late the *Greek*, to the great Displeasure of your female Readers, has usurp'd; for tho' the *Latin* has the Recommendation of being as unintelligible to them as the *Greek*, yet being written of the same Character with their Mother Tongue, by the Assistance of a Spelling-Book it's legible; which Quality the *Greek* wants: And since the Introduction of Operas into this Nation, the Ladies are so charmed with Sounds abstracted from their Ideas, that they adore and honour the Sound of *Latin* as it is old *Italian*. I am a Sollicitor for the fair Sex, and therefore think my self in that Character more likely to be prevalent in this Request, than if I should subscribe my self by my proper Name.

J. M.[2]

'*I desire you may insert this in one of your Speculations, to shew my Zeal for removing the Dissatisfaction of the fair Sex, and restoring you to their Favour.*'

Sir,

'I WAS some time since in Company with a young Officer, who entertained us with the Conquest he had made over a Female Neighbour of his; when a Gentleman who stood by, as, I suppose, envying the Captain's good Fortune, asked him what Reason he had to believe the Lady admired him? Why, says he, my Lodgings are opposite to hers, and she is continually at her Window either at work, reading, taking Snuff, or putting her self in some toying Posture on purpose to draw my Eyes that Way. The Confession of this vain Soldier made me reflect on some of my own Actions; for you must know, Sir, I am often at a Window which fronts the Apartments of several Gentlemen, who I doubt not have the same Opinion of me. I must own I love to look at them all, one for being well dressed, a second for his fine Eye, and one particular one because he is the least Man I ever saw; but there is something so

---

[1] Although Steele had used a Greek motto as early as No. 20 (23 Mar. 1711) they do not become numerous until late in the year 1711; in the month of December seven of the essays were headed by Greek mottoes (all but one in essays by Addison).

[2] For another letter submitted by J. M. and not used see No. 511 (vol. iv).

easy and pleasant in the Manner of my little Man, that I observe he is a Favourite of all his Acquaintance. I could go on to tell you of many others that I believe think I have encouraged them from my Window: But pray let me have your Opinion of the Use of the Window in a beautiful Lady; and how often she may look out at the same Man, without being supposed to have a Mind to jump out to him.

Yours,
Aurelia Careless.'[1]

Twice.

Mr. SPECTATOR,

'I HAVE for some Time made Love to a Lady, who receiv'd it with all the kind Returns I ought to expect. But without any Provocation that I know of, she has of late shunned me with the utmost Abhorrence, insomuch that she went out of Church last *Sunday* in the midst of Divine Service, upon my coming into the same Pew. Pray, Sir, what must I do in this Business?

Your Servant,
Euphues.'

Let Her alone Ten Days.

York, January the 20th, 1711–12.

Mr. SPECTATOR,

'WE have in this Town a sort of People who pretend to Wit and write Lampoons: I have lately been the Subject of one of them. The Scribbler had not Genius enough in Verse to turn my Age, as indeed I am an Old Maid, into Raillery, for affecting a youthier[2] Turn than is consistent with my Time of Day; and therefore he makes the Title to his Madrigal, The Character of Mrs. *Judith Lovebane*, born in the Year 1680. What I desire of you is, That you disallow that a Coxcomb who pretends to write Verse, should put the most malicious thing he can say in Prose. This I humbly

---

[1] A letter signed Cloe and dated from Hampshire, 13 Feb. 1712 (Lillie, ii. 193–5), requests the *Spectator* to make an example of the Captain described here by Aurelia Careless. 'I am resolved to stop up that window and work, take snuff, and put my self in those toying postures (as he calls them) in a backroom two pair of stairs higher.'

[2] *Youthy*, described by Johnson as 'a bad word', is marked rare or obsolete by *OED*; this is the earliest quotation given.

conceive will disable our Country Wits, who indeed take a great deal of Pains to say any thing in Rhime, tho' they say it very ill.

> I *am*, SIR,
> *Your Humble Servant*,
> Susanna Lovebane.'

Mr. SPECTATOR,

'WE are several of us, Gentlemen and Ladies, who board in the same House, and after Dinner one of our Company (an agreeable Man enough otherwise) stands up and reads your Paper to us all. We are the civillest People in the World to one another, and therefore I am forced to this way of desiring our Reader, when he is doing this Office, not to stand afore the Fire. This will be a general Good to our Family this cold Weather. He will, I know, take it to be our common Request when he comes to these Words, *Pray Sir sit down*; which I desire you to insert, and you will particularly oblige

> *Your Daily Reader*,
> Charity Frost.'

Sir,

'I AM a great Lover of Dancing, but cannot perform so well as some others: However by my Out-of-the-Way Capers, and some original Grimaces, I don't fail to divert the Company, particularly the Ladies, who laugh immoderately all the Time. Some, who pretend to be my Friends, tell me they do it in Derision, and would advise me to leave it off, withall that I make my self ridiculous. I don't know what to do in this Affair, but am resolved not to give over upon any Account till I have the Opinion of the SPECTATOR.

> *Your humble Servant*,
> John Trott.'[1]

'IF Mr. *Trott* is not awkard out of Time, he has a Right to dance let who will laugh: But if he has no Ear he will interrupt others; and I am of Opinion he should sit still. Given under my Hand this Fifth of *February*, 1711–12.

> *The* SPECTATOR.'

T

---

[1] John Trott is the name of Sir Fopling Flutter's one English servant (Etherege, *The Man of Mode*, III. iii).

No. 297   *Saturday, February* 9, 1712[1]
[ADDISON]

> . .   . .   *velut si*
> *Egregio inspersos reprendas corpore nævos.*
>   Hor.

AFTER what I have said in my last *Saturday*'s Paper, I shall enter
on the Subject of this without farther Preface, and remark
the several Defects which appear in the Fable, the Characters, the
Sentiments, and the Language of *Milton*'s *Paradise Lost*; not doubting but the Reader will pardon me, if I alledge at the same time
whatever may be said for the Extenuation of such Defects. The
first Imperfection which I shall observe in the Fable is, that the
Event of it is unhappy.[2]

The Fable of every Poem is according to *Aristotle*'s Division
either *Simple* or *Implex*.[3] It is called Simple when there is no change of
Fortune in it, Implex when the Fortune of the chief Actor changes
from Bad to Good, or from Good to Bad. The Implex Fable is
thought the most perfect; I suppose, because it is more proper
to stir up the Passions of the Reader, and to surprize him with
a greater variety of Accidents.

The Implex Fable is therefore of two kinds: In the first the chief
Actor makes his way through a long Series of Dangers and Difficulties, 'till he arrives at Honour and Prosperity, as we see in the
Story of *Ulysses*.[a] In the second, the chief Actor in the Poem falls
from some eminent pitch of Honour and Prosperity, into Misery
and Disgrace. Thus we see *Adam* and *Eve* sinking from a State of
Innocence and Happiness, into the most abject Condition of Sin
and Sorrow.

The most taking Tragedies among the Ancients were built on
this last sort of Implex Fable,[4] particularly the Tragedy of *OEdipus*,

---

[a] Story of *Ulysses*.] Stories of *Achilles*, *Ulysses* and *Æneas*. Fol. *Corrected in Errata*,
No. 315: '*dele* Achilles.'

---

[1] *Motto.* Horace, *Satires* I. 6. 66–67:
As perfect Beauties often have a Mole. CREECH.
[2] Dryden (Dedication of *Aeneis*) thought Milton would have had a better place
among the list of heroic poets 'if the giant had not foiled the knight, and driven him
out of his stronghold, to wander through the world with his lady errant' (Ker, ii. 165).
[3] *Poetics*, 10. I. Dacier (p. 159) translates: 'Fables are either Simple or Implex, for
all those Actions which Fables imitate, have either one, or t'other of these qualities.'
[4] Aristotle, *Poetics*, II. 2–3. Dacier has a long note elaborating this point (pp. 166–7).

which proceeds upon a Story, if we may believe *Aristotle*, the most proper for Tragedy that could be invented by the Wit of Man. I have taken some pains in a former Paper[1] to shew, that this kind of Implex Fable, wherein the Event is unhappy, is more apt to affect an Audience than that of the first kind; notwithstanding many excellent Pieces among the Ancients, as well as most of those which have been written of late Years in our own Country, are raised upon contrary Plans. I must however own, that I think this kind of Fable, which is the most perfect in Tragedy, is not so proper for an Heroic Poem.[2]

Milton seems to have been sensible of this Imperfection in his Fable, and has therefore endeavoured to cure it by several Expedients; particularly by the Mortification which the great Adversary of Mankind meets with upon his return to the Assembly of Infernal Spirits, as it is described in a[a] beautiful Passage of the tenth Book;[3] and likewise by the Vision, wherein *Adam* at the close of the Poem sees his Off-spring triumphing over his great Enemy, and himself restored to a happier *Paradise* than that from which he fell.[4]

There is another Objection against *Milton*'s Fable, which is indeed almost the same with the former, tho' placed in a different Light, namely, That the Hero in the *Paradise Lost* is unsuccessful, and by no means a Match for his Enemies. This gave occasion to Mr. *Dryden*'s Reflection, that the Devil was in reality *Milton*'s Hero.[5] I think I have obviated this Objection in my first Paper. The *Paradise Lost* is an Epic, or a Narrative Poem, and he[b] that looks for an Hero in it, searches for that which *Milton* never intended; but[c] if he will needs fix the Name of an Hero upon any Person in it, 'tis certainly the *Messiah* who is the Hero, both in the Principal Action, and in the chief Episodes.[d] Paganism could not furnish out a real Action for a Fable greater than that of the *Iliad* or *Æneid*, and therefore an Heathen could not form a higher Notion of a Poem than one of that kind, which they call an Heroic. Whether *Milton*'s is not

[a] a] that *Fol.*   [b] an Epic, or a Narrative Poem, and he] *19*; an Epic, Narrative Poem, he *Fol.*; an Epic, or a Narrative Poem, he *8vo, 12mo*   [c] but] or *Fol.*
[d] the chief Episodes.] the Episode. *Fol.*

[1] No. 40 (vol. i).
[2] In the epic, writes Le Bossu (book ii, chap. xvii), 'all the Poets seem to conspire for a happy Catastrophe' (i. 211).
[3] *PL*, x. 504 ff.   [4] *PL*, xii. 325 ff.
[5] Dedication of *Aeneis* (Ker, ii. 165). Dennis (in *The Grounds of Criticism*, 1704) also thought 'the Devil is properly his Hero, because he gets the better' (*Works*, ed. Hooker, i. 334).

of a sublimer[a] Nature I will not presume to determine: It[b] is sufficient that I shew there is in the *Paradise Lost* all the Greatness of Plan, Regularity of Design, and masterly Beauties which we discover in *Homer* and *Virgil*.

I must in the next Place observe, that *Milton* has interwoven in the Texture of his Fable some Particulars which do not seem to have Probability enough for an Epic Poem, particularly in the Actions which he ascribes to *Sin* and *Death*,[1] and the Picture which he draws of the *Lymbo of Vanity*,[2] with other Passages in the second Book. Such Allegories rather savour of the Spirit of *Spencer* and *Ariosto*, than of *Homer* and *Virgil*.

In the Structure of his Poem he has likewise admitted of too many Digressions. It is finely observed by *Aristotle*, that the Author of an Heroic Poem should seldom speak himself, but throw as much of his Work as he can into the Mouths of those who are his Principal Actors.[3] *Aristotle* has given no Reason for this Precept; but I presume it is because the Mind of the Reader is more awed and elevated when he hears *Æneas* or *Achilles* speak, than when *Virgil* or *Homer* talk in their own Persons. Besides that assuming the Character of an eminent Man is apt to fire the Imagination, and raise the Ideas of the Author. *Tully* tells us, mentioning his Dialogue of Old Age, in which *Cato* is the chief Speaker, that upon a Review of it he was agreeably imposed upon, and fancied that it was *Cato*, and not he himself, who utter'd his Thoughts on that Subject.[4]

If the Reader would be at the pains to see how the Story of the *Iliad* and the *Æneid* is delivered by those Persons who act in it, he will be surprized to find how little in either of these Poems proceeds from the Authors. *Milton* has, in the general disposition of his Fable, very finely observed this great Rule, insomuch, that there is scarce a third[c] part of it which comes from the Poet; the rest is spoken either by *Adam* and *Eve*, or by some Good or Evil Spirit who is engaged either in their Destruction or Defence.

From what has been here observed it appears, that Digressions are by no means to be allowed of in an Epic Poem. If the Poet, even

---

[a] sublimer] greater *Fol.*   [b] determine: It] determine, it *Fol.*   [c] third] tenth *Fol. Corrected in Errata (No. 315) to* third

---

[1] *PL*, ii. 648–889.   [2] *PL*, iii. 444–97.
[3] *Poetics*, 24. 7. Dacier (p. 406) translates: 'The Poet ought to say little himself, for in that he is not an Imitator.'
[4] *De Amicitia*, 1. 4.

in the ordinary course of his Narration, should speak as little as possible, he should certainly never let his Narration sleep for the sake of any Reflections of his own. I have often observed, with a secret Admiration, that the longest Reflection in the *Æneid* is in that Passage of the Tenth Book, where *Turnus* is represented as dressing himself in the Spoils of *Pallas*, whom he had slain. *Virgil* here lets his Fable stand still for the sake of the following Remark. *How is the Mind of Man ignorant of Futurity, and unable to bear prosperous Fortune with Moderation? The time will come when* Turnus *shall wish that he had left the Body of* Pallas *untouched, and curse the Day on which he dressed himself in these Spoils.*[1] As the great Event of the *Æneid*, and the Death of *Turnus*, whom *Æneas* slew because he saw him adorned with the Spoils of *Pallas*, turns upon this Incident, *Virgil* went out of his way to make this Reflection upon it, without which so small a Circumstance might possibly have slipped out of his Reader's Memory. *Lucan*, who was an Injudicious Poet, lets drop his Story very frequently for the sake of unnecessary Digressions or his *Diverticula*, as *Scaliger* calls them.[2] If he gives us an Account of the Prodigies which preceded the Civil War, he declaims upon the Occasion, and shews how much happier it would be for Man, if he did not feel his Evil Fortune before it comes to pass, and suffer not only by its real Weight, but by the Apprehension of it.[3] *Milton's* Complaint of his Blindness, his Panegyrick on Marriage, his Reflections on *Adam* and *Eve's* going naked, of the Angels eating, and several other Passages in his Poem, are liable to the same Exception,[4] tho' I must confess there is so great a Beauty in these very Digressions, that I would not wish them out of his Poem.

I have, in a former Paper,[5] spoken of the *Characters* of *Milton's Paradise Lost*, and declared my Opinion, as to the Allegorical Persons who are introduced in it.

If we look into the *Sentiments*, I think they are sometimes defective under the following Heads; First, as there are several[a] of them too much pointed, and some that degenerate even into Punns. Of this

---

[a] several] some *Fol.*

---

[1] *Aeneid*, 10. 501–5.
[2] J. C. Scaliger, *Poetices*, 6. 6 (Lyons, 1561, p. 326).
[3] Lucan, *Pharsalia*, 2. 1–15.
[4] Milton's complaint: *PL*, iii. 1–55; his panegyric: *PL*, iv. 750–70; his reflections: *PL*, iv. 312–20; the angels eating: *PL*, v. 404–33.
[5] No. 273 (vol. ii).

last kind I am afraid is that in the First Book, where, speaking of the Pigmies, he calls them

> . . . *The small* Infantry
> *Warr'd on by Cranes* . . .[1]

Another Blemish that[a] appears in some of his Thoughts, is his frequent Allusion to Heathen Fables, which are not certainly of a Piece with the Divine Subject, of which he treats. I do not find fault with these Allusions, where the Poet himself represents them as fabulous, as he does in some Places, but where he mentions them as Truths and Matters of Fact. The Limits of my Paper will not give me leave to be particular in Instances of this kind: the Reader will easily remark them in his Perusal of the Poem.

A third Fault in his Sentiments, is an unnecessary Ostentation of Learning, which likewise occurs very frequently.[2] It is certain that both *Homer* and *Virgil* were Masters of all the Learning of their Times, but it shews it self in their Works after an indirect and concealed manner. *Milton* seems ambitious of letting us know, by his Excursions on Free-Will and Predestination, and his many Glances upon History, Astronomy, Geography and the like, as well as by the Terms and Phrases he sometimes makes use of, that he was acquainted with the whole Circle of Arts and Sciences.

If, in the last place, we consider the *Language* of this great Poet, we must allow what I have hinted in a former Paper, that it is often too[b] much laboured, and sometimes obscured by old Words, Transpositions, and Foreign Idioms. *Seneca's* Objection to the Stile of a great Author, *Riget ejus oratio, nihil in eâ placidum nihil lene*,[3] is what many Criticks make to *Milton*: as I cannot wholly refute it, so I have already apologized for it in another Paper;[4] to which I may further add, that *Milton's* Sentiments and Ideas were so wonderfully Sublime, that it would have been impossible for him to have represented them in their full Strength and Beauty, without having recourse to these Foreign Assistances. Our Language sunk under him, and was

---

[a] that] which *Fol.*   [b] is often too] is too *Fol.*

[1] *PL*, i. 575–6 ('That small Infantry').
[2] Le Bossu (book vi, chap. vi) warns against pedantry and undue display of learning. 'The desire of appearing learned, makes a Poem smell of it from one end to the other' (ii. 283).
[3] Seneca the Elder, *Controversies*, 7. 4. 8 (altered). The 'great author' is Calvus, who waged with Cicero a very unequal contest for supremacy among Roman orators.
[4] No. 285.

unequal to that greatness of Soul, which furnished him with such glorious Conceptions.

A second Fault in his Language is, that he often affects a kind of Jingle in his Words,[1] as in the following Passages, and many others:

> *And brought into the* World *a* World *of woe.*
> . . . *Begirt th' Almighty throne*
> *Beseeching or besieging . . .*
> *This* tempted *our* attempt . . .
> *At one Slight* bound *high overleapt all* bound.[2]

I know there are Figures for this kind of Speech, that some of the greatest Ancients have been guilty of it, and that *Aristotle* himself has given it a place in his Rhetorick among the Beauties of that Art.[3] But as it is in its self poor and trifling, it is I think at present universally exploded by all the Masters of Polite Writing.

The last Fault which I shall take notice of in *Milton*'s Stile, is the frequent use of what the Learned call *Technical Words*, or Terms of Art.[4] It is one of the great Beauties of Poetry, to make hard things intelligible, and to deliver[a] what is abstruse of it self[b] in such easy Language as may be understood by ordinary Readers: Besides that the Knowledge of a Poet should rather seem born with him, or inspired, than drawn from Books and Systems. I have often

---

a and to deliver] and deliver *Fol.*   b of it self] in it self *Fol.*

[1] Cf. No. 61 (vol. i), where punning is described as 'a jingle of words'. In his notes on Ovid's *Metamorphoses* Addison remarks that Homer, Virgil, and Horace all scorned mixed wit and that 'one would wonder therefore how so sublime a genius as Milton could sometimes fall into it, in such a work as an Epic Poem. But we must attribute it to his humouring the vicious taste of the age he lived in, and the false judgment of our unlearned English readers in general, who have few of them a relish of the more masculine and noble beauties of Poetry' (Guthkelch, i. 144).

[2] *PL*, ix. 11; v. 868–9; i. 642; iv. 181. P. Hume (1695), in his note on the third of these quotations, adds: 'Words, thô well chosen, and significative enough, yet of Gingling and Unpleasant Sound, and like Marriages between Persons too near of Kin, to be avoided.'

[3] Aristotle, *Rhetoric*, 3. 11. 7.

[4] Hobbes, in his *Answer to Davenant* (1650), had objected to 'Metaphors or Comparisons as cannot come into mens thoughts but by mean conversation and experience of humble or evil Arts, which the Person of an *Epique* Poem cannot be thought acquainted with' (Spingarn, ii. 54). In the Preface to *Annus Mirabilis* (1667) Dryden approves of their use (Ker, i. 13), but in the Dedication of *Aeneis* (1697) he admits that he has not written in 'the proper terms of navigation, land-service, or in the cant of any profession'. Virgil, he continues, 'writ not to mariners, soldiers, astronomers, gardeners, peasants, etc., but to all in general, and in particular to men and ladies of the first quality, who have better bred than to be too nicely knowing in the terms. In such cases, it is enough for a poet to write so plainly, that he may be understood by his readers; to avoid impropriety, and not affect to be thought learned in all things' (Ker, ii. 236).

wondered how Mr. *Dryden* could translate a Passage out of[a] *Virgil* after the following manner.

> *Tack to the Larboard, and stand off to Sea.*
> *Veer Star-board Sea and Land . . .*[1]

Milton makes use of *Larboard* in the same manner.[2] When he is upon Building he mentions *Doric Pillars, Pilasters, Cornice, Freeze, Architrave.*[3] When he talks of Heavenly Bodies, you meet with *Eccliptick*, and *Eccentric*, the *trepidation, Stars dropping from the Zenith, Rays culminating from the Equator.*[4] To which might be added many Instances of the like kind in several other Arts and Sciences.

I shall in my next Papers[b] give an Account of the many particular Beauties in *Milton*, which would have been too long to insert under those general Heads I have already treated of, and with which I intend to conclude this Piece of Criticism.   L

No. 298   *Monday, February 11, 1712*[5]
[STEELE]

Nusquam Tuta fides . . .
Virg.[c]

Mr. SPECTATOR,   *London, Feb. 9. 1711–12.*

'I AM a Virgin, and in no Case despicable; but yet such as I am I must remain, or else become, 'tis to be feared, less happy: For I find not the least good Effect from the just Correction you some time since gave, that too free, that looser Part of our Sex which spoils the Men;[6] the same Connivance at the Vices, the same easy Admittance of Addresses, the same vitiated Relish of the Conversation of the greatest of Rakes (or in a more fashionable Way of

---

[a] Passage out of] *19;* Passage of *Fol., 8vo, 12mo*   [b] next Papers] next *Saturday's* Paper *Fol.*   [c] *Motto.* Virg. *added in 8vo, 12mo*

---

[1] Dryden's *Aeneis*, iii. 526–7.   [2] *PL*, ii. 1019.
[3] *PL*, i. 713–16.
[4] *PL*, iii. 740; iii. 575; iii. 483; i. 745; iii. 616–17.
[5] *Motto.* Virgil, *Aeneid*, 4. 373:

Truth is now no more. DRYDEN
[6] See Nos. 198, 266, 274 (vol. ii).

expressing one's self, of such as have seen the World most) still abounds, increases, multiplies.

'The humble Petition therefore of many of the most strictly virtuous, and of my self, is, That you'll once more exert your Authority, and that, according to your late Promise, your full, your impartial Authority, on this sillier Branch of our Kind: For why should they be the uncontroulable Mistresses of our Fate? Why should they with Impunity indulge the Males in Licenciousness whilst single, and we have the dismal Hazard and Plague of reforming them when married? Strike home, Sir, then, and spare not, or all our maiden Hopes, our guilded Hopes of nuptial Felicity are frustrated, are vanished; and you your self, as well as Mr. *Courtly*,[1] will, by smoothing over immodest Practices with the Gloss of soft and harmless Names, for ever forfeit our Esteem. Nor think that I'm herein more severe than need be: If I have not reason more than enough, do you and the World judge from this ensuing Account, which, I think, will prove the Evil to be universal.

'You must know then, that since your Reprehension of this Female Degeneracy came out, I've had a Tender of Respects from no less than five Persons, of tollerable Figure too as Times go: But the Misfortune is, that four of the five are professed Followers of the Mode. They would face me down, that all Women of good Sense ever were, and ever will be, Latitudinarians in Wedlock; and always did, and will, give and take what they profanely term Conjugal Liberty of Conscience.

'The two first of them, a Captain and a Merchant, to strengthen their Argument, pretend to repeat after a Couple, a Brace of Ladies of Quality and Wit, That *Venus* was always kind to *Mars*; and what Soul that has the least spark of Generosity, can deny a Man of Bravery any thing? And how pitiful a Trader, that whom no Woman but his own Wife will have Correspondence and Dealings with? Thus these; whilst the third, the Country Squire, confess'd, That indeed he was surpriz'd into good Breeding, and enter'd into the Knowledge of the World unawares. That dining t'other Day at a Gentleman's House, the Person who entertained, was obliged to leave him with his Wife and Neices; where they spoke with so much Contempt of an absent Gentleman for being slow at a Hint, that he had resolved never to be drowsy, unmannerly, or stupid for the future at a Friend's House; and on an hunting Morning, not to

---

[1] Francis Courtly's letter appeared in No. 276 (vol. ii). See also No. 286.

pursue the Game either with the Husband abroad, or with the Wife at home.

'The next that came was a Tradesman, nor less full of the Age than the former; for he had the Gallantry to tell me, that at a late Junket which he was invited to, the Motion being made, and the Question being put, 'twas by Maid, Wife and Widow resolv'd, *nemine contradicente*, That a young sprightly Journeyman is absolutely necessary in their Way of Business: To which they had the Assent and Concurrence of the Husbands present. I dropp'd him a Curtsy, and gave him to understand that was his Audience of Leave.

'I am reckoned pretty, and have had very many Advances besides these; but have been very averse to hear any of them, from my Observation on these above-mentioned, till I hoped some Good from the Character of my present Admirer, a Clergyman. But I find even among them there are indirect Practices in Relation to Love, and our Treaty is at present a little in Suspence, till some Circumstances are cleared. There is a Charge against him among the Women, and the Case is this: It is alledged, That a certain endowed Female would have appropriated her self to and consolidated her self with a Church, which my Divine now enjoys; (or, which is the same thing, did prostitute her self to her Friend's doing this for her): That my Ecclesiastick, to obtain the one, did engage himself to take off the other that lay on Hand; but that on his Success in the Spiritual, he again renounced the Carnal.

'I put this closely to him, and tax'd him with Disingenuity. He to clear himself made the subsequent Defence, and that in the most solemn Manner possible: That he was applied to and instigated to accept of a Benefice: That a conditional Offer thereof was indeed made him at first, but with Disdain by him rejected: That when nothing (as they easily perceived) of this Nature could bring him to their Purpose, Assurance of his being entirely unengaged beforehand, and safe from all their After-Expectations (the only Stratagem left to draw him in) was given him: That pursuant to this, the Donation it self was without Delay, before several reputable Witnesses, tender'd to him *gratis*, with the open Profession of not the least Reserve, or most minute Condition; but that yet immediately after Induction, his insidious Introducer (or her crafty Procurer, which you will) industriously spread the Report; which had reach'd my Ears not only in the Neighbourhood of that said Church, but in *London*, in the University, in mine and his own County, and where-ever else it might probably obviate his Application to any other Woman, and so confine him to this alone: And in a Word, That as he never did make any previous Offer of his Service, or the least Step to her Affection; so on his Discovery of these Designs thus laid to trick him, he could not but afterwards, in Justice to himself, vindicate both his Innocence and Freedom by keeping his proper Distance.

'This is his Apology, and I think I shall be satisfied with it. But I cannot conclude my tedious Epistle, without recommending to you not only to resume your former Chastisement, but to add to your Criminals the simoniacal Ladies, who seduce the sacred Order into the Difficulty of either breaking a mercenary Troth made to them whom they ought not to deceive, or by breaking or keeping it offending against him whom they cannot deceive. Your Assistance and Labours of this Sort would be of great Benefit, and your speedy Thoughts on this Subject would be very seasonable to,

> SIR,
> *Your most obedient Servant,*
> Chastity Loveworth.'

T

No. 299   *Tuesday, February* 12, 1712[1]

[ADDISON]

Malo Venusinam, quam te, Cornelia, Mater
Gracchorum si cum magnis virtutibus affers
Grande supercilium, & numeras in dote triumphos.
Tolle tuum[a] *precor Annibalem victumque Syphacem*
In castris, & cum totâ Carthagine migra.

                                        Juv.

IT is observed, that a Man improves more by reading the Story of a Person eminent for Prudence and Virtue, than by the finest

---

[a] *tuum*] *suum* Fol.; *corrected in Errata* (No. 301)

[For note 1 see following page.

Rules and Precepts of Morality. In the same manner a Representation of those Calamities and Misfortunes which a weak Man suffers from wrong Measures, and ill-concerted Schemes of Life, is apt to make a deeper Impression upon our Minds, than the wisest Maxims and Instructions that can be given us, for avoiding the like Follies and Indiscretions in our own private Conduct. It is for this Reason that I lay before my Reader the following Letter, and leave it with him to make his own use of it, without adding any Reflections of my own upon the Subject-Matter.

Mr. SPECTATOR,

'HAVING carefully perused a Letter sent you by *Josiah Fribble*, Esq; with your subsequent Discourse upon *Pin-money*,[1] I do presume to trouble you with an Account of my own Case, which I look upon to be no less deplorable than that of Squire *Fribble*. I am a Person of no Extraction, having begun the World with a small parcel of Rusty Iron, and was for some Years commonly known by the Name of *Jack Anvil*.[2] I have naturally a very happy Genius for getting Money, insomuch that by the Age of Five and twenty I had scraped together Four thousand two hundred Pounds, Five Shillings, and a few odd Pence. I then launched out into considerable Business, and became a bold Trader both by Sea and Land, which in a few Years raised me a very great[a] Fortune. For these my good Services I was Knighted in the thirty fifth Year of my Age, and lived with great Dignity among my City-Neighbours by the Name of Sir *John Anvil*. Being in my Temper very Ambitious, I was now bent upon making a Family, and accordingly resolved that my Descendants should have a Dash of good Blood in their Veins. In order to this

[a] great] considerable *Fol. (corrected in Errata No. 301), 8vo, 12mo*

[1] No. 295.
[2] According to Nichols the story told in this letter refers to the wealthy iron-monger Sir Ambrose Crowley who 'changed his name from Crowley to Crawley'. For Sir Ambrose, who died on 7 Oct. 1713, see A. L. Reade, *Johnsonian Gleanings*, i. 9–10; iii. 148; also *Victoria County History of Durham*, ii. 281–7.

[1] *Motto*. Juvenal, *Satires*, 6. 167–71:

Some Country-Girl, scarce to a Curt'sey bred,
Wou'd I much rather than *Cornelia* wed:
If Supercilious, Haughty, Proud, and Vain,
She brought her Father's Triumphs in her Train.
Away with all your *Carthaginian* State,
Let vanquish'd *Hannibal* without-doors wait,
Too burly and too big, to pass my narrow gate. DRYDEN.

I made Love to the Lady *Mary Oddly*, an Indigent young Woman of Quality. To cut short the Marriage Treaty, I threw her a *Charte Blanche*,[1] as our News Papers call it, desiring her to write upon it her own Terms. She was very concise in her Demands, insisting only that the Disposal of my Fortune, and the Regulation of my Family, should be entirely in her Hands. Her Father and Brothers appear'd exceedingly averse to this Match, and would not see me for some time; but at present are so well reconciled, that they Dine with me almost every Day, and have borrowed considerable Sums of me; which my Lady *Mary* very often twits me with, when she would shew me how kind her Relations are to me. She had no Portion, as I told you before, but what she wanted in Fortune, she makes up in Spirit. She at first changed my Name to Sir *John Envil*, and at present writes her self *Mary Enville*. I have had some Children by her, whom she has Christen'd with the Sirnames of her Family, in order, as she tells me, to wear out the Homeliness of their Parentage by the Father's Side. Our eldest Son is the Honourable *Oddly Enville*, Esq; and our eldest Daughter *Harriot Enville*. Upon her first coming into my Family, she turned off a parcel of very careful Servants, who had been long with me, and introduced in their stead a couple of Black-a-moors, and three or four very genteel Fellows in Laced Liveries, besides her *French*-woman, who is perpetually making a Noise in the House in a Language which no body understands, except my Lady *Mary*. She next set her self to reform every Room of my House, having glazed all my Chimney-pieces with Looking-glass, and planted every Corner with such heaps of *China*, that I am obliged to move about my own House with the greatest Caution and Circumspection, for fear of hurting some of our Brittle Furniture. She makes an Illumination once a Week with Wax-candles in one of the largest Rooms, in order, as she phrases it, to see Company. At which time she always desires me to be Abroad, or to confine my self to the Cock-loft, that I may not disgrace her among her Visitants of Quality. Her Footmen, as I told you before, are such Beaus that I do not much care for asking them Questions; when I do, they answer me with a sawcy Frown, and say that every thing, which I find Fault with, was done by my Lady *Mary*'s Order. She tells me that she intends they shall wear Swords with their next Liveries, having lately observed the Footmen of two or three Persons of Quality hanging behind the Coach with Swords by their

[1] See No. 165 (vol. ii).

Sides. As soon as the first Honey-moon was over, I represented to her the Unreasonableness of those daily Innovations which she made in my Family, but she told me I was no longer to consider my self as Sir *John Anvil*, but as her Husband; and added, with a Frown, that I did not seem to know who she was. I was surprized to be treated thus, after such Familiarities as had passed between us. But she has since given me to know, that whatever Freedoms she may sometimes indulge me in, she expects in general to be treated with the Respect that is due to her Birth and Quality. Our Children have been trained up from their Infancy with so many Accounts of their Mother's Family, that they know the Stories of all the great Men and Women it has produced. Their Mother tells them, that such an one commanded in such a Sea Engagement, that their Great Grandfather had a Horse shot under him at *Edgehill*,[1] that their Unkle was at the Siege of *Buda*,[2] and that her Mother danced in a Ball[a] at Court with the Duke of *Monmouth*; with abundance of Fiddle faddle of the same nature. I was, the other Day, a little out of Countenance at a Question of my little Daughter *Harriot*, who asked me, with a great deal of Innocence, why I never told them of the Generals and Admirals that had been in *my* Family. As for my Eldest Son *Oddly*, he has been so spirited up[3] by his Mother, that if he does not mend his Manners I shall go near to disinherit him. He drew his Sword upon me before he was Nine Years old, and told me, that he expected to be used like a Gentleman; upon my offering to correct him for his Insolence, my Lady *Mary* stept in between us, and told me, that I ought to consider there[b] was some difference between his Mother and mine. She is perpetually finding out the Features of her own Relations in every one of my Children, tho', by the way, I have a little Chub-faced[4] Boy as like me as he can stare, if I durst say so; but what most angers me, when she sees me playing with any of them upon my Knee, she has begg'd me more than once to converse with the Children as little as possibly, that they may not learn any of my awkward Tricks.

<hr />

[a] in a Ball] at a Ball *Fol.* (*corrected in Errata, No. 301*)   [b] consider there]
consider that there *Fol.*

<hr />

[1] The first battle of the Civil War in 1642.
[2] Buda, the capital of Hungary, was taken by the troops of the Emperor in 1686, after 145 years of occupation by the Turks.
[3] The first example of this combination in *OED* is from *Spectator* 482 (vol. iv).
[4] Having chubby cheeks or face (from the obese appearance of the fish of this name).

'You must farther know, since I am opening my Heart to you, that she thinks her self my superior in Sense, as much as she is in Quality, and therefore treats me like a plain well-meaning Man, who does not know the World. She dictates to me in my own Business, sets me right in point of Trade, and if I disagree with her about any of my Ships at Sea, wonders that I will dispute with her, when I know very well that her Great Grandfather was a Flag-Officer.

'To compleat my Sufferings, she has teazed me for this Quarter of an Year last past, to remove into one of the Squares at the other End of the Town, promising for my Encouragement, that I shall have as good a Cock-loft as any Gentleman in the Square; to which the Honourable *Oddly Enville*, Esq; always adds, like a Jack-a-napes as he is, that he hopes 'twill be as near the Court as possible.

'In short, Mr. SPECTATOR, I am so much out of my natural Element, that to recover my old way of Life, I would be content to begin the World again, and be plain *Jack Anvil*; but alas! I am in for Life, and am bound to Subscribe my self, with great Sorrow of Heart,

Your Humble Servant,
John Enville, *Knt.*'[1]

L

No. 300　　　　　*Wednesday, February 13*, 1712[2]

[STEELE]

. . . *Diversum vitio vitium prope majus.*

Hor.

Mr. SPECTATOR,

'WHEN you talk of the Subject of Love, and the Relations arising from it, methinks you should take Care to leave no Fault unobserved which concerns the State of Marriage. The great

---

[1] A letter from 'Fungoso Stich' (Lillie. ii. 212–14) tells of an experience similar to 'the deplorable case of poor Sir John Enville'. He complains that his father, a merchant-tailor, 'is just now on the point of marrying me to a woman of a family, and is to make abatements in her fortune, and advances in her pin-money, in proportion to the excess of her quality'.

[2] *Motto.* Horace, *Epistles*, I. 18. 5:

But stay my Friend there is another Vice
Just opposite, and almost worse than this. CREECH.

Vexation that I have observed in it, is, that the wedded Couple seem to want Opportunities of being often enough alone together, and are forced to quarrel and be fond before Company. Mr. *Hotspur* and his Lady, in a Room full of their Friends, are ever saying something so smart to each other, and that but just within Rules, that the whole Company stand in the utmost Anxiety and Suspence for Fear of their falling into Extremities which they could not be present at. On the other Side, *Tom Faddle* and his pretty Spouse wherever they come are billing at such a Rate, as they think must do our Hearts good who behold 'em. Cannot you possibly propose a Mean between being Wasps and Doves in Publick? I should think if you advised to hate or love sincerely it would be better: For if they would be so discreet as to hate from the very Bottom of their Hearts, their Aversion would be too strong for little Gibes every Moment; and if they loved with that calm and noble Value which dwells in the Heart, with a Warmth like that of Life-Blood, they would not be so impatient of their Passion as to fall into observable Fondness. This Method, in each Case, would save Appearances; but as those who offend on the fond Side are by much the fewer, I would have you begin with them, and go on to take Notice of a most impertinent Licence married Women take, not only to be very loving to their Spouses in Publick, but also make nauseous Allusions to private Familiarities and the like. *Lucina*[1] is a Lady of the greatest Discretion you must know in the World; and withal very much a Physician:[2] Upon the Strength of these two Qualities there is nothing she will not speak of before us Virgins; and she every Day talks with a very grave Air in such a Manner, as is very improper so much as to be hinted at but to obviate the greatest Extremity. Those whom they call good Bodies, notable People, hearty Neighbours, and the purest goodest Company in the World, are the great Offenders in this Kind. Here I think I have laid before you an open Field for Pleasantry; and hope you will shew these People that at least they are not witty: In which you will save from many a Blush a daily Sufferer, who is very much

Your most humble Servant,
Susanna Decent.'[a]

<hr>

[a] Susanna Decent.] *8vo*; Susanna Loveworth. *Fol., 12mo*

<hr>

[1] One of the names of Juno, as the goddess presiding over childbirth. See Ovid, *Fasti*, 2. 429–52.
[2] Here used in the obsolete sense of a student of natural science or physics.

Mr. SPECTATOR,

'IN yours of *Wednesday* the 30th past, you and your Correspondent are very severe on a sort of Men, whom you call Male Coquets; but without any other Reason, in my Apprehension, than that of paying a shallow Compliment to the fair Sex, by accusing some Men of imaginary Faults, that the Women may not seem to be the more faulty Sex; though at the same time you suppose there are some so weak as to be imposed upon by fine things and false Addresses. I can't perswade my self that your Design is to debar the Sexes the Benefit of each other's Conversation within the Rules of Honour; nor will you, I dare say, recommend to 'em, or encourage the common Tea-Table Talk, much less that of Politicks and Matter of State: And if these are forbidden Subjects of Discourse, then, as long as there are any Women in the World who take a Pleasure in hearing themselves praised, and can bear the Sight of a Man prostrate at their Feet, so long I shall make no Wonder that there are those of the other Sex who will pay them those impertinent Humiliations. We should have few People such Fools as to practise Flattery, if all were so wise as to despise it. I don't deny but you would do a meritorious Act, if you could prevent all Impositions on the Simplicity of young Women; but I must confess I don't apprehend you have laid the Fault on the proper Person, and if I trouble you with my Thoughts upon it I promise my self your Pardon. Such of the Sex as are raw and innocent, and most exposed to these Attacks, have, or their Parents are much to blame if they have not, one to advise and guard 'em, and are obliged themselves to take Care of 'em; but if these, who ought to hinder Men from all Opportunities of this sort of Conversation, instead of that encourage and promote it, the Suspicion is very just that there are some private Reasons for it; and I'll leave it to you to determine on which Side a Part is then acted. Some Women there are who are arrived at Years of Discretion, I mean are got out of the Hands of their Parents and Governours, and are set up for themselves, who yet are liable to these Attempts; but if these are prevail'd upon, you must excuse me if I lay the Fault upon them that their Wisdom is not grown with their Years. My Client, Mr. *Strephon*, whom you summoned to declare himself, gives you Thanks however for your Warning; and begs the Favour only to inlarge his Time for a Week, or to the last Day of the Term, and then he'll appear *gratis* and pray no Day over. *Yours*, Philanthropos.'

Mr. SPECTATOR,

'I WAS last Night to visit a Lady who I much esteem, and always took for my Friend; but met with so very different a Reception from what I expected, that I cannot help applying my self to you on this Occasion. In the Room of that Civility and Familiarity I used to be treated with by her, an affected Strangeness in her Looks and Coldness in her Behaviour, plainly told me I was not the welcome Guest which the Regard and Tenderness she has often expressed for me gave me Reason to flatter my self to think I was. Sir, this is certainly a great Fault, and I assure you a very common one; therefore I hope you will think it a fit Subject for some Part of a *Spectator*. Be pleased to acquaint us how we must behave our selves towards this valetudinary[1] Friendship, subject to so many Heats and Colds; and you will oblige,

SIR,

Your humble Servant,

Miranda.'

Sir,

'I CANNOT forbear acknowledging the Delight your late *Spectators* on *Saturdays* have given me; for it is writ in the honest Spirit of Criticism, and called to my Mind the following four Lines I had read long since in a Prologue to a Play called *Julius Cæsar*, which has deserved a better Fate.[2] The Verses are addressed to the little Criticks.

> *Shew your small Talent, and let that suffice ye;*
> *But grow not vain upon it, I advise ye.*
> *For every Fop can find out Faults in Plays:*
> *You'll ne'er arrive at Knowing when to praise.*

Yours,

D. G.'

T

---

[1] This is the only example in *OED* of the word used in a figurative sense.

[2] The lines are from the adaptation of Shakespeare's *Julius Caesar* by John Sheffield, Duke of Buckinghamshire (see H. B. Charlton in *Modern Language Review*, xvi (1921), 171–2). This version, in two parts (*Julius Caesar* and *Marcus Brutus*), seems never to have been publicly acted and was not printed until 1722. The manuscript may have been in circulation, however (cf. Giles Jacob, *Historical Account of . . . our most considerable English Poets*, 1720, Dedication, page iv). John Dennis a short time earlier,

Thursday, February 14, 1712[1]

> *Possent ut Juvenes visere fervidi*
> *Multo non sine risu,*
> *Dilapsam in cineres facem.*
>
> Hor.

WE are generally so much pleased with any little Accomplishments, either of Body or Mind, which have once made us remarkable in the World, that we endeavour to perswade our selves it is not in the Power of Time to rob us of them. We are eternally pursuing the same Methods which first procured us the Applauses of Mankind. It is from this Notion that an Author writes on, tho' he is come to Dotage; without ever considering that his Memory is impair'd, and that he has lost that Life, and those Spirits, which formerly raised his Fancy, and fired his Imagination. The same Folly hinders a Man from submitting his Behaviour to his Age, and makes *Clodius*, who was a celebrated Dancer at Five and twenty, still love to hobble in a Minuet, tho' he is past Threescore. It is this, in a word, which fills the Town with elderly Fops, and superannuated Coquets.

Canidia, a Lady of this latter Species, passed by me yesterday in her Coach.[2] *Canidia* was an haughty Beauty of the last Age, and was followed by Crowds of Adorers, whose Passions only pleased her, as they gave her Opportunities of playing the Tyrant. She then contracted that awful Cast of the Eye and forbidding Frown, which she has not yet laid aside, and has still all the Insolence of Beauty

in his *Essay on . . . Shakespear* (1711), had referred to Buckinghamshire as 'that great Man, who some Years ago, I hear, alter'd the *Julius Caesar*' (*Works*, ed. Hooker, ii. 12). The lines, as printed by Pope in *The Works of John Sheffield, Duke of Buckingham* (1723, i. 333), come at the end of the Prologue to 'The Tragedy of Marcus Brutus' and read:

> Shew your small Talent then, let that suffice ye,
> But grow not vain upon it, I advise ye;
> Each petty Critic can Objections raise,
> The greatest Skill is knowing when to praise.

Since Pope knew the Duke as early as 1709 (*Correspondence*, ed. Sherburn, i. 17) and contributed choruses to the *Julius Caesar* (ibid. i. 386), this note signed 'D. G.' may be by Pope.

[1] *Motto*. Horace, *Odes*, 4. 13. 26–28:

> When our hot Youths shall come, and laugh to see
> The Torch that burnt before;
> And kindled aged Lechery,
> To Ashes fall'n, and warm no more. CREECH.

[2] Canidia is the aged and repulsive sorceress in Horace (*Satires*, I. 8, and *Epode* 5).

without its Charms. If she now attracts the Eyes of any Beholders, it is only by being remarkably ridiculous; even her own Sex laugh at her Affectation; and the Men, who always enjoy an ill-natured Pleasure in seeing an imperious Beauty humbled and neglected, regard her with the same Satisfaction that a free Nation sees a Tyrant in Disgrace.

WILL. HONEYCOMB, who is a great Admirer of the Gallantries in King *Charles* the Second's Reign, lately communicated to me a Letter written by a Wit of that Age to his Mistress, who, it seems, was a Lady of *Canidia*'s Humour; and tho' I do not always approve of my Friend WILL's Taste, I liked this Letter so well, that I took a Copy of it, with which I shall here present my Reader.

To CLOE.

Madam,

'SINCE my waking Thoughts have never been able to influence you in my Favour, I am resolved to try whether my Dreams can make any Impression on you. To this end I shall give you an Account of a very odd one which my Fancy presented to me last Night, within a few Hours after I left you.

'Methought I was unaccountably conveyed into the most delicious Place mine Eyes ever beheld, it was a large Valley divided by a River of the purest Water I had ever seen. The Ground on each side of it rose by an easie Ascent, and was cover'd with Flowers of an infinite Variety, which as they were reflected in the Water, doubled the Beauties of the Place, or rather formed an Imaginary Scene more beautiful than the real. On each side of the River was a Range of lofty Trees, whose Boughs were loaden with almost as many Birds as Leaves. Every Tree was full of Harmony.

'I had not gone far in this pleasant Valley, when I perceived that it was terminated by a most magnificent Temple. The Structure was ancient, and Regular. On the Top of it was figured the God *Saturn*, in the same Shape and Dress that the Poets usually represent *Time*.

'As I was advancing to satisfie my Curiosity by a nearer View, I was stopped by an Object far more beautiful than any I had before discovered in the whole Place. I fancy, Madam, you will easily guess, that this could hardly be any thing but your self; in reality it was so; you lay extended on the Flowers by the side of the River, so that your Hands, which were thrown in a negligent Posture, almost touched the Water. Your Eyes were closed; but if your Sleep deprived me of the Satisfaction of seeing them, it left me at leasure to contemplate several other Charms, which disappear when your Eyes are open. I could not but admire the Tranquility you slept in, especially when I considered the Uneasiness you produce in so many others.

'While I was wholly taken up in these Reflections, the Doors of the Temple flew open, with a very great Noise; and lifting up my Eyes, I saw two Figures, in Human Shape, coming into the Valley. Upon a nearer Survey, I found them to be YOUTH and LOVE. The First was encircled with a kind of Purple Light, that spread a Glory over all the Place; the other held a flaming Torch in his Hand. I could observe, that all the way as they came towards us, the Colours of the Flowers appeared more lively, the Trees shot out in Blossoms, the Birds threw themselves into Pairs, and Serenaded them as they passed: The whole Face of Nature glowed with new Beauties. They were no sooner arrived at the Place where you lay, when they seated themselves on each Side of you. On their Approach, methought I saw a new Bloom arise in your Face, and new Charms diffuse themselves over your whole Person. You appeared more than Mortal; but, to my great Surprise, continued fast asleep, tho' the two Deities made several gentle Efforts to awaken you.

'After a short time, YOUTH (displaying a Pair of Wings, which I had not before taken notice of,) flew off. LOVE still remained, and holding the Torch which he had in his Hand before your Face, you still appeared as beautiful as ever. The glaring of the Light in your Eyes at length awaken'd you, when, to my great Surprise, instead of acknowledging the Favour of the Deity, you frowned upon him, and struck the Torch out of his Hand into the River. The God, after having regarded you with a Look that spoke at once[a] his Pity and Displeasure, flew away. Immediately a kind of Gloom overspread the whole Place. At the same time I saw an hideous Spectre enter at one end of the Valley. His Eyes were sunk into his Head, his Face was pale and withered, and his Skin puckered up in Wrinkles. As he walked on the sides of the Bank the River froze, the Flowers faded, the Trees shed their Blossoms, the Birds dropp'd from off the Boughs, and fell dead at his Feet. By these Marks I knew him to be OLD-AGE: You were seized with the utmost Horror

[a] at once] at the same time Fol.

and Amazement at his Approach. You endeavoured to have fled, but the Phantome caught you in his Arms. You may easily guess at the Change you suffered in this Embrace. For my own Part, tho' I am still too full of the dreadful Idea, I will not Shock you with a Description of it: I was so startled at the Sight that my Sleep immediately left me, and I found my self awake, at leasure to consider of a Dream which seems too extraordinary to be without a Meaning. I am, Madam, with the greatest Passion,

Your most Obedient,

most Humble Servant, &c.'

X

No. 302

[HUGHES]

Friday, February 15, 1712[1]

> . . . *Lachrymæque decoræ,*
> *Gratior & pulchro veniens in corpore Virtus.*
>
> Vir. Æn. 5.

I READ what I give for the Entertainment of this Day with a great deal of Pleasure, and publish it just as it came to my Hands. I shall be very glad to find there are many guessed at for *Emilia.*[2]

[1] *Motto.* Virgil, *Aeneid,* 5. 343–4:

> The lovely Grief to Pity won,
> And Virtue, grac'd with Beauty, brighter shone.

[2] Many attempts have been made to discover the original. Among those 'guessed at for Emilia' have been Anne, wife of the 2nd Earl of Coventry, author of *Meditations and Reflections, moral and divine* (1707), who died in 1763 in her ninetieth year; and a lady described by Nichols:

She was the mother of Mrs. Ascham of Connington in Cambridgeshire, and grandmother of the present Lady Hatton. This very amiable Lady was a great benefactress to Mrs. Ockley, the daughter of Dr. Simon Ockley, who was left at the death of her father, not in very easy circumstances. Mrs. Ockley, on whose unsuspicious testimony this information rests, affirms from her own personal knowledge of the real lady, that the character is faithfully delineated. An internal circumstance in the Paper itself, the repeated mention of the name of *Bromius,* seems to corroborate the testimony of Mrs. Ockley, and to vouch for the propriety of the assignment of this Paper to Dr. Brome.

The Lady Hatton referred to is presumably Harriet, the wife of Sir Thomas Hatton, Bart. of Long Stanton (d. 1787), and daughter of Dingley Ascham of Connington (John and John Bernard Burke, *Extinct and Dormant Baronetcies of England,* 1838, pp. 248–50). Another source has been found in the essay by Saint-Evremond, 'Idée de la Femme, qui ne se trouve point, & qui ne se trouvera jamais', in his *Œuvres* published by Tonson in 1711, ii. 241–9 (Walter M. Daniels, *Saint-Evremond en Angleterre*

Mr. SPECTATOR,

'IF this Paper has the good Fortune to be honoured with a Place in your Writings, I shall be the more pleased, because the Character of *Emilia* is not an imaginary but a real one. I have industriously obscured the whole by the Addition of one or two Circumstances of no Consequence, that the Person it is drawn from might still be concealed; and that the Writer of it might not be in the least suspected, and for some other Reasons, I chuse not to give it the Form of a Letter: But if, besides the Faults of the Composition, there be any thing in it more proper for a Correspondent than the SPECTATOR himself to write, I submit it to your better Judgment, to receive any other Model you think fit.

I am,

SIR,

Your very humble Servant.

There is nothing which gives one so pleasing a Prospect of humane Nature, as the Contemplation of Wisdom and Beauty: The latter is the peculiar Portion of that Sex which is therefore called Fair; but the happy Concurrence of both these Excellencies in the same Person, is a Character too celestial to be frequently met with. Beauty is an over-weaning self-sufficient thing, careless of providing it self any more substantial Ornaments; nay so little does it consult its own Interests, that it too often defeats it self, by betraying that Innocence which renders it lovely and desirable. As therefore Virtue makes a beautiful Woman appear more beautiful, so Beauty makes a virtuous Woman really more virtuous. Whilst I am considering these two Perfections gloriously united in one Person, I cannot help representing to my Mind the Image of *Emilia*.

Who ever beheld the charming *Emilia*, without feeling in his Breast at once the Glow of Love and the Tenderness of virtuous Friendship? The unstudied Graces of her Behaviour, and the pleasing Accents of her Tongue, insensibly draw you on to wish for

(Versailles, 1907), p. 126). The character there is called Emilie, but otherwise there is little similarity. According to Nichols, 'the real writer was Dr. Brome, the clergyman of the parish in which the lady lived . . .'. It is listed, however, by Duncombe among Hughes's contributions to the *Spectator*, and Steele's opening words imply that it is a contributed piece which he is publishing 'just as it came to my Hands'. It became one of the most popular essays in the periodical: as late as 1801 the *Gentleman's Magazine* published a paraphrase in verse (April 1801, pp. 348–9), beginning:

Who can behold Emilia, and not feel
Love's warmest glow, and Friendship's kindred zeal?

a nearer Enjoyment of them; but even her Smiles carry in them a silent Reproof to the Impulses of licentious Love. Thus, tho' the Attractives[1] of her Beauty play almost irresistibly upon you and create Desire, you immediately stand corrected not by the Severity but the Decency of her Virtue. That Sweetness and Good-humour which is so visible in her Face, naturally diffuses it self into every Word and Action: A Man must be a Savage, who, at the Sight of *Emilia*, is not more inclined to do her Good than gratify himself: Her Person as it is thus studiously embellished by Nature, thus adorned with unpremeditated Graces, is a fit Lodging for a Mind so fair and lovely; there dwell rational Piety, modest Hope, and chearful Resignation.

Many of the prevailing Passions of Mankind do undeservedly pass under the Name of Religion; which is thus made to express it self in Action, according to the Nature of the Constitution in which it resides: So that were we to make a Judgment from Appearances, one would imagine Religion in some is little better than Sullenness and Reserve, in many Fear, in others the Despondings[2] of a melancholly Complexion, in others the Formality of insignificant unaffecting Observances, in others Severity, in others Ostentation. In *Emilia* it is a Principle founded in Reason and enlivened with Hope; it does not break forth into irregular Fits and Sallies of Devotion, but is an uniform and consistent Tenour of Action: It is strict without Severity, compassionate without Weakness; it is the Perfection of that good Humour which proceeds from the Understanding, not the Effect of an easy Constitution.

By a generous Sympathy in Nature, we feel our selves disposed to mourn when any of our Fellow Creatures are afflicted; but injured Innocence and Beauty in Distress, is an Object that carries in it something inexpressibly moving: It softens the most manly Heart with the tenderest Sensations of Love and Compassion, till at length it confesses its Humanity and flows out into Tears.

Were I to relate that Part of *Emilia*'s Life which has given her an Opportunity of exerting the Heroism of Christianity, it would make too sad, too tender a Story: But when I consider her alone in the Midst of her Distresses, looking beyond this gloomy Vale of Affliction and Sorrow in the Joys of Heaven and Immortality, and when

[1] The attractives, i.e. attractive personal qualities. A 'very favourite word' in the seventeenth and eighteenth centuries, now replaced by *attraction* (*OED*).
[2] The only example of this verbal substantive in *OED* is dated 1818.

I see her in Conversation thoughtless and easy as if she were the most happy Creature in the World, I am transported with Admiration. Surely never did such a Philosophic Soul inhabit such a beauteous Form! For Beauty is often made a Privilege against Thought and Reflexion; it laughs at Wisdom, and will not abide the Gravity of its Instructions.

Were I able to represent *Emilia*'s Virtues in their proper Colours and their due Proportions, Love or Flattery might perhaps be thought to have drawn the Picture larger than Life; but as this is but an imperfect Draught of so excellent a Character, and as I cannot, will not hope to have any Interest in her Person, all that I can say of her is but impartial Praise extorted from me by the prevailing Brightness of her Virtues. So rare a Pattern of Female Excellence ought not to be concealed, but should be set out to the View and Imitation of the World; for how amiable does Virtue appear thus as it were made visible to us in so fair an Example!

Honoria's Disposition is of a very different Turn: Her Thoughts are wholly bent upon Conquest and arbitrary Power. That she has some Wit and Beauty no Body denies, and therefore has the Esteem of all her Acquaintance as a Woman of an agreeable Person and Conversation; but (whatever her Husband may think of it) that is not sufficient for *Honoria*: She waves that Title to Respect as a mean Acquisition, and demands Veneration in the Right of an Idol; for this Reason her natural Desire of Life is continually checked with an inconsistent Fear of Wrinkles and old Age.

Emilia cannot be supposed ignorant of her personal Charms, tho' she seems to be so; but she will not hold her Happiness upon so precarious a Tenure, whilst her Mind is adorned with Beauties of a more exalted and lasting Nature. When in the full Bloom of Youth and Beauty we saw her surrounded with a Croud of Adorers, she took no Pleasure in Slaughter and Destruction, gave no false deluding Hopes which might encrease the Torments of her disappointed Lovers; but having for some Time given to the Decency of a Virgin Coyness, examined the Merit of their several Pretensions, she at length gratified her own, by resigning herself to the ardent Passion of *Bromius*. *Bromius* was then Master of many good Qualities and a moderate Fortune, which was soon after unexpectedly encreased to a plentiful Estate. This for a good while prov'd his Misfortune, as it furnish'd his unexperienc'd Age with the Opportunities of evil Company and a sensual Life. He might have longer wander'd in the

Labyrinths of Vice and Folly, had not *Emilia*'s prudent Conduct won him over to the Government of his Reason. Her Ingenuity has been constantly employed in humanizing his Passions and refining his Pleasures. She has shew'd him by her own Example, that Virtue is consistent with decent Freedoms and good Humour, or rather, that it cannot subsist without 'em. Her good Sense readily instructed her, that a silent Example and an easy unrepining Behaviour, will always be more perswasive than the Severity of Lectures and Admonitions; and that there is so much Pride interwoven into the Make of Humane Nature, that an obstinate Man must only take the Hint from another, and then be left to advise and correct himself. Thus by an artful Train of Management and unseen Perswasions, having at first brought him not to dislike, and at length to be pleased with that which otherwise he would not have bore to hear of, she then knew how to press and secure this Advantage, by approving it as his Thought, and seconding it as his Proposal. By this Means she has gain'd an Interest in some of his leading Passions, and made them accessary to his Reformation.

There is another Particular of *Emilia*'s Conduct which I can't forbear mentioning: To some perhaps it may at first Sight appear but a trifling inconsiderable Circumstance; but for my Part, I think it highly worthy of Observation, and to be recommended to the Consideration of the fair Sex. I have often thought wrapping Gowns and dirty Linnen, with all that huddled Oeconomy of Dress which passes under the general Name of a Mob,[1] the Bane of conjugal Love, and one of the readiest Means imaginable to alienate the Affection of an Husband, especially a fond one. I have heard some Ladies who have been surprized by Company in such a Deshabille, apologize for it after this Manner; *Truly I am ashamed to be caught in this Pickle; but my Husband and I were sitting all alone by our selves, and I did not expect to see such good Company*—This by the Way is a fine Compliment to the good Man, which 'tis ten to one but he returns in dogged Answers and a churlish Behaviour, without knowing what it is that puts him out of Humour.

Emilia's Observation teaches her, that as little Inadvertencies and Neglects cast a Blemish upon a great Character; so the Neglect of Apparel, even among the most intimate Friends, does insensibly lessen their Regards to each other, by creating a Familiarity too

---

[1] This is the last quotation in *OED* for this word ('a négligé attire, a dishabille'). For *deshabille*, used in the next sentence, cf. No. 49 (vol. i).

low and contemptible. She understands the Importance of those things which the Generality account Trifles; and considers every thing as a Matter of Consequence, that has the least Tendency towards keeping up or abating the Affection of her Husband; him she esteems a fit Object to employ her Ingenuity in pleasing, because he is to be pleased for Life.

By the Help of these, and a thousand other nameless Arts, which 'tis easier for her to practise than for another to express, by the Obstinacy of her Goodness and unprovoked Submission, in spight of all her Afflictions and ill Usage, *Bromius* is become a Man of Sense and a kind Husband, and *Emilia* a happy Wife.

Ye guardian Angels to whose Care Heaven has entrusted its dear *Emilia*, guide her still forward in the Paths of Virtue, defend her from the Insolence and Wrongs of this undiscerning World; at length when we must no more converse with such Purity on Earth, lead her gently hence innocent and unreprovable to a better Place, where by an easy Transition from what she now is, she may shine forth an Angel of Light.   T

No. 303   *Saturday, February* 16, 1712[1]
[ADDISON]

> . . . *volet hæc sub luce videri,*
> *Judicis argutum quæ non formidat acumen.*
>   Hor.

I HAVE seen in the Works of a Modern Philosopher, a Map of the Spots in the Sun. My last Paper of the Faults and Blemishes in *Milton's Paradise Lost,* may be consider'd as a Piece of the same Nature. To pursue the Allusion: As it is observ'd, that among the bright parts of the Luminous Body above-mentioned, there are some which glow more intensely, and dart a stronger Light than others; so, notwithstanding I have already shewn *Milton's* Poem to be very beautiful in general, I shall now proceed to take notice of such

---

[1] *Motto.* Horace, *Ars poetica,* 363–4:
Poems like *Pictures,* some when near delight,
At distance some, some ask the clearest light. CREECH.

Beauties as appear to me more exquisite than the rest. *Milton* has proposed the Subject of his Poem in the following Verses.

> *Of Mans first disobedience, and the fruit*
> *Of that forbidden tree, whose mortal taste*
> *Brought Death into the World and all our woe,*
> *With loss of Eden, 'till one greater Man*
> *Restore us, and regain the blissful Seat,*
> *Sing Heav'nly Muse . . .*

These Lines are perhaps as plain, simple and unadorned as any of the whole Poem, in which particular the Author has conform'd himself to the Example of *Homer*, and the Precept of *Horace*.[1]

His Invocation to a Work which turns in a great measure upon the Creation of the World, is very properly made to the Muse who inspired *Moses* in those Books from whence our Author drew his Subject, and to the Holy Spirit who is therein represented as operating after a particular manner in the first Production of Nature. This whole Exordium rises very happily into noble Language and Sentiment, as I think the Transition to the Fable is exquisitely beautiful and natural.

The nine Days Astonishment,[2] in which the Angels lay entranced after their dreadful Overthrow and Fall from Heaven, before they could recover either the use of Thought or Speech, is a noble *Circumstance*, and very finely imagined. The Division of Hell into Seas of Fire, and into firm Ground impregnated with the same furious Element,[3] with that particular Circumstance of the exclusion of *Hope*[4] from those Infernal Regions, are Instances of the same great and fruitful Invention.

Vid. Hesiod.[a]

The Thoughts in the first Speech and Description of *Satan*, who is one of the principal Actors in this Poem, are wonderfully proper to give us a full Idea of him.[5] His Pride, Envy and Revenge, Obstinacy, Despair and Impenitence, are all of them very artfully interwoven. In short, his first Speech is a Complication of all those Passions which discover themselves separately in several other of his Speeches in the Poem. The whole part of this great Enemy of

---

[a] *Vid. Hesiod.* added in *19*

[1] Simplicity and modesty, according to Le Bossu (book iii, chap. iii), are the two characteristics of the propositions in the *Odyssey*, the *Aeneid*, and even the *Iliad*. For the precept of Horace see *Ars poetica*, 136–45.
[2] *PL*, i. 50–53.
[3] *PL*, i. 61–64, 228–9.
[4] *PL*, i. 66.
[5] *PL*, i. 84–124.

Mankind is filled with such Incidents as are very apt to raise and terrifie the Reader's Imagination. Of this Nature, in the Book now before us, is his being the first that awakens out of the general Trance, with his Posture on the burning Lake, his rising from it, and the Description of his Shield and Spear.

> *Thus* Satan *talking to his nearest mate,*
> *With head up-lift above the wave, and eyes*
> *That sparkling blazed, his other parts beside*
> *Prone on the Flood, extended long and large,*
> *Lay floating many a rood . . .*
> *Forthwith upright he rears from off the pool*
> *His mighty Stature; on each hand the flames*
> *Driv'n backward slope their pointing Spires, and rowl'd*
> *In Billows, leave i'th'midst a horrid vale.*
> *Then with expanded wings he steers his flight*
> *Aloft, incumbent on the dusky Air*
> *That felt unusual weight . . .*
> *. . . His pondrous Shield,*
> *Ethereal temper, massie, large and round,*
> *Behind him cast; the broad circumference*
> *Hung on his Shoulders like the Moon, whose orb*
> *Thro' Optick Glass the* Tuscan *Artists view*
> *At Ev'ning from the top of* Fesole,
> *Or in* Valdarno *to descry new Lands,*
> *Rivers or Mountains on her spotty Globe.*
> *His Spear to equal which the tallest pine*
> *Hewn on* Norwegian *Hills to be the Mast*
> *Of some great Ammiral, were but a wand,*
> *He walk'd with to support uneasie Steps*
> *Over the burning Marl . . .*[1]

To which we may add his Call to the fallen Angels that lay plunged and stupified in the Sea of Fire.

> *He call'd so loud, that all the hollow deep*
> *Of Hell resounded . . .*[2]

But there is no single Passage in the whole Poem worked up to a greater Sublimity, than that wherein his Person is described in those celebrated Lines:

[1] *PL*, i. 192-6, 221-7, 284-96.   [2] *PL*, i. 314-15.

> . . . *He, above the rest*
> *In shape and gesture proudly eminent*
> *Stood like a Tower,* &c.[1]

His Sentiments are every way answerable to his Character, and suitable[a] to a created Being of the most exalted and most depraved Nature. Such is that in which he takes Possession of his Place of Torments.

> . . . *Hail Horrors, hail*
> *Infernal World, and thou profoundest Hell*
> *Receive thy new Possessor, one who brings*
> *A mind not to be changed by place or time.*[2]

And afterwards,

> . . . *Here at least*
> *We shall be free; th' Almighty hath not built*
> *Here for his envy, will not drive us hence:*
> *Here we may reign secure, and in my choice*
> *To reign is worth ambition, tho' in Hell:*
> *Better to reign in Hell, than serve in Heaven.*[3]

Amidst those Impieties which this Enraged Spirit utters in other places of the Poem, the Author has taken care to introduce none that is not big with absurdity, and incapable of shocking a Religious Reader; his Words, as the Poet describes[b] them, bearing only a *Semblance of Worth, not Substance.*[4] He is likewise with great Art described as owning his Adversary to be Almighty.[5] Whatever perverse Interpretation he puts on the Justice, Mercy, and other Attributes of the Supreme Being, he frequently confesses his Omnipotence, that being the Perfection he was forced to allow him, and the only Consideration which could support his Pride under the Shame of his Defeat.

Nor must I here omit that beautiful Circumstance of his bursting out in Tears, upon his Survey of those innumerable Spirits whom he had involved in the same Guilt and Ruin with himself.

---

[a] and suitable] and are suitable *Fol.* describes *Fol., 8vo, 12mo*

[b] Poet describes] *19*; Poet himself

---

[1] *PL,* i. 589–91.
[2] *PL,* i. 250–3.
[3] *PL,* i. 258–63.
[4] *PL,* i. 529.
[5] *PL,* i. 144.

> .... *He now prepared*
> *To speak; whereat their doubled ranks they bend*
> *From wing to wing, and half enclose him round*
> *With all his Peers: Attention held them mute.*
> *Thrice he assay'd, and thrice in spite of Scorn*
> *Tears, such as Angels weep, burst forth . . .*[1]

The Catalogue of Evil Spirits[2] has Abundance[a] of Learning in it, and a very agreeable turn of Poetry, which rises in a great measure from its[b] describing the Places where they were worshipped, by those beautiful marks of Rivers so frequent among the Ancient Poets. The Author had doubtless in this place *Homer's* Catalogue of Ships, and *Virgil's* List of Warriors in his view.[3] The Characters of *Moloch* and *Belial*[4] prepare the Reader's Mind for their respective Speeches and Behaviour in the second and sixth Book. The account of *Thammuz* is finely Romantick, and suitable to what we read among the Ancients of the Worship which was paid to that Idol.

> [c] *. . . Thammuz came next behind,*
> *Whose annual Wound in* Lebanon *allur'd*
> *The Syrian Damsels to lament his fate,*
> *In am'rous Ditties all a Summer's day,*
> *While smooth* Adonis *from his native Rock*
> *Ran purple to the Sea, suppos'd with Blood*
> *Of* Thammuz *yearly wounded: the Love-tale,*
> *Infected* Sion's *Daughters with like Heat,*
> *Whose wanton Passions in the sacred Porch*
> Ezekiel *saw, when by the Vision led*
> *His Eye survey'd the dark Idolatries*
> *Of alienated* Judah. . . .[c][5]

---

[a] Abundance] a great deal *Fol.*   [b] its] *19*; his *Fol., 8vo, 12mo*   [c-c] added in *19*

---

[1] *PL*, i. 615–20.   [2] *PL*, i. 376–521.
[3] *Iliad*, 2. 494 ff. Virgil's list: *Aeneid*, 7. 647 ff. In a note on Ovid (Book iii, Fable ii) Addison comments on these catalogues of proper names:
The smoothness of our *English* verse is too much lost by the repetition of proper names, which is otherwise very natural and absolutely necessary in some cases; as before a battel, to raise in our minds an answerable expectation of the event, and a lively Idea of the numbers that are engaged. For had *Homer* or *Virgil* only told us in two or three lines before their fights, that there were forty thousand of each side, our imagination could not possibly have been so affected, as when we see every Leader singled out, and every Regiment in a manner drawn up before our eyes (Guthkelch, i. 142–3).
[4] *PL*, i. 392–405, 490–505.   [5] *PL*, i. 446–57.

ᵃThe Reader will pardon me if I insert as a Note on this beautiful Passage, the Account given us by the late ingenious Mr. *Maundrell*[1] of this Antient Piece of Worship, and probably the first Occasion of such a Superstition. 'We came to a fair large River—doubtless the Antient River *Adonis*, so famous for the Idolatrous Rites perform'd here in Lamentation of *Adonis*. We had the Fortune to see what may be supposed to be the Occasion of that Opinion which *Lucian* relates, concerning this River, *viz.* That this Stream, at certain Seasons of the Year, especially about the Feast of *Adonis*, is of a bloody Colour; which the Heathens looked upon as proceeding from a kind of Sympathy in the River for the Death of *Adonis*, who was killed by a wild Boar in the Mountains, out of which this Stream rises. Something like this we saw actually come to pass; for the Water was stain'd to a surprising redness; and, as we observ'd in Travelling, had discolour'd the Sea a great way into a reddish Hue, occasion'd doubtless by a sort of Minium, or red Earth, washed into the River by the violence of the Rain, and not by any stain from *Adonis*'s Blood.'ᵃ

The Passage in the Catalogue, explaining the manner how Spirits transform themselves by Contraction, or Enlargement of their Dimensions,[2] is introduced with great Judgement, to make way for several surprizing Accidents in the Sequel of the Poem. There follows one, at the very End of the First Book, which is what the *French* Critics call *Marvellous*, but at the same time *probable* by reason of the Passage last mentioned. As soon as the Infernal Palace is finished, we are told the Multitude and Rabble of Spirits immediately shrunk themselves into a small Compass, that there might be Room for such a numberless Assembly in this capacious Hall. But it is the Poet's Refinement upon this Thought, which I most admire, and which is indeed very noble in its self. For he tells us, that notwithstanding the vulgar, among the fallen Spirits, contracted their Forms, those of the first Rank and Dignity still preserved their natural Dimensions.

ᵃ⁻ᵃ *added in 19*

[1] *A Journey from Aleppo to Jerusalem at Easter, A.D. 1697*, by Henry Maundrell, 'Chaplain to the Factory at *Aleppo*', was published at Oxford in 1703. The brief account of his journey is in the form of a journal, and the passage quoted is under the dates 15–16 Mar. (5th ed., Oxford, 1732, pp. 34–35). The stream he identifies with the Adonis was called, according to Maundrell, by the Turks Ibrahim Pasha.
[2] *PL*, i. 423–31.

> *Thus incorporeal Spirits to smallest Forms*
> *Reduc'd their Shapes immense, and were at large,*
> *Though without Number still amidst the Hall*
> *Of that infernal Court. But far within,*
> *And in their own Dimensions like themselves,*
> *The Great Seraphick Lords and Cherubim,*
> *In close recess and Secret conclave sate,*
> *A thousand Demy Gods on Golden Seats,*
> *Frequent and full . . .*[1]

The Character of *Mammon*,[2] and the Description of the *Pandæmonium*,[3] are full of Beauties.

There are several other Strokes in the First Book wonderfully poetical, and Instances of that Sublime Genius so peculiar to the Author. Such is the Description[4] of *Azazel*'s Stature, and of the Infernal Standard, which he unfurls; as also[a] of that ghastly Light, by which the Fiends appear to one another in their Place of Torments.

> *The Seat of Desolation, void of Light,*
> *Save what the glimmering of those livid Flames*
> *Casts pale and dreadful . . .*[5]

The Shout of the whole Host of fallen Angels when drawn up in Battel Array:

> *. . . The Universal Host up sent*
> *A Shout that tore Hells Concave, and beyond*
> *Frighted the reign of* Chaos *and old* Night.[6]

The Review, which the Leader makes of his Infernal Army:

> *. . . He thro' the armed files*
> *Darts his experienc'd eye, and soon traverse*
> *The whole Battalion views, their order due,*
> *Their Vizages and Stature as of Gods,*
> *Their number last he sums. And now his Heart*
> *Distends with Pride, and hard'ning in his strength*
> *Glories . . .*[7]

The Flash of Light, which appeared upon the drawing of their Swords;

[a] unfurls; as also] unfurls, and *Fol.*

[1] *PL*, i. 789–97.   [2] *PL*, i. 678–88.   [3] *PL*, i. 710–30.
[4] *PL*, i. 533–9.   [5] *PL*, i. 181–3 ('these vivid Flames').
[6] *PL*, i. 541–3.   [7] *PL*, i. 567–73.

He spake: and to confirm his words outflew
Millions of flaming Swords, drawn from the Thighs
Of mighty Cherubim; *the sudden blaze*
Far round illumin'd Hell . . .[1]

The sudden Production of the *Pandæmonium*;

Anon out of the Earth a Fabrick huge
Rose like an Exhalation, with the Sound
Of dulcet Symphonies and Voices sweet.[2]

The Artificial Illuminations made in it.

. . . From the arched Roof
Pendent by subtle Magick, many a Row
Of Starry Lamps and blazing Crescets, fed
With Naphtha *and* Asphaltus *yielded Light*
As from a Sky . . .[3]

There are also several noble Similes and Allusions in the first Book of *Paradise Lost*. And here I must observe, that when *Milton* alludes either to Things or Persons, he never quits his Simile till it rises to some very great Idea, which is often foreign to the Occasion that[a] gave Birth to it. The Resemblance does not, perhaps, last above a Line or two, but the Poet runs on with the Hint, till he has raised out of it some glorious Image or Sentiment, proper to inflame the Mind of the Reader, and to give it that sublime kind of Entertainment, which is suitable to the Nature of an Heroic Poem. Those, who are acquainted with *Homer's* and *Virgil's* way of Writing, cannot but be pleased with this kind of Structure in *Milton's* Similitudes. I am the more particular on this Head, because ignorant Readers, who have formed their Taste upon the quaint Similes, and little Turns of Wit, which are so much in Vogue among Modern Poets, cannot relish these Beauties which are of a much higher nature, and are therefore apt to censure *Milton's* Comparisons, in which they do not see any surprizing Points of Likeness. Monsieur *Perrault* was a Man of this viciated Relish, and for that very Reason has endeavoured to turn into Ridicule several of *Homer's* Similitudes, which he calls *Comparaisons a longue queue, Long-tail'd Comparisons.* I shall conclude this Paper on the First Book of *Milton* with the

[a] that] which *Fol.*

---

[1] *PL*, i. 663–6.   [2] *PL*, i. 710–12.
[3] *PL*, i. 726–30. Cf. Addison's use of these lines in *Guardian* 103.

Answer which Monsieur *Boileau* makes to *Perrault* on this Occasion; 'Comparisons, says he, in Odes and Epic Poems are not introduced only to illustrate and embellish the Discourse, but to amuse and relax the Mind of the Reader, by frequently disengaging him from too painful an Attention to the Principal Subject, and by leading him into other agreeable Images. *Homer*, says he, excelled in this Particular, whose Comparisons abound with such Images of Nature as are proper to relieve and diversifie his Subjects. He continually instructs the Reader, and makes him take notice, even in Objects which are every Day before our Eyes, of such Circumstances as we should not otherwise have observed. To this he adds, as a Maxim universally acknowledged, that it is not necessary in Poetry for the Points of the Comparison to correspond with one another exactly, but that a general Resemblance is sufficient, and that too much nicety in this Particular savours of the Rhetorician and Epigrammatist.'[1]

In short, if we look into the Conduct of *Homer*, *Virgil*, and *Milton*, as the great Fable is the Soul of each Poem, so to give their Works an agreeable Variety, their Episodes are so many short Fables, and their Similes so many short Episodes; to which you may add, if you please, that their Metaphors are so many short Similes. If the Reader considers the Comparisons in the First Book of *Milton*, of the Sun in an Eclipse, of the Sleeping *Leviathan*, of the Bees swarming about their Hive, of the Fairy Dance,[2] in the view wherein I have here placed them, he will easily discover the great Beauties that are in each of those Passages.   L

[1] See Boileau's 'Critical Reflections on Longinus', Reflection V (Boileau's *Works*, 1711–12, ii. 103). Addison's quotation from Boileau is from Reflection VI (pp. 110–13). This translation of Boileau, 'by several hands', is advertised by E. Sanger and E. Curll in No. 272 as 'This Day' published. Vol. I is dated 1712 and Vol. II 1711. A life of Boileau, 'Written to Joseph Addison, Esq; By Mr. Des Maizeaux', is prefixed to the first volume.

[2] *PL*, i. 594–9, 200–8, 768–75, 781–8.

No. 304
[STEELE]

Monday, February 18, 1712[1]

Vulnus alit venis & cæco Carpitur igni.
Virg.

THE Circumstances of my Correspondent, whose Letter I now insert, are so frequent, that I cannot want Compassion so much as to forbear laying it before the Town. There is something so mean and inhumane in a direct *Smithfield* Bargain[2] for Children, that if this Lover carries his Point, and observes the Rules he pretends to follow, I do not only wish him Success, but also that it may animate others to follow his Example. I know not one Motive relating to this Life which would produce so many honourable and worthy Actions, as the Hopes of obtaining a Woman of Merit; there would ten thousand Ways of Industry and honest Ambition be pursued by young Men, who believed that the Persons admired had Value enough for their Passion to attend the Event of their good Fortune in all their Applications, in order to make their Circumstances fall in with the Duties they owe to themselves, their Families, and their Country: All these Relations a Man should think of who intends to go into the State of Marriage, and expects to make it a State of Pleasure and Satisfaction.

Mr. SPECTATOR,

'I HAVE for some Years indulged a Passion for a young Lady of Age and Quality suitable to my own, but very much superiour in Fortune. It is the Fashion with Parents (how justly I leave you to judge) to make all Regards give way to the Article of Wealth. From this one Consideration it is that I have concealed the ardent Love I have for her; but I am beholden to the Force of my Love for many Advantages which I reaped from it towards the better Conduct of my Life. A certain Complacency to all the World, a strong Desire to oblige where-ever it lay in my Power, and a circumspect Behaviour in all my Words and Actions, have rendered me more particularly acceptable to all my Friends and Acquaintance. Love has had the

---

[1] *Motto.* Virgil, *Aeneid,* 4. 2:
   She fed within her Veins a Flame unseen. DRYDEN.

[2] A sharp or roguish bargain; also *transf.* a marriage of interest, in which money is the chief consideration (*OED*). This quotation seems to be the earliest known in this transferred sense.

same good Effect upon my Fortune; and I have encreased in Riches in Proportion to my Advancement in those Arts which make a Man agreeable and amiable. There is a certain Simpathy which will tell my Mistress from these Circumstances, that it is I who write this for her Reading, if you will please to insert it. There is not a downright Enmity, but a great Coldness between our Parents; so that if either of us declared any kind Sentiments for each other, her Friends would be very backward to lay an Obligation upon our Family, and mine to receive it from hers. Under these delicate Circumstances it is no easy Matter to act with Safety. I have no Reason to fancy my Mistress has any Regard for me, but from a very disinterested Value which I have for her. If from any Hint in any future Paper of yours she gives me the least Encouragement, I doubt not but I shall surmount all other Difficulties; and inspired by so noble a Motive for the Care of my Fortune, as the Belief she is to be concerned in it, I will not despair of receiving her one Day from her Father's own Hand.

> *I am, SIR,*
> *Your most obedient humble Servant,*
> Clytander.'

To his *Worthy the* SPECTATOR.

The humble Petition of *Anthony Title-Page*, Stationer, in the Centre of *Lincolns-Inn Fields*,

Sheweth,

THAT your Petitioner and his Fore-fathers have been Sellers of Books for Time immemorial: That your Petitioner's Ancestor, *Crouchback Title-Page*, was the first of that Vocation in *Britain*; who keeping his Station (in fair Weather) at the Corner of *Lothbury*,[1] was by way of Eminency call'd *the Stationer*, a Name which from him all succeeding Booksellers have affected to bear: That the Station of your Petitioner and his Father has been in the Place of his present Settlement ever since that Square has been built: That your Petitioner has formerly had the Honour of your Worship's Custom, and hopes you never had Reason to complain of your Pennyworths; that particularly he sold you your first *Lilly*'s Grammar,[2] and at the

---

[1] A short street north of Stocks-Market, inhabited chiefly, according to Hatton (p. 49), by merchants and warehouse-keepers.
[2] William Lilly's *Brevissima Institutio, seu ratio grammatices cognoscendae*, originally written for St. Paul's School in the sixteenth century.

same Time a *Wit's Common-Wealth*[1] almost as good as new: Moreover, that your first rudimental Essays in Spectatorship were made in your Petitioner's Shop, where you often practis'd for Hours together sometimes on his Books upon the Rails, sometimes on the little Hieroglyphicks either gilt, silver'd, or plain, which the *Egyptian* Woman on the other Side of the Shop had wrought in Ginger-bread, and sometimes on the *English* Youth, who in sundry Places there were exercising themselves in the traditional Sports of the Field.

From these Considerations it is, that your Petitioner is encouraged to apply himself to you, and to proceed humbly to acquaint your Worship, That he has certain Intelligence that you receive great Numbers of defamatory Letters design'd by their Authors to be publish'd, which you throw aside and totally neglect: Your Petitioner therefore prays, that you would please to bestow on him those Refuse Letters,[2] and he hopes by printing them to get a more plentiful Provision for his Family; or at the worst, he may be allowed to sell them by the Pound Weight to his good Customers the Pastry-Cooks of *London* and *Westminster*.

And your Petitioner shall ever pray, &c.

To the SPECTATOR.

The humble Petition of *Bartholomew Ladylove*, of *Round-Court*[3] in the Parish of St. *Martins in the Fields*, in Behalf of himself and Neighbours, Sheweth,

THAT your Petitioners have with great Industry and Application arrived at the most exact Art of Invitation or Entreaty: That by a beseeching Air and perswasive Address, they have for many Years last past peaceably drawn in every tenth Passenger, whether they intended or not to call at their Shops, to come in and buy; and from that Softness of Behaviour, have arrived among Tradesmen at the gentle Appellation of *the Fawners*.

That there have of late set up amongst us certain Persons from

---

[1] *Politeuphuia: Wit's Commonwealth*, by John Bodenham (1598), was a collection of phrases, anecdotes, jests, forms of expression, and other 'helps to discourse'.

[2] Some of these were printed by Charles Lillie in two volumes in 1725, under the title, *Original and Genuine Letters sent to the Tatler and Spectator, during the time those works were publishing. None of which have been before printed. Printed by R. Harbin, for Charles Lillie, Perfumer, at the Corner of Beaufort-Buildings in the Strand*.

[3] On the north-west side of the Strand, almost against Buckingham Street end (Hatton, p. 71). Several shops selling cloth and wearing apparel were situated here.

Monmouth-street[1] and *Long-lane*, who by the Strength of their Arms and Loudness of their Throats, draw off the Regard of all Passengers from your said Petitioners; from which Violence they are distinguished by the Name of *the Worriers*.[2]

That while your Petitioners stand ready to receive Passengers with a submissive Bow, and repeat with a gentle Voice, *Ladies what do you want? pray look in here*, the Worriers reach out their Hands at Pistol-shot, and sieze the Customers at Arm's Length.

That while the Fawners strain and relax the Muscles of their Faces, in making Distinction between a Spinster in a coloured Scarf, and an Hand-maid in a Straw-Hat, the Worriers use the same Roughness to both, and prevail[a] upon the Easiness of the Passengers to the Impoverishment of your Petitioners.

Your Petitioners therefore most humbly pray, that the Worriers may not be permitted to inhabit the politer Parts of the Town; and that *Round-Court* may remain a Receptacle for Buyers of a more soft Education.

And your Petitioners, &c.

The Petition of the New-Exchange[3] *concerning the Arts of Buying and Selling, and particularly valuing Goods by the Complexion of the Seller, will be considered on another Occasion.*　　　　　　　　　　T

No. 305　　　　　　　　　　*Tuesday, February* 19, 1712[4]
[ADDISON]

Non tali auxilio, nec defensoribus istis
Tempus eget . . .
　　　　　　　　　　　　　　　　　　Virg.

OUR late News-Papers being full of the Project now on foot in the Court of *France*, for Establishing a Political Academy, and

---

[a] prevail] prevails *Fol.*

[1] Monmouth Street extended from St. Giles south-west to the end of Grafton Street. Long-Lane ran east from West Smithfield to Aldersgate Street and formed a western continuation of Barbican. It was a place where old clothes were sold (cf. No. 264, vol. ii).　　[2] This is the earliest quotation in *OED* for this word.　　[3] See No. 96 (vol. i).
[4] *Motto.* Virgil, *Aeneid*, 2. 521–2:
What Arms are these, and to what use design'd?
These Times want other Aids. DRYDEN.

I my self having received Letters from several Vertuoso's among my Foreign Correspondents, which give some Light into that Affair, I intend to make it the Subject of this Day's Speculation. A general Account of this Project may be met with in the *Daily Courant* of last *Friday* in the following Words, translated from the Gazette of *Amsterdam*.[1]

Paris, February 12. "'Tis confirmed, that the King has resolv'd to establish a new Academy for Politics, of which the Marquis *de Torcy*,[2] Minister and Secretary of State, is to be Protector. Six Academicians are to be chosen, endow'd with proper Talents, for beginning to form this Academy, into which no Person is to be admitted under Twenty five Years of Age: They must likewise have each an Estate of Two thousand Livres a Year, either in Possession, or to come to 'em by Inheritance. The King will allow to each a Pension of a thousand Livres. They are likewise to have able Masters to teach 'em the necessary Sciences, and to instruct them in all the Treaties of Peace, Alliance, and others which have been made in several Ages past. These Members are to meet twice a Week at the *Louvre*. From this Seminary are to be chosen Secretaries to Ambassies, who by degrees may advance to higher Employments.'

Cardinal *Richelieu*'s Politicks made *France* the Terror of *Europe*. The Statesmen who have appeared in that Nation of late Years, have on the contrary rendered it either the Pity or Contempt of its Neighbours. The Cardinal erected that famous Academy[3] which has carried all the Parts of Polite Learning to the greatest height. His chief Design in that Institution was to divert the Men of Genius from meddling with Politicks, a Province in which he did not care to have any one else interfere with him. On the contrary, the Marquis *de Torcy* seems resolved to make several young Men in *France* as Wise as himself, and is therefore taken up at present in establishing a Nursery of Statesmen.

Some private Letters add, that there will also be erected a

[1] The passage from the *Daily Courant* is headed: 'From the Amsterdam Gazette, dated Feb. 19 [N.S.].'

[2] Jean-Baptiste Colbert, Marquis de Torcy (1665–1746), who at this time was carrying on secret negotiations with Bolingbroke in regard to the Peace—and the Restoration of the Pretender.

[3] Cardinal Richelieu founded the Académie Française in 1635. Among the statutes and rules of the Academy, No. 22 reads: 'Les matières politiques ou morales ne seront traitées dans l'Académie que conformément à l'autorité du Prince, à l'état du gouvernement et aux lois du royaume.' Cf. Sir William Temple, 'Of Poetry' (1690): 'The Academy set up by Cardinal *Richlieu* to amuse the Wits of that Age and Country, and divert them from raking into his Politicks and Ministery . . .' (Spingarn, iii. 102).

Seminary of Petticoat Politicians, who are to be brought up at the Feet of Madam *de Maintenon*,[1] and to be dispatched into Foreign Courts upon any Emergencies of State; but as the News of this last Project has not been yet confirmed, I shall take no farther notice of it.

Several of my Readers may doubtless remember, that upon the Conclusion of the last War,[2] which had been carried on so successfully by the Enemy, their Generals were many of them transformed into Ambassadors; but the Conduct of those who have commanded in the present War, has, it seems, brought so little Honour and Advantage to their great Monarch, that he is resolved to trust his Affairs no longer in the Hands of those Military Gentlemen.

The Regulations of this new Academy very much deserve our Attention. The Students are to have in Possession, or Reversion, an Estate of Two thousand *French* Livres[3] *per Annum*, which, as the present Exchange runs, will amount to at least one Hundred and twenty six Pounds *English*. This, with the Royal Allowance of a Thousand Livres, will enable them to find themselves in Coffee and Snuff; not to mention News Papers, Pen and Ink, Wax and Wafers, with the like Necessaries for Politicians.

A Man must be at least Five and twenty before he can be initiated into the Mysteries of this Academy, tho' there is no question but many grave Persons of a much more advanced Age, who have been constant Readers of the *Paris* Gazette, will be glad to begin the World a-new, and enter themselves upon this List of Politicians.

The Society of these hopeful young Gentlemen is to be under the Direction of six Professors, who, it seems, are to be Speculative Statesmen, and drawn out of the Body of the Royal Academy. These six Wise Masters, according to my private Letters, are to have the following Parts allotted them.

The first is to instruct the Students in *State Legerdemain*, as how to take off the Impression of a Seal, to split a Wafer, to open a Letter, to fold it up again, with other the like ingenious Feats of Dexterity and Art. When the Students have accomplished themselves in this part of their Profession, they are to be delivered into the Hands of their second Instructor, who is a kind of *Posture-master*.

This Artist is to teach them how to nod judiciously, to shrug up

---

[1] Madame de Maintenon, secretly married to Louis XIV in 1684, was thought to exercise great political power behind the scenes, particularly in the King's last years.

[2] The Peace of Ryswick was drawn up in 1697.

[3] The livre was worth roughly a little less than a shilling.

their Shoulders in a dubious Case, to connive with either Eye, and in a word, the whole Practice of *Political Grimace*.

The Third is a sort of *Language Master*, who is to instruct them in the Stile proper for a Foreign Minister in his ordinary Discourse. And to the End that this College of Statesmen may be thoroughly practised in the Political Stile, they are to make use of it in their common Conversations, before they are employed either in Foreign or Domestick Affairs. If one of them asks another, what a Clock it is, the other is to answer him indirectly, and, if possible, to turn off the Question. If he is desired to change a *Louis d'or*, he must beg time to consider of it. If it be enquired of him, whether the King is at *Versailles* or *Marly*,[1] he must answer in a Whisper. If he be ask'd the News of the last *Gazette*, or the Subject of a Proclamation, he is to reply, that he has not yet read it: Or if he does not care for explaining himself so far, he needs only draw his Brow up in Wrinkles, or elevate the Left Shoulder.

The Fourth Professor is to teach the whole Art of Political Characters and Hieroglyphics; and to the End that they may be perfect also in this Practice, they are not to send a Note to one another (tho' it be but to borrow a *Tacitus* or a *Machiavil*) which is not written in Cypher.

Their Fifth Professor, it is thought, will be chosen out of the Society of Jesuits, and is to be well Read in the Controversies of probable Doctrines, mental Reservations, and the Rights of Princes. This Learned Man is to instruct them in the Grammar, Syntax, and construing part of *Treaty-latin*;[2] how to distinguish between the Spirit and the Letter, and likewise demonstrate how the same Form of Words may lay an Obligation upon any Prince in *Europe*, different from that which it lays upon his Most Christian Majesty. He is likewise to teach them the Art of finding Flaws, Loop-holes and Evasions, in the most solemn Compacts, and particularly a great *Rabbinical Secret*, revived of late Years by the Fraternity of Jesuits, namely, that contradictory Interpretations of the same Article, may both of them be true and valid.

When our Statesmen are sufficiently improved by these several

---

[1] The palace at Versailles was constructed shortly after 1670 by order of Louis XIV. Toward the end of the century a château, originally designed as a simple retreat from the palace, was built at Marly-le-Roi, about five miles north-west of Versailles.

[2] The implications of this paper, published while secret negotiations were going on between the Tory leaders and the French, would not be lost on contemporary readers.

Instructors, they are to receive their last Polishing from one who is to act among them as *Master of the Ceremonies*. This Gentleman is to give them Lectures upon those important Points of the *Elbow Chair*, and the *Stair-head*, to instruct them in the different Situations of the Right-Hand, and to furnish them with Bows and Inclinations of all Sizes, Measures and Proportions. In short, this Professor is to give the Society their *stiffening*, and infuse into their Manners that Beautiful Political Starch, which may qualifie them for Levées, Conferences, Visits, and make them shine in what vulgar Minds are apt to look upon as Trifles.

I have not yet heard any further Particulars, which are to be observed in this Society of unfledged Statesmen; but I must confess, had I a Son of five and twenty, that shou'd take it into his Head at that Age to set up for a Politician, I think I shou'd go near to disinherit him for a Block-head. Besides, I should be apprehensive least the same Arts which are to enable him to negotiate between Potentates might a little infect his ordinary Behaviour between Man and Man. There is no Question but these young *Machiavils* will, in a little time, turn their College upside-down with Plots and Stratagems, and lay as many Schemes to Circumvent one another in a Frog or a Sallad, as they may hereafter put in practice to over-reach a Neighbouring Prince or State.

We are told that the *Spartans*, tho' they punish'd Theft in their young-Men, when it was discovered, looked upon it as Honourable if it succeeded.[1] Provided the Conveyance was clean and unsuspected, a Youth might afterwards boast of it. This, say the Historians, was to keep them sharp, and to hinder them from being imposed upon, either in their Publick or private Negociations. Whether any such Relaxations of Morality, such little *jeux d'esprit*,[2] ought not to be allow'd in this intended Seminary of Politicians, I shall leave to the Wisdom of their Founder.

In the mean time we have fair Warning given us by this doughty Body of Statesmen; and as *Sylla* saw many *Marius's* in *Cæsar*,[3] so I think we may discover many *Torci's* in this College of Academicians.

---

[1] Plutarch, 'Ancient Customs of the Spartans', *Moralia* 237E; *Life of Lycurgus*, 17. 3.

[2] This is the earliest example of this word in English in the *OED*.

[3] Caesar's father's sister Julia had married the great Marius, and Caesar himself at the age of seventeen married Cornelia, daughter of one of the leaders in the Marian party. He was consequently proscribed by Sulla and in danger of being condemned to death; when the question of his pardon came up before Sulla, the latter commented that they knew little who did not see in this boy many Mariuses (Plutarch, *Life of Caesar*, I. 3).

Whatever we think of our selves, I am afraid neither our *Smyrna* or *St. James's* will be a Match for it.[1] Our Coffee-houses are, indeed, very good Institutions, but whether or no these our *British* Schools of Politics may furnish out as able Envoys and Secretaries as an Academy that is set apart for that purpose, will deserve our serious Consideration; especially if we remember that our Country is more famous for producing Men of Integrity than Statesmen; and that, on the contrary *French* Truth and *British* Policy make a Conspicuous Figure *in* NOTHING, as the Earl of *Rochester* has very well observed in his admirable Poem upon that Barren Subject.[2]   L3

No. 306   *Wednesday, February 20, 1712*[4]
[STEELE]

> ... *Quæ forma, ut se tibi semper*
> *Imputet?* ...
>
>   Juv.

Mr. SPECTATOR,

'I WRITE this to communicate to you a Misfortune which frequently happens, and therefore deserves a consolatory Discourse on the Subject. I was within this Half-Year in the Possession of as

---

[1] Smyrna coffee-house, on the north side of Pall Mall, opposite Marlborough House, had a reputation for political intrigue. Swift and Prior made appointments in it (*Journal to Stella*, 15 Oct. 1710, 19 Feb. 1710/11), and the 'Cluster of Wise Heads' there is referred to in *Tatler* 10. *Tatler* 78 announces that gentlemen who wish instruction in music, poetry, and politics are urged to repair to the Smyrna: 'If any young Student gives Indication of Parts, by listening attentively, or asking a pertinent Question, one of the Professors shall distinguish him, by taking Snuff out of his Box in the Presence of the whole Audience.' For the St. James's, the coffee-house frequented by Whig statesmen, see No. 1 (vol. i).

[2] Rochester's poem on Nothing, Stanza 16. The poem was first printed *c.* 1679. A separate edition 'now first Correctly Printed' is advertised by J. Morphew and Edmund Curll in *Examiner* 46 (14 June 1711) as 'this day' published.

[3] Swift wrote an *Examiner* (No. 14, 9 Nov. 1710) on 'the art of political lying', devoted to a defence of the new Tory ministry. Arbuthnot's *Proposals for printing . . . A Treatise of the Art of Political Lying* is advertised by John Morphew in the *Post Boy* of 16 Oct. 1712 as 'this day' published. Cf. No. 507 (vol. iv).

[4] *Motto.* Juvenal, *Satires*, 6. 178–9:
> What Beauty or what Chastity can bear
> So great a Price, if stately and severe
> She still insults, and you must still adore. DRYDEN.

much Beauty and as many Lovers as any young Lady in *England*. But my Admirers have left me, and I cannot complain of their Behaviour. I have within that Time had the Small-Pox;[1] and this Face, which (according to many amorous Epistles which I have by me) was the Seat of all that is beautiful in Woman, is now disfigured with Scars. It goes to the very Soul of me to speak what I really think of my Face; and tho I think I did not over-rate my Beauty while I had it, it has extremely advanced in its Value with me now it is lost. There is one Circumstance which makes my Case very particular; the ugliest Fellow that ever pretended to me, was, and is most in my Favour, and he treats me at Present the most unreasonably. If you could make him return an Obligation which he owes me, in liking a Person that is not amiable;—But there is, I fear, no Possibility of making Passion move by the Rules of Reason and Gratitude. But say what you can to one who has survived her self, and knows not how to Act in a new Being. My Lovers are at the Feet of my Rivals, my Rivals are every Day bewailing me, and I cannot enjoy what I am, by Reason of the distracting Reflexion upon what I was. Consider the Woman I was did not dye of Old Age, but I was taken off in the Prime of my Youth, and according to

[1] In No. 82 is advertised as 'this day' published: 'A short but full Account of the Rise, Nature and Management of the Small Pox, and other putrid Feavers, with their proper Remedies. Sold by J. Morphew near Stationer's-Hall. Pr. 2d.' The literature of the time constantly refers to the ravages of this disease. It was not until later that Lady Mary Wortley Montagu, who returned from Turkey in 1718, introduced inoculation. Meanwhile, various 'cures' were offered the public. The following advertisement appears in Nos. 64 and 65:

Concerning the Small-Pox. R. Stoughton, Apothecary, at the Unicorn in Southwark, having about Christmas last published in the Postman, Tatler and Courant, a long Advertisement of his large Experience and great Success in curing the Small-Pox, even of the worst Kind and Circumstances, having had a Reputation for it almost 30 Years, and can say, that not 3 in 20 miscarry under his Hands; doth now contract it, and only repeats, That he thinks he has attain'd to as great a Certainty therein (and the Measles, which are near of Kin) as hath been acquired in curing any one Disease, (an intermitting Fever with the Bark only excepted) which he conceives may at this Time, when the Small-Pox so prevails, and is so mortal, justify his Publication, being pressed by several so to do, and hopes it may be for the Good of many. He has had many Patients since his last Publication, and but one of all dy'd. He hath also Certificates from above 20 in a small Time cured, and of the worst Sort. What is here offered is Truth and Matter of Fact; and he will, if desired, go with any one to the Persons themselves who have been cured, many of whom are People of Value and Figure. 'Tis by a correct Management, more than a great deal of Physick, by which also the Face and Eyes are much secured; tho' one Secret he has, (obtained only by Experience, and which few or none know besides) that when they suddenly strike in, very rarely fails of raising them again in few Hours, when many other things, and proper too, have not answered. He does not desire, nor aim at, the supplanting any Physician or Apothecary concerned; but gives his assisting Advice if desired, and in such a Way not dishonourable or injurious to either.

the Course of Nature may have Forty Years After-Life to come.
I have nothing of my self left which I like, but that

I am, SIR,

Your most Humble Servant,

Parthenissa.'[1]

When *Lewis* of *France* had lost the Battle of *Ramelies*,[2] the Addresses
to him at that time were full of his Fortitude, and they turned his
Misfortunes to his Glory; in that, during his Prosperity, he could
never have manifested his heroick Constancy under Distresses, and
so the World had lost the most eminent Part of his Character.
Parthenissa's Condition gives her the same Opportunity; and to
resign Conquests is a Task as difficult in a Beauty as an Hero. In the
very Entrance upon this Work she must burn all her Love-Letters;
or since she is so candid[3] as not to call her Lovers who follow her no
longer unfaithful, it would be a very good Beginning of a new Life
from that of a Beauty, to send them back to those who writ them,
with this honest Inscription, *Articles of a Marriage Treaty broken off
by the Small-Pox.* I have known but one Instance where a Matter of
this Kind went on after a like Misfortune; where the Lady, who was
a Woman of Spirit, writ this Billet to her Lover.

SIR,

'IF you flattered me before I had this terrible Malady, pray come
and see me now: But if you sincerely liked me, stay away; for
I am not the same   *Corinna.*'

The Lover thought there was something so sprightly in her
Behaviour, that he answered,

Madam,

'I AM not obliged since you are not the same Woman, to let you
know whether I flattered you or not; but I assure you, I do not,

---

[1] The heroine of the Earl of Orrery's romance (1654–69). According to Nichols
and 'J. D.' (*Gent. Mag.*, April 1780), this letter was written by John Hughes, and
Parthenissa was 'Miss Rotherham', sister to the second lady of the 6th Lord Effingham,
afterwards married to the Rev. Mr. Wyatt, master of Felsted School in Essex.
Thomas Howard, 6th Baron Howard of Effingham (1682–1725), married on 25 Jan.
1721/2 Elizabeth, widow of Sir Theophilus Napier, and daughter of John Rotheram
of Much Waltham, Essex (G.E.C.). There is no other indication that Hughes wrote
this letter; it is not in Duncombe's list of Hughes's contributions to the *Spectator*.

[2] Louis XIV lost the battle of Ramillies on 23 May 1706 (N.S.), in what the Duc de
Villars called 'the most shameful, humiliating and disastrous of defeats' (Trevelyan,
ii. 119).

[3] Candid, in the obsolete sense of 'favourably disposed, kindly'. Defined by
Johnson as 'free from malice; not desirous to find faults'. The last quotation in *OED*
in this sense is dated 1800.

when I tell you I now like you above all your Sex, and hope you will bear what may befall me when we are both one, as well as you do what happens to your self now you are single; therefore I am ready to take such a Spirit for my Companion as soon as you please.   *Amilcar.*'

If *Parthenissa* can now possess her own Mind, and think as little of her Beauty as she ought to have done when she had it, there will be no great Diminution of her Charms; and if she was formerly affected too much with them, an easy Behaviour will more than make up for the Loss of them. Take the whole Sex together, and you find those who have the strongest Possession of Mens Hearts are not eminent for their Beauty: You see it often happen that those who engage Men to the greatest Violence, are such as those who are Strangers to them would take to be remarkably defective for that End. The fondest Lover I know, said to me one Day in a Crowd of Women at an Entertainment of Musick, You have often heard me talk of my Beloved; That Woman there, continued he, smiling when he had fixed my Eye, is her very Picture. The Lady he showed me was by much the least remarkable for Beauty of any in the whole Assembly; but having my Curiosity extremely raised, I could not keep my Eyes off of her. Her Eyes at last met mine, and with a sudden Surprize she looked round her to see who near her was remarkably handsome that I was gazing at. This little Act explain'd the Secret: She did not understand her self for the Object of Love, and therefore she was so. The Lover is a very honest plain Man; and what charmed him was a Person that goes along with him in the Cares and Joys of Life, not taken up with her self, but sincerely attentive with a ready and chearful Mind to accompany him in either.

I can tell *Parthenissa* for her Comfort, That the Beauties, generally speaking, are the most impertinent and disagreeable of Women. An apparent Desire of Admiration, a Reflexion upon their own Merit, and a precious Behaviour in their general Conduct, are almost inseparable Accidents in Beauties. All you obtain of them is granted to Importunity and Sollicitation for what did not deserve so much of your Time, and you recover from the Possession of it, as out of a Dream.

You are asham'd of the Vagaries of Fancy which so strangely misled you, and your Admiration of a Beauty, merely as such, is inconsistent with a tolerable Reflexion upon your self: The chearful good humoured Creatures, into whose Heads it never entered that they could make any Man unhappy, are the Persons formed for making Men happy. There's Miss *Liddy* can dance a Jigg, raise Paste,[1] write a good Hand, keep an Accompt, give a reasonable Answer, and do as she is bid, while her elder Sister Madam *Martha* is out of Humour, has the Spleen, learns by Reports of People of higher Quality new Ways of being uneasy and displeas'd. And this happens for no Reason in the World, but that poor *Liddy* knows she has no such thing as a certain Negligence *that is so becoming*, that there is not I know not what in *her Air*: And that if she talks like a Fool, there is no one will say, Well! I know not what it is, but *every Thing pleases when she speaks it.*

Ask any of the Husbands of your great Beauties, and they'll tell you that they hate their Wives Nine Hours of every Day they pass together. There is such a Particularity for ever affected by them, that they are incumbered with their Charms in all they say or do. They pray at publick Devotions as they are Beauties; they converse on ordinary Occasions as they are Beauties. Ask *Bellinda* what it is a Clock, and she is at a Stand whether so great a Beauty should answer you. In a Word, I think instead of offering to administer Consolation to *Parthenissa*, I should congratulate her Metamorphosis; and however she thinks she was not in the least insolent in the Prosperity of her Charms, she was enough so to find she may make her self a much more agreeable Creature in her present Adversity. The Endeavour to please is highly promoted by a Consciousness that the Approbation of the Person you would be agreeable to, is a Favour you do not deserve; for in this Case Assurance of Success is the most certain way to Disappointment. Good-Nature will always supply the Absence of Beauty, but Beauty cannot long supply the Absence of Good-Nature.

P. S.

Madam,   February 18.
'I HAVE yours of this Day, wherein you twice bid me not disoblige you, but you must explain your self further before I know what to do.

Your most Obedient Servant
The SPECTATOR.'   T

---

[1] Philospec, writing from the Temple, 11 Nov. 1712 (Lillie, ii. 32), deplores 'the loss of one of the most necessary arts which used to make our mothers and grandmothers so much valued; I mean, the art of raising paste, and making conserves'.

> . . . *Versate diu quid ferre recusent*
> *Quid valeant humeri* . . .
>
> Hor.

I AM so well pleased with the following Letter, that I am in hopes it will not be a disagreeable Present to the Publick.

SIR,

'THOUGH I believe none of your Readers more admire your agreeable manner of working up Trifles than my self, yet as your Speculations are now swelling into Volumes,[2] and will in all probability pass down to future Ages, methinks I would have no single Subject in them, wherein the general Good of Mankind is concern'd, left unfinished.

'I have a long time expected with great Impatience, that you would enlarge upon the ordinary Mistakes which are committed in the Education of our Children. I the more easily flatter'd my self that you would one time or other resume this Consideration, because you tell us that your 168th Paper was only composed of a few broken Hints; but finding my self hitherto disappointed, I have ventured to send you my own Thoughts on this Subject.

'I remember *Pericles*, in his famous Oration at the Funeral of those *Athenian* young Men who perished in the *Samian* Expedition, has a Thought very much celebrated by several Ancient Criticks, namely, That the Loss which the Common-wealth suffered by the Destruction of its Youth, was like the Loss which the Year would suffer by the Destruction of the Spring.[3] The Prejudice which the Publick sustains from a wrong Education of Children, is an Evil of the same Nature, as it in a manner starves Posterity, and defrauds

---

[1] *Motto.* Horace, *Ars poetica*, 39–40:

> You *Writers* try the Vigour of your Muse,
> And what her strength will bear, and what refuse. CREECH.

[2] The first two volumes of the *Spectator* had been published the preceding month—in octavo on 8 January and in duodecimo on the 18th.

[3] The sole authority for this is Aristotle, who commends it in the *Rhetoric* (1. 7. 34; 30. 10. 7). It is one of two fragments surviving from a speech of Pericles in 439 B.C. after the conquest of Samos. Budgell has apparently confused this obscure funeral oration with the celebrated one in 431 B.C. and reported in Thucydides (2. 35–46).

our Country of those Persons, who, with due care, might make an eminent Figure in their respective Posts of Life.

'I have seen a Book written by *Juan Huartes*, a *Spanish* Physician, Entitled, *Examen de Ingenios*,[1] wherein he lays it down as one of his first Positions, that Nothing but Nature can qualifie a Man for Learning; and that without a proper Temperament for the particular Art or Science which he studies, his utmost Pains and Application, assisted by the ablest Masters, will be to no purpose.

'He illustrates this by the Example of *Tully's* Son *Marcus*.

'*Cicero*, in order to accomplish his Son in that sort of Learning which he designed him for, sent him to *Athens*, the most celebrated Academy at that time in the World, and where a vast Concourse, out of the most Polite Nations, could not but furnish the young Gentleman with a Multitude of great Examples, and Accidents that might insensibly have instructed him in his designed Studies:[2] He placed him under the Care of *Cratippus*,[3] who was one of the greatest Philosophers of the Age, and, as if all the Books which were at that time written, had not been sufficient for his use, he composed others[4] on purpose for him; Notwithstanding all this, History informs us, that *Marcus* proved a meer Blockhead, and that Nature (who it seems was even with the Son for her Prodigality to the Father) rendered him incapable of improving by all the Rules of Eloquence, the Precepts of Philosophy, his own Endeavours, and the most refined Conversation in *Athens*. This Author therefore proposes, that there should be certain Tryers or Examiners appointed by the State to inspect the Genius of every particular Boy, and to allot him the Part that is most suitable to his natural Talents.[5]

[1] The book mentioned here, by Juan de San Huarte, was published in 1575. It was translated into English by Richard Carew in 1594, and by Edward Bellamy in 1698. Budgell uses Bellamy's translation, and here paraphrases two chapter heads. Chap. iv is entitled 'Nature only qualifies a Man for Learning', and chap. iii bears the title: 'The Child who has neither Wit nor Ability requisite to the intended Science, cannot prove a great Proficient, though he have the best Masters, many Books, and should labour at it all the Days of his Life.'

[2] This anecdote comes, with only slight verbal alterations, from chap. iii of Huarte in Bellamy's translation (pp. 31–32).

[3] A Peripatetic philosopher who settled at Athens soon after 48 B.C.

[4] Cicero wrote *De Officiis* for his son's use.

[5] This proposal is made in Huarte's Dedication to Philip II, and is not the conclusion to an argument, as Budgell seems to suggest:

And that accordingly none might err in the Choice of that which was most agreeable to the Bent of his Natural Inclination, there should be *Triers* appointed by the State ... to search and sound the Abilities of Youth, and after due Search, to oblige them to the Study of that Science their Heads leaned most to, instead of abandoning them to their own Choice (sig. a3).

'*Plato* in one of his Dialogues tells us, that *Socrates*, who was the Son of a Midwife, used to say, that as his Mother, tho' she was very Skillful in her Profession, could not deliver a Woman, unless she was first with Child; so neither could he himself raise Knowledge out of a Mind, where Nature had not planted it.[1]

'Accordingly the Method this Philosopher took, of instructing his Scholars by several Interrogatories or Questions, was only help-ing the Birth, and bringing their own Thoughts to light.

'The *Spanish* Doctor abovementioned, as his Speculations grow more refined, asserts that every kind of Wit has a particular Science corresponding to it, and in which alone it can be truly Excellent. As to those Genius's, which may seem to have an equal Aptitude for several things, he regards them as so many unfinished Pieces of Nature wrought off in haste.[2]

'There are, indeed, but very few to whom Nature has been so unkind, that they are not capable of shining in some Science or other. There is a certain Byass towards Knowledge in every Mind, which may be strengthened and improved by proper Applications.[3]

'The Story of *Clavius*[4] is very well known; he was entered in a Colledge of Jesuits, and, after having been tryed at several Parts of Learning, was upon the Point of being dismissed as an hopeless Blockhead, till one of the Fathers took it into his Head to make an assay of his Parts in Geometry, which it seems hit his Genius so luckily that he afterwards became one of the greatest Mathema-ticians of the Age. It is commonly thought that the Sagacity of these Fathers, in discovering the Talent of a young Student, has not a little contributed to the Figure which their Order has made in the World.

'How different from this manner of Education is that which pre-

---

[1] Bellamy's translation, p. 34. The dialogue in question is the *Theaetetus*.

[2] Actually it is in the Proem to his treatise, before his 'speculations grow more refined', that Huarte makes these observations:

Of all the different Wits of Men, there is but one (as predominant) can fall to thy share, unless Nature straining hard as it were to form two or three Excellencies more in thee, and being unable to effect what she designed, has left thee off unwrought in haste, as a rude Essay of an unfinish'd Piece. . . . To each different kind of Wit corresponds one Science only transcendently, and no more . . . (sig. a5ᵛ).

[3] 'There is no Man', writes Huarte in chap. ii, 'how gross and imperfect soever formed, but Nature has design'd him for something' (ed. Bellamy, p. 26).

[4] Christopher Clavius (1538–1612), a Bavarian who entered the Jesuit order in 1555, distinguished himself as a mathematician and astronomer. Budgell's anecdote may be found in Obadiah Walker's *Of Education* (5th ed., Oxford, 1687), p. 109.

vails in our own Country? Where nothing is more usual than to see Forty or Fifty Boys of several Ages, Tempers and Inclinations, ranged together in the same Class, employed upon the same Authors, and enjoyned the same Tasks? Whatever their natural Genius may be, they are all to be made Poets, Historians, and Orators alike. They are all obliged to have the same Capacity, to bring in the same Tale of Verse, and to furnish out the same Portion of Prose. Every Boy is bound to have as good a Memory as the Captain of the Form. To be brief, instead of adapting Studies to the particular Genius of a Youth, we expect from the young Man, that he should adapt his Genius to his Studies. This, I must confess, is not so much to be imputed to the Instructor, as to the Parent, who will never be brought to believe, that his Son is not capable of performing as much as his Neighbours, and that he may not make him whatever he has a Mind to.

'If the present Age is more laudable than those which have gone before it in any single Particular, it is in that generous Care which several well-disposed Persons have taken in the Education of poor Children; and as in these Charity Schools[1] there is no Place left for the over-weening Fondness of a Parent, the Directors of them would make them beneficial to the Publick, if they consider'd the Precept which I have been thus long inculcating. They might easily, by well examining the Parts of those under their Inspection, make a just Distribution of them into proper Classes and Divisions, and allot to them this or that particular Study, as their Genius qualifies them for Professions, Trades, Handicrafts, or Service by Sea or Land.

'How is this kind of Regulation wanting in the three great Professions![2]

'Dr. *South* complaining of Persons who took upon them Holy Orders, tho' altogether unqualified for the Sacred Function, says somewhere, that many a Man runs his Head against a Pulpit, who might have done his Country excellent Service at a Plough-tail.[3]

---

[1] See No. 294.

[2] Cf. Huarte (sig. a3ᵛ) on the lack of natural talent in the 'three great professions':

And for want of such Caution at this day, the Christian Religion is in danger by Pretenders to Divinity, who want proper *Genius's* for it; nay, unskilful Physicians have destroyed Mens Bodies; nor has the Skill of the Law arrived at that Pitch it ought, for want of knowing to what Rational Faculty the Use and true Interpretation of the Laws belong.

[3] In a sermon preached at Westminster Abbey on 22 Feb. 1684/5, 'on chance in the affairs of men', South writes: 'One Man perhaps proves miserable in the Study of the Law, which might have flourished in that of Physick, or Divinity.

'In like manner many a Lawyer, who makes but an indifferent Figure at the Bar, might have made a very elegant Waterman, and have shined at the *Temple* Stairs, tho' he can get no Business in the House.

'I have known a Corn-cutter, who with a right Education would have been an excellent Physician.

'To descend lower, are not our Streets filled with sagacious Draymen, and Politicians in Liveries? We have several Taylors of six Foot high, and meet with many a broad pair of Shoulders that are thrown away upon a Barber, when perhaps at the same time we see a pigmy Porter reeling under a Burthen, who might have managed a Needle with much Dexterity, or have snapped his Fingers with great Ease to himself, and Advantage to the Publick.

'The *Spartans*, tho' they acted with the Spirit which I am here speaking of, carried it much farther than what I propose: Among them it was not lawful for the Father himself to bring up his Children after his own Fancy. As soon as they were seven Years old they were all listed in several Companies, and disciplined by the Publick. The old Men were Spectators of their Performances, who often raised Quarrels among them, and set them at strife with one another, that by those early Discoveries they might see how their several Talents lay, and without any regard to their Quality,[1] dispose of them accordingly for the Service of the Common-wealth. By this means *Sparta* soon became the Mistress of *Greece*, and famous through the whole World for her Civil and Military Discipline.

'If you think this Letter deserves a Place among your Speculations, I may perhaps trouble you with some other Thoughts on the same Subject.[2]

I am, &c.'

X

Another runs his Head against the Pulpit, who might have been very serviceable to his Country at the Plough' (*Twelve Sermons Preached upon Several Occasions*, 6th ed., 1727, i. 323–4).

[1] Plutarch, *Life of Lycurgus*, 16. 4.

[2] This is the first of a series of four essays by Budgell on education (see Nos. 313, 337, 353).

No. 308
[STEELE]

Friday, February 22, 1712[1]

> . . . *Jam proterva*
> *Fronte petet Lalage maritum.*
>
> Hor.

Mr. SPECTATOR,

'I GIVE you this Trouble in order to propose my self to you as an Assistant in the weighty Cares which you have thought fit to undergo for the publick Good. I am a very great Lover of Women, that is to say honestly; and as it is natural to study what one likes, I have industriously applied my self to understand them. The present Circumstance relating to them, is, that I think there wants under you, as SPECTATOR, a Person to be distinguished and vested in the Power and Quality of a Censor on Marriages. I lodge at the *Temple*, and know, by seeing Women come hither, and afterwards observing them conducted by their Council to Judges Chambers, that there is a Custom in Case of making Conveyance of a Wife's Estate, that she is carried to a Judge's Apartment and left alone with him, to be examined in private whether she has not been frightened or sweetned by her Spouse into the Act she is going to do, or whether it is of her own free Will. Now if this be a Method founded upon Reason and Equity, why should there not be also a proper Officer for examining such as are entering into the State of Matrimony, whether they are forced by Parents on one Side, or moved by Interest only on the other, to come together, and bring forth such awkard Heirs as are the Product of half Love and constrained Compliances? There is no Body, though I say it my self, would be fitter for this Office than I am; for I am an ugly Fellow of great Wit and Sagacity. My Father was an hail Country-'Squire, my Mother a witty Beauty of no Fortune: The Match was made by Consent of my Mother's Parents against her own; and I am the Child of the Rape on the Wedding-Night; so that I am as healthy and homely as my Father, but as sprightly and agreeable as my Mother. It would be of great Ease to you if you would use me under you, that Matches might be better regulated for the future, and we might

---

[1] *Motto.* Horace, *Odes*, 2. 5. 15–16:

. . . Lalage shall soon proclaim
Her Love, nor blush to own her Flame. CREECH.

have no more Children of Squabbles. I shall not reveal all my Pretentions till I receive your Answer; and am,

SIR,

Your most humble Servant,
Mules Palfrey.'

Mr. SPECTATOR,

'I AM one of those unfortunate Men within the City-Walls who am married to a Woman of Quality, but her Temper is something different from that of Lady *Anvill*.[1] My Lady's whole Time and Thoughts are spent in keeping up to the Mode both in Apparel and Furniture. All the Goods in my House have been changed three times in seven Years. I have had seven Children by her; and by our Marriage-Articles she was to have her Apartment new furnished as often as she lay in. Nothing in our House is useful but that which is fashionable; my Pewter holds out generally half a Year, my Plate a full Twelve-month; Chairs are not fit to sit in that were made two Years since, nor Beds fit for any thing but to sleep in that have stood up above that Time. My Dear is of Opinion that an old-fashion Grate consumes Coals, but gives no Heat: If she drinks out of Glasses of last Year, she cannot distinguish Wine from Small-Beer. Oh dear Sir you may guess all the rest.

Yours.

'P. S. I could bear even all this, if I were not obliged also to eat *fashionably*. I have a plain Stomach, and have a constant loathing of whatever comes to my own Table; for which Reason I dine at the *Chop-House* three Days a Week: Where the good Company wonders they never see you of late. I am sure by your unprejudiced Discourses you love Broth better than Soup.'

Mr. SPECTATOR,   *Will's, Feb.* 19.

'YOU may believe you are a Person as much talked of as any Man in Town. I am one of your best Friends in this House, and have laid a Wager you are so candid a Man and so honest a Fellow, that you will print this Letter, tho' it is in Recommendation of a new Paper called *The Historian*.[2] I have read it carefully, and find it written with Skill, good Sense, Modesty, and Fire. You must

---

[1] No. 299.
[2] A periodical essay published on Tuesdays, Thursdays, and Saturdays; the first number had appeared on Saturday, 2 Feb. 1712. It ran for only thirteen numbers—until 1 Mar. (*CBEL*, ii. 661). The imprint reads, 'LONDON, Printed: And Sold by A. Baldwin in Warwick-Lane; where Advertisements are taken in.' The typography and advertisements suggest that Tonson may have been the printer.

allow the Town is kinder to you than you deserve; and I doubt not but you have so much Sense of the World, Change of Humour, and Instability of all humane Things, as to understand, that the only Way to preserve Favour, is to communicate it to others with Good-Nature and Judgment. You are so generally read, that what you speak of will be read. This with Men of Sense and Taste is all that is wanting to recommend *The Historian*.

> *I am,*
> SIR,
> *Your daily Advocate,*
> Reader Gentle.'

I was very much surprized this Morning, that any one should find out my Lodging, and know it so well, as to come directly to my Closet-Door, and knock at it, to give me the following Letter. When I came out I opened it, and saw by a very strong Pair of Shooes and a warm Coat the Bearer had on, that he walked all the Way to bring it me, tho' dated from *York*. My Misfortune is that I cannot talk, and I found the Messenger had so much of me, that he could think better than speak. He had, I observed, a polite Discerning hid under a shrewd Rusticity: He delivered the Paper with a *Yorkshire* Tone and a Town Leer.

Mr. SPECTATOR,

'THE Privilege you have indulg'd *John Trot*[1] has prov'd of very bad Consequence to our illustrious Assembly, which, besides the many excellent Maxims it is founded upon, is remarkable for the extraordinary Decorum always observed in it. One Instance of which is, that the *Carders*,[2] (who are always of the first Quality) never begin to play till the *French*-Dances are finish'd and the Country-Dances begin: But *John Trot* having now got your Commission in his Pocket, (which every one here has a profound Respect for) has the Assurance to set up for a Minuit-Dancer. Not only so, but he has brought down upon us the whole Body of the *Trots*, which are very numerous, with their Auxiliaries the Hobblers and the Skippers; by which Means the Time is so much wasted, that unless we break all Rules of Government, it must redound to the utter Subversion of the *Brag-Table*,[3] the discreet Members of which

---

[1] No. 296.
[2] An obsolete term for card-players. This quotation is the last in *OED*.
[3] Brag was a game at cards, in which bragging was an ingredient of success. Theophilus Lucas (*Memoirs of the Lives . . . of the most famous Gamesters*, 1714, p. 112)

value Time as *Frible*'s Wife[1] does her Pin-Money. We are pretty well assur'd that your Indulgence to *Trot* was only in Relation to Country-Dances; however we have deferred the issuing an Order of Council upon the Premisses, hoping to get you to joyn with us, that *Trot*, nor any of his Clan, presume for the future to dance any but Country-Dances, unless a Horn Pipe upon a Festival Day. If you will do this you will oblige a great many Ladies, and particularly

Your most humble Servant,

York, Feb. 16.   Eliz. Sweepstakes.'

'I NEVER meant any other than that Mr. *Trot* should confine himself to Country-Dances: And I further direct, that he shall take out none but his own Relations according to their Nearness of Blood, but any Gentlewoman may take out him.

London, Feb. 21.   The SPECTATOR.'

T

No. 309   *Saturday, February 23,* 1712[2]

[ADDISON]

Dî, quibus imperium est animarum, umbræque silentes,
Et Chaos, & Phlegethon, loca nocte silentia late;
Sit mihi fas audita loqui: sit numine vestro
Pandere res alta terra & caligine mersas.

Virg.

I HAVE before observed[3] in general, that the Persons whom *Milton* introduces into his Poem always discover such Sentiments

tells us that Patrick Hurley was an expert at brag, 'which Game being the main thing by which the second Stake is to be won by the Ingenuity of its Management, it takes from Thence its Name; for you are to endeavor to impose upon the Judgment of the rest that play, and particularly on the Person that chiefly offers to oppose you, by boasting of Cards in your Hand, that are better than his or hers that plays against you'. For the rules see Richard Seymour, *The Compleat Gamester* (5th ed., 1734), pt. ii, pp. 19–25.   [1] No. 295.

   [2] *Motto.* Virgil, *Aeneid,* 6. 264–7 (altered):

Ye Realms, yet unreveal'd to human sight,
Ye Gods, who rule the Regions of the Night,
Ye gliding Ghosts, permit me to relate
The mystic Wonders of your silent State. DRYDEN.

Addison had used these lines as the motto of *Tatler* 152.
   [3] No. 279 (vol. ii).

and Behaviour, as are in a peculiar manner conformable to their respective Characters. Every Circumstance in their Speeches and Actions, is with great justness and delicacy adapted to the Persons who speak and act. As the Poet very much excels in this Consistency of his Characters, I shall beg leave to consider several Passages of the Second Book in this Light. That superior Greatness and Mock-Majesty, which is ascribed to the Prince of the fallen Angels, is admirably preserved in the beginning of this Book. His opening and closing the Debate; his taking on himself that great Enterprize at the Thought of which the whole Infernal Assembly trembled; his encountring the hideous Phantom who guarded the Gates of Hell, and appeared to him in all his Terrors, are Instances of that proud and daring Mind which could not brook Submission even to Omni-potence.[1]

> Satan *was now at hand, and from his Seat*
> *The Monster moving onward came as fast*
> *With horrid strides, Hell trembled as he strode*
> *Th'undaunted Fiend what this might be admir'd,*
> *Admir'd, not fear'd . . .*[2]

The same Boldness and Intrepidity of Behaviour discovers it self in the several Adventures which he meets with during his Passage through the Regions of unform'd Matter, and particularly in his Address[3] to those tremendous Powers who are described as presiding over it.

The Part of *Moloch*[4] is likewise in all its Circumstances full of that Fire and Fury which distinguish this Spirit from the rest of the fallen Angels. He is described in the first Book as besmear'd with the Blood of Human Sacrifices, and delighted with the Tears of Parents, and the Cries of Children.[5] In the second Book he is marked out as the fiercest Spirit that fought in Heaven;[6] and if we consider the Figure which he makes in the Sixth Book, where the Battel of the Angels is described, we find it every way answerable to the same furious enraged Character.

> *. . . Where the might of* Gabriel *fought,*
> *And with fierce Ensigns pierc'd the deep array*
> *Of* Moloc, *furious King, who him defy'd,*

---

[1] PL, ii. 11 ff., 465–7, 629 ff., 666 ff.
[3] PL, ii. 968–87.
[5] PL, i. 392–3.
[2] PL, ii. 674–8.
[4] PL, ii. 43–108.
[6] PL, ii. 44–45.

And at his chariot wheels to drag him bound
Threaten'd, nor from the Holy one of Heav'n
Refrain'd his tongue blasphemous; but anon
Down cloven to the waste, with shatter'd arms
And uncouth pain fled bellowing. . . .[1]

It may be worth while to observe, that *Milton* has represented this violent impetuous Spirit, who is hurried on by such precipitate Passions, as the *first* that rises in the Assembly, to give his Opinion upon their present Posture of Affairs. Accordingly he declares himself abruptly for War,[2] and appears incensed at his Companions, for losing so much time as even to deliberate upon it. All his Sentiments are Rash, Audacious and Desperate. Such is that of arming themselves with their Tortures, and turning their Punishments upon him who inflicted them.

> *. . . No, let us rather chuse,*
> *Arm'd with Hell flames and fury, all at once*
> *O'er Heavens high tow'rs to force resistless way,*
> *Turning our tortures into horrid arms*
> *Against the Torturer; when to meet the Noise*
> *Of his almighty Engine he shall hear*
> *Infernal Thunder, and for Lightning see*
> *Black fire and horror shot with equal rage*
> *Among his Angels; and his throne it self*
> *Mixt with* Tartarean *Sulphur, and strange fire,*
> *His own invented Torments . . .*[3]

His preferring Annihilation[4] to Shame or Misery, is also highly suitable to his Character; as the Comfort he draws from their disturbing the Peace of Heaven,[5] that[a] if it be not Victory it is Revenge, is a Sentiment truly Diabolical, and becoming the Bitterness of this implacable Spirit.

Belial is described, in the First Book, as the Idol of the Lewd and Luxurious. He is in the Second Book, pursuant to that Description, characterized as timorous and slothful;[6] and if we look into the Sixth Book, we find him celebrated in the Battel of Angels for nothing but that Scoffing Speech[7] which he makes to *Satan*, on their

---

[a] Heaven, that] *8vo, 12mo, 19;* Heaven, namely, that *Fol.*

[1] *PL*, vi. 355–62.	[2] *PL*, ii. 51.	[3] *PL*, ii. 60–70.
[4] *PL*, ii. 92–98.	[5] *PL*, ii. 101–5.	[6] *PL*, ii. 117.
[7] *PL*, vi. 620–7.		

supposed Advantage over the Enemy. As his Appearance is uniform, and of a Piece, in these three several Views, we find his Sentiments in the Infernal Assembly every way conformable to his Character. Such are his Apprehensions of a second Battel, his Horrors of Annihilation, his preferring to be miserable rather than *not to be*.[1] I need not observe, that the Contrast of Thought in this Speech, and that which precedes it, gives an agreeable Variety to the Debate.

Mammon's Character is so fully drawn in the First Book, that the Poet adds nothing to it in the Second. We were before told, that he was the first who taught Mankind to ransack the Earth for Gold and Silver, and that he was the Architect of *Pandæmonium*, or the Infernal Palace, where the Evil Spirits were to meet in Council.[2] His Speech in this Book is every way suitable to so depraved a Character. How proper is that Reflection,[3] of their being unable to taste the Happiness of Heaven were they actually there, in the Mouth of one, who while he was in Heaven, is said to have had his Mind dazled with the outward Pomps and Glories of the Place, and to have been more intent on the Riches of the Pavement, than on the Beatifick Vision. I shall also leave the Reader to judge how agreeable the following Sentiments are to the same Character.

> ... *This deep world*
> *Of Darkness do we dread? How oft amidst*
> *Thick cloud and dark doth Heav'ns all-ruling Sire*
> *Chuse to reside, his Glory unobscured,*
> *And with the Majesty of darkness round*
> *Covers his Throne; from whence deep thunders roar*
> *Mustring their rage, and Heav'n resembles Hell?*
> *As he our darkness, cannot we his light*
> *Imitate when we please? This desart Soil,*
> *Wants not her hidden lustre, Gems and Gold;*
> *Nor want we Skill or Art, from whence to raise*
> *Magnificence; and what can Heav'n shew more?*[4]

Beëlzebub, who is reckon'd the second in Dignity that fell, and is in the First Book, the second that awakens out of the Trance, and confers with *Satan* upon the situation of their Affairs, maintains his Rank in the Book now before us.[5] There is a wonderful Majesty

[1] *PL*, ii. 143–51.
[2] *PL*, i. 678–88, 732–51.
[3] *PL*, ii. 237–49.
[4] *PL*, ii. 262–73 ('Thick clouds', line 264).
[5] *PL*, i. 79–191.

described in his rising up to speak. He acts as a kind of Moderator between the two opposite Parties, and proposes a third Undertaking, which the whole Assembly gives into.[1] The Motion he makes of detaching one of their Body in search of a new World is grounded upon a Project devised by *Satan*, and cursorily proposed by him in the following Lines of the first Book.

> *Space may produce new Worlds, whereof so rife*
> *There went a fame in Heav'n, that he e'er long*
> *Intended to create, and therein plant*
> *A generation, whom his choice regard*
> *Should favour equal to the Sons of Heaven:*
> *Thither, if but to pry, shall be perhaps*
> *Our first eruption, thither or elsewhere:*
> *For this infernal Pit shall never hold*
> *Celestial Spirits in bondage, nor th'Abyss*
> *Long under Darkness cover. But these thoughts*
> *Full Counsel must mature: . . .*[2]

It is on this Project that *Beëlzebub* grounds his Proposal.

> *. . . What if we find*
> *Some easier enterprize? There is a place*
> *(If ancient and prophetic fame in Heav'n*
> *Err not) another World, the happy Seat*
> *Of some new Race call'd* MAN, *about this time*
> *To be created like to us, though less*
> *In power and excellence, but favoured more*
> *Of him who rules above; so was his Will*
> *Pronounc'd among the Gods, and by an oath,*
> *That shook Heav'ns whole circumference, confirm'd.*[3]

The Reader may observe how just it was, not to omit in the First Book the Project upon which the whole Poem turns: As also that the Prince of the fall'n Angels was the only proper Person to give it Birth, and that the next to him in Dignity was the fittest to second and support it.

There is besides, I think, something wonderfully beautiful, and very apt to affect the Reader's Imagination in this ancient Prophecy or Report in Heaven, concerning the Creation of Man. Nothing could shew more the Dignity of the Species, than this Tradition

[1] *PL*, ii. 299–416.   [2] *PL*, i. 650–60.   [3] *PL*, ii. 344–53.

which ran of them before their Existence. They are represented to have been the Talk of Heaven, before they were created. *Virgil*, in compliment to the *Roman* Common-Wealth, makes the Heroes of it appear in their State of Pre-existence;[1] But *Milton* does a far greater Honour to Mankind in general, as he gives us a Glimpse of them even before they are in Being.

The rising of this great Assembly is described in a very Sublime and Poetical manner.

> *Their rising all at once was as the sound*
> *Of Thunder heard remote . . .*[2]

The Diversions of the fallen Angels, with the particular Account of their Place of Habitation, are described with great Pregnancy of Thought, and Copiousness of Invention.[3] The Diversions are every way suitable to Beings who had nothing left them but Strength and Knowledge misapplied. Such are their Contentions at the Race, and in Feats of Arms, with their Entertainment in the following Lines.

> *Others with vast* Typhæan *rage more fell*
> *Rend up both Rocks and Hills, and ride the Air*
> *In Whirlwind; Hell scarce holds the wild uproar.*[4]

Their Musick[5] is employed in celebrating their own criminal Exploits, and their Discourse in sounding the unfathomable Depths of Fate, Free-will and Fore-knowledge.[6]

The several Circumstances[7] in the Description of Hell are finely[a] imagined; as the four Rivers which disgorge themselves into the Sea of Fire, the Extreams of Cold and Heat, and the River of

---

[a] are finely] *19*; are very finely *Fol.*, *8vo, 12mo*

---

[1] *Aeneid*, 6. 752–886.

[2] *PL*, ii. 476–7.

[3] *PL*, ii. 528 ff. Dennis, in *The Grounds of Criticism in Poetry* (1704), had praised Milton's skill in depicting his infernal characters. 'The Passions of *Milton*'s Devils have enough of Humanity in them to make them delightful, but then they have a great deal more to make them admirable, and may be said to be the true Passions of Devils . . .' (*Works*, ed. Hooker, i. 370).

[4] *PL*, ii. 539–41.

[5] *PL*, ii. 546–55.

[6] *PL*, ii. 555–69. In No. 114 of the *Tatler* Addison had praised this passage for its 'excellent Turns'. Milton 'describes the Fallen Angels engaged in the intricate Disputes of Predestination, Free-will, and Fore-knowledge; and to humour the Perplexity, makes a Kind of Labyrinth in the very Words that describe it'. Addison also quotes these lines in *Spectator* 237, as descriptive of the vain pursuit of knowledge on the part of those excluded from the bliss of Heaven.

[7] *PL*, ii. 575–81, 596–603, 583–6.

Oblivion. The monstrous Animals produced in that infernal World are represented by a single Line, which gives us a more horrid Idea of them, than a much longer Description would have done.

> *. . . Nature breeds,*
> *Perverse, all monstrous, all prodigious things,*
> *Abominable, inutterable, and* worse
> Than Fables yet have feign'd, or fear conceiv'd,
> *Gorgons, and Hydra's, and Chimera's dire.*[1]

This Episode[2] of the fallen Spirits, and their Place of Habitation, comes in very happily to unbend the Mind of the Reader from its Attention to the Debate. An ordinary Poet would indeed have spun out so many Circumstances to a great Length, and by that means have weaken'd, instead of illustrated, the principal Fable.

The Flight of Satan to the Gates of Hell is finely imaged.[3]

I have already declared my Opinion of the Allegory concerning *Sin* and *Death*,[4] which is however a very finished Piece in its kind, when it is not considered as a Part[a] of an Epic Poem. The Genealogy of the several Persons is contrived with great Delicacy.[5] *Sin* is the Daughter of *Satan*, and *Death* the Offspring of *Sin*. The incestuous Mixture between *Sin* and *Death* produces those Monsters and Hellhounds which from time to time enter into their Mother, and tear the Bowels of her who gave them Birth. These are the Terrors of an evil Conscience, and the proper Fruits of *Sin*, which naturally rise from the Apprehensions of *Death*. This last beautiful Moral is, I think, clearly intimated in the Speech of *Sin*, where complaining of this her dreadful Issue, she adds,

> Before mine eyes in opposition sits
> Grim Death my Son and foe, who sets them on.
> *And me his Parent would full soon devour*
> *For want of other prey, but that he knows*
> *His end with mine involv'd . . .*[6]

I need not mention to the Reader the beautiful Circumstance in the last Part of this Quotation. He will likewise observe how naturally the three Persons concerned in this Allegory are tempted

---

[a] as a Part] *19*; as Part *Fol., 8vo, 12mo*

[1] *PL*, ii. 624–8.   [2] *PL*, ii. 614–28.   [3] *PL*, ii. 629–43.
[4] No. 273 (vol. ii).   [5] *PL*, ii. 746–814.   [6] *PL*, ii. 803–7.

by one common Interest to enter into a Confederacy together, and how properly *Sin* is made the Portress of Hell, and the only Being that can open the Gates to that World of Tortures.[1]

The descriptive Part of this Allegory is likewise very strong, and full of Sublime Ideas. The Figure of Death, the Regal Crown upon his Head,[a] his Menace of[b] Satan, his advancing to the Combat,[2] the Outcry[3] at his Birth, are Circumstances too noble to be past over in Silence, and extreamly suitable to this *King of Terrors.* I need not mention the Justness of Thought which is observed in the Generation of these several Symbolical Persons; that *Sin* was produced upon the first Revolt of Satan, that *Death* appeared soon after he was cast into Hell, and that the Terrors of Conscience were conceived at the Gate of this Place of Torments. The Description of the Gates is very poetical, as the opening of them is full of *Milton*'s Spirit.

> *. . . On a sudden open fly*
> *With impetuous recoil and jarring sound*
> *Th'infernal doors, and on their hinges grate*
> *Harsh Thunder, that the lowest bottom shook*
> *Of Erebus. She open'd, but to shut*
> *Excell'd her power; the Gates wide open stood,*
> *That with extended wings a banner'd Host*
> *Under spread Ensigns marching might pass through*
> *With Horse and Chariots rank'd in loose array;*
> *So wide they stood, and like a furnace mouth*
> *Cast forth redounding smoak and ruddy flame.*[4]

[c]In *Satan*'s Voyage[5] through the *Chaos* there are several Imaginary Persons[6] described, as residing in that immense Waste of Matter. This may perhaps be conformable to the Taste of those Criticks who are pleased with nothing in a Poet which has not Life and Manners ascribed to it; but for my own part, I am pleased most with those Passages in this Description which carry in them a greater Measure of Probability, and are such as might possibly have happened. Of this kind[7] is his first mounting in the Smoak that

---

[a] the Regal Crown upon his Head, *added in 8vo, 12mo, 19*; the Royal Crown upon his Head, *12mo*   [b] of] *19; to Fol., 8vo, 12mo*   [c] *No new paragraph in Folio*

[1] *PL*, ii. 746, 774–7.   [2] *PL*, ii. 666–76.   [3] *PL*, ii. 787–9.
[4] *PL*, ii. 879–89.   [5] *PL*, ii. 927–1055.
[6] Addison returns to this in No. 315.
[7] *PL*, ii. 928–38, 1013.

rises from the infernal Pit, his falling into a Cloud of Nitre, and the like combustible Materials, that by their Explosion still hurried him forward in his Voyage; his springing upward like a Pyramid of Fire, with his laborious Passage through that Confusion of Elements, which the Poet calls

The Womb of Nature and perhaps her Grave.[1]

The Glimmering Light[2] which shot into the *Chaos* from the utmost Verge of the Creation, with the distant Discovery of the Earth[3] that hung close by the Moon, are wonderfully beautiful and poetical.   L

No. 310   *Monday, February 25, 1712*[4]

[STEELE]

Connubio Jungam stabili . . .
                               Virg.

Mr. SPECTATOR,
'I AM a certain young Woman that love a certain young Man very heartily; and my Father and Mother were for it a great while, but now they say I can do better, but I think I cannot. They bid me love him, and I cannot unlove him. What must I do? Speak quickly.

                                        Biddy Dobake.'

Dear SPEC.   *Feb.* 19. 1712.
'I HAVE lov'd a Lady entirely for this Year and Half, tho' for a great Part of the Time (which has contributed not a little to my Pain) I have been debarred the Liberty of conversing with her. The Grounds of our Difference was this; That when we had enquired into each other's Circumstances, we found that at our first setting out into the World we should owe five hundred Pounds more than her Fortune would pay off. My Estate is seven hundred Pounds a Year, besides the Benefit of Tin-Mines. Now, dear SPEC. upon this

---

[1] *PL*, ii. 911.   [2] *PL*, ii. 1034–7.
[3] *PL*, ii. 1051–3. Thomas Newton, in his edition of *Paradise Lost* (1749), notes that it is not the earth which Satan discovers, but rather the universe.
[4] *Motto.* Virgil, *Aeneid*, 1. 73:
                    In lasting wedlock I will join them.

State of the Case, and the Lady's positive Declaration that there is still no other Objection, I beg you'll not fail to insert this, with your Opinion, as soon as possibly, whether this ought to be esteemed a just Cause or Impediment why we should not be join'd; and you will for ever oblige

Yours sincerely,
Dick Lovesick.

'P. S. Sir, if I marry this Lady by the Assistance of your Opinion, you may expect a Favour for it.'

Mr. SPECTATOR,

'I HAVE the Misfortune to be one of those unhappy Men who are distinguished by the Name of discarded Lovers; but I am the less mortified at my Disgrace, because the young Lady is one of those Creatures who set up for Negligence of Men, are forsooth the most rigidly virtuous in the World, and yet their Nicety will permit them, at the Command of Parents, to go to Bed to the most utter Stranger that can be proposed to them. As to me my self, I was introduced by the Father of my Mistress; but find I owe my being at first received to a Comparison of my Estate with that of a former Lover, and that I am now in like manner turned off, to give Way to an humble Servant still richer than I am. What makes this Treatment the more extravagant, is, that the young Lady is in the Management of this way of Fraud, and obeys her Father's Orders on these Occasions without any Manner of Reluctance, but does it with the same Air that one of your Men of the World would signify the Necessity of Affairs for turning another out of Office. When I came home last Night I found this Letter from my Mistress.

SIR,

"I HOPE you will not think it is any manner of Disrespect to your Person or Merit, that the intended Nuptials between us are interrupted. My Father says he has much a better Offer for me than you can make, and has ordered me to break off the Treaty between us. If it had proceeded, I should have behaved my self with all suitable Regard to you, but as it is, I beg we may be Strangers for the Future. Adieu. *Lydia.*"

'This great Indifference on this Subject, and the mercenary Motives for making Alliances, is what I think lies naturally before you, and I beg of you to give me your Thoughts upon it. My

Answer to *Lydia* was as follows, which I hope you will approve; for you are to know the Woman's Family affect a wonderful Ease on these Occasions, tho' they expect it should be painfully received on the Man's Side.'

Madam
"I HAVE received yours, and knew the Prudence of your House so well, that I always took Care to be ready to obey your Commands, tho' they should be to see you no more. Pray give my Service to all the good Family.

The Opera Subscription is full.

Adieu,
Clitophon."'

Memorandum. *The Censor of Marriage*[1] *to consider this Letter, and report the common Usages on such Treaties, with how many Pounds or Acres are generally esteemed sufficient Reason for preferring a new to an old Pretender; with his Opinion what is proper to be determined in such Cases for the future.*

Mr. SPECTATOR,
'THERE is an elderly Person, lately left off Business and settled in our Town, in order, as he thinks, to retire from the World; but he has brought with him such an Inclination to Tale-bearing, that he disturbs both himself and all our Neighbourhood. Notwithstanding this Frailty, the honest Gentleman is so happy as to have no Enemy: At the same time he has not one Friend who will venture to acquaint him with his Weakness. It is not to be doubted but if this Failing were set in a proper Light, he would quickly perceive the Indecency and evil Consequences of it. Now, Sir, this being an Infirmity which I hope may be corrected, and knowing that he pays much Deference to you, I beg that, when you are at Leisure to give us a Speculation on Gossiping, you would think of my Neighbour: You will hereby oblige several who will be glad to find a Reformation in their grey-hair'd Friend: And how becoming will it be for him, instead of pouring forth Words at all Adventures, to set a Watch before the Door of his Mouth, to refrain his *Tongue*, to check its Impetuosity, and guard against the Sallies of that *little, pert, forward, busy Person;*[2] which, under a sober Conduct, might prove

---

[1] See No. 308.
[2] This sounds like a quotation, but it has not been identified.

a useful Member of a Society. In Complyance with whose Intimations, I have taken the Liberty to make this Address to you.

I am, SIR,

Your most obscure Servant,

Philanthropos.'

Mr. SPECTATOR,   *Feb.* 16. 1712.

'THIS is to petition you, in Behalf of my self and many more of your gentle Readers, that at any time when you may have private Reasons against letting us know what you think your self, you would be pleased to pardon us such Letters of your Correspondents as seem to be of no Use but to the Printer.[1]

'It is further our humble Request, that you would substitute Advertisements in the Place of such Epistles; and that in order hereunto Mr. *Buckley* may be authorized to take up of your zealous Friend Mr. *Charles Lillie,* any Quantity of Words he shall from time to time have occasion for.

'The many useful Parts of Knowledge which may be communicated to the Publick this Way, will, we hope, be a Consideration in Favour of your Petitioners.

And your Petitioners, &c.'

Note, That particular Regard be had to this Petition; and the Papers marked Letter R[2] may be carefully examined for the future.

T

No. 311   *Tuesday, February 26, 1712*[3]
[ADDISON]

Nec Veneris pharetris macer est; aut lampade fervet:
Inde faces ardent, veniunt a dote sagittæ.

Juv.

Mr. SPECTATOR,

'I AM amazed that among all the Variety of Characters, with which you have enriched your Speculations, you have never

[1] Cf. No. 304.

[2] The signature R—one of Steele's—is not used after No. 134 (vol. ii).

[3] *Motto.* Juvenal, *Satires,* 6. 138–9 (altered):

The Darts of Venus and her Torch he scorns:
The Fortune charms him, 'tis for that he burns.

given us a Picture of those audacious young Fellows among us, who commonly go by the Name of *Fortune-Stealers*. You must know, Sir, I am one who live in a continual Apprehension of this sort of People, that lie in wait, Day and Night, for our Children, and may be considered as a kind of Kidnappers within the Law. I am the Father of a Young Heiress, whom I begin to look upon as Marriageable, and who has looked upon her self as such for above these Six Years. She is now in the Eighteenth Year of her Age. The Fortune-hunters have already cast their Eyes upon her, and take care to plant themselves in her View whenever she appears in any Publick Assembly. I have my self caught a young Jackanapes, with a pair of Silver Fringed Gloves, in the very Fact. You must know, Sir, I have kept her as a Prisoner of State ever since she was in her Teens. Her Chamber Windows are cross-barr'd, she is not permitted to go out of the House but with her Keeper, who is a stay'd Relation of my own; I have likewise forbid her the use of Pen and Ink for this Twelve-Month last past, and do not suffer a Ban-box to be carried into her Room before it has been searched. Notwithstanding these Precautions, I am at my Wits End for fear of any sudden Surprize. There were, two or three Nights ago, some Fiddles heard in the Street, which I am afraid portend me no Good; not to mention a tall *Irish*-Man,[1] that has been seen walking before my House more than once this Winter. My Kinswoman likewise informs me, that the Girl has talked to her twice or thrice of a Gentleman in a Fair Wig, and that she loves to go to Church more than ever she did in her Life. She gave me the Slip about a Week ago, upon which my whole House was in Alarm. I immediately dispatched a Hue and Cry after her to the Change,[2] to her Mantua-maker, and to the young Ladies that Visit her; but after above an Hours search she returned of her self, having been taking a Walk, as she told me, by *Rosamond*'s Pond.[3] I have hereupon turned off her Woman, doubled her Guards, and given new Instructions to my Relation, who, to give her her due, keeps a watchful Eye over all her Motions. This, Sir, keeps me in

---

[1] Almost a stock figure for the fortune-hunter (cf. No. 282, vol. ii). A letter in Lillie (i. 243–5) dated 'Pall-mall-coffee-house, S. Patrick's day, 1712' and signed Patrick O Neil, complains of the distance and caution with which Irishmen are treated in London. 'I am an Irishman, though no very tall one in your acceptation . . . . We cannot but think it pretty odd, that a short Irishman who has warm'd his shins by the fire-sides of two English wives, should cry out to the town to have a care of the tall ones.'

[2] Probably the New Exchange, in the Strand. See No. 96 (vol. i).

[3] Rosamond's Pond, in the south-west corner of St. James's Park, frequently mentioned in plays as a place of assignation. It was filled up in 1770.

a perpetual Anxiety, and makes me very often watch when my Daughter sleeps, as I am afraid she is even with me in her Turn. Now, Sir, what I would desire of you, is, to represent to this Fluttering Tribe of young Fellows, who are for making their Fortunes by these indirect Means, that stealing a Man's Daughter for the sake of her Portion, is but a kind of Tolerated Robbery; and that they make but a poor Amends to the Father, whom they plunder after this Manner, by going to Bed with his Child. Dear Sir, be speedy in your Thoughts on this Subject, that, if possible they may appear before the Disbanding of the Army.

I am, SIR,

Your Most Humble Servant

Tim. Watchwell.'[1]

Themistocles, the great *Athenian* General, being asked whether he wou'd chuse to marry his Daughter to an Indigent Man of Merit, or to a Worthless Man of an Estate, reply'd, That he should prefer a Man without an Estate, to an Estate without a Man.[2] The worst of it is, our Modern Fortune-Hunters are those who turn their Heads that way, because they are good for nothing else. If a young Fellow finds he can make nothing of *Cook* and *Littleton*, he provides himself with a Ladder of Ropes, and by that means very often enters upon the Premises.

The same Art of Scaling has likewise been practised with good Success by many Military Ingineers. Stratagems of this Nature make Parts and Industry superfluous, and cut short the way to Riches.

Nor is Vanity a less Motive than Idleness to this kind of mercenary Pursuit. A Fop who admires his Person in a Glass, soon enters into a Resolution of making his Fortune by it, not questioning but every Woman that falls in his way will do him as much Justice as he does himself. When an Heiress sees a Man throwing particular Graces into his Ogle, or talking loud within her Hearing, she ought to look to her self; but if with-all she observes a Pair of Red-Heels, a Patch, or any other Particularity in his Dress, she cannot take too much care of her Person. These are Baits not to be trifled with, Charms that have done a world of Execution, and made their way into Hearts which have been thought impregnable. The Force of a Man with these Qualifications is so well known, that I am credibly

---

[1] This letter is by John Hughes (in Duncombe's list, vol. i, p. xxxv).
[2] Plutarch, *Life of Themistocles*, 18. 5; Cicero, *De Officiis*, 2. 20. 71.

inform'd there are several Female Undertakers about the Change, who upon the Arrival of a likely Man out of a neighb'ring Kingdom, will furnish him with proper Dress from Head to Foot, to be paid for at a double Price on the Day of Marriage.

We must however distingush between Fortune-Hunters and Fortune-Stealers. The first are those assiduous Gentlemen who employ their whole Lives in the Chace, without ever coming at the Quarry. *Suffenus* has comb'd and powder'd at the Ladies for thirty Years together, and taken his Stand in a Side Box, 'till he is grown wrinkled under their Eyes. He is now laying the same Snares for the present Generation of Beauties, which he practised on their Mothers. *Cottilus*, after having made his Applications to more than you meet with in Mr. *Cowley*'s Ballad of Mistresses,[1] was at last smitten with a City Lady of 20000 *l.* Sterling; but died of old Age before he cou'd bring Matters to bear. Nor must I here omit my worthy Friend Mr. HONEYCOMB, who has often told us in the Club, that for twenty Years successively, upon the Death of a Childless rich Man, he immediately drew on his Boots, called for his Horse, and made up to the Widow. When he is rallied upon his ill Success, WILL. with his usual Gaiety tells us, that he always found her[a] Præ-engaged.

Widows are indeed the great Game of your Fortune-Hunters. There is scarce a young Fellow in the Town of six Foot high, that has not passed in Review before one or other of these wealthy Relicts. *Hudibrass*'s *Cupid*, who

> . . . *took his Stand*
> *Upon a Widow's Jointure-Land,*[2]

is daily employed in throwing Darts, and kindling Flames. But as for Widows, they are such a Subtle Generation of People, that they may be left to their own Conduct; or, if they make a false Step in it, they are answerable for it to no body but themselves. The young innocent Creatures who have no Knowledge and Experience of the World, are those whose Safety I would principally consult in this Speculation. The Stealing of such an one should, in my Opinion, be as punishable as a Rape. Where there is no Judgment there is no

---

[a] her] them *Fol.*

---

[1] 'The Chronicle: a Ballad' (*Poems*, ed. Waller, pp. 39–42).
[2] *Hudibras*, I. iii. 311–12.

Choice; and why the inveigling a Woman before she is come to Years of Discretion, should not be as Criminal as the seducing of her before she is ten Years old, I am at a Loss to comprehend.

L

No. 312   *Wednesday, February 27, 1712*[1]
[STEELE]

> *Quod huic Officium, quæ laus, quod Decus erit tanti, quod*
> *adipisci cum dolore Corporis velit, qui dolorem summum*
> *malum sibi esse persuaserit? Quam porro quis igno-*
> *miniam quam turpitudinem non pertulerit, ut effugiat*
> *dolorem, si id summum malum esse decreverit?*
>
>   Tull. De dolore Tolerando.

IT is a very melancholly Reflexion, that Men are usually so weak, that it is absolutely necessary for them to know Sorrow and Pain to be in their right Senses. Prosperous People, (for happy there are none) are hurried away with a fond Sense of their present Condition, and thoughtless of the Mutability of Fortune; Fortune is a Term which we must use in such Discourses as these, for what is wrought by the unseen Hand of the Disposer of all Things. But methinks the Disposition of a Mind which is truly great, is that which makes Misfortunes and Sorrows little when they befall our selves, great and lamentable when they befall other Men. The most unpardonable Malefactor in the World, going to his Death and bearing it with Composure, would win the Pity of those who should behold him; and this not because his Calamity is deplorable, but because he seems himself not to deplore it: We suffer for him who is less sensible of his own Misery, and are inclined to despise him who sinks under the Weight of his Distresses. On the other Hand, without any Touch of Envy, a temperate and well-governed Mind looks down on such as are exalted with Success, with a certain Shame for the Imbecillity of humane Nature, that can so far forget how liable

---

[1] *Motto.* Cicero, *Tusculan Disputations*, 2. 6. 16: What Preferment, what Praise, what Honour will be sufficient for him to obtain with bodily Pain, who imagines Pain to be the greatest Evil? and who would not endure any Ignominy and Disgrace to avoid Pain, if he judge Pain to be the greatest of all Evils?

it is to Calamity, as to grow giddy with only the Suspence of Sorrow, which is the Portion of all Men. He therefore who turns his Face from the unhappy Man, who will not look again when his Eye is cast upon modest Sorrow, who shuns Affliction like a Contagion, does but pamper himself up for a Sacrifice, and contract in himself a greater Aptitude to Misery by attempting to escape it. A Gentleman where I happened to be last Night, fell into a Discourse which I thought shewed a good Discerning in him: He took Notice, that whenever Men have looked into their Heart for the Idea of true Excellency in humane Nature, they have found it to consist in suffering after a right Manner and with a good Grace. Heroes are always drawn bearing Sorrows, struggling with Adversities, undergoing all Kinds of Hardships, and having in the Service of Mankind a Kind of Appetite to Difficulties and Dangers. The Gentleman went on to observe, that it is from this secret Sense of the high Merit which there is in Patience under Calamities, that the Writers of Romances, when they attempt to furnish out Characters of the highest Excellence, ransack Nature for things terrible; they raise a new Creation of Monsters, Dragons, and Giants: Where the Danger ends, the Hero ceases; when he won an Empire, or gained his Mistress, the rest of his Story is not worth relating. My Friend carried his Discourse so far as to say, that it was for higher Beings than Men to join Happiness and Greatness in the same Idea; but that in our Condition we have no Conception of superlative Excellence, or Heroicism, but as it is surrounded with a Shade of Distress.

It is certainly the proper Education we should give our selves, to be prepared for the ill Events and Accidents we are to meet with in a Life sentenced to be a Scene of Sorrow: But instead of this Expectation, we soften our selves with Prospects of constant Delight, and destroy in our Minds the Seeds of Fortitude and Virtue, which should support us in Hours of Anguish. The constant Pursuit of Pleasure has in it something insolent and improper for our Being. There is a pretty sober Liveliness in the Ode of *Horace* to *Delius*, where he tells him, loud Mirth, or immoderate Sorrow, Inequality of Behaviour either in Prosperity or Adversity, are alike ungraceful in Man that is born to die.[1] Moderation in both Circumstances is peculiar to generous Minds: Men of that Sort ever taste the Gratifications of Health, and all other Advantages of Life, as if they were liable to part with them; and when bereft of them, resign them with

---

[1] Horace, *Odes*, 2. 3.

a Greatness of Mind which shews they knew their Value and Duration. The Contempt of Pleasure is a certain Preparatory for the Contempt of Pain: Without this, the Mind is as it were taken suddenly by any unforeseen Event; but he that has always, during Health and Prosperity, been abstinent in his Satisfactions, enjoys, in the worst of Difficulties, the Reflexion, that his Anguish is not aggravated with the Comparison of past Pleasures which upbraid his present Condition. *Tully* tells us a Story after *Pompey*, which gives us a good Taste of the pleasant Manner the Men of Wit and Philosophy had in old Times, of alleviating the Distresses of Life by the Force of Reason and Philosophy.[1] *Pompey*, when he came to *Rhodes*, had a Curiosity to visit the famous Philosopher *Possidonius*;[2] but finding him in his sick Bed, he bewailed the Misfortune that he should not hear a Discourse from him: But you may, answered *Possidonius*; and immediately entered into the Point of Stoical Philosophy, which says Pain is not an Evil. During the Discourse, upon every Puncture he felt from his Distemper, he smiled and cried out, Pain, Pain, be as impertinent and troublesome as you please, I shall never own thou art an Evil.

Mr. SPECTATOR,

'HAVING seen, in several of your Papers, a Concern for the Honour of the Clergy, and their doing every thing as becomes their Character, and particularly performing the publick Service with a due Zeal and Devotion; I am the more encouraged to lay before them, by your Means, several Expressions used by some of them in their Prayers before Sermon, which I am not well satisfied in: As their giving some Titles and Epithets to great Men, which are indeed due to them in their several Ranks and Stations, but not properly used, I think, in our Prayers. Is it not Contradiction to say, Illustrious, Right Reverend, and Right Honourable poor Sinners? These Distinctions are suited only to our State here, and have no Place in Heaven: We see they are omitted in the Liturgy, which I think the Clergy should take for their Pattern in their own Forms of Devotion. There[a] is another Expression which I would not men-

---

[a] Devotion. There] 'Devotion. Another Expression which I take to be improper, is this, the whole Race of Mankind, when they pray for all Men; for Race signifies Lineage or Descent; and if the Race of Mankind may be used for the present Genera-

[1] *Tusculan Disputations*, 2. 25. 61.
[2] Posidonius (*c.* 135–51 B.C.), head of the Stoic school at Rhodes.

tion, but that I have heard it several times before a learned Congregation, to bring in the last Petition of the Prayer in these Words, *O let not the Lord be angry and I will speak but this once;*[1] as if there was no Difference between *Abraham's* interceding for *Sodom,* for which he had no Warrant as we can find, and our asking those things which we are required to pray for; they would therefore have much more Reason to fear his Anger if they did not make such Petitions to him. There is another pretty Fancy: When a young Man has a Mind to let us know who gave him his Scarf, he speaks a Parenthesis to the Almighty, Bless, *as I am in Duty bound to pray,* the right honourable the Countess; is not that as much as to say, Bless her, for thou knowest I am her Chaplain?

Your humble Servant,

J. O.'[2]

T[3]

tion, (tho' I think not very fitly) the whole Race takes in all from the Beginning to the End of the World. I don't remember to have met with that Expression in their Sense any where but in the old Version of *Psal.* 14.[4] which those Men, I suppose, have but little Esteem for. And some, when they have prayed for all Schools and Nurserys of good Learning and true Religion, especially the two Universities, add these Words, Grant that from them and all other Places dedicated to thy Worship and Service, may come forth such Persons. But what do they mean by all other Places? It seems to me that this is either a Tautology, as being the same with all Schools and Nurseries before expressed, or else it runs too far; for there are several Places dedicated to the divine Service which cannot properly be intended here. There'] *Fol.*

---

[1] Gen. xviii. 32.

[2] There seems to be no evidence for Aitken's suggestion that these initials may stand for John Oldmixon, the Whig journalist and historian.

[3] A letter from Richard Careful, dated London, 1 Apr. 1712 (Lillie, ii. 214–15), comments on 'the success and the reformation which the letter (published about a month ago) touching the parson's prayer before sermon has effected' and speaks of 'another imperfection' in this prayer, in the thanksgiving: 'And lest our unthankfulness for mercies already received should put a stop to the current of thy blessings, &c. From whence (in my humble opinion) it plainly follows, that it is not the mercies themselves, but the prevailing fear of losing them, which occasions the thanksgiving.'

[4] I have not found the allusion here.

No. 313
[BUDGELL]

Thursday, February 28, 1712[1]

Exigite ut mores teneros ceu pollice ducat,
Ut si quis cerâ vultum facit . . .

Juv.

I SHALL give the following Letter no other Recommendation, than by telling my Readers that it comes from the same Hand with that of last *Thursday*.

SIR,

'I SEND you, according to my Promise, some farther Thoughts on the Education of Youth, in which I intend to discuss that famous Question, *Whether the Education at a publick School, or under a private Tutor, is to be preferr'd?*

'As some of the greatest Men in most Ages have been of very different Opinions in this Matter, I shall give a short Account of what I think may be best urged on both sides, and afterwards leave every Person to determine for himself.

'It is certain from *Suetonius*, that the *Romans* thought the Education of their Children a business properly belonging to the Parents themselves; and *Plutarch*, in the Life of *Marcus Cato* tells us, that as soon as his Son was capable of Learning, *Cato* would suffer no body to Teach him but himself, tho' he had a Servant named *Chilo*, who was an excellent Grammarian, and who taught a great many other Youths.[2]

'On the contrary, the *Greeks* seemed more enclined to Publick Schools and Seminaries.

'A private Education promises in the first place Vertue and Good-Breeding; a publick School Manly Assurance, and an early Knowledge in the Ways of the World.

'Mr. *Locke*[3] in his celebrated Treatise *of Education*, confesses that there are Inconveniences to be feared on both sides; *if*, says he, *I keep my Son at Home, he is in danger of becoming my young Master; if I send him Abroad, it is scarce possible to keep him from the reigning Con-*

---

[1] *Motto.* Juvenal, *Satires*, 7. 237–8:

So form the tender Manners of the Boy,
And work him like a waxen Babe with Art.

[2] *Life of Marcus Cato* [Cato Major], 20. 3.

[3] *Some Thoughts concerning Education*, sec. 70 (5th ed., 1705), pp. 93, 103–4.

tagion of Rudeness and Vice. He will perhaps be more Innocent at Home, but more ignorant of the World, and more sheepish when he comes Abroad. However, as this learned Author asserts, That Vertue is much more difficult to be attained than a Knowledge of the World; and that Vice is a much more stubborn, as well as a more dangerous Fault than Sheepishness, he is altogether for a private Education; and the more so, because he does not see why a Youth, with right Management, might not attain the same Assurance in his Father's House, as at a publick School. To this end he advises Parents to accustom their Sons to whatever strange Faces come to the House; to take them with them when they Visit their Neighbours, and to engage them in Conversation with Men of Parts and Breeding.

'It may be objected to this Method, that Conversation is not the only thing necessary, but that unless it be a Conversation with such as are in some measure their Equals in Parts and Years, there can be no room for Emulation, Contention, and several of the most lively Passions of the Mind; which, without being sometimes moved by these means, may possibly contract a Dulness and Insensibility.

'One of the greatest Writers our Nation ever produced observes, That a Boy who forms Parties, and makes himself Popular in a School or a College, would act the same Part with equal ease in a Senate or a Privy-Council; and Mr. *Osborn* speaking like a Man versed in the ways of the World, affirms, that the well laying and carrying on of a design to rob an Orchard, trains up a Youth insensibly to Caution, Secrecy and Circumspection, and fits him for Matters of greater Importance.[1]

'In short, a private Education seems the most natural Method for the forming of a Vertuous Man; a Publick Education for making a Man of Business. The first would furnish out a good Subject for *Plato*'s Republick, the latter a Member for a Community over-run with Artifice and Corruption.

'It must however be confessed, that a Person at the head of a publick School has sometimes so many Boys under his Direction, that it is impossible he should extend a due proportion of his Care to each of them. This is, however, in reality the Fault of the Age, in which we often see twenty Parents, who tho' each expects his Son should be made a Scholar, are not contented all together to make it worth while for any Man of a liberal Education to take upon him the care of their Instruction.

---

[1] Francis Osborne, *Advice to a Son* (Oxford, 1656), p. 2.

'In our great Schools indeed this Fault has been of late Years rectified, so that we have at present not only Ingenious Men for the chief Masters, but such as have proper Ushers and Assistants under them. I must nevertheless own, that for want of the same Encouragement in the Country, we have many a promising Genius spoiled and abused in those little Seminaries.

'I am the more inclined to this Opinion, having my self experienced the Usage of two Rural Masters, each of them very unfit for the Trust they took upon them to discharge. The first imposed much more upon me than my Parts, tho' none of the weakest, could endure; and used me barbarously for not performing Impossibilities. The latter was of quite another Temper; and a Boy, who would run upon his Errands, wash his Coffee-pot, or ring the Bell, might have as little Conversation with any of the Classicks as he thought fit. I have known a Lad at this Place excused his Exercise for assisting the Cookmaid; and remember a Neighbouring Gentleman's Son was among us Five Years, most of which time he employ'd in airing and watering our Master's grey Pad. I scorned to Compound for my Faults, by doing any of these Elegant Offices, and was accordingly the best Scholar, and the worst used of any Boy in the School.

'I shall conclude this Discourse with an Advantage mentioned by *Quintilian*, as accompanying a Publick way of Education, which I have not yet taken notice of; namely, That we very often contract such Friendships at School, as are of Service to us all the following Parts of our Lives.[1]

'I shall give you, under this Head, a Story very well known to several Persons, and which you may depend upon as a real Truth.

'Every one, who is acquainted with *Westminster*-School, knows that there is a Curtain which used to be drawn a-cross the Room, to separate the upper School from the lower. A Youth happened, by some Mischance, to tear the abovementioned Curtain; The Severity of the Master was too well known for the Criminal to expect any Pardon for such a Fault;[2] so that the Boy, who was of a meek Temper, was terrified to Death at the Thoughts of his Appearance, when his Friend, who sat next to him, bad him be of good Cheer, for that he would take the Fault on himself. He kept his word accordingly. As soon as they were grown up to be Men the Civil

---

[1] Quintilian, *Institutio Oratoria*, 1. 2. 20.
[2] The Master of Westminster School was the famous Dr. Richard Busby (1606–95), who was in charge there throughout the Civil War.

War broke out, in which our two Friends took the opposite Sides, one of them followed the Parliament, the other the Royal Party.

'As their Tempers were different, the Youth, who had torn the Curtain, endeavoured to raise himself on the Civil List, and the other, who had born the Blame of it, on the Military: The first succeeded so well, that he was in a short time made a Judge under the Protector. The other was engaged in the unhappy Enterprize of *Penruddock* and *Groves* in the West.[1] I suppose, Sir, I need not acquaint you with the event of that Undertaking. Every one knows that the Royal Party was routed, and all the Heads of them, among whom was the Curtain Champion, imprisoned at *Exeter*. It happened to be his Friend's Lot at that time to go the Western Circuit: The Tryal of the Rebels, as they were then called, was very short, and nothing now remained but to pass Sentence on them; when the Judge hearing the Name of his old Friend, and observing his Face more attentively, which he had not seen for many Years, asked him, if he was not formerly a *Westminster*-Scholar? By the Answer, he was soon convinced that it was his former generous Friend; and, without saying any thing more at that time, made the best of his Way to *London*, where employing all his Power and Interest with the Protector, he saved his Friend from the Fate of his unhappy Associates.

'The Gentleman, whose Life was thus preserved by the Gratitude of his School-fellow, was afterwards the Father of a Son, whom he lived to see promoted in the Church, and who still deservedly fills one of the highest Stations in it.'[2]   X

[1] John Penruddock, the royalist, who took part in a rising on behalf of Charles II in Mar. 1655, was taken prisoner and beheaded at Exeter on 16 May, together with Col. Hugh Grove. Sir John Glynne (an old Westminster boy) presided at the trial, and among the commissioners were Justices Rolle and Nicholas.

[2] The gentleman whose life was saved has traditionally been identified as Col. William Wake, of Shapwick, Blandford, the father of Archbishop Wake. J. D., in the *Gentleman's Magazine*, April 1780, p. 175, quotes the following note by Zachary Grey to *Hudibras* (II. ii. 407–8):

The Spectator (No. 313) gives a remarkable Instance of the good Nature of Mr. Wake, Father to the late Archbishop of Canterbury, who took upon himself the Fault of a Schoolfellow, and was whipp'd for him at Westminster-School. Mr. Wake was a Cavalier, and was engaged in Penruddock's Affair; for which he was tried for his Life at Exeter, by the very Gentleman for whom he had been whipped. The Judge discovering him to be the Humane Person, to whom he had formerly been so much oblig'd, made the best of his way to London: where employing his Power and Interest with the Protector, he saved his Friend from the Fate of his unhappy Associates.

The justice has been identified alternatively as Sir John Glynne and Mr. Justice Nicholas. See further W. W. Ravenhill, 'Records of the Rising in the West', *Wiltshire Archaeological and Natural History Magazine*, xiii (1872), 119–88; xiv (1874), 38–67; J. Sargeaunt, *Annals of Westminster School* (1898), pp. 98–99. The late Dean Sykes

No. 314
[STEELE]

Friday, February 29, 1712[1]

Tandem desine Matrem
Tempestiva sequi viro.
Hor. Od. 23.

Mr. SPECTATOR,   *Feb.* 7. 1711–12.

'I AM a young Man about eighteen Years of Age, and have been in Love with a young Woman of the same Age about this half Year. I go to see her six Days in the Week, but never could have the Happiness of being with her alone. If any of her Friends are at home, she will see me in their Company; but if they be not in the Way, she flies to her Chamber. I can discover no Signs of her Aversion; but either a Fear of falling into the Toils of Matrimony, or a childish Timidity, deprives us of an Interview apart, and drives us upon the Difficulty of languishing out our Lives in fruitless Expectation. Now, Mr. SPECTATOR, if you think us ripe for Oeconomy,[2] perswade the dear Creature, that to pine away into Barrenness and Deformity under a Mother's Shade, is not so honourable, nor does she appear so amiable, as she would in full Bloom. [*There is a great deal left out before he concludes.*]

Mr. SPECTATOR,
Your humble Servant,
Bob. Harmless.'

'IF this Gentleman be really no more than Eighteen, I must do him the Justice to say he is the most knowing Infant I have yet met with. He does not, I fear, yet understand, that all, he thinks of, is another Woman; therefore, till he has given a further Account of

kindly wrote to me on this point: 'Tradition certainly supports the identification of Wake's father, Colonel Wake, with the story.... The archbishop wrote to his friend Browne Willis anent this matter on 15 Sept. 1716 (Add. MSS. Bodleian Library, A. 64, f. 300): "I believe I need not tell you that if I may believe my own parents, I was certainly born in Blandford, Dorset. My father was then a State prisoner in Exeter castle. My mother left him to go home and lie in of me; and so returned again to him." ' See also Sykes, *William Wake, Archbishop of Canterbury, 1657–1737* (Cambridge, 1957), i. 7–8.

[1] *Motto.* Horace, *Odes*, I. 23. 11–12:

> Attend thy Mother's heels no more,
> Now grown mature for Man, and ripe for Joy. CREECH.

[2] Here used in the archaic sense, 'the manner in which a household, or a person's private expenditure, is ordered' (*OED*).

himself, the young Lady is hereby directed to keep close to her Mother.

The SPECTATOR.'

I cannot comply with the Request in Mr. *Trott*'s Letter; but let it go just as it came to my Hands, for being so familiar with the old Gentleman, as rough as he is to him. Since Mr. *Trott* has an Ambition to make him his Father-in-Law, he ought to treat him with more Respect; besides, his Stile to me might have been more distant than he has thought fit to afford me: Moreover, his Mistress shall continue in her Confinement, till he has found out which Word in his Letter is not wrightly spelt.

Mr. SPECTATOR,

'I SHALL ever own my self your obliged humble Servant for the Advice[1] you gave me concerning my Dancing; which unluckily came too late: For, as I said, I would not leave off Capering till I had your Opinion of the Matter; was at our famous Assembly the Day before I received your Papers, and there was observed by an old Gentleman, who was informed I had a Respect for his Daughter; told me I was an insignificant little Fellow, and said that for the Future he would take Care of his Child, so that he did not doubt but to crosse my amerous Inclinations. The Lady is confin'd to her Chamber, and for my Part, am ready to hang my self with the Thoughts that I have danced my self out of Favour with her Father. I hope you will pardon the Trouble I give; but shall take it for a mighty Favour, if you will give me a little more of your Advice to put me in a write Way to cheat the old Dragon and obtain my Mistress. I am once more,

SIR,

York, Feb. 23,   *Your obliged humble Servant,*

1711–12.   John Trott.

'Let me desire you to make what Alterations you please, and insert this as soon as possible. Pardon Mistakes by Haste.'

'I NEVER do pardon Mistakes by Haste.

The SPECTATOR.'

[1] No. 296.

SIR,   *Feb.* 27, 1711–12.
'PRAY be so kind as to let me know what you esteem to be the
chief Qualification of a good Poet, especially of one who writes
Plays; and you will very much oblige,
                                        SIR,
                                        Your very humble Servant,
                                                    N. B.'

'TO be a very well-bred Man.

                                                    The SPECTATOR.'

Mr. SPECTATOR,
'YOU are to know that I am naturally brave, and love Fighting
as well as any Man in *England.* This gallant Temper of mine
makes me extremely delighted with Battles on the Stage. I give you
this Trouble to complain to you, that *Nicolini* refused to gratify me
in that Part of the Opera for which I have most Taste. I observe its
become a Custom, that whenever any Gentlemen are particularly
pleased with a Song, at their crying out *Encore* or *Altro Volto,*[1] the
Performer is so obliging as to sing it over again. I was at the Opera
the last time *Hydaspes* was performed.[2] At that Part of it where the
Heroe engages with the Lion, the graceful Manner with which he
put that terrible Monster to Death gave me so great a Pleasure, and
at the same time so just a Sense of that Gentleman's Intrepidity and
Conduct, that I could not forbear desiring a Repetition of it, by
crying out *Altro Volto* in a very audible Voice; and my Friends

[1] The following letter from John Grott, dated from Pall-mall, 7 Apr. 1712, is
printed in Lillie (ii. 204–5):

   I am footman to a lady of quality, who constantly frequents the opera's, and by
   so doing, I my self am become a mighty lover of them as well as my mistress: but
   the grievance I am going to complain of, is concerning a French or Dutch word,
   (I cannot well tell which) called *Ancore,* or thereabouts, which when repeated in
   the front-boxes, the performers immediately return'd and sung the same over
   again, which I suppose you your self allow was but their duty to do, and I could
   not greatly complain of whilst it was done by them: but they growing weary of it,
   their servants in general have took it up; so that upon every extraordinary squeak
   of a fiddle, or any other noise vocal or instrumental, that either happens not to be
   in tune, or some other misfortune of not agreeing with the rest, the footmen all in
   a body immediately cry out *Ancore, Ancore:* I at the same time, willing that I should
   not be laugh'd at, bawl out as loud as I can, no more, no more; but am unfortunately over-power'd by a great majority: whilst the strutting performer, whoever
   it happens to be, returns again with his wonted pride, and repeats his last song or
   saying, though perhaps as harsh and unagreable as the squeak of a cat-call.... By
   this frequent imposition we are kept at the playhouse till eleven, from supper till
   one, and out of bed till three. I beg of you, when you are not too busy with the
   devil and Milton, you would insert this in one of your papers. . . .

[2] At the Haymarket, on Wednesday, 20 Feb. For Nicolini's fight with the lion
see No. 13 (vol. i).

flatter me that I pronounced those Words with a tollerable good Accent, considering that was but the third Opera I had ever seen in my Life. Yet, notwithstanding all this, there was so little Regard had to me, that the Lion was carried off, and went to Bed, without being kill'd any more that Night. Now, Sir, pray consider that I did not understand a Word of what Mr. *Nicolini* said to this cruel Creature; besides, I have no Ear for Musick; so that during the long Dispute between 'em, the whole Entertainment I had was from my Eye: Why then have not I as much Right to have a graceful Action repeated as another has a pleasing Sound, since he only hears as I only see, and we neither of us know that there is any reasonable thing a doing? Pray Sir settle the Business of this Claim in the Audience, and let us know when we may cry *Altro Volto Anglice*, *again*, *again*, for the Future. I am an *English*-Man, and expect some Reason or other to be given me, and perhaps an ordinary one may serve; but I expect your Answer.

> *I am, SIR,*
> *Your most humble Servant,*
> Toby Rentfree.'

Mr. SPECTATOR,   *Nov.* 29.

'YOU must give me Leave, amongst the rest of your Female Correspondents, to address you about an Affair which has already given you many a Speculation; and which, I know, I need not tell you have had a very happy Influence over the adult Part of our Sex: But as many of us are either too old to learn, or too obstinate in the Pursuit of the Vanities which have been bred up with us from our Infancy, and all of us quitting the Stage whilst you are prompting us to act our Part well; you ought, methinks, rather to turn your Instructions for the Benefit of that Part of our Sex, who are yet in their native Innocence, and ignorant of the Vices and that Variety of Unhappinesses that reign amongst us.

'I must tell you, Mr. SPECTATOR, that it is as much a Part of your Office to oversee the Education of the female Part of the Nation, as well as of the Male; and to convince the World you are not partial, pray proceed to detect the Male-Administration of Governesses as successfully as you have expos'd that of Pedagogues; and rescue our Sex from the Prejudice and Tyranny of Education as well as that of your own, who without your seasonable Interposition are like to improve upon the Vices that are now in vogue.

'I who know the Dignity of your Post, as SPECTATOR, and the Authority a skillful Eye ought to bear in the Female World, could not forbear consulting you, and beg your Advice in so critical a Point, as is that of the Education of young Gentlewomen: Having already provided my self with a very convenient House in a good Air, I'm not without Hope but that you will promote this generous Design. I must farther tell you, Sir, that all who shall be committed to my Conduct, beside the usual Accomplishments of the Needle, Dancing, and the *French* Tongue, shall not fail to be your constant Readers. It is therefore my humble Petition, that you will entertain the Town on this important Subject, and so far oblige a Stranger, as to raise a Curiosity and Enquiry in my Behalf, by publishing the following Advertisement. I am,

SIR,
Your constant Admirer,
M. W.'

ADVERTISEMENTS.

The Boarding-School for young Gentlewomen, which was formerly kept on Mile-End Green, *being laid down, there is now one set up almost opposite to it at the two Golden-Balls, and much more convenient in every Respect; where, beside the common Instructions given to young Gentlewomen, they will be taught the whole Art of Paistrey and Preserving, with whatever may render them accomplished. Those who please to make Tryal of the Vigilance and Ability of the Persons concerned, may enquire at the two Golden-Balls on* Mile-End Green *near* Stepney, *where they will receive further Satisfaction.*

This is to give Notice, that the SPECTATOR *has taken upon him to be Visitant of all Boarding-Schools where young Women are educated; and designs to proceed in the said Office after the same Manner that the Visitants of Colleges do in the two famous Universities of this Land.*

All Lovers who write to the SPECTATOR, *are desired to forbear one Expression which is in most of the Letters to him, either out of Laziness or want of Invention, and is true of not above two thousand Women in the whole World: viz.* She has in her all that is valuable in Woman.

T

No. 315   *Saturday, March 1, 1712*[1]
[ADDISON]

> *Nec deus intersit, nisi dignus vindice nodus*
> *Inciderit . . .*
>
>   Hor.

*H*ORACE advises a Poet to consider thoroughly the Nature and Force of his Genius.[2] *Milton* seems to have known, perfectly well, wherein his Strength lay, and has therefore chosen a Subject entirely conformable to those Talents, of which he was Master. As his Genius was wonderfully turned to the Sublime, his Subject is the noblest that could have entered into the Thoughts of Man. Every thing that is truly great and astonishing, has a place in it. The whole System of the intellectual World; the *Chaos*, and the Creation; Heaven, Earth and Hell; enter into the Constitution of his Poem.

Having in the First and Second Book represented the Infernal World with all its Horrours, the Thread of his Fable naturally leads him into the opposite Regions of Bliss and Glory.

If *Milton*'s Majesty forsakes him any where, it is in those Parts of his Poem, where the Divine Persons are introduced as Speakers.[3] One may, I think, observe that the Author proceeds with a kind of Fear and Trembling, whilst he describes the Sentiments of the Almighty. He dares not give his Imagination its full play, but chuses to confine himself to such Thoughts as are drawn from the Books of the most Orthodox Divines, and to such Expressions as may be met with in Scripture. The Beauties, therefore, which we are to look for in these Speeches, are not of a Poetical nature, nor[a] so proper to fill the Mind with Sentiments of Grandeur, as with Thoughts of Devotion. The Passions, which they are designed to raise, are a Divine Love and Religious Fear. The particular Beauty

---

[a] nor] *19*; or *Fol., 8vo, 12mo*

[1] *Motto.* Horace, *Ars poetica*, 191–2:
> Never presume to make a God appear,
> But for a Business worthy of a God. ROSCOMMON.

[2] *Ars poetica*, 38–40 (the motto of No. 307).

[3] Cf. Dryden, Preface to *Sylvae* (1685): 'Milton's *Paradise Lost* is admirable; but am I therefore bound to maintain, that there are no flats amongst his elevations, when 'tis evident he creeps along sometimes for above an hundred lines together?' (Ker, i. 268).

of the Speeches in the Third Book, consists in that Shortness and Perspicuity of Stile, in which the Poet has couched the greatest Mysteries of Christianity, and drawn together, in a regular Scheme, the whole Dispensation of Providence, with respect to Man. He has represented all the abstruse Doctrines of Predestination, Free-Will and Grace, as also the great Points of Incarnation and Redemption, (which naturally grow up in a Poem that treats of the Fall of Man,) with great Energy of Expression, and in a clearer and stronger Light than I ever met with in any other Writer. As these Points are dry in themselves to the generality of Readers, the concise and clear manner in which he has treated them, is very much to be admired, as is likewise that particular Art which he has made use of in the interspersing of all those Graces of Poetry, which the Subject was capable of receiving.

The Survey of the whole Creation, and of every thing that is transacted in it, is a Prospect worthy of Omniscience; and as much above that, in which *Virgil* has drawn his *Jupiter*,[1] as the Christian Idea of the Supream Being is more rational and Sublime than that of the Heathens. The particular Objects on which he is described to have cast his Eye, are represented in the most beautiful and lively manner.

> *Now had th' Almighty Father from above,*
> *From the pure Empyrean where he sits*
> *High thron'd above all height, bent down his Eye*
> *His own Works and their Works at once to view.*
> *About him all the Sanctities of Heav'n*
> *Stood thick as Stars, and from his Sight receiv'd*
> *Beatitude past utterance: On his right*
> *The radiant image of his Glory sat,*
> *His only Son; On earth he first beheld*
> *Our two first Parents, yet the only two*
> *Of Mankind, in the happy garden plac'd,*
> *Reaping immortal fruits of Joy and Love,*
> *Uninterrupted joy, unrival'd love*
> *In blissful Solitude; he then survey'd*
> *Hell and the Gulf between, and* Satan *there*
> *Coasting the Wall of Heav'n on this side night*
> *In the dun air sublime, and ready now*
> *To stoop with wearied wings, and willing feet*

[1] *Aeneid,* I. 223-6.

On the bare outside of this world, that seem'd
Firm land imbosom'd without firmament,
Uncertain which, in Ocean or in Air.
Him God beholding from his prospect high,
Wherein past, present, future he beholds,
Thus to his only Son foreseeing spake.[1]

Satan's Approach to the Confines of the Creation,[2] is finely imaged in the beginning of the Speech, which immediately follows. The Effects of this Speech in the blessed Spirits, and in the Divine Person, to whom it was addressed, cannot but fill the Mind of the Reader with a secret Pleasure and Complacency.

Thus while God spake, ambrosial fragrance fill'd
All Heav'n, and in the blessed Spirits elect
Sense of new Joy ineffable diffus'd:
Beyond compare the Son of God was seen
Most glorious, in him all his Father shone
Substantially express'd, and in his face
Divine Compassion visibly appear'd,
Love without end, and without measure Grace.[3]

I need not point out the Beauty of that Circumstance, wherein the whole Host of Angels are represented as standing Mute;[4] nor shew how proper the Occasion was to produce such a Silence in Heaven. The Close of this Divine Colloquy, with the Hymn of Angels that follows upon it,[5] are so wonderfully beautiful and poetical, that I should not forbear inserting the whole Passage, if the bounds of my Paper would give me leave.

No sooner had th' Almighty ceas'd, but all
The multitude of Angels with a shout
Loud as from numbers without number, sweet
As from blest Voices, uttering Joy, Heav'n rung
With Jubilee, and loud Hosanna's fill'd
Th' eternal regions; &c, &c, . . .[6]

Satan's Walk upon the Outside of the Universe,[7] which, at a Distance, appeared to him of a globular Form, but, upon his nearer Approach, looked like an unbounded Plain, is natural and noble: As his roaming upon the Frontiers of the Creation, between that Mass

---

[1] *PL*, iii. 56–79.   [2] *PL*, iii. 80–89.   [3] *PL*, iii. 135–42.
[4] *PL*, iii. 217–18.   [5] *PL*, iii. 274–415.
[6] *PL*, iii. 344–9.   [7] *PL*, iii. 418–41.

of Matter, which was wrought into a World, and that shapeless unform'd Heap of Materials, which still lay in Chaos[a] and Confusion, strikes the Imagination with something astonishingly great and wild. I have before spoken[1] of the *Limbo of Vanity*,[b] which the Poet places upon this outermost Surface of the Universe, and shall here explain my self more at large on that, and other Parts of the Poem, which are of the same Shadowy nature.

Aristotle observes, that the Fable of an Epic Poem should abound in Circumstances that are both credible and astonishing;[2] or as the *French* Critics chuse to phrase it, the Fable should be filled with the Probable and the Marvellous.[3] This Rule is as fine and just as any in *Aristotle*'s whole Art of Poetry.

If the Fable is only Probable, it differs nothing from a true History; if it is only Marvellous, it is no better than a Romance. The great Secret therefore of Heroic Poetry is to relate such Circumstances, as may produce in the Reader at thes ame time both Belief and Astonishment. This is brought to pass[c] in a *well chosen* Fable,[4] by the Account of such things as have really happened, or at least of such things as have happen'd according to the received Opinions of Mankind. *Milton*'s Fable is a Master-piece of this Nature; as the War in Heaven, the Condition of the fallen Angels, the State of Innocence, the Temptation of the Serpent, and the Fall of Man, though they are very astonishing in themselves, are not only credible, but actual Points of Faith.

The next Method of reconciling Miracles with Credibility, is by a happy Invention of the Poet; as in particular, when he introduces Agents of a superior Nature, who are capable of effecting what is wonderful, and what is not to be met with in the ordinary course of

---

[a] Chaos] 19; *Chaos* Fol., 8vo, 12mo   [b] *Limbo of Vanity*,] 19; Limbo of Vanity, *Fol.*, *8vo*, *12mo*   [c] is brought to pass] often happens *Fol. Corrected in Errata (No. 327):* 'for happens *read* comes to pass'

---

[1] No. 297.
[2] *Poetics*, 24. 8, 10.
[3] Cf. Dacier's note on the above passage in Aristotle (p. 419):

Since Tragedy and Epopœia imitate that which is more Excellent, they ought to expose only admirable and extraordinary Incidents. . . . However we must not think that he advises the Poets to put things evidently false and impossible into Epopœia, and give them an entire liberty to run to such an excess, as would plainly destroy the Probability, and offend our Reason. And as in Tragedy, the Probable exceeds the Admirable, without excluding it; so in Epopœia, the Wonderful should excel the Probable, without destroying it. . . .

[4] Le Bossu (book i, chap. vii) advises the writer of the epic first 'to chuse the Instruction, and the point of Morality, which is to serve as its Foundation . . .'.

things. *Ulysses*'s Ship being turned into a Rock, and *Æneas*'s Fleet into a Shoal of Water Nymphs; though they are very surprizing Accidents, are nevertheless probable, when we are told that they were the Gods who thus transformed them.[1] It is this kind of Machinery which fills the Poems both of *Homer* and *Virgil* with such Circumstances as are wonderful, but not impossible, and so frequently produce in the Reader the most pleasing Passion that can rise in the Mind of Man, which is Admiration.[2] If there be any Instance in the *Æneid* liable to Exception upon this Account, it is in the beginning of the third Book, where *Æneas* is represented as tearing up the Myrtle that dropped Blood.[3] To qualifie this wonderful Circumstance, *Polydorus* tells a Story from the Root of the Myrtle, that the barbarous Inhabitants of the Country having pierced him with Spears and Arrows, the Wood which was left in his Body took root in his Wounds, and gave birth to that bleeding Tree. This Circumstance seems to have the Marvellous without the Probable, because it is represented as proceeding from Natural Causes, without the Interposition of any God, or other Supernatural Power capable of producing it. The Spears and Arrows grow of themselves, without so much as the Modern help of an Enchantment. If we look into the Fiction of *Milton*'s Fable, though we find it full of surprizing Incidents, they are generally suited to our Notions of the Things and Persons described, and temper'd with a due measure of Probability. I must only make an Exception to the *Lymbo of Vanity*,[a] with his Episode of *Sin* and *Death*,[b] and some of the imaginary Persons in his *Chaos*.[4] These Passages are astonishing, but not credible; the Reader cannot so far impose upon himself as to see a Possibility in them, they are the Description of Dreams and

---

[a] *Lymbo of Vanity*,] Italics added in *19*   [b] *Sin* and *Death*,] Italics added in *19*

[1] *Odyssey*, 13. 146–83; *Aeneid*, 9. 107–22. These are cited together in Le Bossu (book v, chap. iii).

[2] According to Le Bossu (book iii, chap. ix) the passion most peculiar to the Epic is admiration. 'We admire with Joy things that surprize us pleasingly, and we admire with Terrour and Grief such things as terrify and make us sad' (ii. 56). Dennis, in his *Advancement and Reformation of Modern Poetry* (1701), calls admiration 'the reigning Passion in Epick Poetry' (*Works*, ed. Hooker, i. 229); he means, however, approval of the hero 'heighten'd by Revelations, by Machines, and the Ministration of the Gods'. Addison is clearly thinking of astonishment and the marvellous. On the two meanings of the term see the references collected by Hooker (i. 455). Dacier, in a note on chapter ix of the *Poetics*, observes that admiration is too soft for tragedy: 'Tragedy employs only Terror and Compassion, and leaves Admiration for an Epick Poem, to which it is more necessary and proper, and where it has more time to act on Habitudes and Manners' (p. 153).   [3] *Aeneid*, 3. 19–48.

[4] Cf. Nos. 297, 273, 309.

Shadows, not of Things or Persons. I know that many Critics[1] look upon the Stories of *Circe*, *Polypheme*, the *Sirens*,[2] nay the whole *Odissey* and *Iliad*, to be Allegories; but allowing this to be true, they are Fables, which considering the Opinions of Mankind that prevailed in the Age of the Poet, might possibly have been according to the Letter. The Persons are such as might have acted what is ascribed to them, as the Circumstances in which they are represented, might possibly have been Truths and Realities. This appearance of Probability is so absolutely requisite in the greater kinds of Poetry, that *Aristotle* observes the Ancient Tragick Writers made use of the Names of such great Men as had actually lived in the World, tho' the Tragedy proceeded upon Adventures they were never engaged in,[a] on purpose to make the Subject more Credible.[3] In a Word, besides the hidden Meaning of an Epic Allegory, the plain literal Sense ought to appear probable. The Story should be such as an ordinary Reader may acquiesce in, whatever Natural, Moral, or Political Truth may be discovered in it by Men of greater Penetration.

Satan, after having long wandered upon the Surface, or outmost Wall of the Universe, discovers at last a wide Gap in it, which led into the Creation, and is described[b] as the Opening through which the Angels pass to and fro into the lower World, upon their Errands to Mankind.[4] His Sitting upon the brink of this Passage, and taking a Survey of the whole Face of Nature that appeared to him new and fresh in all its Beauties, with the Simile[5] illustrating this Circumstance, fills the Mind of the Reader with as surprising and glorious an Idea as any that arises in the whole Poem. He looks down into that vast hollow of the Universe with the Eye, or (as *Milton* calls it in his first Book) with the Kenn of an Angel.[6] He surveys all the Wonders in this immense Amphitheatre that lie between both the

---

[a] upon Adventures . . . in,] *8vo*, *12mo*, *19*; upon such Adventures were never engaged in, *Fol.* Corrected in Errata (*No. 327*): 'after Adventures *add* as they'   [b] and is described] *8vo*, *12mo*, *19*; and which is described *Fol.*

---

[1] Cf. Le Bossu (book v, chap. iii):

Now the *Episodes* of *Circe*, the *Syrens*, *Polypheme*, and the like, are necessary to the Action of the *Odysseis*, and yet they are not humanly probable. *Homer* artificially brings them under the *Human Probability*, by the Simplicity of those before whom he causes these fabulous Recitals to be made. . . . But even here the Poet is not unmindful of his more understanding Readers. He has in these Fables given them all the Pleasure that can be reaped from *Moral Truths*, so pleasantly disguised under these miraculous *Allegories* (ii. 223–4).

[2] *Odyssey*, books 10–12.   [3] *Poetics*, 9. 6.
[4] *PL*, iii. 498–561.   [5] *PL*, iii. 543–51.   [6] *PL*, i. 59.

Poles of Heaven, and takes in at one View the whole Round of the Creation.

His Flight between the several Worlds that shined on every side of him, with the particular Description of the Sun, are set forth in all the wantonness of a luxuriant Imagination.[1] His Shape, Speech and Behaviour upon his transforming himself into an Angel of Light,[2] are touched with exquisite Beauty. The Poet's Thought of directing *Satan* to the Sun, which in the Vulgar Opinion of Mankind is the most conspicuous Part of the Creation, and the placing in it an Angel, is a Circumstance very finely contriv'd, and the more adjusted to a Poetical Probability, as it was a receiv'd Doctrine among the most famous Philosophers, that every Orb had its *Intelligence*;[3] and as an Apostle in Sacred Writ is said to have seen such an Angel in the Sun.[4] In the Answer which this Angel returns to the disguised Evil Spirit, there is such a becoming Majesty as is altogether suitable to a Superior Being.[5] The part of it in which he represents himself as present at the Creation, is very noble in it self, and not only proper where it is introduced, but requisite to prepare the Reader for what follows in the Seventh Book.

> *I saw when at his word the formless Mass,*
> *This worlds material mould, came to a heap:*
> *Confusion heard his voice, and wild uproar*
> *Stood rul'd, stood vast infinitude confin'd;*
> *Till at his second bidding darkness fled,*
> *Light shon, &c.*[6]

In the following part of the Speech he points out the Earth with such Circumstances, that the Reader can scarce forbear fancying himself employ'd on the same distant view of it.

> *Look downward on that Globe whose hither side*
> *With light from hence, tho' but reflected, shines;*
> *That place is Earth the Seat of man, that light*
> *His day, &c.*[7]

I must not conclude my Reflections upon this Third Book of *Paradise Lost*, without taking notice of that celebrated Complaint[8]

[1] *PL*, iii. 561–633. [2] *PL*, iii. 634–4.
[3] Cf. Cowley's note on *Davideis* (iv. 359): 'According to the old senseless opinion, that the Heavens were divided into several *Orbes* or *Spheres*, and that a particular *Intelligence* or *Angel* was assigned to each of them, to turn it round . . . to all eternity' (*Poems*, ed. Waller, p. 398). [4] Rev. xix. 17.
[5] *PL*, iii. 694–736. [6] *PL*, iii. 708–13.
[7] *PL*, iii. 722–5. [8] *PL*, iii. 1–55.

of *Milton* with which it opens, and which certainly deserves all the Praises that have been given it; tho' as I have before hinted, it may rather be looked upon as an Excrescence, than as an essential Part of the Poem. The same Observation might be applied to that beautiful Digression upon Hypocrisie, in the same Book.[1]   L

No. 316   *Monday, March* 3, 1712[2]

Libertas; quæ sera tamen respexit Inertem.

Virg. Ecl. 1.

Mr. SPECTATOR,

'IF you ever read a Letter which is sent with the more Pleasure for the Reality of its Complaints, this may have Reason to hope for a favourable Acceptance; and if Time be the most irretreivable Loss, the Regrets which follow will be thought, I hope, the most justifiable. The regaining of my Liberty from a long State of Indolence and Inactivity, and the Desire of resisting the farther Encroachments of Idleness, make me apply to you; and the Uneasiness with which I recollect the past Years, and the Apprehensions with which I expect the Future, soon determin'd me to it.

'Idleness is so general a Distemper, that I cannot but imagine a Speculation on this Subject will be of universal use. There is hardly any one Person without some Allay of it; and thousands besides my self spend more Time in an idle Uncertainty which to begin first of two Affairs, than wou'd have been sufficient to have ended them both. The Occasion of this seems to be the Want of some necessary Employment, to put the Spirits in Motion, and awaken them out of their Lethargy. If I had less Leisure, I should have more; for I shou'd then find my Time distinguish'd into Portions, some for Business, and others for the indulging of Pleasures: But now one Face of Indolence over-spreads the whole, and I have no Land-mark to direct my self by. Were one's Time a little straitned by Business, like Water inclos'd in its Banks, it would have some determin'd Course; but unless it be put into some

[1] *PL*, iii. 682–9.
[2] *Motto.* Virgil, *Eclogues*, 1. 27:

> Freedom, which came at length, tho' slow to come
> Long slighted by me.

Channel it has no Current, but becomes a Deluge without either Use or Motion.

'When *Scanderbeg* Prince of *Epirus* was dead, the *Turks*, who had but too often felt the Force of his Arm in the Battles he had won from them, imagin'd that by wearing a Piece of his Bones near their Heart, they shou'd be animated with a Vigour and Force like to that which inspir'd him when living.[1] As I am like to be but of little use whilst I live, I am resolv'd to do what Good I can after my Decease; and have accordingly order'd my Bones to be dispos'd of in this Manner for the Good of my Countrymen, who are troubled with too exorbitant a Degree of Fire. All Fox-hunters upon wearing me, would in a short Time be brought to endure their Beds in a Morning, and perhaps even quit them with Regret at Ten: Instead of hurrying away to teaze a poor Animal, and run away from their own Thoughts, a Chair or a Chariot would be thought the most desirable Means of performing a Remove from one Place to another. I should be a Cure for the unnatural Desire of *John Trott*[2] for Dancing, and a Specifick to lessen the Inclination Mrs. *Fidget* has to Motion, and cause her always to give her Approbation to the present Place she is in. In fine, no *Egyptian* Mummy[3] was ever half so useful in Physick, as I should be to these feaverish Constitutions, to repress the violent Sallies of Youth, and give each Action its proper Weight and Repose.

'I can stifle any violent Inclination, and oppose a Torrent of Anger, or the Sollicitations of Revenge, with Success. But Indolence is a Stream which flows slowly on, but yet undermines the Foundation of every Virtue. A Vice of a more lively Nature were a more desirable Tyrant than this Rust of the Mind,[4] which gives a Tincture of its Nature to every Action of ones Life. It were as little Hazard to be lost in a Storm, as to lay thus perpetually becalm'd: And it is to no Purpose to have within one the Seeds of a thousand good Qualities, if we want the Vigour and Resolution necessary for the exerting them. Death brings all Persons back to an Equality; and this Image

[1] George Castriota, known as Alexander Bey or Scanderbeg (1403–68), was an Albanian prince who warred against the Turks. In 1478 his tomb at Alessio was opened, and the Turks used his bones as talismans. References to Scanderbeg in French prose fiction are collected in Clarence D. Rouillard, *The Turk in French History, Thought, and Literature* (*1520–1660*) (Paris, 1940), pp. 571–5.

[2] No. 296.

[3] 'The mummy of an Egyptian king' is one of the items in the virtuoso's will printed in *Tatler* 216. Hatton (p. 666) describes the Egyptian mummy given by the Duke of Norfolk to Gresham College.

[4] Cf. No. 624 (vol. iv).

of it, this Slumber of the Mind, leaves no Difference between the greatest Genius and the meanest Understanding: A Faculty of doing things remarkably praise-worthy thus conceal'd, is of no more use to the Owner, than a Heap of Gold to the Man who dares not use it.

'To-Morrow is still the fatal Time when all is to be rectified: To-Morrow comes, it goes, and still I please my self with the Shadow, whilst I lose the Reality; unmindful that the present Time alone is ours, the future is yet unborn, and the past is dead, and can only live (as Parents in their Children) in the Actions it has produced.

'The Time we live ought not to be computed by the Number of Years, but by the Use has been made of it; thus 'tis not the Extent of Ground, but the yearly Rent which gives the Value to the Estate. Wretched and thoughtless Creatures, in the only Place where Covetousness were a Virtue we turn Prodigals! Nothing lies upon our Hands with such Uneasiness, nor has there been so many Devices for any one thing, as to make it slide away imperceptibly and to no Purpose. A Shilling shall be hoarded up with Care, whilst that which is above the Price of an Estate, is flung away with Disregard and Contempt. There is nothing now-a-days so much avoided, as a sollicitous Improvement of every Part of Time; 'tis a Report must be shun'd as one tenders the Name of a Wit and a fine Genius, and as one fears the dreadful Character of a laborious Plodder: But notwithstanding this, the greatest Wits any Age has produced thought far otherwise; for who can think either *Socrates* or *Demosthenes* lost any Reputation, by their continual Pains both in overcoming the Defects and improving the Gifts of Nature.[1] All are acquainted with the Labour and Assiduity with which *Tully* acquired his Eloquence.[2] *Seneca* in his Letters to *Lucelius* assures him, there was not a Day in which he did not either write something, or read and epitomize some good Author;[3] and I remember *Pliny* in one of his Letters, where he gives an Account of the various Methods he used to fill up every Vacancy of Time, after several Imployments, which he enumerates; Sometimes, says he, I hunt; but even then I carry with me a Pocket-Book, that whilst my Servants are busied in disposing of the Nets and other Matters, I may be employed in something that may be useful to me in my Studies; and that if I miss of my Game, I may at least bring home

[1] Plutarch, *Life of Demosthenes*, 6–11. [2] Plutarch, *Life of Cicero*, 5. 3.
[3] Seneca, *Epistles*, 2.

some of my own Thoughts with me, and not have the Mortification of having caught nothing all Day.[1]

'Thus, Sir, you see how many Examples I recall to Mind, and what Arguments I use with my self to regain my Liberty: But as I am afraid 'tis no ordinary Perswasion that will be of Service, I shall expect your Thoughts on this Subject with the greatest Impatience, especially since the Good will not be confined to me alone, but will be of universal Use. For there is no Hopes of Amendment where Men are pleased with their Ruin, and whilst they think Laziness is a desirable Character: Whether it be that they like the State it self, or that they think it gives them a new Lustre when they do exert themselves, seemingly to be able to do that without Labour and Application, which others attain to but with the greatest Diligence. I am,

> SIR,
> *Your most obliged humble Servant,*
> Samuel Slack.'

Clytander to Cleone.

Madam,

'PERMISSION to love you is all that I desire, to conquer all the Difficulties those about you place in my Way to surmount and acquire all those Qualifications you expect in him who pretends to the Honour of being,

> *Madam,*
> *Your most devoted humble Servant,*
> Clytander.'[2]

Z3

---

[1] Pliny, *Letters*, I. 6.
[2] Clytander. See No. 304.
[3] A letter signed 'Your new correspondent, but old admirer, INCOGNITO' (Lillie, ii. 224–5), contains some of the ideas in this paper apropos of men who are idle and unprofitable to themselves.

They are soon weary with their own company, and cannot support its conversation for an hour together. They are very unlike that noble Roman, (I think Scipio) and act very contrary to his opinion, which was, *Nunquam minus solus, quam cum solus.* They are like a becalm'd ship, they never move but by the wind of other mens breath, and have no oars of their own to steer withal; and, in my opinion, it is very contradictory in human nature, that men should love themselves above all the rest of the world, and yet endure to converse least with themselves.

The authorship of this number remains uncertain. Nichols thought that it, as well as Nos. 286 and 292, might be 'by Mr. Carey, of New College in Oxford', or 'Mr. Parker, of Merton College'. Hughes has also been suggested as the author (by Morley and Gregory Smith), although it is not in Duncombe's list of Hughes's contributions.

No. 317
[ADDISON]

. . . fruges consumere nati.
Hor.

AUGUSTUS, a few Moments before his Death, asked his Friends who stood about him, if they thought he had acted his Part well; and upon receiving such an Answer as was due to his extraordinary Merit, *Let me then*, says he, *go off the Stage with your Applause;*[2] using the Expression with which the *Roman* Actors made their *Exit* at the Conclusion of a Dramatick Piece. I could wish that Men, while they are in Health, wou'd consider well the Nature of the Part they are engaged in, and what Figure it will make in the Minds of those they leave behind them: whether it was worth coming into the World for, whether it be suitable to a reasonable Being, in short, whether it appears Graceful in this Life, or will turn to Advantage in the next. Let the Sycophant, or Buffoon, the Satyrist, or the Good Companion, consider with himself, when his Body shall be laid in the Grave, and his Soul pass into another State of Existence, how much it will redound to his Praise to have it said of him, that no Man in *England* Eat better, that he had an admirable Talent at turning his Friends into Ridicule, that no body out-did him at an Ill-natured Jest, or that he never went to Bed before he had dispatched his third Bottle. These are, however, very common Funeral Orations, and Elogiums on deceased Persons who have acted among Mankind with some Figure and Reputation.

But if we look into the Bulk of our Species, they are such as are not likely to be remember'd a Moment after their Disappearance. They leave behind them no Traces of their Existence, but are forgotten as tho' they had never been. They are neither wanted by the Poor, regretted by the Rich, nor[a] celebrated by the Learned. They are neither miss'd in the Commonwealth, nor lamented by private Persons. Their Actions are of no Significancy to Mankind, and might have been performed by Creatures of much less Dignity,

<hr>

[a] nor] or *Fol.*

<hr>

[1] *Motto.* Horace, *Epistles*, 1. 2. 27: Born to eat and drink.
[2] Suetonius, *Lives of the Caesars*, 2. 99. 1. Bayle quotes this in the article Elizabeth, Remark Q. The words used by the Roman actors were 'Vos valete et plaudite' (cf. No. 555, vol. iv).

than those who are distinguished by the Faculty of Reason. An eminent *French* Author speaks somewhere to the following Purpose: I have often seen from my Chamber-window two noble Creatures, both of them of an erect Countenance, and endow'd with Reason. These two intellectual Beings are employ'd from Morning to Night, in rubbing two smooth Stones one upon another; that is, as the Vulgar phrase it, in polishing Marble.[1]

My Friend, Sir ANDREW FREEPORT, as we were sitting in the Club last Night, gave us an Account of a sober Citizen, who died a few Days since.[2] This honest Man being of greater Consequence in his own Thoughts, than in the Eye of the World, had for some Years past kept a Journal of his Life. Sir ANDREW shewed us one Week of it. Since[a] the Occurrences set down in it mark out such a Road of Action, as that I have been speaking of, I shall present my Reader with a faithful Copy of it; after having first informed him, that the Deceased Person had in his Youth been bred to Trade, but finding himself not so well turned for Business, he had for several Years last past lived altogether upon a moderate Annuity.

MONDAY, *Eight a Clock.* I put on my Cloaths and walked into the Parlour.

Nine a Clock, ditto. Tied my Knee-strings, and washed my Hands.

Hours Ten, Eleven and Twelve. Smoaked three Pipes of *Virginia*. Read the *Supplement*[3] and *Daily Courant*. Things go ill in the North. Mr. *Nisby*'s Opinion thereupon.

One a Clock in the Afternoon. Chid *Ralph* for mislaying my Tobacco-Box.

Two a Clock. Sat down to Dinner. *Mem.* Too many Plumbs, and no Sewet.

From Three to Four. Took my Afternoon's Nap.

---

[a] Since] As *Fol.*

---

[1] This seems to be a recollection of the passage in La Bruyère ('Of Judgment', *Characters*, ed. 1702, p. 288):

There are a sort of Gods Creatures which are call'd Men, who have a Soul, which is a Spirit; whose whole Life is employ'd in, and whose most vigorous attention is taken up in sawing of Marble; this is very foolish and trivial. But there are others more astonishing, for they are intirely useless, and spend their days in doing nothing: this is yet less than sawing Marble.

[2] 'It is said that this journal was a banter on a member of a congregation of Independents. A Mr. Nesbit—who is referred to in Dunton's "Life and Errors"—was the minister of this congregation, and was constantly consulted on every subject by the journalist' (Nichols).

[3] See No. 269 (vol. ii).

From Four to Six. Walked into the Fields. Wind, S. S. E.

From Six to Ten. At the Club. Mr. *Nisby*'s Opinion about the Peace.

Ten a Clock. Went to Bed, slept sound.

TUESDAY, BEING HOLLIDAY, *Eight a Clock.* Rose as usual.

Nine a Clock. Washed Hands and Face, shaved, put on my double soaled Shoes.

Ten, Eleven, Twelve. Took a Walk to *Islington.*

One. Took a Pot of Mother *Cob*'s Mild.

Between Two and Three. Returned, dined on a Knuckle of Veal and Bacon. *Mem.* Sprouts wanting.

Three. Nap as usual.

From Four to Six. Coffee-house. Read the News. A Dish of Twist.[1] Grand Vizier strangled.[2]

From Six to Ten. At the Club. Mr. *Nisby*'s Account of the great Turk.

Ten. Dream of the Grand Vizier. Broken Sleep.

WEDNESDAY, *Eight a Clock.* Tongue of my Shooe Buckle broke. Hands but not Face.

Nine. Paid off the Butchers Bill. *Mem.* To be allowed for the last Leg of Mutton.

Ten, Eleven. At the Coffee-house. More Work in the North. Stranger in a black Wigg asked me how Stocks went.

From Twelve to One. Walked in the Fields. Wind to the South.

From One to Two. Smoaked a Pipe and a half.

Two. Dined as usual. Stomach good.

Three. Nap broke by the falling of a Pewter Dish. *Mem.* Cook-maid in Love, and grown careless.

---

[1] Twist was a mixture of two liquors or ingredients, such as tea and coffee, gin and brandy, &c. (*OED*).

[2] Speculations on the fate of the Grand Vizier (Mehemet Bashaw) are frequent in the newspapers at this time. Rumours that he had been deposed and the Aga of the Janissaries promoted to his office had appeared in the *Post-Man* on 27 Dec. 1711. The *Daily Courant* (1 Jan. 1712) reported a dispatch from Vienna that the Grand Vizier was still in the Sultan's favour: 'Yet Advices from the Frontier of Turkey confirm his being deposed, adding, that he has been stripped of all his Riches, except three Purses of 500 Crowns each which are left him; that besides he is in Hazard of being Strangled, though he was not when the last Courier came from Constantinople....' The same paper of 10 Jan. quotes a further dispatch from Vienna: 'We have at length received Letters from M. Talman Resident for this Court at Constantinople, dated the 2d of this Month, which confirm, that the Grand Vizier was deposed, and the Aga of the Janisaries put into his Place: But he does not say the first was Strangled, as has been reported.' It was not until April that final news came: 'We have Advice, That Hali Bassaw, formerly Grand Visier, has been beheaded at Mitylene ...' (*Post Boy*, 29 Apr. 1712).

From Four to Six. At the Coffee-house. Advice from *Smyrna*, that the Grand Vizier was first of all strangled, and afterwards beheaded.

Six a Clock in the Evening. Was half an Hour in the Club before any Body else came. Mr. *Nisby* of Opinion, that the Grand Vizier was not strangled the Sixth Instant.

Ten at Night. Went to Bed. Slept without waking till Nine next Morning.

THURSDAY, *Nine a Clock.* Staid within till Two a Clock for Sir *Timothy*. Who did not bring me my Annuity according to his Promise.

Two in the Afternoon. Sate down to Dinner. Loss of Appetite. Small Beer sowr. Beef overcorn'd.

Three. Could not take my Nap.

Four and Five. Gave *Ralph* a Box on the Ear. Turn'd off my Cook-maid. Sent a Message to Sir *Timothy*. *Mem.* I did not go to the Club to Night. Went to Bed at Nine a Clock.

FRIDAY. Pass'd the Morning in Meditation upon Sir *Timothy*, who was with me a Quarter before Twelve.

Twelve a Clock. Bought a new Head to my Cane, and a Tongue to my Buckle. Drank a Glass of Purl[1] to recover Appetite.

Two and Three. Dined, and Slept well.

From Four to Six. Went to the Coffee-house. Met Mr. *Nisby* there. Smoaked several Pipes. Mr. *Nisby* of opinion that laced Coffee is bad for the Head.[2]

Six a Clock. At the Club as Steward. Sat late.

Twelve a Clock. Went to Bed, dreamt that I drank Small-beer with the Grand Vizier.

SATURDAY. Waked at Eleven, walked in the Fields, Wind N.E.

Twelve. Caught in a Shower.

One in the Afternoon. Returned home, and dryed my self.

Two. Mr. *Nisby* dined with me. First Course Marrow-bones, Second Ox Cheek, with a Bottle of *Brooks* and *Hellier*.[3]

Three a Clock. Overslept my self.

Six. Went to the Club. Like to have faln into a Gutter. Grand Vizier certainly Dead.

&c.

[1] See No. 88 (vol. i).
[2] To 'lace' coffee was to mix in sugar or spirits.
[3] Thomas Brook and John Hellier, the leading wine-merchants, of Basing Lane, Bread Street. See No. 362.

I question not, but the Reader will be surprized to find the above-mentioned Journalist taking so much care of a Life that was filled with such inconsiderable Actions, and received so very small Improvements; and yet, if we look into the Behaviour of many whom we daily converse with, we shall find that most of their Hours are taken up in those three Important Articles of Eating, Drinking and Sleeping. I do not suppose that a Man loses his Time, who is not engaged in Publick Affairs, or in an Illustrious Course of Action. On the contrary, I believe our Hours may very often be more profitably laid out in such Transactions as make no Figure in the World, than in such as are apt to draw upon them the Attention of Mankind. One may become wiser and better by several Methods of Employing ones self in Secrecy and Silence, and do what is laudable without Noise or Ostentation. I would, however, recommend to every one of my Readers, the keeping a Journal of their Lives for one Week, and setting down punctually their whole Series of Employments during that Space of Time.[1] This kind of Self-Examination would give them a true State of themselves, and incline them to consider seriously what they are about. One Day would rectifie the Omissions of another, and make a Man weigh all those indifferent Actions, which, though they are easily forgotten, must certainly be accounted for.   L

[1] Lillie (i. 346–50) prints a journal of four days, kept by T. T., the hint of which was derived 'from your excellent paper'. The following is a typical entry:

From six to ten at the playhouse: bowed to all the ladies in the boxes, though I had never seen some of them before. Frighted by the hissing and cat-calls, made so much hast out of the house for fear of a quarrel, that I broke my shins against the seats; tore a lady's gown, and burnt my lac'd-cravat against a footman's link. Mem. this unfortunate accident made me forget my visit to the lady that writ me billet-deux (p. 348).

The following note also appears in Lillie (ii. 225):

The journal you gave us in your last Tuesday's paper was very diverting, but methinks a little imperfect without the account of his Sunday's behaviour. I cannot imagine how that day was spent? though I have bestowed some hours in considering of it, therefore if you know, pray inform

Your admirer,
CYDARIA.

. . . *non omnia possumus omnes.*

Virg.

Mr. SPECTALOR,

'A CERTAIN Vice which you have lately attacked, has not yet been considered by you as growing so deep in the Heart of Man, that the Affectation outlives the Practice of it.[2] You must have observed, that Men who have been bred in Arms preserve to the most extreme and feeble old Age a certain Daring in their Aspect: In like Manner, they who have past their Time in Gallantry and Adventure, keep up, as well as they can, the Appearance of it, and carry a petulant Inclination to their last Moments. Let this serve for a Preface to a Relation I am going to give you[3] of an old Beau in

---

[1] *Motto.* Virgil, *Eclogues,* 8. 63: Every man cannot do every thing.
In the Folio sheets the motto was: *Rideat & pulset Lasciva decentius Ætas* (Men in years ridicule wantonness with the best grace; Horace, *Epistles,* 2. 2. 216).

[2] Cf. Nos. 266, 274, 276 (vol. ii), 286, 298.

[3] The story of Escalus and Isabella is an adaptation of a similar account in Justus Van Effen's periodical, *Le Misantrope,* of 14 Sept. 1711: 'Histoire d'un Vieillard amoureux qui trouva sa Maîtresse trop favorable' (*Le Misantrope: pour l'Annee M.DCC.XI* (La Haye: T. Johnson, 1712), pp. 144–8). Ariste, at eighty, has 'l'esprit charmant, une grande routine de savoir vivre, & toutes les maniéres polies & flateuses de la vieille Cour'. He falls in love with Doriméne, who confides in her husband. When Ariste finally makes a direct proposal, 'Doriméne fit semblant de céder à une tendresse si pressante, & elle affecta tout l'air d'une Femme qui se rend, d'une manière si peu équivoque, qu'en vain le pauvre Homme eut voulu feindre de ne pas entendre le François'. Ariste thereupon became confused and silent, and finally departed. To save his reputation he sent the following letter to Doriméne:

 Tant que vous avez résisté à ma tendresse, *Madame,* votre résistance a si fort animé ma Passion, que je n'avois pas le loisir de songer à rapeller ma Vertu pour ne plus combattre la vôtre; mais dès que cette résistance a paru se relâcher en ma faveur, ma Raison a fait un éfort sur mon Amour, & m'a fait voir la lâcheté de ma conduite à l'égard d'une Personne vertueuse, à qui je m'éforçois d'ôter un tître si précieux & si rare. Je n'ai pas remporté cette Victoire sur moi-même, sans de violens combats, & peut-être ne la dois-je qu'à mon départ précipité. Je vous prie, *Madame,* de croire que ce seul moment de foiblesse ne détruit pas dans mon esprit l'estime pour vous que vous y avez établie par tant d'années de Vertu. Quel malheur eut été le vôtre, si vous aviez eu affaire avec quelque jeune étourdi, qui selon l'usage du Siécle, se seroit fait une gloire de la brutalité de ses sentimens. *Je suis, &.*

Whoever wrote No. 318—Steele or a correspondent—has translated Ariste's letter but rather spoilt the story by changing the incident which precipitated it. In the *Spectator* the concluding letter by Isabella is again a condensation of a fourteen-stanza poem which Doriméne, assisted by her husband, composed by way of reply to Ariste. The first stanza reads:

  En effet, je suis fort heureuse,
  D'avoir Ariste pour Amant:
  Ah! que son Ame est généreuse!
  Qu'il sait écrire joliment.

Town, that has not only been amorous, and a Follower of Women in general, but also, in spite of the Admonition of grey Hairs, been from his sixty third Year to his present seventieth, in an actual Pursuit of a young Lady, the Wife of his Friend, and a Man of Merit. The gay old *Escalus* has Wit, good Health, and is perfectly well bred; but from the Fashion and Manners of the Court when he was in his Bloom, has such a natural Tendency to amorous Adventure, that he thought it would be an endless Reproach to him to make no use of a Familiarity he was allowed at a Gentleman's House, whose good Humour and Confidence exposed his Wife to the Addresses of any who should take in their Head to do him the good Office. It is not impossible that *Escalus* might also resent that the Husband was particularly negligent of him; and tho' he gave many Intimations of a Passion towards the Wife, the Husband either did not see them, or put him to the Contempt of overlooking them. In the mean Time *Isabella*, for so we shall call our Heroine, saw his Passion, and rejoyced in it as a Foundation for much Diversion, and an Opportunity of indulging herself in the dear Delight of being admired, addressed to, and flattered, with no ill Consequence to her Reputation. This Lady is of a free and disengaged Behaviour, ever in good Humour, such as is the Image of Innocence with those who are innocent, and an Encouragement to Vice with those who are abandoned. From this kind of Carriage, and an apparent Approbation of his Gallantry, *Escalus* had frequent Opportunities of laying amorous Epistles in her Way, of fixing his Eyes attentively upon her Action, of performing a thousand little Offices which are neglected by the Unconcerned, but are so many Approaches towards Happiness with the Enamoured. It was now, as is above hinted, almost the End of the seventh Year of his Passion, when *Escalus* from general Terms, and the ambiguous Respect which criminal Lovers retain in their Addresses, began to bewail that his Passion grew too violent for him to answer any longer for his Behaviour towards her; and that he hoped she would have Consideration for his long and patient Respect, to excuse the Motions of a Heart now no longer under the Direction of the unhappy Owner of it. Such for some Months had been the Language of *Escalus* both in his Talk and his Letters to *Isabella*; who returned all the Profusion of kind things which had been the Collection of fifty Years with *I must not hear you; you will make me forget that you are a Gentleman; I would not willingly lose you as a Friend*, and the like Expressions, which the

Skillful interpret to their own Advantage, as well knowing that a feeble Denial is a modest Assent. I should have told you, that *Isabella*, during the whole Progress of this Amour, communicated it to her Husband; and that an Account of *Escalus*'s Love was their usual Entertainment after Half a Day's Absence: *Isabella* therefore, upon her Lover's late more open Assaults, with a Smile told her Husband she could hold out no longer, but that his Fate was now come to a Crisis. After she had explained her self a little farther, with her Husband's Approbation she proceeded in the following Manner. The next Time that *Escalus* was alone with her, and repeated his Importunity, the crafty *Isabella* looked on her Fan with an Air of great Attention, as considering of what Importance such a Secret was to her; and upon the Repetition of a warm Expression, she looked at him with an Eye of Fondness, and told him he was past that Time of Life which could make her fear he would boast of a Lady's Favour; then turned away her Head with a very well-acted Confusion, which favoured the Escape of the aged *Escalus*. This Adventure was Matter of great Pleasantry to *Isabella* and her Spouse; and they had enjoyed it two Days before *Escalus* could recollect himself enough to form the following Letter.

Madam,

"WHAT happened the other Day, gives me a lively Image of the Inconsistency of humane Passions and Inclinations. We pursue what we are denied, and place our Affections on what is absent, tho' we neglected it when present. As long as you refused my Love, your Refusal did so strongly excite my Passion, that I had not once the Leisure to think of recalling my Reason to aid me against the Design upon your Virtue. But when that Virtue began to comply in my Favour, my Reason made an Effort over my Love, and let me see the Baseness of my Behaviour in attempting a Woman of Honour. I own to you, it was not without the most violent Struggle that I gained this Victory over my self; nay I will confess my Shame, and acknowledge I could not have prevailed but by Flight. However, Madam, I beg that you will believe a Moment's Weakness has not destroyed the Esteem I had for you, which was confirmed by so many Years of obstinate Virtue. You have Reason to rejoice that this did not happen within the Observation of one of the young Fellows, who would have exposed your Weakness, and gloried in his own Brutish Inclinations.

I am,

Madam,

Your most devoted humble Servant."

'*Isabella,* with the Help of her Husband, returned the following Answer.

SIR,

"I CANNOT but account my self a very happy Woman, in having a Man for a Lover that can write so well, and give so good a Turn to a Disappointment. Another Excellence you have above all other Pretenders I ever heard of, on Occasions where the most reasonable Men lose all their Reason, you have yours most powerful. We are each of us to thank our Genius, that the Passion of one abated in Proportion as that of the other grew violent. Does it not yet come into your Head, to imagine that I knew my Compliance was the greatest Cruelty I could be guilty of towards you? In Return for your long and faithful Passion, I must let you know that you are old enough to become a little more Gravity; but if you will leave me and coquet it any where else, may your Mistress yield.

Isabella."'

T

No. 319

[BUDGELL]

Thursday, March 6, 1712[1]

Quo teneam vultus mutantem Protea nodo?

Hor.

I HAVE endeavoured, in the course of my Papers, to do Justice to the Age, and have taken care as much as possible to keep my self a Neuter between both Sexes. I have neither spared the Ladies out of Complaisance, nor the Men out of Partiality; but notwithstanding the great Integrity with which I have acted in this Parti-

[1] *Motto.* Horace, *Epistles,* I. I. 90:
   What Chain can hold this varying *Proteus* fast? CREECH.

cular, I find my self taxed with an Inclination to favour my own half of the Species. Whether it be that the Women afford a more fruitful Field for Speculation, or whether they run more in my Head than the Men, I cannot tell, but I shall set down the Charge as it is laid against me in the following Letter.

Mr. SPECTATOR,

'I ALWAYS make one among a Company of young Females, who peruse your Speculations every Morning. I am at present Commissioned, by our whole Assembly, to let you know, that we fear you are a little enclined to be partial towards your own Sex. We must however acknowledge, with all due Gratitude, that in some Cases you have given us our Revenge on the Men, and done us Justice. We could not easily have forgiven you several Strokes in the Dissection of the *Coquet's Heart,* if you had not, much about the same time, made a Sacrifice to us of a *Beau's Scull.*[1]

'You may, however, Sir, please to remember, that not long since you attacked our Hoods and Commodes in such manner, as, to use your own Expression, made very many of us ashamed to shew our Heads.[2] We must, therefore, beg leave to represent to you, that we are in Hopes, if you would please to make a due Enquiry, the Men in all Ages would be found to have been little less whimsical in adorning that Part, than our selves. The different Forms of their Wiggs, together with the various Cocks of their Hats, all flatter us in this Opinion.

'I had an Humble Servant last Summer, who the first time he declared himself, was in a Full-Bottom Wigg;[3] but the Day after, to my no small Surprize, he accosted me in a thin Natural one. I receiv'd him, at this our Second Interview, as a perfect Stranger, but was extreamly confounded, when his Speech discovered who he was. I resolved, therefore, to fix his Face in my Memory for the future; but as I was walking in the Park the same Evening, he appeared to me in one of those Wiggs that I think you call a *Night-cap,*[4] which had alter'd him more effectually than before. He

---

[1] Nos. 275, 281 (vol. ii).

[2] No. 265 (vol. ii). The making 'very many of us ashamed to shew our Heads' is quoted from Tom Trippit's letter in No. 271 (vol. ii).

[3] The huge French periwig of the Restoration period had by now become unfashionable, except for very formal occasions. See Francis M. Kelly and Randolph Schwabe, *A Short History of Costume & Armour chiefly in England,* ii (1931), 43–44.

[4] A close-fitting wig resembling a night-cap. See No. 129 (vol. ii). It is referred to in *Tatler* 26.

afterwards played a Couple of Black Riding-Wiggs[1] upon me, with the same Success; and, in short, assumed a new Face almost every Day in the First Month of his Courtship.

'I observed afterwards, that the variety of Cocks into which he moulded his Hat, had not a little contributed to his Impositions upon me.

'Yet, as if all these ways were not sufficient to distinguish their Heads, you must, doubtless, Sir, have observed, that great Numbers of young Fellows have, for several Months last past, taken upon them to wear Feathers.[2]

'We hope, therefore, that these may, with as much Justice, be called *Indian Princes*, as you have stiled a Woman in a Coloured Hood an *Indian* Queen;[3] and that you will, in due time, take these airy Gentlemen into Consideration.

'We the more earnestly beg that you would put a stop to this Practice, since it has already lost us one of the most agreeable Members of our Society, who after having refused several good Estates, and two Titles, was lured from us last Week by a *mix'd Feather*.

'I am ordered to present you the Respects of our whole Company, and am,

SIR,

Your very humble Servant,

DORINDA.'

Note, *The Person wearing the Feather, tho' our Friend took him for an Officer in the Guards, has proved to be an arrant Linnen-Draper.*[a4]

I am not now at leisure to give my Opinion upon the Hat and Feather; however, to wipe off the present Imputation, and gratifie my Female Correspondent, I shall here print a Letter which I lately

---

^a *an arrant Linnen-Draper.*] 8vo; *an arrant Linnen Draper.* 12mo; *only an Ensign in the Train-bands.* Fol.

---

[1] 'Old Richard Nutt, one of the first printers of these papers, assured this writer, that Steele paid 50 *l. per annum* to his barber, and that he never rode out on airing, which he did often; but in a black full-bottomed dress periwig, the price of one of which, at that time, nearly amounted to this sum' (Nichols, *Tatler*, ed. 1786, i. 413).
[2] A plume of feathers is referred to in No. 281 (vol. ii).
[3] No. 265 (vol. ii).
[4] Gregory Smith suggested that Budgell here may have been thinking of the advertisement in No. 259 which describes a deserter from the First Regiment of Foot Guards: 'Jonathan Burton, 5 Foot 10 Inches high, dark brown hair, aged about 25 Years, a Linnen-draper by Trade.'

received from a Man of Mode, who seems to have a very extra-ordinary Genius in his way.

SIR,

'I PRESUME I need not inform you, that among Men of Dress it is a common Phrase to say *Mr.* Such an one *has struck a bold Stroke*; by which we understand, that he is the first Man who has had Courage enough to lead up a Fashion. Accordingly, when our Taylors take Measure of us, they always Demand *whether we will have a plain Suit, or strike a bold Stroke*. I think I may without Vanity say, that I have struck some of the boldest and most successful Strokes of any Man in *Great Britain*. I was the first that Struck the Long Pocket about two Years since: I was likewise the Author of the Frosted Button, which when I saw the Town came readily into, being resolved to strike while the Iron was hot, I produced much about the same time the Scollop Flap,[1] the knotted Cravat, and made a fair push for the Silver-clock'd Stocking.

'A few Months after I brought up *the modish Jacket*, or the Coat with close Sleeves. I Struck this at first in a plain *Doily*;[2] but that failing, I Struck it a second time in blue Camlet;[3] and repeated the Stroke in several kinds of Cloth, till at last it took effect. There are two or three young Fellows at the other end of the Town, who have always their Eye upon me, and answer me Stroke for Stroke. I was once so unwary as to mention my Fancy in relation to a new-fashion'd *Surtout* before one of these Gentlemen, who was disingenuous enough to steal my Thought, and by that means prevented my intended Stroke.

'I have a design this Spring to make very considerable Innovations in the Wastcoat, and have already begun with a *Coup d'essai* upon the Sleeves,[4] which has succeeded very well.

'I must further inform you, if you will promise to Encourage, or at least to connive at me, that it is my Design to Strike such a Stroke the Beginning of the next Month, as shall surprize the whole Town.

'I do not think it prudent to acquaint you with all the Particulars of my intended Dress; but will only tell you as a small Sample of it, that I shall very speedily appear at *White*'s[5] in a *Cherry-coloured Hat*.

[1] Cf. No. 128 (vol. ii) for 'scollop tops of shoes'. The scallop of the pocket is referred to in *Guardian* 149.
[2] An inexpensive woollen stuff. For the linen-draper of this name see No. 283.
[3] See No. 104 (vol. i).
[4] Waistcoats, down to the end of the reign of George II, usually had sleeves.
[5] No. 49 (vol. i).

I took this Hint from the Ladies Hoods, which I look upon as the boldest Stroke that Sex has Struck for these hundred Years last past.

I am,

SIR,

Your most Obedient,

most Humble Servant,

Will. Sprightly.'[1]

ᵃI have not Time at present to make any Reflections on this Letter, but must not however omit, that having shewn it to WILL HONEYCOMB, he desires to be acquainted with the Gentleman who writ it.ᵃ

X

No. 320   *Friday, March 7, 1712*[2]
[STEELE]

. . . non pronuba Juno,
Non Hymenæus adest, non illi Gratia lecto,
Eumenides stravere torum . . .

Ovid.

Mr. SPECTATOR,

'YOU have given many Hints in your Papers to the Disadvantage of Persons of your own Sex, who lay Plots upon Women.

ᵃ⁻ᵃ *Added in 8vo, 12mo*

[1] Another letter from Will Sprightly is printed in Lillie (ii. 226–8):

In order to put in execution my intended stroke, I have just made my escape to town from a near relation's, who has the misfortune of having a great estate in a country so unpolish'd, that the spectator is very rarely or never seen; and upon my looking over those which have come out since I went, I am not a little surprized to find myself outstruck by that old-fashioned blade Sir Roger de Coverly. I have been under some apprehensions from my two youngsters in the city, with whom I am in a state of war; but I think Sir Roger would have been the last man I should have suspected to have done me any prejudice in my way. How the whim of setting up a beard came into the knight's head I cannot conceive; but he has, I believe, outdone all the barbers in Great Britain, for, in short, he has taken off mine at one stroke. . . . That my misfortune may no longer be a secret, you will please to observe, that, besides the cherry-colour'd-hat (which I mentioned only as a trifle) I designed to have made my entry at White's in a full-bottom'd flaxen beard, for which expedition I have had one by me some time, and have practised upon it best part of the winter. I struck likewise a pair of very odd mustachoes at the same heat; but I had no design of publishing these till my beard had taken root, and began to sprout out pretty thick, at this end of the town. . . .

[For note 2 see opposite page.

Among other hard Words you have published the Term Male-Coquets,[1] and been very severe upon such as give themselves the Liberty of a little Dalliance of Heart, and playing fast and loose, between Love and Indifference, till perhaps an easy young Girl is reduced to Sighs, Dreams and Tears; and languishes away her Life for a careless Coxcomb who looks astonished, and wonders at such an effect from what in him was all but common Civility. Thus you have treated the Men who are irresolute in Marriage; but if you design to be impartial, pray be so honest as to print the Information I now give you, of a certain Set of Women who never Coquet for the Matter, but with an high Hand Marry whom they please to whom they please. As for my part, I should not have concerned my self with them, but that I understand I am pitched upon by them, to be Marryed, against my Will, to one I never saw in my Life. It has been my Misfortune, Sir, very innocently to rejoice in a plentiful Fortune, of which I am Master, to bespeak a fine Chariot,[2] to give Direction for two or three handsome Snuff-Boxes, and as many Suits of fine Cloaths; but before any of these were ready, I heard Reports of my being to be Marryed to two or three different young Women. Upon my taking Notice of it to a young Gentleman who is often in my Company he told me smiling, I was in the Inquisition. You may believe I was not a little startled at what he meant, and more so when he asked me if I had bespoke any thing of late that was fine. I told him several; upon which he produced a Description of my Person from the Tradesmen whom I had employed, and told me that they had certainly informed against me. Mr. SPECTATOR, Whatever the World may think of me, I am more Coxcomb than Fool, and I grew very inquisitive upon this Head, not a little pleased with the Novelty. My Friend told me, there were a certain Set of Women of Fashion, whereof the Number of Six made a Committee, who sate thrice a Week, under the Title of the Inquisition

---

[1] No. 288.
[2] Applied in the eighteenth century to a light four-wheeled carriage with only back seats, and differing from the post-chaise in having a coach-box (*OED*).

---

[2] *Motto.* Ovid, *Metamorphoses*, 6. 428–9, 431:

> Unhappy Feast unbless'd with Juno's Care;
> Nor were the Graces, nor was Hymen there,
> The Furies spread the fatal Bed at Night.

The motto in the Folio sheets was Juvenal, *Satires*, 6. 259: *Hae sunt quae tenui sudant in Cyclade* (Yet these are they, that cannot bear the Heat/Of figur'd Silks, and under Sarcenet sweat. DRYDEN).

on Maids and Batchelours. It seems, whenever there comes such an unthinking gay thing as my self to Town, he must want all manner of Necessaries, or be put into the Inquisition by the first Tradesman he employs. They have constant Intelligence with Cane-Shops, Perfumers, Toy-men,[1] Coach-makers, and China-Houses. From these several Places these Undertakers for Marriages have as constant and regular Correspondence, as the Funeral-men have with Vintners and Apothecaries. All Batchelors are under their immediate Inspection, and my Friend produced to me a Report given into their Board, wherein an old Unkle of mine, who came to Town with me and my self, were inserted, and we stood thus; the Unkle smoaky,[2] rotten, poor; the Nephew raw, but no Fool, sound at present, very rich. My Information did not end here, but my Friend's Advices are so good, that he could shew me a Copy of the Letter sent to the young Lady who is to have me; which I enclose to you.'

Madam,
'THIS is to let you know, that you are to be Marryed to a Beau that comes out on *Thursday* Six in the Evening. Be at the *Park*: You cannot but know a Virgin-Fop; they have a Mind to look saucy, but are out of Countenance. The Board has denyed him to several good Families. I wish you Joy.

Corinna.'

What makes my Correspondent's Case the more deplorable, is, that as I find by the Report from my Censor of Marriages,[3] the Friend he speaks of is employed by the Inquisition to take him in, as the Phrase is. After all that is told him, he has Information only of one Woman that is laid for him, and that the wrong one; for the Lady-Commissioners have devoted him to another than the Person against whom they have employed their Agent his Friend to alarm him. The Plot is laid so well about this young Gentleman, that he has no Friend to retire to, no Place to appear in, or Part of the Kingdom to fly into, but he must fall into the Notice, and be subject to the Power of the Inquisition. They have their Emissaries and Substitutes in all Parts of this united Kingdom. The first Step they

---

[1] I.e. proprietors of toy-shops, where trinkets and fancy goods were sold.
[2] For this word see No. 132 (vol. ii). The sense here seems to be 'shrewd suspicious'.
[3] No. 308.

usually take, is to find from a Correspondence, by their Messengers and Whisperers with some Domestick of the Batchelor (who is to be hunted into the Toils they have laid for him) what are his Manners, his Familiarities, his good Qualities, or Vices; not as the Good in him is a Recommendation, or the ill a Diminution, but as they affect or contribute to the main Enquiry, What Estate he has in him? When this Point is well reported to the Board, they can take in a wild roaring Fox-hunter, as easily as a soft gentle young Fop of the Town. The Way is to make all Places uneasy to him, but the Scenes[a] in which they have allotted him to act. His Brother Huntsmen, Bottle Companions, his Fraternity of Fops, shall be brought into the Conspiracy against him. Then this Matter is not laid in so bare-fac'd a Manner before him, as to have it intimated Mrs. Such-a-one would make him a very proper Wife; but by the Force of their Correspondence they shall make it (as Mr. *Waller* said of the Marriage of the Dwarfs) as impracticable to have any Woman besides her they design him, as it would have been in *Adam* to have refused *Eve*.[1] The Man named by the Commission for Mrs. Such-a-one, shall neither be in Fashion, nor dare ever to appear in Company, should he attempt to evade their Determination.

The female Sex wholly govern domestick Life; and by this Means, when they think fit, they can sow Dissentions between the dearest Friends, nay make Father and Son irreconcilable Enemies, in spite of all the Ties of Gratitude on one Part, and the Duty of Protection to be paid on the other. The Ladies of the Inquisition understand this perfectly well; and where Love is not a Motive to a Man's chusing one whom they allot, they can, with very much Art, insinuate Stories to the Disadvantage of his Honesty or Courage, till the Creature is too much dispirited to bear up against a general ill Reception, which he every where meets with, and in due time falls into their appointed Wedlock for Shelter. I have a long Letter bearing Date the 4th Instant, which gives me a large Account of the Policies of this Court; and find there is now before them a very

---

[a] Scenes] Science *Fol., 12mo*

[1] Waller, *Of the Marriage of the Dwarfs*, 1–6:

> Design, or chance, makes others wive;
> But Nature did this match contrive;
> Eve might as well have Adam fled,
> As she denied her little bed
> To him, for whom Heaven seemed to frame,
> And measure out, this only dame.

refractory Person who has escaped all their Machinations for two Years last past: But they have prevented two successive Matches which were of his own Inclination, the one, by a Report that his Mistress was to be married and the very Day appointed, Wedding-Clothes bought, and all things ready for her being given to another; the second time, by insinuating to all his Mistress's Friends and Acquaintance, that he had been false to several other Women, and the like. The poor Man is now reduced to profess he designs to lead a single Life; but the Inquisition give out to all his Acquaintance, that nothing is intended but the Gentleman's own Welfare and Happiness. When this is urged, he talks still more humbly, and protests he aims only at a Life without Pain or Reproach: Pleasure, Honour, or Riches, are things for which he has no Taste. But not-withstanding all this and what else he may defend himself with, as that the Lady is too old or too young, of a suitable Humour, or the quite contrary, and that it is impossible they can ever do other than wrangle from *June* to *January*, Every Body tells him all this is Spleen, and he must have a Wife; while all the Members of the Inquisition are unanimous in a certain Woman for him, and they think they all together[a] are better able to judge, than he or any other private Person whatsoever.

SIR   *Temple, March 3, 1711.*

'YOUR Speculation this Day on the Subject of Idleness has employed me ever since I read it, in sorrowful Reflections on my having loitered away the Term (or rather the Vacation) of 10 Years in this Place, and unhappily suffered a good Chamber and Study to lie idle as long. My Books (except those I have taken to sleep upon) have been totally neglected, and my Lord *Coke* and other Venerable Authors were never so slighted in their Lives. I spend most of the Day at a Neighbouring Coffee-House, where we have, what I may call a lazy Club. We generally come in Night-Gowns,[1] with our Stockings about our Heels, and sometimes but one on. Our Salutation at Entrance is a Yawn and a Stretch,[2] and then with-out more Ceremony we take our Place at the Lolling Table; where our Discourse is, what I fear you would not read out, therefore shall

---

[a] all together] altogether *Fol.*

[1] I.e. dressing-gowns (the usual sense).
[2] This is the first example in *OED* of this particular use of the word, 'An act of drawing up the body and extending the arms, indicating weariness or languor'.

not insert. But I assure you, Sir, I heartily lament this Loss of Time, and am now resolved, (if possible, with double Diligence) to retrieve it, being effectually awaken'd by the Arguments of Mr. *Slack*[1] out of the Senseless Stupidity that has so long possessed me. And to demonstrate, that Penitence accompanies my Confession, and Constancy my Resolutions, I have lock'd my Door for a Year, and desire you would let my Companions know I am not within. I am with great Respect,

SIR,

Your most Obedient Servant,

N. B.'

T

No. 321

[ADDISON]

Saturday, March 8, 1712[2]

Non satis est pulchra esse poemata, dulcia sunto.

Hor.

THOSE, who know how many Volumes have been written on the Poems of *Homer* and *Virgil*, will easily pardon the Length of my Discourse upon *Milton*. *The Paradise Lost* is look'd upon, by the best Judges, as the greatest Production, or at least the noblest Work of Genius, in our Language, and therefore deserves to be set before an *English* Reader in its full Beauty. For this Reason, tho' I have endeavoured to give a general Idea of its Graces and Imperfections in my Six First Papers, I thought my self obliged to bestow one upon every Book in particular. The Three First Books I have already dispatched, and am now entring upon the Fourth. I need not acquaint my Reader, that there are Multitudes of Beauties in this great Author, especially in the Descriptive Parts of his Poem, which I have not touched upon, it being my Intention to point out those only, which appear to me the most exquisite, or those which are not so obvious to ordinary Readers. Every one that has read the

[1] No. 316.
[2] *Motto.* Horace, *Ars poetica*, 99:
Nor is it enough that Poems please the Ear,
They should please true Taste.

Criticks, who have written upon the *Odissy*, the *Iliad* and the *Æneid*, knows very well, that though they agree in their Opinions of the great Beauties in those Poems, they have nevertheless each of them discovered several Master-Stroaks, which have escaped the Observation of the rest. In the same manner, I question not, but any Writer, who shall treat of this Subject after me, may find several Beauties in *Milton*, which I have not taken notice of. I must likewise observe, that as the greatest Masters of Critical Learning differ among one another, as to some particular Points in an Epic Poem, I have not bound my self scrupulously to the Rules, which any one of them has laid down upon that Art, but have taken the Liberty sometimes to join with one, and sometimes with another, and sometimes to differ from all of them, when I have thought that the Reason of the thing was on my side.

We may consider the Beauties of the Fourth Book under three Heads. In the First are those Pictures of Still-Life, which we meet with in the Descriptions of *Eden*, *Paradise*, *Adam*'s Bower, &c. In the next are the Machines, which comprehend the Speeches and Behaviour of the good and bad Angels. In the last is the Conduct of *Adam* and *Eve*, who are the principal Actors in the Poem.

In the Description of *Paradise*,[1] the Poet has observed *Aristotle*'s Rule of lavishing all the Ornaments of Diction on the weak unactive Parts of the Fable, which are not supported by the Beauty of Sentiments and Characters.[2] Accordingly the Reader may observe, that the Expressions are more florid and elaborate in these Descriptions, than in most other Parts of the Poem. I must further add, that tho' the Drawings of Gardens, Rivers, Rainbows, and the like dead Pieces of Nature, are justly censured in an Heroic Poem, when they run out into an unnecessary length; the Description of *Paradise* would have been faulty, had not the Poet been very particular in it, not only as it is the Scene of the Principal Action, but as it is requisite to give us an Idea of that Happiness from which our first Parents fell. The Plan of it is wonderfully beautiful, and formed upon the short Sketch which we have of it, in Holy Writ. *Milton*'s Exuberance of Imagination, has pour'd forth such a redundancy of

---

[1] In No. 418 Addison cites Milton's description of Paradise as more 'refreshing to the Imagination' than his description of Hell.

[2] *Poetics*, 24. 11: 'Thus ought we to reserve all the Ornaments of the Diction, for these weak parts: Those that have either good Sentiments, or Manners, have no occasion for them. A Brillant, or Glorious Expression, damages them rather, and serves only to hide their Beauty' (Dacier's trans., pp. 408–9).

Ornaments on this Seat of Happiness and Innocence, that it would be endless to point out each Particular.

I must not quit this Head, without further observing, that there is scarce a Speech of *Adam* or *Eve* in the whole Poem, wherein the Sentiments and Allusions are not taken from this their delightful Habitation. The Reader, during their whole Course of Action, always finds himself in the Walks of *Paradise*. In short, as the Criticks have remarked, that in those Poems, wherein Shepherds are Actors, the Thoughts ought always to take a Tincture from the Woods, Fields and Rivers; so we may observe, that our First Parents seldom lose Sight of their happy Station in any thing they speak or do; and, if the Reader will give me leave to use the Expression, that their Thoughts are always *Paradisiacal*.[1]

We are in the next place to consider the Machines of the Fourth Book. *Satan* being now within Prospect of *Eden*, and looking round upon the Glories of the Creation, is filled with Sentiments different from those which he discovered whilst he was in Hell. The Place inspires him with Thoughts more adapted to it: He reflects upon the happy Condition from whence he fell, and breaks forth into a Speech that is softned with several transient Touches of Remorse and Self-accusation:[2] But at length he confirms himself in Impenitence, and in his design of drawing Man into his own State of Guilt and Misery. This Conflict of Passions is raised with a great deal of Art, as the opening of his Speech to the Sun is very bold and noble.

> *O thou that with surpassing Glory crown'd*
> *Look'st from thy Sole Dominion like the God*
> *Of this new World, at whose Sight all the Stars*
> *Hide their diminish'd heads, to thee I call*
> *But with no Friendly Voice, and add thy name*
> *O Sun, to tell thee how I hate thy beams*
> *That bring to my remembrance from what State*
> *I fell, how glorious once above thy Sphere.*[3]

This Speech is, I think, the finest that is ascribed to *Satan* in the whole Poem. The Evil Spirit afterwards proceeds to make his Discoveries concerning our first Parents, and to learn after what manner they may be best attacked. His bounding over the Walls of *Paradise*; his sitting in the Shape of a Cormorant upon the Tree of Life, which

---

[1] Actually not a new 'expression'. Examples are given in *OED* from 1649.
[2] *PL*, iv. 18–113. [3] *PL*, iv. 32–39.

stood in the Center of it, and over-topp'd all the other Trees of the Garden; his alighting among the Herd of Animals, which are so beautifully represented as playing about *Adam* and *Eve*, together with his transforming himself into different Shapes, in order to hear their Conversation,[1] are Circumstances that give an agreeable Surprize to the Reader, and are devised with great Art, to connect that Series of Adventures in which the Poet has engaged this great Artificer of Fraud.

[a]The Thought of *Satan*'s Transformation into a Cormorant, and placing himself on the Tree of Life, seems raised upon that Passage in the *Iliad*,[2] where two Deities are described, as perching on the Top of an Oak in the Shape of Vulturs.[a]

His planting himself at the Ear of *Eve* under the Form[b] of a Toad, in order to produce vain Dreams and Imaginations,[3] is a Circumstance of the same Nature; as his starting up in his own Form is wonderfully fine, both in the Literal Description, and in the Moral which is concealed under it. His Answer upon his being discovered, and demanded to give an Account of himself, is[c] conformable to the Pride and Intrepidity of his Character.

> *Know ye not then, said Satan, fill'd with Scorn,*
> *Know ye not me? ye knew me once no mate*
> *For you, there sitting where you durst not soare;*
> *Not to know me argues your-selves unknown,*
> *The lowest of your throng; . . .*[4]

Zephon's Rebuke, with the Influence it had on *Satan*, is exquisitely Graceful and Moral.[5] *Satan* is afterwards led away to *Gabriel*, the chief of the Guardian Angels, who kept watch in *Paradise*. His disdainful Behaviour on this occasion is so remarkable a Beauty, that the most ordinary Reader cannot but take notice of it. *Gabriel*'s discovering his approach at a distance, is drawn with great strength and liveliness of Imagination.

> *O Friends, I hear the tread of nimble Feet*
> *Hastening this way, and now by glimps discern*
> *Ithuriel and Zephon through the shade;*

[a-a] om. Fol.   [b] under the Form] in the shape *Fol.*   [c] is] *8vo, 19*; are *Fol., 12mo*

[1] PL, iv. 179–83, 194–6, 395–7, 340–50, 397–408.
[2] 7. 58–60.
[3] PL, iv. 799–819. This 'inimitable' account is quoted in *Tatler* 237.
[4] PL, iv. 827–31.   [5] PL, iv. 834–50.

And with them comes a third of Regal Port,
But faded splendor wan; who by his gait
And fierce demeanor seems the Prince of Hell,
Not likely to part hence without contest;
Stand firm, for in his look defiance lours.[1]

The Conference between *Gabriel* and *Satan* abounds with Sentiments proper for the Occasion, and suitable to the Persons of the two Speakers.[2] *Satan*'s cloathing himself with Terror when he prepares for the Combat is truly sublime, and at least equal to *Homer*'s Description[3] of Discord celebrated by *Longinus*,[4] or to that of Fame in *Virgil*,[5] who are both represented with their Feet standing upon the Earth, and their Heads reaching above the Clouds.

While thus he spake, th' Angelic Squadron bright
Turn'd fiery red, sharpning in mooned Horns
Their Phalanx, and began to hem him round
With ported Spears, &c.
. . . On th' other side, Satan alarm'd,
Collecting all his might dilated stood
Like Teneriff *or* Atlas *unremov'd.*
His Stature reach'd the Sky, and on his Crest
Sat horrour plum'd; . . .[6]

I must here take notice, that[a] *Milton* is every where full of Hints, and sometimes literal Translations, taken from the greatest of the *Greek* and *Latin* Poets.[7] But this I may[b] reserve for a Discourse by it self, because I would not break the Thread of these Speculations that are designed for *English* Readers, with such Reflections as would be of no use but to the Learned.

I must however observe in this Place, that the breaking off the Combat between *Gabriel* and *Satan*, by the hanging out of the Golden Scales[8] in Heaven, is a Refinement upon *Homer*'s Thought, who tells us, that before the Battel between *Hector* and *Achilles*, *Jupiter* weighed the Event of it in a pair of Scales. The Reader may see the whole Passage in the 22d *Iliad*.[9]

---

[a] take notice, that] take notice by the way, that *Fol.*   [b] may] shall *Fol.*

---

[1] *PL*, iv. 866–73.   [2] *PL*, iv. 877–976.   [3] *Iliad*, 4. 441–5.
[4] *On the Sublime*, 9. 4 (Boileau's trans., chap. vii).
[5] *Aeneid*, 4. 176–7.   [6] *PL*, iv. 977–80, 985–9.
[7] In No. 12 (vol. i) Addison had pointed out one of these borrowings (in *PL*, iv. 675–88) from Hesiod.   [8] *PL*, iv. 996–1004.
[9] *Iliad*, 22. 208 ff.; *Aeneid*, 12. 725–7. Both these parallels are pointed out by

Virgil, before the last decisive Combat, describes *Jupiter* in the same manner, as weighing the Fates of *Turnus* and *Æneas*. *Milton*, though he fetched this beautiful Circumstance from the *Iliad* and *Æneid*, does not only insert it as a Poetical Embellishment, like the Authors above-mentioned; but makes an artful use of it, for the proper carrying on of his Fable, and for the breaking off the Combat between the two Warriors, who were upon the point of engaging.[1] ªTo this we may further add, that *Milton* is the more justified in this Passage, as we find the same noble Allegory in Holy Writ, where a wicked Prince, ᵇsome few Hours before he was assaulted and slain,ᵇ is said to have been *weigh'd in the Scales, and to have been found wanting.*ª[2]

I must here take Notice under the Head of the Machines, that *Uriel's*ᶜ gliding down to the Earth upon a Sun-beam,[3] with the Poet's Device to make him *descend*, as well in his return to the Sun, as in his coming from it, is a Prettiness that might have been admired in a little fanciful Poet, but seems below the Genius of *Milton*. The Description of the Host of armed Angels walking their nightly Round in *Paradise*, is of another Spirit.

> *So saying, on he led his radiant files,*
> *Dazling the Moon;* . . .[4]

asᵈ that Account of the Hymns[5] which our first Parents used to hear them Sing in these their Midnight Walks, is altogether Divine, and inexpressibly amusing to the Imagination.[6]

We are, in the last place, to consider the Parts which *Adam* and *Eve* act in the Fourth Book. The Description of them as they first appear'd to *Satan*, is exquisitely drawn, and sufficient to make the fallen Angel gaze upon them with all that Astonishment, and those Emotions of Envy, in which he is represented.

> *Two of far nobler Shape erect and tall*
> *God-like erect, with native honour clad*
> *In naked majesty seem'd lords of all,*

ª⁻ª To . . . *wanting.*] *Om. Fol.*   ᵇ⁻ᵇ some . . . slain,] *Added in 19*   ᶜ *Uriel's*] *Gabriel's Fol. Corrected in Errata* (No. 327)   ᵈ as] *8vo, 19*; As (*new paragraph*) *Fol., 12mo*

P.H. (1695) in his note on *PL*, iv. 1002. Dryden, in the Dedication of the *Aeneis*, also quotes the lines from Virgil to illustrate *PL* (Ker, ii. 212).

[1] Dryden also makes the point that in Virgil this machine is used only for ornament and not out of necessity (Ker, ii. 212–13).

[2] Dan. v. 27.   [3] *PL*, iv. 555–6, 589–92.

[4] *PL*, iv. 797–8.   [5] *PL*, iv. 680–8.

[6] *OED* defines *amusing* in this sense as 'engaging the mind or attention in a pleasing way; interesting' and quotes from No. 463 (vol. iv) as the first example.

And worthy seem'd, for in their[a] *looks divine*
The image of their glorious Maker shon,
Truth, Wisdom, Sanctitude severe and pure;
Severe, but in true filial freedom plac'd:
For contemplation he and valour form'd,
For softness she and sweet attractive Grace;
He for God only, she for God in him:
His fair large front, and eye sublime declar'd
Absolute rule; and Hyacinthin *Locks*
Round from his parted forelock manly hung
Clustring, but not beneath his Shoulders broad:
She as a Vail down to her slender waste
Her unadorned golden tresses wore
Dis-shevel'd, but in wanton ringlets wav'd.
So pass'd they naked on, nor shun'd the Sight
Of God or Angel, for they thought no ill:
So hand in hand they pass'd, the loveliest pair
That ever since in loves embraces met.[1]

There is a fine Spirit of Poetry in the Lines which follow, wherein they are describ'd as sitting on a Bed of Flowers by the side of a Fountain, amidst a mixed Assembly of Animals.[2]

The Speeches of these two first Lovers flow equally from Passion and Sincerity. The Professions they make to one another are full of Warmth; but at the same time founded on Truth. In a word, they are the Gallantries of *Paradise*.

. . . When Adam *first of Men, . . .*
Sole partner and sole part of all these joys
Dearer thy self than all; . . .
But let us ever praise him, and extol
His bounty, following our delightful task,
To prune those growing plants, and tend these flowers,
Which were it toilsome, yet with thee were sweet.
To whom thus Eve *repli'd, O thou for whom*
And from whom I was form'd, flesh of thy flesh,
And without whom am to no end, my Guide
And head, what thou hast said is just and right.

[a] *their*] *them* Fol.

---

[1] *PL*, iv. 288–94, 297–306, 319–22.   [2] *PL*, iv. 325–52.

For we to him indeed all praises owe,
And daily thanks, I chiefly who enjoy
So far the happier Lot, enjoying thee
Præeminent by so much odds, while thou
Like consort to thy self canst no where find, &c.[1]

The remaining part of *Eve*'s Speech, in which she gives an Account of her self upon her first Creation, and the manner in which she was brought to *Adam*, is I think as beautiful a Passage as any in *Milton*, or perhaps in any other Poet whatsoever.[2] These Passages are all work'd off with so much Art, that they are capable of pleasing the most delicate Reader, without offending the most severe.

That day I oft remember, when from Sleep, &c.[3]

A Poet of less Judgment and Invention than this great Author, would have found it very difficult to have filled these[a] tender parts of the Poem with Sentiments proper for a State of Innocence; to have described the warmth of Love, and the Professions of it, without Artifice or Hyperbole; to have made the Man speak the most endearing things, without descending from his natural Dignity, and the Woman receiving them without departing from the Modesty of her Character; in a word, to adjust the Prerogatives of Wisdom and Beauty, and make each appear to the other in its proper Force and Loveliness. This mutual Subordination of the two Sexes is wonderfully kept up in the whole Poem, as particularly in the Speech of *Eve* I have before-mentioned, and upon the Conclusion of it in the following Lines.

So spake our general Mother, and with eyes
Of Conjugal attraction unreprov'd,
And meek surrender, half embracing lean'd

[a] these] those *Fol.*

---

[1] *PL*, iv. 408, 411–12, 436–48.

[2] *PL*, iv. 449–91. P. H. (1695) in his note on iv. 461 observes that Milton has improved upon Ovid's fable of Narcissus here. In his notes on the *Metamorphoses* Addison quotes these lines from Milton and adds:

This passage of *Narcissus* probably gave *Milton* the hint of applying it to *Eve*, though I think her surprize at the sight of her own face in the water, far more just and natural, than this of *Narcissus*. She was a raw unexperienced Being, just created, and therefore might easily be subject to the delusion; but *Narcissus* had been in the world sixteen years, was brother and son to the water-nymphs, and therefore to be supposed conversant with fountains long before this fatal mistake (Guthkelch, i. 145).

[3] *PL*, iv. 449.

On our first father, half her swelling breast
Naked met his under the flowing Gold
Of her loose tresses hid; he in delight
Both of her beauty and submissive charms
Smil'd with Superiour Love, . . .[1]

The Poet adds, that the Devil turn'd away with Envy at the sight of so much Happiness.

We have another View of our First Parents in their Evening Discourses, which is full of pleasing Images and Sentiments suitable to their Condition and Characters.[2] The Speech of *Eve*, in particular, is dress'd up in such a soft and natural Turn of Words and Sentiments, as cannot be sufficiently admired.[3]

I shall close my Reflections upon this Book, with observing the Masterly Transition which the Poet makes to their Evening Worship, in the following Lines.

Thus at their shadie lodge arriv'd, both stood,
Both turn'd, and under open Sky ador'd
The God that made both Sky, Air,[a] *Earth and Heav'n,*
Which they beheld, the Moons resplendent Globe
And Starry Pole: Thou also mad'st the night,
Maker omnipotent, and thou the Day. *&c.*[4]

Most of the Modern Heroic Poets have imitated the Ancients, in beginning a Speech without premising, that the Person said thus or thus; but as it is easie to imitate the Ancients in the Omission of two or three Words, it requires Judgment to do it in such a manner as they shall not be miss'd, and that the Speech may begin naturally without them. There is a fine Instance of this Kind out of *Homer*, in the Twenty Third Chapter of *Longinus*.[5]   L

---

[a] *both Sky, Air,*] *both Air*, Fol. *Corrected in Errata (No. 327)*

---

[1] *PL*, iv. 492–9.

[2] *PL*, iv. 610–88.

[3] *PL*, iv. 635–58. Addison quotes lines 639–56 in *Tatler* 114 with praise for the 'infinitely pleasing' variety of images.

[4] *PL*, iv. 720–5.

[5] Longinus, *On the Sublime*, 27. Addison's reference shows that he is citing Boileau's version, where it is chapter 23. The quotation from Homer is *Iliad*, 15. 346–9.

No. 322   *Monday, March* 10, 1712[1]
[STEELE]

> *. . . Ad humum mærore gravi deducit & angit.*
>   Hor.

IT is often said, after a Man has heard a Story with extraordinary
Circumstances, it is a very good one if it be true: But as for the
following Relation, I should be glad were I sure it were false. It is
told with such Simplicity, and there are so many artless Touches of
Distress in it, that I fear it comes too much from the Heart.

Mr. SPECTATOR,

'SOME Years ago it happened that I lived in the same House with
a young Gentleman of Merit; with whose good Qualities I was
so much taken, as to make it my[a] Endeavour to shew as many as
I was able in my self. Familiar Converse improved general Civilities
into an unfeigned Passion on both Sides. He watched an Opportunity to declare himself to me; and I, who could not expect a Man
of so great an Estate as his, received his Addresses in such Terms,
as gave him no Reason to believe I was displeased with them, tho'
I did nothing to make him think me more easy than was decent.
His Father was a very hard worldly Man, and proud; so that there
was no Reason to believe he would easily be brought to think there
was any thing in any Woman's Person or Character that could[b]
ballance the Disadvantage of an unequal Fortune. In the mean Time
the Son continued his Application to me, and omitted no Occasion
of demonstrating the most disinterested Passion imaginable to me;
and in plain direct Terms offer'd to marry me privately, and keep
it so till he should be so happy as to gain his Father's Approbation,
or become possessed of his Estate. I passionately loved him, and you
will believe I did not deny such a one what was my Interest also to
grant. However I was not so young as not to take the Precaution of
carrying with me a faithful Servant, who had been also my Mother's
Maid, to be present at the Ceremony. When that was over, I
demanded a Certificate, signed by the Minister, my Husband, and

---

ᵃ make it my] *8vo*; make my *Fol., 12mo*   ᵇ Character that could] Character
could *Fol.*

---

¹ *Motto.* Horace, *Ars poetica*, 110:
    And Grief dejects, and wrings the tortur'd Soul. ROSCOMMON.

178

the Servant I just now spoke of. After our Nuptials we conversed[1] together very familiarly in the same House; but the Restraints we were generally under, and the Interviews we had being stolen and interrupted, made our Behaviour to each other have rather the impatient Fondness which is visible in Lovers, than the regular and gratified Affection which is to be observed in Man and Wife. This Observation made the Father very anxious for his Son, and press him to a Match he had in his Eye for him. To relieve my Husband from this Importunity, and conceal the Secret of our Marriage, which I had Reason to know would not be long in my Power in Town, it was resolved that I should retire into a remote Place in the Country, and converse under feigned Names by Letter. We long continued this Way of Commerce; and I with my Needle, a few Books, and reading over and over my Husband's Letters, passed my Time in a resigned Expectation of better Days. Be pleased to take Notice, that within four Months after I left my Husband I was delivered of a Daughter, who died within few Hours after her Birth. This Accident, and the retired Manner of Life I led,[a] gave criminal Hopes to a neighbouring Brute of a Country Gentleman, whose Folly was the Source of all my Affliction. This Rustick is one of those rich Clowns, who supply the want of all manner of Breeding by the Neglect of it, and with noisy Mirth, half Understanding, and ample Fortune, force themselves upon Persons and things without any Sense of Time or Place. The poor ignorant People where I lay concealed, and now passed for a Widow, wondered I could be so shy and strange, as they called it, to the Squire; and were bribed by him to admit him whenever he thought fit. I happened to be sitting in a little Parlour which belonged to my own Part of the House, and musing over one of the fondest of my Husband's Letters, in which I always kept the Certificate of my Marriage, when this rude Fellow came in, and with the nauseous Familiarity of such unbred Brutes, snatched the Papers out of my Hand. I was immediately under so great a Concern, that I threw my self at his Feet, and begged of him to return them. He, with the same odious Pretence to Freedom and Gayety, swore he would read them. I grew more importunate, he more curious, till at last, with an Indignation arising from a Passion I then first discovered in him, he threw the Papers[b] into the Fire, swearing that

---

[a] led,] lead, *Fol.*   [b] Papers] Paper *Fol.*

[1] Here used in the special sense of holding sexual intercourse.

since he was not to read them, the Man who writ them should never be so happy as to have me read them over again. It is insignificant to tell you my Tears and Reproaches made the boisterous Calf leave the Room ashamed and out of Countenance, when I had leisure to ruminate on this Accident with more than ordinary Sorrow: However such was then my Confidence in my Husband, that I writ to him the Misfortune, and desired another Paper of the same Kind. He deferred writing two or three Posts, and at last answered me in general, That he could not then send me what[a] I asked for, but when he could find a proper Conveyance, I should be sure to have it: From this Time his Letters were more cold every Day than other,[1] and as he grew indifferent I grew jealous. This has at last brought me to Town, where I find both the Witnesses of my Marriage dead, and that my Husband, after three Months Cohabitation, has buried a young Lady whom he married in Obedience to his Father. In a Word, he shuns and disowns me: Should I come to the House and confront him, the Father would join in supporting him against me, though he believed my Story. Should I talk it to the World, what Reparation can I expect for an Injury I cannot make out? I believe he means to bring me, through Necessity, to resign my Pretentions to him for some Provision for my Life; but I will dye first. Pray bid him remember what he said, and how he was charmed when he laughed at the heedless Discovery I often made of my self; let him remember how awkard I was in my dissembled Indifference towards him before Company; ask him how I, who could never conceal my Love for him, at his own Request, can part with him for ever? Oh, Mr. SPECTATOR, Sensible Spirits know no Indifference in Marriage; what then do you think is my piercing Affliction—I leave you to represent my Distress your own Way, in which I desire you to be speedy, if you have Compassion for Innocence exposed to Infamy.

Octavia.'

T

a send me what] send what *Fol.*

---

[1] 'The simple *other* was formerly used in the sense "each preceding one (in turn)"' (*OED*). The last example given in *OED* is from Tillotson (d. 1694).

   ... *modò Vir, modò Fœmina* ...

               Virg.

THE Journal with which I presented my Reader on *Tuesday* last,[2] has brought me in several Letters with Accounts[a] of many private Lives cast into that form. I have the *Rake's Journal*; the *Sot's Journal*; the *Whore-master's Journal*, and among several others a very curious Piece, Entituled, *The Journal of a Mohock*.[3] By these Instances I find that the Intention of my last *Tuesday's* Paper has been mistaken by many of my Readers. I did not design so much to expose Vice as Idleness, and aimed at those Persons who pass away their Time rather in Trifle and Impertinence, than in Crimes and Immoralities. Offences of this latter kind are not to be dallied with, or treated in so ludicrous a manner. In short, my Journal only holds up Folly to the Light, and shews the Disagreeableness of such Actions as are indifferent in themselves, and blameable only as they proceed from Creatures endow'd with Reason.

My following Correspondent, who calls her self *Clarinda*, is such a Journalist as I require: She seems by her Letter to be placed in a modish State of Indifference between Vice and Vertue, and to be susceptible of either, were there proper Pains taken with her. Had her Journal been filled with Gallantries, or such Occurrences as had shewn her wholly divested of her natural Innocence, notwithstanding it might have been more pleasing to the Generality of Readers, I should not have published it; but as it is only the Picture of a Life filled with a fashionable kind of Gaiety and Laziness, I shall set down five Days of it, as I have received it from the hand of my fair Correspondent.

Dear Mr. SPECTATOR,

'YOU having set your Readers an Exercise in one of your last Week's Papers, I have perform'd mine according to your Orders, and herewith send it you enclosed. You must know,

------

  [a] with Accounts] *12mo*; with the Accounts *Fol.*; with Account *8vo*

  [1] *Motto.* Ovid, *Metamorphoses*, 4. 280:
            One while a Man, another while a Woman.
  [2] No. 317.   [3] The Mohocks are the subject of the following number.

181

Mr. SPECTATOR, that I am a Maiden Lady of a good Fortune, who have had several Matches offer'd me for these ten Years last past, and have at present warm Applications made to me by a very pretty Fellow.[1] As I am at my own disposal I come up to Town every Winter, and pass my time in it after the manner you will find in[a] the following Journal, which I began[b] to write upon the very Day after your *Spectator* upon that Subject.'

TUESDAY *Night*. Could not go to Sleep till one in the Morning for thinking of my Journal.

WEDNESDAY. *From Eight till Ten*. Drank two Dishes of Chocolate in Bed, and fell asleep after 'em.

From Ten to Eleven. Eat a slice of Bread and Butter, drank a Dish of Bohea,[2] read the *Spectator*.

From Eleven to One. At my Toilet, try'd a new Head. Gave Orders for *Veny*[3] to be combed and washed. *Mem*. I look best in Blue.

From One till half an Hour after Two. Drove to the *Change*.[4] Cheapned a couple of Fans.

Till Four. At Dinner. *Mem*. Mr. *Froth* passed by in his new Liveries.

From Four to Six. Dressed, paid a Visit to old Lady *Blithe* and her Sister, having before heard they were gone out of Town that Day.

From Six to Eleven. At *Basset*.[5] *Mem*. Never set again upon the Ace of Diamonds.

THURSDAY. *From Eleven at Night to Eight in the Morning*. Dream'd that I punted to Mr. *Froth*.

---

[a] in] within *Fol.*   [b] began] begun *Fol.*

[1] Cf. No. 261 (vol. ii).

[2] For kinds of tea see No. 328.

[3] Veny seems to have been a fairly common name. Teresia in Shadwell's *Volunteers* (1693) has a dog Venny (I. i), and a song by Nancia in Richard Estcourt's interlude *Prunella* (1708) laments the loss of her little dog Veny (p. 10). The *Daily Courant* of 29 Mar. 1706 advertises the loss from a house on Dowgate-Hill of 'a little Black and White Spanel Bitch . . ., her Name Vene'.

[4] Here probably the New Exchange. See No. 96 (vol. i).

[5] A card game, in which the dealer or 'banker' had considerable opportunities for making money. Richard Seymour (*The Compleat Gamester*, 5th ed., 1734, pp. 113–25) gives a list of the terms used, the rules for playing, and the 'frauds' practised. It is 'one of the most Polite Games on the Cards; and only fit for Persons of the First Rank to play at; by reason of such great Losses, or Advantages, as may possibly fall on one Side or other' (p. 113). The players are called punters: 'our *Punters* in *England* have the Liberty to stake whatever they please, from one Guinea, to one 100 or higher, upon a Card, as is often seen at Court' (Seymour, p. 119).

From Eight to Ten. Chocolate. Read two Acts in *Aurenzebe* a-bed.

From Ten to Eleven. Tea Table. Sent to borrow Lady *Faddle*'s *Cupid* for *Veny*. Read the Play Bills. Received a Letter from Mr. *Froth*. *Mem.* Locked it up in my strong Box.

Rest of the Morning. Fontange,[1] the Tire-woman, Her Account of my Lady *Blithe*'s Wash. Broke a Tooth in my little Tortoise shell Comb. Sent *Frank* to know how my Lady *Hectick* rested after her Monky's leaping out at Window. Looked pale. *Fontange* tells me my Glass is not true. Dressed by Three.

From Three to Four. Dinner cold before I sate down.

From Four to Eleven. Saw Company. Mr. *Froth*'s Opinion of *Milton*. His Account of the *Mohocks*. His Fancy for a Pin-cushion. Picture in the Lid of his Snuff-box. Old Lady *Faddle* promises me her Woman to cut my Hair. Lost five Guineas at Crimp.[2]

Twelve a Clock at Night. Went to Bed.

FRIDAY. *Eight in the Morning. A-bed,* read over all Mr. *Froth*'s Letters. *Cupid* and *Veny*.

Ten a Clock. Stay'd within all Day, not at home.

From Ten to Twelve. In Conference with my Mantua-Maker. Sorted a Suit of Ribbands. Broke my Blue China Cup.

From Twelve to One. Shut my self up in my Chamber, practised Lady *Betty Modely*'s Skuttle.[3]

One in the Afternoon. Called for my flowered Handkerchief. Worked half a violet Leaf in it. Eyes aked and Head out of Order. Threw by my Work, and read over the remaining Part of *Aurenzebe*.

From Three to Four. Dined.

From Four to Twelve. Changed my Mind, dressed, went abroad, and play'd at Crimp till Midnight. Found Mrs. *Spitely* at home. Conversation: Mrs. *Brilliant*'s Necklace false Stones. Old Lady *Loveday* going to be married to a young Fellow that is not worth a Groat. Miss *Prue* gone into the Country. *Tom. Townley* has red Hair. *Mem.* Mrs. *Spitely* whispered in my Ear, that she had something to tell me about Mr. *Froth.* I am sure it is not true.

Between Twelve and One. Dreamed that Mr. *Froth* lay at my Feet, and called me *Indamora*.[4]

---

[1] A fontange was one of the names for the tall head-dress (see No. 98, vol. i), the name derived from *Fontanges*, the territorial title of a mistress of Louis XIV (*OED*).

[2] A card game popular in the seventeenth century, but by this time apparently somewhat old-fashioned. Cf. *Tatler* 250.

[3] Defined by Johnson as 'a quick pace; a short run; a pace of affected precipitation'.

[4] In Dryden's *Aurengzebe*, referred to shortly before.

SATURDAY. Rose at Eight a Clock in the Morning. Sat[a] down to my Toilet.

From Eight to Nine. Shifted a patch for half an Hour before I could determine it. Fixed it above my Left Eyebrow.

From Nine to Twelve. Drank my Tea, and dressed.

From Twelve to Two. At Chappel. A great deal of good Company. *Mem.* The third Air in the new Opera. Lady *Blithe* dressed frightfully.

From Three to Four. Dined. Miss *Kitty* called upon me to go to the Opera before I was risen from Table.

From Dinner to Six. Drank Tea. Turned off a Footman for being rude to *Veny.*

Six a Clock. Went to the Opera. I did not see Mr. *Froth* till the beginning of the Second Act. Mr. *Froth* talked to a Gentleman in a black Wigg. Bowed to a Lady in the Front Box. Mr. *Froth* and his Friend clapt *Nicolini* in the third Act. Mr. *Froth* cryed out *Ancora.*[1] Mr. *Froth* led me to my Chair, I think he squeezed my Hand.

Eleven at Night. Went to Bed. Melancholy Dreams. Methought *Nicolini* said he was Mr. *Froth.*

SUNDAY. Indisposed.

MONDAY. *Eight a Clock.* Waked by Miss *Kitty. Aurenzebe* lay upon the Chair by me. *Kitty* repeated, without Book, the Eight best Lines in the Play. Went in our Mobbs[2] to the Dumb Man,[3] according to Appointment. Told me, that my Lover's Name began with a *G. Mem.* The Conjuror was within a Letter of Mr. *Froth*'s Name. *&c.*

'Upon looking back into this my Journal, I find that I am at a loss to know whether I pass my Time well or ill; and indeed never

---

[a] Sat] Set *Fol.*

---

[1] Cf. No. 314.

[2] 'A huddled oeconomy of dress so called' (Nichols). See No. 302.

[3] This was Duncan Campbell (1680?–1730), a Scotch fortune-teller, who had come to London at an early age and become a fashionable consultant. In *The History of the Life and Adventures of Mr. Duncan Campbell* (1720) Defoe noted that his unusual talent 'was celebrated in some of the most witty weekly papers that ever appeared in public', notably by Isaac Bickerstaff in the *Tatler.*

And when that bright author, who joined the uttermost facetiousness with the most solid improvements of morality and learning in his works, laid aside the title of a Tatler, and assumed the name of a Spectator and censor of men's actions, he still, every now and then, thought our Duncan Campbell a subject worthy enough to employ his farther considerations upon (Defoe, *Novels and Miscellaneous Works,* Bohn's Standard Library, 1893, vi. 139).

thought of Considering how I did it, before I perused your Speculation upon that Subject. I scarce find a single Action in these Five Days, that I can thoroughly approve of, except the working upon the Violet Leaf, which I am resolved to finish the first Day I am at leisure. As for Mr. *Froth* and *Veny*, I did not think they took up so much of my Time and Thoughts, as I find they do upon my Journal. The latter of them I will turn off, if you insist upon it; and if Mr. *Froth* does not bring matters to a Conclusion very suddenly, I will not let my Life run away in a Dream.

Your Humble Servant
Clarinda.'

To resume one of the Morals of my First Paper,[a] and to confirm *Clarinda* in her good Inclinations, I would have her consider what a pretty Figure she would make among Posterity, were the History of her whole Life published like these Five Days of it. I shall conclude my Paper with an Epitaph written by an uncertain Author[b][1] on Sir *Philip Sidney*'s Sister, a Lady who seems to have been of a Temper very much different from that of *Clarinda*. The last Thought of it is so very noble, that I dare say my Reader will pardon me the Quotation.

On the Countess Dowager of *Pembroke*.

Underneath this Marble Hearse
Lies the Subject of all Verse,
Sydney's Sister, Pembroke's Mother;
Death, ere thou hast Kill'd another,
Fair and learn'd, and good as she,
Time shall throw a Dart at thee.

L

[a] Paper,] Papers, *Fol. Corrected in Errata (No. 325)*   [b] written by an uncertain Author] which *Ben Johnson* has written *Fol.*

[1] William Browne of Tavistock. The poem seems to have been first published anonymously in the third edition (1623) of Camden's *Remaines* (p. 340). See 'Poems ascribed to Jonson' in Herford and Simpson's edition of Ben Jonson, vol. viii, pp. 433–4. It is interesting to note that Addison first attributed the poem to Jonson and then substituted 'an uncertain author'. According to Herford and Simpson it was Whalley who first (1756) printed the poem as Jonson's.

No. 324   *Wednesday, March 12, 1712*[1]
[STEELE]

O curvæ in terris animæ, & cœlestium inanes.

Pers.

Mr. SPECTATOR,

'THE Materials you have collected together towards a general
History of Clubs, make so bright a Part of your Speculations,
that I think it is but a Justice we all owe the learned World, to
furnish you with such Assistances as may promote that useful Work.
For this Reason I could not forbear communicating to you some
imperfect Informations of a Set of Men (if you will allow them
a Place in that Species of Being) who have lately erected themselves
into a nocturnal Fraternity, under the Title of *The Mohock Club*;[2]

---

[1] *Motto.* Persius, *Satires,* 2. 61:

    O Souls, in whom no heav'nly Fire is found,
    Fat Minds, and ever grov'ling on the ground. DRYDEN.

In the Folio sheets the motto was *Sævis inter se convenit Ursis* (Juvenal, *Satires,*
15. 164), already used for No. 9 (vol. i).

[2] On the same day in which this number appeared Swift wrote to Stella of the
excitement caused in London by the Mohocks: 'Grubstreet Papers about them fly
like Lightning.' Hearne noted on 30 Mar., 'There are great Numbers of them & their
Custom is to make themselves drunk and in the Night-time go about the Streets in
great Droves & to abuse after a most inhumane Manner all Persons they meet, by
beating down their Noses, pricking the fleshy Parts of their Bodys with their swords,
not sparing even the Women . . .' (*Remarks & Collections,* ed. C. E. Doble, iii. 326).
See also Defoe's *Review* of 15 Mar., which dissents from the opinion of 'the Ingenious
Spectator' as to the origin of the name. *The History of the Mohocks* (Dublin: Re-Printed
in Fish-shamble-street, n.d.) attacks the *Review* and identifies the Mohocks with the
Puritans. *The Mohocks: A Poem, in Miltonic Verse: Address'd to the Spectator* (1712)
describes these outrages and then pays tribute to the reforms achieved by the
Spectator among the vintners, the hackney coachmen, and the 'Dames who feed on
hireling Lust'. Gay's 'tragi-comical farce, as it was acted near the Watch-House in
Covent-Garden', *The Mohocks,* was published by Lintott on 15 Apr. (advertised in
the *Post Boy* and *Daily Courant*). A broadside ballad entitled 'The Mohocks Revel',
beginning 'We *Mohocks* Rule the World by Night', appears as No. 299 in *The
Rothschild Library* (Cambridge, 1954). For other items see R. J. Allen, *The Clubs of
Augustan London* (Cambridge, Mass., 1933), pp. 105–18, and Louis C. Jones, *The
Clubs of the Georgian Rakes* (New York, 1942), chap. ii ('The Tradition of the
Mohocks').

In the high state of political tension at this time it was easy for rumours to spread
that an organized insurrection was under way on the part of persons disaffected to
the government, and the Tory leaders seem to have industriously spread these
rumours (see Sir Winston Churchill's *Marlborough,* vi. 518). Hearne was ready
(30 Mar.) to believe that the Mohocks were 'young, lewd, debauch'd Sparks, all
of the Whiggish Gang', and on 1 Apr. mentions the report that Bishop Burnet's son
was one of the ringleaders. Thomas Burnet himself, in a letter of 15 Mar., after describing the Mohocks, says, 'The Town, because I have gone sometimes to Nando's
Coffeehouse and have a sort of innate fierceness in my Looks, will have it that I am

a Name borrowed it seems from a sort of *Cannibals* in *India*, who subsist by plundering and devouring all the Nations about them. The President is stiled *Emperor of the Mohocks*; and his Arms are a *Turkish* Crescent, which his Imperial Majesty bears at present in a very extraordinary Manner engraven upon his Forehead. Agreeable to their Name, the avowed Design of their Institution is Mischief; and upon this Foundation all their Rules and Orders are framed. An outragious Ambition of doing all possible Hurt to their Fellow-Creatures, is the great Cement of their Assembly, and the only Qualification required in the Members. In order to exert this Principle in its full Strength and Perfection, they take Care to drink themselves to a Pitch, that is, beyond the Possibility of attending to any Motions of Reason or Humanity; then make a general Sally, and attack all that are so unfortunate as to walk the Streets thro' which they patroll. Some are knock'd down, others stabb'd, others cut and carbonado'd. To put the Watch to a total Rout, and mortify some of those inoffensive Militia, is reckon'd a *Coup d'eclat*.[1] The particular Talents by which these *Misanthropes* are distinguish'd from one another, consist in the various kinds of Barbarities which they execute upon their Prisoners. Some are celebrated for a happy Dexterity in tipping the Lion[2] upon them; which is perform'd by squeezing the Nose flat to the Face, and boring out the Eyes with their Fingers: Others are call'd the Dancing-Masters, and teach their Scholars to cut Capers by running Swords thro' their Legs; a new Invention, whether originally *French* I cannot tell: A third Sort are the Tumblers,[3] whose Office it is to set Women upon their Heads, and commit certain Indecencies, or rather Barbarities, on

---

one of this gang' (*Letters*, ed. D. Nichol Smith, Oxford, 1914, p. 2). On 17 Mar. a proclamation was issued for the suppressing of riots and the discovery of offenders (London *Gazette*, 18 Mar.; *British Mercury*, 19 Mar.). A list of persons assaulted during February and March in Covent Garden, the Strand, Tavistoke-Court, and elsewhere, is printed in the *Gazette* of 19 Apr. The Tory attempt to make political capital out of these outrages seems to have come to naught, in spite of efforts to magnify 'this pretended Combination of *Mohocks* and *Hawkubites*, in order to throw the Odium of it upon the *Whiggs*; whom, by all possible means, they endeavour to asperse and render obnoxious to the People' (*Political State*, Mar. 1712, p. 237). Lillie (ii. 228–32) prints a letter from Hackney on the outrages of the Mohocks, with a petition from the Gentlemen of the Temple asking that the rumour that they are Mohocks be stopped.

[1] This is the only quotation in *OED* to illustrate this word.

[2] I.e., 'squeezing a person's nose flat to his face with the thumb' (Aitken).

[3] Defined by *OED* as 'a class of street ruffians', with this as the earliest quotation. Cf. Gay's *Trivia* (iii. 326):

> How matrons, hoop'd within the hogshead's womb,
> Were tumbled furious thence.

the Limbs which they expose. But these I forbear to mention, because they can't but be[a] very shocking to the Reader as well as the SPECTATOR. In this Manner they carry on a War against Mankind; and by the standing Maxims of their Policy, are to enter into no Alliances but one, and that is offensive and defensive with all Bawdy-Houses in general, of which they have declar'd themselves Protectors and Guarantees.

'I must own, Sir, these are only broken incoherent Memoirs of this wonderful Society, but they are the best I have been yet able to procure; for being but of late Establishment, it is not ripe for a just History: And to be serious, the chief Design of this Trouble is to hinder it from ever being so. You have been pleas'd, out of a Concern for the Good of your Countrymen, to act under the Character of SPECTATOR not only the Part of a Looker-on, but an Overseer of their Actions; and whenever such Enormities as this infest the Town, we immediately fly to you for Redress. I have reason to believe, that some thoughtless Youngsters, out of a false Notion of Bravery, and an immoderate Fondness to be distinguished for Fellows of Fire, are insensibly hurried into this senseless scandalous Project: Such will probably stand corrected by your Reproofs, especially if you inform them, that it is not Courage for half a Score Fellows, mad with Wine and Lust, to set upon two or three soberer than themselves; and that the Manners of *Indian* Savages are no becoming Accomplishments to an *English* fine Gentleman. Such of them as have been Bullies and Scowrers[1] of a long standing, and are grown Veterans in this Kind of Service, are I fear too hardned to receive any Impressions from your Admonitions. But I beg you would recommend to their Perusal your Ninth Speculation: They may there be taught to take Warning from the Club of Duellists; and be put in Mind, that the common Fate of those Men of Honour was to be hang'd.

I am,

SIR,

Your most humble Servant,

Philanthropos.'

March the 10*th,*
1711–12.

The following Letter is of a quite contrary Nature; but I add it here that the Reader may observe at the same View, how amiable

---

[a] but be] be but *Fol.*

[1] See No. 276 (vol. ii).

Ignorance may be when it is shewn in its Simplicities, and how detestable in Barbarities. It is written by an honest Countryman to his Mistress, and came to the Hands of a Lady of good Sense wrapped about a Thread-Paper,[1] who has long kept it by her as an Image of artless Love.

To her I very much respect, Mrs. Margaret Clark.

'LOVELY, and oh that I could write loving Mrs. *Margaret Clark*, I pray you let Affection excuse Presumption. Having been so happy as to enjoy the Sight of your sweet Countenance and comely Body, sometimes when I had Occasion to buy Treacle or Liquorish Powder at the Apothecary's Shop, I am so enamoured with you, that I can no more keep close my flaming Desire to become your Servant. And I am the more bold now to write to your sweet self, because I am now my own Man, and may match where I please; for my Father is taken away; and now I am come to my Living, which is Ten Yard Land, and a House; and there is never a Yard of Land[2] in our Field but is as well worth ten Pound a Year as a Thief's worth a Halter; and all my Brothers and Sisters are provided for: Besides I have good Houshold-stuff, though I say it, both Brass and Pewter, Linnens and Woollens; and though my House be thatched, yet if you and I match, it shall go hard but I will have one Half of it slated. If you shall think well of this Motion I will wait upon you as soon as my new Cloaths is made and Hay-Harvest is in. I could, though I say it, have good——' The rest is torn off;[3] and Posterity

[1] The earliest quotation for this word in *OED* is dated 1761.
[2] 'A yard land (*virgata terrae*) in some counties contains 20 acres, in some 24, and in others 30 acres of land' (*Les Termes de la Ley*, revised by Thomas Blount, 1667, p. 613).
[3] The continuation will be found in No. 328*. The following note by Percy appears in Nichols's edition:

This letter was really conveyed in the manner here mentioned to a Mrs. Cole, the wife of a churlish attorney in or near Northampton, who would not suffer her to correspond with any body. It was written by a substantial freeholder in Northamptonshire, whose name was Gabriel Bullock, and given to Steele by his friend the ingenious antiquary Mr. Browne Willis. Mrs. Cantrell, niece to Mrs. Cole, fortunately remembered what was torn off from the letter by a child at play, so that it is given here entire on good authority.

—'good matches amongst my neighbours. My mother, peace be with her soul, the good old gentlewoman has left me good store of houshold linen of her own spinning, a chest full. If you and I lay our means together, it shall go hard but I will pave the way to [do] well. Your loving servant till death, Mister Gabriel Bullock, now my father is dead.'

Nichols adds: 'The curious may see another edition of this letter in Spect. No. 328*, and is left at entire liberty to take whichever he likes best for the *genuine* copy. . . .'

must be contented to know that Mrs. *Margaret Clark* was very pretty, but are left in the Dark as to the Name of her Lover.

T

No. 325
[BUDGELL]

Thursday, March 13, 1712[1]

> . . . *Quid frustra Simulacra fugacia captas?*
> *Quod petis, est nusquam: quod amas avertere, perdes.*
> *Ista repercussæ quam cernis imaginis umbra est,*
> *Nil habet ista sui; tecum venitque, manetque,*
> *Tecum discedat si tu discedere possis.*

Ovid.

WILL. HONEYCOMB diverted us last Night with an Account of a young Fellow's first discovering his Passion to his Mistress. The young Lady was one, it seems, who had long before conceived a favourable Opinion of him, and was still in Hopes that he would some time or other make his Advances. As he was one Day talking with her in Company of her two Sisters, the Conversation happening to turn upon Love, each of the young Ladies was, by way of Railery, recommending a Wife to him; when, to the no small Surprize of her who languished for him in secret, he told them with a more than ordinary Seriousness, That his Heart had been long engaged to one whose Name he thought himself obliged in Honour to conceal; but that he could shew her Picture in the Lid of his Snuff-Box. The young Lady, who found her self most sensibly touched by this Confession, took the first Opportunity that offered of snatching his Box out of his Hand. He seemed desirous of recovering it, but finding her resolved to look into the Lid, begged her,

---

[1] *Motto.* Ovid, *Metamorphoses*, 3. 432–6:

> What could, fond youth, this helpless passion move?
> What kindle in thee this unpity'd love?
> Thy own warm blush within the water glows,
> With thee the colour'd shadow comes and goes,
> Its empty being on thy self relies;
> Step thou aside, and the frail charmer dies. ADDISON.

that if she should happen to know the Person she would not reveal her Name. Upon carrying it to the Window she was very agreeably surprized to find there was nothing within the Lid but a little looking Glass;[1] in which, after she had viewed her own Face, with more Pleasure than she had ever done before, she returned the Box with a Smile, telling him, She could not but admire at his Choice.

WILL. fancying that his Story took, immediately fell into a Dissertation on the Usefulness of looking-Glasses, and applying himself to me, asked If there were any Looking-Glasses in the Times of the *Greeks* and *Romans*; for that he had often observed in the Translations of Poems out of those Languages, that People generally talked of seeing themselves in Wells, Fountains, Lakes and Rivers: Nay, says he, I remember Mr. *Dryden* in his *Ovid* tells us of a swingeing Fellow called *Polypheme*, that made use of the Sea for his Looking-Glass, and could never dress himself to Advantage but in a Calm.[2]

My Friend WILL. to shew us the whole Compass of his Learning upon this Subject, further informed us, that there were still several Nations in the World so very barbarous as not to have any Looking-Glasses among them; and that he had lately read a Voyage to the South-Sea, in which it is said, that the Ladies of *Chili* always dress their Heads over a Bason of Water.

I am the more particular in my Account of WILL's last Night's Lecture on these natural Mirrors, as it seems to bear some Relation to the following Letter, which I received the Day before.

SIR,

'I HAVE read your last *Saturday*'s Observations, on the fourth Book of *Milton* with great Satisfaction, and am particularly pleased with the hidden Moral, which you have taken notice of in several Parts of the Poem. The Design of this Letter is to desire your Thoughts, whether there may not also be some Moral couched under that Place in the same Book where the Poet lets us know, that the first Woman immediately after her Creation, ran to a Looking-glass, and became so enamoured of her own Face, that she had never removed to view any of the other Works of Nature, had not she been led off to a Man. If you think fit to set down the whole Passage from *Milton*, your Readers will be able to judge for

---

[1] In William Burnaby's *Modish Husband* (1702) Lionel reveals his love for Lady Cringe in this manner (II. iii). In the *Post Boy* of 17 Apr. 1712 appears an advertisement for a lost snuff-box 'with a very small Looking-Glass on the Inside of the Lid'.

[2] Ovid, *Metamorphoses* 13. 30–33.

themselves, and the Quotation will not a little contribute to the filling up of your Paper.

Your Humble Servant,
R. T.'

The last Consideration urged by my Querist, is so strong, that I cannot forbear closing with it. The Passage he alludes to is Part of *Eve*'s Speech to *Adam*, and one of the most Beautiful Passages in the whole Poem.

> *That day I oft remember, when from sleep*
> *I first awak'd, and found my self repos'd*
> *Under a shade of flours, much wondering where*
> *And what I was, whence thither brought, and how.*
> *Not distant far from thence a murmuring sound*
> *Of waters issu'd from a Cave and spread*
> *Into a liquid Plain, then stood unmov'd*
> *Pure as th' expanse of Heav'n; I thither went*
> *With unexperienc'd thought, and laid me down*
> *On the green bank, to look into the clear*
> *Smooth Lake, that to me seem'd another Skie.*
> *As I bent down to look, just opposite,*
> *A shape within the watry gleam appear'd*
> *Bending to look on me, I started back,*
> *It started back, but pleas'd I soon return'd,*
> *Pleas'd it return'd as soon with answering looks*
> *Of sympathy and love; there I had fixt*
> *Mine eyes till now, and pin'd with vain desire,*
> *Had not a voice thus warn'd me, What thou seest,*
> *What there thou seest fair Creature is thy self,*
> *With thee it came and goes: but follow me,*
> *And I will bring thee where no shadow stays*
> *Thy coming, and thy soft imbraces he*
> *Whose image thou art, him thou shalt enjoy*
> *Inseperably thine, to him shalt bear*
> *Multitudes like thy self, and thence be call'd*
> *Mother of human Race: what could I doe,*
> *But follow streight, invisibly thus led;*
> *Till I espy'd thee, fair indeed and tall,*
> *Under a Platan, yet methought less fair,*
> *Less winning soft, less amiably mild,*

Than that smooth watry image; back I turn'd,
Thou following cryd'st aloud, Return fair Eve,
Whom fly'st thou; whom thou fly'st, of him thou art,
His flesh, his bone; to give thee being I lent
Out of my side to thee, nearest my heart
Substantial Life, to have thee by my side
Henceforth an individual solace dear;
Part of my Soul I seek thee, and thee claim
My other half: with that thy gentle hand
Seis'd mine, I yielded, and from that time see
How beauty is excell'd by manly grace
And wisdom, which alone is truly fair.
So spake our general Mother, . . .[1]

X

No. 326
[STEELE]

Friday, March 14, 1712[2]

Inclusam Danaen turris ahenea
Robustæque fores, & vigilum canum
Tristes excubiæ munierant satis
Nocturnis ab adulteris:
Si non . . .

Hor.

Mr. SPECTATOR,

'YOUR Correspondent's Letter[3] relating to Fortune-Hunters, and your subsequent Discourse upon it, have given me Encouragement to send you a State of my Case; by which you will

---

[1] *PL* iv. 449-92.
[2] *Motto.* Horace, *Odes*, 3. 16. 1-5:
> A Tower of Brass, Gates strong and barr'd,
> And watchful Dogs suspicious Guard
> From creeping Night Adulterers,
> That sought imprison'd *Danae's* Bed,
> Might have secur'd one Maiden-Head,
> Had not ...   CREECH.

[3] No. 311.

see, that the Matter complain'd of is a common Grievance both to City and Country.

'I am a Country Gentleman of between five and six thousand a Year. It is my Misfortune to have a very fine Park and an only Daughter; upon which Account I have been so plagu'd with Deer-Stealers and Fops, that for these four Years past I have scarce enjoy'd a Moment's Rest. I look upon my self to be in a State of War; and am forc'd to keep as constant Watch in my Seat, as a Governour would do that commanded a Town on the Frontier of an Enemy's Country. I have indeed pretty well secur'd my Park, having for this Purpose provided my self of four Keepers, who are Left-handed,[1] and handle a Quarter-staff beyond any other Fellows in the Country. And for the Guard of my House, besides a Band of Pensioner-Matrons and an old Maiden Relation, whom I keep on constant Duty, I have Blunderbusses always charg'd, and Fox-Gins planted in private Places about my Garden, of which I have given frequent Notice in the Neighbourhood; yet so it is, that in spite of all my Care, I shall every now and then have a sawcy Rascal ride by *reconnoitring*[2] (as I think you call it) under my Windows, as sprucely drest as if he were going to a Ball. I am aware of this Way of attacking a Mistress on Horseback, having heard that it is a common Practice in *Spain*; and have therefore taken Care to remove my Daughter from the Road Side of the House, and to lodge her next the Garden. But to cut short my Story: What can a Man do after all? I durst not stand for Member of Parliament last Election, for fear of some ill Consequence from my being off of my Post. What I would therefore desire of you, is, to promote a Project I have set on Foot, and upon which I have writ to some of my Friends; and that is, that Care may be taken to secure our Daughters by Law as well as our Deer; and that some honest Gentleman of a publick Spirit, would move for Leave to bring in a Bill *for the better preserving of the female Game*.

I am,

SIR,

Your humble Servant.'

[1] In *Tatler* 59 Steele had observed of the Greenhats: 'It is remarkable, that they are all Left-handed, and have always been very expert at Single Rapier. A Man must be very much used to their Play to know how to defend himself; for their Posture is so different from that of the Right-handed, that you run upon their Swords if you push forward. . . .'

[2] This is the earliest example in *OED* of the verb used intransitively. In the transitive sense it is one of the French words cited in No. 165 (vol. ii).

Mr. SPECTATOR, *Mile-End Green,*[1] *March* 6, 1711–12.

'HERE is a young Man walks by our Door every Day about the Dusk of the Evening. He looks up at my Window as if to see me; and if I steal towards it to peep at him, he turns another way, and looks frighted at finding what he was looking for. The Air is very cold; and pray let him know that, if[a] he knocks at the Door he will be carried to the Parlour Fire; and I will come down soon after, and give him an Opportunity to break his Mind.

> I am,
> SIR,
> *Your humble Servant,*
> Mary Comfitt.

'If I observe he cannot speak, I'll give him Time to recover himself, and ask him how he does.'

Dear SIR,

'I BEG you[b] to print this without Delay, and by the first Opportunity give us the natural Causes of Longing in Women;[2] or put me out of Fear that my Wife will one Time or other be delivered of something as monstrous as any thing that has yet[c] appeared to the World; for they say the Child is to bear a Resemblance of what was desired by the Mother. I have been married upwards of six Years, have had four Children, and my Wife is now big with the fifth. The Expences she has put me to in procuring what she has longed for during her Pregnancy with them, would not only have handsomly defrayed the Charges of the Month, but of their Education too; her Fancy being so exorbitant for the first Year or two, as not to confine it self to the usual Objects of Eatables and Drinkables, but running out after Equipage and Furniture, and the like Extravagancies. To trouble you only with a few of them: When she was with Child of *Tom* my eldest Son, she came home one Day just fainting, and told me she had been visiting a Relation, whose Husband had made her a Present of a Chariot and a stately Pair of Horses; and that she was positive she could not breathe a Week longer, unless she took the

---

a know that, if] *8vo*; know if *Fol.*; know that if *12mo*   b Beg you] Beg of you *Fol.*   c has yet] yet has *Fol.*

---

[1] Cf. No. 314.
[2] Sir Thomas Browne, *Pseudodoxia epidemica* (book vi, chap. x), gives examples. For a list of the innumerable treatises on the subject see Heinrich Laehr, *Die Literatur der Psychiatrie . . . von 1459–1799* (Berlin, 1900), s.v. 'Imagination'.

Air in the Fellow to it of her own within that Time. This, rather than lose an Heir, I readily complied with. Then the Furniture of her best Room must be instantly changed, or she should mark the Child with some of the frightful Figures in the old-fashion'd Tapestry. Well, the Upholsterer was called, and her Longing saved that Bout. When she went with *Molly*, she had fix'd her Mind upon a new Set of Plate, and as much China as would have furnish'd an *India* Shop. These also I chearfully granted, for fear of being Father to an *Indian Pagod*.[1] Hitherto I found her Demands rose upon every Concession; and had she gone on I had been ruined: But by good Fortune, with her third, which was *Peggy*, the Heighth of her Imagination came down to the Corner of a Venison-Pasty, and brought her once even upon her Knees to gnaw off the Ears of a Pig from the Spit. The Gratifications of her Palate were easily preferred to those of her Vanity; and sometimes a Partridge or a Quail, a Wheat-Ear or the Pestle[2] of a Lark were chearfully purchased; nay I could be contented tho' I were to feed her with green Pease in *April* or[a] Cherries in *May*. But with the Babe she now goes she is turned Girl again, and fallen to eating of Chalk, pretending 'twill make the Child's Skin white; and nothing will serve her but I must bear her Company, to prevent its having a Shade of my Brown. In this however I have ventured to deny her. No longer ago than Yesterday, as we were coming to Town, she saw a Parcel of Crows so heartily at Breakfast upon a Piece of Horse-flesh, that she had an invincible Desire to partake with them, and (to my infinite Surprize) begg'd the Coachman to cut her off a Slice as if 'twere for himself; which the Fellow did; and as soon as she came home she fell to it with such an Appetite, that she seem'd rather to devour than eat it. What her next Sally will be I cannot guess; but in the mean Time my Request to you is, that if there be any way to come at these wild unaccountable Rovings of Imagination by Reason and Argument, you'd speedily afford us your Assistance. This exceeds the Grievance of Pin-Money;[3] and I think in every Settlement there ought to be a Clause inserted, that the Father should be answerable

---

[a] or] and *Fol*.

---

[1] An image of a deity, an idol (1582–). *OED*.
[2] In figurative use, as a trifle, something very small. This is the last quotation in this sense in *OED*.
[3] No. 295.

for the Longings of his Daughter. But I shall impatiently expect your Thoughts in this Matter; and am,

SIR,
Your most obliged,
And most faithful
Humble Servant,
T. B.

'Let me know whether you think the next Child will love Horses as much as *Molly* does China-Ware.'   T

No. 327
[ADDISON]

Saturday, March 15, 1712[1]

. . . *major rerum mihi nascitur ordo.*
Virg.

WE were told in the foregoing Book how the Evil Spirit practised upon *Eve* as she lay asleep, in order to inspire her with Thoughts of Vanity, Pride and Ambition.[2] The Author, who shews a wonderful Art throughout his whole Poem, in preparing the Reader for the several Occurrences that arise in it, founds upon the above-mentioned Circumstance the first part of the Fifth Book. *Adam* upon his awaking finds *Eve* still asleep with an unusual Discomposure in her Looks. The Posture in which he regards her, is described with a wonderful Tenderness,[a] as the Whisper with which he awakens her, is the softest that ever was conveyed to a Lover's Ear.

> *His wonder was to find unwaken'd* Eve
> *With Tresses discompos'd, and glowing cheek*
> *As through unquiet rest: he on his side*
> *Leaning half rais'd, with looks of cordial love*

[a] a wonderful Tenderness,] a Tenderness not to be expressed, *all edd. Corrected in Errata in Fol.* (*No. 369*): '*after* a *read* wonderful, *dele* not to be expressed.'

[1] *Motto.* Virgil, *Aeneid*, 7. 44:
A larger Scene of Action is display'd,
And, rising hence, a greater Work is weigh'd. DRYDEN.

[2] *PL,* iv. 799–819.

Hung over her enamour'd, and beheld
Beauty, which whether waking or asleep,
Shot forth peculiar Graces; then with voice
Mild, as when Zephyrus *on*^a *Flora breathes,*
Her hand soft touching, whisper'd thus. Awake
My fairest, my espous'd, my latest found,
Heav'ns last best gift, my ever new delight,
Awake, the morning shines, and the fresh field
Calls us, we lose the prime, to mark how spring
Our tended plants, how blows the Citron Grove,
What dropp's the Myrrhe, and what the balmie Reed,
How Nature paints her colours, how the Bee
Sits on the bloom, extracting liquid sweet.
Such Whispring wak'd her, but with startled Eye
On Adam, *whom embracing, thus she spake.*
  O Sole in whom my thoughts find all repose,
My Glory, my perfection, glad I see
Thy face, and morn return'd . . .[1]

I cannot but take notice that *Milton*, in the^b Conferences between *Adam* and *Eve*, had his Eye very frequently upon the Book of *Canticles*, in which there is a noble Spirit of Eastern Poetry, and very often not unlike what we meet with in *Homer*, who is generally placed near the Age of *Solomon*. I think there is no question but the Poet in the preceding Speech remembred those two Passages which are spoken on the like occasion, and fill'd with the same pleasing Images of Nature.

My beloved spake, and said unto me, Rise up, my love, my fair one, and come away; For lo, the winter is past, the rain is over and gone; the Flowers appear on the earth; the time of the singing of birds is come, and the Voice of the Turtle is heard in our Land. The Fig-tree putteth forth her green figs, and the Vines with the tender grape give a good smell. Arise, my love, my fair one, and come away.[2]

Come, my beloved, let us go forth into the Field; let us get up early to the Vineyards, let us see if the Vine flourish, whether the tender Grape appear, and the Pomegranates bud forth.[3]

----

^a *on*] 19; *or* Fol., 8vo, 12mo   ^b the] his *Fol.*

----

[1] *PL*, v. 9–30. In *Tatler* 263 Steele had quoted lines 1–30, Milton's 'inimitable Description of *Adam's* awakening his *Eve* in Paradise'.
[2] Song of Sol. ii. 10–13.   [3] Ibid. vii. 11–12.

His preferring the Garden of *Eden* to that

> ... *Where the* Sapient *King*
> *Held dalliance with his fair* Egyptian *Spouse*,[1]

shews that the Poet had this delightful Scene in his mind.

Eve's Dream is full of those *high Conceits engendring Pride*,[2] which we are told the Devil endeavoured to instil into her. Of this kind is that part of it where she fancies her self awaken'd by *Adam* in the following beautiful Lines.

> *Why sleep'st thou* Eve? *now is the pleasant time,*
> *The cool, the silent, save where silence yields*
> *To the night-warbling bird, that now awake*
> *Tunes sweetest his Love-labour'd song; now reigns*
> *Full orb'd the moon, and with more pleasing*[a] *light*
> *Shadowy sets off the face of things; in vain*
> *If none regard; Heav'n wakes with all his eyes*
> *Whom to behold but thee, Natures desire,*
> *In whose sight all things joy, with ravishment*
> *Attracted by thy beauty still to gaze.*[3]

An injudicious Poet would have made *Adam* talk through the whole Work, in such Sentiments as these.[b] But Flattery and Falshood are not the Courtship of *Milton*'s *Adam*, and cou'd not be heard by *Eve* in her State of Innocence, excepting only in a Dream produced on purpose to taint her Imagination. Other vain Sentiments of the same kind in this relation of her Dream, will be obvious to every Reader. Tho' the Catastrophe[c] of the Poem is finely presaged on this occasion, the Particulars of it are so artfully shadow'd, that they do not anticipate the Story which follows in the Ninth Book. I shall only add, that tho' the Vision it self is founded upon Truth, the Circumstances of it are full of that Wildness and Inconsistency which are natural to a Dream. *Adam*, conformable to his superior Character for Wisdom, instructs and comforts *Eve* upon this occasion.

> *So chear'd he his fair Spouse, and she was chear'd,*
> *But silently a gentle tear let fall*
> *From either eye, and wiped them with her hair;*

---

[a] *pleasing*] *pleasant* Fol.   [b] these.] this. *Fol*.   [c] the Catastrophe] the great Catastrophe *Fol*.

---

[1] *PL*, ix. 442-3.   [2] *PL*, iv. 809.   [3] *PL*, v. 38-47.

Two other precious drops that ready stood,
Each in their chrystal sluice, he e'er they fell
Kiss'd as the gracious Signs of sweet remorse
And pious awe, that fear'd to have offended.[1]

The Morning Hymn[2] is written in Imitation of one of those Psalms,[3] where, in the Overflowings of Gratitude[a] and Praise, the Psalmist calls not only upon the Angels, but upon the most conspicuous parts of the inanimate Creation, to join with him in extolling their Common Maker. Invocations of this Nature fill the Mind with glorious Ideas of God's Works, and awaken that Divine Enthusiasm, which is so natural to Devotion. But if this calling upon the dead parts of Nature, is at all times a proper kind of Worship, it was in a particular manner suitable to our first Parents, who had the Creation fresh upon their Minds, and had not seen the various Dispensations of Providence, nor consequently could be acquainted with those many Topicks of Praise which might afford matter to the Devotions of their Posterity. I need not remark the[b] beautiful Spirit of Poetry which runs through this whole Hymn, nor the Holiness of that Resolution with which it concludes.

Having already mentioned those Speeches which are assigned to the Persons in this Poem, I proceed to the Description which the Poet gives of[c] *Raphael*. His Departure from before the Throne, and his Flight thro' the Quires of Angels,[4] is finely imaged. As *Milton* every where fills his Poem with Circumstances that are marvellous and astonishing, he describes the Gate of Heaven as framed after such a manner, that it open'd of it self upon the approach of the Angel who was to pass through it.

> *. . . 'till at the gate*
> *Of Heav'n arriv'd, the gate self-open'd wide,*
> *On golden Hinges turning, as by work*
> *Divine the Sovereign Architect had fram'd.*[5]

The Poet here seems to have regarded two or three Passages in

---

[a] of Gratitude] of his Gratitude *Fol.*
8vo, 19; gives us of *Fol., 12mo*   [b] the] that *Fol.*   [c] gives of]

---

[1] *PL*, v. 129–35.   [2] *PL*, v. 153–208.
[3] e.g. Ps. cxlviii.   [4] *PL*, v. 247–53.
[5] *PL*, v. 253–6.

the eighteenth *Iliad*, as that[a] in particular where, speaking of *Vulcan*, *Homer* says, that he had made Twenty *Tripodes* running on Golden Wheels, which, upon Occasion, might go of themselves to the Assembly of the Gods, and, when there was no more use for them, return again after the same manner.[1] *Scaliger* has rallied *Homer* very severely upon this Point, as Mons. *Dacier* has endeavoured to defend it.[2] I will not pretend to determine, whether in this Particular of *Homer*, the Marvellous does not lose sight of the Probable. As the miraculous Workmanship of *Milton*'s Gates is not so extraordinary as this of the *Tripodes*, so I am perswaded he would not have mentioned it, had not he been supported in it by a Passage in the Scripture, which speaks of Wheels in Heaven that had Life in them, and moved of themselves, or stood still, in Conformity with the Cherubims, whom they accompanied.[3]

There is no question but *Milton* had this Circumstance in his Thoughts, because in the following Book he describes the Chariot of the *Messiah* with *living* Wheels, according to the Plan in *Ezekiel*'s Vision.

> . . . *Forth rush'd with whirlwind sound*
> *The Chariot of Paternal Deity*
> *Flashing thick flames, wheel within wheel undrawn,*
> *It self instinct with Spirit* . . .[4]

I question not but *Bossu*, and the two *Daciers*, who are for vindicating every thing that is censured in *Homer*, by something Parallel in Holy Writ, would have been very well pleased had they thought of confronting *Vulcan*'s *Tripodes* with *Ezekiel*'s Wheels.

Raphael's Descent to the Earth, with the Figure of his Person, is represented in very lively Colours.[5] Several of the *French*, *Italian* and *English* Poets have given a loose to their Imaginations in the Description of Angels: But I do not remember to have met with any, so finely drawn and so conformable to the Notions which are given of them in Scripture, as this in *Milton*. After having set him forth in

---

[a] as that] as to that *Fol. Corrected in Errata (No. 369)*

[1] *Iliad*, 18. 372–7. As Newton pointed out (1749) in his note on this passage in *Paradise Lost*, the reference is more likely to 'Homer's making the gates of Heaven open of their own accord to the Deities who passed thro' them, *Iliad*, V. 749'.

[2] For Scaliger's criticism and Dacier's defence of Homer see the latter's note on Aristotle's *Poetics*, 25. 17: 'If *Vulcan* had made ordinary Trevits, they would not have been fit for a Poem [i.e. an epic], and had not answered the Greatness, Power, and Skill of a God' (p. 480).   [3] Ezek. i. 21, X. 17.

[4] *PL*, vi. 749–52.   [5] *PL*, v. 266–87.

all his Heavenly Plumage, and represented him as alighting upon the Earth, the Poet concludes his Description with a Circumstance, which is altogether new, and imagined with the greatest Strength of Fancy.

> . . . *Like Maia's Son he stood,*
> *And shook his plumes, that Heav'nly fragrance fill'd*
> *The Circuit wide.* . . .[1]

Raphael's Reception by the Guardian Angels; his passing through the Wilderness of Sweets; his distant Appearance to *Adam*, have all the Graces that Poetry is capable of bestowing.[2] The Author afterwards gives us a particular Description of *Eve* in her Domestick Employments.

> *So saying, with dispatchful looks in haste*
> *She turns, on hospitable thoughts intent,*
> *What choice to chuse for delicacy best,*
> *What order, so contriv'd as not to mix*
> *Tastes, not well joyn'd, inelegant, but bring*
> *Taste after taste, upheld with kindliest change;*
> *Bestirs her then &c.* . . .[3]

Though in this, and other Parts of the same Book, the Subject is only the Housewifry of our First Parent, it is set off with so many pleasing Images and strong Expressions, as make it none of the least agreeable Parts in this Divine Work.

The natural Majesty of *Adam*,[4] and at the same time his submissive Behaviour to the Superiour Being, who had vouchsafed to be his Guest; the solemn Hail[5] which the Angel bestows upon the Mother of Mankind, with the Figure of *Eve*[6] ministring at the Table, are Circumstances which deserve to be admir'd.

Raphael's Behaviour is every way suitable to the dignity of his Nature, and to that Character of a sociable Spirit, with which the Author has so judiciously introduced him. He had received Instructions to converse with *Adam*, as one Friend converses with another, and to warn him of the Enemy, who was contriving his Destruction: Accordingly he is represented as sitting down at Table with *Adam*, and eating of the Fruits of *Paradise*.[7] The Occasion naturally leads

---

[1] *PL*, v. 285–7. Maia's son was Hermes.　　[2] *PL*, v. 287–300.
[3] *PL*, v. 331–7. Addison quotes this 'beautiful description' in *Guardian* 138.
[4] *PL*, v. 350–60.　　　　　　　　　　　[5] *PL*, v. 388.
[6] *PL*, v. 443–5.　　　　　　　　　　　　[7] *PL*, v. 433.

him to his Discourse on the Food of Angels. After having thus entered into Conversation[1] with Man upon more indifferent Subjects, he warns him of his Obedience,[2] and makes a natural Transition to the History of that fallen Angel, who was employed in the Circumvention of our First Parents.

Had I followed Monsieur *Bossu's*[3] Method in my First Paper on *Milton*, I should have dated the Action of *Paradise Lost* from the Beginning of *Raphael's* Speech in this Book, as he supposes the Action of the *Æneid* to begin in the second Book of that Poem. I could alledge many Reasons for my drawing the Action of the *Æneid*, rather from its immediate Beginning in the first Book, than from its remote Beginning in the Second, and shew why I have considered the Sacking of *Troy* as an *Episode*, according to the common Acceptation of that Word. But as this would be a dry un-entertaining Piece of Criticism, and perhaps unnecessary to those who have read my First Paper, I shall not enlarge upon it. Which-ever of the Notions be true, the Unity of *Milton's* Action is preserved according to either of them; whether we consider the Fall of Man in its immediate Beginning, as proceeding from the Resolutions taken in the Infernal Council, or in its more remote Beginning, as proceeding from the First Revolt of the Angels in Heaven. The Occasion which *Milton* assigns for this Revolt, as it is founded on Hints in Holy Writ, and on the Opinion of some great Writers, so it was the most proper that the Poet could have made use of.

The Revolt in Heaven is described with great Force of Imagination, and a fine Variety of Circumstances. The Learned Reader cannot but be pleased with the Poet's Imitation of *Homer* in the last of the following Lines.

> *At length into the limits of the North*
> *They came, and Satan took his Royal Seat*
> *High on a hill, far blazeing, as a mount*
> *Rais'd on a Mount, with Pyramids and tow'rs*
> *From Diamond quarries hewn, and rocks of Gold*
> *The palace of great* Lucifer, *(so call*
> *That Structure in the Dialect of men*
> *Interpreted)* . . .[4]

Homer[5] mentions Persons and Things, which he tells us in the

[1] *PL*, v. 404–33.   [2] *PL*, v. 519–43.   [3] Book ii, chap. xi.
[4] *PL*, v. 755–62.   [5] *Iliad*, 1. 403; 2. 813; 14. 291; 20. 74.

Language of the Gods are call'd by different Names from those they go by in the Language of Men. *Milton* has imitated him with his usual Judgment in this particular place, wherein he has likewise the Authority of Scripture to justify him. The part of *Abdiel*, who was the only Spirit that in this Infinite Host of Angels preserved his Allegiance to his Maker, exhibits to us a noble Moral of religious Singularity.[1] The Zeal of the Seraph[a] breaks forth in a becoming Warmth of Sentiments and Expressions, as the Character which is given us of him denotes that generous Scorn and Intrepidity which attends Heroic Vertue. The Author, doubtless, designed it as a Pattern to those who live among Mankind in their present State of Degeneracy and Corruption.

> *So spake the Seraph* Abdiel *faithful found,*
> *Among the faithless, faithful only he;*
> *Among innumerable false, unmov'd,*
> *Unshaken, unseduc'd, unterrify'd;*
> *His Loyalty he kept, his Love, his Zeal:*
> *Nor Number, nor example with him wrought*
> *To swerve from truth, or change his constant mind*
> *Though Single. From amidst them forth he pass'd,*
> *Long way through hostile Scorn,[b] which he sustain'd*
> *Superior, nor of violence fear'd aught;*
> *And with retorted Scorn his back he turn'd*
> *On those proud Tow'rs to swift Destruction doom'd.*[2]

L

No. 328   *Monday, March* 17, 1712[3]
[STEELE]

Nullum a labore me reclinat otium.

Hor.

Mr. SPECTATOR,

'AS I believe this is the first Complaint that ever was made to you of this Nature, so you are the first Person I ever could prevail

---

ª Seraph] *19*; Seraphim *Fol., 8vo, 12mo*   ᵇ *through hostile Scorn,*] *through Scorn,* Fol.

[1] *PL*, v. 805–907.   [2] *PL*, v. 896–907.   [*For note 3 see opposite page.*

upon my self to lay it before. When I tell you I have a healthy vigorous Constitution, a plentiful Estate, no inordinate Desires, and am married to a very virtuous lovely Woman, who neither wants Wit nor good Nature, and by whom I have a numerous Offspring to perpetuate my Family, you will naturally conclude me a happy Man. But, notwithstanding these promising Appearances, I am so far from it, that the Prospect of being ruin'd and undone, by a Sort of Extravagance which of late Years is in a less Degree crept into every fashionable Family, deprives me of all the Comforts of my Life, and renders me the most anxious miserable Man on Earth. My Wife, who was the only Child and darling Care of an indulgent Mother, employ'd her early Years in learning all those Accomplishments we generally understand by good Breeding and a polite Education. She sings, dances, plays on the Lute and Harpsichord, paints prettily, is a perfect Mistress of the *French* Tongue, and has made a considerable Progress in *Italian*. She is besides excellently skill'd in all domestick Sciences, as Preserving, Pickling, Pastry, making Wines of Fruits of our own Growth, Embroidering, and Needle-works of every Kind. Hitherto you will be apt to think there is very little Cause of Complaint; but suspend your Opinion till I have further explain'd my self, and then I make no Question you will come over to mine. You are not to imagine I find Fault that she either possesses or takes Delight in the Exercise of those Qualifications I just now mention'd; 'tis the immoderate Fondness she has to them that I lament, and that what is only design'd for the innocent Amusement and Recreation of Life, is become the whole Business and Study of hers. The six Months we are in Town (for the Year is equally divided between that and the Country) from almost Break of Day 'till Noon, the whole Morning is laid out in practising with her several Masters; and to make up the Losses occasion'd by her Absence in Summer, every Day in the Week their Attendance is requir'd; and as they all are People eminent in their Professions, their Skill and Time must be recompensed accordingly:

[3] *Motto.* Horace, *Epodes*, 17. 24:

No Ease doth lay me down from Pain. CREECH.

This paper was substituted in 8vo and 12mo for No. 328* in Folio. Morley and Gregory Smith assign it to Addison. It was not, however, reprinted in Tickell's edition of Addison's works, and it is signed with Steele's signature T. It is very likely a genuine letter, chosen by Steele from the numerous letters which had accumulated by the time the 8vo and 12mo editions came to be printed.

So how far these Articles extend, I leave you to judge. Limning,[1] one would think, is no expensive Diversion, but as she manages the Matter, 'tis a very considerable Addition to her Disbursements; which you will easily believe when you know she paints Fans for all her female Acquaintance, and draws all her Relations Pictures in Miniature; the first must be mounted by no Body but *Colmar*,[2] and the other set by no Body but *Charles Mather*.[3] What follows is still much worse than the former; for, as I told you, she is a great Artist at her Needle, 'tis incredible what Sums she expends in Embroidery: For besides what is appropriated to her personal Use, as Mantuas, Petticoats, Stomachers, Handkerchiefs, Purses, Pin-cushions, and Working-Aprons, she keeps four *French* Protestants[4] continually employ'd in making divers Pieces of superfluous Furniture, as Quilts, Toilets, Hangings for Closets, Beds, Window-Curtains, easy Chairs, and Tabourets: Nor have I any Hopes of ever reclaiming her from this Extravagance, while she obstinately persists in thinking it a notable Piece of good Housewifry, because they are made at Home, and she has had some Share in the Performance. There would be no End of relating to you the Particulars of the annual Charge in furnishing her Store-room with a Profusion of Pickles and Preserves; for she is not contented with having every Thing, unless it be done every Way, in which she consults an hereditary Book of Receipts; for her female Ancestors have been always fam'd for good House-wifry, one of whom is made immortal by giving her Name to an Eye-Water and two Sorts of Puddings. I cannot undertake to recite all her medicinal Preparations, as Salves, Cerecloths,[5] Powders, Confects, Cordials, Ratafia,[6] Persico,[7] Orange-flower, and Cherry-

---

[1] Formerly used specifically for painting in water-colour or distemper (*OED*).

[2] Colmar's advertisement does not appear among those of the *Spectator*. Cf. Pope, *Letter to a Noble Lord* (1733): 'Does your Lordship use *Hinchcliff* as a proper name? or as the ladies say a *hinchcliff* or a *colmar*, for a silk or a fan?' (Elwin–Courthope,v. 435–6).

[3] A toyman near the Temple Bar in Fleet Street. He is referred to in Nos. 503 and 570 (vol. iv). *Tatler* 142 prints a long letter praising Mather, 'the first that brought Toys in Fashion, and Bawbles to Perfection'; he is described as 'admirably well versed in Screws, Springs, and Hinges, and deeply read in Knives, Combs or Scissars, Buttons or Buckles'. An advertisement for a peruke-maker's shop to be let at Temple-Bar (*Post Boy*, 3 May 1709) concludes: 'Note, it faces the Rainbow and Nando's Coffee-Houses, and Mr. Mathers's, the great Toy-shop.'

[4] The French Protestants, who had fled from France in 1685 upon the Revocation of the Edict of Nantes, were known for their work in embroidery and weaving.

[5] Cerecloths were waxed cloths used as plasters in surgery.

[6] 'A delicious Liquor made of Apricocks, or Cherries, with their Kernels bruis'd and steept in Brandy' (John Kersey, *Dictionary*, 1713).

[7] Persico, or persicot, like ratafia, was a cordial prepared by macerating the kernels of peaches, apricots, &c., in spirit (Lat. *persicum*, peach). *OED*. Paul Girard, at the

Brandy, together with innumerable Sorts of simple Waters. But there is nothing I lay so much to Heart, as that detestable Catalogue of counterfeit Wines, which derive their Names from the Fruits, Herbs, or Trees of whose Juices they are chiefly compounded: They are loathsome to the Taste, and pernicious to the Health; and as they seldom survive the Year, and then are thrown away, under a false Pretence of Frugality, I may affirm they stand me in more than if I entertain'd all our Visiters with the best Burgundy and Champaign. Coffee, Chocolate, Green, Imperial, Peco, and Bohea Tea[1] seem to be Trifles; but when the proper Appurtenances of the Tea-Table are added, they swell the Account higher than one would imagine. I cannot conclude without doing her Justice in one Article; where her Frugality is so remarkable I must not deny her the Merit of it, and that is in Relation to her Children, who are all confin'd, both Boys and Girls, to one large Room in the remotest Part of the House, with Bolts on the Doors, and Barrs to the Windows, under the Care and Tuition of an old Woman who had been dry Nurse to her Grandmother. This is their Residence all the Year round; and as they are never allow'd to appear, she prudently thinks it needless to be at any Expence in Apparel or Learning. Her eldest Daughter to this Day would have neither read nor writ, if it had not been for the Butler, who being the Son of a Country Attorney, has taught her such a Hand as is generally used for engrossing Bills in Chancery. By this Time I have sufficiently tired your Patience with my

'3 Flower de Luces', at Charing-Cross, advertises in No. 335 and later numbers chests of distilled waters from Italy: 'Every Chest containing 24 Bottles (3 of which is a full Quart) and consists only of the 4 most select Sorts (i.e.) Millefleur, Orangiat, Burgamot, and Persicot, and are all of a double Spirit, and drown off in the same manner as the Citron Waters of Barbadoes, which they excel in every Quality. . . .' They were sold at three guineas per chest.

[1] According to Thomas Short, *A Dissertation upon Tea* (1730), 'we have only two Sorts imported to us, *viz. Green* and *Bohea*' (p. 13). Of the green he enumerates six varieties, ranging from 13 to 36 shillings a pound, one of which is Imperial Green at 18 shillings. Of bohea he specifies Common Bohea at 12 shillings, Congo at 14 shillings, and Pekoe at 15 shillings a pound. According to *OED* the name Bohea derives from 'the Wu-i hills, whence black tea was first brought to England', and Pekoe from the Mandarin word for white hair or down, pekoe tea being so called 'from the leaves being picked young with the down still on them'. This quotation is the earliest in *OED* for Pekoe. An advertisement in *Tatler* 112 is of interest for relative prices:

Turkey Coffee, 6s. 4d. with allowance to them that buy Quantities. Bohee from 12 to 24s. All Sorts of Green, the lowest, 12s. Chocolate with Sugar, 2s. 2d. All Nut, 3s. 6d. The finest Brazil 48s. and 3s. 4d. an Ounce. Portugal, 18s. and 1s. 4d. an Ounce. Right Amazona, Barcelona, and Port St. Lucas. Sold very cheap by Wholesale, or Retail; and Orange-Flower water; at the Star in Bedford-Court, near Bedford-street, Covent Garden.

domestick Grievances; which I hope you will agree could not well be contain'd in a narrower Compass, when you consider what a Paradox I undertook to maintain in the Beginning of my Epistle, and which manifestly appears to be but too melancholy a Truth. And now I heartily wish the Relation I have given of my Misfortunes may be of Use and Benefit to the Publick. By the Example I have set before them, the truly virtuous Wives may learn to avoid those Errors which have so unhappily misled mine, and which are visibly these three. First, In mistaking the proper Objects of her Esteem, and fixing her Affections upon such Things as are only the Trappings and Decorations of her Sex. Secondly, In not distinguishing what becomes the different Stages of Life. And, Lastly, The Abuse and Corruption of some excellent Qualities, which, if circumscrib'd within just Bounds, would have been the Blessing[a] and Prosperity of her Family, but by a vicious Extream are like to be the Bane and Destruction of it.'   T

No. 328*
[STEELE]

Monday, March 17, 1712[1]

Delectata illa Urbanitate tam stulta.
Petron. Arb.

THAT useful Part of Learning which consists in Emendations, Knowledge of different Readings, and the like, is what in all Ages Persons extremely wise and learned have had in great Veneration. For this Reason I cannot but rejoyce at the following Epistle, which lets us into the true Author of the Letter to Mrs. *Margaret Clark*, Part of which I did my self the Honour to publish in a former Paper. I must confess I do not naturally affect critical Learning; but

---

[a] Blessing] *12mo*; Blessings *8vo*

---

[1] *Motto.* Petronius Arbiter, *Satyricon* 7. 1:
Delighted with unaffected Plainness.

'In a MS. written by Dr. Birch, now before the Annotator, it is said, that an original number of the Spectator *in folio* was withdrawn at the time of its republication in volumes, on the remonstrance of a family who conceived themselves injured by its appearance in print. It was, most probably, this very Paper' (Nichols). A part of the letter to Mrs. Margaret Clark appears in No. 324. I have not been able to make any further identification of the originals.

finding my self not so much regarded as I am apt to flatter my self I may deserve from some professed Patrons of Learning, I could not but do my self the Justice to shew I am not a Stranger to such Erudition as they smile upon, if I were duly encouraged. However this only to let the World see what I could do; and shall not give my Reader any more of this Kind, if he will forgive the Ostentation I shew at present.

SIR,   *March* 13, 1711.[1]

'UPON reading your Paper of Yesterday, I took the Pains to look out a Copy I had formerly taken, and remember'd to be very like your last Letter: Comparing them, I found they were the very same; and have underwritten sent you that Part of it which you say was torn off. I hope you will insert it, that Posterity may know 'twas *Gabriel Bullock* that made Love in that natural Stile of which you seem to be so fond. But to let you see I have other Manuscripts in the same way, I have sent you enclosed three Copies, faithfully taken by my own Hand from the Originals, which were writ by a *Yorkshire* Gentleman of a good Estate to Madam *Mary*, and an Uncle of her's, a Knight very well known by the most ancient Gentry in that and several other Counties of *Great Britain*. I have exactly followed the Form and Spelling. I have been credibly informed that Mr. *William Bullock*,[2] the famous Comedian, is the Descendant of this *Gabriel*, who begot Mr. *William Bullock*'s Great Grandfather on the Body of the above-mention'd Mrs. *Margaret Clark*: But neither *Speed*, nor *Baker*, nor *Selden*[3] taking Notice of it, I will not pretend to be positive; but desire that the Letter may be reprinted, and what is here recovered may be in Italick.

I am, SIR,
Your daily Reader.

To her I very much respect, Mrs. Margaret Clark.

"LOVELY, and oh that I could write loving Mrs. *Margaret Clark*, I pray you let Affection excuse Presumption. Having been so happy as to enjoy the Sight of your sweet Countenance and comely Body, sometimes when I had Occasion to buy Treacle or Liquorish

---

[1] I.e. 1711/12.   [2] See No. 36 (vol. i).
[3] John Speed's *Theatre of the Empire of Great Britain*, with its continuation, *The History of Great Britaine*, was published in 1611, and often reprinted. For Sir Richard Baker's *Chronicle of the Kings of England* (1643) see No. 37 (vol. i). John Selden's *Titles of Honour* appeared in 1614.

Powder at the Apothecary's Shop, I am so enamoured with you, that I can no more keep close my flaming Desire to become your Servant. And I am the more bold now to write to your sweet self, because I am now my own Man, and may match where I please; for my Father is taken away; and now I am come to my Living, which is Ten Yard Land, and a House; and there is never a Yard of Land in our Field but is as well worth ten Pound a Year as a Thief's worth a Halter; and all my Brothers and Sisters are provided for: Besides I have good Houshold-stuff, though I say it, both Brass and Pewter, Linnens and Woollens; and though my House be thatched, yet if you and I match, it shall go hard but I will have one Half of it slated. If you shall think well of this Motion, I will wait upon you as soon as my new Cloaths is made and Hay-Harvest is in. I could, though I say it, have good *Matches in our Town*; *but my Mother,* (*God's Peace be with her*) *charg'd me upon her Death-Bed to marry a Gentlewoman, one who had been well train'd up in Sowing and Cookery. I do not think but that if you and I can agree to marry, and lay our Means together, I shall be made Grand-Jury-man e'er two or three Years come about, and that will be a great Credit to us. If I could have got a Messenger for Sixpence, I wou'd have sent one on purpose, and some Trifle or other for a token of my Love; but I hope there is nothing lost for that neither. So hoping you will take this Letter in good part, and answer it with what care and speed you can, I rest and remain,*

Yours, if my own,

Swepson,[1] *Leistershire.*   Mr. *Gabriel Bullock,*

now my Father is dead.

"When the Coal Carts come, I shall send oftener; and may come in one of them my self."

For Sir William to go to london at westmister remember a parlement.

SIR

"William, i hope that you are well. i write to let you know that i am in troubel about a lady you nease; and I do desire that you will be my frend; for when i did com to see her at your hall, i was mighty Abuesed. i woud fain a see you at topecliff,[2] and thay would not let me go to you; but i desire that you will be our frends, for it is no dishonor neither for you nor she, for God did make us all. i wish that i might see you, for thay say that you are a good man;

---

[1] Swepstone is a village in Leicestershire, five miles north-west of Bosworth.
[2] Topcliff is a village in the North Riding of Yorkshire near Thirsk.

and many doth wounder at it, but madam norton is abuesed and
ceated two i beleive. i might a had many a lady, but i con have none
but her with a good consons, for there is a God that know our harts.
if you and madam norton will come to York, there i shill meet you
if God be willing and if you pleased. so be not angterie till you
know the trutes of things.

I give my to me lady, and to Mr.
Aysenby, and to madam norton.
March the 19th, 1706."

George Nillson.

This is for madam mary norton disforth Lady she went to York.

"MADAM Mary. Deare loving sweet lady, i hope you are well.
Do not go to london, for they will put you in the nunnery;
and heed not Mrs. Lucy what she saith to you, for she will ly and ceat
you. go from to another Place, and we will gate wed so with speed.
mind what I write to you, for if they gate you to london they will
keep you there; and so let us gate wed, and we will both go. so if you
go to london, you rueing your self. so heed not what none of them
saith to you. let us gate wed, and we shall lie to gader any time.
i will do any thing for you to my poore. i hope the devill will faile
them all, for a hellish Company there be. from there cursed trick
and mischeifus ways good lord bless and deliver both you and me.

I think to be at york the 24 day."

This is for madam mary norton to go to london for
a lady that belongs to dishforth.

"MADAM Mary, i hope you are well. i am soary that you went
away from York. deare loving sweet lady, i writt to let you
know that i do remain faithfull; and if can let me know where i can
meet you, i will wed you, and i will do any thing to my poor; for
you are a good woman, and will be a loving Misteris. i am in troubel
for you, so if you will come to york i will wed you. so with speed
come, and i will have none but you. so, sweet love, heed not what
to say to me, and with speed come; heed not what none of them say
to you; your Maid makes you believe ought.

"So deare love think of Mr. george Nillson with speed; i sent you
2 or 3 letters before.

"I gave misteris elcock some nots, and thay put me in pruson
all the night for me pains, and non new whear i was, and i did
gat cold.

"But it is for mrs. Lucy to go a good way from home, for in York and round about she is known; to writ any more her deeds, the same will tell hor soul is back within, hor corkis stinks of hell.

March 19th, 1706."'

T[1]

No. 329   *Tuesday, March 18, 1712*[2]
[ADDISON]

Ire tamen restat Numa quo devenit & Ancus.

Hor.

MY Friend Sir ROGER DE COVERLY told me t'other[a] Night, that he had been reading my Paper upon *Westminster-Abby*,[3] in which, says he, there are a great many Ingenious Fancies. He told me at the same time, that he observed I had promised another Paper upon *the Tombs*, and that he should be glad to go and see them with me, not having visited them since he had read History. I could not at first imagine how this came into the Knight's Head, till I recollected that he had been very busie all last Summer upon *Baker*'s Chronicle,[4] which he has quoted several times in his Disputes with Sir ANDREW FREEPORT since his last coming to Town. Accordingly I promised to call upon him the next Morning, that we might go together to the *Abby*.

I found the Knight under his Butler's Hands, who always shaves him. He was no sooner dressed, than he called for a Glass of the Widow *Trueby*'s Water,[5] which he told me he always drank before he went Abroad. He recommended to me a Dram of it at the same time, with so much heartiness, that I could not forbear drinking it. As soon as I had got it down I found it very unpalatable, upon which

---

[a] t'other] last *Fol.*

[1] For T. Trash's comment on this paper see No. 330.
[2] *Motto.* Horace, *Epistles* 1. 6. 27:

    Thither we must go, where Numa and where Ancus went before.
[3] No. 26 (vol. i).
[4] Cf. No. 37 (vol. i).
[5] Apparently not a well-known water but one made by a Mrs. Trueby in Sir Roger's neighbourhood.

the Knight observing that I had made[a] several wry Faces, told me that he knew I should not like it at first, but that it was the best thing in the World against the Stone or Gravel.

I could have wished indeed that he had acquainted me with the Vertues of it sooner; but it was too late to complain, and I knew what he had done was out of Good-will. Sir ROGER told me further, that he looked upon it to be very good for a Man whilst he staid in Town to keep off Infection, and that he got together a quantity of it upon the first News of the Sickness being at *Dantzick*:[1] When of a sudden turning short to one of his Servants who stood behind him, he bid him call an Hackney-Coach, and take care it was an elderly Man that drove it.

He then resumed his Discourse upon Mrs. *Trueby*'s Water, telling me that the Widow *Trueby* was one who did more Good than all the Doctors and Apothecaries in the County: That she distilled every Poppy that grew within five Miles of her, that she distributed her Water *gratis* among all sorts of People; to which the Knight added, that she had a very great Jointure, and that the whole Country would fain have it a Match between him and her; and truly, says Sir ROGER, if I had not been engaged, perhaps I could not have done better.

His Discourse was broken off by his Man's telling him he had call'd a Coach. Upon our going to it, after having cast his Eye upon the Wheels, he asked the Coachman if his Axle-tree was good; upon the Fellow's telling him he would warrant it, the Knight turned to me, told me he looked like an honest Man, and went in without further Ceremony.

We had not gone far, when Sir ROGER popping out his Head, called the Coachman down from his Box, and upon his presenting himself at the Window, asked him if he Smoaked; as I was considering what this would end in, he bid him stop by the way at any good Tobacconist's, and take in a Roll of their best *Virginia*.[2] Nothing material happened in the remaining part of our Journey, till we were set down at the West end of the *Abby*.

As we went up the Body of the Church, the Knight pointed at

---

[a] had made] made *Fol.*

[1] During the year 1709 Danzig was the scene of a great plague. The *Post-Man* of 14 Jan. 1709/10 reported that about 24,000 persons died of the disease during the year. Other estimates have placed the number as high as 40,000.

[2] 'Right Virginia' tobacco is mentioned in No. 134 (vol. ii).

the Trophies upon one of the new Monuments, and cry'd out A brave Man I warrant him. Passing afterwards by Sir *Cloudsly Shovel*[1] he flung his hand that way, and cry'd Sir *Cloudsly Shovel*! a very gallant Man! As we stood before *Busby*'s Tomb the Knight utter'd himself again after the same manner, Dr. *Busby*, a great Man, he whipp'd my Grandfather, a very great Man. I should have gone to him my self, if I had not been a Blockhead; a very great Man![2]

We were immediately conducted into the little Chappel[3] on the Right Hand. Sir ROGER planting himself at our Historian's Elbow, was very attentive to every thing he said, particularly to the Account he gave us of the Lord, who had cut off the King of *Morocco*'s Head.[4] Among several other Figures, he was very well pleased to see the Statesman *Cecil*[5] upon his Knees, and, concluding them all to be Great Men, was conducted to the Figure which represents that Martyr to good-Housewifery, who dyed by the Prick of a Needle.[6] Upon our Interpreter's telling us, that she was a Maid of Honour to Queen *Elizabeth*, the Knight was very inquisitive into her Name and Family, and after having regarded her Finger for some time,

---

[1] See No. 26 (vol. i).

[2] Dr. Richard Busby, headmaster of Westminster School from 1640 to his death in 1695, is buried in the South Transept. 'His pupils', wrote Tom Brown, 'when they come by, look as pale as his Marble, in remembrance of his severe Execution on their Posteriors' ('A Walk round London and Westminster', *Works*, 3rd ed. 1715, iii. 313).

[3] St. Edmund's Chapel.

[4] This was Sir Bernard Brocas (d. 1395), for whom see *DNB*. The crest represents what is heraldically called 'a Moor's head orientally crowned.' Although he served in the Moorish wars, the story of his cutting off the king's head seems to be only legendary.

[5] William Cecil, Lord Burleigh (1520–98). In his *Historical Memorials of Westminster Abbey* (chap. iv) Dean Stanley comments: 'It shows the degree of superhuman majesty which he had attained in English history, that "Sir Roger de Coverley was very well pleased to see the statesman Cecil on his knees"' (p. 187).

[6] Elizabeth Russell (d. 1601), daughter of John, Lord Russell, second son of the 2nd Earl of Bedford. The monument, which represents her as seated erect in an osier chair on a floridly decorated pedestal, 'has bred one of "the vulgar errors" of Westminster mythology. Her finger pointing to the skull, the emblem of mortality at her feet, had already, within seventy years from her death, led to the legend that she had "died of the prick of a needle," sometimes magnified into a judgment on her for working on Sunday' (Stanley, *Historical Memorials*, chap. iv, p. 185). It was one of the favourite sights in the Abbey. Tom Brown (iii. 314) describes it, and Von Uffenbach, who visited the Abbey on 3 July 1710, notes: 'Among other monuments we found that of Elizabeth, "daughter of John Russel," who, only pricking her finger with a pin, bled to death. She is portrayed holding her finger towards the ground with the blood dripping from it' (p. 92). As early as 1676 Horace Wiseman (*Several Chirurgicall Treatises*, p. 278) reflected that this monument 'may serve to show you that in ill habits of body small wounds are mortall'. In William Burnaby's *Reform'd Wife* (1700) Dr. Safety, who objects to drawing blood from a finger, says, 'I shake when I think of the Lady in *Westminster-Abbey*, that looks so ghastly with her Finger thus—And a drop of Life-blood hanging at the end of it' (II. iv).

I wonder, says he, that Sir *Richard Baker* has said nothing of her in his Chronicle.

We were then conveyed to the two Coronation Chairs,[1] where my old Friend, after having heard that the Stone[2] underneath the most ancient of them, which was brought from *Scotland*, was called *Jacob's Pillow*, sat himself down in the Chair; and looking like the Figure of an old *Gothic* King, asked our Interpreter, What Authority they had to say, that *Jacob* had ever been in *Scotland*? The Fellow, instead of returning him an Answer, told him that he hoped his Honour would pay his Forfeit. I could observe Sir ROGER a little ruffled upon being thus trepanned; but our Guide not insisting upon his Demand, the Knight soon recovered his good Humour, and whispered in my Ear, that if WILL. WIMBLE were with us, and saw those two Chairs, it would go hard but he would get a Tobacco-Stopper out of one or t'other of them.

Sir ROGER, in the next place, laid his Hand upon *Edward* the Third's Sword,[3] and leaning upon the Pummel of it, gave us the whole History of the *Black Prince*; concluding, that in Sir *Richard Baker*'s Opinion,[4] *Edward* the Third was one of the greatest Princes that ever sate upon the *English* Throne.

We were then shewn *Edward* the Confessor's Tomb;[5] upon which Sir ROGER acquainted us, that he was the First who touched for the Evil, and afterwards *Henry* the Fourths;[6] upon which he shook his Head, and told us, there was fine reading in the Casualties of that Reign.

Our Conductor then pointed to that Monument, where there is the Figure of one of our *English* Kings[7] without an Head; and upon

[1] Von Uffenbach also noted these as among the notable sights of the Abbey. 'One is liable to punishment for even sitting on one of these chairs' (p. 93).

[2] The Stone of Scone, brought to England from Scotland by Edward I early in the fourteenth century. 'Here was the Pillar of old *Jacob*, brought to *Scotland* by *Pharaoh's* Daughter' (Tom Brown, *Works*, iii. 314).

[3] 'The sword he used in Battel, is yet to be seen, being eight pound in weight, and seven foot in length' (Baker, *Chronicle*, ed. 1684, p. 133). Von Uffenbach describes it as nine spans long, three fingers wide, and very heavy (p. 93).

[4] Baker's *Chronicle* devotes twenty folio pages to the reign of Edward III, a king 'no less fortunate than valiant' (ed. 1684, p. 133).

[5] Tom Brown describes it as 'the chief piece of Antiquity' and Edward 'the firstRoyal Empirick for Scabs and Scrophulous Humours' (*Works*, iii. 315). Edward the Confessor, who died in 1066, was canonized in 1161. A shrine was prepared for his body in 1163, and later a new shrine was prepared by Henry III; on 13 Oct. 1269 the body was placed here, to the east of the altar.

[6] The tomb of Henry IV is in Canterbury Cathedral. The reference is probably to the tomb of Henry III, which was on the north side of the Confessor's Shrine.

[7] The tomb of Henry V, at the eastern end of the Confessor's Chapel, one of

giving us to know, that the Head, which was of beaten Silver, had been stolen away several Years since: Some Whig, I'll warrant you, says Sir ROGER, You ought to lock up your Kings better. They will carry off the Body too, if you don't take care.

The Glorious Names of *Henry* the Fifth and Queen *Elizabeth*, gave the Knight great Opportunities of shining, and of doing Justice to Sir *Richard Baker*, who, as our Knight observed with some Surprise, had a great many Kings in him, whose Monuments he had not seen in the Abby.

For my own part, I could not but be pleased to see the Knight shew such an honest Passion for the Glory of his Country, and such a respectful Gratitude to the Memory of its Princes.

I must not omit, that the Benevolence of my good old Friend, which flows out towards every one he converses with, made him very kind to our Interpreter, whom he looked upon as an extraordinary Man, for which reason he shook him by the Hand at Parting, telling him, that he should be very glad to see him at his Lodgings in *Norfolk-Buildings*,[1] and talk over these Matters with him more at leasure.   L

No. 330   *Wednesday, March* 19, 1712[2]
[STEELE]

Maxima Debetur pueris reverentia . . .
                                                          Juv.

THE following Letters, written by two very considerate Correspondents, both under twenty Years of Age, are very good Arguments of the Necessity of taking into Consideration the many Incidents which affect the Education of Youth.

---

the most magnificent in the Abbey. The effigy was cut from oak, plated with silver gilt, with a head of solid silver, which was carried off by robbers in the sixteenth century. Cf. Tom Brown: 'There was a Conqueror without a Head; for they were so vile to make that of Silver, and his Body of Brass, so the Thief stole the Head, and left the Trunk unattempted' (*Works*, 1715, iii. 314).

[1] A general term for the houses erected on the old Norfolk palace grounds, which included the streets of Arundel, Norfolk, and Surrey, with the spaces between them. Norfolk Street, Strand, was built *c.* 1682.

[2] *Motto.* Juvenal, *Satires*, 14. 47 (altered):
          Children do our greatest reverence claim.

SIR,

'I HAVE long expected, that in the Course of your Observations upon the several Parts of humane Life, you would one Time or other fall upon a Subject which, since you have not, I take the Liberty to recommend to you. What I mean is the Patronage of young modest Men, to such as are able to countenance and introduce them into the World. For want of such Assistances, a Youth of Merit languishes in Obscurity or Poverty when his[a] Circumstances are low, and runs[b] into Riot and Excess when his[c] Fortunes are plentiful. I cannot make my self better understood, than by sending you an History of my self, which I shall desire you to insert in your Paper, it being the only Way I have of expressing my Gratitude for the highest Obligations imaginable.

'I am the Son of a Merchant of the City of *London,* who, by many Losses was reduced from a very Luxuriant[1] Trade and Credit, to very narrow Circumstances in comparison to that his former abundance. This took away the Vigour of his mind, and all manner of attention to a fortune, which he now thought desperate, insomuch, that he died without a Will, having before buried my Mother in the midst of his other Misfortunes. I was sixteen Years of Age when I lost my Father, and an Estate of 200 *l.* a year came into my Possession, without Friend or Guardian to instruct me in the management or Enjoyment of it. The natural Consequence of this, was, [d](though I wanted no director, and soon had Fellows who found me out for a smart young Gentleman, and led me into all the Debaucheries of which I was capable,)[d] that my[e] Companions and I could not well be supplied without running[f] in Debt, which I did very frankly, till I was arrested and conveyed with a Guard strong enough for the most desperate Assassine to a Bayliff's House, where I lay four days surrounded with very merry, but not very agreeable Company. As soon as I had extricated my self from this shameful Confinement, I reflected upon it with so much Horror, that I deserted all my old Acquaintance, and took Chambers in an Inn of Court, with a resolution to study the Law with all possible Application. But I trifled away a whole year in looking over a thousand intricacies without Friend to apply to in any case of doubt; so that

---

 a his] their *Fol.*   b runs] run *Fol.*   c his] their *Fol.*   d-d *Parenthesis marks added in 8vo, 12mo*   e that my] my *Fol.*   f without running] without my running *Fol.*

1 In the obsolete sense of excessively prosperous.

I only lived there among Men as little Children are sent to School before they are capable of Improvement, only to be out of harm's way. In the midst of this State of Suspense, not knowing how to dispose of my self, I was sought for by a relation of mine, who upon observing a good inclination in me, used me with great Familiarity, and carried me to his Seat in the Country. When I came there he introduced me to all the good Company in the County, and the great Obligation I have to him for this kind notice, and residence with him ever since, has made so strong an impression upon me, that he has an Authority of a Father over me, founded upon the Love of a Brother. I have a good Study of Books, a good Stable of Horses always at my command; and tho' I am not now quite Eighteen Years of Age, familiar Converse on his part, and a strong Inclination to exert my self on mine, have had an effect upon me, that makes me acceptable wherever I go. Thus, Mr. SPECTATOR, by this Gentleman's Favour and Patronage, it is my own Fault if I am not wiser and richer every Day I live. I speak this as well by subscribing the initial Letters of my Name to thank him, as to incite others to an Imitation of his Virtue. It would be a worthy Work to shew what great Charities are to be done without Expence, and how many noble Actions are lost out of Inadvertency in Persons capable of performing them if they were put in Mind of it. If a Gentleman of Figure in a County would make his Family a Pattern of Sobriety, good Sense, and Breeding, and would kindly endeavour to influence the Education and growing Prospects of the younger Gentry about him, I am apt to believe it would save him a great deal of stale Beer on a publick Occasion, and render him the Leader of his Country from their Gratitude to him, instead of being a Slave to their Riots and Tumults in order to be made their Representative. The same thing might be recommended to all who have made any Progress in any Parts of Knowledge, or arrived at any Degree in a Profession; others may gain Preferments and Fortunes from their Patrons, but I have, I hope, received from mine good Habits and Virtues. I repeat to you, Sir, my Request to print this, in return for all the Evil an helpless Orphan shall ever escape, and all the Good he shall receive in this Life; both which are wholly owing to this Gentleman's Favour to,

SIR,

Your most obedient humble Servant,

S. P.'

Mr. SPECTATOR,

'I AM a Lad of about 14. I find a mighty pleasure in Learning. I have been at the *Latin*-Shool 4 Years. I don't know I ever play'd at trouant, or neglected any task my Master[a] set me in my Life. I think on what I read in School as I go home at Noon and Night, and so intently that I have often gone half a mile out of my way, not minding whither I went. Our Maid tells me, she often hears me talk *Latin* in my Sleep. And I dream two or three Nights in the Week I am reading *Juvenal* and *Homer*. My Master seems as well pleased with my performances as any Boy's in the same Class. I think if I know my own mind, I would chuse rather to be a Scholar, than a Prince without Learning. I have a very good[b] affectionate Father, but though very rich, yet so mighty near, that he thinks much of the Charges of my Education. He often tells me, he believes my Schooling will ruin him, that I cost him God knows what in Books. I tremble to tell him I want one. I am forced to keep my Pocket-Money, and lay it out for a Book now and then that he don't know of. He has ordered my Master to buy no more Books for me, but says he will buy them himself. I asked him for *Horace* t'other Day, and he told me in a Passion, he did not believe I was fit for it, but only my Master had a mind to make him think I had got a great way in my Learning. I am sometimes a Month behind other Boys in getting the Books my Master gives orders for. All the Boys in the School but I, have the Classic Authors, *in usum Delphini*,[1] guilt and letter'd on the Back. My Father is often reckoning up how long I have been at School, and tells me he fears I do little good. My Father's carriage so discourages me, that he makes me grow dull and melancholy. My Master wonders what is the matter with me; I am afraid to tell him; for he is a Man that loves to encourage Learning, and would be apt to chide my Father, and not knowing my Father's Temper, may make him worse. Sir, if you have any Love for Learning, I beg you would give me some Instructions in this Case, and perswade Parents to encourage their Children when they find them diligent and desirous of Learning. I have heard

Master] Maker *Fol.*   [b] good] loving *Fol.*

---

[1] The famous series of Latin classics edited in 1674 for the use of the Dauphin, prepared under the supervision of Pierre Daniel Huet, with the assistance of Anne Lefèvre (the future Madame Dacier).

some Parents say, they would do any thing for their Children, if they would but mind their Learning. I would be glad to be in their Place. Dear Sir, pardon my Boldness. If you will but consider and pity my case, I will pray for your prosperity as long as I live.

London, March
2, 1711.

Your Humble Servant,
James Discipulus.'ᵃ1

ᵃ Mr. SPECTATOR, *March the* 18*th.*
'THE Ostentation you shew'd Yesterday wou'd have been pardonable, had you provided better for the two Extremities of your Paper, and plac'd in one the Letter R, in the other *Nescio quid meditans nugarum; & totus in illis.*² A Word to the Wise.

I am your most humble Servant,
T. Trash.'

According to the Emendation of the above Correspondent, the Reader is desired in the Paper of the 17th to read R for T. *Fol.* T

---

¹ A letter from Nobilis Junius (Lillie, ii. 40–44) refers to the motto of this paper. 'There is a general neglect of good management in publick schools, and there is no care taken at home, to insinuate the social and useful virtues into the minds of children, and to preserve modesty in youth. . . . I went the other day to see a neighbour of mine, and from his carriage . . . I learned the true meaning of your lemma, *summa debetur pueris reverentia*' (p. 41).
² Horace, *Satires,* 1. 9. 2 (musing after my fashion on I know not what trifle, and wholly occupied thereon).

No. 331

[BUDGELL]

Thursday, March 20, 1712³

. . . Stolidam præbet tibi vellere barbam.

Pers.

WHEN I was last with my Friend Sir ROGER in *Westminster-Abby,* I observed that he stood longer than ordinary before the Bust of a Venerable old Man. I was at a loss to guess the Reason of it, when after some time he pointed to the Figure, and asked me if I did not think that our Forefathers looked much wiser in their Beards than we do without them? For my part, says he, when I am walking in my Gallery in the Country, and see my Ancestors, who many of them died before they were of my Age, I cannot forbear

³ *Motto.* Persius, *Satires,* 2. 28:
And to your hold a bushy Beard presents.

regarding them as so many old Patriarchs, and at the same time looking upon my self as an idle Smock-faced young Fellow. I love to see your *Abrahams*, your *Isaacs* and your *Jacobs*, as we have them in old Pieces of Tapestry, with Beards below their Girdles, that cover half the Hangings. The Knight added, if[a] I would recommend Beards in one of my Papers, and endeavour to restore Human Faces to their Ancient Dignity, that upon a Month's warning he would undertake to lead up the Fashion himself in a pair of Whiskers.

I smiled at my Friend's Fancy; but after we parted could not forbear reflecting on the Metamorphoses our Faces have undergone in this Particular.

The Beard, conformable to the Notion of my Friend, Sir ROGER, was for many Ages looked upon as the Type of Wisdom. *Lucian* more than once rallies the Philosophers of his Time who endeavoured to rival one another in Beard; and represents a learned Man who stood for a Professorship in Philosophy as unqualified for it by the Shortness of his Beard.[1]

Ælian in his Account of *Zoilus*, the pretended Critick, who wrote against *Homer* and *Plato*, and thought himself wiser than all who had gone before him, tells us that this *Zoilus* had a very long Beard that hung down upon his Breast, but no Hair upon his Head, which he always kept close shaved; regarding, it seems, the Hairs of his Head as so many Suckers, which if they had been suffered to grow, might have drawn away the Nourishment from his Chin, and by that means have starved his Beard.[2]

I have read somewhere that one of the Popes refused to accept an Edition of a Saint's Works, which were presented to him, because the Saint, in his Effigies before the Book, was drawn without a Beard.[3]

We see by these Instances what Homage the World has formerly paid to Beards; and that a Barber was not then allowed to make

---

[a] added, if] added, that if *Fol.*

[1] 'The Eunuch' (*Works*, 1711, iii. 6–7).

Budgell is indebted here to Boileau's 'Critical Reflections on Longinus', section v. Boileau quotes from book xi of Aelian's *Divers Histories*: '*Zoilus*, he who wrote against *Homer*, *Plato*, and several other Illustrious Persons, was a Native of *Amphipolis*. . . . He had a long Beard that hung down upon his Breast but no Hair upon his Head, which he always kept close Shav'd . . .' (Boileau, *Works*, ii (London, 1711), p. 105. The *Variae Historiae* (in Greek) of Claudius Aelianus date from the second century.

[3] I have not identified this.

those Depredations on the Faces of the Learned, which have been permitted him of later Years.

Accordingly several wise Nations have been so extreamly Jealous of the least Ruffle offered to their Beards, that they seem to have fix'd the Point of Honour principally in that part. The *Spaniards* were wonderfully tender in this Particular. *Don Quevedo*, in his third Vision on the last Judgment, has carried the Humour very far, when he tells us that one of his vain-glorious Countrymen, after having received Sentence, was taken into Custody by a couple of Evil Spirits; but that his Guides happening to disorder his Musta-choes, they were forced to recompose them with a pair of Curling-Irons before they could get him to file off.[1]

If we look into the History of our own Nation, we shall find that the Beard flourished in the *Saxon* Heptarchy, but was very much discouraged under the *Norman* Line. It shot out, however, from time to time in several Reigns, under different Shapes. The last Effort it made seems to have been in Queen *Mary*'s Days, as the curious Reader may find, if he pleases to peruse the Figures of Cardinal *Poole* and Bishop *Gardiner*; tho' at the same time, I think, it may be questioned, if Zeal against Popery has not induced our Protestant Painters, to extend the Beards of these two Persecutors beyond their natural Dimensions, in order to make them appear the more terrible.

I find but few Beards, worth taking notice of, in the Reign of King *James* the First.

During the Civil Wars there appeared one, which makes too great a Figure in Story to be passed over in Silence; I mean that of the redoubted *Hudibras*, an Account of which *Butler* has transmitted to Posterity in the following Lines.

> *His tawny Beard was th' equal Grace,*
> *Both of his Wisdom, and his Face.*
> *In Cut and Dye so like a Tyle,*
> *A sudden View it would beguile.*
> *The upper Part thereof was Whey,*
> *The nether Orange mixt with Grey.*[2]

The Whisker continued for some time among us, after the

---

[1] See *The Visions of Dom Francisco de Quevedo Villegas*, trans. L'Estrange (9th ed., 1702), p. 88.
[2] *Hudibras*, I. i. 239–44.

Extirpation of Beards; but this is a Subject which I shall not here enter upon, having discussed it at large in a distinct Treatise, which I keep by me in Manuscript upon the *Mustachoe.*

If my Friend Sir ROGER's Project, of introducing Beards, should take Effect, I fear the Luxury of the present Age would make it a very expensive Fashion. There is no question but the Beaux would soon provide themselves with false ones of the lightest Colours, and the most immoderate Lengths. A fair Beard, of the Tapestry-Size Sir ROGER seems to approve, could not come under Twenty Guineas. The Famous Golden Beard of *Esculapius*[1] would hardly be more Valuable, than one made in the Extravagance of the Fashion.

Besides, we are not certain that the Ladies would not come into the Mode, when they take the Air on Horse-back. They already appear in Hats and Feathers,[2] Coats and Perriwigs; and I see no Reason, why we may not suppose that they would have their *riding Beards* on the same Occasion.

I may give the Moral of this Discourse in another Paper.

X

No. 332
[STEELE]

Friday, March 21, 1712[3]

> . . . *Minus aptus acutis*
> *Naribus horum hominum* . . .
> Hor.

Dear Short-Face,
'IN your Speculation of *Wednesday* last,[4] you have given us some Account of that worthy Society of Brutes the *Mohocks*; wherein you have particularly specified the ingenious Performances of the Lion-Tippers, the Dancing-Masters, and the Tumblers: But as you

---

[1] Cicero, *De natura deorum,* 3. 34. 83.   [2] Cf. No. 104 (vol. i).
[3] *Motto.* Horace, *Satires,* I. 3. 29–30:
　　　　　He cannot bear the Raillery of the Age. CREECH.
This had also been used as the motto of No. 268 (vol. ii).
[4] No. 324.

acknowledge you had not then a perfect History of the whole Club, you might very easily omit one of the most notable Species of it, the Sweaters,[1] which may be reckon'd a sort of Dancing-Masters too. It is, it seems, the Custom for Half a Dozen, or more, of these well-disposed Savages, as soon as they have inclosed the Person upon whom they design the Favour of a Sweat, to whip out their Swords, and holding them parallel to the Horizon, they describe a sort of Magick Circle round him with the Points. As soon as this Piece of Conjuration is perform'd, and the Patient without Doubt already beginning to wax warm, to forward the Operation, that Member of the Circle towards whom he is so rude as to turn his Back first, runs his Sword directly into that Part of the Patient wherein School-boys are punished; and, as it is very natural to imagine, this will soon make him tack about to some other Point, every Gentleman does himself the same Justice as often as he receives the Affront. After this Gig has gone two or three times round, and the Patient is thought to have sweat sufficient, he is very handsomly rubb'd down by some Attendants, who carry with them Instruments for that Purpose, and so discharged. This Relation I had from a Friend of mine, who has lately been under this Discipline. He tells me he had the Honour to dance before the Emperor himself, not without the Applause and Acclamations both of his Imperial Majesty and the whole Ring; tho', I dare say, neither I or any of his Acquaintance ever dreamt he wou'd have merited any Reputation by his Activity.

'I can assure you, Mr. SPEC. I was very near being qualified to have given you a faithful and painful Account of this walking Bagnio, if I may so call it, my self: For going the other Night along *Fleet-street*, and having, out of Curiosity, just enter'd into Discourse with a wandering Female who was travelling the same Way, a Couple of Fellows advanced towards us, drew their Swords, and cry'd out to each other, A Sweat! a Sweat! Whereupon, suspecting they were some of the Ringleaders of the Bagnio, I also drew my Sword, and demanded a Parly; but finding none wou'd be granted me, and perceiving others behind them filing off with great Diligence to take me in Flank, I began to sweat for fear of being forced to it; but very luckily betaking my self to a Pair of Heels, which I had

---

[1] 'One of a set of street ruffians in the eighteenth century, who threatened or attacked people so as to make them sweat' (*OED*). This is the earliest example of the word in *OED*.

good Reason to believe wou'd do me Justice, I instantly got Possession of a very snug Corner in a neighbouring Alley that lay in my
Rear; which Post I maintained for above Half an Hour with great
Firmness and Resolution, tho' not letting this Success so far overcome me, as to make me unmindful of the Circumspection that was
necessary to be observed upon my advancing again toward the
Street; by which Prudence and good Management I made a handsome and orderly Retreat, having suffer'd no other Damage in this
Action than the Loss of my Baggage, and the Dislocation of one of
my Shooe-heels, which last I am just now inform'd is in a fair way
of Recovery. These Sweaters, by what I can learn from my Friend,
and by as near a View as I was able to take of them my self, seem to
me to have at present but a rude kind of Discipline amongst them.
It is probable, if you wou'd take a little Pains with them, they
might be brought into better Order. But I'll leave this to your own
Discretion; and will only add, that if you think it worth while to
insert this by way of Caution to those who have a Mind to preserve
their Skins whole from this sort of Cupping, and tell them at the
same Time the Hazard of treating with Night-Walkers,[1] you will
perhaps oblige others, as well as

Your very humble Servant,
Jack Lightfoot.

'*P.S.* My Friend will have me acquaint you, That tho' he wou'd not
willingly detract from the Merit of that extraordinary Strokes-Man
Mr. *Sprightly*,[2] yet it is his real Opinion, that some of these Fellows
who are employ'd as Rubbers to this new-fashion'd Bagnio, have
struck as bold Strokes as ever he did in his Life.

'I had sent this four and twenty Hours sooner, if I had not had the
Misfortune of being in a great Doubt about the Orthography of the
Word Bagnio. I consulted several Dictionaries, but found no Relief;
at last having Recourse both to the Bagnio in *Newgate-street* and to
that in *Chancery-lane*,[3] and finding the original Manuscripts upon

---

[1] Cf. No. 8 (vol. i).
[2] See No. 319.
[3] Hatton (pp. 784–98) lists six: the Royal Bagnio in Newgate Street, Hummums
in Covent Garden, Queen's in Long Acre, one in Chancery Lane, Pierault's in St.
James's Street, and Castle-Yard Bagnio (called Trimnels) in Castle-Yard. The Royal
Bagnio is 'a very spacious and commodious place', said to be 'the only true Bagnio
built after the *Turkish* Model', and was opened in 1679 (p. 797). 'The Charge of the
House for Sweating, Rubbing, Shaving, Cupping and Bathing is 4s. each Person.
There are 9 Servants who attend' (ibid.).

the Sign-Posts of each to agree literally with my own Spelling, I returned home full of Satisfaction in order to dispatch this Epistle.'

Mr. SPECTATOR,

'AS you have taken most of the Circumstances of humane Life into your Consideration, we, the under-written, thought it not improper for us also to represent to you our Condition. We are three Ladies who live in the Country, and the greatest Improvements we make is by reading. We have taken a small Journal of our Lives, and find it extremely opposite to your last *Tuesday*'s Speculation.[1] We rise by seven, and pass the Beginning of each Day in Devotion and looking into those Affairs that fall within the Occurrences of a retired Life; in the Afternoon, we sometimes enjoy the good Company of some Friend or Neighbour, or else work or read; at Night, we retire to our Chambers, and take Leave of each other for the whole Night at Ten of Clock. We take particular Care never to be sick of a *Sunday*. Mr. SPECTATOR, We are all very good Maids; but are ambitious of Characters which we think more laudable, that of being very good Wives. If any of your Correspondents enquire for a Spouse for an honest Country Gentleman, whose Estate is not dipped,[2] and wants a Wife that can save half his Revenue, and yet make a better Figure than any of his Neighbours of the same Estate with finer bred Women, you shall have further Notice from,

SIR,

Your courteous Readers,

Martha Busie,
Deborah Thrifty,
Alice Early.'

T[a]

[a]*ADVERTISEMENTS.*

The Boarding-School[3] *for young Gentlewomen, which was formerly kept on* Mile-End Green, *being laid down, there is now one set up almost opposite to it at the two Golden-Balls, and much more convenient in every Respect; where, beside the common Instructions given to young Gentlewomen, they will be taught the whole Art of Paistrey and Preserving, with whatever may render them accomplished.* Fol.

---

[1] No. 323.
[2] A colloquial term for 'involved in debt, mortgaged' (*OED*).
[3] See No. 314.

. . . *vocat in Certamina Divos.*
Virg.

WE are now entering upon the Sixth Book of *Paradise Lost*, in which the Poet describes the Battel of Angels; having raised his Reader's Expectation, and prepared him for it by several Passages in the preceding Books. I omitted quoting these Passages in my Observations on the former Books, having purposely reserved them for the opening of this, the Subject of which gave occasion to them. The Author's Imagination was so inflamed with this great Scene of Action, that where-ever he speaks of it, he rises, if possible, above himself. Thus where he mentions Satan in the beginning of his Poem,

> . . . *Him the Almighty power*
> *Hurl'd headlong flameing from th' Ethereal Skie,*
> *With hideous ruin and combustion down*
> *To bottomless perdition, there to dwell*
> *In Adamantine Chains and penal fire,*
> *Who durst defie th' Omnipotent to Arms.*[2]

We have likewise several noble Hints of it in the Infernal Conference.

> *O Prince, O Chief of many throned Powers*
> *That led th' imbattel'd Seraphim to War,*
> *Too well I see and rue the dire event,*
> *That with sad overthrow and foul defeat*
> *Hath lost us Heav'n, and all this mighty host*
> *In horrible destruction laid thus low.*
> *But see the angry victor hath recall'd*
> *His Ministers of Vengeance and pursuit*
> *Back to the Gates of Heav'n: The Sulphurous hail*
> *Shot after us in Storm, o'erblown hath laid*
> *The fiery Surge, that from the precipice*
> *Of Heav'n receiv'd us falling, and the thunder*
> *Wing'd with red lightning and impetuous rage,*

---

[1] *Motto.* Virgil, *Aeneid*, 6. 172:
    And to Contention calls the Gods.

[2] *PL*, i. 44–49.

Perhaps hath spent his Shafts, and ceases now
To bellow through the vast and boundless deep.[1]

There are several other very Sublime Images on the same Subject in the First Book, as also in the Second.

What when we fled amain, pursu'd and strook
With Heav'ns afflicting Thunder, and besought
The deep to shelter us; this Hell then seem'd
A refuge from those wounds . . .[2]

In short, the Poet never mentions any thing of this Battel but in such Images of Greatness and Terrour, as are suitable to the Subject. Among several others, I cannot forbear quoting that Passage where the Power, who is describ'd as presiding over the Chaos, speaks in the Third Book.[3]

Thus Satan; and him thus the Anarch old
With faultring speech and visage incompos'd
Answer'd. I know thee, stranger, who thou art,
That mighty leading Angel, who of late
Made head against Heav'ns King, though overthrown.
I saw and heard, for such a numerous host
Fled not in Silence through the frighted deep
With ruin upon ruin, rout on rout,
Confusion worse confounded; and Heav'n Gates
Pour'd out by Millions her victorious bands
Pursuing. . . .[4]

It required great Pregnancy of Invention, and Strength of Imagination, to fill this Battel with such Circumstances as should raise and astonish the Mind of the Reader; and, at the same time, an exactness of Judgment to avoid every thing that might appear light or trivial. Those, who look into *Homer*, are surprised to find his Battels still rising one above another, and improving in Horrour, to the Conclusion of the *Iliad*. *Milton's* Fight of Angels is wrought up with the same Beauty. It is ushered in with such Signs of Wrath as are suitable to Omnipotence incensed.[5] The First Engagement is carried on under a Cope of Fire, occasion'd by the Flights of innumerable burning Darts and Arrows, which are discharged from either Host.[6]

[1] *PL*, i. 128–9, 134–7, 169–77.
[3] Actually Book II.
[5] *PL*, vi. 56–60.

[2] *PL*, ii. 165–8.
[4] *PL*, ii. 988–98.
[6] *PL*, vi. 212–17.

The Second Onset is still more terrible, as it is filled with those artificial Thunders, which seem to make the Victory doubtful, and produce a kind of Consternation, even in the Good Angels.[1] This is followed by the tearing up of Mountains and Promontories;[2] till, in the last place, *Messiah*[a] comes forth in the fulness of Majesty and Terrour. The Pomp of his Appearance, amidst the Roarings of his Thunders, the Flashes of his Lightnings, and the Noise of his Chariot Wheels, is described with the utmost Flights of Human Imagination.[3]

There is nothing in the first and last Days Engagement, which does not appear natural and agreeable enough to the Ideas most Readers would conceive of a Fight between two Armies of Angels.

The Second Day's Engagement is apt to startle an Imagination, which has not been raised and qualified for such a Description, by the reading of the Ancient Poets, and of *Homer* in particular. It was certainly a very bold Thought in our Author, to ascribe the first use of Artillery to the Rebel Angels. But as such a pernicious Invention may be well supposed to have proceeded from such Authors, so it enters[b] very properly into the Thoughts of that Being, who is all along described as aspiring to the Majesty of his Maker. Such Engines were the only Instruments he could have made use of to imitate those Thunders, that in all Poetry, both Sacred and Prophane, are represented as the Arms of the Almighty. The tearing up the[c] Hills was not altogether so daring a Thought as the former. We are, in some measure, prepared for such an Incident by the Description of the Gyants War, which we meet with among the Ancient Poets. What still made this Circumstance the more proper for the Poets use, is the Opinion of many Learned Men, that the Fable of the Gyants War, which makes so great a Noise in Antiquity, and gave Birth to the sublimest Description in *Hesiod's* Works,[d] was[e] an Allegory founded upon this very Tradition of a Fight between the good and bad Angels.[4]

It may, perhaps, be worth while to consider with what Judgment *Milton*, in this Narration, has avoided every thing that is mean and trivial in the Descriptions of the *Latin* and *Greek* Poets; and, at the

---

^a *Messiah*] 19; the Messiah *Fol., 8vo, 12mo*   ^b enters] entered *all edd. Corrected in Folio Errata (No. 369): 'for* entered *read* enters.'   ^c the] *8vo,* 19; of the *Fol., 12mo*   ^d and gave . . . Works,] *om. Fol.*   ^e was] is *Fol.*

¹ *PL,* vi. 582–90.   ² *PL,* vi. 639–69.   ³ *PL,* vi. 749–72.
⁴ *Theogony,* 664–745. In Winterton, pp. 97–101.

same time, improved every great Hint which he met with in their Works upon this Subject. *Homer*[1] in that Passage, which *Longinus* has celebrated for its Sublimeness,[2] and which *Virgil* and *Ovid* have copied after him, tells us, that the Gyants threw *Ossa* upon *Olympus*, and *Pelion* upon *Ossa*. He adds an Epithete to *Pelion*, (εἰνοσίφυλλον) which very much swells the Idea, by bringing up to the Reader's Imagination all the Woods that grew upon it. There is further a great Beauty in his singling out by Name these three remarkable Mountains so well known to the *Greeks*.[3] This last is such a Beauty as the Scene of *Milton*'s War could not possibly furnish him with. *Claudian* in his Fragment upon the Gyants War, has given full Scope to that wildness of Imagination which was natural to him. He tells us, that the Gyants tore up whole Islands by the Roots, and threw them at the Gods. He describes one of them in particular taking up *Lemnos* in his Arms, and whirling it to the Skies, with all *Vulcan*'s Shop in the midst of it. Another tears up Mount *Ida*, with the River *Enipeus* which ran down the sides of it; but the Poet, not content to describe him with this Mountain upon his Shoulders, tells us that the River flowed down his Back, as he held it up in that Posture.[4] It is visible to every judicious Reader, that such Ideas savour more of Burlesque[a] than of the Sublime. They proceed from a Wantonness of Imagination, and rather divert the Mind than astonish it. *Milton* has taken every thing that is Sublime in these several Passages, and composes out of them the following great Image.

> *From their Foundations loosning to and fro*
> *They pluck'd the seated Hills with all their load,*
> *Rocks, Waters, Woods, and by the shaggy tops*
> *Up-lifting bore them in their Hands: . . .*[5]

We have the full Majesty of *Homer* in this short Description, improved by the Imagination of *Claudian*, without its Puerilities.

[a] of Burlesque] of the Burlesque *Fol.*

[1] *Odyssey*, II. 315–16.
[2] *On the Sublime*, 8. 2 (Boileau's translation, chap. vi).
[3] Addison makes this point also in the *Discourse on Ancient and Modern Learning*: the habitations of the ancients 'lay among the Scenes of the *Æneid*; they cou'd find out their own Country in *Homer*, and had every Day perhaps in their Sight the Mountain or Field where such an Adventure happen'd, or such a Battle was fought' (Guthkelch, ii. 455).
[4] Claudian, *Gigantomachia*, 62–91. In Nos. 279 (vol. ii) and 285 Claudian is mentioned in illustration of the false sublime.
[5] *PL*, vi. 643–6.

I need not point out the Description of the fallen Angels, seeing the Promontories hanging over their Heads in such a dreadful manner, with the other numberless Beauties in this Book, which are so conspicuous, that they cannot escape the Notice of the most ordinary Reader.

There are indeed so many wonderful stroaks of Poetry in this Book, and such a variety of Sublime Ideas, that it would have been impossible to have given them a place within the bounds of this Paper. Besides that, I find it in a great measure done to my Hand, at the end of my Lord *Roscommon*'s Essay on Translated Poetry.[1] I shall refer my Reader thither for some of the Master-Stroaks in the Sixth Book of *Paradise Lost*, tho' at the same time there are many others which that noble Author has not taken notice of.

Milton, notwithstanding the Sublime Genius he was Master of, has in this Book drawn to his Assistance all the helps he could meet with among the Ancient Poets. The Sword of *Michael*, which makes so great an havock among the bad Angels, was given him, we are told, out of the Armory of God.

> *. . . But the Sword*
> *Of* Michael *from the Armory of God*
> *Was giv'n him temper'd so, that neither keen*
> *Nor solid might resist that edge: it met*
> *The Sword of* Satan *with steep force to smite*
> *Descending, and in half cut sheere . . .*[2]

This Passage is a Copy of that in *Virgil*, wherein the Poet tells us, that the Sword of *Æneas*, which was given him by a Deity, broke into pieces the Sword of *Turnus*, which came from a Mortal Forge:[3] As the Moral in this place is Divine, so by the way we may observe, that the bestowing on a Man who is favour'd by Heaven such an Allegorical Weapon, is very conformable to the old Eastern way of Thinking. Not only *Homer* has made use of it, but we find the *Jewish* Hero in the Book of *Maccabees*,[4] who had fought the Battels of the chosen People with so much Glory and Success, receiving in his

---

[1] Near the end of the Earl of Roscommon's *Essay on Translated Verse* (1684) is a passage of 27 lines added to the 2nd edition (1685) headed in the margin, 'An Essay on blanc verse out of the 6th Book of *Paradise Lost*' (for text see Spingarn, ii. 308–9).
[2] *PL*, vi. 320–5.
[3] *Aeneid*, 12. 728–41. It is the armour of Aeneas, not his sword, which shatters the weapon of Turnus.
[4] 2 Macc. 15.15

Dream a Sword from the hand of the Prophet *Jeremiah*.[a] The following Passage, wherein *Satan* is described as wounded by the Sword of *Michael*, is in imitation of *Homer*.

> *The griding Sword with discontinuous wound*
> *Pass'd through him, but th' Ethereal substance closed*
> *Not long divisible, and from the gash*
> *A stream of Nectarous humour issuing flow'd*
> *Sanguin, such as celestial Spirits may bleed,*
> *And all his Armour stain'd . . .*[1]

Homer tells us in the same manner, that upon *Diomedes* wounding the Gods, there flow'd from the Wound an *Ichor*, or pure kind of Blood, which was not bred from Mortal Viands; and that tho' the Pain was exquisitely great, the Wound soon closed up and healed in those Beings who are vested with Immortality.[2]

I question not but *Milton* in his Description of his furious *Moloch*[3] flying from the Battel, and bellowing with the Wound he had receiv'd, had his Eye on[b] *Mars* in the *Iliad*, who upon his being wounded, is represented as retiring out of the Fight, and making an Outcry louder than that of a whole Army when it begins the Charge.[4] *Homer* adds, that the *Greeks* and *Trojans*, who were engaged in a general Battel, were terrified on each side with the bellowing of this wounded Deity. The Reader will easily observe how *Milton* has kept all the horrour of this Image without running into the Ridicule of it.

> *. . . Where the might of* Gabriel *fought,*
> *And with fierce Ensigns pierc'd the deep array*
> *Of Moloc furious King, who him defy'd,*
> *And at his Chariot wheels to drag him bound*
> *Threaten'd, nor from the Holy One of Heav'n*
> *Refrain'd his tongue blasphemous; but anon*
> *Down clov'n to the waste, with shatter'd Arms*
> *And uncouth pain fled bellowing. . . .*[5]

Milton has likewise rais'd his Description in this Book with many Images taken out of the Poetical Parts of Scripture. The Messiah's Chariot, as I have before taken notice, is form'd upon a Vision of

---

[a] *Jeremiah*.] *Jeremy. Fol.*   [b] on] upon *Fol.*

---

[1] PL, vi. 329–34.   [2] *Iliad*, 5. 334–42.   [3] PL, vi. 360–2.
[4] *Iliad*, 5. 855–63.   [5] PL, vi. 355–62.

Ezekiel,[1] who, as *Grotius*[2] observes, has very much in him of *Homer*'s Spirit in the Poetical Parts of his Prophecy.

The following Lines in that glorious Commission which is given the Messiah to extirpate the Host of Rebel Angels, is drawn from a Sublime Passage in the Psalms.[3]

> *Go then thou mightiest in thy Father's might*
> *Ascend my Chariot, guide the rapid wheels*
> *That shake Heav'ns basis, bring forth all my War*
> *My Bow, my thunder, my almighty arms,*
> *Gird on thy sword on thy puissant thigh.*[4]

The Reader will easily discover many other Stroaks of the same nature.

There is no question but *Milton* had heated his Imagination with the Fight of the Gods in *Homer*, before he entered upon this Engagement of the Angels. *Homer* there gives us a Scene of Men, Heroes and Gods mixed together in Battel. *Mars* animates the contending Armies, and lifts up his Voice in such a manner, that it is heard distinctly amidst all the Shouts and Confusion of the Fight.[5] *Jupiter* at the same time Thunders over their Heads; while *Neptune* raises such a Tempest, that the whole Field of Battel, and all the tops of the Mountains shake about them. The Poet tells us, that *Pluto* himself, whose Habitation was in the very Center of the Earth, was so afrighted at the shock, that he leapt from his Throne. *Homer* afterwards describes *Vulcan* as pouring down a Storm of Fire upon the River *Xanthus*, and *Minerva* as throwing a Rock at *Mars*; who, he tells us, covered seven Acres in his Fall.[6]

As *Homer* has introduced into his Battel of the Gods every thing that is great and terrible in Nature, *Milton* has filled his Fight of Good and Bad Angels with all the like Circumstances of Horrour. The Shout of Armies, the Rattling of Brazen Chariots, the Hurling of Rocks and Mountains, the Earthquake,[a] the Fire, the Thunder, are all of them employed to lift up the Reader's Imagination, and give him a suitable Idea of so great an Action. With what Art has

---

[a] Earthquake,] Earthquakes, *Fol.*

[1] Ezek., i. 19 ff.   [2] I have not identified this.   [3] Ps. xlv. 3.
[4] *PL*, vi. 710–14. In Milton the last two lines read:
    My Bow and Thunder, my Almightie Arms
    Gird on, and Sword upon thy puissant Thigh.
[5] *Iliad*, 20. 51–66.   [6] *Iliad*, 21. 328–82, 403–14 ('seven roods').

the Poet represented the whole Body of the Earth trembling, even before it was created.

> *All Heaven resounded, and had Earth been then*
> *All Earth had to its Center shook . . .*[1]

In how sublime and just a manner does he afterwards describe the whole Heaven shaking under the Wheels of the Messiah's Chariot, with that Exception to the Throne of God?

> *. . . Under his burning Wheels*
> *The steadfast* Empyrean *shook throughout,*
> *All but the Throne it self of God . . .*[2]

Notwithstanding the Messiah appears cloathed with so much Terrour and Majesty, the Poet has still found means to make his Readers conceive an Idea of him, beyond what he himself was able to describe.

> *Yet half his strength he put not forth, but checkt*
> *His thunder in mid volly, for he meant*
> *Not to destroy, but root them out of Heaven.*[3]

In a word, *Milton*'s Genius which was so great in it self, and so strengthened by all the helps of Learning, appears in this Book every way Equal to his Subject, which was the most Sublime that could enter into the Thoughts of a Poet. [a]As he knew all the Arts of Affecting the Mind, he knew it was necessary to give it certain Resting-places and Opportunities of recovering it self from Time to Time: He has therefore with great Address interspersed several Speeches, Reflections, Similitudes, and the like Reliefs, to diversifie his Narration, and ease the Attention of the Reader, that he might come fresh to his great Action; and by such a Contrast of Ideas, have a more lively Taste of the nobler Parts of his Description.[a]

L

[a-a] As . . . Description.] As he knew all the Arts of affecting the Mind, had he not given it certain resting places and Opportunities of recovering it self from time to time: He has with great Address interspersed several Speeches, Reflections, Similitudes, and the like Reliefs to diversifie his Narration, and ease the Attention of his Reader, that he might come fresh to his great Action, and by such a Contrast of

---

[1] *PL*, vi. 217–19:

> all Heav'n
> Resounded, and had Earth bin then, all Earth
> Had to her Center shook.

[2] *PL*, vi. 832–4.   [3] *PL*, vi. 853–5.

*. . . Voluisti, in suo Genere, unumquemque nostrum quasi
quendam esse Roscium, dixistique non tam ea quæ recta
essent probari, quam quæ prava sunt fastidiis adhærescere.*
Cicero de Gestu.

IT is very natural to take for our whole Lives a light Impression
of a thing which at first fell into Contempt with us for want of
Consideration. The real Use of a certain Qualification (which the
wiser part of Mankind look upon as at best an indifferent thing, and
generally a frivolous Circumstance) shews the ill Consequence of
such Prepossessions. What I mean is the Art, Skill, Accomplishment,
or whatever you will call it, of Dancing. I knew a Gentleman of
great Abilities, who bewailed the Want of this part of his Education
to the End of a very honourable Life. He observed that there was not
occasion for the common Use of great Talents; that they are but
seldom in Demand; and that these very great Talents were often
rendered useless to a Man for want of small Attainments. A good
Mein (a becoming Motion, Gesture and Aspect) is natural to some
Men; but even these would be highly more graceful in their Carriage,
if what they do from the Force of Nature were confirmed and
heighten'd from the Force of Reason. To one who has not at all
considered it, to mention the Force of Reason on a Subject, will
appear fantastical; but when you have a little attended to it, an
Assembly of Men will have quite another View; and they will tell
you, it is evident from plain and infallible Rules, why this Man
with those beautiful Features, and well-fashioned Person, is not so
agreeable as he who sits by him without any of those Advantages.
When we read we do it without any exerted Act of Memory that
presents the Shape of the Letters; but Habit makes us do it

Ideas, have a more lively taste of the nobler parts of his Description. *Fol. Corrected in
Errata (No. 369) to read*: As he knew all the Arts of affecting the Mind, he has given
it certain resting places and Opportunities of recovering it self from time to time:
several Speeches, Reflections, Similitudes, and the like Reliefs being interspersed to
diversifie his Narration, and ease the Attention of his Reader.

---

[1] *Motto.* Cicero, *De Oratore*, 1. 61. 258 (altered): You would recommend each of
us, in his way, as a second Roscius, and take notice not only of those Excellencies
which deserve Praise, but ascribe ev'n that which deserves Censure to an agreeable
Pride.

mechanically without staying, like Children, to recollect and join those Letters. A Man who has not had the Regard of his Gesture in any part of his Education, will find himself unable to act with Freedom before new Company, as a Child that is but now learning would be to read without Hesitation. It is for the Advancement of the Pleasure we receive in being agreeable to each other in ordinary Life, that one would wish Dancing were generally understood as conducive as it really is to a proper Deportment in Matters that appear the most remote from it.[1] A Man of Learning and Sense is distinguished from others as he is such, tho' he never runs upon Points too difficult for the rest of the World; in like Manner the reaching out of the Arm, and the most ordinary Motion, discovers whether a Man ever learnt to know what is the true Harmony and Composure of his Limbs and Countenance. Whoever has seen *Booth* in the Character of *Pyrrhus*[2] march to his Throne to receive *Orestes*, is convinced that majestick and great Conceptions are expressed in the very Step; but perhaps, tho' no other Man could perform that Incident as well as he does, he himself would do it with a yet greater Elevation were he a Dancer. This is so dangerous a Subject to treat with Gravity, that I shall not at present enter into it any further: But the Author of the following Letter[3] has treated it in the Essay he speaks of in such a Manner, that I am beholden to him for a Resolution, that I will never hereafter think meanly of any thing, till I have heard what they who have another Opinion of it have to say in its Defence.

Mr. SPECTATOR,

'SINCE there are scarce any of the Arts or Sciences that have not been recommended to the World by the Pens of some of the

[1] Cf. Pope, *Essay on Criticism*, 363: 'As those move easiest who have learned to dance.'

[2] In Philips's *Distrest Mother*, referred to in the next paper. It had first been given on the preceding Monday, 17 Mar. The scene referred to here is Act I, scene ii. Barton Booth (1681–1733) had been 'kept in the background by Wilks, who perpetually subordinated him to Mills, an actor in every way his inferior' (*DNB*); apart from the title roles in *Othello* and *Oroonoko* he had recently had such relatively minor parts as the Ghost in *Hamlet*, Hotspur in *Henry the Fourth*, and Guyomar in *The Indian Emperor*. In 1713 he was to achieve a great success in the title role of Addison's *Cato*.

[3] This is almost certainly John Weaver, whose *Essay towards an History of Dancing* was published a few months later, on 11 Sept. (advertisement in No. 481). The quotation from Macrobius is not in the book which, however, does quote (pp. 151–5) from Macrobius' *Saturnalia*. Pantomimes form the subject of chapter vi. Weaver was a dancing master who resided in Shrewsbury and died in 1760 (E. F. Rimbault in *N & Q*, 2nd ser., iii. 297).

Professors, Masters, or Lovers of them, whereby the Usefulness, Excellence, and Benefit arising from them, both as to the speculative and practical Part, have been made publick, to the great Advantage and Improvement of such Arts and Sciences; why should Dancing, an Art celebrated by the Ancients in so extraordinary a Manner, be totally neglected by the Moderns, and left destitute of any Pen to recommend its various Excellencies and substantial Merit to Mankind?

'The low Ebb to which Dancing is now fallen, is altogether owing to this Silence. The Art is esteem'd only as an amusing Trifle; it lies altogether uncultivated, and is unhappily fall'n under the Imputation of Illiterate and Mechanic: And as *Terence*, in one of his Prologues, complains of the Rope-dancers drawing all the Spectators from his Play,[1] so may we well say, that Capering and Tumbling is now preferred to, and supplies the Place of, just and regular Dancing on our Theatres. It is therefore, in my Opinion, high Time, that some one should come in to its Assistance, and relieve it from the many gross and growing Errors that have crept into it, and overcast its real Beauties; and to set Dancing in its true Light, would shew the Usefulness and Elegancy of it, with the Pleasure and Instruction produc'd from it; and also lay down some fundamental Rules, that might so tend to the Improvement of its Professors and Information of the Spectators, that the first might be the better enabled to perform, and the latter rendred more capable of judging, what is (if there be any thing) valuable in this Art.

'To encourage therefore some ingenious Pen capable of so generous an Undertaking, and in some Measure to relieve Dancing from the Disadvantages it at present lies under, I who teach to dance have attempted a small Treatise as an Essay towards an History of Dancing; in which I have enquired into its Antiquity, Original, and Use, and shewn what Esteem the Ancients had for it: I have likewise considered the Nature and Perfection of all its several Parts, and how beneficial and delightful it is, both as a Qualification and[a] an Exercise; and endeavour'd to answer all Objections that have been maliciously rais'd against it. I have proceeded to give an Account of the particular Dances of the *Greeks* and *Romans*, whether Religious, Warlike, or Civil; and taken particular Notice of that Part of Dancing relating to the ancient Stage, and in which the *Pantomimes* had

[a] and] or *Fol.*

[1] Prologue I to *Hecyra* ('The Mother-in-Law').

so great a Share: Nor have I been wanting in giving an historical Account of some particular Masters excellent in that surprizing Art; after which I have advanc'd some Observations on the modern Dancing, both as to the Stage, and that Part of it so absolutely necessary for the Qualification of Gentlemen and Ladies; and have concluded with some short Remarks on the Origin and Progress of the Character by which Dances are writ down, and communicated to one Master from another. If some great Genius after this would arise, and advance this Art to that Perfection it seems capable of receiving, what might not be expected from it? For if we consider the Origin of Arts and Sciences, we shall find that some of them took Rise from Beginnings so mean and unpromising, that it is very wonderful to think that ever such surprizing Structures should have been rais'd upon such ordinary Foundations. But what cannot a great Genius effect? Who would have thought that the clangorous Noise of a Smith's Hammers should have given the first Rise to Musick? Yet *Macrobius* in his 2d Book relates, that *Pythagoras*, in passing by a Smith's Shop, found, that the Sounds proceeding from the Hammers were either more grave or acute, according to the different Weights of the Hammers. The Philosopher, to improve this Hint, suspends different Weights by Strings of the same Bigness, and found in like Manner that the Sounds answer'd to the Weights. This being discovered, he finds out those Numbers which produced Sounds that were Consonants: As, that two Strings of the same Substance and Tension, the one being double the Length of the other, give that Interval which is call'd *Diapason*, or an Eighth; the same was also effected from two Strings of the same Length and Size, the one having four times the Tension of the other. By these Steps, from so mean a Beginning, did this great Man reduce, what was only before Noise, to one of the most delightful Sciences, by marrying it to the Mathematicks; and by that means caus'd it to be one of the most abstract and demonstrative of Sciences.[1] Who knows therefore but Motion, whether Decorous or Representative, may not (as it seems highly probable it may) be taken into Consideration by some Person capable of reducing it into a regular Science, tho' not so demonstrative as that proceeding from Sounds, yet sufficient to entitle it to a Place among the magnify'd Arts.

[1] Macrobius, *Somnium Scipionis*, 2. See Diogenes Laertius, 8. 12. Dacier (*Life of Pythagoras*, 1707, pp. 82–84) relates this story, and cites Macrobius, book II, chap. i, in a footnote, along with other authorities.

'Now, Mr. SPECTATOR, as you have declared your self Visitor of Dancing-Schools,[1] and this being an Undertaking which more immediately respects them; I think my self indispensably oblig'd, before I proceed to the Publication of this my Essay, to ask your Advice; and hold it absolutely necessary to have your Approbation; and in order to recommend my Treatise to the Perusal of the Parents of such as learn to Dance, as well as of the young Ladies to whom, as Visitor, you ought to be Guardian.

Salop, March 19,   *I am SIR,*

   1711-12.   *Your most humble Servant.*'

                                         T

No. 335   *Tuesday, March 25, 1712*[2]
[ADDISON]

Respicere exemplar vitæ morumque jubebo
Doctum imitatorem, & veras hinc ducere voces.
                             Hor.

MY Friend Sir ROGER DE COVERLY, when we last met together at the Club, told me, that he had a great mind to see the new Tragedy[3] with me, assuring me at the same time, that he had not been at a Play these twenty Years. The last I saw, says Sir ROGER, was the *Committee*, which I should not have gone to neither, had not I been told before-hand that it was a good Church of *England* Comedy.[4] He then proceeded to enquire of me who this Distrest Mother was, and upon hearing that she was *Hector's*

[1] Nos. 296, 308, 314.

[2] *Motto.* Horace, *Ars poetica*, 317-18 (altered):
           Study the Manners and the Lives of Men,
           And thence by Imitation form the Scene.

[3] *The Distrest Mother*, by Ambrose Philips, first produced at Drury Lane on Monday, 17 Mar. 1712, and again on the 18th, the 20th, the 22nd, the 24th, the 25th, the 27th, and the 29th—a total of eight performances. It was published by Buckley and Tonson on 28 Mar. (advertisement in No. 338), and the cast is given as follows: Pyrrhus, Mr. Booth; Phoenix, Mr. Bowman; Orestes, Mr. Powell; Pylades, Mr. Mills; Andromache, Mrs. Oldfield; Cephisa, Mrs. Knight; Hermione, Mrs. Porter; and Cleone, Mrs. Cox. The Prologue was by Steele and the Epilogue by Budgell.

[4] *The Committee*, by Sir Robert Howard, first given in 1662 and popular because of its satire on the Commonwealth régime. The most recent performance at Drury Lane had been on 10 Dec. 1711.

Widow, he told me that her Husband was a brave Man, and that when he was a School-Boy he had read his Life at the end of the Dictionary. My Friend asked me, in the next place, if there would not be some danger in coming home late, in case the *Mohocks* should be Abroad.[1] I assure you, says he, I thought I had fallen into their Hands last Night, for I observed two or three lusty black Men that followed me half way up *Fleetstreet*, and mended their pace behind me, in proportion as I put on to get away from them. You must know, continued the Knight with a Smile, I fancied they had a mind to *hunt* me; for I remember an honest Gentleman in my Neighbourhood, who was serv'd such a Trick in King *Charles* the Second's time; for which reason he has not ventur'd himself in Town ever since. I might have shown them very good Sport, had this been their Design, for as I am an old Fox-hunter, I should have turned and dodged, and have played them a thousand Tricks, they had never seen in their Lives before. Sir ROGER added, that if these Gentlemen had any such Intention, they did not succeed very well in it, for I threw them out, says he, at the end of *Norfolk-street*,[2] where I doubled the Corner and got shelter in my Lodgings before they could imagine what was become of me. However, says the Knight, if Captain SENTRY will make one with us to Morrow Night, and if you will both of you call upon me about four a-Clock, that we may be at the House before it is full, I will have my own Coach in readiness to attend you, for *John* tells me he has got the fore-Wheels mended.

The Captain, who did not fail to meet me there at the appointed Hour, bid Sir ROGER fear nothing, for that he had put on the same Sword which he made use of at the Battel of *Steenkirk*.[3] Sir ROGER's Servants, and among the rest my old Friend, the Butler, had I found provided themselves with good Oaken Plants, to attend their Master upon this occasion. When we had placed him in his Coach, with my self at his Left Hand, the Captain before him, and his Butler at the head of his Footmen, in the Rear, we convoy'd him in safety to the Playhouse; where after having marched up the Entry in good Order, the Captain and I went in with him, and seated him betwixt us in the Pit. As soon as the House was

[1] No. 324.

[2] Norfolk Street ran south from the Strand to the Thames between Arundel and Surrey Streets.

[3] Here, in 1692, William III was defeated by the French under the Marshal of Luxemburg.

full, and the Candles lighted, my old Friend stood up and looked about him with that Pleasure, which a Mind seasoned with Humanity naturally feels in it self, at the sight of a multitude of People who seem pleased with one another, and partake of the same common Entertainment. I could not but fancy to my self, as the old Man stood up in the middle of the Pit, that he made a very proper Center to a Tragick Audience. Upon the entring of *Pyrrhus*, the Knight told me, that he did not believe the King of *France* himself had a better Strut. I was indeed very attentive to my old Friend's Remarks, because I looked upon them as a piece of Natural Criticism, and was well pleased to hear him at the conclusion of almost every Scene, telling me that he could not imagine how the Play would end. One while he appeared much[a] concerned for *Andromache*; and a little while after as much for *Hermione*; and was extremely puzzled to think what would become of *Pyrrhus*.

When Sir ROGER saw *Andromache*'s obstinate Refusal to her Lover's Importunities, he whispered me in the Ear, that he was sure she would never have him; to which he added, with a more than ordinary Vehemence, You can't imagine, Sir, what 'tis to have to do with a Widow. Upon *Pyrrhus* his threatning afterwards to leave her, the Knight shook his Head, and muttered to himself, Ay, do if you can. This Part dwelt so much upon my Friend's Imagination, that at the close of the Third Act, as I was thinking of something else, he whispered in my Ear, These Widows, Sir, are the most perverse Creatures in the World. But pray, says he, you that are a Critick, is this Play according to your Dramatick Rules, as you call them? Should your People in Tragedy always talk to be understood? Why, there is not a single Sentence in this Play, that I do not know the Meaning of.

The Fourth Act very luckily begun before I had time to give the old Gentleman an Answer; Well, says the Knight, sitting down with great Satisfaction, I suppose we are now to see *Hector*'s Ghost. He then renewed his Attention, and, from time to time, fell a praising the Widow. He made, indeed, a little Mistake as to one of her Pages, whom, at his first entring, he took for *Astyanax*; but he quickly set himself right in that Particular, though, at the same time, he owned he should have been very glad to have seen the little Boy, who, says he, must needs be a very fine Child by the Account that is given of him. Upon *Hermione*'s going off with a

<hr />

[a] much] very much *Fol*.

Menace to *Pyrrhus*, the Audience gave a loud Clap, to which Sir ROGER added, On my Word, a notable young Baggage.

As there was a very remarkable Silence and Stillness in the Audience during the whole Action,[a] it was natural for them to take the Opportunity of these Intervals between the Acts, to express their Opinion of the Players, and of their[b] respective Parts. Sir ROGER hearing a Cluster of them praise *Orestes*, struck in with them and told them, that he thought his Friend *Pylades* was a very sensible Man; As they were afterwards applauding *Pyrrhus*, Sir ROGER put in a second time, And let me tell you, says he, though he speaks but little, I like the old Fellow in Whiskers as well as any of them.[1] Captain SENTRY, seeing two or three Waggs who sat near us, lean with an attentive Ear towards Sir ROGER, and fearing least they should Smoak[2] the Knight, pluck'd him by the Elbow, and whispered something in his Ear, that lasted till the opening of the Fifth Act. The Knight was wonderfully attentive to the Account which *Orestes* gives of *Pyrrhus* his Death, and at the Conclusion of it, told me it was such a bloody piece of Work, that he was glad it was not done upon the Stage. Seeing afterwards *Orestes* in his raving Fit, he grew more than ordinarily serious, and took Occasion to moralize (in his way) upon an Evil Conscience, adding, that *Orestes, in his Madness, looked as if he saw something*.

As we were the first that came into the House, so we were the last that went out of it; being resolved to have a clear Passage for our old Friend, whom we did not care to venture among the justling of the Crowd. Sir ROGER went out fully satisfied with his Entertainment, and we guarded him to his Lodgings in the same manner that we brought him to the Playhouse; being highly pleased, for my own part, not only with the Performance of the Excellent Piece which had been presented,[c] but with the Satisfaction which it had given to the good old Man.   L

---

[a] Stillness . . . Action,] Stillness during the Action, *Fol.*   [b] and of their] and their *Fol.*   [c] presented,] represented, *Fol.*

---

[1] The 'old fellow in whiskers' is Phoenix, the counsellor to Pyrrhus, who speaks only about sixty-five lines.
[2] Here used, apparently, in the now archaic sense of 'to ridicule or banter' (*OED*).

> . . . *Clament periisse pudorem*
> *Cuncti pœne patres: ea cum reprehendere coner,*
> *Quæ gravis Æsopus, quæ doctus Roscius egit:*
> *Vel quia nil rectum, nisi quod placuit sibi, ducunt;*
> *Vel quia turpe putant parere minoribus, & quæ*
> *Imberbes didicere, senes perdenda fateri.*
>
> Hor. Lib. 2. Epist. 1. v. 80.

Mr. SPECTATOR,

'AS you are the daily Endeavourer to promote Learning and good Sense, I think my self obliged to suggest to your Consideration whatever may promote or prejudice them. There is an Evil which has prevailed from Generation to Generation, which grey Hairs and tyrannical Custom continue to support; I hope your spectatorial Authority will give a seasonable Check to the Spread of the Infection; I mean old Men's overbearing the strongest Sense of their Juniors by the meer Force of Seniority; so that for a young Man in the Bloom of Life and Vigour of Age to give a reasonable Contradiction to his Elders, is esteemed an unpardonable Insolence, and regarded as a reversing the Decrees of Nature. I am a young Man I confess, yet I honour the grey Head as much as any one; however, when in Company with old Men I hear them speak obscurely or reason preposterously (into which Absurdities Prejudice, Pride, or Interest will sometimes throw the wisest) I count it no Crime to rectify their Reasonings, unless Conscience must truckle to Ceremony, and Truth fall a Sacrifice to Complaisance. The strongest Arguments are enervated, and the brightest Evidence disappears, before those tremendous Reasonings and dazzling Discoveries of venerable old Age: You are young giddy-headed Fellows,

---

[1] *Motto.* Horace, *Epistles,* 2. 1. 80–85:
> The old ones straight will cry the Youngster's proud,
> He's impudent, nor thinks those Plays exact,
> Which Roscius and grave Æsop us'd to act:
> Because they judge by their own Appetites,
> And think nought right but what their Taste delights,
> Perhaps all Junior Judgments they disdain
> Or scorn to think what once they learnt was vain,
> And only fit to be forgot again. CREECH.

you have not yet had Experience of the World. Thus we young Folks find our Ambition cramp'd and our Laziness indulg'd, since, while young, we have little Room to display our selves, and, when old, the Weakness of Nature must pass for Strength of Sense, and we hope that hoary Heads will raise us above the Attacks of Contradiction. Now, Sir, as you would enliven our Activity in the Pursuit of Learning, take our Case into Consideration; and with a Gloss on brave *Elihu's* Sentiments, assert the Rights of Youth, and prevent the pernicious Incroachments of Age. The generous Reasonings of that gallant Youth would adorn your Paper; and I beg you would insert them, not doubting but that they will give good Entertainment to the most intelligent of your Readers.

'So these three Men ceased to answer Job, because he was righteous in his own Eyes. Then was kindled the Wrath of Elihu the Son of Barachel the Buzite, of the Kindred of Ram: Against Job was his Wrath kindled, because he justified himself rather than God. Also against his three Friends was his Wrath kindled, because they had found no Answer, and yet had condemned Job. Now Elihu had waited till Job had spoken, because they were elder than he. When Elihu saw there was no Answer in the Mouth of these three Men, then his Wrath was kindled. And Elihu the Son of Barachel the Buzite answered and said, I am young, and ye are very old, wherefore I was afraid, and durst not shew you mine Opinion. I said, Days should speak, and Multitude of Years should teach Wisdom. But there is a Spirit in Man: And the Inspiration of the Almighty giveth them Understanding. Great Men are not always wise: Neither do the aged understand Judgment. Therefore I said, hearken to me, I also will shew mine Opinion. Behold I waited for your Words; I gave Ear to your Reasons, whilest you searched out what to say. Yea, I attended unto you: And behold there was none of you that convinced Job, or that answered his Words: Lest ye should say, we have found out Wisdom: God thrusteth him down, not Man. Now he hath not directed his Words against me: Neither will I answer him with your Speeches. They were amazed, they answered no more: They left off speaking. When I had waited, (for they spake not, but stood still and answered no more,) I said, I will answer also my Part, I also will shew mine Opinion. For I am full of Matter, the Spirit within me constraineth me. Behold, my Belly is as Wine which hath no Vent, it is ready to burst like new Bottles. I will speak that I may be refreshed: I will open my Lips, and answer. Let me not, I pray you, accept any Man's Person, neither let me give flattering Titles unto Man. For I know *not to give flattering Titles, in so doing my Maker would soon take me away.*[1]

Mr. SPECTATOR,

'I HAVE formerly read with great Satisfaction, your Papers about Idols, and the Behaviour of Gentlemen in those Coffee-houses where Women officiate,[2] and impatiently waited to see you take India and China Shops into Consideration: But since you have pass'd us over in Silence, either that you have not as yet thought us worth your Notice, or that the Grievances we lie under have escap'd your discerning Eye, I must make my Complaints to you, and am encourag'd to do it because you seem a little at leisure at this present Writing. I am, dear Sir, one of the top China-Women about Town; and though I say it, keep as good things, and receive as fine Company as any o' this end of the Town, let the other be who she will: In short, I am in a fair way to be easy, were it not for a Club of Female Rakes, who, under Pretence of taking their innocent Rambles forsooth, and diverting the Spleen, seldom fail to plague me twice or thrice a Day, to cheapen Tea or buy a Screen, *what else should they mean?* as they often repeat it. These Rakes are your idle Ladies of Fashion, who having nothing to do, employ themselves in tumbling over my Ware. One of these No-Customers[3] (for by the way they seldom or never buy any thing) calls for a Set of Tea Dishes, another for a Bason, a third for my best Green Tea, and even to the Punch-Bowl there's scarce a Piece in my Shop but must be displac'd, and the whole agreeable Architecture disorder'd, so that I can compare 'em to nothing but to the Night-Goblins that take a Pleasure to over-turn the Disposition of Plates and Dishes in the Kitchens of your housewifely Maids. Well, after all this Racket and Clutter, this is too dear, that is their Aversion, another thing is charming but not wanted: The Ladies are cur'd of the Spleen, but I am not a Shilling the better for it: Lord! what signifies one poor Pot of Tea, considering the Trouble they put me to? Vapours,[4] Mr. SPECTATOR, are terrible things; for tho' I am not possess'd by 'em my self, I suffer more from 'em than if I were. Now I must beg you to admonish all such Day-Goblins, to make fewer Visits, or to be less troublesome when they come to one's Shop; and to convince 'em, that we honest Shop-keepers have something better to do, than to

---

[1] Job xxxii. 1–22.   [2] See Nos. 73, 87 (vol. i), 155 (vol. ii).
[3] For examples of this type of combination, 'very common after 1600', see *OED*.
[4] See No. 115 (vol. i). Here used more generally for depression of spirits.

cure Folks of the Vapours *gratis*. A young Son of mine, a School-Boy, is my Secretary; so I hope you'll make Allowances. I am Sir,

Your constant Reader

and very humble Servant,

Rebecca *the distress'd.'*

T

March the 22d.

No. 337
[BUDGELL]

Thursday, March 27, 1712[1]

Fingit equum tenerâ docilem cervice Magister
Ire viam quam monstret eques . . .

Hor.

I HAVE lately received a third Letter from the Gentleman, who has already given the Publick two Essays upon Education.[2] As his Thoughts seem to be very just and new[a] upon this Subject, I shall communicate them to the Reader.

SIR,

'IF I had not been hindred by some extraordinary Business, I should have sent you sooner my further Thoughts upon Education. You may please to remember, that in my last Letter I endeavoured to give the best Reasons that could be urged in favour of a Private or Publick Education. Upon the whole it may perhaps be thought that I seemed rather enclin'd to the latter, tho' at the same time I confessed that Vertue, which ought to be our first and principal Care, was more usually acquir'd in the former.

'I intend, therefore in this Letter, to offer at Methods, by which I conceive Boys might be made to improve in Vertue as they advance in Letters.

'I know that in most of our Publick Schools Vice is punished and discouraged whenever it is found out; but this is far from being

---

[a] very just and new] wholly new *Fol.*

[1] *Motto.* Horace, *Epistles,* 1. 2. 64–65:
The Jocky trains the young and tender Horse,
Whilst yet soft-mouth'd he breeds him to the Course. CREECH.

[2] Nos. 307, 313.

sufficient, unless our Youth are at the same time taught to form a right Judgment of Things, and to know what is properly Virtue.

'To this end, whenever they read the Lives and Actions of such Men as have been famous in their Generation, it should not be thought enough to make them barely understand so many *Greek* or *Latin* Sentences, but they should be asked their Opinion of such an Action or Saying, and obliged to give their Reasons why they take it to be good or bad. By this means they would insensibly arrive at proper Notions of Courage, Temperance, Honour and Justice.

'There must be great Care taken how the Example of any particular Person is recommended to them in gross; instead of which they ought to be taught wherein such a Man, tho' great in some Respects, was weak and faulty in others. For want of this Caution, a Boy is often so dazzled with the Lustre of a great Character, that he confounds its Beauties with its Blemishes, and looks even upon the faulty parts of it with an Eye of Admiration.

'I have often wondered how *Alexander*, who was naturally of a generous and merciful Disposition, came to be guilty of so barbarous an Action as that of dragging the Governor of a Town after his Chariot.[1] I know this is generally ascribed to his Passion for *Homer*; but I lately met with a Passage in *Plutarch*, which, if I am not very much mistaken, still gives us a clearer light into the Motives of this Action. *Plutarch* tells us, that *Alexander* in his Youth had a Master named *Lysimachus*, who though he was a Man destitute of all Politeness, ingratiated himself both with *Philip* and his Pupil, and became the second Man at Court, by calling the King *Peleus*, the Prince *Achilles*, and himself *Phœnix*.[2] It is no wonder if *Alexander*, having been thus used not only to admire, but to personate *Achilles*, should think it glorious to imitate him in this Piece of Cruelty and Extravagance.

'To carry this Thought yet further, I shall submit[a] it to your Consideration, whether instead of a Theam or Copy of Verses, which are the usual Exercises, as they are called in the School phrase, it would not be more proper that a Boy should be tasked once or twice a Week to write down his Opinion of such Persons and Things

---

[a] shall submit] shall therefore submit *Fol.*

---

[1] Alexander caused Betis, the governor of Gaza, to be bound to the king's chariot, and the horses dragged him around the city. See Quintus Curtius, 4. 6. 29.
[2] *Life of Alexander*, 5. 5.

as occur to him in his Reading; that he should descant upon the Actions of *Turnus* or *Æneas*, shew wherein they excelled or were defective, censure or approve any particular Action, observe[a] how it might have been carried to a greater degree of Perfection, and how[b] it exceeded or fell short of another. He might at the same time mark what was moral in any Speech, and how far it agreed with the Character of the Person speaking. This Exercise would soon strengthen his Judgment in what is blameable or praise-worthy, and give him an early Seasoning of Morality.

'Next to those Examples which may be met with in Books, I very much approve *Horace*'s way of setting before Youth the infamous or honourable Characters of their Contemporaries; that Poet tells us this was the Method his Father made use of to incline him to any particular Virtue, or give him an Aversion to any particular Vice. If, says *Horace*, my Father advised me to live within Bounds, and be contented with the Fortune he should leave me; Do not you see (says he) the miserable Condition of *Barrus*, and the Son of *Albus*? Let the Misfortunes of those two Wretches teach you to avoid Luxury and Extravagance. If he would inspire me with an Abhorrence to Debauchery, Do not (says he) make your self like *Sectanus*, when you may be happy in the Enjoyment of lawful Pleasures. How Scandalous (says he)[c] is the Character of *Trebonius*, who was lately caught in bed with another Man's Wife? To illustrate the Force of this Method, the Poet adds, that as a headstrong Patient, who will not at first follow his Physician's Prescriptions, grows orderly when he hears that his Neighbours dye all about him, so Youth is often frighted from Vice by hearing the ill Report it brings upon others.[1]

'*Xenophon*'s Schools of Equity, in his Life of *Cyrus* the Great, are sufficiently famous;[2] he tells us that the *Persian* Children went to School, and employed their time as diligently in learning the Principles of Justice and Sobriety, as the Youth in other Countries did, to acquire the most difficult Arts and Sciences; their Governours spent most part of the Day in hearing their mutual Accusations one against the other, whether for Violence, Cheating, Slander, or Ingratitude, and taught them how to give Judgment against those

[a] observe] and observe *Fol.*   [b] Perfection, and how] Perfection; how *Fol.*
[c] Scandalous (says he)] Scandalous, says he, *Fol.*

[1] Horace, *Satires*, I. 4. 105–26. (Properly Baius, Albius, and Scetanus.)
[2] *Cyropaedia*, I. 2. 6, 7.

who were found to be any ways guilty of these Crimes. I omit the Story of the long and short Coat,[1] for which *Cyrus* himself was punished, as a Case equally known with any in *Littleton*.

'The Method which *Apuleius* tells us the *Indian Gymnosophists* took to educate their Disciples is still more curious and remarkable. His Words are as follow. When their Dinner is ready, before it is served up, the Masters inquire of every particular Scholar, how he has employed his Time since Sun-rising; some of them answer, that having been chosen as Arbiters between two Persons they have composed their Differences, and made them Friends; some, that they have been executing the Orders of their Parents; and others, that they have either found out something new, by their own Application, or learnt it from the Instructions of their Fellows: But if there happens to be any one among them, who cannot make it appear that he has employed the Morning to advantage, he is immediately excluded from the Company, and obliged to work, while the rest are at Dinner.[2]

'It is not impossible that from these several ways of producing Virtue in the Minds of Boys, some general Method might be invented. What I would endeavour to inculcate is, that our Youth cannot be too soon taught the Principles of Virtue, seeing the first Impressions which are made on the Mind are always the strongest.

'The Arch-bishop of *Cambray* makes *Telemachus* say, that tho' he was young in Years he was old in the Art of knowing how to keep both his own and his Friends Secrets.[3] When my Father, says the Prince, went to the Siege of *Troy*, he took me on his Knees, and after having embraced and blessed me, as he was surrounded by the Nobles of *Ithaca*, O my Friends, says he, into your Hands I commit the Education of my Son; If ever you lov'd his Father shew it in your Care towards him, but above all, do not omit to form him just, sincere, and faithful in keeping a Secret. These Words of my Father, says *Telemachus*, were continually repeated to me by his Friends in his Absence; who made no scruple of communicating to me their Uneasiness to see my Mother surrounded with Lovers, and the measures they designed to take on that Occasion. He adds, that he was so ravished at being thus treated like a Man, and at the Confidence reposed in him, that he never once abused it; nor could

---

[1] *Cyropaedia*, 1. 3. 16, 17.
[2] Apuleius, *Florida*, 1. 6. See Bayle, art. 'Gymnosophists' and Remark C, which quotes the passage from *Florida*.
[3] Fénelon, *Adventures of Telemachus* (1699), pp. 69–72.

all the Insinuations of his Father's Rivals ever get him to betray what was committed to him under the Seal of Secrecy.

'There is hardly any Virtue which a Lad might not thus learn by Practice and Example.

'I have heard of a good Man, who used at certain times to give his Scholars Six Pence a-piece, that they might tell him the next Day how they had employ'd it. The third part was always to be laid out in Charity, and every Boy was blamed or commended as he could make it appear that he had chosen a fit Object.

'In short, nothing is more wanting to our Publick Schools, than that the Masters of them should use the same Care in fashioning the Manners of their Scholars, as in forming their Tongues to the learned Languages. Where-ever the former is omitted, I cannot help agreeing with Mr. *Lock*, That a Man must have a very strange value for Words, when preferring the Languages of the *Greeks* and *Romans* to that which made them such brave Men, he can think it worth while to hazard the Innocence and Virtue of his Son for a little *Greek* and *Latin*.[1]

'As the Subject of this Essay is of the highest Importance, and what I do not remember to have yet seen treated by any Author, I have sent you what occurr'd to me on it from my own Observation or Reading, and which you may either suppress or publish as you think fit.

I am, SIR, Yours, &c.'

X

No. 338   *Friday, March 28, 1712*[2]

. . . Nil fuit unquam
Tam dispar sibi . . .

Hor.

I FIND the Tragedy of the *Distrest Mother*[3] is publish'd to Day: The Author of the Prologue, I suppose, pleads an old Excuse

---

[1] *Of Education*, 47.   [For notes 2 and 3 see opposite page.

I have read somewhere, of being *dull with design*;[1] and the Gentleman who writ the Epilogue,[2] has, to my Knowledge, so much of greater Moment to value himself upon, that he will easily forgive me for publishing the Exceptions made against Gayety at the end of serious Entertainments, in the following Letter: I should be more unwilling to pardon him than any body, a Practice which cannot have any ill Consequence, but from the Abilities of the Person who is guilty of it.

Mr. SPECTATOR,

'I HAD the Happiness the other Night of sitting very near you, and your worthy Friend Sir ROGER, at the Acting of the new Tragedy, which you have in a late Paper or two so justly recommended.[3] I was highly pleas'd with the advantagious Situation Fortune had given me, in placing me so near two Gentlemen, from one of which I was sure to hear such Reflections on the several

---

[1] Steele had concluded *Tatler* 38 with the words, 'It is to be noted, That when any Part of this Paper appears dull, there is a Design in it'—a statement frequently quoted against him, e.g. by the *Examiner* No. 50 (12 July 1711) and by Defoe in the *Review* of 18 Aug. 1711. Addison promised to give over the *Spectator* when it should grow dull (No. 10), and Steele forecast (No. 19) that he would 'sometimes be dull' in order to satisfy the envy of his detractors. In No. 124 Addison writes: 'Authors have established it as a Kind of Rule, That a Man ought to be dull sometimes.'

[2] In his life of Ambrose Philips Johnson calls this 'the most successful Epilogue that was ever yet spoken on the English theatre. . . .

Of this distinguished Epilogue the reputed author was the wretched Budgel, whom Addison used to denominate *the man who calls me cousin*; and when he was asked how such a silly fellow could write so well, replied, *The Epilogue was quite another thing when I saw it first*. It was known in Tonson's family, and told to Garrick, that Addison was himself the author of it, and that when it had been at first printed with his name, he came early in the morning, before the copies were distributed, and ordered it to be given to Budgel, that it might add weight to the solicitation which he was then making for a place (*Lives of the Poets*, World's Classics ed., ii. 387–8).

Nichols (note to No. 341) repeats the substance of this, as does Joseph Warton in vol. ii of his *Essay on Pope* (1782): 'I have heard Mr. Garrick say, that Addison wrote the celebrated epilogue to this tragedy, published in the name of Budgell: that this was a fact he received from some of the Tonsons' (p. 303n.). According to William Egerton's *Memoirs of Mrs. Oldfield* (1731), p. 35, it was this actress's manner of speaking the Epilogue which greatly contributed to the success of this play, 'and which whenever revived, the Audience always have insisted on'.

[3] See No. 335.

---

[2] *Motto.* Horace, *Satires*, i. 3. 18–19 (altered): None was ever so unlike itself.

The motto in the Folio sheets was Horace, *Ars poetica*, 126–7, which had been used as the motto for No. 162 (vol. ii).

The letter which forms the main part of this number may be a genuine contribution, or it may be an 'attack' especially written by Budgell, Steele, or Addison, in order to give Budgell the opportunity of writing the reply in No. 341. The first paragraph is doubtless by Steele.

[3] *The Distrest Mother* is advertised in this issue as 'this day' published. The author of the Prologue is Steele.

Incidents of the Play as pure Nature suggested, and from the other such as flow'd from the exactest Art and Judgment: Tho' I must confess that my Curiosity led me so much to observe the Knight's Reflections, that I was not so well at leisure to improve my self by yours. Nature I found play'd her Part in the Knight pretty well, till at the last concluding Lines she intirely forsook him. You must know, Sir, that it is always my Custom, when I have been well entertained at a new Tragedy, to make my Retreat before the facetious Epilogue enters; not but that those Pieces are often very well writ, but having paid down my Half Crown, and made a fair Purchase of as much of the pleasing Melancholy as the Poet's Art can afford me, or my own Nature admit of, I am willing to carry some of it home with me, and can't endure to be at once trick'd out of all, tho' by the wittiest Dexterity in the World. However, I kept my Seat t'other Night, in hopes of finding my own Sentiments of this Matter favour'd by your Friends; when, to my great Surprize, I found the Knight entering with equal Pleasure into both Parts, and as much satisfied with Mrs. *Oldfield*'s Gaiety,[1] as he had been before with *Andromache*'s Greatness. Whether this were no other than an Effect of the Knight's peculiar Humanity, pleas'd to find at last, that after all the Tragical Doings, every thing was safe and well, I don't know. But for my own part, I must confess, I was so dissatisfied, that I was sorry the Poet had sav'd *Andromache*, and could heartily have wish'd that he had left her stone-dead upon the Stage. For you cannot imagine, Mr. SPECTATOR, the Mischief she was reserv'd to do me. I found my Soul, during the Action, gradually work'd up to the highest Pitch; and felt the exalted Passion which all generous Minds conceive at the Sight of Virtue in Distress. The Impression, believe me Sir, was so strong upon me,

---

[1] The Epilogue, spoken by Mrs. Oldfield, begins:

> I hope you'll own that with becoming Art
> I've play'd my Game, and topp'd the Widow's Part;
> My Spouse, poor Man! could not live out the Play,
> But dy'd commodiously on Wedding-Day,
> While I his Relict made at one bold Fling
> My self a Princess, and young *Sty* a King.

Anne Oldfield (1683–1730), who played the part of Andromache, was the most talented actress of the day. Her first notable role was that of Lady Betty Modish in Cibber's *Careless Husband* (1704). She played Ismena in *Phaedra and Hippolitus*. In chap. ix of the *Apology* Cibber pays tribute to her versatility as an actress and to her willingness to learn from others, even at the height of her powers. Steele's portrait of Flavia in *Tatler* 212 is taken by William Egerton (*Memoirs of Mrs. Oldfield*, 1731, p. 60) as a picture of Mrs. Oldfield. At this time she was mistress of Addison's friend Arthur Maynwaring (d. 13 Nov. 1712), to whom she bore a son.

that I am perswaded, if I had been let alone in it, I could at an Extremity have ventured to defend your self, and Sir ROGER, against half a Score of the fiercest *Mohocks*: But the ludicrous Epilogue in the Close, extinguish'd all my Ardour, and made me look upon all such noble Atchievements as downright silly and romantick. What the rest of the Audience felt, I can't so well tell: For my self I must declare, that at the end of the Play I found my Soul uniform, and all of a Piece; but at the end of the Epilogue it was so jumbled together, and divided between Jest and Earnest, that if you will forgive me an extravagant Fancy, I will here set it down. I could not but fancy, if my Soul had at that Moment quitted my Body, and descended to the Poetical Shades, in the Posture it was then in, what a strange Figure it would have made among them. They would not have known what to have made of my mottley Spectre, half Comic and half Tragic, all over resembling a ridiculous Face, that at the same Time laughs on one side, and cries o' t'other. The only Defence, I think, I have ever heard made for this, as it seems to me, most unnatural Tack of the Comic Tail to the Tragic Head, is, this, that the Minds of the Audience must be refreshed, and Gentlemen and Ladies not sent away to their own Homes with too dismal and melancholy Thoughts about them.[1] For who knows the Consequence of this? We are much obliged indeed to the Poets for the great Tenderness they express for the Safety of our Persons, and heartily thank them for it. But if that be all, pray, good Sir, assure them, that we are none of us like to come to any great Harm; and that, let them do their best, we shall in all Probability live out the Length of our Days, and frequent the Theatres more than ever. What makes me more desirous to have some Reformation of this Matter, is because of an ill Consequence or two attending it: For a great many of our Church-Musicians being related to the Theatre, they have, in Imitation of these Epilogues, introduc'd in their fare-well Voluntaries a sort of Musick quite foreign to the Design of Church-Services, to the great Prejudice of well-dispos'd People. Those fingering Gentlemen should be inform'd, that they ought to suit their Airs to the Place and Business; and that the Musician is oblig'd to keep to the Text as much as the Preacher. For want of this, I have found by Experience a great deal of Mischief: For when

---

[1] Thomas Burnet writes (18 Mar. 1714), apropos of the Epilogue to *Cato*, 'the Town is now wholly gone into the Fancy of having a merry one to divert them after a Grave Tragedy' (*Letters*, ed. D. Nichol Smith, p. 57).

the Preacher has often, with great Piety and Art enough, handled his Subject, and the judicious Clark has with utmost Diligence cull'd out two Staves proper to the Discourse, and I have found in my self, and in the rest of the Pew, good Thoughts and Dispositions, they have been all in a Moment dissipated by a merry Jigg from the Organ-Loft. One knows not what further ill Effects the Epilogues I have been speaking of may in Time produce: But this I am credibly inform'd of, that *Paul Lorrain* has resolv'd upon a very sudden Reformation in his tragical Dramas; and that at the next monthly Performance, he designs, instead of a Penitential Psalm, to dismiss his Audience with an excellent new Ballad of his own composing.[1] Pray Sir do what you can to put a Stop to these growing Evils, and you will very much oblige

Your humble Servant,
Physibulus.'[a]

No. 339   *Saturday, March* 29, 1712[2]
[ADDISON]

. . . *Ut his exordia primis*
Omnia & ipse tener Mundi concreverit orbis.
Tum durare solum & discludere Nerea ponto
Cœperit, & rerum paullatim sumere formas.

Virg.[b]

*L*ONGINUS has observed, that there may be a Loftiness in Sentiments, where there is no Passion, and brings Instances out of Ancient Authors to support this his Opinion.[3] The Pathetick,

---

[a] *No. 338 is unsigned in Fol., 8vo, 12mo*
The Boarding-School for young Gentlewomen, which was formerly kept on Mile-End Green,[4] *being laid down, there is now one set up almost opposite to it at the two Golden-Balls, and much more convenient in every Respect; where, beside the common Instructions given to young Gentlewomen, they will be taught the whole Art of Paistrey and Preserving, with whatever may render them accomplished.* Fol.
[b] Virg.] *19;* Ovid. Fol., 8vo, 12mo. *Corrected in Folio Errata (No. 369) to* Virgil

[1] Paul Lorrain, the ordinary of Newgate Prison, compiled the accounts of the 'penitential' dying speeches of executed criminals (cf. *Tatler* 63).
[2] *Motto.* Virgil, *Eclogues*, 6. 33–36:
He sung the secret Seeds of Nature's Frame;
How Seas, and Earth, and Air, and active Flame,
Fell through the mighty Void; and in their fall
Were blindly gather'd in this goodly Ball. DRYDEN.
[3] *On the Sublime*, 8 (Boileau's translation, chap. vi).
[4] No. 314.

as that great Critick observes, may animate and inflame the Sublime, but is not essential to it. Accordingly, as he further remarks, we very often find that those, who excell most in stirring up the Passions, very often want the Talent of Writing in the Great and Sublime manner; and so on the contrary. *Milton* has shewn himself a Master in both these ways of Writing. The Seventh Book, which we are now entering upon, is an Instance of that Sublime, which is not mixt and work'd up with Passion. The Author appears in a kind of composed and sedate Majesty; and tho' the Sentiments do not give so great an Emotion[a] as those in the former Book, they abound with as magnificent Ideas. The Sixth Book, like a troubled Ocean, represents Greatness in Confusion; the Seventh affects the Imagination like the Ocean in a Calm, and fills the Mind of the Reader without producing in it any thing like Tumult or Agitation.

The Critick abovementioned, among the Rules which he lays down for succeeding in the Sublime way of Writing, proposes to his Reader, that he should imitate the most celebrated Authors who have gone before him, and have been engaged in Works of the same nature; as in particular that if he writes on a Poetical Subject, he should consider how *Homer* would have spoken on such an Occasion.[1] By this means one great Genius often catches the Flame from another, and writes in his Spirit, without copying servilely after him. There are a thousand Shining Passages in *Virgil*, which have been lighted up by *Homer*.

Milton, though his own natural Strength of Genius was capable of furnishing out a perfect Work, has doubtless very much raised and ennobled his Conceptions, by such an Imitation as that which *Longinus* has recommended.

In this Book, which gives us an Account of the Six Days Works, the Poet received but very few Assistances from Heathen Writers, who were Strangers to the Wonders of Creation. But as there are many Glorious Stroaks of Poetry upon this Subject in Holy Writ, the Author has numberless Allusions to them through the whole Course of this Book. The great Critick,[2] I have before mentioned, tho' an Heathen, has taken notice of the Sublime manner in which the Law-giver of the *Jews* has described the Creation in the First

---

[a] so great an Emotion] so great Emotion *Fol.*

---

[1] Longinus, 14. 1 (Boileau, chap. xii). Addison refers to this at the beginning of *Guardian* 152: 'There is no rule in Longinus which I more admire . . . .'

[2] Longinus, 9. 9 (Boileau, chap. vii).

Chapter of *Genesis*; and there are many other Passages in Scripture, which rise up to the same Majesty, where this Subject is toucht upon. *Milton* has shewn his Judgment very remarkably, in making use of such of these as were proper for his Poem, and in duly qualifying those high Strains of Eastern Poetry, which were suited to Readers whose Imaginations were set to an higher pitch than those of colder Climates.

Adam's Speech to the Angel, wherein he desires an Account of what had passed within the Regions of Nature before the Creation,[a] is very great and solemn.[1] The following Lines, in which he tells him that the Day is not too far spent for him to enter upon such a Subject, are exquisite in their kind.

> *And the Great light of day yet wants to run*
> *Much of his race though steep, suspens in Heav'n*
> *Held by thy voice, thy potent voice he hears,*
> *And longer will delay to hear thee tell*
> *His Generation, &c. . . .*[2]

The Angel's encouraging our first Parents[b] in a modest pursuit after Knowledge, with the Causes which he assigns for the Creation of the World, are very just and beautiful. The Messiah, by whom, as we are told in Scripture,[3] the Worlds[c] were made, comes[d] forth in the Power of his Father, surrounded with an Host of Angels, and cloathed with such a Majesty as becomes his entering upon a Work, which, according to our Conceptions, appears[e] the utmost exertion of Omnipotence. What a beautiful Description has our Author raised upon that Hint in one of the Prophets;[f] *And behold there came four Chariots out from between two Mountains, and the Mountains were Mountains of Brass?*[g][4]

> *About his Chariot numberless were pour'd*
> Cherub *and* Seraph, *Potentates and Thrones,*
> *And virtues, winged Spirits, and Chariots wing'd,*
> *From the Armoury of God, where stand of old*
> *Myriads between two brazen mountains lodg'd*

---

[a] before the Creation,] before his Creation, *Fol.*   [b] Parents] Parent *Fol.*
[c] Worlds] *19;* Heavens *Fol., 8vo, 12mo*   [d] comes] *all edd. Corrected in Folio Errata* (*No. 369*) *to* goes   [e] appears] looks like *Fol.*   [f] Prophets;] *19;* Prophets. *Fol., 8vo, 12mo*   [g] Brass?] *19;* Brass. Fol., 8vo, 12mo

[1] *PL,* vii. 70–108.   [2] *PL,* vii. 98–102.
[3] John i. 3; Ephes. iii. 9; Heb. i. 2, &c.   [4] Zech. vi. 1.

Against a solemn day, harnest at hand;
Celestial Equipage, and now came forth
Spontaneous, for within them spirit liv'd
Attendant on their lord: Heav'n open'd wide
Her ever-during Gates, Harmonious sound
On golden Hinges moving . . .[1]

I have before taken notice of these Chariots of God, and of these Gates of Heaven,[2] and shall here only add, that *Homer* gives us the same Idea of the latter as opening of themselves, tho' he afterwards takes off from it, by telling us, that the Hours first of all removed those prodigious heaps of Clouds which lay as a Barrier before them.[3]

I do not know any thing in the whole Poem more Sublime than the Description which follows, where the Messiah is represented at the head of his Angels, as looking down into the *Chaos*, calming its Confusion, riding into the midst of it, and drawing the first Out-Line of the Creation.

On Heav'nly ground they stood, and from the shore
They view'd the vast immeasurable Abyss
Outragious as a Sea, dark, wasteful, wild,
Up from the bottom turn'd by furious winds
And surging waves, as Mountains to assault
Heav'ns height, and with the Center mix the Pole.
Silence ye troubled waves, and thou Deep, Peace,
Said then th' Omnific word, your Discord end:
Nor staid, but on the wings of Cherubim
Up-lifted, in Paternal Glory rode
Far into Chaos, and the world unborn;
For Chaos heard his voice: him all his train
Follow'd in bright Procession to behold
Creation, and the wonders of his might.
Then staid the fervid wheels, and in his hand
He took the golden Compasses, prepared
In Gods eternal Store, to circumscribe
This Universe, and all created things:
One foot he Center'd, and the other turn'd,
Round through the vast profundity obscure,

---

[1] *PL*, vii. 197–207.　　　　　　　　　　　　　[2] See Nos. 327, 333.
[3] *Iliad*, 5. 748–51; 8. 393–5.

And said, thus far extend, thus far thy bounds,
This be thy just Circumference, O World.[1]

The Thought of the Golden Compasses is conceiv'd altogether in *Homer*'s Spirit, and is a very noble Incident in this wonderful Description. *Homer*, when he speaks of the Gods, ascribes to them several Arms and Instruments with the same greatness of Imagination. Let the Reader only peruse the Description of *Minerva*'s *Ægis*,[2] or Buckler, in the Fifth Book of the Iliad,[a] with her Spear, which would[b] overturn whole Squadrons, and her Helmet, that was sufficient to cover an Army, drawn out of an hundred Cities: The Golden Compasses, in the above-mentioned Passage appear a very natural Instrument in the Hand of him, whom *Plato* somewhere calls the Divine Geometrician.[3] As Poetry delights in cloathing abstracted Ideas in Allegories and sensible Images,[4] we find a magnificent Description of the Creation form'd after the same manner in one of the Prophets, wherein he describes the Almighty Architect as measuring the Waters in the hollow of his Hand, meting out the Heavens with his Span, comprehending the Dust of the Earth in a Measure, weighing the Mountains in Scales, and the Hills in a Ballance.[5] Another of them describing the Supreme Being in this great Work of Creation, represents him as laying the Foundations of the Earth, and stretching a Line upon it.[6] And in another place as garnishing the Heavens, stretching out the North over the empty place, and hanging the Earth upon nothing.[7] This last noble Thought *Milton* has express'd in the following Verse.

And Earth self-ballanc'd on her Center hung.[8]

The Beauties of Description in this Book lie so very thick, that it is impossible to enumerate them in this Paper. The Poet has employed on them the whole Energy of our Tongue. The several great Scenes of the Creation rise up to view one after another, in such a manner that the Reader seems present at this wonderful

---

[a] of the Iliad,] *added in 19*   [b] would] could *Fol.*

[1] *PL*, vii. 210–31.   [2] *Iliad*, 5. 738–47.
[3] Plutarch, *Symposiaca*, 8. 2. Bayle, art. 'Zeno the Epicurean', Remark D, cites the passage from Plutarch, 'which turns on a Maxim of Plato, that God is continually Employed in Geometrical Exercises'.
[4] In his *Essay on Virgil's Georgics* (1697) Addison had praised Virgil's art in clothing precepts of morality and objects of natural philosophy with beautiful descriptions and images, 'which are the spirit and life of poetry' (Guthkelch, i. 4).
[5] Isa. xl. 12.   [6] Job xxxviii. 4, 5.
[7] Job xxvi. 13, 7.   [8] *PL*, vii. 242.

Work, and to assist among the Quires of Angels, who are the Spectators of it. How glorious is the Conclusion of the first Day.

> *. . . Thus was the first day Ev'n and Morn.*
> *Nor past uncelebrated, nor unsung*
> *By the Celestial Quires when Orient light*
> *Exhaling first from Darkness they beheld;*
> *Birth-day of Heav'n and Earth; with joy and shout*
> *The hollow universal Orb they fill'd.*[1]

We have the same elevation of Thought in the third Day, when the Mountains were brought forth, and the Deep was made.

> *Immediately the mountains huge appear*
> *Emergent, and their broad bare backs up heave*
> *Into the Clouds, their tops ascend the Sky.*
> *So high as heav'd the tumid hills, so low*
> *Down sunk a hollow bottom broad and deep,*
> *Capacious bed of Waters . . .*[2]

We have also the rising of the whole vegetable World described in this Day's Work, which is fill'd with all the Graces that other Poets have lavished on their Descriptions of the Spring, and leads the Reader's Imagination into a Theatre equally surprizing and beautiful.[3]

The several Glories of the Heav'ns make their appearance on the Fourth Day.

> *First in his East the glorious lamp was seen*
> *Regent of day, and all th' Horizon round*
> *Invested with bright rays, jocond to run*
> *His Longitude through Heav'ns high rode: the Gray*
> *Dawn, and the Pleiades before him danced*
> *Shedding sweet influence: less bright the moon,*
> *But opposite in level'd West was set,*
> *His Mirror, with full face borrowing her light*
> *From him, for other light she needed none*
> *In that aspect, and still that distance keeps*
> *Till night; then in the East her turn she shines*
> *Revolv'd on Heav'ns great Axle, and her reign*
> *With thousand lesser lights dividual holds,*

[1] *PL*, vii. 252–7. [2] *PL*, vii. 285–90. [3] *PL*, vii. 309–38.

With thousand thousand stars, that then appear'd
Spangling the Hemisphere . . .[1]

One would wonder how the Poet could be so concise in his Description of the Six Days Works, as to comprehend them within the bounds of an Episode, and at the same time so particular, as to give us a lively Idea of them. This is still more remarkable in his Account of the Fifth and Sixth Days,[a] in which he has drawn out to our view the whole Animal Creation, from the Reptil to the Behemoth.[2] As the Lion and the Leviathan are two of the noblest Productions in the World[b] of living Creatures, the Reader will find a most exquisite Spirit of Poetry, in the Account which our Author gives us of them.[3] The Sixth Day concludes with the Formation of Man,[4] upon which the Angel takes occasion, as he did after the Battel in Heaven, to remind *Adam* of his Obedience, which was the principal Design of this his Visit.

The Poet afterwards represents the Messiah returning into Heaven, and taking a Survey of his great Work. There is something inexpressibly Sublime in this Part of the Poem, where the Author describes that great Period of Time, fill'd with so many Glorious Circumstances; when the Heavens and Earth[c] were finished; when the Messiah ascended up in Triumph through the Everlasting Gates; when he look'd down with pleasure upon his new Creation; when every Part of Nature seemed to rejoice in its Existence; when the Morning Stars sang together, and all the Sons of God shouted for Joy.[5]

So Ev'n and Morn accomplish'd the Sixth day:
Yet not till the Creator from his Work
Desisting, tho' unwearied, up return'd,
Up to the Heav'n of Heav'ns his high abode,
Thence to behold this new created world
Th' addition of his empire; how it shew'd
In prospect from his throne, how good, how fair
Answering his great Idea. Up he rode
Follow'd with acclamation and the Sound
Symphonious of ten thousand harps that tun'd

[a] Days,] Day, *Fol.*   [b] the World] this World *Fol.*   [c] and Earth] and the Earth *Fol.*

[1] *PL*, vii. 370–84.   [2] *PL*, vii. 387–504.   [3] *PL*, vii. 463–6, 412–16.
[4] *PL*, vii. 505–47.   [5] Job xxxviii. 7.

Angelic Harmonies: the earth, the air
Resounded, (thou remember'st, for thou heard'st)
The Heavens and all the Constellations rung,
The Planets in their Station list'ning stood,
While the bright pomp ascended jubilant.
Open, ye everlasting gates, they sung,
Open, ye Heav'ns, your living doors, let in
The great Creator from his work return'd
Magnificent, his six days work, a World.[1]

I cannot conclude this Book upon the Creation, without mentioning a Poem which has lately appeared under that Title.[2] The Work was undertaken with so good an Intention, and is executed with so great a Mastery, that it deserves to be looked upon as one of the most useful and noble Productions in our *English* Verse. The Reader cannot but be pleased to find the Depths of Philosophy enlivened with all the Charms of Poetry, and to see so great a Strength of Reason, amidst so beautiful a Redundancy[3] of Imagination. The Author has shewn us that Design in all the Works of Nature, which necessarily leads us to the Knowledge of its first Cause. In short, he has illustrated, by numberless and incontestable Instances, that Divine Wisdom, which the Son of *Sirach* has so nobly ascribed to the Supreme Being in his Formation of the World, when he tells us, that *He created her, and saw her, and numbered her, and poured her out upon all his Works.*[4]   L[5]

---

[1] *PL*, vii. 550–68 (line 563, 'stations').

[2] It was advertised in No. 313:

This Day is Publish'd, Creation. A Philosophical Poem. Demonstrating the Existence and Providence of a God. In Seven Books. By Sir Richard Blackmore, Knt. M.D. and Fellow of the College of Physicians in London. Printed for Sam. Buckley, at the Dolphin in little Britain, and Jacob Tonson, at Shakespear's Head over against Catherine-street in the Strand.

For the generally favourable reception of the poem see Albert Rosenberg, *Sir Richard Blackmore* (Lincoln, Nebr., 1953), pp. 100–4.

[3] I.e. superabundance.

[4] Ecclus. i. 9.

[5] On the same date of this essay Defoe wrote in the *Review*: 'If anything could heighten the imagination or move the passions and affections in the subject which Milton wrote upon, more than reading Milton himself, I should think the world beholden to the Spectator for his extraordinary notes upon that sublime work.'

No. 340
[STEELE]

Monday, March 31, 1712[1]

Quis novus hic nostris successit sedibus Hospes?
Quem sese Ore ferens! quam forti Pectore & Armis!
Virg.

I TAKE it to be the highest Instance of a noble Mind, to bear great Qualities without discovering in a Man's Behaviour any Consciousness that he is superiour to the rest of the World: Or, to say it otherwise, it is the Duty of a great Person so to demean himself, as that whatever Endowments he may have, he may appear to value himself upon no Qualities but such as any Man may arrive at: He ought to think no Man valuable but for his publick Spirit, Justice, and Integrity; and all other Endowments to be esteemed only as they contribute to the exerting those Virtues. Such a Man, if he is wise or valiant, knows it is of no Consideration to other Men that he is so, but as he employs those high Talents for their Use and Service. He who affects the Applauses and Addresses of a Multitude, or assumes to himself a Pre-eminence upon any other Consideration, must soon turn Admiration into Contempt. It is certain that there can be no Merit in any Man who is not conscious of it; but the Sense that it is valuable only according to the Application of it, makes that Superiority amiable which would otherwise be invidious. In this Light it is considered as a thing in which every Man bears a Share: It annexes the Ideas of Dignity, Power, and Fame in an agreeable and familiar Manner to him who is Possessor of it; and all Men who were Strangers to him are naturally incited to indulge a Curiosity in beholding the Person, Behaviour, Feature and Shape, of him in whose Character, perhaps, each Man had formed something in common with himself. Whether such, or any other, are the Causes, all Men have a yearning[a] Curiosity to behold a Man of heroick Worth; and I have had many[b] Letters from all Parts of this Kingdom, that request I would give them an exact Account of the

---

[a] a yearning] an earning *Fol.*   [b] have had many] have very many *Fol.*

---

[1] *Motto.* Virgil, *Aeneid,* 4. 10–11:
  Who is this Stranger in our Palace seen?
  How great in Arms, of what a godlike Mien?

Stature, the Mein, the Aspect, of the Prince who lately visited *England*, and has done such Wonders for the Liberty of *Europe*.[1] It would puzzle the most Curious to form to himself the Sort of Man my several Correspondents expect to hear of, by the Action mentioned, when they desire a Description of him: There is always something that concerns themselves, and growing out of their own Circumstances, in all their Enquiries. A Friend of mine in *Wales* beseeches me to be very exact in my Account of that wonderful Man who had marched an Army and all its Baggage over the *Alps*; and, if possible, to learn whether the Peasant who shewed him the Way,[2] and is drawn in the Map, be yet living. A Gentleman from the University, who is deeply intent on the Study of Humanity, desires me to be as particular, if I had Opportunity, in observing the whole Interview between his Highness and our late General. Thus do Mens Fancies work according to their several Educations and Circumstances; but all pay a Respect, mixed with Admiration, to this illustrious Character. I have waited for his Arrival in *Holland*,[3] before I would let my Corespondents know, that I have not been so uncurious a Spectator, as not to have seen Prince *Eugene*. It would be very difficult, as I said just now, to answer every Expectation of those who have writ to me on that Head; nor is it possible for me to find Words to let one know, what an artful Glance there is in his Countenance who surprized *Cremona*; how daring he appears who forced the Trenches of *Turin*:[4] But in general can say, that he who beholds him, will easily expect from him any thing that is to be imagined or executed by the Wit or Force of Man. The Prince is of that Stature which makes a Man most easily become all Parts of

[1] Prince Eugene of Savoy (1663–1736), the friend and colleague of Marlborough in the wars against Louis XIV, had been in England from 5 Jan. to 18 Mar. of this year (cf. No. 269, vol. ii). According to Burnet, 'That Prince's character was so justly high, that all people for some weeks pressed about the places, where he was to be seen, to look on him . . .' (*History*, ed. 1753, iv. 350). The *Political State of Great Britain*, Mar. 1712 (iii. 231–5), quotes from this essay by 'the ingenious and famous Author of the *Philological* Paper call'd the *Spectator*', and concludes: 'I shall not pretend to add any thing to this finish'd Piece: But only observe, that you ought not to suspect in it any Artful Heightnings: Since the Author, with the Character, he sustains, with deserv'd Applause, of *Censor* of *Great Britain*, professes an utter Abhorrence of Flattery' (p. 235).

[2] I have not identified this.

[3] 'Yesterday Morning Prince Eugene of Savoy imbark'd at Greenwich for Holland' (*Post-Man*, Tues., 18 Mar. 1712).

[4] In February 1702 Eugene surprised the French garrison at Cremona and captured the commander, Marshal Villeroi. In September 1706, by marching through the valley of the Po, he came to the relief of Turin (which had been besieged by nearly 60,000 French) and succeeded in routing the French, thus securing Italy for the Allies. See Trevelyan, ii. 140–4.

Exercise; has Height to be graceful on Occasions of State and Ceremony, and no less adapted for Agility and Dispatch: His Aspect is
erect and compos'd; his Eye lively and thoughtful, yet rather
vigilant than sparkling: His Action and Address the most easy
imaginable, and his Behaviour in an Assembly peculiarly graceful
in a certain Art of mixing insensibly with the rest, and becoming
one of the Company, instead of receiving the Courtship of it. The
Shape of his Person, and Composure of his Limbs, are remarkably
exact and beautiful.[1] There is in his Look something sublime, which
does not seem to arise from his Quality or Character, but the innate
Disposition of his Mind. It is apparent that he suffers the Presence
of much Company, instead of taking Delight in it; and he appeared
in Publick while with us, rather to return Good-will, or satisfy
Curiosity, than[a] to gratify any Taste he himself had of being popular.
As his Thoughts are never tumultuous in Danger, they are as little
discomposed on Occasions of Pomp and Magnificence: A great Soul
is affected in either Case, no further than in considering the properest Methods to extricate it self from them. If this Heroe has the
strong Incentives to uncommon Enterprizes that were remarkable
in *Alexander*, he prosecutes and enjoys the Fame of them with the
Justness, Propriety, and good Sense of *Cæsar*. It is easy to observe in
him a Mind as capable of being entertained with Contemplation
as Enterprize; a Mind ready for great Exploits, but not impatient
for Occasions to exert it self. The Prince has Wisdom and Valour in
as high Perfection as Man can enjoy it; which noble Faculties in
conjunction, banish all Vain-Glory, Ostentation, Ambition, and all
other Vices which might intrude upon his Mind to make it unequal.
These Habits and Qualities of Soul and Body render this Personage
so extraordinary, that he appears to have nothing in him but what
every Man should have in him, The Exertion of his very self,
abstracted from the Circumstances in which Fortune has placed
him. Thus were you to see Prince *Eugene*, and were told he was
a private Gentleman, you would say he is a Man of Modesty and

[a] satisfy Curiosity, than] satisfy a Curiosity, more than *Fol.*

---

[1] Swift, who saw Eugene at court on 13 Jan., wrote to Stella, 'I don't think him an
ugly faced fellow, but well enough, and a good shape' (*Journal to Stella*, ed. Williams,
p. 463). Burnet describes him in even more complimentary language: 'He has a most
unaffected modesty, and does scarcely bear the acknowledgments that all the
world pay him: He descends to an easy equality with those, with whom he converses; and seems to assume nothing to himself, while he reasons with others'
(*History*, ed. 1753, iv. 350).

Merit: Should you be told that was Prince *Eugene*, he would be diminished no otherwise, than that Part of your distant Admiration would turn into familiar Good-will. This I thought fit to entertain my Reader with, concerning an Heroe who never was equalled but by one Man;[1] over whom also he has this Advantage, that he has had an Opportunity to manifest an Esteem for him in his Adversity.

T[2]

No. 341   *Tuesday, April 1, 1712*[3]

[BUDGELL]

> . . . *Revocate animos mœstumque timorem*
> *Mittite* . . .
>
>   Virg.

HAVING, to oblige my Correspondent *Physibulus*, Printed his Letter last *Friday*, in Relation to the New Epilogue, he cannot take it amiss, if I now publish another, which I have just received from a Gentleman,[4] who does not agree with him in his Sentiments upon that matter.

SIR,

'I AM amazed to find an Epilogue attacked in your last *Friday*'s Paper, which has been so generally applauded by the Town,

---

[1] The Duke of Marlborough, who had been dismissed from his employments on 31 Dec. 1711. Steele's third child was born on 4 Mar., during the Prince's visit to England, and was christened on 2 Apr. Eugene.

[2] A brief comment on this paper by J. C. is printed in Lillie (ii. 235), praising Marlborough, 'worthy of his great mistress's favours by his faithfulness, and Britain's unalterable veneration by noblest actions and more signal services'.

[3] *Motto.* Virgil, *Aeneid*, I. 202–3:

> Resume your Courage, and dismiss your Care. DRYDEN.

[4] Budgell, the author of the Epilogue. Many years later, in *The Bee* (No. 20, July 1733), Budgell defends this epilogue against the charge that it was 'smutty'. It was spoken no less than nine times by Mrs. Oldfield, he says, on the three first performances, and after the exchange of letters in *Spectators* 338 and 341 Lord Halifax sent for Budgell and told him that 'From thence forward, he must be acquainted with him, and desired to be ranked among the Number of his Friends' (*The Bee*, vol. ii, p. 855).

and received such Honours as were never before given to any in an *English* Theatre.

'The Audience would not permit Mrs. *Oldfield* to go off the Stage the First Night, till she had repeated it twice. The Second Night the Noise of *Ancoras* was as loud as before, and she was again obliged to speak it twice. The Third Night it was still called for a Second time; and, in short, contrary to all other Epilogues, which are dropp'd after the third Representation of the Play, this has already been repeated nine times.

'I must own, I am the more surprised to find this Censure in Opposition to the whole Town, in a Paper which has hitherto been famous for the Candour of its Criticisms.

'I can by no means allow your melancholy Correspondent, that the new Epilogue is unnatural, because it is gay. If I had a mind to be learned I could tell him, that the Prologue and Epilogue were real Parts of the ancient Tragedy; but every one knows that on the *British* Stage they are distinct Performances by themselves, Pieces intirely detached from the Play, and no way essential to it.

'The Moment the Play ends, Mrs. *Oldfield* is no more *Andromache*, but Mrs. *Oldfield*; and tho' the Poet had left *Andromache stone-dead upon the Stage*, as your ingenious Correspondent phrases it, Mrs. *Oldfield* might still have spoke a merry Epilogue. We have an Instance of this in a Tragedy, where there is not only a Death, but a Martyrdom.[1] St. *Catherine* was there personated by *Nell Gwin*, she lies *Stone-dead upon the Stage*, but upon those Gentlemens offering to remove her Body, whose business it is to carry off the Slain in our *English* Tragedies, she breaks out into that abrupt beginning, of what was a very ludicrous, but at the same time thought a very good Epilogue.

> *Hold, are you mad? you damn'd confounded Dog,*
> *I am to rise and speak the Epilogue.*

[1] Dryden's *Tyrannick Love* (1669), in which Nell Gwynn, playing the part of Valeria, stabs herself and dies. The part of St. Catherine was actually played by Mrs. Boutell, and Budgell's reference may derive from the concluding lines of Dryden's epilogue:

> As for my Epitaph when I am gone,
> I'le trust no Poet, but will write my own.
> Here *Nelly* lies, who, though she liv'd a Slater'n,
> Yet dy'd a Princess, acting in *S. Cathar'n.*

For earlier examples of facetious epilogues to tragedies see Autrey Nell Wiley, 'Female Prologues and Epilogues in English Plays', *PMLA*, xlviii (1933), 1060–79, especially pp. 1074–9 ('Merry Prologues and Epilogues').

'This diverting manner was always practised by Mr. *Dryden*, who, if he was not the best Writer of Tragedies in his Time, was allowed by every one to have the happiest Turn for a Prologue or an Epilogue. The Epilogues to *Cleomenes*, *Don Sebastian*, *The Duke of Guise*, *Aurenge Zebe*, and *Love Triumphant*, are all Presidents of this nature.

'I might further justifie this Practice by that Excellent Epilogue which was spoken a few Years since, after the Tragedy of *Phædra* and *Hippolitus*;[1] with a great many others, in which the Authors have endeavour'd to make the Audience merry. If they have not all succeeded so well as the Writer of this, they have, however, shewn that it was not for want of Good-will.

'I must further observe, that the Gayety of it may be still the more proper, as it is at the End of a *French* Play; since every one knows that Nation, who are generally esteemed to have as polite a Taste as any in *Europe*, always close their Tragic Entertainments with what they call a *Petite Piece*, which is purposely design'd to raise Mirth, and send away the Audience well pleased. The same Person, who has supported the chief Character in the Tragedy, very often plays the Principal Part in the *Petite Piece*, so that I have my self seen at *Paris*, *Orestes* and *Lubin*[2] acted the same Night by the same Man.

'Tragi-Comedy, indeed, you have your self in a former Speculation[3] found fault with very justly, because it breaks the Tide of the Passions while they are yet flowing; but this is nothing at all to the present Case, where they have already had their full Course.

'As the new Epilogue is written conformably to the Practice of our best Poets, so it is not such an one which, as the Duke of *Buckingham* says in his *Rehearsal*,[4] might serve for any other Play, but wholly rises out of the Occurrences of the Piece it was Composed for.

'The only Reason your Mournful Correspondent gives against this *facetious Epilogue*, as he calls it, is, that he has a mind to go home *Melancholy*. I wish the Gentleman may not be more Grave than

[1] By Edmund Smith, produced at the Haymarket on 21, 22, 25, and 26 Apr. 1707. See No. 18 (vol. i). Mrs. Oldfield played the part of Ismena, the captive princess, and the Epilogue was by Prior.
[2] In Racine's *Andromaque* and Molière's *George Dandin*.
[3] No. 40 (vol. i).
[4] In the opening scene Bayes announces: 'I have made a prologue and an epilogue which may both serve for either—do you mark? Nay, they may both serve too, I gad, for any other play as well as this.'

Wise: For my own part, I must confess I think it very sufficient to have the Anguish of a fictitious Piece remain upon me while it is representing, but I love to be sent home to Bed in a good Humour. If *Physibulus* is however resolved to be inconsolable, and not to have his Tears dried up, he need only continue his old Custom, and when he has had his half Crowns worth of Sorrow, slink out before the Epilogue begins.

'It is pleasant enough to hear this Tragical Genius complaining of the *great mischief Andromache* had done him: What was that? Why, she made him laugh. The poor Gentleman's Sufferings put me in mind of *Harlequin's* Case, who was tickled to Death. He tells us soon after, thro' a small Mistake of Sorrow for Rage, that during the whole Action he was so very Sorry, that he thinks he could have attack'd *half a Score of the fiercest Mohocks* in the excess of his Grief. I cannot but look upon it as an happy Accident, that a Man who is so bloody-minded in his Affliction, was diverted from this Fit of outragious Melancholy. The Valour of this Gentleman in his Distress, brings to ones Memory the *Knight of the Sorrowful Countenance,*[1] who lays about him at such an unmerciful rate in an old Romance. I shall readily grant him, that his Soul, as he himself says, *would have made a very ridiculous figure, had it quitted the Body, and descended to the Poetical Shades* in such an Encounter.

'As to his Conceit of tacking a *Tragic Head* with *a Comic Tail,* in order to *refresh the Audience,* it is such a Piece of *Jargon,* that I don't know what to make of it.

'The Elegant Writer makes a very sudden Transition from the Play-house to the Church, and from thence to the Gallows.

'As for what relates to the Church, he is of Opinion that these Epilogues have given occasion to those *merry Jiggs from the Organ-Loft, which have dissipated those good Thoughts and Dispositions he has found in himself, and the rest of the Pew, upon the singing of two Staves cull'd out by the judicious and diligent Clark.*

'He fetches his next Thought from *Tyburn*; and seems very apprehensive least there should happen any Innovations in the Tragedies of his Friend *Paul Lorrain.*

'In the mean time, Sir, this gloomy Writer, who is so mightily scandalized at a gay Epilogue after a serious Play, speaking of the Fate of those unhappy Wretches who are Condemned to suffer an Ignominious Death by the Justice of our Laws, endeavours to make

[1] Don Quixote.

the Reader merry on so improper an Occasion, by those poor Burlesque Expressions of *Tragical Drama's* and *Monthly Performances.*

I am, SIR,

with great Respect,

your most obedient,

most humble Servant,

Philomeides.'[1]

X

No. 342   *Wednesday, April 2, 1712*[2]

[STEELE]

*Justitiæ partes sunt non violare homines: Verecundiæ, non
offendere.*

Tull.

AS Regard to Decency is a great Rule of Life in general, but more
especially to be consulted by the Female World; I cannot
overlook the following Letter, which describes an egregious
Offender.

Mr. SPECTATOR,

'I WAS this Day looking over your Papers; and reading in that of
December 6th[3] with great Delight, the amiable Grief of *Asteria*
for the Absence of her Husband, it threw me into a great deal of
Reflection. I cannot say but this arose very much from the Circumstances of my own Life, who am a Soldier, and expect every Day to
receive Orders; which will oblige me to leave behind me a Wife that
is very dear to me, and that very deservedly. She is, at present,
I am sure, no way below your *Asteria* for Conjugal Affection: But
I see the Behaviour of some Women so little suited to the Circumstances wherein my Wife and I shall soon be, that it is with a
Reluctance I never knew before, I am going to my Duty. What puts
me to present Pain, is the Example of a young Lady, whose Story

---

[1] I.e. laughter-loving, the epithet of Aphrodite (*Odyssey*, 8. 362, &c.). The Greek
form of the word is cited at the end of No. 249 (vol. ii).

[2] *Motto.* Cicero, *De Officiis*, 1. 28. 99: It belongs to *Justice* not to *wrong* men; and
to *Modesty*, not to *offend* them. L'ESTRANGE.

[3] No. 241 (vol. ii).

you shall have as well as I can give it you. *Hortensius*, an Officer of good Rank in Her Majesty's Service, happened in a certain Part of *England* to be brought to a Country-Gentleman's House, where he was received with that more than ordinary Welcome, with which Men of domestick Lives entertain such few Soldiers whom a military Life, from the Variety of Adventures, has not rendered over-bearing, but humane, easy, and agreeable. *Hortensius* stay'd here some Time, and had easy Access at all Hours, as well as unavoidable Conversation at some Parts of the Day with the beautiful *Sylvana*, the Gentleman's Daughter. People who live in Cities are wonderfully struck with every little Country Aboad they see when they take the Air; and 'tis natural to such to fancy they could live in every neat Cottage (by which they pass) much happier than in their present Circumstances. The turbulent way of Life which *Hortensius* was used to, made him reflect with much Satisfaction on all the Advantages of a sweet Retreat one Day; and among the rest, you'll think it not improbable, it might enter into his Thought, that such a Woman as *Sylvana* would consummate the Happiness. The World is so debauched with mean Considerations, that *Hortensius* knew it would be received as an Act of Generosity, if he asked for a Woman of the highest Merit, without further Questions, of a Parent who had nothing to add to her personal Qualifications. The Wedding was celebrated at her Father's House: When that was over, the generous Husband did not proportion his Provision for her to the Circumstances of her Fortune, but considered his Wife as his Darling, his Pride, and his Vanity; or rather that it was in the Woman he had chosen that a Man of Sense could shew Pride or Vanity with any Excuse, and therefore adorned her with rich Habits and valuable Jewels. He did not however omit to admonish her that he did his very utmost in this, that it was an Ostentation he could not but be guilty of to a Woman he had so much Pleasure in, desiring her to consider it as such; and begged of her also to take these Matters rightly, and believe the Gems, the Gowns, the Laces, would still become her better, if her Air and Behaviour was such, that it might appear she dressed thus rather in Complyance to his Humour that Way, than out of any Value she herself had for the Trifles. To this Lesson, too hard for Woman, *Hortensius* added, that she must be sure to stay with her Friends in the Country till his Return. Assoon as *Hortensius* departed, *Sylvana* saw in her Looking-glass that the Love he conceived for her was wholly owing to the

Accident of seeing her; and she is convinced it was only her Misfortune the rest of Mankind had not beheld her, or Men of much greater Quality and Merit had contended for one so genteel, tho' bred in Obscurity; so very witty, tho' never acquainted with Court or Town. She therefore resolved not to hide so much Excellence from the World, but without any Regard to the Absence of the most generous Man alive, she is now the gayest Lady about this Town, and has shut out the Thoughts of her Husband by a constant Retinue of the vainest young Fellows this Age has produced; to entertain whom she squanders away all *Hortensius* is able to supply her with, tho' that Supply is purchased with no less Difficulty than the Hazard of his Life.

'Now, Mr. SPECTATOR, would it not be a Work becoming your Office, to treat this Criminal as she deserves? You should give it the severest Reflexions you can: You should tell Women, that they are more accountable for behaviour in absence, than after Death. The dead are not dishonoured by their Levities; the living may return, and be laughed at by empty Fops; who will not fail to turn into Ridicule the good Man, who is so unseasonable as to be still alive, and come and spoil good Company.

> *I am,*
> SIR,
> *Your most Obedient,*
> *Humble Servant.'*

All strictness of behaviour is so unmercifully laughed at in our Age, that the other much worse Extreme is the more common Folly. But let any Woman consider which of the two Offences an Husband would the more easily forgive, that of being less entertaining than she could to please Company, or raising the desires of the whole Room to his disadvantage; and she will easily be able to form her Conduct: We have indeed carryed Womens Characters too much into publick Life, and you shall see them now a-Days affect a sort of Fame: But I cannot help venturing to disoblige them for their service, by telling them, that the utmost of a Woman's Character is contained in Domestick Life;[1] she is Blameable or Praise-worthy according as her carriage affects the House of her Father or her

---

[1] Cf. Rae Blanchard, 'Richard Steele and the Status of Women', *Studies in Philology*, xxvi (1929), 325–55. Vol. ii of *The Ladies Library*, which Steele brought out in 1714, is divided into the following sections: The Daughter, The Wife, The Mother, The Widow, and The Mistress.

Husband. All she has to do in this World, is contained within the Duties of a Daughter, a Sister, a Wife, and a Mother: All these may be well performed tho' a Lady should not be the very finest Woman at an Opera, or an Assembly. They are likewise consistent with a moderate share of Wit, a plain Dress, and a modest Air. But when the very Brains of the Sex are turned, and they place their Ambition on Circumstances wherein to excell, 'tis no addition to what is truly Commendable. Where can this end, but as it frequently does in their placing all their Industry, Pleasure and Ambition on things, which will naturally make the Gratifications of Life last, at best no longer than Youth and good Fortune? And when we consider the least ill Consequence, it can be no less, than looking on their own condition as Years advance, with a disrelish of Life, and falling into Contempt of their own Persons, or being the derision of others. But when they consider themselves, as they ought, no other than an additional Part of the Species, (for their own Happiness and Comfort, as well as that[a] of those for whom they were born) their Ambition to excell will be directed accordingly; and they will in no part of their Lives want Opportunities of being shining Ornaments to their Fathers, Husbands, Brothers or Children.   T

No. 343
[ADDISON]

Thursday, April 3, 1712[1]

> *. . . Errat, & illinc*
> *Huc venit, hinc illuc, & quoslibet occupat artus*
> *Spiritus: éque feris humana in corpora transit,*
> *Inque feras noster . . .*
>
> Pythag. ap. Ov.

WILL. HONEYCOMB, who loves to shew upon occasion all the little Learning he has picked up, told us yesterday at the Club, that he thought there might be a great deal said for the

---

[a] as well as that] as well that *Fol.*

[1] *Motto.* Ovid, *Metamorphoses,* 15. 165–8:
> From Seat to Seat the wand'ring Spirit strays,
> From Man to Beast at certain times it roams,
> Thence back to Man its former Mansion comes.

Transmigration of Souls, and that the Eastern parts of the World believed in that Doctrine to this Day. Sir *Paul Rycaut*, says he, gives us an account of several well-disposed Mahometans that purchase the Freedom of any little Bird they see confined to a Cage, and think they merit as much by it, as we shou'd do here by ransoming any of our Countrymen from their Captivity at *Algiers*.[1] You must know, says WILL. the reason is, because they consider every Animal as a Brother or a Sister in disguise, and therefore think themselves obliged to extend their Charity to them, tho' under such mean Circumstances. They'll tell you, says WILL. that the Soul of a Man, when he dies, immediately passes into the Body of another Man, or of some Brute, which he resembled in his Humour, or his Fortune, when he was one of *us*.

As I was wondring what this profusion of Learning would end in, WILL. told us, that *Jack Freelove*, who was a Fellow of Whim, made Love to[a] one of those Ladies who throw away all their Fondness on[b] Parrots, Monkeys and Lap-dogs. Upon going to pay her a Visit one Morning, he writ a very pretty Epistle upon this Hint. *Jack*, says he, was conducted into the Parlour, where he diverted himself for some time with her Favourite Monkey, which was chained in one of the Windows; 'till at length observing a Pen and Ink lie by him, he writ the following Letter to his Mistress in the Person of the Monkey, and upon her not coming down so[c] soon as he expected, left it in the Window, and went about his Business.

The Lady soon after coming into the Parlour, and seeing her Monkey look upon a Paper with great Earnestness, took it up, and to this Day is in some doubt, says WILL. whether it was written by *Jack*, or the Monkey.

[a] to] with *Fol.*   [b] on] upon *Fol.*   [c] so] as *Fol.*

---

[1] Sir Paul Rycaut, *The Present State of the Ottoman Empire* (1668), writes (book ii, chap. xxvi): 'Those who would appear of a compassionate and tender nature, hold it a pious work to buy a Bird from a cage to give him his liberty; and hold it a merciful action to buy bread and feed the Dogs . . .' (p. 167). He says nothing, however, at this point of transmigration. The discussion of this comes in book ii, chap. xii, where he describes the Munashi sect (pp. 132–3). Addison is doubtless quoting from memory and confusing the two passages—or attributing something read elsewhere to Rycaut. The *Voyages and Travels of John Albert de Mandelslo into the East Indies* (1638) associates the belief in transmigration with mercy toward animals. 'What is yet more superstitious, they do not onely redeem the Birds, which the *Mahumetans* had taken, but they also built Hospitals for Beasts that are hurt and wounded' (book i, p. 68).

Madam,

'NOT having the Gift of Speech, I have a long time waited in vain for an Opportunity of making my self known to you, and having at present the Conveniencies of Pen, Ink and Paper by me, I gladly take the Occasion of giving you my History in Writing, which I could not do by Word of Mouth. You must know, Madam, that about a thousand Years ago I was an *Indian* Brachman, and versed in all those mysterious Secrets which your *European* Philosopher, called *Pythagoras*,[1] is said to have learned from our Fraternity. I had so ingratiated my self by my great Skill in the Occult Sciences with a Dæmon whom I used to converse with, that he promised to grant me whatever I should ask of him. I desired that my Soul might never pass into the Body of a Brute Creature; but this he told me was not in his Power to grant me. I then begg'd that into whatever Creature I should chance to Transmigrate, I might still retain my Memory, and be conscious that I was the same Person who lived in different Animals. This he told me was within his Power, and accordingly promised on the Word of a Dæmon, that he would grant me what I desired. From that time forth I lived so very unblameably, that I was made President of a College of Brachmans; an Office which I discharged with great Integrity 'till the Day of my Death.

'I was then shuffled into another Human Body, and acted my part so very well in it, that I became first Minister to a Prince who reigned upon the Banks of the *Ganges*. I here lived in great Honour for several Years, but by degrees lost all the Innocence of the Brachman, being obliged to rifle and oppress the People to enrich my Sovereign; till at length I became so odious, that my Master, to recover his Credit with his Subjects, shot me through the Heart with an Arrow, as I was one Day addressing my self to him at the head of his Army.

'Upon my next Remove I found my self in the Woods, under the Shape of a Jack-call, and soon listed my self in the Service of a Lion. I used to yelp near his Den about Midnight, which was his time of rouzing and seeking after his Prey. He always followed me in the Rear, and when I had run down a fat Buck, a wild Goat, or an Hare, after he had feasted very plentifully upon it himself, would now and then throw me a Bone that was but half picked for my Encourage-

---

[1] His views on transmigration are outlined in Dacier's *Life of Pythagoras* (1707), pp. 43-50.

ment; but upon my being unsuccessful in two or three Chaces, he gave me such a confounded gripe in his Anger, that I died of it.

'In my next Transmigration I was again set upon two Legs, and became an *Indian* Tax-gatherer; but having been guilty of great Extravagancies, and being married to an expensive Jade of a Wife, I ran so cursedly in Debt that I durst not shew my Head. I could no sooner step out of my House, but I was arrested by some body or other that lay in wait for me. As I ventured abroad one Night in the Dusk of the Evening, I was taken up and hurried into a Dungeon, where I died a few Months after.

'My Soul then entered into a flying-fish, and in that State led a most melancholy Life for the space of Six Years. Several Fishes of Prey pursued me when I was in the Water, and if I betook my self to my Wings it was ten to one but I had a Flock of Birds aiming at me. As I was one Day flying amidst a Fleet of *English* Ships, I observed an huge Sea-Gull whetting his Bill and hovering just over my Head: Upon my dipping into the Water to avoid him, I fell into the Mouth of a monstrous Shark that swallowed me down in an Instant.

'I was some Years afterwards, to my great surprise, an eminent Banker in *Lombard-Street*, and remembring how I had formerly suffered for want of Mony, became so very sordid and avaritious, that the whole Town cryed shame of me. I was a miserable little old Fellow to look upon, for I had in a manner starved my self, and was nothing but Skin and Bone when I dyed.

'I was afterwards very much troubled and amazed, to find my self dwindled into an Emmet. I was heartily concerned to make so insignificant a Figure, and did not know but, some time or other, I might be reduced to a Mite, if I did not mend my Manners. I therefore applied my self, with great Diligence, to the Offices that were allotted me, and was generally looked upon as the notablest Ant in the whole Molehill. I was at last picked up, as I was groaning under a Burden, by an unlucky Cock-sparrow that lived in the Neighbourhood, and had before made great Depredations upon our Common-wealth.

'I then bettered my Condition a little, and lived a whole Summer in the Shape of a Bee; but being tired with the painful and penurious Life I had undergone in my two last Transmigrations, I fell into the other Extream, and turned Drone. As I one Day headed a Party to plunder an Hive, we were received so warmly by the Swarm which defended it, that we were most of us left dead upon the Spot.

'I might tell you of many other Transmigrations which I went through; how I was a Town-Rake, and afterwards did Penance in a Bay-Gelding for Ten Years; as also how I was a Taylor, a Shrimp, and a Tom-Tit. In the last of these my Shapes[a] I was shot in the Christmas Hollydays by a young Jack-a-napes, who would needs try his new Gun upon me.

'But I shall pass over these and several other Stages of Life, to remind you of the young Beau who made Love to you about Six Years since. You may remember, Madam, how he masked, and danced, and sung, and played a thousand Tricks to gain you; and how he was at last carried off by a Cold that he got under your Window one Night in[b] a Serenade. I was that unfortunate young Fellow, whom you were then so cruel to. Not long after my shifting that unlucky Body, I found my self upon a Hill in *Æthiopia*, where I lived in my present Grotesque Shape, till I was caught by a Servant of the *English* Factory, and sent over into *Great Britain*: I need not inform you how I came into your Hands. You see, Madam, this is not the first time that you have had me in a Chain; I am however very happy in this my Captivity, as you often bestow on me those Kisses and Caresses which I would have given the World for when I was a Man. I hope this Discovery of my Person will not tend to my Disadvantage, but that you will still continue your accustomed Favours to

Your most Devoted
Humble Servant,
Pugg.

'*P. S.* I would advise your little Shock-dog to keep out of my way, for as I look upon him to be the most formidable of my Rivals, I may chance one time or other to give him such a Snap as he wont like.'

L

---

[a] these my Shapes] these Shapes *Fol*.　　[b] in] at *Fol*.

> . . . *In solo vivendi causa palato est.*
>   Juv.

Mr. SPECTATOR,

'I THINK it has not yet fallen in your Way to discourse on little Ambition, or the many whimsical Ways Men fall into, to distinguish themselves among their Acquaintance: Such Observations, well pursued, would make a pretty History of low Life. I myself am got into a great Reputation, which arose (as most extraordinary Occurrences in a Man's Life seem to do) from a meer Accident. I was some Days ago unfortunately engaged among a Set of Gentlemen, who esteem a Man according to the Quantity of Food he throws down at a Meal.[2] Now I, who am ever for distinguishing my self according to the Notions of Superiority which the rest of the Company entertain, eat so immoderately for their Applause, as had like to have cost me my Life: What added to my Misfortune was, that having naturally a good Stomach, and having lived soberly for some time, my Body was as well prepared for this Contention, as if it had been by Appointment. I had quickly vanquished every Glutton in Company but one, who was such a Prodigy in his Way, and withal so very merry during the whole Entertainment, that he insensibly betrayed me to continue his Competitor, which in a little time concluded in a compleat Victory over my Rival; after which, by Way of Insult, I eat a considerable Proportion beyond what the Spectators thought me obliged in Honour to do. The Effect, however, of this Engagement, has made me resolve never to eat more for Renown; and I have, pursuant to this Resolution, compounded three Wagers I had depending on the Strength of my Stomach, which happened very luckily, because it was stipulated in our Articles either to play or pay. How a Man of common Sense could be thus engaged is hard to determine; but the Occasion of this is to desire you, to inform several Gluttons of my Acquaintance, who look on me with Envy, that they had best moderate their Ambition in time, lest Infamy or Death attend their Success. I forgot to tell

---

[1] *Motto.* Juvenal, *Satires*, 11. 11:

> Whose sole Bliss is eating. CONGREVE.

[2] Excessive eating and drinking are frequently commented on in the *Tatler*, Nos. 205, 241, 252, &c.

you, Sir, with what unspeakable Pleasure I received the Acclamations and Applause of the whole Board, when I had almost eat my
Antagonist into Convulsions: It was then that I returned his Mirth
upon him, with such Success as he was hardly able to swallow,
though prompted by a Desire of Fame, and a passionate Fondness
for Distinction: I had not endeavoured to excell so far, had not the
Company been so loud in their Approbation of my Victory. I don't
question but the same Thirst after Glory, has often caused a Man
to drink Quarts without taking Breath, and prompted Men to many
other as difficult Enterprizes; though, if otherwise pursued, might
turn very much to a Man's Advantage. This Ambition of mine was
indeed extravagantly pursued: However I can't help observing, that
you hardly ever see a Man commended for a good Stomach, but
he immediately falls to eating more (though he had before dined) as
well to confirm the Person that commended him in his good Opinion
of him, as to convince any other at the Table, who may have been
unattentive enough not to have done Justice to his Character.

I am,

SIR,

Your most humble Servant,

Epicure Mammon.'[1]

Mr. SPECTATOR,

'I HAVE writ to you three or four Times, to desire you would take
Notice of an impertinent Custom the Women, the fine Women,
have lately fallen into, of taking Snuff.[2] This silly trick is attended
with such a Coquet Air in some Ladies, and such a sedate Masculine
one in others, that I cannot tell which most to complain of; but they

---

[1] In Jonson's *Alchemist*. It had recently (19 Feb.) been produced at Drury Lane;
Sir Epicure Mammon was one of Estcourt's roles.

[2] See No. 73 (vol. i). Various kinds of snuff are frequently advertised in the
Spectator—by Francis Zouch, in Thames–street, corner of Garlick-Hill, at the bottom
of Bow-lane, Cheapside (Nos. 10, 12); at Sam's Coffee-house, Ludgate-street (Nos. 27,
181); by Robert Tate, Druggist, at the Star in Bedford-Court, Covent-Garden (Nos.
33, 39) and later against York Buildings in the Strand (No. 108, &c.); by Tho.
Burges, Druggist, at the Blue Anchor in Fleet-street (Nos. 418, 422, &c.); and at
Elford's Coffee-house in George-yard, Lombard-street (No. 502). Plain Spanish seems
to have varied in price from 4 to 8 shillings a pound, Portugal snuff to have sold at
about 24 shillings a pound, and Brazil snuff from 20 to 50 shillings a pound.

There are also many advertisements of 'snuff' for medical purposes—Sir Theodore
Maynern's Imperial Snuff, 'each Paper 6d.', sold at 'Mr. Garretts under the Royal
Exchange', and at other places (Nos. 48, &c.); Angelick Snuff, 'removing all
manner of Disorders of the Head and Brain', sold at Mr. Payn's Toyshop at the
Angel and Crown in St. Paul's Church Yard, 'Price 1s. a Paper, with Directions'
(Nos. 68, 92, &c.); the True Royal Snuff for Purging the Head, 'Price 9d. a
Paper', at Edmund Calverley's, Stationer, at the Lyon and Lamb, near the Kings-

are to me equally disagreeable. Mistress *Saunter* is so impatient of being without it, that she takes it as often as she does Salt at Meals; and as she affects a wonderful Ease and Negligence in all her Manner, an upper Lip mixed with Snuff and the Sauce, is what is presented to the Observation of all who have the Honour to Eat with her. The pretty Creature, her Niece, does all she can to be as disagreeable as her Aunt; and if she is not as offensive to the Eye, she is quite as much to the Ear, and makes up all she Wants in a confident Air, by a nauseous Rattle of the Nose when the Snuff is delivered, and the Fingers make the Stops and Closes on the Nostrils. This, perhaps, is not a very courtly Image in speaking of Ladies, that is very true; but where arises the Offence? Is it in those who commit, or those who observe it? As for my part, I have been so extremely Disgusted with this filthy Physick hanging on the Lip, that the most agreeable Conversation, or Person, has not been able to make up for it. As to those who take it for no other end but to give themselves Occasion for pretty Action, or to fill up little Intervals of Discourse, I can bear with them; but then they must not use it when another is speaking, who ought to be heard with too much Respect, to admit of offering at that Time from Hand to Hand the Snuff-Box. But *Flavilla* is so far taken with her Behaviour in this Kind, that she pulls out her Box (which is indeed full of good *Brazile*)[1] in the middle of the Sermon; and to shew she has the Audacity of a well-bred Woman, she offers it the Men as well as the Women who sit near her: But since by this Time all the World knows she has a fine Hand, I am in hopes she may give herself no further Trouble in this Matter. On *Sunday* was sennight, when they came about for the Offering, she gave her Charity with a very good Air; but at the same Time asked the Church-warden if he would take a Pinch. Pray Sir, think of these Things in Time, and you will oblige,

SIR,

Your most humble Servant.'

T[2]

Head-Inn in the Borough of Southwark, and at three other places (Nos. 386, 392); Dr. Tyson's Apoplectick Snuff, at St. James's Coffee-House at St. James's, and elsewhere, at 3s. 6d. a Box (No. 348); and a snuff 'which cures the Head-ach', offered by a 'Gentlewoman' at the Golden Heart and Golden Ball next Door to Mr. Ridout's, Surgeon, in Salisbury-Court, Fleet-street (No. 593).

[1] Charles Lillie's *British Perfumer, Snuff Manufacturer, and Colourman's Guide* (1822), chap. lx, describes this superior type of snuff 'made in the Brazils'. Here the tobacco is 'gently dried, not washed, in order not to destroy entirely the green color of the leaf' (pp. 321–2).

[2] *The Medley* of this date comments: 'I heard t'other Day some sowr-fac'd Criticks

No. 345   *Saturday, April 5, 1712*[1]
[ADDISON]

> *Sanctius his animal, mentisque capacius altæ*
> *Deerat adhuc, & quod dominari in cætera posset.*
> *Natus homo est . . .*
>
>   Ov. Met.

THE Accounts which *Raphael* gives of the Battel of Angels, and the Creation of the World, have in them those Qualifications which the Criticks judge requisite to an Episode.[2] They are nearly related to the principal Action, and have a just Connection with the Fable.

The Eighth Book opens with a beautiful Description of the Impression which this Discourse of the Archangel made on our first Parents.[a] *Adam* afterwards, by a very natural Curiosity, enquires concerning the Motions of those Celestial Bodies which make the most glorious Appearance among the six Days Works. The Poet here, with a great deal of Art, represents *Eve* as withdrawing from this part of their Conversation to Amusements more suitable[b] to her Sex. He well knew, that the Episode in this Book, which is filled with *Adam*'s Account of his Passion and Esteem for *Eve*, would have been improper for her hearing, and has therefore devised very just and beautiful Reasons for her Retiring.

[a] Parents.] *19*; Parent. *Fol., 8vo, 12mo*   [b] Amusements more suitable] Amusements that seem more suitable *Fol.*

---

complain, that the *Spectator* writes about *Nothing*; and yet who is there so remarkable in any sort of Learning, that would not be content to part with all his past Reputation, to be able for the future to write like the *Spectator*?'

[1] Motto. Ovid, *Metamorphoses*, I. 76–78:

> A creature of a more exalted kind
> Was wanting yet, and then was man designed;
> Conscious of thought, of more capacious breast,
> For empire formed and fit to rule the rest. DRYDEN.

[2] See Le Bossu, book ii, chap. ii–vi. Le Bossu defines episodes as 'necessary Parts of the Action, extended by probable Circumstances' (II. vi). Dennis, who quotes this definition without acknowledgement in his *Remarks on Prince Arthur* (1696), goes on to name the three qualities which episodes must have (again borrowing from Le Bossu): they are to be derived from the first plan of the action, they are to have a necessary or probable dependence one upon another, and they are not to be complete in themselves (*Works*, ed. Hooker, i. 58). Rapin calls the episode 'a kind of Digression from the Subject' and stipulates that it be proportionately short, closely related to the subject, and not used too often ('A Comparison of Homer and Virgil', chap. vi, *Whole Critical Works*, 1706, i. 151).

So spake our Sire, and by his Countenance seem'd
Entring on studious thoughts abstruse, which Eve
Perceiving where she sat retired in sight,
With lowliness Majestick from her Seat
And Grace that won who saw to wish her stay,
Rose, and went forth among her fruits and flowers
To visit how they prosper'd, bud and bloom,
Her Nursery; they at her coming sprung,
And toucht by her fair tendance gladlier grew.
Yet went she not, as not with such discourse
Delighted, or not capable her ear
Of what was high: Such pleasure she reserv'd
Adam *relating, she sole Auditress;*
Her Husband the relater she preferr'd
Before the Angel, and of him to ask
Chose rather: he, she knew, would intermix
Grateful digressions, and solve high dispute
With conjugal Caresses, from his Lip
Not words alone pleased her. O when meet now
Such pairs in Love, and mutual honour join'd?[1]

The Angel's returning a doubtful Answer to *Adam*'s Enquiries, was not only proper for the Moral Reason which the Poet assigns, but because it would have been highly absurd to have given the Sanction of an Archangel to any particular System of Philosophy. The chief Points in the *Ptolomaick* and *Copernican* Hypothesis are described with great Conciseness and Perspicuity, and at the same time dressed in very pleasing and Poetical Images.

Adam, to detain the Angel, enters afterwards upon his own History, and relates to him the Circumstances in which he found himself upon his Creation; as also his Conversation with his Maker, and his first Meeting with *Eve*. There is no part of the Poem more apt to raise the attention of the Reader, than this Discourse of our great Ancestor; as nothing can be more surprizing and delightful to us, than to hear the Sentiments that arose in the first Man while he was yet new and fresh from the hands of his Creator. The Poet has interwoven every thing which[a] is delivered upon this Subject

[a] which] that *Fol.*

[1] *PL*, viii. 39–58. Steele quotes this passage in *Tatler* 149 'as a Lecture to those of my own Sex, who have a Mind to make their Conversation agreeable as well as instructive, to the Fair Partners who are fallen into their Care'.

in Holy Writ with so many beautiful Imaginations of his own, that nothing can be conceived more just and natural than this whole Episode. As our Author knew this Subject could not but be agreeable to his Reader, he would not throw it into the relation of the six Days Works, but reserved it for a distinct Episode, that he might have an opportunity of expatiating upon it more at large. Before I enter on this part of the Poem, I cannot but take notice of two shining Passages in the Dialogue between *Adam* and the Angel.[1] The first is that wherein our Ancestor gives an Account of the Pleasure he took in conversing with him, which contains a very noble Moral.

> *For while I sit with thee, I seem in Heav'n,*
> *And sweeter thy discourse is to my ear*
> *Than fruits of Palm-tree pleasantest to thirst*
> *And hunger both, from labour, at the hour*
> *Of sweet repast; they satiate, and soon fill,*
> *Tho' pleasant, but thy words with Grace divine*
> *Imbu'd, bring to their sweetness no satiety.*[2]

The other I shall mention is that in which the Angel gives a reason why he should be glad to hear the Story *Adam* was about to relate.

> *For I that day was absent, as befell,*
> *Bound on a Voyage uncouth and obscure,*
> *Far on excursion towards the Gates of Hell;*
> *Squar'd in full Legion (such command we had)*
> *To see that none thence issued forth a Spy,*
> *Or enemy, while God was in his work,*
> *Lest he incenst at such eruption bold,*
> *Destruction with Creation might have mix'd.*[3]

There is no question but our Poet drew the Image in what follows from that in *Virgil's* Sixth Book, where *Æneas* and the Sybil stand before the *Adamantine* Gates which are there describ'd as shut upon the place of Torments, and listen to the Groans, the clank of Chains, and the noise of Iron Whips that were heard in those Regions of Pain and Sorrow.[4]

> *... Fast we found, fast shut*
> *The dismal gates, and barricadoed strong;*

[1] *PL*, viii. 250–520.
[3] *PL*, viii. 229–36.
[2] *PL*, viii. 210–16.
[4] *Aeneid*, 6. 552–8.

But long e'er our approaching heard within
Noise, other than the sound of Dance or Song,
Torment, and loud lament, and furious rage.[1]

Adam then proceeds to give an Account of his Condition and Sentiments immediately after his Creation. How agreeably does he represent the posture in which he found himself, the delightful[a] Landskip that surrounded him, and the gladness of Heart which grew up in him on that occasion.

. . . As new waked from soundest sleep
Soft on the flowry herb I found me laid
In balmy sweat, which with his beams the Sun
Soon dried, and on the reaking moisture fed.
Streight toward Heav'n my wondering eyes I turn'd,
And gaz'd a while the ample Sky, 'till rais'd
By quick instinctive motion up I sprung
As thitherward endeavouring, and upright
Stood on my feet; about me round I saw
Hill, Dale, and shady woods and sunny plains,
And liquid lapse of murmuring streams; by these
Creatures that liv'd, and mov'd, and walk'd, or flew,
Birds on the branches warbling; all things smil'd:
With fragrance, and with Joy my heart o'erflow'd.[b][2]

Adam is afterwards describ'd as surpriz'd at his own Existence, and taking a Survey of himself, and of all the Works of Nature. He[3] likewise is represented as discovering by the Light of Reason, that he and every thing about him must have been the effect of some Being infinitely good and powerful, and that this Being had a Right to his Worship and Adoration. His first address to the Sun, and to those parts of the Creation which made the most distinguished Figure, is very natural and amusing to the Imagination.[4]

. . . Thou Sun, said I, fair Light,
And thou enlight'ned earth, so fresh and gay,
Ye Hills and Dales, ye Rivers, Woods and Plains,

---

[a] delightful] *19*; beautiful *Fol., 8vo, 12mo*　　　[b] o'erflow'd.] *overflow'd. Fol.*

---

[1] PL, viii. 240–4.　　　　　　　　　[2] PL, viii. 253–66.
[3] PL, viii. 267–77; 278–82.
[4] See No. 321 (above, p. 174). In No. 351 (below, p. 309) and elsewhere 'amusement' is used in the modern sense of 'diversion'.

And ye that live and move, fair creatures tell,
Tell if you saw, how came I thus, how here?[1]

His next Sentiment, when upon his first going to Sleep he fancies himself losing his Existence, and falling away into nothing, can never be sufficiently admired.[2] His Dream, in which he still preserves the Consciousness of his Existence, together with his removal into the Garden which was prepared for his Reception, are also Circumstances finely imagined, and grounded upon what is delivered in Sacred Story.[3]

These and the like wonderful Incidents, in this Part of the Work, have in them all the Beauties of Novelty, at the same time that they have all the Graces of Nature. They are such as none but a great Genius could have thought of, though, upon the perusal of them, they seem to rise of themselves from the Subject of which he treats. In a Word, though they are natural they are not obvious, which is the true Character of all fine Writing.

The Impression which the Interdiction of the Tree of Life left in the Mind of our First Parent, is described with great Strength and Judgment,[4] as the Image of the several Beasts and Birds passing in review before him is very beautiful and lively.

> *. . . Each Bird and Beast behold*
> *Approaching two and two, these cowring low*
> *With blandishment, each bird stoop'd on his Wing:*
> *I nam'd them as they pass'd . . .*[5]

Adam, in the next place, describes a Conference which he held with his Maker upon the Subject of Solitude.[6] The Poet here represents the Supreme Being, as making an Essay of his own Work, and putting to the tryal that reasoning Faculty, with which he had endued his Creature. *Adam* urges, in this divine Colloquy, the Impossibility of his being happy, tho' he was the Inhabitant of *Paradise*, and Lord of the whole Creation, without the Conversation and Society of some rational Creature, who should partake those Blessings with him. This Dialogue, which is supported chiefly by the Beauty of the Thoughts, without other Poetical Ornaments, is as fine a part as any in the whole Poem: The more the Reader

---

[1] *PL*, viii. 273–7.
[2] *Tatler* 6 had quoted lines 283–91, with praise for the 'wonderfully just and natural' thoughts contained therein.
[3] *PL*, viii. 292–451.
[4] *PL*, viii. 333–6.
[5] *PL*, viii. 349–52.
[6] *PL*, viii. 357–451.

examines the justness and delicacy of its Sentiments, the more he will find himself pleased with it. The Poet has wonderfully preserved the Character of Majesty and Condescention in the Creator, and at the same time that of Humility and Adoration in the Creature, as particularly in the following Lines,[a]

> *Thus I presumptuous; and the Vision bright,*
> *As with a smile more brightned, thus reply'd. &c.*
>   *. . . I with leave of speech implor'd*
> *And humble deprecation thus reply'd,*
> *Let not my Words offend thee, Heav'nly power,*
> *My maker, be propitious while I speak. &c.*[1]

Adam then proceeds to give an account of his second Sleep, and of the Dream in which he beheld the Formation of *Eve*.[2] The new Passion that was awakened in him at the sight of her is touched very finely.

> *Under his forming hands a Creature grew,*
> *Manlike, but different Sex; so lovely fair,*
> *That what seem'd fair in all the World seem'd now*
> *Mean, or in her summ'd up, in her contain'd,*
> *And in her looks, which from that time infus'd*
> *Sweetness into my heart, unfelt before,*
> *And into all things from her air inspir'd*
> *The spirit of Love and amorous delight.*[3]

Adam's Distress upon losing sight of this beautiful Phantom, with his Exclamations of Joy and Gratitude at the Discovery of a real Creature, who resembled the Apparition which had been presented to him in his Dream; the Approaches he makes to her, and his manner of Courtship, are all laid together in a most exquisite Propriety of Sentiments.[4]

Tho' this part of the Poem is work'd up with great Warmth and Spirit, the Love, which is described in it, is every way suitable to a State of Innocence. If the Reader compares the Description which *Adam* here gives of his leading *Eve* to the Nuptial Bower, with that which Mr. *Dryden*[5] has made on the same Occasion in a Scene

---

[a] in the following Lines,] *19*; in those beautiful Lines. *Fol., 8vo, 12mo*

[1] *PL*, viii. 367–8, 377–80.   [2] *PL*, viii. 452–77.
[3] *PL*, viii. 470–7. In No. 89 (vol. i) Addison had quoted lines 469–511.
[4] *PL*, viii. 478–520.
[5] *The State of Innocence, and Fall of Man* (1678), III. i.

of his *Fall of Man*, he will be sensible of the great Care which *Milton* took to avoid all Thoughts on so delicate a Subject, that might be offensive to Religion or Good-manners. The Sentiments are chaste, but not cold, and convey to the Mind Ideas of the most transporting Passion, and of the greatest Purity. What a noble Mixture of Rapture and Innocence has the Author joined together, in the Reflection which *Adam* makes on the Pleasures of Love, compared to those of Sense.

> *Thus have I told thee all my State, and brought*
> *My Story to the Sum of earthly bliss*
> *Which I enjoy, and must confess to find*
> *In all things else delight indeed, but such*
> *As us'd or not, works in the mind no change,*
> *Nor vehement desire, these delicacies*
> *I mean of taste, sight, smell, herbs, fruits and flowers,*
> *Walks, and the melody of Birds; but here*
> *Far otherwise, transported I behold,*
> *Transported touch; here passion first I felt,*
> *Commotion strange, in all enjoyments else*
> *Superiour and unmov'd, here only weak*
> *Against the Charm of beauties powerfull glance.*
> *Or nature fail'd in me, and left some part*
> *Not proof enough such object to sustain,*
> *Or from my side subducting, took perhaps*
> *More than enough; at least on her bestow'd*
> *Too much of ornament, in outward shew*
> *Elaborate, of inward less exact.*
> *. . . When I approach*
> *Her loveliness, so absolute she seems*
> *And in herself compleat, so well to know*
> *Her own, that what she wills to do or say,*
> *Seems wisest, vertuousest, discreetest, best:*
> *All higher knowledge in her presence falls*
> *Degraded: Wisdom in discourse with her*
> *Loses discountenanc'd, and like folly shews;*
> *Authority and reason on her wait,*
> *As one intended first, not after made*
> *Occasionally; and to consummate all,*
> *Greatness of mind and nobleness their Seat*

Build in her loveliest, and create an awe
About her, as a guard Angelick plac'd.[1]

These Sentiments of Love, in our First Parent, gave the Angel such an Insight into Humane Nature, that he seems apprehensive of the Evils which might befall the Species in general, as well as *Adam* in particular, from the Excess of this Passion. He therefore fortifies him against it by timely Admonitions;[2] which very artfully prepare the Mind of the Reader for the Occurrences of the next Book, where the Weakness of which *Adam* here gives such distant discoveries, brings about that fatal Event which is the Subject of the Poem. His Discourse, which follows the gentle Rebuke he receiv'd from the Angel, shews that his Love, however violent it might appear, was still founded in Reason, and consequently not improper for *Paradise*.

> *Neither her outside form so fair, nor aught*
> *In procreation common to all kinds*
> *(Though higher of the genial bed by far,*
> *And with mysterious reverence I deem)*
> *So much delights me as those graceful acts,*
> *Those thousand decencies that daily flow*
> *From all her words and actions mixt with love*
> *And sweet compliance, which declare unfeign'd*
> *Union of mind, or in us both one Soul;*
> *Harmony to behold in wedded pair.*[3]

Adam's Speech, at parting with the Angel, has in it a Deference and Gratitude agreeable to an Inferior Nature, and at the same time a certain Dignity and Greatness, suitable to the Father of Mankind in his State of Innocence.[4]   L

[1] *PL*, viii. 521–39, 546–59. Addison had quoted lines 546–59 in *Tatler* 102; lines 546–54 he quotes later in *Free-Holder* 32, adding: 'If there is such a native Loveliness in the Sex, as to make them Victorious even when they are in the wrong, how resistless is their Power when they are on the Side of Truth!'
[2] *PL*, viii. 561–94.
[3] *PL*, viii. 596–605 ('Neither her outside found so fair').
[4] *PL*, viii. 645–51.

No. 346   *Monday, April* 7, 1712[1]
[STEELE]

*Consuetudinem benignitatis largitioni Munerum longe
antepono. Hæc est Gravium hominum atque Magnorum:
Illa quasi assentatorum populi, multitudinis levitatem
voluptate quasi titillantium.*

Tull.

WHEN we consider the Offices of humane Life, there is,
methinks, something in what we ordinarily call Generosity,
which, when carefully examined, seems to flow rather from a loose
and unguarded Temper, than an honest and liberal Mind. For this
Reason it is absolutely necessary, that all Liberality should have for
its Basis and Support Frugality. By this Means the beneficent Spirit
works in a Man from the Convictions of Reason, not from the
Impulses of Passion. The generous Man, in the ordinary Acceptation, without respect to the Demands of his own Family, will soon
find, upon the Foot[2] of his Account, that he has sacrificed to Fools,
Knaves, Flatterers, or the deservedly unhappy, all the Opportunities
of affording any future Assistance where it ought to be. Let him
therefore reflect, that if to bestow be in it self laudable, should not
a Man take Care to secure an Ability to do things Praise-worthy as
long as he lives? Or could there be a more cruel Piece of Rallery
upon a Man who should have reduced his Fortune below the
Capacity of acting according to his natural Temper, than to say of
him, *That Gentleman was generous.* My beloved Author therefore has,
in the Sentence on the Top of my Paper, turned his Eye with
a certain Satiety from beholding the Addresses to the People by
Largesses and publick Entertainments, which he asserts to be in
general vicious, and are always to be regulated according to the
Circumstances of Time and a Man's own Fortune.[3] A constant
Benignity in Commerce with the rest of the World, which ought to
run through all a Man's Actions, has Effects more useful to those

---

[1] *Motto.* Cicero, *De Officiis*, 2. 18. 63: I prefer an habitual Benignity before a
Prodigality in Gifts. The one is peculiar to great and wise Men; the other to such as
court the Mob, and would win upon their Levity, by tickling their Vanity.

[2] I.e. the sum or total (of an account). This is the last quotation in *OED* of this
sense.

[3] In this and the following three sentences Steele paraphrases Cicero, *De Officiis*,
2. 18. 64.

whom you oblige, and less ostentatious in your self. He turns his Recommendation of this Virtue in commercial Life; and according to him, a Citizen who is frank in his Kindnesses, and abhors Severity in his Demands; he who in buying, selling, lending, doing acts of good Neighbourhood, is just and easy; he who appears naturally averse to Disputes, and above the Sense of little Sufferings, bears a nobler Character, and does much more Good to Mankind than any other Man's Fortune without Commerce can possibly support. For the Citizen above all other Men has Opportunities of arriving at *that highest Fruit of Wealth, to be liberal without the least Expence of a Man's own Fortune.* It is not to be denied but such a Practice is liable to Hazard; but this therefore adds to the Obligation, that, among Traders, he who obliges is as much concerned to keep the Favour a Secret, as he who receives it. The unhappy Distinctions among us in *England* are so great, that to celebrate the Intercourse of commercial Friendship (with which I am daily made acquainted) would be to raise the virtuous Man so many Enemies of the contrary Party. I am obliged to conceal all I know of *Tom the Bounteous*,[1] who lends at the ordinary Interest, to give Men of less Fortune Opportunities of making greater Advantages. He conceals under a rough Air and distant Behaviour a bleeding Compassion and womanish Tenderness. This is governed by the most exact Circumspection, that there is no Industry wanting in the Person whom he is to serve, and that he is guilty of no improper Expences. This I know of *Tom*, but who dares say it of so known a Tory? The same Care I was forced to use some Time ago in the Report of another's Virtue, and said Fifty instead of an Hundred,[2] because the Man I pointed at was a Whigg. Actions of this Kind are popular without being invidious, for every Man of ordinary Circumstances looks upon a Man who has this known Benignity in his Nature, as a Person ready to be his Friend upon such Terms as he ought to expect it; and the Wealthy, who may envy such a Character, can do no Injury to its Interests but by the Imitation of it, in which the good Citizens will rejoyce to be rivalled. I know not how to form to my self a greater Idea of Humane Life, than in what is the Practice

---

[1] Nichols quotes from Blundel's manuscript notes in a copy of the 12mo edition of 1712: 'Tom Colson. This gentleman is represented in a very different light in the Tatler No. 46, under the name of Aurenzebe.' The satiric picture of Aurengezebe in *Tatler* 46, sometimes taken for Governor Pitt, was designed for the goldsmith or banker, Sir Stephen Evance, who superintended the cutting of the Pitt diamond and who was afterwards a bankrupt (Nichols).

[2] Steele may refer to the letter by W. S. in No. 248 (vol. ii).

of some wealthy Men whom I could name, that make no Step to
the improvement of their own Fortunes, wherein they do not also
advance those of other Men, who would languish in Poverty without that Munificence. In a Nation where there are so many publick
Funds to be supported, I know not whether he can be called a good
Subject, who does not imbark some Part of his Fortune with the
State to whose Vigilance he owes the security of the whole. This
certainly is an immediate Way of laying an Obligation upon many,
and extending your Benignity the furthest a Man can possibly, who
is not engaged in Commerce. But he who Trades, besides giving
the State some part of this sort of Credit he gives his Banker, may
in all the Occurrences of his Life, have his Eye upon removing Want
from the Door of the Industrious, and defending the unhappy
upright Man from Bankrupcy. Without this Benignity, Pride or
Vengeance will precipitate a Man to chuse the Receipt of half his
Demands from one whom he has undone, rather than the whole
from one to whom he has shewn Mercy. This Benignity is essential
to the Character of a fair Trader, and any Man who designs to
enjoy his Wealth with Honour and Self-Satisfaction: Nay it would
not be hard to maintain, that the Practice of supporting good and
industrious Men, would carry a Man further, even to his Profit,
than indulging the Propensity of serving and obliging the Fortunate.
My Author argues on this Subject, in order to incline Men's minds
to those who want them most, after this Manner. *We must always
consider the Nature of things, and govern our selves accordingly. The
wealthy Man when he has repaid you, is upon a Balance with you; but the
Person whom you favoured with a Loan, if he be a good Man, will think
himself in your Debt after he has paid you. The Wealthy and the Conspicuous
are not obliged by the benefits you do them, they think they conferred a
Benefit when they receive one. Your good Offices are always suspected, and it
is with them the same thing to expect their favour as to receive it. But the
Man below you, who knows in the good you have done him, you respected
himself more than his Circumstances, does not act like an obliged Man
only to him from whom he has received a Benefit, but also to all who
are capable of doing him one. And whatever little Offices he can do for
you, he is so far from magnifying it, that he will labour to extenuate it
in all his Actions and Expressions. Moreover the regard to what you do
to a great Man, at best is taken Notice of no further than by himself or
his Family; but what you do to a Man of an humble Fortune, (provided
always that he is a good and a modest Man) raises the Affections to-*

wards you, of all Men of that Character (of which there are many) in the whole City.[1]

There is nothing gains a Reputation to a Preacher so much as his own Practice; I am therefore casting about what Act of Benignity is in the Power of a SPECTATOR. Alass that lies but in a very narrow Compass, and I think the most immediately under my Patronage, are either Players, or such whose Circumstances bear an affinity with theirs: All therefore I am able to do at this Time of this Kind, is to tell the Town, that on *Friday* the Eleventh of this Instant *April,* there will be performed in *York-Buildings,*[2] a Consort of Vocal and instrumental Musick, for the Benefit of Mr. *Edward Keen,*[3] the Father of Twenty Children; and that this Day the haughty *George Powell*[4] hopes all the Good-natured Part of the Town, will favour him whom they Applauded in *Alexander*, *Timon*, *Lear* and *Orestes,*[5] with their Company this Night, when he hazards all his Heroick Glory for their Approbation in the humbler Condition of honest *Jack Falstaffe.*   T

[1] Cicero, *De Officiis*, 2. 20. 69–70.

[2] The blocks of houses erected on the site of York House, the old palace of the Archbishop of York, when it was pulled down in 1672. Steele lived in Villiers Street, York Buildings, from 1719 until 1724.

[3] Concerts for his benefit were no new thing. The *Post Boy* of 9 May 1699 advertises 'a Consort of New Vocal, and Instrumental Musick, for the benefit of Mr. Edward Keene, who was the first Promoter of the Musical Entertainments in Sommerset-House Garden', to be given at the Music Room in York-Buildings on Friday the 16th. Another is announced in the *Daily Courant* of 26 Mar. 1707 for that date in York Buildings.

[4] An advertisement in this number announces a performance at Drury Lane for this night of *King Henry IV, with the Humours of Sir John Falstaff*. 'The Part of Falstaff to be perform'd by Mr. Powell, for his own Benefit.'

[5] Orestes was Powell's role in *The Distrest Mother*, which had had eight performances in the preceding month. *Lear* had been given at Drury Lane on 26 Feb. 1712, *Timon of Athens* on 30 Oct. 1711. His playing of Alexander in *The Rival Queens*, at Penketh-man's theatre in the summer of 1710 (4 and 6 July), would be still remembered.

No. 347   *Tuesday, April* 8, 1712[1]
[BUDGELL]

Quis furor o Cives! quæ tanta licentia ferri!
                            Lucan.

I DO not question but my Country Readers have been very much surprized at the several Accounts they have met with in our Publick Papers of that Species of Men among us, lately known by the Name of *Mohocks*. I find the Opinions of the Learned, as to their Origin and Designs, are altogether various, insomuch that very many begin to doubt whether indeed there were ever any such Society of Men.[2] The Terror which spread itself over the whole Nation some Years since, on account of the *Irish*, is still fresh in most People's Memories, tho' it afterwards appeared there was not the least ground for that general Consternation.[3]

The late pannick Fear was, in the Opinion of many deep and penetrating Persons, of the same Nature. These will have it, that the *Mohocks* are like those Spectres and Apparitions which frighten several Towns and Villages in her Majesty's Dominions, tho' they were never seen by any of the Inhabitants. Others are apt to think that these *Mohocks* are a kind of Bull-beggars,[4] first invented by prudent married Men, and Masters of Families, in order to deter their Wives and Daughters from taking the Air at unseasonable Hours; and that when they tell them *the* Mohocks *will catch them*, it is a Caution of the same nature with that of our Fore-fathers, when they bid their Children have a care of *Raw-head* and *Bloody-bones*.[5]

---

[1] *Motto.* Lucan, *Pharsalia*, I. 8: What rage was this, O citizens, and whence this licence to the barbarous sword?

[2] The Whig position was that the rumours about the Mohocks were exaggerated and that the Tories were spreading the stories for political purposes. On the Mohocks see Nos. 324, 332.

[3] In the seventeenth century, particularly at the time of the Revolution, rumours were circulated of impending terrorism on the part of the Irish peasants. In Ned Ward's *London Spy*, part iv, some drunkards in a tavern are described as 'staring as if they took us for some of the *Wild-Irish*, that should have cut their Throats in the beginning of the Revolution' (Casanova Society ed., p. 77). According to Misson (p. 251) an alarm was spread in December 1688 that the Irish who were a part of James II's army were to massacre the inhabitants of London.

[4] The obsolete term for bogies or scarecrows (*OED*). A letter in *Tatler* 212 describes a masked man who turns out to be not a robber but 'a harmless Bull-Beggar, who delights to fright innocent People, and set them a gallopping'.

[5] The traditional names of nursery bugbears. Cf. *Hudibras*, III. ii. 687; Shadwell, *Epsom Wells*, IV. i; Ned Ward, *London Spy*, part iv; and John Oldmixon, *British Empire in America*, ii. 119.

For my own part I am afraid there was too much reason for that great Alarm the whole City has been in upon this occasion; tho' at the same time I must own that I am in some doubt whether the following Pieces are Genuine and Authentic, and the more so, because I am not fully satisfied that the Name by which the Emperor subscribes himself, is altogether conformable to the *Indian* Orthography.

I shall only further inform my Readers, that it was some time since I received the following Letter and Manifesto, tho' for particular Reasons I did not think fit to publish them till now.

To the SPECTATOR.

SIR,

'FINDING that our earnest Endeavours for the good of Mankind have been basely and maliciously represented to the World, we send you enclosed our Imperial Manifesto, which it is our Will and Pleasure that you forthwith communicate to the Publick, by inserting it in your next daily Paper. We do not doubt of your ready Compliance in this particular, and therefore bid you heartily farewell.

Sign'd,

Taw Waw Eben Zan Kaladar,[1]

Emperor of the Mohocks.'

The Manifesto of Taw Waw Eben Zan Kaladar, Emperor of the Mohocks.

'WHEREAS we have received Information, from sundry Quarters of this great and populous City, of several Outrages committed on the Legs, Arms, Noses, and other Parts of the good People of *England*, by such as have stiled themselves our Subjects; in order to vindicate our Imperial Dignity from those false Aspersions which have been cast on it, as if we our selves might have encouraged or abetted any such Practices; We have, by these Presents, thought fit to signifie our utmost Abhorrence and Detestation of all such tumultuous and irregular Proceedings; and do hereby further give Notice, that if any Person or Persons has or have suffered any Wound, Hurt, Damage or Detriment in his or their Limb or Limbs, otherwise than shall be hereafter Specified,

---

[1] A name obviously intended to imitate those of the Four Indian Kings (cf. No. 50, vol. i).

the said Person or Persons, upon applying themselves to such as we shall appoint for the Inspection and Redress of the Grievances aforesaid, shall be forthwith committed to the Care of our principal Surgeon, and be cured at our own Expence, in some one or other of those Hospitals which we are now erecting for that purpose.

'And to the end that no one may either thro' Ignorance or Inadvertency incur those Penalties which we have thought fit to inflict on Persons of loose and dissolute Lives, we do hereby notifie to the Publick, that if any Man be knocked down or assaulted while he is imployed in his lawful Business, at proper Hours, that it is not done by our Order; and we do hereby permit and allow any such Person so knocked down or assaulted to rise again, and defend himself in the best manner that he is able.

'We do also command all and every our good Subjects, that they do not presume upon any Pretext whatsoever to issue and sally forth from their respective Quarters till between the Hours of Eleven and Twelve. That they never *Tip the Lion*[1] upon Man, Woman or Child till the Clock at St. *Dunstans* shall have struck One.[2]

'That the *Sweat* be never given but between the Hours of One and Two; always provided, that our *Hunters* may begin to *Hunt* a little after the close of the Evening, any thing to the contrary herein notwithstanding. Provided also that if ever they are reduced to the necessity of *Pinking* it shall always be in the most fleshy Parts, and such as are least exposed to view.

'It is also our Imperial Will and Pleasure, that our good Subjects the *Sweaters* do establish their *Hummums*[3] in such close Places,

---

[1] Tip the lion, &c. For these terms see No. 332.

[2] St. Dunstan's in the West, on the north side of Fleet Street, just east of Chancery Lane, was famed for its clock which hung out into the street, described by Hatton (p. 231) as having 'two Figures of Savages or wild Men, well carved in Wood, and painted natural Colour, appearing as big as the Life, standing erect, with each a knotty Club in his Hand wherewith they alternately strike the Quarters, not only their Arms, but even their Heads, moving at every blow. . . .'

[3] The general term for a bagnio or Turkish bath. It was also the particular name of a bagnio in Covent Garden (cf. No. 332), advertised in the *Post-Man* of 12 Oct. 1706:

> At the Hummums in Covent-Garden are the best Accommodations for Persons of Quality to Sweat or Bath every hour in the year, the conveniencies of all kinds, far exceeding all other Bagnio's or Sweating Houses both for Rich and Poor. Persons of good Reputation may be accommodated with handsome Lodgings to lye all night. There is also a Man and Woman who Cup after the newest and easiest method. In the Garden of the same House is also a large Cold Bath of Spring Water, which for its Coldness and Delicacy deserves an equal Reputation with any in use.

Ward's *London Spy*, part ix, gives a realistic picture of a visit to the Hummums (Casanova Society ed., pp. 218–26).

Alleys, Nookes, and Corners, that the Patient or Patients may not be in danger of catching Cold.

'That the *Tumblers*, to whose Care we chiefly commit the Female Sex, confine themselves to *Drury-lane* and the Purlieus of the *Temple*; and that every other Party and Division of our Subjects do each of them keep within the respective Quarters we have allotted to them. Provided nevertheless, that nothing herein contained shall in any wise be construed to extend to the *Hunters*, who have our full Licence and Permission to enter into any part of the Town wherever their Game shall lead them.

'And whereas we have nothing more at our Imperial Heart than the Reformation of the Cities of *London* and *Westminster*, which to our unspeakable Satisfaction we have in some measure already effected, we do hereby earnestly pray and exhort all Husbands, Fathers, House-keepers, and Masters of Families, in either of the aforesaid[a] Cities, not only to repair themselves to their respective Habitations at early and seasonable Hours; but also to keep their Wives and Daughters, Sons, Servants and Apprentices from appearing in the Streets at those Times and Seasons, which may expose them to Military Discipline, as it is practised by our good Subjects the *Mohocks*; and we do further[b] promise, on our Imperial Word, that as soon as the Reformation aforesaid shall be brought about, we will forthwith cause all Hostilities to cease.

Given from our Court at the Devil
Tavern,[1] March 15, 1712.'   X

---

[a] aforesaid] foresaid *Fol.*   [b] further] farther *Fol.*

---

[1] The Devil Tavern, in Fleet Street, nearly opposite to St. Dunstan's in the West. Its name was originally The Devil and St. Dunstan, and its sign depicted St. Dunstan pulling the devil by the nose. Swift dined here with Garth and Addison on 12 Oct. 1710 (*Journal to Stella*, ed. Williams, p. 51).

No. 348   *Wednesday, April 9, 1712*[1]
[STEELE]

Invidiam placare paras virtute relicta?
Hor.

Mr. SPECTATOR,

'I HAVE not seen you lately at any of the Places where I visit, so
that I am afraid you are wholly unacquainted with what passes
among my part of the World, who are, tho' I say it, without Contro-
versy, the most accomplished and best bred of the Town. Give
me Leave to tell you, that I am extremely discomposed when I hear
Scandal, and am an utter Enemy to all manner of Detraction, and
think it the greatest Meanness that People of Distinction can be
guilty of: However, it is hardly possible to come into Company,
where you do not find them pulling one another to pieces, and that
from no other Provocation but that of hearing any one commended.
Merit, both as to Wit and Beauty, is become no other than the
Possession of a few trifling People's Favour, which you cannot
possibly arrive at, if you have really any thing in you that is
deserving. What they would bring to pass, is, to make all Good and
Evil consist in Report, and with Whispers, Calumnies and Imper-
tinencies, to have the Conduct of those Reports. By this means
Innocents are blasted upon their first Appearance in Town; and
there is nothing more required to make a young Woman the Object
of Envy and Hatred, than to deserve Love and Admiration. This
abominable Endeavour to suppress or lessen every thing that is
Praise-worthy, is as frequent among the Men as the Women. If I can
remember what passed at a Visit last Night, it will serve as an
Instance that the Sexes are equally inclined to Defamation, with
equal Malice, with equal Impotence. *Jack Triplett* came into my
Lady *Airye's* about Eight of Clock: You know the manner we sit
at a Visit, and I need not describe the Circle; but Mr. *Triplett* came
in, introduced by two Tapers supported by a spruce Servant, whose
Hair is under a Cap till my Lady's Candles are all lighted up, and
the Hour of Ceremony begins: I say *Jack Triplett* came in, and
singing (for he is really good Company) *Every Feature, charming
Creature;*[2] he went on, *It is a most unreasonable thing, that People cannot*

---

[1] *Motto.* Horace, *Satires* 2. 3. 13: What, would you your Virtue leave, to live
exempt from Envy?

[2] From Sir Trusty's song in Addison's *Rosamond,* II. iii. 16–17. 'Charming Creature,

go peaceably to see their Friends, but these Murderers are let loose. Such a Shape! such an Air! what a Glance was that as her Chariot passed by mine—My Lady herself interupted him; Pray who is this fine thing— I warrant, says another, 'tis the Creature I was telling your Ladyship of just now. You were telling of? says Jack; I wish I had been so happy as to have come in and heard you, for I have not Words to say what she is: But if an agreeable Height, a modest Air, a Virgin Shame, and Impatience of being beheld, amidst a Blaze of ten thousand Charms—The whole Room flew out—Oh Mr. Triplett!—When Mrs. Lofty, a known Prude, said she believed she knew whom the Gentleman meant; but she was indeed, as he civilly represented her, impatient of being beheld—Then turning to the Lady next to her—The most unbred Creature you ever saw. Another pursued the Discourse: As unbred, Madam, as you may think her, she is extremely belyed if she is the Novice she appears. She was last Week at a Ball till Two in the Morning; Mr. Triplett knows whether he was the happy Man that took Care of her Home; but—This was followed by some particular Exception that each Woman in the Room made to some peculiar Grace or Advantage; so that Mr. Triplett was beaten from one Limb and Feature to another, till he was forced to resign the whole Woman. In the End, I took Notice Triplett recorded all this Malice in his Heart; and saw in his Countenance, and a certain waggish Shrug, that he designed to repeat the Conversation. I therefore let the Discourse die, and soon after took an Occasion to commend a certain Gentleman of my Acquaintance for a Person of singular Modesty, Courage, Integrity, and withal as a Man of an entertaining Conversation, to which Advantages he had a Shape and Manner peculiarly graceful. Mr. Triplett, who is a Woman's Man,[1] seemed to hear me with Patience enough commend the Qualities of his Mind: He never heard indeed but that he was a very honest Man and no Fool, but for a fine Gentleman he must ask Pardon. Upon no other Foundation than this, Mr. Triplett took Occasion to give the Gentleman's Pedigree, by what Methods some Part of the Estate was acquired, how much it was beholden to a Marriage for the present Circumstances of it: After all, he could see nothing but a common Man in his Person, his Breeding, or Understanding.

'Thus, Mr. SPECTATOR, this impertinent Humour of diminishing

every Feature' is one of the songs in *Arsinoe* (No. 14, sung by Mr. Hughes). See *Songs in the Opera call'd Arsinoe Queen of Cyprus* (1705).

[1] See No. 156 (vol. ii).

every one who is produced in Conversation to their Advantage, runs through the World; and I am, I confess, so fearful of the Force of ill Tongues, that I have begged of all those who are my Well-wishers never to commend me, for it will but bring my Frailties in to Examination, and I had rather be unobserved, than conspicuous for disputed Perfections. I am confident a thousand young People who would have been Ornaments to Society, have, from Fear of Scandal, never dared to exert themselves in the polite Arts of Life. Their Lives have passed away in an odious Rusticity, in spite of great Advantages of Person, Genius, and Fortune. There is a vicious Terrour of being blamed in some well inclined People, and a wicked Pleasure in suppressing them in others; both which I recommend to your Spectatorial Wisdom to animadvert upon; and if you can be successful in it, I need not say how much you will deserve of the Town, but new Toasts will owe to you their Beauty, and new Wits their Fame. I am,

SIR,

Your most Obedient,

Humble Servant,

Mary.'

T

No. 349
[ADDISON]

Thursday, April 10, 1712[1]

> . . . *Quos ille timorum*
> *Maximus haud urget lethi metus: inde ruendi*
> *In ferrum mens prona viris, animæque capaces*
> *Mortis . . .*
>
> Luc.

I AM very much pleased with a Consolatory Letter of *Phalaris*, to one who had lost a Son that was a young Man of great Merit.[2]

[1] *Motto.* Lucan, *Pharsalia*, 1. 459–62:
    They whom the worst of Terrors cannot move
    The fear of Death; with Cheerful Hearts can go
    To meet a naked Sword, or armed Foe,
    And dare their Fate . . .

[2] *Epistles*, 10 ('To Lacritus').

The Thought with which he comforts the afflicted Father is, to the best of my Memory, as follows; That he should consider Death, had set a kind of Seal upon his Son's Character, and placed him out of the Reach of Vice and Infamy: That while he lived he was still within the Possibility of falling away from Virtue, and losing the Fame of which he was possessed. Death only closes a Man's Reputation, and determines it as good or bad.

This, among other Motives, may be one Reason why we are naturally averse to the launching out into a Man's Praise till his Head is laid in the Dust. Whilst he is capable of changing, we may be forced to retract our Opinions. He may forfeit the Esteem we have conceived of him, and some time or other appear to us under a different Light from what he does at present. In short, as the Life of any Man cannot be called happy or unhappy,[1] so neither can it be pronounced vicious or virtuous, before the Conclusion of it.

It was upon this Consideration that *Epaminondas*, being asked whether *Chabrias*, *Iphicrates*, or he himself, deserved most to be esteemed; You must first see us dye, said he, before that Question can be answered.[2]

As there is not a more melancholy Consideration to a good Man than his being obnoxious[3] to such a Change, so there is nothing more glorious than to keep up an Uniformity in his Actions, and preserve the Beauty of his Character to the last.

The end of a Man's Life is often compared to the winding up of a well-written Play, where the principal Persons still act in Character, whatever the Fate is which they undergo.[4] There is scarce a great Person in the *Grecian* or *Roman* History whose Death has not been remarked upon by some Writer or other, and censured or applauded according to the Genius or Principles of the Person who has descanted on it. Monsieur *de St. Evremont*[a][5] is very particular in

---

[a] Monsieur *de St. Evremont*] Monsieur *St. Evremont* Fol.

---

[1] A commonplace, to be found in Ovid (*Metamorphoses*, 3. 136–7) and elsewhere.

[2] Epaminondas (*c.* 460–362) was a Theban general; Chabrias and Iphicrates were Athenian commanders. See Plutarch, 'Apophthegms of Kings and Commanders', Epaminondas, 22 (*Moralia*, 194A). Montaigne (*Essays*, I. xviii, 'That Men are not to judge of our happiness till after death') quotes this anecdote (trans. Cotton, 1685, i. 100).

[3] I.e. liable (formerly the prevailing use).

[4] Another commonplace. Cf. Seneca, *Epistles*, 77. 20.

[5] 'The Life and Character of Petronius Arbiter' was included in the English translation of the *Satyricon* (1708), vol. i, pp. i–xvi. The essay here referred to is a translation of part of his *Jugement sur Sénèque, Plutarque et Pétrone*, first published in 1664. According to Saint-Evremond, Petronius 'rather seem'd a Man in perfect

setting forth the Constancy and Courage of *Petronius Arbiter* during his last Moments, and thinks he discovers in them a greater Firmness of Mind and Resolution than in the Death of *Seneca*, *Cato*, or *Socrates*. There is no Question but this polite Author's Affectation of appearing singular in his Remarks, and making Discoveries which had escaped the Observation of others, threw him into this course of Reflection. It was *Petronius* his Merit that he died in the same Gaiety of Temper in which he lived; but as his Life was altogether loose and dissolute, the Indifference which he shewed at the Close of it is to be looked upon as a piece of natural Carelessness and Levity, rather than Fortitude. The Resolution of *Socrates* proceeded[a] from very different Motives, the Consciousness of a well-spent Life, and the Prospect of a happy Eternity. If the Ingenious Author abovementioned was so pleased with Gaiety of Humour in a dying Man, he might have found a much nobler Instance of it in our Countryman, Sir *Thomas More*.

This great and learned Man was famous for enlivening his ordinary Discourses with Wit and Pleasantry, and, as *Erasmus* tells him in an Epistle Dedicatory, acted in all parts of Life like a second *Democritus*.[1]

He died upon a point of Religion, and is respected as a Martyr by that side for which he suffered. That innocent Mirth, which had been so conspicuous in his Life, did not forsake him to the last: He maintain'd the same Chearfulness of Heart upon the Scaffold, which he used to shew at his Table: and upon laying his Head on the Block, gave instances of that good Humour with which he had always entertained his Friends in the most ordinary Occurrences.[2] His Death[b] was of a piece with his Life. There was nothing in it new, forced or affected. He did not look upon the severing of his Head from his Body as a Circumstance that ought to produce any Change in the disposition of his Mind; and as he died under a fix'd and settled hope of Immortality, he thought any unusual degree of

---

ᵃ proceeded] arose *Fol.*　　　　ᵇ His Death] In a word, his Death *Fol.*

Health than one that was dying; so that his Death, tho' *Violent*, appear'd to his Friends as if it had been *Natural*' (p. xv).

[1] In the 'Prefatory Epistle from Erasmus to Sir Tho. Moor' prefixed to *Moriae Encomium: or, a Panegyrick upon Folly* (London: J. Woodward, 1709), p. ii, we read: 'You (Sir) that are wont with this Sort of Jocose Raillery . . . to be mightily pleased, and in your ordinary Converse to approve your self a *Democritus Junior* . . . .'

[2] Upon laying his head on the block More is said to have put aside his beard, saying that it had committed no treason. See Thomas Bayly, *Witty Apophthegms* (1658), p. 168; W. Hickes, *Oxford Jests* (1684), p. 37; &c.

Sorrow and Concern improper on such an occasion as had nothing in it which could deject or terrifie him.

There is no great danger of Imitation from this Example. Mens natural fears will be a sufficient guard against it. I shall only observe that what was Philosophy in this extraordinary Man, would be Frenzy in one who does not resemble him as well in the chearfulness of his Temper, as in the sanctity of his Life and Manners.

I shall conclude this Paper with the instance of a Person who seems to me to have shewn more Intrepidity and greatness of Soul in his dying Moments, than what we meet with among any of the most celebrated *Greeks* and *Romans*. I meet with this instance in the History of the Revolutions in *Portugal*, written by the Abbot *de Vertot*.[1]

When Don *Sebastian*, King of *Portugal*, had invaded the Territories of *Muly Moluc*, Emperor of *Morocco*, in order to dethrone him, and set his Crown upon the Head of his Nephew, *Moluc* was wearing away[a] with a Distemper which he himself knew was incurable. However he prepared for the reception of so formidable an Enemy. He was indeed so[b] far spent with his Sickness that he did not expect to live out the whole Day, when the last decisive Battel was given; but knowing the fatal Consequences that would happen to his Children and People in case he should die before he put an end to that War, he commanded his principal Officers that if he died during the Engagement they should conceal his Death from the Army, and that they should ride up to the Litter in which his Corps was carried, under pretence of receiving Orders from him as usual. Before the Battel begun he was carried thro' all the Ranks of

---

[a] was wearing away] was insensibly worn away *Fol.*   [b] was indeed so] was so *Fol.*

---

[1] The *Histoire de la conjuration de Portugal en 1640*, by René-Aubert de Vertot d'Aubœuf, appeared in 1689. (Dryden drew on this for the background of his play *Don Sebastian*.) It was later brought up to the year 1668 and issued (1712) as the *Histoire des Revolutions de Portugal*, with an English translation in the same year by John Hughes. According to Vertot, the Moorish victory and death of Moley Moluc took place on 4 Aug. 1578. Addison follows Hughes's translation. The Emperor of Morocco,

seeing his Men fly in Disorder before a victorious Enemy, threw himself out of his Litter, transported with Rage, and tho' he was dying woud rally them himself, and lead them on to renew the Charge. His Officers endeavour'd in vain to stop him; he forc'd them with his Sword to give him Way; but his small Remains of Strength being spent by these Efforts, he fainted in the Arms of his Attendants: They replac'd him in his Litter, where immediately laying his Finger on his Mouth, as it were to enjoin them Secrecy, he dy'd before they cou'd carry him to his Tent (p. 12).

his Army in an open Litter, as they stood drawn up in Array, encouraging them to fight valiantly in defence of their Religion and Country. Finding afterwards the Battel to go against him, tho' he was very near his last Agonies, he threw himself out of his Litter, rallied his Army, and led them on to the Charge which afterwards ended in a compleat Victory on the side of the *Moors*. He had no sooner brought his Men to the Engagement, but finding himself utterly spent, he was again re-placed in his Litter, where laying his Finger on his Mouth, to enjoin Secresie to his Officers who stood about him, he died a few Moments after in that posture. L

No. 350   *Friday, April* 11, 1712[1]
[STEELE]

Ea animi elatio quæ cernitur in periculis, si Justitia vacat pugnatque pro suis commodis, in vitio est.

Tull.

CAPTAIN SENTRY was last Night at the Club, and produced a Letter from *Ipswich*, which his Correspondent desired him to Communicate to his Friend the SPECTATOR. It contained an Account of an Engagement between a *French* Privateer Commanded by one *Dominick Pottiere*, and a little Vessel of that Place laden with Corn; the Master whereof, as I remember, was one *Goodwin*.[2] The *English* Man defended himself with incredible Bravery, and beat off the *French*, after having been boarded three or four Times. The Enemy still came on with greater Fury, and hoped by his Number of Men to carry the Prize; till at last the *English* Man finding himself sink a pace, and ready to Perish, struck: But the Effect which this singular Gallantry had upon the Captain of the Privateer, was no other than an unmanly Desire of Vengeance for the Loss he had sustained in his several Attacks. He told the *Ipswich* Man in a speaking Trumpet, that he would not take him aboard; and that he

---

[1] *Motto.* Cicero, *De Officiis*, 1. 19. 62: That elevation of mind which is displayed in dangers, if it wants justice and fights for its own conveniency, is vicious.

[2] The account read by Captain Sentry was apparently based on an actual incident. An advertisement in the *Post Boy* of 12 Aug. 1712 offers ten guineas reward for John Goodwin of Ipswich, 'Master of a Pink, taken, and carried into Calais by one Capt. Potcheare, laden with Corn'. The reward is offered by 'Mr. John Bridges in Harp-Lane, London' (*Post Boy*, 12 Aug., and corrected notice, 14 Aug.).

stay'd to see him sink. The *English* Man at the same Time observed a Disorder in the Vessel, which he rightly judged to proceed from the Disdain which the Ship's Crew had of their Captain's Inhumanity: With this hope he went into his Boat, and approached the Enemy. He was taken in by the Sailors in spite of their Commander, but tho' they received him against his Command, they treated him when he was in the Ship in the Manner he directed. *Pottiere* caused his Men to hold *Goodwin* while he beat him with a Stick, till he fainted with Loss of Blood, and Rage of Heart; after which he ordered him into Irons, without allowing him[a] any Food, but such as one or two of the Men Stole to him under Peril of the like Usage: After having kept him several Days overwhelmed with the Misery of Stench, Hunger and Soreness, he brought[b] him into *Calais*. The Governour of the Place was soon acquainted with all that had passed, dismiss'd *Pottiere* from his Charge with Ignominy, and gave *Goodwin* all the Relief which a Man of Honour would bestow upon an Enemy Barbarously treated, to recover the Imputation of Cruelty upon his Prince and Country.

When Mr. SENTRY had read his Letter, full of many other Circumstances which aggravate the Barbarity, he fell into a sort of Criticism upon Magnanimity and Courage, and argued that they were inseparable; and that Courage, without Regard to Justice and Humanity, was no other than the Fierceness of a wild Beast. A good and truly bold Spirit, continued he, is ever actuated by Reason and a Sense of Honour and Duty: The Affectation of such a Spirit, exerts it self in an impudent Aspect, an overbearing Confidence, and a certain Negligence of giving Offence. This is visible in all the cocking[1] Youths you see about this Town, who are noisy in Assemblies, unawed by the Presence of wise and virtuous Men; in a Word, insensible of all the Honours and Decencies of humane Life. A shameless Fellow takes Advantage of Merit cloathed with Modesty and Magnanimity, and in the Eyes of little People appears sprightly and agreeable; while the Man of Resolution and true Gallantry is overlooked and disregarded, if not despised. There is a Propriety in all things; and I believe what you Scholars call just and sublime, in Opposition to Turgid and bombast Expression, may give you an Idea of what I mean, when I say Modesty is the certain Indication

---

[a] without allowing him] and without giving him *Fol.*   [b] he brought] brought *Fol.*

[1] Here, 'swaggering, strutting; bragging; playing the cock' (*OED*).

of a great Spirit, and Impudence the Affectation of it. He that writes with Judgment, and never rises into improper Warmths, manifests the true Force of Genius; in like Manner, he who is Quiet and Equal in all his Behaviour, is supported in that Deportment by what we may call true Courage. Alass, it is not so easy a thing to be a brave Man as the unthinking Part of Mankind imagine: To dare is not all that there is in it. The Privateer we were just now talking of, had Boldness enough to attack his Enemy, but not Greatness of Mind enough to admire the same Quality exerted by that Enemy in defending himself. Thus his base and little Mind was wholly taken up in the sordid Regard to the Prize, of which he failed, and the Damage done to his own Vessel; and therefore he used[a] an honest Man who defended his own from him, in the Manner as he would a Thief that should rob him.

He was equally disappointed, and had not Spirit enough to consider that one Case would be Laudable, and the[b] other Criminal. Malice, Rancour, Hatred, Vengeance, are what tear the Breasts of mean Men in Fight; but Fame, Glory, Conquests, Desires of Opportunities to pardon and oblige their Opposers, are what glow in the Minds of the Gallant. The Captain ended his Discourse with a Specimen of his Book Learning; and gave us to understand that he had read a *French* Author on the Subject of Justness in Point of Gallantry.[1] I love, said Mr. SENTRY, a Critick who mixes the Rules of Life with Annotations upon Writers. My Author, added he, in his Discourse upon Epick Poem, takes Occasion to speak of the same Quality of Courage drawn in the two different Characters of *Turnus* and *Æneas*: He makes Courage the chief and greatest Ornament of *Turnus*; but in *Æneas* there are many others which out-shine it, among the rest that of Piety. *Turnus* is therefore all along painted by the Poet full of Ostentation, his Language haughty and vain-glorious, as placing his Honour in the Manifestation of his Valour; *Æneas* speaks little, is slow to Action, and shews only a sort of defensive Courage. If Equipage and Address make *Turnus* appear more couragious than *Æneas*; Conduct and Success prove *Æneas* more valiant than *Turnus*. T

[a] he used] used *Fol.*   [b] and the] the *Fol.*

---

[1] Le Bossu, book iv, chap. xiv (ed. 1719, ii. 193–4).

> . . . *In te omnis domus inclinata recumbit.*
> Virg.

IF we look into the three great Heroic Poems which have appear'd in the World, we may observe that they are built upon very slight Foundations. *Homer* lived near 300 Years after the *Trojan* War, and, as the Writing of History was not then in use among the *Greeks*, we may very well suppose, that the Tradition of *Achilles* and *Ulysses* had brought down but very few Particulars to his Knowledge, tho' there is no question but he has wrought into his two Poems such of their remarkable Adventures as were still talked of among his Contemporaries.

The Story of *Æneas*, on which *Virgil* founded his Poem, was likewise very bare of Circumstances, and by that means afforded him an Opportunity of embellishing it with Fiction, and giving a full Range to his own Invention. We find, however, that he has interwoven, in the course of his Fable, the principal Particulars, which were generally believed among the *Romans*, of *Æneas* his Voyage and Settlement in *Italy*.

The Reader may find an Abridgment of the whole Story as collected out of the Ancient Historians, and as it was received among the *Romans*, in *Dionisius Halicarnasseus.*[2]

Since none of the Criticks have considered *Virgil's* Fable, with relation to this History of *Æneas*, it may not, perhaps, be amiss to examine it in this Light, so far as regards my present Purpose. Whoever looks into the Abridgment abovementioned, will find that the Character of *Æneas* is filled with Piety to the Gods, and a superstitious Observation of Prodigies, Oracles, and Predictions. *Virgil* has not only preserved this Character in the Person of *Æneas*, but has given a place in his Poem to those particular Prophecies which he found recorded of him in History and Tradition. The Poet took the matters of Fact as they came down to him, and circumstanced[3]

---

[1] *Motto.* Virgil, *Aeneid,* 12. 59:

> Since on the safety of thy Life alone,
> Depends *Latinus*, and the *Latian* Throne. DRYDEN.

[2] Dionysius of Halicarnassus, *Roman Antiquities,* 1. 45–64.
[3] I.e. furnished with details. The last quotation in *OED* is dated 1774.

them after his own manner, to make them appear the more natural, agreeable or surprising. I believe very many Readers have been shocked at that ludicrous Prophecy, which one of the *Harpyes* pronounces to the *Trojans* in the Third Book, namely, that before they had built their Intended City, they should be reduced by Hunger to eat their very Tables.[1] But, when they hear that this was one of the Circumstances that had been transmitted to the *Romans* in the History of *Æneas*, they will think the Poet did very well in taking notice of it. The Historian abovementioned, acquaints us, a Prophetess[a] had foretold *Æneas*, that he should take his Voyage Westward, till his Companions should eat their Tables, and that accordingly, upon his landing in *Italy*, as they were eating their Flesh upon Cakes of Bread, for want of other Conveniences, they afterwards fed on the Cakes themselves, upon which one of the Company said merrily, 'We are eating our Tables.' They immediately took the Hint, says the Historian, and concluded the Prophecy to be fulfilled. As *Virgil* did not think it proper to omit so material a Particular in the History of *Æneas*, it may be worth while to consider with how much Judgment he has qualified it, and taken off every thing that might have appeared improper for a Passage in an Heroic Poem. The Prophetess who foretells it is an hungry *Harpy*, as the Person who discovers it is young *Ascanius*.

Heus etiam mensas consumimus inquit Iulus![2]

Such an Observation, which is beautiful in the mouth of a Boy, would have been ridiculous from any other of the Company. I am apt to think that the changing of the *Trojan* Fleet into Water-Nymphs, which is the most violent Machine in the whole *Æneid*, and has given Offence to several Critics, may be accounted for the same way.[3] *Virgil* himself, before he begins that Relation, premises that what he was going to tell appeared incredible, but that it was justified by Tradition. What further confirms me that this change of the Fleet was a celebrated Circumstance in the History of *Æneas*, is, that *Ovid* has given a place to the same *Metamorphosis* in his account of the Heathen Mythology.[4]

[a] acquaints us, a Prophetess] acquaints us that a Prophetess *Fol. Corrected in Errata (No. 369)*: 'after Æneas *dele* that'

---

[1] *Aeneid*, 3. 255-7.   [2] *Aeneid*, 7. 116.
[3] *Aeneid*, 9. 107-22. Addison refers to this also in No. 315 and No. 589.
[4] *Metamorphoses*, 14. 530-65.

None of the Criticks, I have met with, having considered the Fable of the *Æneid* in this Light, and taken notice how the Tradition, on which it was founded, authorizes those Parts in it which appear the most Exceptionable; I hope the length of this Reflection will not make it unacceptable to the curious Part of my Readers.

The History, which was the Basis of *Milton*'s Poem, is still shorter than either that of the *Iliad* or *Æneid*. The Poet has likewise taken care to insert every Circumstance of it in the Body of his Fable. The Ninth Book, which we are here to consider, is raised upon that brief Account in Scripture, wherein we are told that the Serpent was more subtile than any Beast of the Field, that he tempted the Woman to eat of the Forbidden Fruit, that she was overcome by this Temptation, and that *Adam* followed her Example. From these few Particulars *Milton* has formed one of the most Entertaining Fables that Invention ever produced. He has disposed of these several Circumstances among so many agreeable[a] and natural Fictions of his own, that his whole Story looks only like a Comment upon sacred Writ, or rather seems to be a full and compleat Relation of what the other is only an Epitome. I have insisted the longer on this Consideration, as I look upon the Disposition and Contrivance of the Fable to be the Principal Beauty of the Ninth Book, which has more *Story* in it, and is fuller of Incidents, than any other in the whole Poem. *Satan*'s traversing the Globe, and still keeping within the Shadow of the Night, as fearing to be discovered by the Angel of the Sun, who had before detected him, is one of those beautiful Imaginations which[b] introduces this his second Series of Adventures.[1] Having examined the Nature of every Creature, and found out one which was the most proper for his Purpose, he again returns to Paradise; and, to avoid Discovery, sinks by Night with a River that ran under the Garden, and rises up again through a Fountain that issued[c] from it by the Tree of Life.[2] The Poet, who, as we have before taken notice, speaks as little as possible in his own Person, and, after the example of *Homer*, fills every Part of his Work with Manners and Characters, introduces a Soliloquy of this Infernal Agent, who was thus restless in the Destruction of Man.[3] He is then describ'd as

---

[a] agreeable] *19*; beautiful *Fol., 8vo, 12mo corrected in Folio Errata (No. 369):* 'dele with, he'

[b] which] with which he *all edd.;*
[c] issued] run *Fol.; corrected in Folio Errata (No. 369)*

---

[1] *PL*, ix. 58–69.   [2] *PL*, ix. 69–96.   [3] *PL*, ix. 99–178.

gliding through the Garden under the resemblance of a Mist, in order to find out that Creature in which he design'd to tempt our first Parents. This Description has something in it very Poetical and Surprizing.

> *So saying, through each thicket Dank or Dry*
> *Like a black Mist, low creeping, he held on*
> *His Midnight Search, where soonest he might find*
> *The Serpent: him fast sleeping soon he found*
> *In Labyrinth of many a round self-roll'd,*
> *His head the midst, well-stor'd with subtle wiles.*[1]

The Author afterwards gives us a Description of the Morning, which is wonderfully suitable to a Divine Poem, and peculiar to that first Season of Nature: He[a] represents the Earth before it was curst, as a great Altar breathing out its Incense from all parts, and sending up a pleasant[b] Savour to the Nostrils of its Creator; to which he adds a noble Idea of *Adam* and *Eve*, as offering their Morning Worship, and filling up the universal Consort of Praise and Adoration.

> *Now when as sacred light began to dawn*
> *In* Eden *on the humid flowers, that breathed*
> *Their morning incense, when all things that breath*
> *From th' Earth's great Altar send up silent praise*
> *To the Creatour, and his nostrils fill*
> *With grateful smell, forth came the human pair*
> *And joyn'd their vocal worship to the Choir*
> *Of Creatures wanting voice . . .*[2]

The Dispute which follows between our two first Parents is represented with great Art:[3] It proceeds[c] from a difference of Judgment, not of Passion, and is managed with Reason, not with Heat: It[d] is such a Dispute as we may suppose might have happened in *Paradise*, had Man continued Happy and Innocent. There is a great Delicacy in the Moralities which are interspersed in *Adam*'s Discourse, and which the most ordinary Reader cannot but take notice of. That force of Love which the Father of Mankind so finely describes in the Eighth Book, and which is inserted in the foregoing

[a] Nature: He] Nature; he *Fol.*   [b] a pleasant] pleasant *Fol. Corrected in Errata (No. 369)*   [c] proceeds] arises *Fol.*   [d] Heat: It] Heat; it *Fol.*

---

[1] *PL,* ix. 179–84.   [2] *PL,* ix. 192–9.   [3] *PL,* ix. 205–384.

Paper,[a] shews it self here in many fine[b] Instances: As in those fond Regards he casts[c] towards *Eve* at her parting from him.

> *Her long with ardent look his eye pursued*
> *Delighted, but desiring more her stay.*
> *Oft he to her his charge of quick return*
> *Repeated, she to him as oft engaged*
> *To be return'd by noon amid the Bowre.*[1]

In his impatience and amusement during her Absence.

> *. . . Adam the while*
> *Waiting desirous her return, had wove*
> *Of choicest flowers a Garland to adorn*
> *Her Tresses, and her rural labours crown,*
> *As Reapers oft are wont their Harvest Queen.*
> *Great Joy he promised to his thoughts, and new*
> *Solace in her return, so long delay'd;*[2]

But particularly in that passionate Speech, where seeing her irrecoverably lost, he resolves to perish with her, rather than to live without her.

> *. . . Some cursed fraud*
> *Or enemy hath beguil'd thee, yet unknown,*
> *And me with thee hath ruin'd, for with thee*
> *Certain my resolution is to die;*
> *How can I live without thee, how forego*
> *Thy sweet converse and love so dearly join'd,*
> *To live again in these wild woods forlorn?*
> *Should God create another Eve, and I*
> *Another rib afford, yet loss of thee*
> *Would never from my heart; no, no, I feel*
> *The link of nature draw me: Flesh of Flesh,*
> *Bone of my bone thou art, and from thy State*
> *Mine never shall be parted Bliss or Woe.*[3]

The beginning of this Speech, and the Preparation to it,[4] are

---

a which is inserted in the foregoing Paper,] *19*; which I incerted in my last *Saturday*'s Paper, *Fol., 8vo, 12mo*   b fine] *19*; beautiful *Fol., 8vo, 12mo*   c casts] cast *all editions. Corrected in Folio Errata (No. 369) to* casts

---

[1] *PL*, ix. 397–401.   [2] *PL*, ix. 838–44.
[3] *PL*, ix. 904–16 ('fraud of enemy').   [4] *PL*, ix. 888–904.

309

animated with the same Spirit as the Conclusion, which I have here quoted.

The several Wiles which are put in Practice by the Tempter, when he found *Eve* separated from her Husband, the many pleasing Images of Nature, which are intermixt in this part of the Story, with its gradual and regular Progress to the fatal Catastrophe, are so very remarkable, that it would be superfluous to point out their respective[a] Beauties.

I have avoided mentioning any particular Similitudes in my Remarks on this great Work, because I have given a general account of them in my Paper on the First Book. There is one, however, in this part of the Poem which I shall here quote, as it is not only very beautiful, but the closest of any in the whole Poem;[b] I mean that where the Serpent is describ'd as rolling forward in all his Pride, animated by the evil Spirit, and conducting *Eve* to her Destruction, while *Adam* was at too great a distance from her, to give her his Assistance. These several Particulars are all of them wrought into the following Similitude.

> *. . . Hope elevates, and Joy*
> *Brighten's his Crest, as when a wand'ring fire*
> *Compact of unctuous vapour, which the night*
> *Condenses, and the cold invirons round,*
> *Kindled through agitation to a flame,*
> *(Which oft, they say, some evil spirit attends)*
> *Hovering and blazing with delusive light,*
> *Misleads th' amaz'd Night-wanderer from his way*
> *To boggs and mires, and oft through pond or pool,*
> *There swallow'd up and lost, from succour far:*[1]

That secret Intoxication of Pleasure, with all those transient flushings of Guilt and Joy which the Poet represents in our first Parents upon their eating the forbidden Fruit,[2] to those flaggings of Spirit, damps of Sorrow and mutual Accusations which succeed it,[3] are conceiv'd with a wonderful Imagination, and described in very natural Sentiments.

---

[a] respective] several *Fol.*   [b] Poem;] Poem. *Fol.*

---

[1] *PL*, ix. 633–42.   [2] *PL*, ix. 1007–1189.
[3] Steele devoted a part of *Tatler* 217 to this subject, with a humorous paraphrase of Adam and Eve's conversation, 'put into Domestick Stile'.

When *Dido* in the Fourth *Æneid* yielded to that fatal Temptation which ruin'd her, *Virgil* tells us, the Earth trembled, the Heavens were filled with flashes of Lightning, and the Nymphs howl'd upon the Mountain Tops.[1] *Milton*, in the same Poetical Spirit, has describ'd all Nature as disturbed upon *Eve*'s eating the forbidden Fruit.

> *So saying, her rash hand in evil hour*
> *Forth reaching to the Fruit, she plucked, she eat:*
> *Earth felt the wound, and nature from her Seat*
> *Sighing through all her works gave signs of Woe*
> *That all was lost . . .*[2]

Upon *Adam*'s falling into the same Guilt, the whole Creation appears a second time in Convulsions.

> *. . . He scrupl'd not to eat*
> *Against his better knowledge, not deceiv'd,*
> *But fondly overcome with Female charm.*
> *Earth trembled from her Entrails, as again*
> *In pangs, and nature gave a second groan,*
> *Sky lowred and muttering thunder some sad drops*
> *Wept at compleating of the mortal Sin . . .*[3]

As all Nature suffer'd by the guilt of our first Parents, these Symptoms of Trouble and Consternation are wonderfully imagin'd, not only as Prodigies, but as Marks of her Sympathizing in the Fall of Man.

Adam's Converse with *Eve*, after having eaten the forbidden Fruit, is an exact Copy of that between *Jupiter* and *Juno*, in the Fourteenth *Iliad*. *Juno* there approaches *Jupiter* with the Girdle which she had receiv'd from *Venus*, upon which he tells her, that she appeared more charming and desirable than she had ever[a] done before, even when their Loves were at the highest. The Poet afterwards describes them as reposing on a Summet of Mount *Ida*, which[b] produced under them a Bed of Flowers, the *Lotos*, the *Crocus*, and the *Hyacinth*, and concludes his Description with their falling a-sleep.[4]

---

    [a] had ever] ever had *Fol.*   [b] which] that *Fol.*

---

[1] *Aeneid*, 4. 166-8.   [2] *PL*, ix. 780-4.
[3] *PL*, ix. 997-1003.   [4] *Iliad*, 14. 292-353.

Let the Reader compare this with the following Passage in *Milton*, which begins with *Adam*'s Speech to *Eve*.

> *For never did thy Beauty since the Day*
> *I saw thee first and wedded thee, adorn'd*
> *With all Perfections so enflame my Sense*
> *With ardor to enjoy thee, fairer now*
> *Than ever, bounty of this virtuous Tree.*
> *So said he, and forebore not glance or toy*
> *Of amorous intent, well understood*
> *Of Eve, whose Eye darted contagious fire.*
> *Her hand he seised, and to a shady bank*
> *Thick over-head with verdant roof embowr'd*
> *He led her nothing loath: Flow'rs were the Couch,*
> *Pansies, and Violets, and Asphodel,*
> *And Hyacinth, Earth's freshest softest lap.*
> *There they their fill of Love, and Loves disport*
> *Took largely, of their mutual guilt the Seal,*
> *The Solace of their Sin, 'till dewy sleep*
> *Oppress'd them . . .*[1]

As no Poet seems ever to have studied *Homer* more, or to have more resembled him in the greatness of Genius than *Milton*, I think I shou'd have given but a very imperfect Account of his Beauties, if I had not observed the most remarkable Passages which look like Parallels in these two great Authors. I might, in the course of these Criticisms, have taken notice of many particular Lines and Expressions which are translated from the *Greek* Poet, but as I thought this would have appeared too minute and over-curious, I have purposely omitted them. The greater Incidents, however, are not only set off by being shown in the same Light, with several of the same Nature in *Homer*, but by that means may be also guarded against the Cavils of the Tasteless or Ignorant. L

---

[1] *PL*, ix. 1029–45.

. . . Si ad honestatem nati sumus, ea aut sola expetenda est, aut certe omni pondere gravior est habenda quam reliqua omnia.

Tull.

WILL HONEYCOMB was complaining to me Yesterday, that the Conversation of the Town is so altered of late Years that a fine Gentleman is at a Loss for Matter to start Discourse, as well as unable to fall in with the Talk he generally meets with. WILL takes Notice, that there is now an Evil under the Sun which he supposes to be intirely new, because not mentioned by any Satyrist or Moralist in any Age: Men, said he, grow Knaves sooner than they ever did since the Creation of the World before. If you read the Tragedies of the last Age, you find the artful Men and Persons of Intrigue are advanced very far in Years, and beyond the Pleasures and Sallies of Youth; but now WILL observes, that the Young have taken in the Vices of the Aged; and you shall have a Man of five and twenty crafty, false and intriguing, not ashamed to over-reach, cousen, and beguile. My Friend adds, that till about the latter End of King *Charles*'s Reign, there was not a Rascal of any Eminence under forty: In the Places of Resort for Conversation, you now hear[a] nothing but what relates to the improving[b] Mens Fortunes, without Regard to the Methods towards it. This is so fashionable, that young Men form themselves upon a certain Neglect of every thing that is candid, simple and worthy of true Esteem; and affect being yet worse than they are, by acknowledging in their general Turn of Mind and Discourse, that they have not any remaining Value for true Honour and Honesty: Preferring the Capacity of being Artful to gain their Ends, to the Merit of despising those Ends when they come in Competition with their Honesty. All this is due to the very silly Pride that generally prevails, of being valued for the Ability of carrying their Point: In a Word, from the Opinion that shallow and unexperienced People entertain of the short lived

[a] you now hear] you hear *Fol.*   [b] to the improving] to improving *Fol.*

[1] *Motto.* Cicero, *De Officiis*, 3. 8. 35 (altered): If we are born to be honest, honesty is alone to be sought after, or certainly a greater stress should be laid upon it than anything else.

force of Cunning. But I shall, before I enter upon the various Faces which Folly covered with Artifice puts on to impose upon the Unthinking, produce a great Authority for asserting, that nothing but Truth and Ingenuity[1] has any lasting good Effect even upon a Man's Fortune and Interest.[a]

'Truth and Reality have all the Advantages of Appearance, and many more.[2] If the shew of any thing be good for any thing, I am sure Sincerity is better; for why does any Man dissemble, or seem to be that which he is not, but because he thinks it good to have such a quality as he pretends to? for to counterfeit and dissemble, is to put on the appearance of some real Excellency. Now the best way in the World for a Man to seem to be any thing, is really to be what he would seem to be. Besides, that it is many times as troublesome to make good the Pretence of a good Quality, as to have it; and if a Man have it not, it is ten to one, but he is discovered to want it; and then all his pains and labour to seem to have it, is lost. There is something unnatural in Painting, which a skillful Eye will easily discern from Native Beauty and Complexion.

'It is hard to personate and act a Part long; for where Truth is not at the Bottom, Nature will always be endeavouring to return, and will peep out and betray herself one time or other. Therefore if any Man think it convenient to seem Good, let him be so indeed, and then his Goodness will appear to every Bodys Satisfaction;[3] so that upon all Accounts Sincerity is true Wisdom. Particularly as to the Affairs of this World, Integrity hath many Advantages over all the fine and artificial ways of Dissimulation and Deceit; it is much the plainer and easier, much the safer and more secure way of dealing in the World; it has less of trouble and difficulty, of entanglement and perplexity, of danger and hazard in it; it is the shortest and nearest way to our end, carrying us thither in a streight line,

[a] *The remainder of the paper is in italics in Folio*

---

[1] Here used in the now rare sense of 'freedom from dissimulation', the current word being 'ingenuousness' (*OED*).

[2] The remainder of the paper is taken from Tillotson's sermon, 'Of Sincerity towards God and Man', preached at Kingston 29 July 1694, said to be the last sermon delivered by the Archbishop. In Tillotson's *Works* (4th ed., 1728) it is the first sermon in vol. ii, and the passage copied by Steele comes near the end (pp. 7–9). Some of the more important variations from Tillotson's text are noted below.

[3] In Tillotson the sentence continues: 'for truth is convincing, and carries its own light and evidence along with it, and will not only commend us to every man's conscience, but which is more, to God, who searcheth and seeth our hearts; so that upon all accounts sincerity is true wisdom'.

and will hold out and last longest. The Arts of Deceit and Cunning do continually grow weaker and less effectual and serviceable to them that use them; whereas Integrity gains strength by use, and the more and longer any Man practiseth it, the greater service it does him, by confirming his Reputation, and encouraging those with whom he hath to do, to repose the greatest trust[1] and confidence in him, which is an unspeakable advantage in the Business and Affairs of Life.[2]

'Truth is always consistent with it self, and needs nothing to help it out; it is always near at hand, and sits upon our Lips, and is ready to drop out before we are aware; whereas a Lye is troublesome, and sets a Man's invention upon the Rack, and one trick needs a great many more to make it good. It is like building upon a false Foundation, which continually stands in need of Props to shoar it up, and proves at last more chargeable, than to have raised a substantial Building at first upon a true and solid Foundation; for Sincerity is firm and substantial, and there is nothing hollow and unsound in it, and because it is plain and open, fears no discovery, of which the crafty Man is always in danger, and when he thinks he walks in the dark, all his Pretences are so transparent, that he that runs may read them; he is the last Man that finds himself to be found out, and whilst he takes it for granted that he makes Fools of others, he renders himself ridiculous.

'Add to all this, that Sincerity is the most compendious Wisdom, and an excellent Instrument for the speedy dispatch of Business; it creates confidence in those we have to deal with, saves the labour of many Enquiries, and brings things to an issue in few Words: It is like travelling in a plain beaten Road, which commonly brings a Man sooner to his Journeys end, than By-ways, in which Men often lose themselves. In a word, whatsoever convenience may be thought to be in Falshood and Dissimulation, it is soon over; but the inconvenience of it is perpetual, because it brings a Man under an everlasting jealousie and suspicion, so that he is not believed when he speaks truth, nor trusted when perhaps he means honestly: When a Man hath once forfeited the Reputation of his Integrity, he is set fast, and nothing will then serve his turn, neither Truth nor Falshood.

'And I have often thought, that God hath in great Wisdom hid

---

[1] In Tillotson 'the greater trust'.
[2] Steele here omits three sentences and part of a fourth.

from Men of false and dishonest Minds the wonderful Advantages of Truth and Integrity to the prosperity even of our worldly Affairs; these Men are so blinded by their Covetousness and Ambition, that they cannot look beyond a present Advantage, nor forbear to seize upon it, tho' by ways never so indirect; they cannot see so far, as to the remote Consequences of a steady Integrity, and the vast Benefit and Advantages which it will bring a Man at last. Were but this sort of Men wise and clear-sighted enough to discern this, they would be honest, out of very Knavery, not out of any love to Honesty and Virtue, but with a crafty design to promote and advance more effectually their own Interests; and therefore the Justice of the Divine Providence hath hid this truest point of Wisdom from their Eyes, that bad Men might not be upon equal Terms with the Just and Upright, and serve their own wicked Designs by honest and lawful Means.

'Indeed, if a Man were only to deal in the World for a Day, and should never have occasion to converse more with Mankind, never more need their good Opinion, or good Word, it were then no great matter (speaking as to the Concernments of this World) if a Man spent his Reputation all at once, and ventured it at one throw: But if he be to continue in the World, and would have the advantage of Conversation whilst he is in it, let him make use of Truth and Sincerity in all his Words and Actions, for nothing but this will last and hold out to the end; all other Arts will fail, but Truth and Integrity will carry a Man through, and bear him out to the last.'[1]

T

No. 353
[BUDGELL]

Tuesday, April 15, 1712[2]

In tenui labor . . .
Virg.

THE Gentleman who obliges the World in general, and me in particular, with his Thoughts upon Education, has just sent me the following Letter.

---

[1] Steele omits the three final paragraphs of Tillotson's sermon.
[2] *Motto.* Virgil, *Georgics*, 4. 6. Nor small the labour of an humble theme. Addison had used this as the motto for *Tatler* 119.

SIR,

'I TAKE the Liberty to send you a Fourth Letter upon the Education of Youth:[1] In my last I gave you my Thoughts about some particular Tasks which I conceived it might not be amiss to mix with their usual Exercises, in order to give them an early Seasoning of Virtue; I shall in this propose some others which I fancy might contribute to give them a right Turn for the World, and enable them to make their way in it.

'The design of Learning is, as I take it, either to render a Man an agreeable Companion to himself, and teach him to support Solitude with Pleasure; or, if he is not born to an Estate, to supply that Defect, and furnish him with the Means of acquiring one. A Person who applies himself to Learning with the first of these Views may be said to study for Ornament, as he who proposes to himself the Second properly studies for Use. The one does it to raise himself a Fortune, the other to set off that which he is already possessed of: But as far the greater part of Mankind are included in the latter Class,[2] I shall only propose some Methods at present for the Service of such who expect to advance themselves in the World by their Learning: In order to which, I shall premise that many more Estates have been acquired by little Accomplishments than by extraordinary ones: those Qualities which make the greatest Figure in the Eye of the World not being always the most useful in themselves, or the most advantagious to their Owners.

'The Posts which require Men of shining and uncommon Parts to discharge them are so very few, that many a great Genius goes out of the World without ever having had an Opportunity to exert it self; whereas Persons of ordinary Endowments meet with Occasions fitted to their Parts and Capacities every Day in the common Occurrences of Life.

'I am acquainted with two Persons who were formerly School-fellows, and have been good Friends ever since:[3] One of them was not only thought an impenetrable Block-head at School, but still maintained his Reputation at the University; the other was the Pride of his Master, and the most celebrated Person in the College

---

[1] See Nos. 307, 313, 337.   [2] I.e. those 'not born to an Estate'.

[3] Nichols identifies these as Swift and Francis Stratford, the Hamburg merchant, who were schoolfellows together at Kilkenny and at Trinity College, Dublin. At this time, however, as Sir Harold Williams points out (Swift's *Journal to Stella*, p. 16), Swift was not 'buried in a country parsonage' and Stratford had been bankrupt for about three months.

of which he was a Member. The Man of Genius is at present buried in a Country Parsonage of eight-score Pounds a Year; while the other, with the bare Abilities of a common Scrivener, has got an Estate of above an hundred thousand Pounds.

'I fancy from what I have said it will almost appear a doubtful case to many a wealthy Citizen, whether or no he ought to wish his Son should be a great Genius; but this I am sure of, that nothing is more absurd than to give a Lad the Education of one, whom Nature has not favour'd with any particular Marks of Distinction.

'The Fault therefore of our Grammar Schools is, that every Boy is pushed on to Works of Genius; whereas it would be far more advantageous for the greatest part of them, to be taught such little Practical Arts and Sciences as do not require any great share of Parts to be master of them, and yet may come often into Play during the course of a Man's Life.

'Such are all the parts of Practical Geometry. I have known a Man contract a Friendship with a Minister of State, upon cutting a Dial in his Window; and remember a Clergy-man who got one of the best Benefices in the West of *England*, by setting a Country Gentleman's Affairs in some Method, and giving him an exact Survey of his Estate.

'While I am upon this Subject, I cannot forbear mentioning a particular which is of use in every Station of Life, and which methinks every Master should teach his Scholars, I mean the Writing of *English* Letters. To this end, instead of perplexing them with *Latin* Epistles, Themes and Verses, there might be a punctual Correspondence established between two Boys, who might act in any imaginary parts of Business, or be allowed sometimes to give a range to their own Fancies, and communicate to each other whatever Trifles they thought fit, provided neither of them ever failed at the appointed time to answer his Correspondent's Letter.

'I believe I may venture to affirm, that the generality of Boys would find themselves more advantaged by this Custom, when they come to be Men, than by all the *Greek* and *Latin* their Masters can teach them in seven or eight Years.

'The want of it is very visible in many learned Persons, who while they are admiring the Stiles of *Demosthenes* or *Cicero*, want Phrases to express themselves on the most common Occasions. I have seen a Letter from one of these *Latin* Orators, which would have been deservedly laughed at by a common Attorney.

'Under this Head of Writing I cannot omit Accounts and Short-hand, which are learnt with little Pains, and very properly come into the number of such Arts as I have been here recommending.

'You must doubtless, Sir, observe, that I have hitherto chiefly insisted upon these things for such Boys as do not appear to have any thing extraordinary in their Natural Talents, and consequently are not qualified for the finer Parts of Learning; yet I believe I might carry this matter still further, and venture to assert, that a Lad of Genius has sometimes occasion for these little Acquirements, to be as it were the Fore-runners of his Parts, and to introduce him[a] into the World.

'History is full of Examples of Persons, who though they have had the largest Abilities, have been obliged to insinuate themselves into the Favour of great Men by these trivial Accomplishments; as the compleat Gentleman, in some of our Modern Comedies, makes his first Advances to his Mistress under the disguise of a Painter or a Dancing-Master.

'The difference is, that in a Lad of Genius these are only so many Accomplishments, which in another are Essentials; the one diverts himself with them, the other works at them. In short, I look upon a great Genius, with these little Additions, in the same Light as I regard the Grand Signior, who is obliged, by an express Command in the Alcoran, to learn and practise some Handy-craft Trade.[1] Tho' I need not have gone for my Instance further than *Germany*, where several Emperors have voluntarily done the same thing. *Leopold* the last[2] worked in Wood, and I have heard there are several Handy-craft Works of his making to be seen at *Vienna* so neatly turned, that the best Joyner in *Europe* might safely own them, without any Disgrace to his Profession.

'I would not be thought, by any thing I have said, to be against improving a Boys Genius to the utmost Pitch it can be carried. What I wou'd endeavour to shew in this Essay is, that there may be Methods taken to make Learning advantageous, even to the meanest Capacities.

I am, SIR,
Yours, &c.'

X

---

[a] him] them *Fol.*

---

[1] I have not been able to discover an express command to the Grand Signior on this matter.   [2] The Emperor Leopold I (died 5 May 1705, N.S.).

No. 354
[STEELE]
Wednesday, April 16, 1712[1]

> . . . *Cum magnis virtutibus affers*
> *Grande supercilium . . .*
>
> Juv.

Mr. SPECTATOR,

'YOU have in some of your Discourses described most sort of Women in their distinct and proper Classes, as the *Ape,* the *Coquet,*[2] and many others; but I think you have never yet said any thing of a *Devotée.* A *Devotée* is one of those who disparage Religion by their indiscreet and unseasonable Introduction of the mention of Virtue on all Occasions: She professes she is what no Body ought to doubt she is, and betrays the Labour she is put to, to be what she ought to be with Chearfullness and Alacrity. She lives in the World and denies her self none of the Diversions of it, with a constant Declaration, how insipid all things in it are to her. She is never her self but at Church; there she displays her Vertue, and is so fervent in her Devotions, that I have frequently seen her Pray her self out of Breath. While other young Ladies in the House are dancing, or playing at Questions and Commands,[3] she reads aloud in her Closet. She says all Love is ridiculous, except it be cœlestial; but she speaks of the Passion of one Mortal to another with too much Bitterness, for one that had no Jealousy mixed with her Contempt of it. If at any Time she sees a Man warm in his Addresses to his Mistress, she will lift up her Eyes to Heaven and cry, What Nonsense is that Fool talking? will the Bell never ring for Prayers? We have an eminent Lady of this Stamp in our County, who pretends to Amusements very much above the rest of her Sex. She never carrys a white shock Dog with Bells under her Arm, nor a Squirrel,[4] or Dormouse, in her Pocket, but always an abridg'd Piece of Morality to steal out when she is sure of being observed. When she went to the famous Ass-Race (which I must confess was but an odd Diversion to be encouraged by People of Rank and Figure) it was not, like other Ladies, to hear those poor Animals bray, nor to see Fellows run

---

[1] *Motto.* Juvenal, *Satires,* 6. 168–9: Such affectation all your virtues stains.
[2] Nos. 209, 247 (vol. ii).
[3] See No. 245 (vol. ii).
[4] In Steele's comedy, *The Funeral,* Lady Brumpton is shown (v. iii) mourning the death of her squirrel Robin.

naked,[1] or to hear Country Squires in bob Wigs and white Girdles make love at the Side of a Coach, and cry Madam this is dainty Weather. Thus she described the Diversion; for she went only to pray heartily that no body might be hurt in the Crowd, and to see if the poor Fellows Face, which was distorted with Grinning, might any Way be brought to it self again. She never chats over her Tea, but covers her Face, and is supposed in an Ejaculation before she taste a Sup. This ostentatious Behaviour is such an Offence to true Sanctity, that it disparages it; and makes Virtue not only unamiable but also ridiculous. The sacred Writings are full of Reflexions which abhor this kind of Conduct; and a *Devotée* is so far from promoting Goodness, that she deters others by her Example. Folly and Vanity in one of these Ladies, is like Vice in a Clergyman; it does not only debase himself, but makes the inconsiderate Part of the World think the worse of Religion.

I am,

SIR,

Your humble Servant,

Hotspur.'

Mr. SPECTATOR,

' XENOPHON in his short Account of the *Spartan* Commonwealth, speaking of the behaviour of their young Men in the Streets, says, There was so much Modesty in their Looks, that you might as soon have turned the Eyes of a marble Statue upon you as theirs; and that in all their behaviour they were more Modest than a Bride when put to Bed upon her wedding Night: This Vertue, which is always joyn'd to Magnanimity, had such an Influence upon their Courage, that in Battle an Enemy could not look them in the Face; and they durst not but Dye for their Country.[2]

'Whenever I walk into the Streets of *London* and *Westminster*, the Countenances of all the young Fellows that pass by me, make me wish my self in *Sparta*: I meet[a] with such blustring Airs, big Looks, and bold Fronts, that to a superficial Observer would bespeak a Courage above those *Grecians*. I am arriv'd to that Perfection in Speculation, that I understand the Language of the Eyes, which would be a great Misfortune to me had I not corrected the testiness

[a] meet] met *Fol.*

---

[1] See Christina Hole, *English Sports and Pastimes* (1949), pp. 25–26.
[2] *On the Policy of Lacedaemon*, 3. 5. Quoted by Longinus, 4. 4.

of old Age by Philosophy. There is scarce a Man in a red Coat who does not tell me, with a full Stare, he's a bold Man: I see several Swear inwardly at me, without any Offence of mine, but the odness of my Person: I meet Contempt in every Street, express'd in different Manners, by the scornful Look, the elevated Eye-brow, and the swelling Nostrils of the Proud and Prosperous. The Prentice speaks his disrespect by an extended Finger, and the Porter by stealing out his Tongue. If a Country Gentleman appears a little Curious in observing the Edifices, Signs, Clocks, Coaches and Dials, it is not to be imagined how the polite Rabble of this Town, who are acquainted with these Objects, ridicule his rusticity. I have known a Fellow with a Burden on his Head steal an Hand down from his Load and slily twirle the Cock of a Squire's Hat behind him; while the offended Person is Swearing, or out of Countenance, all the Wagg-Wits in the Highway are grinning in Applause of the ingenious Rogue that gave him the Tip; and the Folly of him who had not Eyes all round his Head to prevent receiving it. These things arise from a general Affectation of Smartness, Wit and Courage: *Wicherly* somewhere rallies the Pretentions this Way, by making a Fellow say, red Breeches are a certain Sign of Valour;[1] and *Otway* makes a Man to boast his Agility, trip up a Beggar on Crutches.[2] From such Hints I beg a Speculation on this Subject, in the mean time I shall do all in the power of a weak old Fellow in my own Defence; for as *Diogenes* being in quest of an honest Man, sought for him when it was broad Day light with a Lanthorn and Candle,[3] so I intend for the future to walk the Streets with a dark Lanthorn which has a convex Christal in it; and if any Man Stares at me, I give fair warning that I'll direct the Light full into his Eyes; thus despairing to find Men Modest, I hope by this Means to evade their Impudence.

> I am,
> SIR,
> Your most humble Servant,
> Sophrosunius.'

T

[1] *The Plain Dealer*, II. i. The speaker is Mr. Novell, 'a pert railing Coxcomb, and an Admirer of Novelties'.
[2] *Friendship in Fashion*, III. i. Malagene makes this boast of having tripped up a lame fellow who asked charity of him.
[3] Diogenes Laertius, 6. 41.

Non ego mordaci distrinxi carmine quenquam.
Ovid.

I HAVE been very often tempted to write Invectives upon those who have detracted from my Works, or spoken in derogation of my Person; but I look upon it as a particular Happiness that I have always hinder'd my Resentments from proceeding to this Extremity. I once had gone through half a Satyr, but found so many Motions of Humanity rising in me towards the Persons whom I had severely treated, that I threw it into the Fire without ever finishing it. I have been angry enough to make several little Epigrams and Lampoons, and after having admired them a Day or two, have likewise committed them to the Flames. These I look upon as so many Sacrifices to Humanity, and have received much greater Satisfaction from the suppressing such Performances, than I could have done from any Reputation they might have procured me, or from any Mortification they might have given my Enemies, in case I had made them publick. If a Man has any Talent in Writing, it shews a good Mind to forbear answering Calumnies and Reproaches in the same Spirit of Bitterness with which they are offered: But when a Man has been at some pains in making suitable returns to an Enemy, and has the Instruments of Revenge in his Hands, to let drop his Wrath, and stifle his Resentments, seems to have something in it Great and Heroical. There is a particular Merit in such a way of forgiving an Enemy, and the more violent and unprovoked the Offence has been, the greater still is the Merit of him who thus forgives it.

I never met with a Consideration that is more finely spun, and what has better pleased me, than one in *Epictetus*, which places an Enemy in a new Light, and gives us a view of him altogether different from that in which we are used to regard him.[2] The Sense of it is as follows: Does a Man reproach thee for being Proud or Ill-natured; Envious or Conceited; Ignorant or Detracting? consider

---

[1] *Motto.* Ovid, *Tristia,* 2. 563: No one is wounded in the lines I write.
The motto in the original Folio sheets contained the additional line, *Nulla venenato littera mista joco est* (*Tristia,* 2. 566), 'Mongst what I write no venom doth appear—used as the motto for No. 262 (vol. ii).
[2] *Enchiridion,* 42.

with thy self whether his Reproaches are true, if they are not, consider that thou art not the Person whom he reproaches, but that he reviles an Imaginary Being, and perhaps loves what thou really art, tho' he hates what thou appearest to be. If his Reproaches are true, if thou art the envious ill-natured Man he takes thee for, give thy self another turn, become mild, affable and obliging, and his Reproaches of thee naturally cease: his Reproaches may indeed continue, but thou art no longer[a] the Person whom he reproaches.

I often apply this Rule to my self, and, when I hear of a Satyrical Speech or Writing that is aimed at me, I examine my own Heart, whether I deserve it or not. If I bring in a Verdict against my self, I endeavour to rectifie my Conduct for the future in those Particulars, which have drawn the Censure upon me; but if the whole Invective be grounded upon a Falshood, I trouble my self no further about it, and look upon my Name at the Head of it, to signifie no more than one of those fictitious Names made use of by an Author to introduce an Imaginary Character. Why should a Man be sensible of the Sting of a Reproach, who is a Stranger to the Guilt that is implied in it? or subject himself to the Penalty, when he knows he has never committed the Crime? This is a Piece of Fortitude, which every one owes to his own Innocence, and without which it is impossible for a Man of any Merit or Figure to live at peace with himself in a Country that abounds with Wit and Liberty.

The Famous Monsieur *Balzac*,[1] in a Letter to the Chancellour of *France*, who had prevented the Publication of a Book against him, has the following Words, which are a lively Picture of the Greatness of Mind so visible in the Works of that Author. *If it was a new thing, it may be I should not be displeased with the Suppression of the first Libel that should abuse me, but since there are enough of 'em to make a small Library, I am secretly pleased to see the number encreased, and take Delight in raising a Heap of Stones, that Envy has cast at me without doing me any harm.*

The Author here alludes to those Monuments of the Eastern Nations, which were Mountains of Stones raised upon the dead Body by Travellers, that used to cast every one his Stone upon it

[a] no longer] not *Fol.*

[1] Jean-Louis Guez de Balzac (1597–1654), 'le grand épistolier de France'. See Bayle, art. Balzac, Remark H. Addison quotes the English translation of Bayle exactly, except that for Bayle's 'am almost well pleas'd' he substitutes 'am secretly pleased'. The Chancellor of France was Pierre Séguier.

as they passed by.[a] It is certain that no Monument is so glorious as one which is thus raised by the Hands of Envy. For my part, I admire an Author for such a Temper of Mind, as enables him to bear an undeserved Reproach without Resentment, more than for all the Wit of any the finest Satirical Reply.

Thus far I thought necessary to explain my self in relation to those who have animadverted on this Paper, and to shew the Reasons why I have not thought fit to return them any formal Answer. I must further add, that the Work wou'd have been of very little use to the Publick, had it been filled with Personal Reflections and Debates, for which reason I have never once turned out of my way to observe those little Cavils which have been made against it by Envy or Ignorance. The common fry of Scribblers who have no other way of being taken notice of, but by attacking what has gained some Reputation in the World, wou'd have furnished me with Business enough, had they found me disposed to enter the Lists with 'em.

I shall conclude with the Fable of *Boccalini*'s Traveller, who was so pestered with the Noise of Grashoppers in his Ears that he alighted from his Horse in great Wrath to kill them all. This, says the Author, was troubling himself to no manner of purpose: Had he pursued his Journey without taking notice of them, the troublesome Insects would have died of themselves in a very few Weeks, and he would have suffered nothing from them.[1]   L

---

[a] passed by.] passed by it. *Fol.*

[1] See the *Ragguagli di Parnaso*, ed. Giuseppe Rua (Bari, 1910), i. 368. Addison's direct source is L'Estrange's *Fables and Stories Moraliz'd* (1699), Fable 186, p. 174:

Boccalini's *Traveller* was so Disorder'd in the Heat of the Dog-Days with the Noise of *Grass-hoppers* in his Ears, that he alighted from his Horse in great Wrath to kill them all. Now This, says the Author, was only playing the Fool to no Manner of Purpose: for if he had but kept on, his Way, without minding them, they would e'en have gone Sputtering-on till they Burst, and the Man never the Worse for't.

No. 356   *Friday, April* 18, 1712[1]
[STEELE]

> . . . *Aptissima quæque dabunt Dii*
> *Charior est illis homo quam sibi* . . .
>   Juv.

IT is owing to Pride, and a secret Affectation of a certain Self-Existence, that the noblest Motive for Action that ever was proposed to Man, is not acknowledged the Glory and Happiness of their Being. The Heart is treacherous to it self, and we do not let our Reflections go deep enough to receive Religion as the most honourable Incentive to good and worthy Actions. It is our natural Weakness to flatter our selves into a Belief, that if we search into our[a] inmost Thoughts, we find our selves wholly disinterested, and divested of any Views arising from Self-Love and Vain-Glory. But, however Spirits of superficial Greatness may disdain at first Sight to do any thing, but from a noble Impulse in themselves, without any future Regards in this or another Being; upon stricter Enquiry they will find, to act worthily, and expect to be rewarded only in another World, is as heroick a Pitch of Virtue as humane Nature can arrive at. If the Tenour of our Actions have any other Motive than the Desire to be pleasing in the Eye of the Deity, it will necessarily follow that we must be more than Men, if we are not too much exalted in Prosperity and depressed in Adversity: But the Christian World has a Leader, the Contemplation of whose Life and Sufferings must administer Comfort in Affliction, while the Sense of his Power and Omnipotence must give them Humiliation in Prosperity.

It is owing to the forbidding and unlovely Constraint with which Men of low Conceptions act when they think they conform themselves to Religion, as well as to the more odious Conduct of Hypocrites, that the Word Christian does not carry with it at first View all that is Great, Worthy, Friendly, Generous, and Heroick. The

---

[a] search into our] search our *Fol.*

---

[1] *Motto.* Juvenal, *Satires,* 10. 349–50:
>   The Gods will grant
> What their unerring wisdom sees thee want:
> In Goodness as in Greatness they excel;
> Ah that we lov'd our selves but half so well. DRYDEN.

These lines had been used by Addison as the motto of *Tatler* 146.

Man who suspends his Hopes of the Reward of worthy Actions till after Death, who can bestow unseen, who can overlook Hatred, do Good to his Slanderer, who can never be angry at his Friend, never revengeful to his Enemy, is certainly formed for the Benefit of Society: Yet these are so far from heroick Virtues, that they are but the ordinary Duties of a Christian.

When a Man with a steddy Faith looks back on the great Catastrophe of this Day,[1] with what bleeding Emotions of Heart must he contemplate the Life and Sufferings of his Deliverer? When his Agonies occur to him, how will he weep to reflect that he has often forgot them for the Glance of a Wanton, for the Applause of a vain World, for an Heap of fleeting past Pleasures, which are at present[a] aking Sorrows?

How pleasing is the Contemplation of the lowly Steps our Almighty Leader took in conducting us to his heavenly Mansions! In plain and apt Parable,[2] Similitude and Allegory, our great Master enforced the Doctrine of our Salvation; but they of his Acquaintance, instead of receiving what they could not oppose, were offended at the Presumption of being wiser then they: They could not raise their little Ideas above the Consideration of him, in those Circumstances familiar to them, or conceive that he who appeared not more Terrible or Pompous, should have any thing more Exalted than themselves; he in that Place therefore would not longer ineffectually exert a Power which was incapable of Conquering the Prepossession of their narrow and mean Conceptions.

Multitudes follow'd him, and brought him the Dumb, the Blind, the Sick and Maim'd; whom when their Creator had Touch'd, with a second Life they Saw, Spoke, Leap'd and Ran. In[b] Affection to him, and Admiration of his Actions, the Crowd could not leave him, but waited near him till they were almost as faint and helpless as others they brought for Succour: He had Compassion on them, and by a Miracle supplyed their Necessities. Oh the Extatick Entertainment, when they could behold their Food immediately increase, to the Distributer's Hand, and see their God in Person, Feeding and Refreshing his Creatures: Oh Envied Happiness! But why do I say

---

[a] are at present] are present *Fol.*   [b] Ran. In] Ran; in *Fol.*

---

[1] This number was published on Good Friday.
[2] From this point on Steele transcribes, with some omissions and changes, a passage from chap. ii of his early work, *The Christian Hero.* The quotation will be found in *Tracts and Pamphlets,* ed. Rae Blanchard, pp. 32–35.

Envied, as if our God[a] did not still preside over our temperate Meals, chearful Hours, and innocent Conversations.

But tho' the sacred Story is every where full of Miracles, not inferior to this, and tho' in the midst of those Acts of Divinity, he never gave the least hint of a Design to become a Secular Prince, yet had not hitherto the Apostles themselves any other than hopes of Worldly Power, Preferment, Riches and Pomp; for[b] *Peter*, upon an Accident of Ambition among the Apostles, hearing his Master explain that his Kingdom was not of this World; was so scandaliz'd, that he, whom he had so long follow'd, should suffer the Ignominy, Shame and Death which he foretold, that he took him aside and said, *Be it far from thee, Lord, this shall not be unto thee*:[1] For which he suffer'd a severe Reprehension from his Master, as having in his View the Glory of Man, rather than that of God.

The great Change of things began to draw near, when the Lord of Nature thought fit as a Saviour and Deliverer to make his publick Entry into *Jerusalem*, with more than the Power and Joy, but none of the Ostentation and Pomp of a Triumph: He came Humble, Meek and Lowly; with an unfelt new Extasie, Multitudes strow'd his way with Garments and Olive-branches, Crying with loud Gladness and Acclamation, *Hosannah to the Son of* David, *Blessed is he that cometh in the Name of the Lord!*[2] At this Great King's Accession to his Throne, Men were not Ennobled but Sav'd; Crimes were not Remitted, but Sins Forgiven; he did not bestow Medals, Honours, Favours, but Health, Joy, Sight, Speech! The first Object the Blind ever saw, was the Author of Sight, while the Lame Ran before, and the Dumb repeated the *Hosannah!* Thus Attended, he Entered into his own House, the sacred Temple, and by his Divine Authority expelled Traders and Worldlings that prophaned it; and thus did he, for a time, use a great and despotick Power, to let Unbelievers understand, that 'twas not Want of, but Superiority to all Worldly Dominion, that made him not exert it: But is this then the Saviour, is this the Deliverer? Shall this obscure *Nazarine* command *Israel*, and sit in the Throne of *David*? their proud and disdainful Hearts, which were petrifyed with the Love[c] and Pride of this World, were impregnable to the Reception of so mean a Benefactor, and were

[a] our God] our good God *Fol.*   [b] Pomp; for] Pomp: For *Fol.*   [c] with the Love] with Love *Fol.*

[1] Matt. xvi. 22.   [2] Matt. xxi. 9.

now enough exasperated with Benefits to conspire his Death: Our Lord was sensible of their Design, and prepar'd his Disciples for it, by recounting to 'em now more distinctly what should befall him; but *Peter* with an ungrounded Resolution, and in a Flush of Temper, made a sanguine Protestation; that tho' all Men were offended in him, yet would not he be offended.[1] It was a great Article of our Saviour's Business in the World, to bring us to a Sense of our Inability, without God's Assistance, to do any thing great or good; he therefore told *Peter*, who thought so well of his Courage and Fidelity, that they would both fail him, and ev'n he should deny him Thrice that very Night.

But what Heart can conceive? what Tongue utter the Sequel? who is that yonder buffeted, mock'd and spurn'd! whom do they drag like a Felon! Whither do they carry my Lord, my King, my Saviour and my God? And will he Die to Expiate those very Injuries? see where they have nail'd the Lord and Giver of Life! How his Wounds blacken! his Body writhes, and Heart heaves with Pity, and with Agony! Oh Almighty Sufferer, look down, look down from thy Triumphant Infamy; lo he inclines his Head to his sacred Bosom! Hark he Groans, see he Expires! The Earth trembles, the Temple rends, the Rocks burst, the Dead arise; which are the Quick? which are the Dead? Sure Nature, all Nature is departing with her Creator.   T

No. 357   *Saturday, April* 19, 1712[2]
[ADDISON]

. . . quis talia fando . . .
Temperet à lacrymis? . . .
               Virg.

THE Tenth Book of *Paradise Lost* has a greater variety of Persons in it than any other in the whole Poem. The Author upon the winding up of his Action introduces all those who had any Concern in it, and shews with great Beauty the influence which it had upon each of them. It is like the last Act of a well written Tragedy, in which all who had a part in it are generally drawn up

[1] Matt. xxvi. 33-34.
[2] *Motto.* Virgil, *Aeneid*, 2. 6, 8: At such a tale who can forbear to weep?
This had been used as the motto of No. 84 (and of *Tatler* 134). In the original Folio sheets the motto was Horace, *Ars poetica*, 316 (the motto of No. 279, vol. ii).

before the Audience, and represented under those Circumstances in which the determination of the Action places them.

I shall therefore consider this Book under four Heads, in relation to the Celestial, the Infernal, the Human, and the Imaginary Persons, who have their respective Parts allotted in it.

To begin with the Celestial Persons: The Guardian Angels of *Paradise* are described as returning to Heaven upon the Fall of Man, in order to approve their Vigilance; their Arrival, their manner of Reception, with the Sorrow which appeared in themselves, and in those Spirits who are said to Rejoice at the Conversion of a Sinner, are very finely laid together in the following Lines.

> *Up into Heav'n from Paradise in haste*
> *Th' angelick guards ascended, mute and sad*
> *For man, for of his state by this they knew*
> *Much wond'ring how the subtle Fiend had stoln*
> *Entrance unseen. Soon as th' unwelcome news*
> *From earth arriv'd at Heaven Gate, displeas'd*
> *All were who heard, dim sadness did not spare*
> *That time Celestial visages, yet mixt*
> *With pity, violated not their bliss.*
> *About the new-arriv'd, in multitudes*
> *Th' Æthereal people ran, to hear and know*
> *How all befell: They tow'rds the throne supreame*
> *Accountable made haste to make appear*
> *With righteous plea, their utmost vigilance,*
> *And easily approv'd; when the most High*
> *Eternal father from his secret cloud,*
> *Amidst in thunder utter'd thus his voice.*[1]

The same Divine Person who in the foregoing parts of this Poem interceded for our first Parents before their Fall, overthrew the Rebel Angels, and created the World, is now represented as descending to *Paradise*, and pronouncing Sentence upon the three Offenders.[2] The cool of the Evening, being a Circumstance with which Holy Writ introduces this great Scene, it is Poetically described by our Author, who has also kept religiously to the form of Words, in which the three several Sentences were passed upon *Adam*, *Eve* and the Serpent. He has rather chosen to neglect the numerousness of his Verse, than to deviate from those Speeches

[1] *PL*, x. 17-33.　　　　　　　　[2] *PL*, x. 85-102.

which are recorded on this great occasion. The Guilt and Confusion of our first Parents standing naked before their Judge, is touch'd with great Beauty. Upon the arrival of *Sin* and *Death* into the Works of the Creation, the Almighty is again introduced as speaking to his Angels that surrounded him.

> *See with what heat these Dogs of Hell advance*
> *To waste and havock yonder world, which I*
> *So fair and good created, &c.*[1]

The following Passage is formed upon that glorious Image in Holy Writ which compares the Voice of an innumerable Host of Angels, uttering Hallelujahs, to the Voice of mighty Thunderings, or of many Waters.[2]

> *He ended, and the Heav'nly Audience loud*
> *Sung Hallelujah, as the sound of Seas,*
> *Through multitude that sung: Just are thy ways,*
> *Righteous are thy Decrees in all thy Works,*
> *Who can extenuate thee? . . .*[3]

Though the Author in the whole course of his Poem, and particularly in the Book we are now examining, has infinite Allusions to places of Scripture, I have only taken notice in my Remarks of such as are of a Poetical Nature, and which are woven with great Beauty into the Body of his[a] Fable. Of this kind is that Passage in the present Book, where describing *Sin*[b] as marching through the Works of Nature, he adds,

> *. . . Behind her Death*
> *Close following pace for pace, not mounted yet*
> *On his pale horse: . . .*[4]

Which alludes to that Passage in Scripture so wonderfully Poetical, and terrifying to the Imagination. *And I looked, and behold, a pale Horse, and his Name that sat on him was Death, and Hell followed with him: and power was given unto them over the fourth part of the earth, to kill with sword, and with hunger, and with sickness, and with the beasts of the earth.*[5] Under this first head of Celestial Persons we must likewise

[a] his] this *all edd. Corrected in Errata in Folio (No. 369) to* his   [b] *Sin*] Sin and Death *all edd. Corrected in Errata in Folio (No. 369):* 'dele and Death'

[1] *PL*, x. 616–18.   [2] Rev. xix. 6.
[3] *PL*, x. 641–5 ('on all thy Works').   [4] *PL*, x. 588–90.
[5] Rev. vi. 8 (the text reads 'with death' rather than 'with sickness').

take notice of the Command which the Angels received, to produce several[a] Changes in Nature, and sully the Beauty of the Creation.[1] Accordingly they are represented as infecting the Stars and Planets with malignant Influences, weakning the Light of the Sun, bringing down the Winter into the milder Regions of Nature, planting Winds and Storms in several Quarters of the Sky, storing the Clouds with Thunder, and in short, perverting the whole frame of the Universe to the condition of its Criminal Inhabitants. As this is a noble Incident in the Poem, the following Lines, in which we see the Angels heaving up the Earth, and placing it in a different posture to the Sun from what it had before the Fall of Man, is conceived with that sublime Imagination which was so peculiar to this great Author.

> *Some say he bid his angels turn ascanse*
> *The Poles of earth twice ten degrees and more*
> *From the Sun's Axle; they with labour push'd*
> *Oblique the Centrick Globe . . .*[2]

We are in the second place to consider the Infernal Agents under the View which *Milton* has given us of them in this Book. It is observed by those who would set forth the Greatness of *Virgil's* Plan, that he conducts his Reader thro' all the Parts of the Earth which were discover'd in his time. *Asia, Africk* and *Europe* are the several Scenes of his Fable. The Plan of *Milton's* Poem is of an infinitely greater extent, and fills the Mind with many more astonishing Circumstances. *Satan,* having surrounded the Earth seven times,[3] departs at length from *Paradise.* We then[b] see him steering his Course among the Constellations, and after having traversed the whole Creation, pursuing his Voyage through the *Chaos,* and entering into his own Infernal Dominions.[4]

His first appearance in the Assembly of Fallen Angels[5] is work'd up with Circumstances which give a delightful Surprize to the Reader; but there is no Incident in the whole Poem which does this more than the Transformation of the whole Audience, that follows the account their Leader gives them of his Expedition.[6] The gradual change of *Satan* himself is described after *Ovid's* manner, and may

---

[a] produce several] produce the several *all edd. Corrected in Errata in Folio (No. 369)* *to* produce several   [b] then] afterwards *Fol.*

---

[1] *PL,* x. 649–67.   [2] *PL,* x. 668–71.   [3] *PL,* ix. 63–69.
[4] *PL,* x. 325–49, 414–20.   [5] *PL,* x. 441–59.   [6] *PL,* x. 504–47.

vie with any of those celebrated Transformations which are looked upon as the most beautiful parts in that Poet's Works. *Milton* never fails of improving his own Hints, and bestowing the last finishing Touches to every Incident which is admitted into his Poem. The unexpected Hiss which rises in this Episode, the Dimensions and Bulk of *Satan* so much superior to those of the Infernal Spirits who lay under the same Transformation, with the annual Change[1] which they are supposed to suffer, are Instances of this kind. The Beauty of the Diction is very remarkable in this whole Episode, as I have observed in the Sixth Paper[2] of these Remarks[a] the great Judgment with which it was contrived.

The Parts of *Adam* and *Eve*, or the Humane Persons, come next under our Consideration. *Milton's* Art is no where more shewn than in his conducting the parts of these our first Parents. The Representation he gives of them, without falsifying the Story, is wonderfully contrived to influence the Reader with Pity and Compassion towards them. Tho' *Adam* involves the whole Species in Misery, his Crime proceeds from a Weakness which every Man is inclin'd to pardon and commiserate, as it seems rather the frailty of Humane Nature, than of the Person who offended. Every one is apt to excuse a Fault which he himself might have fallen into. It was the Excess of Love for *Eve* that ruined *Adam* and his Posterity. I need not add, that the Author is justified in this particular by many of the Fathers, and the most Orthodox Writers. *Milton* has by this means filled a great part of his Poem with that kind of Writing which the *French* Criticks call the *Tender*, and which is in a particular manner engaging to all sorts of Readers.

Adam and *Eve*, in the Book we are now considering, are likewise drawn with such Sentiments as do not only interest the Reader in their Afflictions; but raise in him the most melting Passions of Humanity and Commiseration. When *Adam* sees the several Changes in Nature produced, about him, he appears in a disorder of Mind suitable to one who had forfeited both his Innocence and his Happiness. He is filled with Horror, Remorse, Despair; in the anguish of his Heart he expostulates with his Creator for having[b] him an unasked Existence.

[a] these Remarks] *19*; these my Remarks *Fol., 8vo, 12mo*   [b] having given] giving *Fol.*

---

[1] *PL*, x. 575-7.   [2] Actually in the fourth paper (No. 285).

Did I request thee, Maker, from my Clay
To mould me, Man, did I solicite thee
From darkness to promote me, or here place
In this delicious Garden? as my will
Concurr'd not to my being, 'twere but right
And equal to reduce me to my dust,
Desirous to resign, and render back
All I receiv'd . . .[1]

He immediately after recovers from his Presumption, owns his Doom to be just, and begs that the Death which is threaten'd him may be inflicted on him.

. . . Why delays
His hand to execute what his decree
Fix'd on this day? Why do I overlive,
Why am I mock'd with Death, and lengthen'd out
To Deathless pain? how gladly would I meet
Mortality my Sentence, and be earth
Insensible, how glad would lay me down
As in my mothers lap? there should I rest
And sleep secure; his dreadful voice no more
Would thunder in my ears, no fear of worse
To me and to my off-spring, would torment me
With cruel expectation . . .[2]

This whole Speech is full of the like Emotion, and varied with all those Sentiments which we may suppose natural to a Mind so broken and disturb'd. I must not omit that generous Concern which our first Father shows in it for his Posterity, and which is so proper to affect the Reader.

. . . Hide me from the face
Of God, whom to behold was then my height
Of Happiness: yet well if here would end
The misery, I deserv'd it, and would bear
My own deservings; but this will not serve;
All that I eat, or drink, or shall beget,
Is propagated Curse. O voice once heard
Delightfully, encrease and multiply,
Now Death to hear! . . .

[1] *PL*, x. 743–50.   [2] *PL*, x. 771–82 (in line 778 'I should').

> *. . . In me all*
> *Posterity stands curst: Fair Patrimony*
> *That I must leave you, Sons; O were I able*
> *To waste it all my self, and leave you none!*
> *So disinherited how would you bless*
> *Me now your curse! Ah, why should all Mankind*
> *For one Mans fault thus guiltless be condemned*
> *If guiltless? But from me what can proceed*
> *But all corrupt . . .*[1]

Who can afterwards behold the Father of Mankind extended upon the Earth, uttering his Midnight Complaints, bewailing his Existence, and wishing for Death, without sympathizing with him in his Distress?

> *Thus Adam to himself lamented loud*
> *Through the still night, not now, as e're man fell*
> *Wholesome and cool and mild, but with black Air*
> *Accompanied, with damps and dreadful gloom*
> *Which to his evil Conscience represented*
> *All things with double terrour: on the Ground*
> *Outstretch'd he lay, on the cold ground, and oft*
> *Curs'd his Creation, Death as oft accus'd*
> *Of tardy execution. . . .*[2]

The Part of *Eve* in this Book is no less passionate, and apt to sway the Reader in her Favour. She is represented with great Tenderness as approaching *Adam*, but is spurn'd from him with a Spirit of Upbraiding and Indignation conformable to the Nature of Man, whose Passions had now gained the Dominion over him.[3] The following Passage, wherein she is described as renewing her Addresses to him, with the whole Speech that follows it, have something in them exquisitely moving and pathetick.

> *He added not, and from her turn'd: but* Eve
> *Not so repulst, with tears that ceas'd not flowing*
> *And tresses all disorder'd, at his Feet*
> *Fell humble, and embracing them, besought*
> *His peace, and thus proceeded*[a] *in her plaint.*

[a] *proceeded*] 19; *proceeding* Fol., 8vo, 12mo

---

[1] *PL*, x. 723-31, 817-25.　　　[2] *PL*, x. 845-53.　　　[3] *PL*, x. 863-908.

Forsake me not thus Adam, *witness Heav'n*
What love sincere and reverence in my heart
I bear thee, and unweeting have offended,
Unhappily deceiv'd; thy Suppliant
I beg, and clasp thy knees; bereave me not,
Whereon I live, thy gentle looks, thy aid,
Thy counsel in this uttermost distress,
My only strength and stay: Forlorn of thee
Whither shall I betake me, where subsist?
While yet we live, scarce one short hour perhaps,
Between us two let there be peace, &c.[1]

Adam's Reconcilement to her is worked up in the same Spirit of Tenderness. *Eve* afterwards proposes to her Husband, in the Blindness of her Despair, that to prevent their Guilt from descending upon Posterity they should resolve to live Childless; or, if that could not be done, they[a] should seek their own Deaths by violent Methods.[2] As those Sentiments naturally engage the Reader to regard the Mother of Mankind with more than ordinary Commiseration, they likewise contain a very fine Moral. The Resolution of dying to end our Miseries does not shew such a degree of Magnanimity as a Resolution to bear them, and submit to the Dispensations of Providence. Our Author has therefore, with great Delicacy, represented *Eve* as entertaining this Thought, and *Adam* as disapproving it.

We are, in the last place, to consider the Imaginary Persons, or *Death* and *Sin*,[b] who act a large part in this Book.[3] Such beautiful extended Allegories are certainly some of the finest Compositions of Genius; but, as I have before observed, are not agreeable to the Nature of an Heroic Poem. This of *Sin* and *Death* is very exquisite in its kind, if not considered as a Part of such a Work. The Truths contained in it are so clear and open that I shall not lose time in explaining them, but shall only observe, that a Reader who knows the strength of the *English* Tongue will be amazed to think how the

---

^a they] that they *Fol.*   ^b *Death* and *Sin*,] *Sin* and *Death Fol.*

[1] *PL*, x. 909–24.
[2] *PL*, x. 979–1006.
[3] Addison here discusses at some length the objection which he had briefly mentioned earlier, in Nos. 273 (vol. ii), 297, 309, and 315. 'This unskilful allegory appears to me one of the greatest faults of the poem' (Johnson, *Life of Milton*, World's Classics ed., i. 134).

Poet could find such apt Words and Phrases to describe the Actions[a] of those[b] two imaginary Persons, and particularly in that Part where *Death* is exhibited as forming a Bridge over the *Chaos*:[1] a Work suitable to the Genius of *Milton*.

Since the Subject I am upon gives me an Opportunity of speaking more at large of such Shadowy and imaginary Persons as may be introduced into Heroic Poems, I shall beg leave to explain my self in[c] a Matter which is curious in its kind, and which none of the Criticks have treated of. It is certain *Homer* and *Virgil* are full of imaginary Persons, who are very beautiful in Poetry when they are just shown, without being engaged in any Series of Action. *Homer* indeed represents *Sleep* as a Person, and ascribes a short Part to him in his *Iliad*;[2] but we must consider that tho' we now regard such a Person as entirely Shadowy and unsubstantial, the Heathens made Statues of him, placed him in their Temples, and looked upon him as a real Deity. When *Homer* makes use of other such Allegorical Persons it is only in short Expressions, which convey an ordinary Thought to the Mind in the most pleasing manner, and may rather be looked upon as Poetical Phrases than allegorical Descriptions.[3] Instead of telling us that Men naturally fly when they are terrified, he introduces the Persons of *Flight* and *Fear*, who he tells us are inseparable Companions.[4] Instead of saying that the Time was come when *Apollo* ought to have received his Recompence, he tells us that the *Hours* brought him his Reward.[5] Instead of describing the Effects which *Minerva*'s *Ægis* produced in Battel, he tells us that the Brims of it were encompassed by *Terrour*, *Rout*, *Discord*, *Fury*, *Pursuit*, *Massacre* and *Death*.[6] In the same Figure of speaking he represents *Victory* as following *Diomedes*;[7] *Discord* as the Mother of Funerals and Mourning,[8] *Venus* as dressed by the *Graces*, *Bellona* as wearing Terrour and Consternation like a Garment.[9] I might give several other Instances out of *Homer*, as well as a great many out of *Virgil*.[10]

---

[a] Actions] Action *Fol.*   [b] those] these *Fol.*   [c] in] on *Fol.*

---

[1] PL, x. 282–324.   [2] *Iliad*, 14. 231–91.
[3] Cf. Le Bossu, book v, chap. iv, on this point.
[4] *Iliad*, 9. 1–3.   [5] *Iliad*, 21. 450.
[6] *Iliad*, 5. 738–42 (cf. also 4. 439–40).
[7] This does not appear to be in Homer; Addison may be recalling *Iliad*, 5. 835–41, where Pallas Athene accompanies Diomedes.
[8] *Iliad*, 4. 440; 11. 73.   [9] *Iliad*, 5. 338.
[10] Dennis, in his *Remarks on Prince Arthur* (1696), had made the same application: '*Virgil* has seldom describ'd any of his Machines; and in those which he has describ'd,

Milton has likewise very often made use of the same way of speaking, as where he tells us that *Victory* sat on the right hand of the Messiah, when he march'd forth against the Rebel Angels;[1] that at the rising of the Sun the *Hours* unbarr'd the Gates of Light;[2] that *Discord* was the Daughter of *Sin*.[3] Of the same nature are those Expressions where describing the singing of the Nightingale he adds, *Silence was pleased*;[4] and upon the Messiah's bidding Peace to the *Chaos*, *Confusion heard his voice*.[5] I might add innumerable Instances[a] of our Poet's writing in this beautiful Figure. It is plain that[b] these I have mentioned, in which Persons of an imaginary Nature are introduced, are such short Allegories as are not designed to be taken in the litteral Sense, but only to convey particular Circumstances to the Reader after an unusual and entertaining Manner. But when such Persons are introduced as principal Actors, and engaged in a Series of Adventures, they take too much upon them, and are by no means proper for an Heroic Poem, which ought to appear credible in its principal Parts. I cannot forbear therefore thinking that *Sin* and *Death* are as improper Agents in a Work of this Nature, as *Strength* and *Necessity*[c] in one of the Tragedies of *Eschylus*,[6] who represented those two Persons nailing down *Prometheus* to a Rock, for which he has been justly censured by the greatest Criticks.[7] I do not know any imaginary Person made use of in a more Sublime manner of thinking than that in one of the Prophets, who describing God as descending from Heaven, and visiting the Sins of Mankind, adds that dreadful Circumstance; *Before him went the Pestilence*.[8] It is certain this imaginary Person might have been de-

---

[a] Instances] other Instances *Fol.*   [b] that] from *Fol. Corrected in Errata (No. 369)*   [c] Necessity] *Violence Fol.*

he has been very short; and even in those short Descriptions, he has describ'd Actions, and not Persons' (*Works*, ed. Hooker, i. 105).

[1] *PL*, vi. 762.   [2] *PL*, vi. 4.   [3] *PL*, x. 707–8.
[4] *PL*, iv. 604.   [5] *PL*, iii. 710.

[6] *Prometheus Bound*. Although there are references in the play to 'strong necessity', the two figures who are introduced as leading in Prometheus are Strength and Force. (The Folio reading, 'Strength and Violence', is more accurate.)

[7] Dacier's note on Aristotle's *Poetics*, 14, criticizes poets who endeavour to excite passions by monstrous decorations:

Nothing can be farther from true Tragedy than this means. *Æschylus* has a great share in this Censure, for as his imagination was vast and quick, but extravagant and irregular, he often ventured at those things, which were not only contrary to Art, but Nature too. His *Prom[e]theus* is full of these Monsters, which *Aristotle* Condemns, for what can be more such, than his Punishment of that God, where *Force and Violence*, two persons Nail him to the Rock with vast Hammers?' (p. 238)

[8] Hab. iii. 5.

scribed in all her purple Spots. The *Fever* might have march'd before her, *Pain* might have stood at her right Hand, *Phrenzy* on her left, and *Death* in her Rear. She might have been introduced as gliding down from the Tail of a Comet, or darted upon the Earth in a Flash of Lightning: She might have tainted the Atmosphere with her Breath; the very glaring of her Eyes might have scattered Infection. But I believe every Reader will think that in such Sublime Writings the mentioning of her as it is done in Scripture has something in it more just, as well as great, than all that the most fanciful Poet could have bestowed upon her in the Richness of his Imagination.

L

No. 358

[STEELE]

Monday, April 21, 1712[1]

Desipere in loco.

Hor.

*C*HARLES LILLIE attended me the other Day, and made me a Present of a large Sheet of Paper, on which is delineated a Pavement in Mosaick Work, lately discovered at *Stunsfeild* near *Woodstock*.[2] A Person who has so much the Gift of Speech as Mr. *Lillie*, and can carry on a Discourse without Reply, had great

---

[1] *Motto.* Horace, *Odes*, 4. 12. 28: To act foolishly in due place.

[2] The pavement, which had been discovered in January at Stunsfield, or Stonesfield, near Woodstock in Oxfordshire, was the object of considerable speculation by Thomas Hearne, who made at least eight visits to it. After much wavering Hearne concluded that it was Roman, and done in the time of Valentinian I. 'A great many People go still to see this Curiosity, especially such as go to Woodstock for the Sake of seeing Blenheim Castle' (*Remarks and Collections*, iii. 369). Steele's allusion to the discovery is doubtless a friendly gesture to Charles Lillie, whose advertisement appears in Nos. 353, 355, 361, and 365:

Whereas about nine Weeks since there was accidentally discovered by an Husbandman at Stimsfield [*sic*] near Woodstock in Oxfordshire, (a large Pavement of rich Mosaick Work of the Ancient Romans, which is adorn'd with several Figures alluding to Mirth and Concord, in particular that of Bacchus seated on a Panther.) This is to give Notice, that an exact Delineation of the same is Engraven and Imprinted on a large Elephant Sheet of Paper; which are to be Sold at Mr. Charles Lillie's, Perfumer, at the corner of Beauford Buildings in the Strand, at 1 s. N.B. There are to be had at the same place at one Guinea each on a superfine Atlas Paper, some painted with the same variety of Colours that the said Pavement is beautified with; this Piece of Antiquity is esteemed by the Learned to be the most considerable ever found in Britain.

Opportunity on that Occasion to expatiate upon so fine[a] a Piece of Antiquity. Among other things, I remember he gave me his Opinion, which he drew from the Ornaments of the Work, That this was the Floor of a Room dedicated to Mirth and Concord. Viewing this Work, made my Fancy run over the many gay Expressions I had read in ancient Authors, which contained Invitations to lay aside Care and Anxiety, and give a Loose to that pleasing Forgetfulness wherein Men put off their Characters of Business, and enjoy their very Selves. These Hours were usually passed in Rooms adorned for that Purpose, and set out in such a Manner, as the Objects all around the Company gladdened their Hearts; which, joined to the chearful Looks of well-chosen and agreeable Friends, gave new Vigour to the Airy, produced the latent Fire of the Modest, and gave Grace to the slow Humour of the Reserved. A judicious Mixture of such Company, crowned with Chaplets of Flowers, and the whole Apartment glittering with gay Lights, cheared with a Profusion of Roses, artificial Falls of Water, and Intervals of soft Notes, to Songs of Love and Wine, suspended the Cares of humane Life, and made a Festival of mutual Kindness. Such Parties of Pleasure as these, and the Reports of the agreeable Passages in their Jollities, have in all Ages awakened the dull Part of Mankind, to pretend to Mirth and good Humour without Capacity for such Entertainments; for if I may be allowed to say so, there are an hundred Men fit for any Employment, to one who is capable of passing a Night in Company of the first Taste, without shocking any Member of the Society, overrating his own Part of the Conversation, but equally receiving and contributing to the Pleasure of the whole Company. When one considers such Collections of Companions in past Times, and such as one might name in the present Age, with how much Spleen must a Man needs reflect upon the awkard Gayety of those who affect the Frolick with an ill Grace? I have a Letter from a Correspondent of mine, who desires me to admonish all loud, mischeivous, airy, dull Companions, that they are mistaken in what they call a Frolick. Irregularity in its self is not what creates Pleasure and Mirth; but to see a Man who knows what Rule and Decency are, descend from them agreeably in our Company, is what denominates him a pleasant Companion. Instead of that, you find many whose Mirth consists only in doing things which do not become them, with a secret Consciousness that all the World know

a fine] great *Fol.*

they know better: To this is always added something mischeivous to themselves or others. I have heard of some very merry Fellows, among whom the Frolick was started, and passed by a great Majority, that every Man should immediately draw a Tooth; after which they have gone in a Body and smoaked[1] a Cobler. The same Company, at another Night, has each Man burned his Cravat; and one perhaps, whose Estate would bear it, has thrown a long Wigg and laced Hat into the same Fire. Thus they have jested themselves stark naked, and ran into the Streets, and frighted Women very successfully.[2] There is no Inhabitant of any standing in *Covent-Garden*, but can tell you a hundred good Humours, where People have come off with little Blood-shed, and yet scowered all the witty Hours of the Night. I know a Gentleman that has several Wounds in the Head by Watch-Poles,[3] and has been thrice run through the Body to carry on a good Jest: He is very old for a Man of so much good Humour; but to this Day he is seldom merry, but he has occasion to be valiant at the same time. But by the Favour of these Gentlemen, I am humbly of Opinion, that a Man may be a very witty Man, and never offend one Statute of this Kingdom, not excepting even that of Stabbing.

The Writers of Plays have what they call Unity of Time and Place to give a Justness to their Representation; and it would not be amiss if all who pretend to be Companions, would confine their Action to the Place of Meeting: For a Frolick carried further may be better performed by other Animals than Men. It is not to rid much Ground, or do much Mischief, that should denominate a pleasant Fellow; but that is truly Frolick which is the Play of the Mind, and consists of various and unforced Sallies of Imagination. Festivity of Spirit is a very uncommon Talent, and must proceed from an Assemblage of agreeable Qualities in the same Person: There are some few whom I think peculiarly happy in it; but it is a Talent one cannot name in a Man, especially when one considers that it is never very graceful but where it is regarded by him who possesses it in the second Place. The best Man that I know of for

[1] For this verb see No. 335. It seems to be used here in the archaic sense of *to banter* (*OED*, sense 9).

[2] The drawing of teeth and the burning of a laced neck-cloth are among the 'frolicks' of Sedley recorded by William Oldys in his manuscript notes on Langbaine, printed in V. de Sola Pinto's *Sir Charles Sedley* (1927), p. 319. The 'jesting themselves stark naked' is one of the better-known stories of Sedley and his companions (see Pinto, pp. 61–66).

[3] A watchman's pole or staff.

heightening the Revel-Gayety of a Company is *Estcourt*,[1] whose jovial Humour diffuses it self from the highest Person at an Entertainment to the meanest Waiter. Merry Tales, accompanied with apt Gestures and lively Representations of Circumstances and Persons, beguile the gravest Mind into a Consent to be as humourous as himself. Add to this, that when a Man is in his good Graces, he has a Mimickry that does not debase the Person he represents; but which, taking from the Gravity of the Character, adds to the Agreeableness of it. This pleasant Fellow gives one some Idea of the antient *Pantomime*,[2] who is said to have given the Audience, in Dumb-show, an exact Idea of any Character or Passion, or make an intelligible Relation of any publick Occurrence with no other Expression than that of his Looks and Gestures. If all who have been obliged to these Talents in *Estcourt*, will be at *Love for Love* to Morrow Night, they will but pay him what they owe him, at so easy a Rate as being present at a Play which no Body would omit seeing that had, or had not ever seen it before.[3]   T

No. 359
[BUDGELL]
Tuesday, April 22, 1712[4]

> *Torva leæna lupum sequitur, lupus ipse capellam.*
> *Florentem cytisum sequitur lasciva capella.*
>
> Virg.

AS we were at the Club last Night, I observ'd that my Friend Sir ROGER, contrary to his usual Custom, sat very silent, and

[1] See No. 264 (vol. ii).

[2] The word is here used in its original sense: a Roman actor who performed in dumb show, representing by mimicry various characters and scenes (*OED*). Danet defines pantomime as 'a *Mimick*, who among the Ancients appeared on the Stage, and by his Signs and Gestures represented all sorts of Actions'. The last quotation in this sense in *OED* is dated 1656.

[3] *Love for Love*, Congreve's comedy, is advertised in this number for performance on the following night at Drury Lane, 'For the Benefit of Mr. Estcourt'. He frequently acted in this play, in the role of Sir Sampson Legend, a part which Addison particularly praises (see No. 189, vol. ii).

[4] *Motto*. Virgil, *Eclogues*, 2. 63–64:
> The greedy Lioness the Wolf pursues,
> The Wolf the Kid, the wanton Kid the Browze. DRYDEN.

instead of minding what was said by the Company, was Whistling to himself in a very thoughtful Mood, and playing with a Cork. I jogg'd Sir ANDREW FREEPORT who sat between us; and as we were both observing him, we saw the Knight shake his Head, and heard him say to himself *A foolish Woman! I can't believe it.* Sir ANDREW gave him a gentle pat upon the Shoulder, and offer'd to lay him a Bottle of Wine that he was thinking of the Widow. My old Friend started, and recovering out of his brown Study, told Sir ANDREW, that once in his Life he had been in the right. In short, after some little Hesitation, Sir ROGER told us in the Fulness of his Heart, that he had just receiv'd a Letter from his Steward, which acquainted him, that his old Rival and Antagonist in the County, Sir *David Dundrum*, had been making a Visit to the Widow. However, says Sir ROGER, I can never think she'll have a Man that's half a Year older than I am, and a noted Republican into the Bargain.

WILL. HONEYCOMB, who looks upon Love as his particular Province, interrupting our Friend with a janty Laugh, I thought, Knight, says he, thou hadst lived long enough in the World, not to pin thy Happiness upon one that is a Woman and a Widow. I think, that without Vanity, I may pretend to know as much of the Female World as any Man in *Great Britain*, tho' the chief of my Knowledge consists in this, that they are not to be known. WILL. immediately, with his usual Fluency, rambled into an Account of his own Amours. I am now, says he, upon the Verge of Fifty, tho' by the way we all knew he was turn'd of Threescore. You may easily guess, continu'd WILL. that I have not lived so long in the World without having had some Thoughts of *settling* in it, as the Phrase is. To tell you truly, I have several times tried my Fortune that way, tho' I can't much boast of my Success.

I made my first Addresses to a young Lady in the Country, but, when I thought things were pretty well drawing to a Conclusion, her Father happening to hear that I had formerly boarded with a Surgeon, the old Put[1] forbid me his House, and within a Fortnight after married his Daughter to a Fox-hunter in the Neighbourhood.

---

[1] 'A stupid man, blockhead', a word just then apparently coming into fashion. In his letter to the *Tatler* (No. 230, 28 Sept. 1710) Swift speaks of 'certain Words invented by some *Pretty Fellows*; such as Banter, Bamboozle, Country Put, and Kidney, . . . some of which are now strugling for the Vogue, and others are in Possession of it'.

I made my next Applications to a Widow, and attacked her so briskly, that I thought my self within a Fortnight of her. As I waited upon her one Morning, she told me, that she intended to keep her ready Mony and Jointure in her own Hand, and desired me to call upon her Attorney in *Lyons-Inn*,[1] who would adjust with me what it was proper for me to add to it. I was so rebuffed by this Overture, that I never enquired either for her or her Attorney afterwards.

A few Months after I addressed my self to a Young Lady, who was an only Daughter, and of a good Family; I danced with her at several Balls, squeezed her by the Hand, said soft things to her, and, in short, made no doubt of her Heart; and though my Fortune was not equal to hers, I was in Hopes that her fond Father would not deny her the Man she had fixed her Affections upon. But as I went one Day to the House, in order to break the matter to him, I found the whole Family in Confusion, and heard, to my unspeakable Surprize, that Miss *Jenny* was that very Morning run away with the Butler.

I then courted a second Widow, and am at a loss, to this Day, how I came to miss her, for she had often commended my Person and Behaviour. Her Maid, indeed, told me one Day, that her Mistress had said, she never saw a Gentleman with such a Spindle Pair of Legs as Mr. HONEYCOMB.

After this I laid Siege to Four Heiresses successively, and being a handsom young Dog in those Days, quickly made a Breach in their Hearts, but I don't know how it came to pass, tho' I seldom failed of getting the Daughters Consent, I could never in my Life get the old People on my side.

I could give you an Account of a thousand other unsuccessful Attempts, particularly of one which I made some Years since upon an old Woman, whom I had certainly bore away with flying Colours, if her Relations had not come pouring in to her Assistance from all Parts of *England*. Nay, I believe I should have got her at last, had not she been carried off by an hard Frost.

As WILL's Transitions are extreamly quick, he turned from Sir ROGER, and applying himself to me, told me, there was a Passage in the Book I had considered last *Saturday*, which deserved to be

---

[1] One of the Inns of Chancery belonging to the Inner Temple. Hatton (p. 700) notes that 'they have a handsome Hall built in the Year 1700'. It was pulled down in 1868.

writ in Letters of Gold; and taking out a Pocket *Milton*,[1] read the following Lines, which are part of one of *Adam*'s Speeches to *Eve* after the Fall.

> . . . *O why did our*
> *Creatour wise, that peopled highest heaven*
> *With Spirits masculine, create at last*
> *This Novelty on Earth, this fair defect*
> *Of nature, and not fill the world at once*
> *With men as angels without feminine?*
> *Or find some other way to generate*
> *Mankind? this mischief had not then befall'n,*
> *And more that shall befall, Innumerable*
> *Disturbances on earth through female Snares,*
> *And strait conjunction with this Sex; for either*
> *He never shall find out fit mate, but such*
> *As some misfortune brings him, or mistake,*
> *Or whom he wishes most shall seldom gain*
> *Through her perverseness; but shall see her gain'd*
> *By a far worse, or if she love, withheld*
> *By parents, or his happiest Choice too late*
> *Shall meet already link'd and Wedlock-bound*
> *To a fell adversary, his hate or shame;*
> *Which infinite calamity shall cause*
> *To human Life, and houshold peace confound.*[2]

Sir ROGER listened to this Passage with great Attention, and desiring Mr. HONEYCOMB to fold down a Leaf at the Place, and lend him his Book, the Knight put it up in his Pocket, and told us that he would read over those Verses again before he went to Bed.

X

[1] In No. 285 and later issues Tonson advertises as 'just published':

A very neat Pocket Edition, Printed with an Elziver Letter, of Paradise Lost, a Poem, in twelve Books. Written by John Milton.

[2] *PL*, x. 888–908 ('O why did God, Creator wise').

No. 360
[STEELE]

Wednesday, April 23, 1712[1]

> . . . *De paupertate tacentes*
> *Plus poscente ferent* . . .
>
> Hor.

I HAVE nothing to do with the Business of this Day, any further than affixing the piece of *Latin* on the head of my Paper; which I think a Motto not unsuitable, since if Silence of our Poverty is a recommendation, still more commendable is his Modesty who conceals it by a decent Dress.

Mr. SPECTATOR,

'THERE is an Evil under the Sun which has not yet come within your Speculation; and is, the Censure, Disesteem, and Contempt, which some young Fellows meet with from particular Persons, for the reasonable Methods they take to avoid them in general. This is by appearing in a better Dress, than may seem to a Relation regularly consistent with a small Fortune; and therefore may occasion a Judgment of a suitable Extravagance in other Particulars: But the disadvantage with which the Man of narrow Circumstances acts and speaks, is so feelingly set forth in a little Book called the *Christian Hero*,[2] that the appearing to be otherwise is not only pardonable but necessary. Every one knows the hurry of Conclusions that are made in Contempt of a Person that appears to be calamitous, which makes it very excusable to prepare one's self for the Company of those that are of a superiour Quality and Fortune, by appearing to be in a better Condition than one is, so far as such appearance shall not make us really of worse.

'It is a Justice due to the Character of one who suffers hard Reflections from any particular Person upon this Account, that such Person would inquire into his manner of spending his Time; of which, tho' no further Information can be had than that he remains

---

[1] *Motto.* Horace, *Epistles*, I. 17. 43–44:
> The Man that's silent, nor proclaims his want,
> Gets more than him that makes a loud complaint. CREECH.

[2] In the opening paragraph of chap. iii Steele had written: 'It is every Body's Observation with what disadvantage a Poor Man enters upon the most Ordinary Affairs . . .; Poverty creates Disesteem, Scorn and Prejudice to all the Undertakings of the Indigent . . .' (*Tracts and Pamphlets*, ed. Rae Blanchard, p. 35).

so many Hours in his Chamber; yet if this is clear'd, to imagine that a reasonable Creature wrung with a narrow Fortune does not make the best use of this Retirement, would be a Conclusion extremely uncharitable. From what has, or will be said, I hope no Consequence can be extorted, implying, that I would have any young Fellow spend more Time than the common leisure which his Studies require, or more Money than his Fortune or Allowance may admit of, in the pursuit of an Acquaintance with his Betters. For as to his Time, the gross of that ought to be sacred to more substantial Acquisitions; for each irrevocable Moment of which he ought to believe he stands religiously Accountable. And as to his Dress, I shall engage my self no further than in the modest Defence of two plain Suits a Year: For being perfectly satisfied in *Eutrapelus*'s Contrivance of making a *Mohock* of a Man by presenting him with lac'd and embroidered Suits,[1] I would by no means be thought to controvert that Conceit, by insinuating the Advantages of Foppery. It is an assertion which admits of much proof, that a Stranger of tolerable Sense, dress'd like a Gentleman, will be better received by those of Quality above him, than one of much better Parts, whose Dress is regulated by the rigid Notions of Frugality. A Man's Appearance falls within the Censure of every one that sees him; his Parts and Learning very few are Judges of; and even upon these few, they can't at first be well intruded, for policy and good breeding will Council him to be reserv'd among Strangers, and to support himself only by the common spirit of Conversation. Indeed, among the Injudicious, the Words Delicacy, Idiom, fine Images, Structure of Periods, Genius, Fire, and the rest, made use of with a frugal and comely Gravity, will maintain the figure of immense Reading and depth of Criticism.

'All Gentlemen of Fortune, at least the young and middle Aged, are apt to pride themselves a little too much upon their Dress, and consequently to value others in some measure upon the same Consideration. With what Confusion is a Man of Figure obliged to return the Civilities of the Hat to a Person whose Air and Attire hardly entitle him to it? For whom nevertheless the other has a particular Esteem tho' he is ashamed to have it challenged in so publick a Manner. It must be allowed, that any young Fellow that

---

[1] Eutrapelus has not been mentioned in earlier papers on the Mohocks. The letter which occupies most of this number may well be a genuine contribution, and the reference to Eutrapelus possibly has to do with an earlier letter submitted to the *Spectator* but not used.

affects to Dress and appear genteely, might with artificial Management save Ten Pound a Year, as instead of fine Holland he might mourn in Sackcloth, and in other particulars be proportionably shabby; but of what great service would this Sum be to avert any misfortune whilst it would leave him deserted by the little good Acquaintance he has, and prevent his gaining any other. As the Appearance of an easy Fortune is necessary towards making one, I don't know but it might be of Advantage sometimes, to throw into ones Discourse certain Exclamations about Bank-stock; and to shew a marvelous Surprize upon its Fall, as well as the most affected Triumph upon its Rise. The Veneration and Respect which the Practice of all Ages has preserved to Appearances, without Doubt suggested to our Tradesmen that wise and politick Custom, to apply and recommend themselves to the Publick by all those Decorations upon their Sign-Posts and Houses, which the most eminent Hands in the Neighbourhood can furnish them with. What can be more attractive to a Man of Letters, than that immense Erudition of all Ages and Languages which a skillful Bookseller, in Conjunction with a Painter, shall image upon his Column and the Extremities of his Shop? The same Spirit of maintaining a handsome Appearance reigns among the grave and solid Apprentices of the Law, (here I could be particularly dull in proving[a] the Word Apprentice to be significant of a Barrister) and you may easily distinguish who has most lately made his Pretentions to Business by the whitest and most ornamental Frame of his Window: If indeed the Chamber is a Ground-room, and has Rails before it, the Finery is of Necessity more extended, and the Pomp of Business better maintained. And what can be a greater Indication of the Dignity of Dress, than that burthensome Finery which is the regular Habit of our Judges, Nobles and Bishops, with which upon certain Days we see them incumbered? And though it may be said this is awful and necessary for the Dignity of the State, yet the wisest of them have been remarkable, before they arrived at their present Stations, for being *very well-dressed Persons*. As to my own Part, I am near thirty; and since I left School have not been idle, which is a modern Phrase for having studied hard. I brought off a clean System of Moral Philosophy, and a tolerable Jargon of Metaphysicks from the University; since that, I have been engaged in the clearing Part of the perplexed Stile and Matter of the Law, which so hereditarily des-

---

[a] proving] clearing *Fol.*

cends to all its Professors: To all which severe Studies I have thrown in, at proper Interims, the pretty Learning of the Classicks. Notwithstanding which I am what *Shakespear* calls *A Fellow of no Mark or Likelihood*;[1] which makes me understand the more fully, that since the regular Methods of making Friends and a Fortune by the meer Force of a Profession is so very slow and uncertain, a Man should take all reasonable Opportunities by enlarging a good Acquaintance, to court that Time and Chance which is said to happen to every Man.'[2]

T

No. 361   *Thursday, April 24, 1712*[3]
[ADDISON]

Tartaream intendit vocem, quâ protinus omne
Contremuit domus . . .

Virg.

I HAVE lately received the following Letter from a Country Gentleman.

Mr. SPECTATOR,

'THE Night before I left *London* I went to see a Play called *The Humorous Lieutenant.*[4] Upon the rising of the Curtain I was very much surprised with the great Consort of Cat-calls which was exhibited that Evening, and began[a] to think with my self that I had made a Mistake, and gone to a Musick Meeting instead of the Play-house. It appeared indeed[b] a little odd to me to see so many Persons of Quality of both Sexes assembled together at a kind of Catter-wawling, for I cannot look upon that Performance to have been any thing better, whatever the Musicians themselves might

---

^a began] begun *Fol.*   ^b appeared indeed] indeed appeared *Fol.*

---

[1] *1 Henry IV*, III. ii. 45.
[2] Eccles. ix. 11.
[3] *Motto.* Virgil, *Aeneid*, 7. 514–15:
            Adds all her Breath, the Rocks and Woods around,
            And Mountains, tremble at th'infernal Sound. DRYDEN.

[4] *The Humorous Lieutenant*, by Beaumont and Fletcher, had been recently given at Drury Lane (on 3 Apr.) for the benefit of Mrs. Oldfield.

think of it. As I had no Acquaintance in the House to ask Questions of, and was forced to go out of Town early the next Morning, I could not learn the Secret of this Matter. What I wou'd therefore desire of you is, to give some Account of this strange Instrument which I found the Company called a Cat-call; and particularly to let me know whether it be a Piece of Musick lately come from *Italy*. For my own part, to be free with you, I wou'd rather hear an *English* Fiddle; tho' I durst not shew my Dislike whilst I was in the Play-house, it being my Chance to sit the very next Man to one of the Performers.

> I *am*, SIR,
>> *Your most Affectionate Friend,*
>>> *and Servant,*
>>>> John Shallow, *Esq*;'

In compliance with Squire *Shallow*'s Request, I design this Paper as a Dissertation upon the Cat-call.[1] In order to make my self a Master of the Subject, I purchased one the beginning of last Week, tho' not without great difficulty, being inform'd at two or three Toyshops that the Players had lately bought them all up. I have since consulted many learned Antiquaries in relation to its Original, and find them very much divided among themselves upon that particular. A Fellow of the Royal Society, who is my good Friend, and a great Proficient in the Mathematical part of Musick, concludes from the Simplicity of its Make, and the Uniformity of its Sound, that the Cat-call is older than any of the Inventions of *Jubal*.[2] He observes very well, that Musical Instruments took their first rise from the Notes of Birds, and other melodious Animals; and what, says he, was more natural than for the first Ages of Mankind to imitate the Voice of a Cat that lived under the same Roof with

---

[1] The cat-call was a kind of whistle. Pepys (7 Mar. 1659/60) speaks of buying one for two groats. D'Urfey dedicated his *Banditti* (1686) to 'Sir Critick Cat-call', and Ned Ward's *London Spy* (Part X) describes 'the Intolerable Squeakings of *Cat-Calls*, and *Penny-Trumpets*' at the entrance to Bartholomew Fair (Casanova Society ed., p. 239). Chetwood (*General History of the Stage*, Dublin, 1749) describes an incident in the theatre some twenty years earlier when a sea-captain was annoyed by two sparks with 'their offensive Instruments, vulgarly term'd *Cat-calls*, which they were often tuning before the Play began'. When the captain complained, one put his whistle in his pocket, but the other persisted. He 'clap'd his troublesome Instrument to his Mouth, with Cheeks swell'd out like a Trumpeter, to give it a redoubled, and louder Noise, but like the broken Crow of a Cock in a Fright, the Squeak was stopt in the Middle by a Blow from the Officer, which he gave him with so strong a Will, that his Child's Trumpet was struck through his Cheek, and his Companion led him out to a Surgeon . . .' (pp. 43–44). See also Pope's *Dunciad*, ii. 223.
[2] Gen. iv. 21.

them? He added, that the Cat had contributed more to Harmony than any other Animal, as we are not only beholden to her for this Wind Instrument, but for our String Musick in general.

Another Virtuoso of my Acquaintance will not allow the Cat-call to be older than *Thespis*,[1] and is apt to think it appear'd in the World soon after the Ancient Comedy; for which reason it has still a place in our Dramatick Entertainments: Nor must I here omit what a very curious Gentleman, who is lately return'd from his Travels, has more than once assured me, namely, that there was lately dug up at *Rome* the Statue of a *Momus*,[2] who holds an Instrument in his Right Hand, very much resembling our Modern Cat-call.

There are others who ascribe this Invention to *Orpheus*, and look upon the Cat-call to be one of those Instruments which that famous Musician made use of to draw the Beasts about him. It is certain, that the roasting of a Cat does not call together a greater Audience of that Species, than this Instrument, if dexterously play'd upon in proper Time and Place.

But notwithstanding these various and learned Conjectures, I cannot forbear thinking that the Cat-call is originally a Piece of *English* Musick. Its Resemblance to the Voice of some of our *British* Songsters, as well as the use of it, which is peculiar to our Nation, confirms me in this Opinion. It has at least received great Improvements among us, whether we consider the Instrument it self, or those several Quavers and Graces which are thrown into the playing of it. Every one might be sensible of this, who heard that remarkable overgrown Cat-call which was placed in the Center of the Pit, and presided over all the rest at that celebrated Performance lately exhibited in *Drury-Lane*.[3]

Having said thus much concerning the Original of the Cat-call, we are in the next place to consider the Use of it. The Cat-call exerts it self to most advantage in the *British* Theatre: It very much improves the sound of Nonsense, and often goes along with the

[1] The Greek poet (6th cent. B.C.), generally regarded as the father of tragedy.
[2] The god of mockery and censure.
[3] This may refer to a disturbance involving a performance of the *Distrest Mother*. According to William Egerton, *Faithful Memoirs of . . . Mrs. Anne Oldfield* (1731), Mrs. Rogers, disappointed at not being given the part of Andromache, 'raised a Posse of Profligates, fond of Tumult and Riot, who made such a Commotion in the House, that the Court hearing of it sent four of the Royal Messengers, and a strong Guard, to suppress all Disorders' (pp. 31–32). Colley Cibber (*Apology*, ed. Lowe, ii. 166) also refers to having to dismiss an audience of 150 l. because of this disturbance, which presumably occurred on the first showing of *The Distrest Mother*. I owe these references to Professor Emmet Avery.

Voice of the Actor who pronounces it, as the Violin or Harpsicord accompanies the *Italian* Recitativo.

It has often supplied the place of the ancient *Chorus*, in the Works of Mr. ★★★a In short, a bad Poet has as great an Antipathy to a Cat-call as many People have to a real Cat.

Mr. *Collier*, in his Ingenious Essay upon Musick, has the following Passage:

I believe 'tis possible to invent an Instrument *that shall have a quite contrary Effect to those Martial ones now in use. An* Instrument *that shall sink the Spirits, and shake the Nerves, and curdle the Blood, and inspire Despair, and Cowardise, and Consternation, at a surprizing rate. 'Tis probable the Roaring of Lions, the Warbling of Cats and Scritch-Owls, together with a mixture of the Howling of Dogs, judiciously imitated and compounded, might go a great way in this Invention. Whether such Anti-musick as this might not be of Service in a Camp, I shall leave to the Military Men to consider.*[1]

What this learned Gentleman supposes in Speculation, I have known actually verified in Practice. The Cat-call has struck a Damp into Generals, and frighted Heroes off the Stage. At the first sound of it I have seen a Crowned Head tremble, and a Princess fall into Fits. The *Humorous Lieutenant* himself could not stand it, nay, I am told that even *Almanzor* looked like a Mouse, and trembled at the Voice of this terrifying Instrument.[2]

As it is of a Dramatick Nature, and peculiarly appropriated to the Stage, I can by no means approve the Thought of that angry Lover; who after an unsuccessful Pursuit of some Years took leave of his Mistress in a Serenade of Cat-calls.

I must conclude this Paper with the Account I have lately received of an ingenious Artist who has long studied this Instrument, and is very well versed in all the Rules of the Drama. He teaches to play on it by Book, and to express by it the whole Art of Criticism. He has his Base and his Treble Cat-call; the former for Tragedy, the latter for Comedy; only in Tragy-Comedies they may both play together in Consort. He has a particular Squeak to denote

---

a ★★★ *Not being yet determined with whose Name to fill up the Gap in this Dissertation which is marked with Asterisks, I shall defer it till this Paper appears with others in a Volume.*

[1] Jeremy Collier, *Essays upon Several Moral Subjects* (6th ed. 1709, part ii, p. 24). The passage, from the essay 'Of Musick', is quoted exactly, except for a shift in punctuation in the second sentence. Collier's text reads: 'and inspire Despair and Cowardise, and Consternation at a surprizing rate'.

[2] In Dryden's *Conquest of Granada*. Cf. No. 167 (vol. ii).

the Violation of each of the Unities, and has different Sounds to shew whether he aims at the Poet or the Player. In short, he teaches the Smut-note, the Fustian-note, the Stupid-note, and has composed a kind of Air that may serve as an Act-tune to an incorrigible[1] Play, and which takes in the whole Compass of the Cat-call.   L

No. 362   *Friday, April 25, 1712*[2]
[STEELE]

Laudibus arguitur Vini vinosus . . .
                                            Hor.

Mr. SPECTATOR,   *Temple, April 24.*

'SEVERAL of my Friends were this Morning got together over a Dish of Tea in very good Health, though we had celebrated Yesterday[3] with more Glasses than we could have dispensed with, had we not been beholden to *Brooke* and *Hillier*.[4] In Gratitude there-

---

[1] I.e. impossible to be improved or set right, said of something faulty or defective, 1541–1804. *Obs.* (*OED*).

[2] *Motto.* Horace, *Epistles*, I. 19. 6: From his praise of it his love of wine appears.

[3] Queen Anne's Coronation Day (23 Apr.).

[4] Thomas Brooke and John Hellier, wine-merchants in Basing-Lane, near Bread Street, advertise frequently in the *Spectator* and in the *Daily Courant*. In *Tatler* 131 Addison had exposed the 'Chymical Operators' who adulterated wines and defrauded the public; throughout 1711 Brooke and Hellier seem to have carried on a vigorous campaign of advertising—warning against the adulterated wines of other importers and advising where their own pure wines were to be had. Politics may have played a part: Brooke and Hellier advertise consistently in the *Spectator* and *Daily Courant*, their rivals in the Tory *Post Boy* (although occasionally in the *Post-Man*). One John Crooke in the *Post Boy* ridicules their claims; in the issue of 20 Nov. 1711 he refers to them as 'dreadful Names to all, who have the Misfortune to have Wines of any Sort upon their Hands'. More important, both merchants seem to have been friends of Addison and Steele, and the names of both Brooke and Hellier are in the list of subscribers to the collected *Spectator*.

The letter by 'Tom Pottle' seems to be a gesture of friendship on behalf of the two merchants, who may already have been in financial difficulties. By the summer of 1712, at any rate, they were bankrupt (*London Gazette*, 26 Aug.). Sales of their wines, for the benefit of creditors, are announced for 4 Dec. 1712 and 22 Jan. 1713 at Lloyd's Coffee-house (*Daily Courant*, 1 Dec.; *Post Boy*, 22 Jan.). On 19 Dec. 1712 were sold at auction 'all the Houshold-Goods of Mr. Brooke and Hilliard, Wine-Merchants, at their late Dwelling-House in Basing-lane by Gerrard's-Hall; consisting of fine Beds and Tapistry Hangings, Peer-Glasses, and all sorts of Houshold-Goods' (*Daily Courant*, 16 Dec.). By the following summer each merchant was in business again for himself. Brooke reopened on 1 Sept. 1713 the Bumper Tavern in James's Street, Covent-Garden. In a long announcement in the *Post Boy* of 27 Aug. 1713 he reviews the course of events and implies that the bankruptcy proceedings in the summer of 1712 had not been carried out with perfect fairness.

Among the pamphlets published in 1712 were *The Quack-Vintners; or, a Satyr*

---

fore to those good Citizens, I am, in the Name of the Company, to accuse you of great Negligence in over-looking their Merit who have imported true and generous Wine, and taken Care that it should not be adulterated by the Retailers before it comes to the Tables of private Families, or the Clubs of honest Fellows. I cannot imagine how a SPECTATOR can be supposed to do his Duty, without frequent Resumption of such Subjects as concern our Health, the first thing to be regarded if we have a Mind to relish any thing else. It would therefore very well become your spectatorial Vigilance to give it in Orders to your Officer for inspecting Signs,[1] that in his March he would look into the Itinerants who deal in Provisions, and inquire where they buy their several Wares. Ever since the Decease of *Cully Mully Puff*[2] of agreeable and noisy Memory, I cannot say I have observed any thing sold in Carts, or carried by Horse or Asse; or in fine, in any moving Market, which is not perished or putrified: Witness the Wheel-barrows of rotten Raisons, Almonds, Figs and Currants, which you see vended by a Merchant dressed in a second-hand Suit of a Foot Soldier. You should consider that a Child may be poisoned for the Worth of a Farthing; but except his poor Parents send to one certain Doctor in Town they can have no Advice for him under a Guinea.[3] When Poisons are thus cheap and Medicines thus dear, how can you be negligent in inspecting what we eat and drink, or take no Notice of such as the above-mentioned Citizens who have been so serviceable to us of late in that Particular? It was a Custom among the old *Romans*, to do him

against *Bad Wine: With Directions where to have Good: Inscrib'd to B——ks and H——r*, 'Sold by the Booksellers of London and Westminster'; and *Brooke and Hellier: a Satyr*, 'London: Printed, and Sold by J. Baker', the latter of which refers to the *Spectator*:

> Tell us in all those Glorious Days,
> What Laureat Reign'd? Who wore the Bays?
> Who wrote *the Drama*? Who *the Satyr*?
> What Genius then adorn'd the Theater?
> Or prithee who *was their Spectator*?
> Where were the bright Sublime Essays,
> For After-times to Read and Praise?

[1] See No. 28 (vol. i).

[2] See No. 251 (vol. ii). 'This little man, who had nothing at all striking in his appearance, and was but just able to support the basket of pastry which he carried on his head, sung in a very peculiar tone the cant words which passed into his name. This singularity was very advantageous to him, as it rendered him one of the most noted of the cries in London' (Nichols).

[3] 'There was a *Doctor* about this time, perhaps, as he said, a regular-bred physician, who advertised his readiness to attend patients at determinate distances all over London, &c. for the small fees of a shilling, &c. to half-a-crown a time each visit . . .' (Nichols).

particular Honours who had saved the Life of a Citizen; how much more does the World owe to those who prevent the Death of Multitudes? As these Men deserve well of your Office, so such as act to the Detriment of our Health, you ought to represent to themselves and their Fellow-Subjects in the Colours which they deserve to wear. I think it would be for the publick Good, that all who vend Wines should be under Oaths in that Behalf. The Chairman at a Quarter Sessions should inform the Country, that the Vintner who mixes Wine to his Customers, shall (upon Proof that the Drinker thereof died within a Year and a Day after taking it) be deemed guilty of wilful Murder; and the Jury should be instructed to enquire and present such Delinquents accordingly. It is no Mitigation of the Crime, nor will it be conceived that it can be brought in Chance-Medley[1] or Man-Slaughter, upon Proof that it shall appear Wine joined to Wine, or right *Herefordshire* poured into *Port O Port*;[2] but his selling it for one thing knowing it to be another, must justly bear the foresaid Guilt of wilful Murder: For that he, the said Vintner, did an unlawful Act willingly in the false Mixture; and is therefore with Equity liable to all the Pains to which a Man would be, if it were proved he designed only to run a Man through the Arm, whom he whipped through the Lungs. This is my third Year at the *Temple*, and this is or should be Law. An ill Intention well proved, should meet with no Alleviation, because it out-run it self. There cannot be too great Severity used against the Injustice as well as Cruelty of those who play with Mens Lives, by preparing Liquors whose Nature, for ought they know, may be noxious when mixed, tho' innocent when apart: And *Brooke* and *Hillier*, who have ensured our Safety at our Meals, and driven Jealousy from our Cups in Conversation, deserve the Custom and Thanks of the whole Town; and it is your Duty to remind them of the Obligation.

I am,

SIR,

Your humble Servant,

Tom Pottle.'

Mr. SPECTATOR,

'I AM a Person who was long immured in a College, read much, saw little; so that I knew no more of the World than what

---

[1] See No. 33 (vol. i).

[2] The old name for port (Portuguese *O Porto*, the Port), derived from Oporto, the town in Portugal (cf. *OED*).

a Lecture or a View of the Map taught me. By this Means I improved in my Study, but became unpleasant in Conversation. By conversing generally with the Dead, I grew almost unfit for the Society of the Living. So by a long Confinement, I contracted an ungainly Aversion to Conversation, and ever discoursed with pain to my self, and little Entertainment to others. At last I was in some Measure made sensible of my failing, and the Mortification of never being spoke to, or speaking, unless the Discourse ran upon Books, put me upon forcing my self amongst Men. I immediately affected the politest Company, by the frequent use of which I hoped to wear off the Rust I had contracted; but by an uncouth Imitation of Men used to act in publick, I got no further than to discover I had a Mind to appear a finer thing than I really was.

'Such I was, and such was my Condition, when I became an ardent Lover, and passionate Admirer of the beauteous *Belinda*: Then it was that I really began to improve. This Passion changed all my Fears and Diffidences in my general Behaviour, to the sole concern of pleasing her. I had not now to study the Action of a Gentleman, but Love possessing all my Thoughts, made me truly be the thing I had a Mind to appear. My Thoughts grew free and generous, and the Ambition to be agreeable to her I admired, produced, in my Carriage a feint similitude of that disengaged Manner of my *Belinda*. The way we are in at present, is that she sees my Passion, and sees I at present forbear speaking of it through prudential Regards. This respect to her she returns with much Civility, and makes my Value for her as little a Misfortune to me, as is consistent with Discretion. She Sings very charmingly, and is readier to do so at my Request, because she knows I love her: She will Dance with me rather than another for the same Reason. My Fortune must alter from what it is before I can speak my Heart to her, and her Circumstances are not considerable enough to make up for the narrowness of mine: But I write to you now only to give you the Character of *Belinda*, as a Woman that has address enough to demonstrate a gratitude to her Lover, without giving him hopes of Success in his Passion. *Belinda* has from a great Wit, governed by as great Prudence, and both adorned with Innocence, the Happiness of always being ready to discover her real Thoughts. She has many of us, who now are her Admirers, but her Treatment of us, is so just and proportioned to our Merit towards her, and what we are in our selves; that I protest to you, I have neither Jealousy nor Hatred toward my Rivals. Such is her Goodness, and the Acknowledgement of every Man who admires her, that he thinks he ought to believe she will take him who best deserves her. I will not say, that this Peace among us is not owing to Self-love, which prompts each to think himself the best deserver. I think there is something uncommon and worthy of Imitation in this Lady's Character. If you will please to Print my Letter, you will oblige the little Fraternity of happy Rivals, and in a more particular Manner,

SIR,

Your most humble Servant,

Will. Cymon.'

T

No. 363
[ADDISON]

Saturday, April 26, 1712[1]

. . . Crudelis ubique
Luctus, ubique pavor, & plurima Mortis Imago.
Virg.

MILTON has shewn a wonderful Art in describing that variety of Passions which arise in our first Parents upon the breach of the Commandment that had been given them. We see them gradually passing from the triumph of their Guilt thro' Remorse, Shame, Despair, Contrition, Prayer, and Hope, to a perfect and compleat Repentance. At the end of the Tenth Book they are represented as prostrating themselves upon the Ground, and watering the Earth with their Tears: To which the Poet joins this beautiful Circumstance, that they offer'd up their Penitential Prayers on the very place where their Judge appeared to them when he pronounced their Sentence.

. . . They forthwith to the place
Repairing, where he judg'd them, prostrate fell
Before him reverent, and both confess'd

---

[1] *Motto.* Virgil, *Aeneid,* 2. 368–9:
  All parts resound with Tumults, Plaints, and Fears,
  And grisly Death in sundry shapes appears. DRYDEN.

Humbly their faults, and pardon begg'd, with tears
Watring the Ground . . .[1]

[a]There is a Beauty of the same kind in a Tragedy of *Sophocles*,[2] where *Oedipus*, after having put out his own Eyes, instead of breaking his Neck from the Palace Battlements (which furnishes so elegant an Entertainment for our *English* Audience)[3] desires that he may be conducted to Mount *Cithæron*, in order to end his Life in that very Place where he was exposed in his Infancy, and where he should then have died, had the Will of his Parents been executed.[a]

As the Author never fails to give a Poetical turn to his Sentiments, he describes in the beginning of this Book the Acceptance which these their Prayers met with, in a short Allegory form'd upon that beautiful Passage in Holy Writ. *And another Angel came and stood at the Altar, having a golden Censer; and there was given unto him much incense, that he should offer it with the prayers of all Saints upon the Golden Altar, which was before the throne: And the smoak of the incense which came with the Prayers of the Saints, ascended up before God.*[4]

> *. . . To Heav'n their prayers*
> *Flew up, nor missed the way, by envious winds*
> *Blown vagabond or frustrate: in they pass'd*
> *Dimentionless through Heav'nly doors, then clad*
> *With incense, where the Golden Altar fumed,*
> *By their great intercessor, came in sight*
> *Before the Father's throne . . .*[5]

We have the same Thought expressed a second time in the Intercession of the Messiah, which is conceived in very Emphatick Sentiments and Expressions.[6]

Among the Poetical parts of Scripture which *Milton* has so finely wrought into this part of his Narration, I must not omit that wherein *Ezekiel* speaking of the Angels who appeared to him in a Vision, adds that *every one had four faces*, and that *their whole bodies, and their backs, and their hands, and their wings were full of eyes round about.*[7]

[a-a] *omitted Fol.*

---

[1] *PL*, x. 1098–1102.
[2] Sophocles, *Oedipus the King*, 1452–7.
[3] At the end of the *Oedipus* of Dryden and Lee, a stage direction reads: 'He [Oedipus] flings himself from the Window: The Thebans gather about his Body.'
[4] Rev. viii. 3, 4.
[5] *PL*, xi. 14–20.
[6] *PL*, xi. 20–44.
[7] Ezek. i. 6; x. 12.

. . . The Cohort bright
Of watchful Cherubim; four faces each
Had, like a double Janus, *all their shape*
Spangled with eyes . . .[1]

The assembling of all the Angels of Heaven to hear the Solemn Decree passed upon Man is represented in very lively Ideas.[2] The Almighty is here describ'd as remembring Mercy in the midst of Judgment, and commanding *Michael* to deliver his Message in the mildest terms, least the Spirit of Man, which was already broken with the Sense of his Guilt and Misery, should fail before him.

. . . Yet least they faint
At the sad Sentence rigorously urg'd,
For I behold them softned and with tears
Bewailing their excess, all terror hide.[3]

The Conference of *Adam* and *Eve* is full of moving Sentiments.[4] Upon their going Abroad after the melancholy Night which they had passed together, they discover the Lion and the Eagle pursuing each of them their Prey towards the Eastern Gates of *Paradise*.[5] There is a double Beauty in this Incident, not only as it presents great and just Omens which are always agreeable in Poetry; but as it expresses that Enmity which was now produced in the Animal Creation. The Poet, to shew the like changes in Nature, as well as to grace his Fable with a noble Prodigy, represents the Sun in an Eclipse. This particular Incident has likewise a fine effect upon the Imagination of the Reader, in regard to what follows; For at the same time that the Sun is under an Eclipse, a bright Cloud descends in the Western quarter of the Heavens, filled with an Host of Angels, and more luminous than the Sun it self. The whole Theatre of Nature is darkned, that this glorious Machine may appear in all its lustre and magnificence.

. . . Why in the East
Darkness ere day's mid-course, and morning light
More orient in that Western cloud that draws
O'er the blue firmament a radiant white,
And slow descends, with something heav'nly fraught?
He err'd not, for by this the Heav'nly bands
Down from a Sky of Jasper lighted now

[1] *PL*, xi. 127-30.　　　[2] *PL*, xi. 72-83.　　　[3] *PL*, xi. 108-11.
[4] *PL*, xi. 141-80.　　　　　[5] *PL*, xi. 184-90.

In Paradise, and on a Hill made halt;
A glorious apparition . . .[1]

I need not observe how properly this Author, who always suits his Parts to the Actors whom he introduces, has employed *Michael* in the Expulsion of our first Parents from *Paradise*. The Arch-angel on this occasion neither appears in his proper Shape, nor in that familiar manner with which *Raphael* the sociable Spirit entertained the Father of Mankind before the Fall. His Person, his Port and Behaviour are suitable to a Spirit of the highest Rank, and exquisitely describ'd in the following Passage.

> *. . . Th' Archangel soon drew nigh*
> *Not in his shape Celestial, but as man*
> *Clad to meet man; over his lucid arms*
> *A military vest of purple flow'd*
> *Livelier than* Melibæan, *or the grain*
> *Of* Sarra, *worn by Kings and Heroes old*
> *In time of truce;* Iris *had dipt the Wooff;*
> *His starry helm, unbuckled, shew'd him prime*
> *In Manhood where Youth ended; by his side*
> *As in a glistring Zodiack hung the Sword,*
> Satan's *dire dread, and in his hand the Spear.*
> Adam *bow'd low, he kingly from his state*
> *Inclined not, but his coming thus declared.*[2]

Eve's Complaint upon hearing that she was to be removed from the Garden of *Paradise* is wonderfully beautiful. The Sentiments are not only proper to the Subject; but have something in them particularly soft and womanish.

> *Must I then leave thee, Paradise? thus leave*
> *Thee, native Soil, these happy walks and shades,*
> *Fit haunt of Gods? Where I had hope to spend*
> *Quiet though sad the respit of that day*
> *That must be mortal to us both. O flow'rs*
> *That never will in other Climate grow,*
> *My early visitation, and my last*
> *At Even, which I bred up with tender hand*
> *From the first opening bud, and gave you names;*

[1] *PL*, xi. 203-11 (line 205: in yon Western cloud).
[2] *PL*, xi. 238-50.

Who now shall rear you to the Sun, or rank
Your tribes, and water from th' ambrosial fount?
Thee lastly, Nuptial bowre, by me adorn'd
With what to sight or smell was sweet; from thee
How shall I part, and whither wander down
Into a lower world, to this obscure
And wild, how shall we breath in other air
Less pure, accustom'd to immortal fruits?[1]

Adam's Speech abounds with Thoughts which are equally moving, but of a more Masculine and elevated Turn. Nothing can be conceived more Sublime and Poetical, than the following Passage in it.

This most afflicts me, that departing hence
As from his face I shall be hid, deprived
His blessed Count'nance; here I could frequent,
With worship, place by place where he vouchsafed
Presence divine, and to my Sons relate;
On this mount he appear'd, under this tree
Stood visible, among these Pines his voice
I heard, here with him at this fountain talk'd:
So many grateful Altars I would rear
Of grassie turf, and pile up every Stone
Of lustre from the brook, in memory,
Or monument to ages, and thereon
Offer sweet smelling Gums and fruits and flowers:
In yonder nether world where shall I seek
His bright appearances, or footsteps trace?
For though I fled him angry, yet recall'd
To life prolong'd and promised race, I now
Gladly behold though but his utmost Skirts
Of Glory, and far off his Steps adore.[2]

The Angel afterwards leads *Adam* to the highest Mount of *Paradise,* and lays before him a whole Hemisphere, as a proper Stage for those Visions which were to be represented on it.[3] I have before observed how the Plan of *Milton's* Poem is in many Particulars greater than that of the *Iliad* or *Æneid. Virgil's* Hero, in the last of these Poems,[4] is entertained with a sight of all those who are to

---

[1] PL, xi. 269–85 (Must I thus leave thee).
[2] PL, xi. 315–33 (line 329: footstep).
[3] PL, xi. 376–411.   [4] Aeneid, 6. 756–885.

descend from him, but tho' that Episode is justly admired as one of the noblest Designs in the whole *Æneid*, every one must allow that this of *Milton* is of a much higher Nature. *Adam*'s Vision is not confined to any particular Tribe of Mankind, but extends to the whole Species.

In this great Review, which *Adam* takes of all his Sons and Daughters, the first Objects he is presented with exhibit to him the Story of *Cain*, and *Abel*, which is drawn together with much Closeness and Propriety of Expression.[1] That Curiosity and natural Horror which arises in *Adam* at the Sight of the first dying Man is touched with great beauty.

> *But have I now seen death, is this the way*
> *I must return to native dust? O Sight*
> *Of terrour foul and ugly to behold,*
> *Horrid to think, how horrible to feel!*[2]

The second Vision sets before him the Image of Death in a great Variety of Appearances.[3] The Angel, to give him a General Idea of those Effects, which his Guilt had brought upon his Posterity, places before him a large Hospital, or Lazar-House, fill'd with Persons lying under all kinds of Mortal Diseases. How finely has the Poet told us that the sick Persons languished under Lingring and Incurable Distempers by an apt and Judicious use of such Imaginary Beings, as those I mentioned in my last[a] Paper.

> *Dire was the tossing, deep the Groans,* Despair
> *Tended the Sick, busie from Couch to Couch;*
> *And over them triumphant* Death *his dart*
> *Shook, but delay'd to strike, though oft invoked*
> *With vows as their chief good and final hope.*[4]

The Passion which likewise rises in *Adam* on this Occasion is very natural.

> *Sight so deform what Heart of rock could long*
> *Dry-eyed behold?* Adam *could not, but wept*
> *Tho' not of Woman born; Compassion quell'd*
> *His best of Man, and gave him up to tears.*[5]

---

[a] last] *19*; last *Saturday's Fol., 8vo, 12mo*

---

[1] *PL*, xi. 429–47.   [2] *PL*, xi. 462–5.   [3] *PL*, xi. 477–93.
[4] *PL*, xi. 489–93 (line 490: busiest).   [5] *PL*, xi. 494–7.

The Discourse between the Angel and *Adam* which follows, abounds with noble Morals.[1]

As there is nothing more delightful in Poetry, than a Contrast and Opposition of Incidents, the Author, after this melancholy Prospect of Death and Sickness, raises up a Scene of Mirth, Love and Jollity.[2] The secret Pleasure that steals into *Adam*'s Heart, as he is intent upon this Vision, is imagined with great Delicacy. I must not omit the Description of the loose Female troupe, who seduced the Sons of God as they are call'd in Scripture.

> *For that fair female troupe thou saw's tthat seem'd*
> *Of Goddesses, so Blithe, so Smooth, so Gay,*
> *Yet empty of all good wherein consists*
> *Womans domestick honour and chief praise;*
> *Bred only and compleated to the taste*
> *Of lustful appetence, to sing, to dance,*
> *To dress, and troule the tongue, and roul the Eye.*
> *To these that sober race of Men, whose lives*
> *Religious titled them the Sons of God,*
> *Shall yield up all their vertue, all their fame*
> *Ignobly, to the trains and to the smiles*
> *Of these fair Atheists . . .*[3]

The next Vision is of a quite contrary Nature, and filled with the Horrours of War.[4] *Adam* at the sight of it, melts into Tears, and breaks out in that passionate Speech;

> *. . . O what are these*
> *Deaths ministers not Men, who thus deal death*
> *Inhumanly to Men, and multiply*
> *Ten thousand fold the Sin of him who slew*
> *His Brother: for of whom such Massacre*
> *Make they but of their Breth'ren, men of men?*[5]

Milton, to keep up an agreeable variety in his Visions, after having raised in the Mind of his Reader the several Ideas of Terror which are conformable to the Description of War, passes on to those softer Images of Triumphs and Festivals, in that Vision of Lewdness and Luxury, which ushers in the Flood.[6]

As it is visible, that the Poet had his Eye upon *Ovid*'s account[7] of

---

[1] *PL*, xi. 500–55. [2] *PL*, xi. 580–97. [3] *PL*, xi. 614–25.
[4] *PL*, xi. 638–73. [5] *PL*, xi. 675–80.
[6] *PL*, xi. 712–18. [7] *Metamorphoses*, I. 260–312.

the universal Deluge, the Reader may observe with how much
Judgment he has avoided every thing that is redundant or puerile
in the *Latin* Poet. We do not here see the Wolf swimming among
the Sheep,[1] nor any of those wanton Imaginations which *Seneca*
found[a] fault with, as unbecoming the[b] great Catastrophe of Nature.[2]
If our Poet has imitated that Verse in which *Ovid* tells us, that there
was nothing but Sea, and that this Sea had no Shoar to it, he has not
set the Thought in such a light as to incur the Censure which
Criticks have passed upon it. The latter part of that Verse in *Ovid*
is idle and superfluous;[3] but just and beautiful in *Milton*.

> *Jamque mare & tellus nullum discrimen habebant,*
> *Nil nisi pontus erat deerant quoque littora ponto.*   Ovid.[4]

> . . . *Sea cover'd Sea,*
> *Sea without Shoar* . . .   Milton.[5]

In *Milton* the former part of the Description does not forestall the
latter. How much more great and solemn on this occasion is that
which follows in our *English* Poet,

> . . . *And in their palaces*
> *Where luxury late reign'd, Sea Monsters whelp'd*
> *And Stabl'd* . . .[6]

than that in *Ovid*, where we are told, that the Sea Calfs lay in those
places where the Goats were used to browze?[7] The Reader may find
several other Parallel Passages in the *Latin* and *English* Description
of the Deluge, wherein our Poet has visibly the Advantage. The
Sky's being over-charged with Clouds, the descending of the Rains,
the rising of the Seas,[8] and the appearance of the Rainbow,[9] are such
Descriptions as every one must take notice of. The Circumstance
relating to *Paradise* is so finely imagined and suitable to the Opinions

---

[a] found] has found *Fol.*   [b] the] this *Fol.*

---

[1] *Metamorphoses*, I. 304.
[2] Seneca, *Natural Questions*, 3. 27. The passage from Ovid, with Seneca's criticism,
is quoted in *Menagiana* (3rd ed. 1715, ii. 120).
[3] Cowley, commenting on this passage in Ovid (in the notes to Book I of *Davideis*),
calls the latter part of the verse 'superfluous, even to ridiculousness' (*Poems*, ed.
Waller, p. 270).
[4] *Metamorphoses*, I. 291–2. (And now the sea and land have no distinction; there
was nothing but sea, and that sea had no shore.)
[5] *PL*, xi. 749–50.   [6] *PL*, xi. 750–2.
[7] *Metamorphoses*, I. 299–300.   [8] *PL*, xi. 738–50.
[9] *PL*, xi. 865–7.

of many learned Authors, that I cannot forbear giving it a place in this Paper.

> *. . . Then shall this mount*
> *Of Paradise by might of Waves be mov'd*
> *Out of his place, push'd by the horned flood,*
> *With all his verdure spoild, and trees a drift*
> *Down the great river to the op'ning Gulf,*
> *And there take root an Island salt and bare,*
> *The haunt of Seals and Orcs, and Sea-Mews clang:*[1]

The Transition which the Poet makes from the Vision of the Deluge, to the Concern it occasioned in *Adam*, is exquisitely graceful, and copied after *Virgil*, tho' the first Thought it introduces is rather in the Spirit of *Ovid*.

> *How didst thou grieve, then* Adam, *to behold*
> *The end of all thy Off-spring, end so sad,*
> *Depopulation; thee another floud,*
> *Of tears and sorrow, a floud thee also drown'd,*
> *And sunk thee as thy Sons: 'till gently rear'd*
> *By th' Angel, on thy feet thou stoodst at last,*
> *Though comfortless, as when a father mourns*
> *His Children, all in view destroy'd at once.*[2]

I have been the more particular in my Quotations out of the Eleventh Book of *Paradise Lost*, because it is not generally reckoned among the most shining Books of this Poem;[3] for[a] which reason, the Reader might be apt to overlook those many Passages in it, which deserve our Admiration. The Eleventh and Twelfth are indeed built upon that single Circumstance of the Removal of our first Parents from *Paradise*, but tho' this is not in it self so great a Subject as that in most of the foregoing Books, it is extended and diversified with so many surprizing Incidents and pleasing Episodes, that these two last Books can by no means be looked upon as unequal Parts of

---

[a] Poem; for] Poem. For *Fol.*

---

[1] *PL*, xi. 829–35. [2] *PL*, xi. 754–61.

[3] Addison may be thinking of Dennis (*Grounds of Criticism in Poetry*, 1704), who remarked that Milton in the first eight books of *Paradise Lost* 'divinely entertain'd us with the wondrous Works of God', but that 'in the latter end of his Poem, and more particularly, in the last Book, he makes an Angel entertain us with the Works of corrupted Man' (*Critical Works*, ed. Hooker, i. 351).

this divine Poem. I must further add, that had not *Milton* represented our first Parents as driven out of *Paradise*, his Fall of Man would not have been compleat, and consequently his Action would have been imperfect.

L

No. 364
[STEELE]

Monday, April 28, 1712[1]

> . . . *Navibus atque*
> *Quadrigis petimus bene vivere.*
>
> Hor.

Mr. SPECTATOR,[2]

'A LADY of my Acquaintance, for whom I have too much Respect to be easy while she is doing an indiscreet Action, has given Occasion to this Trouble: She is a Widow, to whom the

---

[1] *Motto.* Horace, *Epistles,* I. II. 28–29:

> We ride and sail to seek for happiness. CREECH.

In the folio sheets the motto included the first part of line 28: *Strenua nos exercet inertia* (A busy idleness destroys our ease).

[2] 'This letter on *Travelling*, was written by Mr. Philip Yorke, afterwards Earl of Hardwicke, who was likewise the author of another Paper in the *Spectator*, which his son could not particularly remember. This information is given on the authority of Dr. Thomas Birch, in a letter dated June 15, 1764' (Nichols). At the time of Lord Chancellor Hardwicke's death *Lloyd's Evening Post* (7 Mar. 1764) referred to his writing in the *Spectator*:

> His talents as a Speaker in the Senate, as well as on the Bench, have left too strong an impression to need being dilated upon; and those as a Writer were such, as might be expected from one, who had early distinguished himself in that character in *The Spectator*.

This note, repeated the next day in the *London Chronicle*, was followed a few days later by a reprint, in both newspapers, of the letter from *Spectator* 364, as 'Lord Hardwicke's Thoughts on Travelling'. The tradition has been accepted by most writers on Lord Hardwicke (including the *DNB*) and on the *Spectator*, but it seems to have little basis in fact. Richard Cooksey's *Essay on the Life and Character of John Lord Somers, Baron of Evesham: also Sketches of an Essay on the Life and Character of Philip Earl of Hardwicke* (1791) contains (p. 98) a strong denial of the authenticity of the letter from 'an old man of the law, who knew him well'. Dr. Johnson would not allow that the letter had merit. 'He said, "it was quite vulgar, and had nothing luminous"' (Boswell, 10 Apr. 1776; Hill–Powell, iii. 34). On the general subject see William Edward Mead, *The Grand Tour in the Eighteenth Century* (Boston, 1914). With Philip Homebred's letter may be compared *Tatler* 93, on 'our ordinary Method of sending young Gentlemen to travel for their Education'.

Indulgence of a tender Husband has entrusted the Management of a very great Fortune and a Son about sixteen, both which she is extremely fond of. The Boy has Parts of the middle Size, neither shining nor despicable, and has passed the common Exercises of his Years with tolerable Advantage; but is withal what you would call a forward Youth: By the Help of this last Qualification, which serves as a Varnish to all the rest, he is enabled to make the best Use of his Learning, and display it at full Length upon all Occasions. Last Summer he distinguished himself two or three times very remarkably, by puzzling the Vicar before an Assembly of most of the Ladies in the Neighbourhood; and from such weighty Considerations as these, as it too often unfortunately falls out, the Mother is become invincibly perswaded that her Son is a great Scholar; and that to chain him down to the ordinary Methods of Education with others of his Age, would be to cramp his Faculties, and do an irreparable Injury to his wonderful Capacity.

'I happened to visit at the House last Week, and missing the young Gentleman at the Tea-Table, where he seldom fails to officiate, could not upon so extraordinary a Circumstance avoid inquiring after him. My Lady told me, He was gone out with her Woman, in order to make some Preparations for their Equipage; for that she intended very speedily to carry him to travel. The Oddness of the Expression shocked me a little; however, I soon recovered my self enough to let her know, that all I was willing to understand by it, was, that she designed this Summer to shew her Son his Estate in a distant County, in which he has never yet been: But she soon took care to robb me of that agreeable Mistake, and let me into the whole Affair. She enlarged upon young Master's prodigious Improvements, and his comprehensive Knowledge of all Book-Learning; concluding, That it was now high Time he should be made acquainted with Men and Things; That she had resolved he should make the Tour of *France* and *Italy*, but could not bear to have him out of her Sight, and therefore intended to go along with him.

'I was going to rally her for so extravagant a Resolution, but found my self not in fit Humour to meddle with a Subject that demanded the most soft and delicate Touch imaginable. I was afraid of dropping something that might seem to bear hard either upon the Son's Abilities or the Mother's Discretion; being sensible that in both these Cases, though supported with all the Powers of Reason, I should, instead of gaining her Ladyship over to my

Opinion, only expose my self to her Disesteem: I therefore immediately determined to refer the whole Matter to the SPECTATOR.

'When I came to reflect at Night, as my Custom is, upon the Occurrences of the Day, I could not but believe that this Humour of carrying a Boy to travel in his Mother's Lap, and that upon Pretence of learning Men and Things, is a Case of an extraordinary Nature, and carries on it a particular Stamp of Folly. I did not remember to have met with its Parallel within the Compass of my Observation, though I could call to mind some not extremely unlike it: From hence my Thoughts took occasion to ramble into the general Notion of Travelling, as it is now made a Part of Education. Nothing is more frequent than to take a Lad from Grammar and Taw,[1] and under the Tuition of some poor Scholar, who is willing to be banished for thirty Pounds a Year and a little Victuals, send him crying and snivelling into foreign Countries. Thus he spends his Time as Children do at Puppet-Shows, and with much the same Advantage, in staring and gaping at an amazing Variety of strange things; strange indeed to one that is not prepared to comprehend the Reasons and Meaning of them; whilst he should be laying the solid Foundations of Knowledge in his Mind, and furnishing it with just Rules to direct his future Progress in Life under some skillful Master of the Art of Instruction.

'Can there be a more astonishing Thought in Nature, than to consider how Men should fall into so palpable a Mistake? It is a large Field, and may very well exercise a sprightly Genius; but I don't remember you have yet taken a Turn in it. I wish, Sir, you would make People understand, that *Travel* is really the last Step to be taken in the Institution of Youth; and that to set out with it, is to begin where they should end.

'Certainly the true End of visiting forreign Parts, is to look into their Customs and Policies, and observe in what Particulars they excell or come short of our own; to unlearn some odd Peculiarities in our Manners, and wear off such awkard Stiffnesses and Affectations in our Behaviour, as may possibly have been contracted from constantly associating with one Nation of Men, by a more free, general, and mixed Conversation. But how can any of these Advantages be attained by one who is a meer Stranger to the Customs and Policies of his native Country, and has not yet fixed in his Mind the

---

[1] The game played with 'large choice or fancy marbles, often streaked or variegated'. The first quotation in *OED* is from *Tatler* 112.

first Principles of Manners and Behaviour? To endeavour it, is to build a gaudy Structure without any Foundation; or, if I may be allowed the Expression, to work a rich Embroidery upon a Cobweb.

'Another End of Travelling which deserves to be consider'd, is the Improving our Taste of the best Authors of Antiquity, by seeing the Places where they lived, and of which they wrote; to compare the natural Face of the Country with the Descriptions they have given us, and observe how well the Picture agrees with the Original. This must certainly be a most charming Exercise to the Mind, that is rightly turn'd for it; besides, that it may in a good Measure be made Subservient to Morality, if the Person is capable of drawing just Conclusions concerning the Uncertainty of humane Things, from the Ruinous alterations Time and Barbarity have brought upon so many Palaces, Cities, and whole Countries, which make the most illustrious Figures in History. And this Hint may be not a little improv'd by examining every Spot of Ground that we find celebrated as the Scene of some famous Action, or retaining any Foot-steps of a *Cato*, *Cicero* or *Brutus*, or some such great Vertuous Man. A nearer View of any such particular, tho' really little and trifling in its self, may serve the more powerfully to warm a generous Mind to an Emulation of their Virtues, and a greater Ardency of Ambition to imitate their bright Examples, if it comes duly tempered and prepared for the Impression. But this I believe you'll hardly think those to be who are so far from entring into the Sense and Spirit of the Ancients, that they don't yet understand their Language with any Exactness.[a][1]

'But I have wandered from my Purpose, which was only to desire you to save, if possible, a fond *English* Mother, and Mother's *own*

---

[a] *The following paragraph in Folio is omitted in 8vo and 12mo:*

'I can't quit this Head without paying my Acknowledgments to one of the most entertaining Pieces this Age has produc'd, for the Pleasure it gave me. You will easily guess, that the Book I have in my Head is Mr. *A——*'s *Remarks upon Italy*. That Ingenious Gentleman has with so much Art and Judgment applied his exact Knowledge of all the Parts of Classical Learning to illustrate the several Occurrences of his Travels, that his Work alone is a pregnant Proof of what I have said. No Body that has a Taste this way, can read him going from *Rome* to *Naples*, and making *Horace* and *Silius Italicus* his Chart, but he must feel some uneasiness in himself to Reflect that he was not in his Retinue. I am sure, I wish'd it Ten Times in every Page, and that not without a secret Vanity to think in what State I should have Travelled the *Appian* Road with *Horace* for a Guide, and in Company with a Countryman of my own, who of all Men living knows best how to follow his Steps.'

---

[1] The passage complimenting Addison's *Remarks upon Italy* was omitted in the 8vo and 12mo reprints, no doubt at Addison's request.

Son, from being shewn a ridiculous Spectacle thro' the most polite Part of *Europe*. Pray tell them, that tho' to be Seasick or jumbled in an outlandish[1] Stage-Coach may perhaps be healthful for the Constitution of the Body, yet it is apt to cause such a diziness in young empty Heads, as too often lasts their Life-Time.

I am,

SIR,

Your most humble Servant,

Philip Homebred.'

SIR, Bur*chin-Lane*.[2]

'I WAS Married on *Sunday* last, and went peaceably to Bed; but to my surprize was awakened the next Morning by the Thunder of a Set of Drums.[3] These warlike Sounds (methinks) are very improper in a Marriage Consort, and give great Offence; they seem to insinuate, that the Joys of this State are short, and that Jars and Discord soon Ensue. I fear they have been Ominous in many Matches, and sometimes prov'd a prelude to a Battle in the Honey-Moon. A Nod from you may hush them; therefore pray, Sir, let them be silenced, that for the future none but soft Airs may Usher in the Morning of a Bridal Night, which will be a Favour not only to those who come after, but to me who can still Subscribe my self,

Your most humble,

and most obedient Servant,

Robin Bridegroom'.

Mr. SPECTATOR,

'I AM one of that sort of Women whom the gayer Part of our Sex are apt to call a Prude. But to shew them that I have very little Regard to their Railery, I shall be glad to see them all at *The Amorous Widow; or, The Wanton Wife;*[4] which is to be Acted, for the

---

[1] i.e. foreign. Now archaic (cf. *OED*).

[2] Birchin Lane, a short street running from Cornhill south to Lombard Street, somewhat east of the Royal Exchange.

[3] Misson (p. 352) describes the return of a newly wedded couple to their home 'at Night as quietly as Lambs. If the Drums and Fiddles have Notice of it, they will be sure to be with them by Day-break, making a horrible Racket, till they have got the Pence. . . .'

[4] A comedy by Thomas Betterton (based on Molière's *George Dandin*), first played at Lincoln's Inn Fields Theatre about 1670. It had been given three times at Drury Lane in 1711 and on 18 Jan. 1712. The performance here referred to is advertised in this issue of the *Spectator* 'for the Benefit of Mrs. Porter, who is on her Recovery from a serious Feaver'. The part of Philadelphia was played by Mrs. Porter, and that of the 'wanton wife' by Mrs. Oldfield.

Benefit of Mrs. *Porter*, on *Monday* the 28th Instant. I assure you I can Laugh at an Amorous Widow, or Wanton Wife, with as little Temptation to imitate them, as I could at any other vitious Character. Mrs. *Porter* obliged me so very much in the exquisite Sense she seemed to have of the honourable Sentiments and noble Passions in the Character of *Hermione*,[1] that I shall appear in her behalf at a Comedy, tho' I have no great relish for any Entertainments where the Mirth is not seasoned with a certain Severity, which ought to recommend it to People who pretend to keep Reason and Authority over all their Actions.

> *I am,*
> *SIR,*
> *Your frequent Reader,*
> Altamira.'

T

No. 365

[BUDGELL]

Tuesday, April 29, 1712[2]

Vere magis, quia vere calor redit ossibus . . .
Virg.

THE Author of the *Menagiana*[3] acquaints us, that discoursing one Day with several Ladies of Quality about the Effects of the Month of *May*, which infuses a kindly Warmth into the Earth, and all its Inhabitants; the Marchioness of *S——* who was one of the Company, told him that *Tho' she would promise to be Chaste in*

---

[1] Mrs. Porter had created the role of Hermione in *The Distrest Mother* at Drury Lane on 17 Mar. (cf. Nos. 338, 341).

[2] *Motto.* Virgil, *Georgics*, 3. 272:

> For with the Spring their genial Warmth returns. DRYDEN.

[3] Budgell has copied the passage hastily and failed to notice that the saying is not by the Marchioness of S——, but by her mother. As quoted in Bayle, art. Sixtus IV, Remark C, it reads:

> One day as we were discoursing of the Effects of the Month of *May*, which heats anew, not only the Earth, and what's on it, but also revives Love in the very bottom of the Water; after a great deal of talk about that Subject, the Marchioness *de C—— L——* Mother of the Marchioness *de S——* told me, I'll ingage to be Chaste in all the Months of the Year, but I cannot be sure of it in *May*.

See *Menagiana* (3rd ed., Paris, 1715, ii. 349–50). In a marginal note Bayle cites the line from Virgil which is used as the motto for this paper.

every Month besides, she could not engage for her self in May. As the beginning therefore of this Month is now very near, I design this Paper for a Caveat to the fair Sex, and publish it before *April* is quite out, that if any of them should be caught tripping, they may not pretend they had not timely Notice.

I am induced to this, being perswaded the abovementioned Observation is as well calculated for our Climate as for that of *France*, and that some of our *British* Ladies are of the same Constitution with the *French* Marchioness.

I shall leave it among Physicians to determine what may be the Cause of such an Anniversary Inclination, whether or no it is that the Spirits after having been as it were frozen and congealed by Winter, are now turned loose, and set a rambling; or that the gay prospects of Fields and Meadows, with the courtship of the Birds in every Bush, naturally unbend the Mind, and soften it to Pleasure. Or that, as some have imagin'd, a Woman is prompted by a kind of Instinct to throw her self on a Bed of Flowers, and not to let those beautiful Couches which Nature has provided lie useless. However it be, the effects of this Month on the lower part of the Sex, who act without disguise, is very visible. It is at this time that we see the young Wenches in a Country Parish dancing round a *May-pole*, which one of our learned Antiquaries supposes to be a Rellick of a certain Pagan Worship that I do not think fit to mention.

It is likewise on the first Day of this Month that we see the ruddy Milk-Maid exerting her self in a most sprightly manner under a Pyramid of Silver Tankards,[1] and like the Virgin *Tarpeia* oppress'd by the costly Ornaments which her Benefactors lay upon her.

I need not mention the Ceremony of the Green Gown,[2] which is also peculiar to this gay Season.

---

[1] See Marcellus Laroon, *The Cryes of the City of London*, No. 47 ('The Merry Milk Maid'). Misson (p. 307) describes the custom:

> On the first of *May*, and the five and six Days following, all the pretty young Country Girls that serve the Town with Milk, dress themselves up very neatly, and borrow abundance of Silver Plate, whereof they make a Pyramid, which they adorn with Ribbands and Flowers, and carry upon their Heads, instead of their common Milk-Pails. In this Equipage, accompany'd by some of their Fellow Milk-Maids, and a Bagpipe, or Fiddle, they go from Door to Door, dancing before the Houses of their Customers, in the midst of Boys and Girls that follow them in Troops, and every Body gives them something.

See also Strutt, *Sports and Pastimes*, book iv, chap. iii (ed. Cox, 1903, p. 281).
[2] The staining of a girl's dress with green, from rolling on the grass with her lover, is referred to at the end of Gay's 'Thursday; or, the Spell', in his *Shepherd's Week* (lines 135–6).

The same periodical Love-fit spreads thro' the whole Sex, as Mr. *Dryden* well observes in his Description of this merry Month.

> *For thee, sweet Month, the Groves green Liv'ries wear,*
> *If not the first, the fairest of the Year;*
> *For thee the Graces lead the dancing Hours,*
> *And Nature's ready Pencil paints the Flow'rs.*
> *The sprightly* May *commands our Youth to keep*
> *The Vigils of her Night, and breaks their Sleep;*
> *Each gentle Breast with kindly Warmth she moves,*
> *Inspires new Flames, revives extinguish'd Loves.*[1]

Accordingly among the Works of the great Masters in Painting, who have drawn this genial Season of the Year, we often observe *Cupids* confused with *Zephirs*, flying up and down promiscuously in several parts of the Picture. I cannot but add from my own Experience, that about this time of the Year Love-Letters come up to me in great numbers from all Quarters of the Nation.

I receiv'd an Epistle in particular by the last Post from a *Yorkshire* Gentleman, who makes heavy Complaints of one *Zelinda*, whom it seems he has courted unsuccessfully these three Years past. He tells me that he designs to try her this *May*, and if he does not carry his point, he will never think of her more.

Having thus fairly admonished the Female Sex, and laid before them the Dangers they are exposed to in this Critical Month, I shall in the next place lay down some Rules and Directions for their better avoiding those Calentures,[2] which are so very frequent in this Season.

In the first place, I would advise them never to venture abroad in the Fields, but in the Company of a Parent, a Guardian, or some other sober discreet Person. I have before shewn how apt they are to trip in a Flowry Meadow, and shall further observe to them, that *Proserpine* was out a *Maying*, when she met with that fatal Adventure, to which *Milton* alludes when he mentions

> *. . . That fair Field*
> *Of* Enna, *where* Proserpine *gathering flowers*
> *Her self a fairer flower by gloomy* Dis
> *Was gathered . . .*[3]

---

[1] Dryden, *Palamon and Arcite*, ii. 53–56; i. 176–9 (line 176, 'For sprightly May'; line 177, 'breaks their sluggard Sleep').

[2] 'A disease incident to sailors within the tropics, characterized by delirium in which, it is said, they fancy the sea to be green fields and desire to leap into it' (*OED*).

[3] *Paradise Lost*, iv. 268–71.

Since I am got into Quotations, I shall conclude this Head with *Virgil's* Advice to young People, while they are gathering wild Strawberries and Nosegays, that they should have a care of the *Snake in the Grass*.[1]

In the second place I cannot but approve those Prescriptions, which our Astrological Physicians give in their Almanacks for this Month; such as are *a Spare and Simple Diet, with the moderate use of Phlebotomy*.[2]

Under this Head of Abstinence, I shall also advise my fair Readers, to be in a particular manner careful how they meddle with Romances, Chocolate, Novels, and the like Inflamers;[3] which I look upon as very dangerous to be made use of during this great Carnival of Nature.

As I have often declared, that I have nothing more at Heart than the Honour of my dear Country-Women, I would beg them to consider, whenever their Resolutions begin to fail them, that there are but one and thirty Days of this soft Season, and that if they can but weather out this one Month, the rest of the Year will be easie to them. As for that part of the Fair Sex, who stay in Town, I would advise them to be particularly cautious how they give themselves up to their most innocent Entertainments. If they cannot forbear the Play-house, I would recommend *Tragedy* to them, rather than *Comedy*; and should think the *Puppet-show* much safer for them than the *Opera*, all the while the Sun is in *Gemini*.

The Reader will observe, that this Paper is written for the use of those Ladies who think it worth while to war against Nature in the Cause of Honour. As for that abandoned Crew, who do not think Virtue worth contending for, but give up their Reputation at the first Summons, such Warnings and Premonitions are thrown away

---

[1] *Eclogues*, 3. 92–93.

[2] Richard Saunders's *Apollo Anglicanus* (1665) advises, under May: 'In this Moneth *wash* often thy face with fair running Water, but eat not of such meats as be hot in quality; good to bleed especially in the Feet upon occasion; beware of eating stale Fish, or tainted Flesh, but eat your meals in due season, and drink but little Wine this Moneth. . . .' *Pond's Almanack* for 1709 has the following stanza on May:

> Health to preserve, rise early all the *May*,
> And often drink good clarified Whey,
> Refuse not Bleeding, Bathing and Purgation,
> 'Tis very good to use in this our Nation.

[3] *The Natural History of Coffee, Thee, Chocolate, and Tobacco* (1682), a pamphlet in the *Harleian Miscellany* (1808), i. 528–41, describes the dangerous effects of these stimulants to passion. 'The use of chocolate in venery' is dealt with on p. 534: 'If the amorous and martial Turk should ever taste it, he would despise his opium.'

upon them. A Prostitute is the same easie Creature in all Months of the Year, and makes no difference between *May* and *December*.

X[1]

No. 366   *Wednesday, April 30, 1712*[2]

[STEELE]

> *Pone me pigris ubi nulla Campis*
> *Arbor Æstiva recreatur aura*
> *Dulce ridentem Lalagen amabo*
> *Dulce loquentem.*

THERE are such wild Inconsistencies in the Thoughts of a Man in love, that I have often reflected there can be no Reason for allowing him more Liberty than others possessed with Phrenzy; but that his Distemper has no Malevolence in it to any Mortal. That Devotion to his Mistress kindles in his Mind a general Tenderness which exerts it self towards every Object, as well as his Fair one. When this Passion is represented by Writers, it is common with them to endeavour at certain Quaintnesses and Turns of Imagination, which are apparently the Work of a Mind at Ease; but the Men of true Taste can easily distinguish the Exertion of a Mind which overflows with tender Sentiments, and the Labour of one which is only describing Distress. In Performances of this Kind the most absurd of all things is to be witty; every Sentiment must grow out of the Occasion, and be suitable to the Circumstances of the Character. Where this Rule is transgressed the humble Servant, in all the fine things he says, is but shewing his Mistress how well he

---

[1] A letter signed 'Your constant admirer, Jenny Chast, Every month in the year (Lillie, ii. 247), reads:

    I am too much your friend not to inform you, that your paper concerning the effects of the month of May, has given great offence to the best part of our sex; indeed I expected both more wit and more manners from you; but since it is done, I advise you either to make an excuse, or if you are above that, make us amends some other way, if you intend to keep the good opinion of your female readers.

[2] *Motto.* Horace, *Odes,* I. 22. 17–18, 23–24:

> Me where no Sun appears convey,
> Remote from Summer's chearful Ray;
> Love and the Nymph shall ease my Toils,
> Who softly speaks, and sweetly smiles.

can dress, instead of saying how well he loves. Lace and Drapery is as much a Man, as Wit and Turn is Passion.

Mr. SPECTATOR,

'THE following Verses are a Translation of a *Lapland* Love-Song, which I met with in *Scheffer*'s History of that Country.[1] I was agreeably surpriz'd to find a Spirit of Tenderness and Poetry in a Region which I never suspected for Delicacy. In hotter Climates, tho' altogether uncivilized, I had not wondered if I had found some sweet wild Notes among the Natives, where they lie in Groves of Oranges, and hear the Melody of Birds about them: But a *Lapland* Lyric breathing Sentiments of Love and Poetry, not unworthy old *Greece* or *Rome*; a regular Ode from a Climate pinched with Frost, and cursed with Darkness so great a Part of the Year; where 'tis amazing that the poor Natives shou'd get Food, or be tempted to propagate their Species; this, I confess, seemed a greater Miracle to me than the famous Stories of their Drums, their Winds, and Inchantments.

'I am the bolder in commending this Northern Song, because I have faithfully kept to the Sentiments, without adding or diminishing; and pretend to no greater Praise from my Translation, than they who smooth and clean the Furrs of that Country which have suffered by Carriage. The Numbers in the Original[2] are as loose and unequal, as those in which the *British* Ladies sport their *Pindariques*;

[1] John Scheffer's *Lapponia* (Frankfurt, 1673) was translated into English by Acton Cremer as *The History of Lapland* (Oxford, 1674). The English version was reprinted in 1704. The song in this essay and that in No. 408 are poetic versions of those in chap. xxv, 'The manner of Courtship and Marriages of the Laplanders'. Although they have been attributed (by Nichols) to Ambrose Philips they are not included in the edition of his poems by M. G. Segar (Oxford, 1937), nor does Miss Segar discuss the possibility of Philips's authorship. A Harvard University dissertation on Philips by A. J. Bryan (1936) speaks of them as 'possibly by Ambrose Philips'.

[2] In Cremer's translation of Scheffer, the poem, 'communicated to me by Olaus Matthias', begins (ed. 1704, p. 287):

> With brightest Beams let the Sun shine,
> On *Orra Moor*,
> Could I be sure,
> That from the top of th' lofty Pine
> I *Orra Moor* might see,
> I to his highest Bow would climb,
> And with industrious Labour try,
> Thence to descry,
> My Mistress, if that there she be.

Another poetic version of the song will be found in *The Miscellaneous Works in Prose and Verse of Mrs. Elizabeth Rowe*, i (1739), 92–93.

and perhaps the fairest of them might not think it a disagreeable Present from a Lover: But I have ventured to bind it in stricter Measures, as being more proper for our Tongue, tho' perhaps, wilder Graces may better suit the Genius of the *Laponian* Language.

'It will be necessary to imagine that the Author of this Song, not having the Liberty of visiting his Mistress at her Father's House, was in Hopes of spying her at a Distance in the Fields.'

I.

THOU rising Sun, whose gladsome Ray,
Invites my Fair to Rural Play,
Dispel the Mist, and clear the Skies,
And bring my Orra to my Eyes.

II.

Oh! were I sure my Dear to view,
I'd climb that Pine-Tree's topmost Bough,
Aloft in Air, that quivering plays:
And round and round for ever gaze.

III.

My Orra Moor, where art thou laid?
What Wood conceals my sleeping Maid?
Fast by the Roots enrag'd I'll tear
The Trees, that hide my promis'd Fair.

IV.

Oh! I cou'd ride the Clouds and Skies,
Or on the Raven's Pinions rise!
Ye Storks, ye Swans, a Moment stay,
And waft a Lover on his Way.

V.

My Bliss too long my Bride denies,
Apace the wasting Summer flies:
Nor yet the wintry Blasts I fear,
Not Storms, or Night, shall keep me here.

VI.

What may for Strength with Steel compare?
Oh! Love has *Fetters stronger far:*
By Bolts of Steel are Limbs confin'd,
But cruel Love enchains the Mind.

VII.

No longer then perplex thy Breast,
When Thoughts torment, the first are best;
'Tis mad to go, 'tis Death to stay,
Away to Orra, *haste away.*

Mr. SPECTATOR,   *April the* 10*th.*

'I AM one of those despicable Creatures called a Chamber-Maid,
and have lived with a Mistress for some time, whom I love as
my Life; which has made my Duty and Pleasure inseparable. My
greatest Delight has been in being imployed about her Person; and
indeed she is very seldom out of Humour for a Woman of her
Quality: But here lies my Complaint, Sir, To bear with me is all
the Encouragement she is pleased to bestow upon me; for she gives
her cast-off Cloaths from me to others; some she is pleased to bestow
in the House to those that neither wants nor wears them, and
some to Hangers-on that frequents the House daily, who comes
dressed out in them. This, Sir, is a very mortifying Sight to me,
who am a little necessitous for Cloaths, and loves to appear what
I am, and causes an Uneasiness so that I can't serve with that Chearfulness as formerly; which my Mistress takes Notice of, and calls
Envy and ill Temper at seeing others preferred before me. My
Mistress has a younger Sister lives in the House with her that is
some Thousands below her in Estate, who is continually heaping
her Favours on her Maid; so that she can appear every *Sunday*, for
the first Quarter, in a fresh Suit of Cloaths of her Mistress's giving,
with all other things suitable: All this I see without envying, but
not without wishing my Mistress would a little consider what a Dis-
couragement it is to me to have my Perquisites divided between
Fawners and Jobbers, which others enjoy intire to themselves.
I have spoke to my Mistress, but to little Purpose; I have desired
to be discharged (for indeed I fret my self to nothing) but that she

^a *has*] *hath* Fol.

answers with Silence. I beg, Sir, your Direction what to do, for I am
fully resolved to follow your Council; who am,

Your Admirer and humble Servant,

Constantia Comb-brush.

'I beg that you would put it in a better Dress, and let it come
abroad; that my Mistress, who is an Admirer of your Speculations,
may see it.'   T

No. 367   *Thursday, May 1, 1712*[1]
[ADDISON]

. . . perituræ parcite chartæ.

Juv.

I HAVE often pleas'd my self with considering the two kinds of
Benefits which accrue to the Publick from these my Speculations,
and which, were I to speak after the manner of Logicians, I would
distinguish into the *Material* and the *Formal*. By the latter I understand those Advantages which my Readers receive, as their Minds
are either improved or delighted by these my daily Labours; but
having already several times descanted on my Endeavours in this
Light, I shall at present wholly confine my self to the Consideration
of the former. By the Word *Material* I mean those Benefits which
arise to the Publick from these my Speculations, as they consume
a considerable quantity of our Paper Manufacture, employ our
Artisans in Printing, and find Business for great Numbers of Indigent
Persons.

Our Paper Manufacture takes into it several mean Materials
which could be put to no other use, and affords Work for several
Hands in the collecting of them, which are incapable of any other
Employment. Those[a] poor Retailers, whom we see so busie in every
Street, deliver in their respective Gleanings to the Merchant. The
Merchant carries them in Loads to the Paper-Mill,[2] where they

---

a Those] These *Fol.*

[1] *Motto.* Juvenal, *Satires*, 1. 18: Spare a few Sheets already doom'd to dye.
[2] The Company of White Paper Makers was chartered in 1686. On the develop-
ment of paper manufacture in England at the end of the seventeenth century see
Allen T. Hazen, 'Eustace Burnaby's Manufacture of White Paper in England', *Papers
of the Bibliographical Society of America*, xlviii (1954), 315–33.

pass thro' a fresh Sett of Hands, and give Life to another Trade. Those who have Mills on their Estates by this means considerably raise their Rents, and the whole Nation is in a great measure supplied with a Manufacture, for which formerly she was obliged to her Neighbours.

The Materials are no sooner wrought into Paper, but they are distributed among the Presses, where they again set innumerable Artists at Work, and furnish Business to another Mystery. From hence, accordingly as they are stained with News or Politicks, they fly thro' the Town in *Post-Men*, *Post-boys*, *Daily-Courants*, *Reviews*, *Medleys* and *Examiners*.[1] Men, Women and Children contend who shall be the first Bearers of them, and get their daily Sustenance by spreading them. In short, when I trace in my Mind a bundle of Rags to a Quire of *Spectators*, I find so many Hands employ'd in every Step they take thro' their whole Progress, that while I am writing a *Spectator*, I fancy my self providing Bread for a Multitude.

If I do not take care to obviate[2] some of my witty Readers, they will be apt to tell me, that my Paper, after it is thus Printed and Published, is still beneficial to the Publick on several Occasions. I must confess, I have lighted my Pipe with my own Works for this Twelve-month past: My Landlady often sends up her little Daughter to desire some of my old *Spectators*, and has frequently told me, that the[a] Paper they are printed on is the best in the World to wrap Spice in. They likewise make a good Foundation for a Mutton-pye, as I have more than once experienced, and were very much sought for, last *Christmas*, by the whole Neighbourhood.

It is pleasant enough to consider the Changes that a Linnen-fragment undergoes, by passing through the several Hands above-mentioned. The finest Pieces of Holland, when worn to tatters, assume a new Whiteness more beautiful than their first, and often

---

[a] has frequently told me, that the] has told me, more than once, the *Fol.*

[1] *Post-Men*, see No. 1 (vol. i). *Post-boys*, see No. 173 (vol. ii). *Daily-Courants*, see No. 12 (vol. i). Defoe's *Weekly Review of the Affairs of France*, which ran from 19 Feb. 1704 to 11 June 1713, expressed the moderate Tory views of Harley. *Medleys*: The first series of the *Medley*, printed and sold by Anne Baldwin, was published weekly from 5 Oct. 1710 to 6 Aug. 1711; the second series, published semi-weekly, ran from 3 Mar. to 4 Aug. 1712, and was printed by J. Baker (there was also a rival issue printed and sold by Anne Baldwin); the writers for the *Medley* were Arthur Maynwaring, John Oldmixon, Anthony Henley, and Steele. The Tory *Examiner*, conducted by William King, Swift, Mrs. Manley, and others, was published from 3 Aug. 1710 to 26 July 1714.
[2] Here used in the obsolete sense 'to anticipate, forestall'. This quotation is the only example in *OED* of the word in this sense.

return in the shape of Letters to their Native Country. A Lady's Shift may be metamorphosed into Billets doux, and come into her Possession a second time. A Beau may peruse his Cravat after it is worn out, with greater Pleasure and Advantage than ever he did in a Glass. In a word, a piece of Cloath, after having officiated for some Years as a Towel or a Napkin, may by this means be raised from a Dung-hill, and become the most valuable piece of Furniture in a Prince's Cabinet.

The politest Nations of *Europe* have endeavoured to vie with one another for the Reputation of the finest Printing; Absolute Governments, as well as Republicks, have encouraged an Art which seems to be the noblest and most beneficial that was ever invented among the Sons of Men. The Present King of *France*, in his Pursuits after Glory, has particularly distinguished himself by the promoting of this useful Art, insomuch that several Books have been printed in the *Louvre* at his own Expence, upon which he sets so great a value, that he considers them as the noblest Presents he can make to Foreign Princes and Ambassadors.[1] If we look into the Commonwealths of *Holland* and *Venice*, we shall find that in this Particular they have made themselves the Envy of the greatest Monarchies. *Elzevir* and *Aldus* are more frequently mentioned than any Pentioner of the one, or Doge of the other.[2]

The several Presses which are now in *England*, and the great Encouragement which has been given to Learning for some Years last past, has made our own Nation as glorious upon this Account, as for its late Triumphs and Conquests. The new Edition which is given us of *Cæsar's* Commentaries has already been taken notice of in Foreign *Gazettes*, and is a Work that does Honour to the *English* Press.[3] It is no wonder that an Edition should be very correct, which

---

[1] Louis XIV's encouragement of fine printing was acknowledged by English writers. John Oldmixon, writing shortly after the publication of this number, in his *Reflections on Dr. Swift's Letter to the Earl of Oxford, about the English Tongue* (1712), speaks of the 'prodigious Expences he has been at in Printing only at the *Louvre* . . .' (p. 32).

[2] The Elzevir family of printers in Holland in the seventeenth century were noted especially for their small volumes of Latin classics. 'Aldus' refers to the printing-house established at Venice by Aldus Manutius late in the fifteenth century, and carried on there and in other Italian cities through the sixteenth century.

[3] This book, edited by Dr. Samuel Clarke, had just been printed and published by Tonson on 7 Apr. (it is advertised in No. 346 as 'this day' published and 'ready to be deliver'd to the Subscribers'). It contained a dedication to the Duke of Marlborough, an English translation of which (by R. T.) is advertised by Morphew for separate publication on 9 Apr. (No. 347). Hearne comments (6 Apr.) disparagingly on the edition (*Remarks*, iii. 329).

has passed through the Hands of one of the most Accurate, Learned and Judicious Writers this Age has produced. The Beauty of the Paper, of the Character, and of the several Cuts with which this noble Work is Illustrated, makes it the finest Book that I have ever seen; and is a true Instance of the *English* Genius, which, though it does not come the first into any Art, generally carries it to greater heights than any other Country in the World. I am particularly glad that this Author comes from a *British* Printing-house in so great a Magnificence, as he is the first who has given us any tolerable Account of our Country.

My Illiterate Readers, if any such there are, will be surprised to hear me talk of Learning as the Glory of a Nation, and of Printing as an Art that gains a Reputation to a People among whom it flourishes. When Mens Thoughts are taken up with Avarice and Ambition, they cannot look upon any thing as great or valuable, which does not bring with it an extraordinary Power or Interest to the Person who is concerned in it. But as I shall never sink this Paper so far as to engage with *Goths* and *Vandals*, I shall only regard such kind of Reasoners with that Pity which is due to so deplorable a degree of Stupidity and Ignorance.   L

No. 368   *Friday, May 2, 1712*[1]
[STEELE]

> *Nos decebat*
> *Lugere ubi esset aliquis in Lucem editus*
> *Humanæ vitæ varia reputantes mala;*
> *At qui Labores morte finisset graves*
> *Omnes amicos laude & lætitia exequi.*
>   Euripides apud Tull.

AS the *Spectator* is in a Kind a Paper of News from the natural World, as others are from the busy and politick Part of Man-

---

[1] *Motto.* Euripides, *Cresphontes*, quoted by Cicero, *Tusculan Disputations*, i. 48. 115 (altered):

> It is a Duty, when a Child is born,
> In pity of its future Woes to mourn:
> But when in Death's kind Arms his Labours cease,
> We shou'd rejoice to see a Friend in Peace.

kind, I shall translate the following Letter written to an eminent *French* Gentleman in this Town from *Paris*; which gives us the Exit of an Heroine who is a Pattern of Patience and Generosity.[1]

SIR,   *Paris, April* 18. 1712.

'IT is so many Years since you left your native Country, that I am to tell you the Characters of your nearest Relations as much as if you were an utter Stranger to them. The Occasion of this is to give you an Account of the Death of Madam *de Villacerfe*, whose Departure out of this Life I know not whether a Man of your Philosophy will call unfortunate or not, since it was attended with some Circumstances as much to be desired as to be lamented: She was her whole Life happy in an uninterrupted Health, and was always honoured for an Evenness of Temper and Greatness of Mind. On the 10th Instant that Lady was taken with an Indisposition which confined her to her Chamber, but was such as was too slight to make her take a sick Bed, and yet too grievous to admit of any Satisfaction in being out of it. It is notoriously known that some Years ago Monsieur *Festeau*, one of the most considerable Surgeons in *Paris*, was desperately in love with this Lady: Her Quality placed her above any application to her, on the Account of his Passion; but as a Woman always has some regard to the Person whom she believes to be her real Admirer, she now took it in her Head (upon advice of her Physicians, to lose some of her Blood,) to send for Monsieur *Festeau* on that occasion. I happened to be there at that time, and my near Relation gave me the privilege to be present. As soon as her Arm was stripped bare and he began to press it, in order to raise the Vein, his Colour changed, and I observed him seized with a sudden Tremor, which made me take the Liberty to speak of it to my Cousin with some Apprehension: She Smiled and said she knew Mr. *Festeau* had no Inclination to do her Injury. He seemed to recover himself and Smiling also, proceeded in his Work: Immediately after the Operation, he cryed out, that he was the most unfortunate of all Men, for that he had opened an Artery instead of

[1] The tragedy described here is reported in the *British Mercury* of 23 Apr. 1712:

Paris, April 22. Madam de Villacerf is dead, after her Arm, as high as her Shoulder, was cut off, on Account of having an Artery prick'd by the Surgeon, who let her Blood. But this Lady, in her Will, has left a considerable Legacy to the Surgeon, who was the Cause of her Death; her Reason was, that so unfortunate an Accident must necessarily prove his Ruin.

Paul Regnaud, the supposed author of the letter, has not been identified.

a Vein: It is as impossible to express the Artist's Distraction, as the Patients Composure. I will not dwell on little Circumstances, but go on to inform you, that within Three Days Time it was thought necessary to take off her Arm. She was so far from using *Festeau*, as it would be natural to one of a lower Spirit to treat him, that she would not let him be absent from any Consultation about her present Condition, and on every Occasion asked whether he was satisfy'd in the Measures that were[a] taken about her. Before this last Operation she ordered her Will to be drawn, and after having been about a Quarter of an Hour alone, she bid the Surgeons, of whom poor *Festeau* was one, go on in their Work. I know not how to give you the Terms of Art; but there appeared such Symptoms after the Amputation of her Arm, that it was visible she could not live four and twenty Hours. Her behaviour was so Magnanimous throughout this whole Affair, that I was particularly Curious in taking Notice of what passed as her Fate approached nearer and nearer, and took Notes of what she said to all about her, particularly Word for Word what she spoke to Mr. *Festeau*, which was as follows.

SIR,

"YOU give me inexpressible Sorrow for the Anguish with which I see you overwhelmed. I am removed to all Intents and Purposes from the Interests of humane Life, therefore I am to begin to think like one wholly unconcerned in it. I do not consider you as one by whose Errour I have lost my Life: No, you are my Benefactor, as you have hastened my Entrance into a happy Immortality. This is my Sense of this Accident, but the World in which you live may have Thoughts of it to your Disadvantage; I have therefore taken Care to provide for you in my Will, and have placed you above what you have to fear from their ill Nature."

'While this excellent Woman spoke these Words, *Festeau* looked as if he received a Condemnation to dye instead of a Pension for his Life. Madam *de Villacerfe* lived till Eight of Clock the next Night; and though she must have laboured under the most exquisite Torments, she possessed her Mind with so wonderful a Patience, that one may rather say she ceased to breath than she dyed at that Hour. You, who had not the Happiness to be personally known to this Lady, have nothing but to rejoyce in the Honour you had of being related to so great Merit; but we, who have lost her Con-

[a] that were] were *Fol.*

versation, cannot so easily resign our own Happiness by Reflexion upon hers.

I am,

SIR,

Your affectionate Kinsman,
and most obedient humble Servant,

Paul Regnaud.'

There hardly can be a greater Instance of an Heroick Mind, than the unprejudiced manner in which this Lady weighed this Misfortune. The regard of Life it self could not make her overlook the Contrition of the unhappy Man, whose more than Ordinary Concern for her, was all his Guilt. It would certainly be of singular use to Humane Society, to have an exact Account of this Lady's ordinary Conduct, which was Crowned by so uncommon magnanimity. Such Greatness was not to be acquired in her last Article, nor is it to be^a doubted but it was a constant Practice of all that is praiseworthy, which made her capable of beholding Death, not as the Dissolution but Consummation of her Life.   T

No. 369

[ADDISON]

Saturday, May 3, 1712[1]

Segnius irritant animos demissa per aures
Quam quæ sunt oculis subjecta fidelibus . . .

Hor.

*M*ILTON, after having represented in Vision the History of Mankind to the First great Period of Nature, dispatches the remaining Part of it in Narration. He has devised a very handsome Reason for the Angel's proceeding with *Adam* after this manner;[2] tho' doubtless, the true Reason was the difficulty which

---

^a is it to be] *12mo*; is to be *Fol., 8vo*

[1] *Motto.* Horace, *Ars poetica*, 180–1 (altered):
> Things only *told*, though of the same degree,
> Do raise our Passions less than what we *see*. CREECH.

These lines had been used as the motto of *Tatler* 167.
[2] *PL*, xii. 8–10.

the Poet would have found to have shadowed out so mixt and complicated a Story in visible Objects. I could wish, however, that the Author had done it, whatever Pains it might have cost him. To give my Opinion freely, I think that the exhibiting Part of the History of Mankind in Vision, and part in Narrative, is as if an History Painter should put in Colours one half of his Subject, and write down the remaining part of it. If *Milton*'s Poem flags any where, it is in this Narration, where in some places the Author has been so attentive to his Divinity, that he has neglected his Poetry. The Narration, however, rises very happily on several Occasions, where the Subject is capable of Poetical Ornaments, as particularly in the Confusion which he describes among the Builders of *Babel*,[1] and in his short Sketch of the Plagues of *Egypt*.[2] The Storm of Hail and Fire, with the Darkness that overspread the Land for three Days, are described with great Strength. The beautiful Passage, which follows, is raised upon noble Hints in Scripture.

> *. . . Thus with ten wounds*
> *The River-Dragon tamed at length submits*
> *To let his Sojourners depart, and oft*
> *Humbles his stubborn heart, but still as Ice*
> *More harden'd after thaw, till in his rage*
> *Pursuing whom he late dismiss'd, the Sea*
> *Swallows him with his host, but them lets pass*
> *As on dry land between two Chrystal walls,*
> *Aw'd by the rod of* Moses *so to stand*
> *Divided . . .*[3]

The *River-Dragon* is an Allusion to the Crocodile, which inhabits the *Nile*, from whence *Egypt* derives her Plenty. This Allusion is taken from that Sublime Passage in *Ezekiel*. *Thus saith the Lord God, behold, I am against thee* Pharoah *King of* Egypt, *the great Dragon that lieth in the midst of his Rivers, which hath said, My River is mine own, and I have made it for my self*.[4] *Milton* has given us another very noble and Poetical Image in the same Description, which is copied almost Word for Word out of the History of *Moses*.[5]

> *All night he will pursue, but his approach*
> *Darkness defends between till morning watch;*

[1] *PL*, xii. 52–62.   [2] *PL*, xii. 181–8.   [3] *PL*, xii. 190–9.
[4] Ezek. xxix. 3.   [5] Exod. xiv. 19–31.

Then through the fiery pillar and the cloud
God looking forth, will trouble all his hoast,
And craze their Chariot Wheels: *when by command*
Moses *once more his potent Rod extends*
Over the Sea; the Sea his Rod obeys;
On their Embattelled ranks the waves return
And overwhelm their War: . . .[1]

As the Principal Design of this *Episode* was to give *Adam* an Idea
of the Holy Person, who was to reinstate Human Nature in that
Happiness and Perfection from which it had fallen, the Poet confines
himself to the Line of *Abraham*, from whence the *Messiah* was to
Descend. The Angel is described as seeing the Patriarch actually
travelling towards the Land of *Promise*, which gives a particular
Liveliness to this part of the Narration.

> *I see him, but thou canst not, with what faith*
> *He leaves his Gods, his Friends, and native Soil*
> Ur *of* Chaldæa, *passing now the Ford,*
> *To* Haran, *after him a cumbrous train*
> *Of Herds and flocks, and numerous servitude;*
> *Not wand'ring poor, but trusting all his wealth*
> *With God, who call'd him, in a Land unknown.*
> Canaan *he now attains, I see his tents*
> *Pitch't about* Sechem, *and the neighbouring plain*
> *Of* Moreh, *there by promise he receives*
> *Gift to his Progeny of all that Land;*
> *From* Hamath *Northward to the Desart South,*
> (*Things by their names I call, though yet unnam'd.*)[2]

As *Virgil's* Vision in the Sixth *Æneid* probably gave *Milton* the
Hint of this whole *Episode*, the last Line is a Translation of that
Verse, where *Anchises* mentions the Names of Places, which they
were to bear hereafter.

> *Hæc tum nomina erunt, nunc sunt sine nomine terræ.*[3]

The Poet has very finely represented the Joy and Gladness of
Heart, which rises in *Adam* upon his Discovery of the Messiah.[4]
As he sees his Day at a distance through Types and Shadows, he

---

[1] *PL*, xii. 206–14. [2] *PL*, xii. 128–40.
[3] *Aeneid*, 6. 776. (These shall then be names that now are nameless lands.)
[4] *PL*, xii. 372–85.

rejoices in it; but when he finds the Redemption of Man com-
pleated, and *Paradise* again renewed, he breaks forth in Rapture and
Transport,

> *O goodness infinite, goodness immense!*
> *That all this good of evil shall produce. &c.*[1]

I have hinted, in my Sixth Paper[2] on *Milton*, that an Heroic Poem,
according to the Opinion of the best Criticks, ought to end happily,
and leave the Mind of the Reader, after having conducted it
through many Doubts and Fears, Sorrows and Disquietudes, in
a state of Tranquillity and Satisfaction. *Milton*'s Fable, which had
so many other Qualifications to recommend it, was deficient in
this Particular. It is here therefore, that the Poet has shewn a most
exquisite Judgment, as well as the finest Invention, by finding out
a Method to supply this Natural Defect in his Subject. Accordingly
he leaves the Adversary of Mankind, in the last View which he
gives us of him, under the lowest State of Mortification and Disappointment. We see him chewing Ashes, groveling in the Dust,
and loaden with Supernumerary Pains and Torments.[3] On the contrary, our two first Parents are comforted by Dreams and Visions,
cheared with Promises of Salvation, and, in a manner, raised to
a greater Happiness than that which they had forfeited: In short,
Satan is represented miserable in the height of his Triumphs, and
Adam triumphant in the height of Misery.

Milton's Poem ends very nobly. The last Speeches of *Adam* and
the Arch-angel are full of Moral and Instructive Sentiments.[4] The
Sleep that fell upon *Eve*, and the effects it had in quieting the
Disorders of her Mind, produces the same kind of Consolation in
the Reader, who cannot peruse the last beautiful Speech which is
ascrib'd to the Mother of Mankind, without a secret Pleasure and
Satisfaction.

> *Whence thou return'st, and whither went'st, I know;*
> *For God is also in Sleep, and dreams advise,*
> *Which he hath sent propitious, some great good*
> *Presaging, since with Sorrow and Hearts distress*
> *Wearied I fell asleep: but now lead on;*
> *In me is no delay: with thee to go*
> *Is to stay here; without thee here to stay*

---

[1] *PL*, xii. 469–70. [2] See No. 297.
[3] *PL*, x. 566. [4] *PL*, xii. 552–605.

Is to go hence unwilling; thou to me
Art all things under Heav'n, all places thou
Who for my wilful crime art banish'd hence.
This farther Consolation yet secure
I carry hence; though all by me is lost,
Such favour, I unworthy, am vouchsaf'd,
By me the promised Seed shall all restore.[1]

The following Lines which conclude the Poem rise in a most glorious blaze of Poetical Images and Expressions.

Heliodorus in his *Æthiopicks* acquaints us that the Motion of the Gods differs from that of Mortals, as the former do not stir their Feet, nor proceed Step by Step, but slide o'er the Surface of the Earth by an uniform Swimming of the whole Body.[2] The Reader may observe with how Poetical a Description *Milton* has attributed the same kind of Motion to the Angels who were to take Possession of *Paradise*.

So spake our Mother Eve, and Adam heard
Well pleas'd, but answer'd not; for now too nigh
Th' Archangel stood, and from the other hill
To their fix'd station, all in bright array
The Cherubim descended; on the ground
Gliding meteorous, as ev'ning mist
Ris'n from a River, o'er the marish glides,
And gathers ground fast at the lab'rers heel
Homeward returning. High in Front advanc'd,
The brandish'd Sword of God before them blaz'd
Fierce as a Comet . . .[3]

The Author helped his Invention in the following Passage, by reflecting on the Behaviour of the Angel, who, in Holy Writ, has the Conduct of *Lot* and his Family.[4] The Circumstances drawn from that Relation are very gracefully made use of on this Occasion.

In either hand the hastning Angel caught
Our lingring Parents, and to th' Eastern gate

---

[1] *PL*, xii. 610–23.

[2] Heliodorus, *Aethiopian History*, Book 3, translated as *The Triumphs of Love and Constancy* (2nd ed., 1687, p. 118): 'Yet by their going [gods and divine spirits] may be better known [than by their eyes]; for their pace is not made by stepping or transposition of the Feet, but by a certain airy violence and quick even Motion, that they rather sail or cut, than pass the Air.'

[3] *PL*, xii. 624–34.   [4] Gen. xix. 16.

Led them direct; and down the Cliff as fast
To the subjected plain; then disappear'd.
They looking back &c. . . .[1]

The Scene[a] which our first Parents are surprised with upon their looking back on *Paradise*, wonderfully strikes the Reader's Imagination, as nothing can be more natural than the Tears they shed on that Occasion.

They looking back, all th' Eastern side behold
Of Paradise, *so late their happy Seat,*
Wav'd over by that flaming brand, the gate
With dreadful faces throng'd and fiery Arms:
Some natural tears they dropp'd, but wiped them soon;
The world was all before them, where to chuse
Their place of rest, and providence their Guide:[2]

If I might presume to offer at the smallest Alteration in this Divine Work, I should think the Poem would end better with the Passage here quoted, than with the two Verses which follow.

They hand in hand with wandering steps and slow,
Through Eden *took their solitary way.*[3]

These two Verses, though they have their Beauty, fall very much below the foregoing Passage, and renew in the Mind of the Reader that Anguish which was pretty well laid by that Consideration,

The World was all before them, where to chuse
Their place of rest, and providence their Guide.[4]

The number of Books in *Paradise Lost* is equal to those of the *Æneid*. Our Author in his First Edition had divided his Poem into ten Books, but afterwards broke the Seventh and the Eleventh each of them into two different Books, by the help of some small Additions.[5] This second Division was made with great Judgment, as any one may see who will be at the pains of examining it. It was not done for the sake of such a Chimerical Beauty as that of resembling *Virgil* in this particular, but for the more just and regular Disposition of this great Work.

Those who have read *Bossu*,[6] and many of the Criticks who have

[a] Scene] Prospect *Fol.*

---

[1] *PL*, xii. 637–41. [2] *PL*, xii. 641–7.
[3] *PL*, xii. 648–9. [4] *PL*, xii. 646–7.
[5] In the second edition of *Paradise Lost* (1674) Milton divided books vii and x (not book xi) into two books each.
[6] Book i, chap. vii: The Method of Composing a Fable. According to Le Bossu,

written since his time, will not pardon me if I do not find out the particular Moral which is inculcated in *Paradise Lost*. Tho' I can by no means think with the last-mentioned *French* Author, that an Epic Writer first of all pitches upon a certain Moral, as the Groundwork and Foundation of his Poem, and afterwards finds out a Story to it: I am, however, of Opinion, that no just Heroic Poem ever was, or can be made, from whence one great Moral may not be deduced. That which reigns in *Milton* is the most universal and most useful that can be imagined; it is in short this, *that Obedience to the Will of God makes Men happy, and that Disobedience makes them miserable*. This is visibly the Moral of the principal Fable which turns upon *Adam* and *Eve*, who continued in *Paradise* while they kept the Command that was given them, and were driven out of it as soon as they had transgressed. This is likewise the Moral of the principal Episode, which shews us how an innumerable multitude of Angels fell from their State of Bliss, and were cast into Hell upon their Disobedience. Besides this great Moral, which may be looked upon as the Soul of the Fable, there are an infinity of Under-Morals which are to be drawn from the several parts of the Poem, and which make this Work more useful and instructive than any other Poem in any Language.

Those who have criticised on the *Odyssey*, the *Iliad*, and *Æneid*, have taken a great deal of pains to fix the number of Months or Days contain'd in the Action of each of those Poems.[1] If any one thinks it worth his while to examine this Particular in *Milton*, he will find that from *Adam*'s first Appearance in the Fourth Book, to his Expulsion from *Paradise* in the Twelfth, the Author reckons ten Days. As for that part of the Action which is described in the three first Books, as it does not pass within the Regions of Nature, I have before observ'd that it is not subject to any Calculations of Time.

I have now finish'd my Observations on a Work which does an Honour to the *English* Nation. I have taken a general View of it under those four Heads, the Fable, the Characters, the Sentiments and the Language, and made each of them the Subject of a parti-

the first step in composing a fable is 'to chuse the Instruction, and the point of Morality, which is to serve as its Foundation' (i. 28–29).

[1] Addison again is doubtless thinking of Le Bossu, who in book ii, chap. v, traces the number of months and days in these epics (i. 130), a matter which he takes up again in book ii, chap. xviii, and book iii, chap. xii. Addison had referred to this earlier, at the end of No. 267 (vol. ii). *Tatler* 6 (an article from the Grecian coffeehouse) recounts an attempt to put the action of the *Iliad* into an exact journal with the events distributed into days.

cular Paper. I have in the next place spoken of the Censures which our Author may incur under each of these Heads, which I have confined to two Papers, tho' I might have enlarged the number, if I had been disposed to dwell on so ungrateful a Subject. I believe, however, that the severest Reader will not find any little fault in Heroic Poetry, which this Author has fallen into, that does not come under one of those Heads among which I have distributed his several Blemishes. After having thus treated at large of *Paradise Lost*, I could not think it sufficient to have celebrated this Poem in the whole, without descending to Particulars. I have therefore bestowed a Paper upon each Book, and endeavoured not only to prove[a] that the Poem is beautiful in general, but to point out its particular Beauties, and to determine wherein they consist. I have endeavoured to shew how some Passages are beautiful by being Sublime, others by being Soft, others by being Natural; which of them are recommended by the Passion, which by the Moral, which by the Sentiment, and which by the Expression. I have likewise endeavoured[b] to shew how the Genius of the Poet shines by a happy Invention, a distant Allusion, or a judicious Imitation; how he has copied or improved *Homer* or *Virgil*, and raised his own Imaginations by the use which he has made of several Poetical Passages in Scripture. I might have inserted also several[c] Passages of *Tasso*, which our Author has imitated;[d] but as I do not look upon *Tasso* to be a sufficient Voucher, I would not perplex my Reader with such Quotations, as might do more Honour to the *Italian* than the *English* Poet. In short, I have endeavoured to particularize those innumerable Kinds of Beauty, which it would be tedious to recapitulate, but which are essential to Poetry, and which may be met with in the Works of this great Author. Had I thought, at my first engaging in this Design, that it would have led me to so great a length, I believe I should never have entered upon it; but the kind Reception which it has met with among those whose Judgments I have a Value for, as well as the uncommon Demands which my Bookseller tells me has been made for these particular Discourses, give me no Reason to repent of the Pains I have been at in composing them.

L

[a] prove] shew *Fol.*   [b] have likewise endeavoured] have endeavoured *Fol.*
[c] inserted also several] inserted several *Fol.*   [d] has imitated;] has likewise imitated; *Fol.*

Totus mundus agit Histrionem.

MANY of my fair Readers, as well as very gay and well-received Persons of the other Sex, are extremely perplexed at the *Latin* Sentences at the Head of my Speculations; I do not know whether I ought not to indulge them with Translations of each of them: However, I have to Day taken down from the Top of the Stage in *Drury-Lane* a Bit of *Latin* which often stands in their View, and signifies that *the whole World acts the Player.* It is certain that if we look all round us and behold the different Employments of Mankind, you hardly see one who is not, as the Player is, in an assumed Character. The Lawyer who is vehement and loud in a Cause wherein he knows he has not the Truth of the Question on his Side, is a Player, as to the personated Part, but incomparably meaner than he as to the Prostitution of himself for Hire; because the Pleader's Falshood introduces Injustice, the Player feigns for no other End but to divert or instruct you. The Divine whose Passions transport him to say any thing with any View but promoting the Interests of true Piety and Religion, is a Player with a still greater Imputation of Guilt in Proportion to his depreciating a Character more sacred. Consider all the different Pursuits and Employments of Men, and you will find half their Actions tend to nothing else but Disguise and Imposture; and all that is done which proceeds not from a Man's very self is the Action of a Player. For this Reason it is that I make so frequent mention of the Stage: It is, with me, a Matter of the highest Consideration what Parts are well or ill performed, what Passions or Sentiments are indulged or cultivated, and consequently what Manners and Customs are transfused from the Stage to the World, which reciprocally imitate each other. As the Writers of Epick Poems introduce shadowy Persons, and represent Vices and Vertues under the Characters of Men and Women; so I, who am a SPECTATOR in the World, may perhaps sometimes make use of the Names of the Actors on the Stage, to represent or admonish those who transact Affairs in the World. When I am commending *Wilks* for representing the Tenderness of a Husband

---

[1] *Motto.* For sources and variants of this often quoted sentence (translated below by Steele) see *N & Q,* clxxxv (1943), 212–13.

and a Father in *Macbeth*, the Contrition of a reformed Prodigal in *Harry the Fourth*, the winning Emptiness of a young Man of Goodnature and Wealth in *the Trip to the Jubilee*, the Officiousness of an artful Servant in *the Fox*: When I thus celebrate *Wilks*, I talk to all the World who are engaged in any of those Circumstances.[1] If I were to speak of Merit neglected, misapplyed or misunderstood, might not I say *Eastcourt*[2] has a great Capacity, but it is not the Interest of others who bear a Figure on the Stage, that his Talents were understood; it is their Business to impose upon him what cannot become him, or keep out of his Hands any thing in which he would Shine. Were one to raise a suspicion of himself in a Man who passes upon the World for a fine Thing, in order to alarm him, one might say, if Lord *Foppington*[3] were not on the Stage, (*Cibber* acts the false Pretentions to a genteel Behaviour so very Justly) he would have in the generality of Mankind more that would admire than deride him. When we come to Characters directly comical, it is not to be imagined what Effect a well regulated Stage would have upon Men's Manners. The craft of an Usurer, the Absurdity of a rich Fool, the awkard Roughness of a Fellow of half Courage, the ungraceful Mirth of a Creature of half Wit, might be for ever put out of Countenance by proper Parts for *Dogget*.[4] *Johnson*, by acting *Corbacchio* the other Night, must have given all who saw him a thorough Detestation of aged Avarice.[5] The Petulancy[6] of a peevish old Fellow who loves and hates he knows not why, is very excellently performed by the Ingenious Mr. *William Penkethman*[7] in *the Fop's Fortune*; where, in the Character of *Don Cholerick Snap Shorto de*

---

[1] For Robert Wilks, the actor and theatre-manager, see No. 268 (vol. ii). He played the part of Macduff in *Macbeth* (given recently at Drury Lane on 6 Mar.); that of the Prince of Wales in *Henry IV* (Drury Lane, 7 Apr.); that of Sir Harry Wild-Air in *The Constant Couple, or a Trip to the Jubilee* by Farquhar (advertised for the following evening, 6 May); and that of Mosca in Jonson's *Volpone* (Drury Lane, 29 Apr.). His acting in *Macbeth* and *Henry IV* is praised in *Tatlers* 68 and 182.

[2] See Nos. 264 (vol. ii) and 468 (vol. iv).

[3] Cibber's part in his own play, *The Careless Husband* (1704). He had played this role in the recent performance at Drury Lane on 3 Jan.

[4] Thomas Doggett. See No. 235 (vol. ii).

[5] Benjamin Johnson (1665?–1742) had taken the part of Old Corbaccio in Jonson's *Volpone* at Drury Lane on 29 Apr.

[6] Petulance, in the sense of peevishness, pettishness. This is the earliest example in *OED*.

[7] See No. 31 (vol. i). Cibber's *Love Makes a Man; or, The Fop's Fortune*, is advertised in this number for performance on this day, for Penkethman's benefit, 'With a new Epilogue spoken by Mr. Penkethman riding on an Ass'. He played the part of 'Don Lewis, alias Don Cholerick Snap Shorto de Testy'. The part of Carlos was taken by Wilks, and that of 'Clodio, alias Don Dismallo Thick-Scullo de Half-Witto' by Cibber.

Testy, he answers no Questions but to those whom he likes, and wants no Account of any thing from those he approves. Mr. *Penketh-man* is also Master of as many Faces in the Dumb-Scene, as can be expected from a Man in the Circumstances of being ready to perish out of Fear and Hunger: He wonders throughout the whole Scene very masterly without neglecting his Victuals. If it be, as I have heard it sometimes mentioned, a great Qualification for the World to follow Business and Pleasure too, what is it in the Ingenious Mr. *Penkethman* to represent a Sense of Pleasure and Pain at the same time; as you may see him do this Evening?

As it is certain that a Stage ought to be wholly suppressed or judiciously encouraged while there is one in the Nation, Men turned for regular Pleasure cannot employ their Thoughts more usefully, for the Diversion of Mankind, than by convincing them that it is in themselves to raise this Entertainment to the greatest Height. It would be a great Improvement, as well as Embellish-ment to the Theatre, if Dancing were more regarded, and taught to all the Actors. One who has the Advantage of such an agreeable girlish Person as Mrs. *Bicknell*,[1] joyned with her Capacity of Imita-tion, could in proper Gesture and Motion represent all the decent Characters of female Life. An amiable Modesty in one Aspect of a Dancer, an assumed Confidence in another, a sudden Joy in another, a falling off with an Impatience[a] of being beheld, a Return towards the Audience with an unsteady Resolution to approach them, and a well-acted Sollicitude to please, would revive in the Company all the fine Touches of Mind raised in observing all the Objects of Affection or Passion they had before beheld. Such elegant Entertainments as these, would polish the Town into Judgment in their Gratifications; and Delicacy in Pleasure is the first Step People of Condition take in Reformation from Vice. Mrs. *Bicknell* has the only Capacity for this sort of Dancing of any on the Stage; and

---

[a] with an Impatience] with Impatience *Fol.*

[1] For this popular actress (born *c.* 1695) see *Tatler* 3. She is also mentioned by Steele in *Tatler* 11 and *Guardian* 50. Performances of *Volpone* (on 29 Apr.) and *The Constant Couple* (on 6 May) include dancing by Mrs. Bicknell and others. Just a week earlier (No. 364) the *Spectator* had printed a letter advertising a benefit for Mrs. Porter. A letter signed A. B——n in the *British Mercury* of 7 May observes:

The Spectator . . . has lately taken some Pains to flatter the Powerful on the Stage, in order to fill their Benefit-Days; you are therefore desir'd to say something of the Tragedy of Venice preserv'd, and on Mrs. Rogers, for whose Benefit it is acted next Friday. . . .

I dare say all who see her Performance to Morrow Night, when sure the Romp will do her best for her own Benefit, will be of my Mind.

T

No. 371　　　　　　　　　　　　*Tuesday, May* 6, 1712[1]

[ADDISON]

*Jamné igitur laudas quod de sapientibùs unus
Ridebat? . . .*

Juv.

I SHALL communicate to my Reader the following Letter for the Entertainment of this Day.

SIR,

'YOU know very well that our Nation is more famous for that sort of Men who are called *Whims* and *Humorists*,[2] than any other Country in the World, for which reason it is observ'd that our *English* Comedy excells that of all other Nations in the Novelty and Variety of its Characters.[3]

'Among those innumerable Setts of *Whims* which our Country produces, there are none whom I have regarded with more Curiosity than those who have invented any particular kind of Diversion for the Entertainment of themselves or their Friends. My Letter shall single out those who take delight in sorting a Company that has something of Burlesque and Ridicule in its appearance. I shall make my self understood by the following Example. One of the Wits of the last Age, who was a Man of a good Estate, thought he never laid out his Mony better than in a Jest.[4] As he was one Year at the

---

[1] *Motto.* Juvenal, *Satires*, 10. 28–29 (altered):

　　　Do you commend or praise, because a single Sage
　　　Did laugh?

[2] See Ascoli, book ii, chap. vi (pp. 423–46), for a summary of French opinion of English traits.

[3] Sir William Temple ('Of Poetry', 1690) attributes the variety of humour in English comedy to the 'greater variety' in English life. 'We have more Humour, because every Man follows his own, and takes a Pleasure, perhaps a Pride, to shew it' (Spingarn, iii. 104).

[4] Nichols and other editors have taken this as a reference to George Villiers, Duke of Buckingham (1628–87), but offer no evidence other than oral tradition. John H. Wilson, *A Rake and His Times* (1954), says nothing of the jest.

Bath, observing that in the great Confluence of fine People there were several among them with long Chins,[1] a part of the Visage by which he himself was very much distinguished, he invited to Dinner half a Score of these remarkable Persons who had their Mouths in the middle of their Faces. They had no sooner placed themselves about the Table, but they began to stare upon one another, not being able to imagine what had brought them together. Our *English* Proverb says,

> *'Tis merry in the Hall,*
> *When Beards wag all.*[2]

It proved so in the Assembly I am now speaking of, who seeing so many Peaks of Faces agitated with Eating, Drinking and Discourse, and observing all the Chins that were present meeting together very often over the Center of the Table, every one grew sensible of the Jest, and came into it with so much good Humour, that they lived in strict Friendship and Alliance from that Day forward.

'The same Gentleman some time after packed together a Sett of Oglers, as he called them, consisting of such as had an unlucky Cast in their Eyes: His Diversion on this occasion was to see the cross Bows, mistaken Signs, and wrong Connivances[3] that passed amidst so many broken and refracted Rays of Sight.

'The third Feast which this merry Gentleman exhibited was to the Stammerers, whom he got together in a sufficient Body to fill his Table. He had order'd one of his Servants, who was placed behind a Skreen, to write down their Table-Talk, which was very easie to be done, without the help of Short-hand. It appears by the Notes which were taken, that tho' their Conversation never fell, there were not above twenty Words spoken during the first Course; that upon serving up the second, one of the Company was a quarter of an Hour in telling them, that the Ducklins and Sparrow-grass were very good; and that another took up the same time in declaring himself of the same Opinion. This Jest did not, however, go off

---

[1] Buckingham's poem, 'Advice to a Painter, to draw my L. A——ton; Grand Minister of State', contains the following:

> Paint at the door attending night and noon
> *Povey* the Wit, and R —— the Beau-garzon,
> Who at his Entering shews a foot of Chin,
> To let you know his Face is coming in.

(*Miscellaneous Works*, collected by Tho. Brown (1705), ii. 81–82.)

[2] Apperson cites this from the early fourteenth century.

[3] Winking (in literal sense). *OED* gives only two examples, dated 1596 and 1614.

so well as either of the former; for one of the Guests being a brave Man, and fuller of Resentment than he knew how to express, went out of the Room, and sent the facetious Inviter a Challenge in Writing, which tho it was afterwards dropp'd by the Interposition of Friends, put a Stop to these ludicrous Entertainments.

'Now, Sir, I dare say you will agree with me, that as there is no Moral in these Jests they ought to be discouraged, and looked upon rather as Pieces of Unluckiness, than Wit. However as it is natural for one Man to refine upon the Thought of another, and impossible for any single Person, how great soever his Parts may be, to invent an Art, and bring it to its utmost Perfection, I shall here give you an Account of an honest Gentleman of my Acquaintance, who upon hearing the Character of the Wit abovementioned has himself assumed it, and endeavoured to convert it to the Benefit of Mankind. He invited half a dozen of his Friends one day to Dinner, who were each of them famous for inserting several redundant Phrases in their Discourse, as *d'y'hear me, d'y'see, that is, and so Sir*. Each of the Guests making frequent use of his particular Elegance appeared so ridiculous to his Neighbour, that he could not but reflect upon himself as appearing equally ridiculous to the rest of the Company; by this means, before they had sate long together, every one talking with the greatest Circumspection and carefully avoiding his favourite Expletive, the Conversation was cleared of its Redundancies, and had a greater quantity of Sense tho' less of Sound in it.

'The same well-meaning Gentleman took occasion, at another time, to bring together such of his Friends as were addicted to a foolish habitual Custom of swearing. In order to shew them the Absurdity of the Practice, he had recourse to the Invention abovementioned, having placed an *Amanuensis* in a private part of the Room. After the second Bottle, when Men open their Minds without Reserve, my honest Friend begun to take notice of the many sonorous but unnecessary Words that had passed in his House since their sitting down at Table, and how much good Conversation they had lost by giving way to such superfluous Phrases. What a Tax, says he, would they have raised for the Poor, had we put the Laws in execution upon one another! Every one of them took this gentle Reproof in good part: Upon which he told them, that knowing their Conversation would have no Secrets in it, he had ordered it to be taken down in Writing, and for the humour sake would read it to them, if they pleased. There were Ten sheets of it, which might have been reduced to two, had there not been those abominable Interpolations I have before mentioned. Upon the reading of it in cold Blood, it looked rather like a Conference of Fiends than of Men. In short, every one trembled at himself upon hearing calmly what he had pronounced amidst the Heat and Inadvertency of Discourse.

'I shall only mention another Occasion wherein he made use of the same Invention to cure a different kind of Men, who are the Pests of all polite Conversation, and murder Time as much as either of the two former, though they do it more innocently; I mean that dull Generation of Story-tellers. My Friend got together about half a dozen of his Acquaintance, who were infected with this strange Malady. The first Day one of them sitting down, enter'd upon the Siege of *Namur*,[1] which lasted till four a-Clock, their time of parting. The second Day a *North-Britain* took Possession of the Discourse, which it was impossible to get out of his Hands so long as the Company staid together. The third Day was engrossed, after the same manner, by a Story of the same length. They at last begun to reflect upon this barbarous way of treating one another, and by this means awaken'd out of that Lethargy with which each of them had been seized for several Years.

'As you have somewhere declared that extraordinary and uncommon Characters of Mankind are the Game which you delight in,[2] and as I look upon you to be the greatest Sportsman, or, if you please, the *Nimrod* among this Species of Writers, I thought this Discovery would not be unacceptable to you.

I am,

SIR, &c.'

I

---

[1] After nearly three months of siege Namur surrendered to the armies of William III in 1695.   [2] No. 108 (vol. i).

No. 372
[STEELE]

Wednesday, May 7, 1712[1]

> ... *Pudet hæc opprobria nobis*
> *Et dici potuisse & non potuisse refelli.*
> Ovid.

Mr. SPECTATOR,   *May* 6, 1712.

'I AM Sexton of the Parish of *Covent-Garden*, and complained to you some time ago,[2] that as I was tolling in to Prayers at Eleven in the Morning, Crowds of People of Quality hastened to assemble at a Puppet-Show on the other Side of the Garden. I had at the same time a very great Disesteem for Mr. *Powell* and his little thoughtless Commonwealth, as if they had enticed the Gentry into those Wanderings: But let that be as it will, I now am convinced of the honest Intentions of the said Mr. *Powell* and Company; and send this to acquaint you, that he has given all the Profits which shall arise to Morrow Night by his Play to the Use of the poor Charity Children of this Parish.[3] I have been informed, Sir, that in *Holland* all Persons who set up any Show, or act any Stage-Play, be the Actors either of Wood and Wire, or Flesh and Blood, are obliged to pay out of their Gain such a Proportion to the honest and industrious Poor in the Neighbourhood: By this Means they make Diversion and Pleasure pay a Tax to Labour and Industry.[4] I have been told also, that all the Time of *Lent*, in Roman-Catholick Countries, the Persons of Condition administred to the Necessities of the Poor, and attended the Beds of Lazars and diseased Persons. Our Protestant Ladies and Gentlemen are much to seek for proper Ways of

---

[1] *Motto.* Ovid, *Metamorphoses*, 1. 758–9: I am ashamed that this scandal should disgrace my name and yet could not be refuted.

In the Folio sheets only the first line was used. Steele had used these lines as the motto for *Tatler* 187.   [2] In No. 14 (vol. i).

[3] An advertisement for this performance appears in the *Daily Courant* of this date (7 May):

> For the Benefit of the Children of the Charity-School of Paul's Covent-Garden. An Opera call'd, The False Triumph; or, The Destruction of Troy. To which will be added a New Piece of Machinery never before seen, surpasing all his former Performances. To which will be added a Highland Dance, and several other New Decorations. Note, That the Children may have the Benefit of the Day, he will Act twice, viz. Beginning exactly at 6, and also at 8 in the Evening.

[4] Cf. *Tatler* 20: 'The Profits of the Theatre [in Amsterdam] maintain an Hospital: For as here they do not think the Profession of an Actor the only Trade that a Man ought to exercise, so they will not allow any Body to grow rich on a Profession that so little conduces to the Good of the Commonwealth.'

passing Time, that they are obliged to *Punchinello* for knowing what to do with themselves. Since the Case is so, I desire only you would entreat our People of Quality, who are not to be interrupted in their Pleasure to think of the Practice of any moral Duty, that they would at least fine for their Sins, and give something to these poor Children: A little out of their Luxury and Superfluity would attone, in some Measure, for the wanton Use of the rest of their Fortunes. It would not methinks be amiss, if the Ladies who haunt the Cloysters and Passages of the Play-house were upon every Offence obliged to pay to this excellent Institution of Schools of Charity: This Method would make Offenders themselves do Service to the Publick. But in the mean time I desire you would publish this voluntary Reparation which Mr. *Powell* does our Parish, for the Noise he has made in it by the constant rattling of Coaches, Drums, Trumpets, Triumphs, and Battles. The Destruction of *Troy*, adorned with Highland Dances, are to make up the Entertainment of all who are so well disposed as not to forbear a light Entertainment, for no other Reason but that it is to do a good Action.

I am,

SIR,

Your most humble Servant,

Ralph Bellfry.

'I am credibly informed that all the Insinuations which a certain Writer made against Mr. *Powell* at the *Bath*, are false and groundless.'[1]

Mr. SPECTATOR,

'MY Employment, which is that of a Broker, leading me often into Taverns about the *Exchange*, has given me Occasion to observe a certain Enormity, which I shall here submit to your Animadversion. In three or four of these Taverns, I have at different Times taken notice of a precise Set of People, with grave Countenances, short Wiggs, black Cloaths, or dark Camlet trimm'd with Black, and Mourning Gloves and Hatbands, who meet on certain Days at each Tavern successive, and keep a sort of moving Club. Having often met with their Faces, and observ'd a certain slinking Way in their dropping in one after another, I had the Curiosity to enquire into their Characters, being the rather mov'd to it by their

---

[1] See *Tatlers* 44, 50, 77, 115.

agreeing in the singularity of their Dress; and I find upon due Examination they are a Knot of Parish-Clarks, who have taken a Fancy to one another, and perhaps settle the Bills of Mortality over their half Pints. I have so great a Value and Veneration for any who have but even an assenting *Amen* in the Service of Religion, that I am afraid lest these Persons shou'd incur some scandal by this Practice; and wou'd therefore have them, without raillery, advis'd to send the Florence[1] and Pullets home to their own Houses, and not pretend to live as well as the Overseers of the Poor.

I am,

SIR,

Your humble Servant,

Humphry Transfer.'

Mr. SPECTATOR,   *May 6th.*

'I WAS last *Wednesday* Night at a Tavern in the City, amongst a Set of Men who call themselves the Lawyers Club. You must know, Sir, this Club consists only of Attorneys; and at this Meeting every one proposes the Cause he has then in Hand to the Board, upon which each Member gives his Judgment according to the Experience he has met with. If it happens that any one puts a Case, of which they have had no President,[2] it is noted down by their Clerk *Will. Goosequill*, (who Registers all their Proceedings) that one of them may go the next Day with it to a Counsel. This indeed is commendable, and ought to be the principal End of their Meeting; but had you been there to have heard them relate their Methods of managing a Cause, their Manner of drawing out their Bills, and in short, their Arguments upon the several Ways of abusing their Clients, with the Applause that is given to him who has done it most Artfully, you would before now have given your Remarks on them. They are so conscious that their Discourses ought to be kept Secret, that they are very cautious of admitting any Person who is not of their Profession. When any, who are not of the Law, are let in, the Person who introduces him, says, he is a very honest Gentleman; and he is taken in, as their Cant is, to pay Costs. I am admitted upon the recommendation of one of their Principals, as *a very honest good natured Fellow*, that will never be in a Plot, and only desires to drink his Bottle and smoke his Pipe. You have formerly remarked

---

[1] Here a kind of wine brought from Florence.

[2] I.e. precedent. A common spelling in the eighteenth century, 'through practical identity of pronunciation, and consequent confusion, with *President*' (OED).

upon several Sorts of Clubs; and as the Tendency of this is only to increase Fraud and Deceit, I hope you will please to take Notice of it.

I am, (with respect)
Your humble Servant,
H. R.'

T

No. 373   *Thursday, May 8, 1712*[1]
[BUDGELL]

Fallit enim Vitium specie virtutis & umbra.
Juv.

MR. *Lock*, in his Treatise of Human Understanding, has spent two Chapters upon the Abuse of Words.[2] The first and most palpable Abuse of Words, he says, is, when they are used without clear and distinct Ideas. The second, when we are so inconstant and unsteady in the Application of them, that we sometimes use them to signifie one Idea, sometimes another. He adds, that the Result of our Contemplations and Reasonings, while we have no precise Ideas fixed to our Words, must needs be very confused and absurd. To avoid this Inconvenience, more especially in Moral Discourses, where the same Word should constantly be used in the same Sense, he earnestly recommends the use of Definitions. *A Definition,* says he, *is the only way whereby the precise meaning of Moral Words can be known.*[3] He therefore accuses those of great Negligence who discourse of Moral things with the least Obscurity in the Terms they make use of, since upon the foremention'd Ground he does not scruple to

---

[1] *Motto.* Juvenal, *Satires*, 14. 109: Vice oftentimes deceives in Virtue's Cloak.

In the Folio sheets the motto was Horace, *Satires* 1. 3. 44–48:

>   Strabonem
> Appellat paetum pater; & pullum, male parvus
> Si cui filius est; ut abortivus fuit olim
> Sisyphus: hunc varum, distortis cruribus; illum
> Balbutit scaurum, pravis fultum malè talis.

> A Father that hath got a *Squint-ey'd* Boy
> Crys *what a pretty Cast adorns my Joy!*
> And calls his dwarfish Son that's often sick,
> As that Abortive *Sisyphus*, his Chick.   CREECH.

[2] Locke, *Essay*, III. x, xi.   [3] Ibid. III. xi. 17.

say that he thinks *Morality is capable of Demonstration as well as the Mathematicks.*[1]

I know no two Words that[a] have been more abused by the different and wrong Interpretations which are put upon them, than those two, *Modesty* and *Assurance.* To say such an one is *a modest Man,* sometimes indeed passes for a good Character; but at present is very often used to signifie a sheepish, awkard Fellow, who has neither Good-breeding, Politeness, nor any Knowledge of the World.

Again, *A Man of Assurance,* tho' at first it only denoted a Person of a free and open Carriage, is now very usually applied to a profligate Wretch, who can break through all the Rules of Decency and Morality without a Blush.

I shall endeavour therefore in this Essay to restore these Words to their true Meaning, to prevent the Idea of *Modesty* from being confounded with that of *Sheepishness,* and to hinder *Impudence* from passing for *Assurance.*

If I was put to define *Modesty,* I would call it *The Reflection of an Ingenuous Mind, either when a Man has committed an Action for which he Censures himself, or fancies that he is exposed to the Censure of others.*

For this Reason a Man truly Modest is as much so when he is alone, as in Company; and as subject to a Blush in his Closet, as when the Eyes of Multitudes are upon him.

I do not remember to have met with any Instance of Modesty with which I am so well pleased, as that celebrated one of the young Prince, whose Father being a Tributary King to the *Romans,* had several Complaints laid against him before the Senate, as a Tyrant and Oppressor of his Subjects. The Prince went to *Rome* to defend his Father; but coming into the Senate, and hearing a multitude of Crimes proved upon him, was so oppressed when it came to his turn to speak, that he was unable to utter a Word.[2] The Story tells us, that the Fathers were more moved at this Instance of Modesty and Ingenuity,[3] than they could have been by the most Pathetick Oration; and, in short, pardoned the Guilty Father for this early Promise of Virtue in the Son.

I take *Assurance* to be *The Faculty of possessing a Man's self,* or of *saying and doing indifferent things without any Uneasiness or Emotion in the*

---

[a] that] which *Fol.*

---

[1] Locke, *Essay,* III. xi. 16. [2] I have not identified this incident.
[3] I.e. ingenuousness. Cf. No. 352.

Mind. That which generally gives a Man Assurance is a moderate Knowledge of the World, but above all a Mind fixed and determined in it self to do nothing against the Rules of Honour and Decency. An open and assured Behaviour is the natural Consequence of such a Resolution. A Man thus armed, if his Words or Actions are at any time misinterpreted, retires within himself, and from a Consciousness of his own Integrity assumes Force enough to despise the little Censures of Ignorance or Malice.

Every one ought to cherish and encourage in himself the Modesty and Assurance I have here mentioned.

A Man without Assurance is lyable to be made uneasie by the Folly or Ill-nature of every one he converses with. A Man without Modesty is lost to all Sense of Honour and Virtue.

It is more than probable that the Prince above-mentioned possessed both these Qualifications in a very eminent degree. Without Assurance he would never have undertaken to speak before the most august Assembly in the World: Without Modesty he would have pleaded the Cause he had taken upon him, tho' it had appeared never so Scandalous.

From what has been said it is plain, that Modesty and Assurance are both amiable, and may very well meet in the same Person. When they are thus mixed and blended together they compose what we endeavour to express when we say *a modest Assurance*; by which we understand the Just Mean between Bashfulness and Impudence.

I shall conclude, with observing, that as the same Man may be both Modest and Assured, so it is also possible for the same Person to be both Impudent and Bashful.

We have frequent Instances of this odd kind of Mixture in People of depraved Minds and mean Education; who tho' they are not able to meet a Man's Eyes, or pronounce a Sentence without Confusion, can voluntarily commit the greatest Villanies, or most Indecent Action.

Such a Person seems to have made a Resolution to do Ill even in spite of himself, and in defiance of all those Checks and Restraints his Temper and Complection[1] seem to have laid in his way.

Upon the whole, I would endeavour to establish this Maxim, That the Practice of *Virtue* is the most proper Method to give

---

[1] Here used in the obsolete sense of constitution or habit of mind, disposition, temperament, 'nature' (*OED*).

a Man a becoming Assurance in his Words and Actions. *Guilt* always seeks to shelter it self in one of the Extreams; and is sometimes attended with both.   X

No. 374   *Friday, May 9, 1712*[1]
[STEELE]

Nil actum reputans si quid superesset agendum.

Luc.

THERE is a Fault, which tho' common, Wants a Name. It is the very contrary to Procrastination: As we lose the present Hour by delaying from Day to Day to execute what we ought to do immediately; so most of us take Occasion to sit still and throw away the Time in our Possession, by retrospect on what is past, imagining we have already acquitted our selves and established our Characters in the sight of Mankind. But when we thus put a Value upon our selves for what we have already done, any further than to explain our selves in order to assist our future Conduct, that will give us an over-weening Opinion of our Merit to the prejudice of our present Industry. The great Rule, methinks, should be to manage the Instant in which we stand with Fortitude, Æquanimity, and Moderation, according to Mens respective Circumstances. If our past Actions reproach us, they cannot be attoned for by our own severe Reflexions so effectually as by a contrary Behaviour: If they are praise-worthy, the memory of them is of no use but to act suitably to them. Thus a good present Behaviour is an implicit Repentance for any miscarriage in what is past; but present Slackness will not make up for past Activity. Time has swallowed up all that we Contemporaries did Yesterday, as irrevocably as it has the Actions of the Antediluvians: But we are again awake, and what shall we do to Day, to Day which passes while we are yet speaking? Shall we remember the Folly of last Night, or resolve upon the Exercise of Virtue to Morrow? Last Night is certainly gone, and to Morrow may never arrive: This Instant make use of. Can you oblige any Man of Honour and Virtue? Do it immediately. Can you

---

[1] *Motto.* Lucan, *Pharsalia,* 2. 657: Accounting nothing done while anything remained to do.

visit a sick Friend? Will it revive him to see you enter and suspend your own Ease and Pleasure to comfort his Weakness, and hear the impertinences of a Wretch in Pain? Don't stay to take Coach, but be gone. Your Mistress will bring Sorrow, and your Bottle Madness: Go to neither.—Such Vertues and Diversions as these, are mentioned because they occur to all Men. But every Man is sufficiently convinced, that to suspend the use of the present Moment, and resolve better for the future only, is an unpardonable Folly; what I attempted to Consider, was the Mischief of setting such a Value upon what is past, as to think we have done enough. Let a Man have filled all the Offices of Life with the highest Dignity till Yesterday, and begin to live only to himself to Day; he must expect he will in the Effects upon his Reputation, be considered as the Man who dyed Yesterday. The Man who distinguishes himself from the rest, stands in a Press of People; those before him intercept his Progress, and those behind him, if he does not urge on, will tread him down. *Cæsar*, of whom it was said, *that he thought nothing done while there was any thing left for him to do*,[1] went on in performing the greatest Exploits, without assuming to himself a Privilege of taking Rest upon the Foundation of the Merit of his former Actions. It was the manner of that glorious Captain, to write down what Scenes he passed through, but it was rather to keep his Affairs in Method, and capable of a clear review in case they should be examined by others, than that he built a renown upon any thing which was passed. I shall produce two Fragments of his to Demonstrate, that it was his rule of Life to support himself rather by what he should perform, than what he had done already. In the Tablet which he wore about him the same Year in which he obtained the Battle of *Pharsalia*, there were found these loose Notes[2] for his own Conduct. It is supposed by the Circumstances they alluded to, that they might be set down the Evening of the same Night.

'My Part is now but begun, and my Glory must be sustained by the Use I make of this Victory; otherwise, my Loss will be greater

---

[1] Lucan, *Pharsalia*, 2. 657 (the motto of this essay). Bayle, who quotes the passage from Lucan, writes (art. Julius Caesar, Remark C): '*Cæsar* look'd upon what he had done as nothing at all, if anything remain'd to be done: He was for finishing altogether the Wars wherein he was engag'd: He was not willing that Fortune should have any Opportunity to undo all that he had not finish'd.' Cf. Addison, *The Present State of the War* (1708): 'It was a celebrated part in *Cæsar*'s character . . ., that he thought nothing at all was done, while any thing remained undone' (Guthkelch, ii. 248).

[2] Caesar's 'loose notes' and the reflections on the battle are apocryphal. I have not discovered the immediate source.

than that of *Pompey*. Our personal Reputation will rise or fall as we bear our respective Fortunes. All my private Enemies among the Prisoners shall be spared. I will forget this in order to obtain such another Day. *Trebutius* is ashamed to see me: I will go to his Tent and be reconciled in private. Give all the Men of Honour who take Part with me, the Terms I offered before the Battle: Let them owe this to their Friends who have been long in my Interests. Power is weakened by the full Use of it, but extended by Moderation. *Galbinius* is proud, and will be servile in his present Fortune; let him wait. Send for *Stertinius*: He is modest, and his Virtue is worth gaining. I have cooled my Heart with Reflexion; and am fit to rejoice with the Army to Morrow. He is a popular General who can expose himself like a private Man during a Battle; but he is more popular who can rejoice but like a private Man after a Victory.'

What is particularly proper for the Example of all who pretend to Industry in the Pursuit of Honour and Virtue, is, That this Hero was more than ordinarily sollicitous about his Reputation, when a common Mind would have thought it self in Security, and given it self a Loose to Joy and Triumph. But though this is a very great Instance of his Temper, I must confess I am more taken with his Reflexions when he retired to his Closet in some Disturbance, upon the repeated ill Omens of *Calphurnia*'s Dream the Night before his Death. The literal Translation of that Fragment shall conclude this Paper.

'Be it so then. If I am to dye to Morrow, that is what I am to do to Morrow: It will not be then because I am willing it should be then; nor shall I escape it because I am unwilling. It is in the Gods when, but in my self how I shall dye. If *Calphurnia*'s Dreams are Fumes of Indigestion, how shall I behold the Day after to Morrow? If they are from the Gods, their Admonition is not to prepare me to escape from their Decree, but to meet it. I have lived to a Fulness of Days and of Glory; what is there that *Cæsar* has not done with as much Honour as antient Heroes? *Cæsar* has not yet dyed, *Cæsar* is prepared to dye.'

T

Non possidentem multa vocaveris
Rectè beatum: rectiùs occupat
Nomen beati, qui Deorum
Muneribus sapienter uti,
Duramque callet Pauperiem pati,
Pejusque Letho flagitium timet.
Hor.

I HAVE more than once had occasion to mention a Noble Saying
of *Seneca* the Philosopher, that a Virtuous Person struggling with
Misfortunes, and rising above them, is an Object on which the
Gods themselves may look down with Delight.[2] I shall therefore
set before my Reader a Scene of this kind of Distress in private
Life, for the Speculation of this Day.[3]

An eminent Citizen, who had lived in good Fashion and Credit,
was by a Train of Accidents, and by an unavoidable Perplexity in
his Affairs, reduced to a low Condition. There is a Modesty usually

---

[1] *Motto.* Horace, *Odes,* 4. 9. 45–50:

> He is not number'd with the Blest,
>   To whom the Gods large Stores have giv'n;
> But he who of enough possest
>   Can wisely use the Gifts of Heav'n,
> Who fortune's Frowns unmov'd can bear
> And th'hated Weight of Poverty,
> Who more than Death doth Baseness fear.

[2] Seneca. *De Providentia,* 2. 8–9. Quoted also in Nos. 39 (vol. i) and 237 (vol. ii).
[3] Hughes's authorship of this paper is revealed by Steele at the end of No. 537
(vol. iv). It is also in Duncombe's list. Alexander Bayne, writing to Duncombe
14 Jan. 1734/5, suggests that not only Hughes's poems be collected but also some
example of his 'pretty manner of writing prose. . . . There is one piece of this kind,
which would answer my view exactly. It is a picture of distress in low life, which he
sent to the *Spectator,* and stands recorded there under the name of *Amanda,* and is
inferior to none of the kind, in my judgment. I remember, when that *Spectator* came
out, as the paper was generally read at breakfast, it mixed tears with a great deal
of the tea, which was that morning drunk in London and Westminster' (*Letters of
Several Eminent Persons,* ed. Duncombe, 1772, i. 213).
   The similarity to *Pamela* has been noted. William Bowyer writes to Percy (14 June
1764): 'You may observe what elegant compositions have been occasionally formed
out of the Spectators since they were first published; being not only a pattern of
good writing, but affording even materials for it. Mr. Richardson's Pamela is no
other than the story in vol. V. No. 375. And perhaps it appears with as much
advantage in its original brevity, as in its diffused length of a volume' (Nichols,
Literary Anecdotes, ii. 443).

attending faultless Poverty, which made him rather chuse to reduce his manner of Living to his present Circumstances, than sollicit his Friends in order to support the Shew of an Estate when the Substance was gone. His Wife, who was a Woman of Sense and Virtue, behaved her self on this occasion with uncommon Decency, and never appeared so amiable in his Eyes as now. Instead of upbraiding him with the ample Fortune she had brought, or the many great Offers she had refused for his Sake, she redoubled all the Instances of her Affection, while her Husband was continually pouring out his Heart to her in Complaints that he had ruined the best Woman in the World. He sometimes came Home at a time when she did not expect him, and surprised her in Tears, which she endeavoured to conceal, and always put on an Air of Cheerfulness to receive him. To lessen their Expence, their eldest Daughter (whom I shall call *Amanda*) was sent into the Country, to the House of an honest Farmer who had married a Servant of the Family. This young Woman was apprehensive of the Ruin which was approaching, and had privately engaged a Friend in the Neighbourhood to give her an Account of what passed from time to time in her Father's Affairs. *Amanda* was in the Bloom of her Youth and Beauty, when the Lord of the Mannor, who often called in at the Farmer's House as he follow'd his Country Sports, fell passionately in Love with her. He was a Man of great Generosity, but from a loose Education had contracted a hearty Aversion to Marriage. He therefore entertained a Design upon *Amanda*'s Virtue, which at present he thought fit to keep private. The Innocent Creature, who never suspected his Intentions, was pleased with his Person, and having observed his growing Passion for her, hoped by so advantageous a Match she might quickly be in a Capacity of supporting her impoverished Relations. One Day as he called to see her, he found her in Tears over a Letter she had just received from her Friend, which gave an Account that her Father had lately been stripped of every thing by an Execution. The Lover, who with some Difficulty found out the Cause of her Grief, took this occasion to make her a Proposal. It is impossible to express *Amanda*'s Confusion when she found his Pretensions were not honourable. She was now deserted of all her Hopes, and had no Power to speak; but rushing from him in the utmost Disturbance, locked her self up in her Chamber. He immediately dispatched a Messenger to her Father with the following Letter.

SIR,

'I HAVE heard of your Misfortune, and have offered your Daughter, if she will live with me, to settle on her Four hundred Pounds a Year, and to lay down the Sum for which you are now distressed. I will be so ingenuous as to tell you that I do not intend Marriage: But if you are wise, you will use your Authority with her not to be too nice, when she has an opportunity of saving you and your Family, and of making her self happy.

I am, &c.'

This Letter came to the Hands of *Amanda*'s Mother; she opened and read it with great Surprize and Concern. She did not think it proper to explain her self to the Messenger, but desiring him to call again the next Morning, she wrote to her Daughter as follows.

Dearest Child,

'YOUR Father and I have just now received a Letter from a Gentleman who pretends Love to you, with a Proposal that insults our Misfortunes, and would throw us to a lower Degree of Misery than any thing which is come upon us. How could this barbarous Man think, that the tenderest of Parents would be tempted to supply their Want, by giving up the best of Children to Infamy and Ruin? It is a mean and cruel Artifice to make this Proposal at a time when he thinks our Necessities must compel us to any thing; but we will not eat the Bread of Shame; and therefore we charge thee not to think of us, but to avoid the Snare which is laid for thy Virtue. Beware of pitying us: It is not so bad as you have perhaps been told. All things will yet be well, and I shall write my Child better News.

'I have been interrupted. I know not how I was moved to say things would mend. As I was going on, I was startled by a Noise of one that knocked at the Door, and hath brought us an unexpected supply of a Debt which had long been owing. O I will now tell thee all. It is some Days I have lived almost without Support, having conveyed what little Mony I could raise to your poor Father— Thou wilt weep to think where he is, yet be assured he will be soon at Liberty. That cruel Letter would have broke his Heart, but I have concealed it from him. I have no Companion at present besides little *Fanny*, who stands watching my Looks as I write, and is crying for her Sister. She says she is sure you are not well, having discovered that my present Trouble is about you. But do not think

I would thus repeat my Sorrows, to grieve thee; No, it is to entreat thee not to make them insupportable, by adding what would be worse than all. Let us bear chearfully an Affliction, which we have not brought on our selves, and remember there is a Power who can better deliver us out of it than by the Loss of thy Innocence. Heaven preserve my Dear Child.

Thy Affectionate Mother—'

The Messenger, notwithstanding he[a] promised to deliver this Letter to *Amanda*, carried it first to his Master, who he imagined would be glad to have an Opportunity of giving it into her Hands himself. His Master was impatient to know the Success of his Proposal, and therefore broke open the Letter privately, to see the Contents. He was not a little moved at so true a Picture of Virtue in Distress. But at the same time was infinitely surprised to find his Offers rejected. However, he resolved not to suppress the Letter, but carefully Sealed it up again, and carried it to *Amanda*. All his Endeavours to see her were in vain, till she was assured he brought a Letter from her Mother. He would not part with it, but upon Condition that she should read it without leaving the Room. While she was perusing it, he fixed his Eyes on her Face with the deepest Attention: Her Concern gave a new Softness to her Beauty, and when she burst into Tears, he could no longer refrain from bearing a part in her Sorrow, and telling her, that he too had read the Letter, and was resolved to make Reparation for having been the Occasion of it. My Reader will not be displeased to see the[b] Second Epistle, which he now wrote to *Amanda*'s Mother.

MADAM,

'I AM full of Shame, and will never forgive my self, if I have not your Pardon for what I lately wrote. It was far from my Intention to add Trouble to the Afflicted; nor could any thing, but my being a Stranger to you, have betrayed me into a Fault, for which if I live I shall endeavour to make you amends, as a Son. You cannot be unhappy, while *Amanda* is your Daughter; nor shall be, if any thing can prevent it, which is in the power of,

MADAM,
Your most Obedient
Humble Servant—'

[a] he] that he *Fol.*   [b] the] this *Fol.*

This Letter he sent by his Steward, and soon after went up to Town himself, to compleat the generous Act he had now resolved on. By his Friendship and Assistance *Amanda*'s Father was quickly in a Condition of retrieving his perplexed Affairs. To conclude, he Marryed *Amanda*, and enjoyed the double Satisfaction of having restored a worthy Family to their former Prosperity, and of making himself happy by an Alliance to their Virtues.

No. 376   *Monday, May* 12, 1712[1]
[STEELE]

> . . . *Pavone ex Pythagoreo.*
> Persius.

Mr. SPECTATOR,

'I HAVE not observed that the Officer you some time ago appointed as Inspector of Signs,[2] has done his Duty so well as to give you an Account of very many strange Occurrences in the publick Streets, which are worthy of, but have escaped your Notice. Among all the Oddnesses which I have ever met with, that which I am now telling you of gave me most Delight. You must have observed that all the Cryers in the Street[3] attract the Attention of the Passengers, and of the Inhabitants in the several Parts, by something very particular in their Tone it self, in the dwelling upon a Note, or else making themselves wholly unintelligible by a Scream. The Person I am so delighted with has nothing to sell, but very gravely receives the Bounty of the People, for no other Merit but the Homage they pay to his Manner of signifying to them that he wants a Subsidy. You must, sure, have heard speak of an old Man who walks about the City, and that Part of the Suburbs which lies beyond the *Tower*, performing the Office of a *Day-Watchman*, followed by a Goose which bears the Bob[4] of his Ditty, and confirms what he says with a Quack, Quack. I gave little Heed to the Mention of this known Circumstance, till, being the other Day in those Quarters, I passed by a decrepid old Fellow with a Pole in his Hand,

---

[1] *Motto.* Persius, *Satires*, 6. 11: From the Pythagorean peacock.
In the Folio sheets the full line is given: *Maeonides Quintus Pavone ex Pythagorea.*
[2] Nos. 28 (vol. i), 362.   [3] No. 251 (vol. ii).
[4] I.e. the refrain or burden of a song.

who just then was bawling out, Half an Hour after one a Clock, and immediately a dirty Goose behind him made her Response Quack, Quack. I could not forbear attending this grave Procession for the Length of half a Street, with no small Amazement to find the whole Place so familiarly acquainted with a melancholy Mid-night Voice at Noon day, giving them the Hour, and exhorting them of the Departure of Time, with a Bounce at their Doors. While I was full of this Novelty, I went into a Friend's House, and told him how I was diverted with their whimsical Monitor and his Equipage. My Friend gave me the History; and interrupted my Commendation of the Man, by telling me the Livelihood of these two Animals is purchased rather by the good Parts of the Goose than of her Leader: For it seems the Peripatetick who walked before her was a Watch-man in that Neighbourhood; and the Goose of herself by frequent hearing his Tone, out of her natural Vigilance, not only observed but answered it very regularly from Time to Time. The Watchman was so affected with it, that he bought her, and has taken her in Partner, only altering their Hours of Duty from Night to Day. The Town has come into it, and they live very comfortably. This is the Matter of Fact: Now I desire you, who are a profound Philosopher, to consider this Alliance of Instinct and Reason; your Speculation may turn very naturally upon the Force the superiour Part of Man-kind may have upon the Spirits of such as, like this Watchman, may be very near the Standard of Geese. And you may add to this practical Observations, how in all Ages and Times the World has been carried away by odd unaccountable things, which one would think would pass upon no Creature which had Reason; and under the Symbol of this Goose, you may enter into the Manner and Method of leading Creatures, with their Eyes open, through thick and thin, for they know not what they know not why.[1]

'All which is humbly submitted to your spectatorial Wisdom, by

SIR,

Your most humble Servant,

Michael Gander.'

Mr. SPECTATOR,

'I HAVE for several Years had under my Care the Government and Education of young Ladies, which Trust I have endeavoured to discharge with due regard to their several Capacities and Fortunes: I have left nothing undone to imprint in every one of them an

[1] Blind party allegiance is doubtless glanced at here.

humble courteous Mind, accompanied with a graceful becoming Mein, and have made them pretty much acquainted with the Houshold part of Family Affairs; but still I find there is something very wanting in the Air of my Ladies, different from what I observe in those that are esteemed your fine bred Women. Now, Sir, I must own to you, I never suffered my Girls to learn to Dance; but since I have read your Discourse of Dancing,[1] where you have described the Beauty and Spirit there is in regular Motion, I own my self your Convert, and resolve for the future to give my young Ladies that Accomplishment. But upon imparting my Design to their Parents, I have been made very uneasy for some Time, because several of them have declared, that if I did not make use of the Master they recommended, they would take away their Childern. There was Collonel *Jumper*'s Lady, a Collonel of the Train-Bands, that has a great Interest in her Parish; she recommends Mr. *Trott*[2] for the prettiest Master in Town, that no Man teaches a Jigg like him, that she has seen him rise six or seven Capers together with the greatest Ease imaginable, and that his Scholars twist themselves more ways than the Scholars of any Master in Town; besides, there is Madam *Prim* an Alderman's Lady, recommends a Master of her own Name, but she declares he is not of their Family, yet a very extraordinary Man in his way; for besides a very soft Air he has in Dancing, he gives them a particular Behaviour at a Tea-Table, and in presenting their Snuff-Box, to Twerl, Slip, or Flirt a Fan, and how to place Patches to the best Advantage, either for Fat or Lean, Long or Oval Faces; for my Lady says, there is more in these Things than the World Imagines: But I must confess the Major part of those I am concerned with leave it to me. I desire therefore according to the inclosed Direction, you would send your Correspondent who has writ to you on that subject to my House. If proper Application this way can give Innocence new Charms, and make Virtue legible in the Countenance, I shall spare no charge to make my Scholars in their very Features and Limbs bear witness how careful I have been in the other Parts of their Education.

I am,

SIR,

Your most humble Servant,

Rachel Watchfull.'

T

---

[1] No. 334.   [2] Nos. 296, 308, 314, 316.

No. 377
[ADDISON]

Tuesday, May 13, 1712[1]

*Quid quisque vitet, nunquam homini satis
Cautum est in horas . . .*

LOVE was the Mother of Poetry, and still produces, among the most ignorant and barbarous, a thousand imaginary Distresses and Poetical Complaints. It makes a Footman talk like *Oroondates*,[2] and converts a Brutal Rustick into a gentle Swain. The most ordinary Plebeian or Mechanick in Love, bleeds and pines away with a certain Elegance and Tenderness of Sentiments which this Passion naturally inspires.

These inward Languishings of a Mind infected with this Softness, have given Birth to a Phrase which is made use of by all the melting Tribe, from the highest to the lowest, I mean that of *dying for Love*.

Romances, which owe their very Being to this Passion, are full of these metaphorical Deaths. Heroes and Heroines, Knights, Squires and Damsels are all of them in a dying Condition. There is the same kind of Mortality in our Modern Tragedies, where every one gasps, faints, bleeds and dies. Many of the Poets, to describe the Execution which is done by this Passion, represent the fair Sex as *Basilisks* that destroy with their Eyes; but I think Mr. *Cowley* has with greater Justness of Thought compared a beautiful Woman to a *Porcupine*, that sends an Arrow from every part.[3]

I have often thought that there is no way so effectual for the Cure of this general Infirmity, as a Man's reflecting upon the Motives that produce it. When the Passion proceeds from the Sense of any Virtue or Perfection in the Person beloved, I would by no means discourage it; but if a Man considers that all his heavy Complaints of Wounds and Deaths rise from some little Affectations of Coquetry, which are improved into Charms by his own fond Imagination,

---

[1] *Motto*. Horace, *Odes*, 2. 13. 13–14:

What each should fly is seldom known,
We unprovided are undone. CREECH.

The motto of *Tatler* 172.

[2] In La Calprenède's *Cassandra*. Cf. No. 199 (vol. ii).

[3] Cowley, *Anacreontiques*, iii (*Poems*, ed. Waller, p. 52):

They are *all weapon*, and they dart
Like *Porcupines* from every part.

the very laying before himself the Cause of his Distemper, may be sufficient to effect the Cure of it.

It is in this view that I have looked over the several Bundles of Letters which I have received from Dying People, and composed out of them the following Bill of Mortality, which I shall lay before my Reader without any further Preface, as hoping that it may be useful to him in discovering those several Places where there is most Danger, and those fatal Arts which are made use of to destroy the Heedless and Unwary.

Lysander, slain at a Puppet-Show on the 3d of *September*.

Thyrsis, shot from a Casement in *Pickadilly*.

T. S. wounded by *Zelinda*'s Scarlet Stocking, as she was stepping out of a Coach.

Will. Simple, smitten at the Opera by the Glance of an Eye that was aimed at one who stood by him.

Tho. Vainlove lost his Life at a Ball.

Tim. Tattle, killed by the tap of a Fan on his Left Shoulder by *Coquetilla*, as he was talking carelessly with her in a Bow-window.

Sir *Simon Softly*, murder'd at the Play-house in *Drury-lane* by a Frown.

Philander, mortally wounded by *Cleora*, as she was adjusting her Tucker.[1]

Ralph Gapely, Esq; hit by a Random Shot at the Ring.[2]

F. R. caught his Death upon the Water, *April* the 31st.

W. W. killed by an unknown Hand, that was playing, with the Glove off, upon the side of the front Box in *Drury-lane*.

Sir *Christopher Crazy*, Bar. hurt by the brush of a Whalebone Petticoat.

Sylvius, shot through the Sticks of a Fan at St. *James*'s Church.[3]

Damon, struck through the Heart by a Diamond Necklace.

Thomas Trusty, *Francis Goosequill*, *William Meanwell*, *Edward Callow* Esqrs; standing in a Row, fell all Four at the same time by an Ogle of the Widow *Trapland*.

Tom Rattle chancing to tread upon a Lady's Tail, as he came out of the Play-House, she turned full upon him, and laid him dead upon the Spot.

[1] Cf. No. 38 (vol. i).
[2] No. 15 (vol. i).
[3] St. James's Church, in Piccadilly, the most fashionable London church in Addison's day. 'St. James within the Liberty of Westminster Church' is described by Hatton (pp. 298–301).

Dick Tastewell, slain by a Blush from the Queen's Box in the Third Act of the *Trip to the Jubilee*.[1]

Samuel Felt, Haberdasher, wounded in his Walk to *Islington*, by Mrs. *Susannah Crossstitch*, as she was clambering over a Stile.

R. F, T. W, S. I, M. P, &c. Put to Death in the last Birth-Day Massacre.[2]

Roger Blinko cut off in the Twenty First Year of his Age by a White-wash.[3]

Musidorus, slain by an Arrow that flew out of a Dimple in *Belinda's* Left Cheek.

Ned Courtly presenting *Flavia* with her Glove (which she had dropped on purpose) she received it, and took away his Life with a Curtsie.

John Gosselin, having received a slight Hurt from a pair of Blue Eyes, as he was making his Escape, was dispatch'd by a Smile.

Strephon, kill'd by *Clarinda* as she looked down into the Pit.

Charles Careless, shot flying by a Girl of Fifteen, who unexpectedly popped her Head upon him out of a Coach.

Josiah Wither, aged Threescore and Three, sent to his long Home by *Elizabeth Jett-well*, Spinster.

Jack Freelove, murder'd by *Melissa* in her Hair.

William Wiseaker, Gent. drowned in a flood of Tears by *Moll. Common*.

John Pleadwell, Esq; of the *Middle Temple*, Barrister at Law, Assassinated in his Chambers the 6th Instant by *Kitty Sly*, who pretended to come to him for his Advice.   I

---

[1] Farquhar's play had been given at Drury Lane on the preceding Tuesday (6 May) with Wilks and Mrs. Oldfield in the principal roles.

[2] The Queen's birthday ball, on 6 Feb.

[3] In *Guardian* 116 Addison writes: 'I have heard a whole Sermon against a White-wash, and have known a coloured Ribbon made the Mark of the Unconverted.' One of the popular whitewashes frequently advertised in the *Spectator* is the following (from No. 374):

The Chrystal Cosmetick approv'd of by the worthy Dr. Paul Chamberline, viz. By washing Morning or Evening, cures all red Faces proceeding from what Cause soever, it takes off all Morphews, Pimples and Freckles; it's of a soft Nature, cleansing and adorning the Face and Hands of both Sexes in a very beautiful Manner, and may be used with as much safety as Milk, having in it no Mercury (so frequently made use off) or any other thing that may be prejudicial to the Body, being the best of this Nature now extant. Price of the larger Bottle 6s. the lesser 3s. Note, To prevent Counterfets, each single Bottle is Tied and Sealed with this Coat of Arms prefix'd; at the Blue Coat-Boy near the Royal-Exchange, Cornhill; at Mr. John Jackson's the Corner of Wood-street, Cheapside; at the Seven-Stars under St. Dunstan's Church, Fleet-street; at Mrs. Bracknocks the upper End of St. James's-street, Piccadilly.

Aggredere, O magnos, aderit jam tempus, honores.

Virg.

I WILL make no Apology for entertaining the Reader with the
following Poem, which is written by a great Genius, a Friend of
mine, in the Country; who is not ashamed to employ his Wit in
the Praise of his Maker.

MESSIAH.[2]

A sacred Eclogue, compos'd of several Passages

of *Isaiah* the Prophet.

Written in Imitation of Virgil's POLLIO.

[a]*YE Nymphs of* Solyma! *begin the Song:*
To heav'nly Themes sublimer Strains belong.
The Mossie Fountains and the Sylvan Shades,
The Dreams of Pindus *and th'* Aonian *Maids,*

[a] *The text of the poem is in roman type in Fol.*

---

[1] *Motto.* Virgil, *Eclogues*, 4. 48:
     Mature in years, to ready Honours move,
     O of Cœlestial Seed! DRYDEN.

[2] This is the first printing of Pope's poem. In a letter to Pope (1 June 1712) Steele
comments on the poem:

     I have turn'd to every verse and chapter, and think you have preserv'd the
sublime heavenly spirit throughout the whole, especially at—*Hark a glad voice*—
and—*The lamb with wolves shall graze*—There is but one line which I think below
the original,
            He wipes the tears for ever from our eyes.
You have express'd it with a good and pious, but not with so exalted and
poetical a spirit as the prophet. *The Lord God will wipe away tears from off all faces.*
If you agree with me in this, alter it by way of paraphrase or otherwise, that when
it comes into a volume it may be amended. Your Poem is already better than the
Pollio. (Pope, *Correspondence*, ed. Sherburn, i. 146.)

As the textual notes show, Pope revised the passage, substituting four lines for the
two in the original.
     In reprinting the poem in his own *Works* Pope made a few further revisions: line 50,
'Seeks freshest pasture'; line 55, 'Thus shall mankind'; and line 84, 'And with their
forky tongue shall innocently play'.
     Two weeks after the publication of this number Pope wrote to Caryll (28 May):
'The eclogue on the Messiah in imitation of Pollio, I had transcribed a week since
with design to send it to you; but finding it printed in the *Spectator* of the fourteenth
(which paper I know is constantly sent down to you) I gave it to Mr Englefield'
(*Corresp.* i. 144).
     A poetical paraphrase of Isaiah lv, inspired by 'your paper of the 14th instant', is
printed in Lillie (ii. 248–52), signed A. B. and dated 'London, May 26, 1712'.

Delight no more—O Thou my Voice inspire
Who touch'd Isaiah's hallow'd Lips with Fire!
   Rapt into future Times, the Bard begun;
A Virgin shall conceive, a Virgin bear a Son!
From Jesse's Root behold a Branch arise,   Isaiae. Cap. 11. v. 1.
Whose sacred Flow'r with Fragrance fills the Skies.
Th' Æthereal Spirit o'er its Leaves shall move,
And on its Top descends the Mystic Dove.
Ye Heav'ns! from high the dewy Nectar pour,   Cap. 45. v. 8.
And in soft Silence shed the kindly Show'r!
The Sick and Weak the healing Plant shall aid;   Cap. 25. v. 4.
From Storms a Shelter, and from Heat a Shade.
All Crimes shall cease, and ancient Fraud shall fail;
Returning Justice lift aloft her Scale;   Cap. 9. v. 7.
Peace o'er the World her Olive-Wand extend,
And white-roab'd Innocence from Heav'n descend.
Swift fly the Years, and rise th' expected Morn!
Oh spring to Light, Auspicious Babe, be born!
See Nature hasts her earliest Wreaths to bring,
With all the Incence of the breathing Spring:
See lofty Lebanon his Head advance,   Cap. 35. v. 2.
See nodding Forests on the Mountains dance,
See spicy Clouds from lowly Saron rise,
And Carmel's flow'ry Top perfumes the Skies!
Hark! a glad Voice the lonely Desert chears: Cap. 40. v. 3-4.
Prepare the Way! a God, a God appears.
A God, a God! the vocal Hills reply,
The Rocks proclaim th' approaching Deity.
Lo Earth receives him from the bending Skies!
Sink down ye Mountains, and ye Vallies rise:
With Heads declin'd, ye Cedars, Homage pay;
Be smooth ye Rocks, ye rapid Floods give way!
The SAVIOR comes! by ancient Bards foretold:
Hear him ye Deaf, and all ye Blind behold!   Cap. 42. v. 18.
He from thick Films shall purge the visual Ray,   Cap. 35. v. 5, 6.
And on the sightless Eye-ball pour the Day.
'Tis he th' obstructed Paths of Sound shall clear,
And bid new Musick charm th' unfolding Ear.
The Dumb shall sing, the Lame his Crutch foregoe,
And leap exulting like the bounding Roe.

^a*No Sigh, no Murmur the wide World shall hear,*
From ev'ry Face he wipes off ev'ry Tear.
In Adamantine Chains shall Death be bound,   Cap. 25. v. 8.
And Hell's grim Tyrant feel th' eternal Wound.^a
As the good Shepherd tends his fleecy Care,   Cap. 40. v. 11.
Seeks freshest Pastures, and the purest Air,
Explores the lost, the wand'ring Sheep directs,
By Day o'ersees them, and by Night protects;
The tender Lambs he raises in his Arms,
Feeds from his Hand, and in his Bosom warms:
Mankind shall thus his Guardian Care ingage,
The promis'd Father of the future Age.   Cap. 9. v. 6.
No more shall Nation against Nation rise,   Cap. 2. v. 4.
Nor ardent Warriors meet with hateful Eyes,
Nor Fields with gleaming Steel be cover'd o'er;
The Brazen Trumpets kindle Rage no more:
But useless Lances into Scythes shall bend,
And the broad Faulchion in a Plow-share end.
Then Palaces shall rise; the joyful Son   Cap. 65. v. 21, 22.
Shall finish what his short-liv'd Sire begun;
Their Vines a Shadow to their Race shall yield;
And the same Hand that sow'd, shall reap the Field.
The Swain in barren Desarts with surprize   Cap. 35. v. 1, 7.
Sees Lillies spring, and sudden Verdure rise;
And Starts, amidst the thirsty Wilds, to hear
New Falls of Water murm'ring in his Ear:
On rifted Rocks, the Dragon's late Abodes,
The green Reed trembles, and the Bulrush nods.
Waste sandy Vallies, once perplex'd with Thorn,   Cap. 41. v. 19. and
The spiry Firr and shapely Box adorn;   Cap. 55. v. 13.
To leaf-less Shrubs the flow'ring Palms succeed,
And od'rous Myrtle to the noisome Weed.
The Lambs with Wolves shall graze the verdant   Cap. 11. v. 6, 7, 8.
    Mead,
And Boys in flow'ry Bands the Tyger lead;
The Steer and Lion at one Crib shall meet;
And harmless Serpents lick the Pilgrim's Feet.

    ^a *No Sigh, . . . Wound.*] *These four lines are substituted in 8vo and 12mo for the following*
two in Folio:
        Before him Death, the grisly Tyrant, flies;   Cap. 25. v. 8.
        He wipes the Tears for ever from our Eyes.

The smiling Infant in his Hand shall take
The crested Basilisk and speckled Snake;
Pleas'd, the green Lustre of the Scales survey,
And with their forky Tongue, and pointless Sting shall play.
Rise, crown'd with Light, Imperial Salem *rise!*　　Cap. 60. v. 1.
Exalt thy Tow'ry Head, and lift thy Eyes!
See, a long Race thy spatious Courts adorn;　　Cap. 60. v. 4.
See future Sons, and Daughters yet unborn
In crowding Ranks on ev'ry Side arise,
Demanding Life, impatient for the Skies!
See barb'rous Nations at thy Gates attend,　　Cap. 60. v. 3.
Walk in thy Light, and in thy Temple bend.
See thy bright Altars throng'd with prostrate Kings,
And heap'd with Products of Sabæan *Springs!*　　Cap. 60. v. 6.
For thee, Idume's *spicy Forests blow;*
And Seeds of Gold in Ophyr's *Mountains glow.*
See Heav'n its sparkling Portals wide display,
And break upon thee in a Flood of Day!
No more the rising Sun *shall gild the Morn,*　　Cap. 60. v. 19, 20.
Nor Evening Cynthia *fill her silver Horn,*
But lost, dissolv'd in thy superior Rays;
One Tyde of Glory, one unclouded Blaze,
O'erflow thy Courts: The LIGHT HIMSELF *shall shine*
Reveal'd; and God's *eternal Day be thine!*
The Seas shall waste; the Skies in Smoke decay;　　Cap. 51. v. 6. and
Rocks fall to Dust, and Mountains melt away;　　Cap. 54. v. 10.
But fix'd His *Word,* His *saving Pow'r remains:*
Thy Realm *for ever lasts! thy own* Messiah *reigns.*

T

No. 379　　　　　　　　　　*Thursday, May* 15, 1712[1]
[BUDGELL]

Scire tuum nihil est nisi te scire hoc sciat alter.

Pers.

I HAVE often wonder'd at that Ill-natur'd Position which has been sometimes maintained in the Schools, and is comprised in

[1] *Motto.* Persius, *Satires,* 1. 27: A Man's Knowledge is worth nothing unless he communicates it to the World; for Science is not Science 'till reveal'd.

an old *Latin* Verse, namely, that *A Man's Knowledge is worth nothing, if he communicates what he knows to any one besides.*[1] There is certainly no more sensible Pleasure to a Good-natured Man, than if he can by any means gratifie or inform the Mind of another. I might add, that this Virtue naturally carries its own Reward along with it, since it is almost impossible it should be exercised without the Improvement of the Person who practises it. The Reading of Books, and the daily Occurrences of Life, are continually furnishing us with Matter for Thought and Reflection. It is extremely natural for us to desire to see such our Thoughts put into the Dress of Words, without which indeed we can scarce have a clear and distinct Idea of them our-selves: When they are thus cloathed in Expressions, nothing so truly shews us whether they are Just or False, as those Effects which they produce in the Minds of others.

I am apt to flatter my self, that in the Course of these my Speculations, I have treated of several Subjects, and laid down many such Rules for the Conduct of a Man's Life, which my Readers were either wholly ignorant of before, or which at least those few who were acquainted with them, looked upon as so many Secrets they had found out for the Conduct of themselves, but were resolved never to have made publick.

I am the more confirmed in this Opinion from my having received several Letters, wherein I am censured for having prostituted Learning to the Embraces of the Vulgar; and made her, as one of my Correspondents phrases it, a Common Strumpet; I am charged by another with laying open the *Arcana*, or Secrets of Prudence to the Eyes of every Reader.

The narrow Spirit, which appears in the Letters of these my Correspondents, is the less surprising, as it has shewn it self in all Ages; there is still extant an Epistle written by *Alexander* the Great, to his Tutor *Aristotle*, upon that Philosopher's publishing some part of his Writings, in which the Prince complains of his having made known, to all the World, those Secrets in Learning, which he had before communicated to him in private Lectures; concluding, *That he had rather excell the rest of Mankind in Knowledge than in Power.*[2]

Luisa de Padilla, a Lady of great Learning, and Countess of *Aranda*, was in like manner angry with the Famous *Gratian*, upon

---

[1] This has not been identified.
[2] Aulus Gellius, *Noctes Atticae*, 20. 5. 7–12; Plutarch, *Alexander*, 7. 4–5.

his publishing his Treatise of the *Discreto*, wherein she fancied that he had laid open those Maxims to common Readers, which ought only to have been reserved for the knowledge of the Great.[1]

These Objections are thought by many of so much weight, that they often defend the abovementioned Authors, by affirming they have affected such an Obscurity in their Stile and Manner of Writing, that, tho' every one may read their Works, there will be but very few who can comprehend their Meaning.

Persius, the *Latin* Satirist, affected Obscurity for another Reason,[2] with which however Mr. *Cowley* is so offended, that writing to one of his Friends, You, says he, tell me, that you do not know whether *Persius* be a good Poet or no, because you cannot understand him, for which very Reason I affirm that he is not so.[3]

However, this Art of *writing unintelligibly* has been very much Improved, and followed by several of the Moderns, who observing the general Inclination of Mankind to dive into a Secret, and the Reputation many have acquired by concealing their Meaning under obscure Terms and Phrases, resolve, that they may be still more abstruse, to write without any Meaning at all: This Art, as it is at present practised by many eminent Authors, consists in throwing so many Words at a venture into different Periods, and leaving the Curious Reader to find out the Meaning of them.

The *Egyptians*, who made use of Hieroglyphicks to signifie several things, expressed a Man who confined his Knowledge and Discoveries altogether within himself, by the Figure of a Dark-Lanthorn closed on all sides, which, tho' it was illuminated within, afforded no manner of Light or Advantage to such as stood by it.[4] For my own part, as I shall from time to time communicate to the Publick whatever Discoveries I happen to make, I should much rather be compared to an ordinary Lamp which consumes and wastes it self for the benefit of every Passenger.

I shall conclude this Paper with the Story of *Rosicrucius*'s Sepul-

[1] The story is told by John Lastanosa, in his Preface to the *Discreto* of Gracián (1655), quoted in the English version (Gracián's *Art of Prudence: or, a Companion for a Man of Sense*, 1702), Preface, A3ᵛ. Budgell probably found it in Bayle, 'Padilla, Louise de', Remark F, where it is quoted.

[2] Dryden discusses this at some length in the *Discourse concerning Satire* (*Essays*, ed. Ker, ii. 69 ff.).

[3] Cowley, Essay 10, 'The Danger of Procrastination' (ed. Waller, p. 454).

[4] A popular symbol for wisdom which is self-contained. Cf. *The Turkish Spy*, ed.1702, v. 77; Voltaire's *English Notebook*, ed. Theodore Besterman (Geneva, 1952), i. 40; &c. Steele repeats it in the Dedication to the original Volume II of the collected *Spectator*.

cher. I suppose I need not inform my Readers that this Man was the Founder of the *Rosicrucian* Sect, and that his Disciples still pretend to new Discoveries, which they are never to Communicate to the rest of Mankind.

A certain Person having occasion to dig somewhat deep in the Ground where this Philosopher lay Interr'd, met with a small Door having a Wall on each side of it. His Curiosity, and the hopes of finding some hidden Treasure, soon prompted him to force open the Door. He was immediately surprized by a sudden blaze of Light, and discovered a very fair Vault: At the upper end of it was the Statue of a Man in Armour sitting by a Table, and leaning on his Left Arm. He held a Truncheon in his Right Hand, and had a Lamp burning before him. The Man had no sooner set one Foot within the Vault, than the Statue erecting it self from its leaning Posture, stood bolt upright; and upon the Fellow's advancing another Step, lifted up the Truncheon in its Right Hand. The Man still ventured a third Step, when the Statue with a furious Blow broke the Lamp in a thousand pieces, and left his Guest in a sudden Darkness.

Upon the Report of this Adventure the Country People soon came with Lights to the Sepulchre, and discovered that the Statue, which was made of Brass, was nothing more than a piece of Clockwork; that the Floor of the Vault was all loose, and underlaid with several Springs, which upon any Man's entring, naturally produced that which had happened.

Rosicrucius, say his Disciples, made use of this Method to shew the World that he had re-invented the ever-burning Lamps of the Ancients, tho' he was resolved no one should reap any Advantage from the Discovery.[1]   X

---

[1] Cowley, in a note to *Davideis* iv, writes of 'the *Lamps* burning in the *Sepulchres* of the Ancients, and going out as soon as ever the *Sepulchres* were opened and air let in' (*Poems*, ed. Waller, p. 380). The *Comte de Gabalis* of the Abbé de Villars had popularized the legends connected with the Rosicrucians. Sir Kenelm Digby (*Of Bodies and of Mans Soul*, chap. viii, sect. 9) writes of the 'lamps pretended to have been found in Tombes with inconsumptive lights'.

A letter from Emilia Lovetruth, dated 14 May (Lillie, ii. 252–6), says of this story: 'What you relate I remember to have read a great while ago, in a history of the invasion of Spain by the Moors, to have happened to their last king of the gothick race. Roderigo, upon opening a supposed enchanted cave, in hopes of finding vast treasures, as the rumour went, were hid there, . . . there was this farther particular, That the cave and all vanished upon extinguishing the light, and left the king so despirited with his disappointment and the consciousness of his crime in ravishing Count Julian's daughter (who in revenge brought in the Moors) that he was easily overcome. It happens I have just done reading the Rosicrucian story in the Fame and Confession, a book published by the fraternity' (pp. 252–3).

No. 380   *Friday, May 16, 1712*[1]
[STEELE]

Rivalem patienter habe . . .
Ovid.

SIR,   *Thursday, May the 8th,* 1712.

'THE Character you have in the World of being the Ladies Philosopher, and the pretty Advice I have seen you give to others in your Papers, makes me address my self to you in this abrupt Manner; and do desire your Opinion what in this Age a Woman may call a Lover. I have lately had a Gentleman that I thought made Pretentions to me, insomuch that most of my Friends took Notice of it, and thought we were really married; which I did not take much Pains to undeceive them, and especially a young Gentlewoman of my particular Acquaintance which was then in the Country. She coming to Town, and seeing our Intimacy so great, she gave her self the liberty of taking me to task concerning it: I ingeniously told her we were not married, but I did not know what might be the Event. She soon got acquainted with the Gentleman, and was pleased to take upon her to examine him about it. Now whether a new Face had made a greater conquest than the old, I'll leave you to judge, but I am informed that he utterly denied all Pretentions to Courtship: But withal profess'd a sincere Friendship for me; but whether Marriages are proposed by way of Friendship or not, is what I desire to know, and what I may really call a Lover. There are so many who talk in a Language, fit only for that Character, and yet guard themselves against speaking in direct Terms to the Point, that it is impossible to distinguish between Courtship and Conversation. I hope you will do me Justice both upon my Lover and my Friend, if they provoke me further; in the mean time I carry it with so equal a Behaviour, that the Nymph and the Swain too are mightily at a loss; each believes, I who know them both well, think my self revenged in their Love to one another, which creates an irreconcilable Jealousy. If all comes right again you shall hear further from,

SIR,   Your most obedient Servant,
Mirtilla.'

---

[1] *Motto.* Ovid, *Ars amatoria,* 2. 539: Patiently your rival bear.

Mr. SPECTATOR, *April* 28. 1712.

'YOUR Observations on Persons that have behaved themselves
irreverently at Church, I doubt not have had[a] a good Effect
on some that have read them:[1] But there is another Fault which[b]
has hitherto escaped your Notice. I mean of such Persons as are
very zealous and punctual to perform an Ejaculation, that is only
preparatory to the Service of the Church, and yet neglect to joyn
in the Service it self. There is an Instance of this in a Friend of WILL.
HONEYCOMB's, who sits opposite to me: He seldom comes in till
the Prayers are about half over; and when he has entered his Seat
(instead of joyning with the Congregation) he devoutly holds his
Hat before his Face for three or four Moments, then bows to all his
Acquaintance, sits down, takes a Pinch of Snuff, (if it be Evening-
Service, perhaps a Nap) and spends the remaining Time in surveying the Congregation. Now, Sir, what I would desire is, that you
will animadvert a little on this Gentleman's Practice. In my Opinion,
this Gentleman's Devotion, Cap in Hand, is only a Complyance to
the Custom of the Place, and goes no further than a little ecclesiastical
good Breeding. If you will not pretend to tell us the Motives that
bring such Triflers to solemn Assemblies, yet let me desire that you
will give this Letter a Place in your Paper; and I shall remain,

SIR,

Your obliged humble Servant,

J. S.'

Mr. SPECTATOR, *May the* 5*th*.

'THE Conversation at a Club, of which I am a Member, last
Night falling upon Vanity and the Desire of being admired,
put me in Mind of relating how agreeably I was entertained at my
own Door last *Thursday* by a clean fresh-coloured Girl, under the
most elegant and the best furnished Milk-Pail I had ever observed.
I was glad of such an Opportunity of seeing the Behaviour of a
Coquet in Low Life, and how she received the extraordinary Notice
that was taken of her; which I found had affected every Muscle of
her Face in the same Manner as it does the Feature of a first Rate
Toast at a Play, or in an Assembly. This Hint of mine made the
Discourse turn upon the Sense of Pleasure; which ended in a general

---

[a] have had] has had *Fol.* [b] which] that *Fol.*

[1] Irreverent behaviour in church is a topic frequently discussed. See especially
No. 259 (vol. ii).

Resolution, that the Milk-Maid enjoys her Vanity as exquisitly as the Woman of Quality. I think it would not be an improper Subject for you to examine this Frailty, and trace it to all Conditions of Life; which is recommended to you as an Occasion of obliging many of your Readers, among the rest,

Your most humble Servant,

T. B.'

SIR,

'COMING last Week into a Coffee-house not far from the *Exchange* with my Basket under my Arm, a *Jew* of considerable Note, as I am informed, takes half a Dozen Oranges of me; and at the same time slides a Guinea into my Hand.[1] I made him a Courtesy and went my Way: He followed me, and finding I was going about my Business, he came up with me and told me plainly, that he gave me the Guinea with no other Intent but to purchase my Person for an Hour. Did you so, Sir, says I? You gave it me then to make me be wicked? I'll keep it to make me honest. However, not to be in the least ungrateful, I promise you I'll lay it out in a couple of Rings, and wear them for your Sake. I am so just, Sir, besides, as to give every Body that asks how I came by my Rings, this Account of my Benefactor: But to save me the Trouble of telling my Tale over and over again, I humbly beg the Favour of you so to tell it once for all, and you will extremely oblige,

Your humble Servant,

May 12, 1712.   Betty Lemon.'

SIR,   St. *Bride's, May* 15. 1712.

'TIS a great deal of pleasure to me, and I dare say will be no less Satisfaction to you, that I have an Opportunity of informing you, that the Gentlemen and others of the Parish of St. *Bride's* have raised a Charity School of fifty Girls, as before of fifty Boys. You were so kind to recommend the Boys to the charitable World;[2] and the other Sex hope you will do them the same Favour in *Friday's Spectator* for *Sunday* next; when they are to appear with their humble Airs, at the Parish Church of St. *Bride's.* Sir, the mention of this may

---

[1] J. J. Welker (*Studies in Philology*, xxviii [1931], 519–21) makes the improbable suggestion that this is a reference to Sir Solomon de Medina, the noted contractor for supplying bread and bread wagons to the allied army and one of the subscribers to the collected *Spectator*.

[2] See No. 294.

possibly be serviceable to the Children; and sure no one will omit a good Action attended with no Expence.

I am,

SIR,

Your very humble Servant,

The Sexton.'

T

No. 381

[ADDISON]

Æquam memento rebus in arduis
Servare mentem, non secùs in bonis
Ab insolenti temperatam
Lætitiâ, moriture Deli.

Hor.

I HAVE always preferred Chearfulness to Mirth. The latter I consider as an Act, the former as an Habit of the Mind. Mirth is short and transient, Chearfulness fixt and permanent. Those are often raised into the greatest Transports of Mirth, who are subject to the greatest Depressions of Melancholy. On the contrary, Chearfulness, tho' it does not give the Mind such an exquisite Gladness, prevents us from falling into any Depths of Sorrow. Mirth is like a Flash of Lightning that breaks thro' a gloom of Clouds, and glitters for a moment: Chearfulness keeps up a kind of Day-light in the Mind, and fills it with a steady and perpetual Serenity.

Men of austere Principles look upon Mirth as too wanton and dissolute for a state of Probation, and as fill'd[a] with a certain Triumph and Insolence of Heart, that is inconsistent with a Life which is every moment obnoxious[2] to the greatest Dangers. Writers

---

[a] and as fill'd] and fill'd *Fol.*

---

[1] *Motto.* Horace, *Odes,* 2. 3. 1–4:

An even Mind in every State,
Amidst the Frowns and Smiles of Fate,
Dear mortal *Delius* always show;
Let not too much of cloudy Fear,
Nor too intemperate Joys appear
Or to contract, or to extend thy Brow. CREECH.

[2] I.e. liable (cf. No. 349).

of this Complexion have observed, that the Sacred Person who was the great Pattern of Perfection was never seen to Laugh.[1]

Chearfulness of Mind is not liable to any of these Exceptions; it is of a serious and composed Nature, it does not throw the Mind into a Condition improper for the present State of Humanity, and is very conspicuous in the Characters of those who are look'd upon as the greatest Philosophers among the Heathens, as well as among those who have been deservedly esteemed as Saints and Holy Men among Christians.

If we consider Chearfulness in three Lights, with regard to our selves, to those we Converse with, and to the great Author of our Being, it will not a little recommend it self on each of these Accounts. The Man who is possessed of this excellent frame of Mind, is not only easie in his Thoughts, but a perfect Master of all the Powers and Faculties of his Soul: His Imagination is always clear, and his Judgment undisturbed: His Temper is even and unruffled, whether in Action or in Solitude. He comes with a Relish to all those Goods which Nature has provided for him, tastes all the Pleasures of the Creation which are poured about him, and does not feel the full weight of those accidental Evils which may befal him.

If we consider him in relation to the Persons whom he converses with, it naturally produces Love and Good-will towards him. A chearful Mind is not only disposed to be affable and obliging, but raises the same good Humour in those who come within its Influence. A Man finds himself pleased, he does not know why, with the Chearfulness of his Companion: It is like a sudden Sun-shine that awakens a secret Delight in the Mind, without her attending to it. The Heart rejoices of its own accord, and naturally flows out into[a] Friendship and Benevolence towards the Person who has so kindly an effect upon it.

When I consider this chearful State of Mind in its third Relation, I cannot but look upon it as a constant habitual Gratitude to the great Author of Nature. An inward Chearfulness is an implicit Praise and Thanksgiving to Providence under all its Dispensations. It is a kind of Acquiescence in the State wherein we are placed, and a secret Approbation of the Divine Will in his Conduct towards Man.

[a] into] in *Fol.*

[1] Donne refers to this tradition in his *Letters* (ed. 1654), pp. 46–47. Other references are collected in *N & Q*, 3rd ser., ix (1866).

There are but two things which, in my Opinion, can reasonably deprive us of this Chearfulness of Heart. The first of these is, the Sense of Guilt: A Man who lives in a State of Vice and Impenitence, can have no Title to that Evenness and Tranquillity of Mind which is the Health of the Soul, and the natural effect of Virtue and Innocence. Chearfulness in an ill Man deserves a harder Name than Language can furnish us with, and is many degrees beyond what we commonly call Folly or Madness.

Atheism, by which I mean a Disbelief of a Supreme Being, and consequently of a future State, under whatsoever Titles it shelters it self, may likewise very reasonably deprive a Man of this Chearfulness of Temper. There is something so particularly gloomy and offensive to Human Nature in the Prospect of Non-Existence,[1] that I cannot but wonder, with many Excellent Writers, how it is possible for a Man to outlive the Expectation of it. For my own part, I think the Being of a God is so little to be doubted, that it is almost the only Truth we are sure of, and such a Truth as we meet with in every Object, in every Occurrence, and in every Thought. If we look into the Characters of this Tribe of Infidels, we generally find they are made up of Pride, Spleen and Cavil: It is, indeed, no wonder that Men, who are uneasie to themselves, should be so to the rest of the World; and how is it possible for a Man to be otherwise than uneasie in himself, who is in Danger every Moment of losing his entire Existence, and dropping into nothing?

The vicious Man and Atheist have therefore no Pretence to Chearfulness, and would act very unreasonably, should they endeavour after it. It is impossible for any one to live in good Humour, and enjoy his present Existence, who is apprehensive either of Torment or of Annihilation; of being miserable, or of not being at all.

After having mentioned these two great Principles, which are destructive of Chearfulness in their own Nature, as well as in right Reason, I cannot think of any other that ought to banish this happy Temper from a Virtuous Mind. Pain and Sickness, Shame and Reproach, Poverty and Old Age, nay Death it self, considering the shortness of their Duration, and the Advantage we may reap from them, do not deserve the Name of Evils. A good Mind may bear up under them with Fortitude, with Indolence, and with Chearfulness

[1] A favourite theme of Tillotson, e.g. Sermon 12, 'Of the Inward Peace and Pleasure which attends Religion' (Works, ed. 1728, i. 102-10). John Scott, in *The Christian Life* (part i, chap. iv), emphasizes 'Chearfulness' as one of the Christian's essential characteristics (ed. 1700, i. 286 ff.).

of Heart. The tossing of a Tempest does not discompose him, which he is sure will bring him to a Joyful Harbour.

A Man, who uses his best Endeavours to live according to the Dictates of Virtue and right Reason has two perpetual Sources of Chearfulness; In the Consideration of his own Nature, and of that Being on whom he has a Dependance. If he looks into himself, he cannot but rejoice in that Existence, which is so lately bestowed upon him, and which, after Millions of Ages, will be still new, and still in its beginning. How many Self-Congratulations naturally arise in the Mind, when it reflects on this its Entrance into Eternity, when it takes a View of those improveable Faculties, which in a few Years, and even at its first setting out, have made so considerable a Progress, and which will be still receiving an increase of Perfection, and consequently an increase of Happiness. The Consciousness of such a Being spreads a perpetual Diffusion of Joy through the Soul of a virtuous Man, and makes him look upon himself every Moment as more happy than he knows how to conceive.

The second Source of Chearfulness to a good Mind, is its Consideration of that Being on whom we have our Dependance, and in whom, though we behold him as yet but in the first faint Discoveries of his Perfections, we see every thing that we can imagine as great, glorious or amiable. We find our selves every where upheld by his Goodness, and surrounded with an Immensity of Love and Mercy. In short, we depend upon a Being, whose Power qualifies him to make us happy by an Infinity of Means, whose Goodness and Truth engage him to make those happy who desire it of him, and whose Unchangeableness will secure us in this Happiness to all Eternity.

Such Considerations, which every one should perpetually cherish in his Thoughts, will banish from us all that secret Heaviness of Heart, which unthinking Men are subject to when they lie under no real Affliction, all that Anguish which we may feel from any Evil that actually oppresses us, to which I may likewise add those[a] little Cracklings of Mirth and Folly that are apter to betray Virtue than support it; and establish in us such an even and chearful Temper, as makes us pleasing to our selves, to those with whom we converse, and to him whom we were made to please.[1]   I

---

a add those] add all those *Fol.*

---

[1] No. 387 serves as a sequel to this number.

Habes confitentem reum.
Tull.

I OUGHT not to have neglected a Request of one of my Correspondents so long as I have; but I dare say I have given him Time
to add Practice to Profession. He sent me some time ago a Bottle or
two of excellent Wine to drink the Health of a Gentleman, who had
by the Penny-Post advertised him of an egregious Errour in his
Conduct. My Correspondent received the Obligation from an
unknown Hand with the Candour which is natural to an ingenuous
Mind; and promises a contrary Behaviour in that Point for the
future: He will offend his Monitor with no more Errours of that
Kind, but thanks him for his Benevolence. This frank Carriage
makes me reflect upon the amiable Atonement a Man makes in an
ingenuous Acknowledgment of a Fault: All such Miscarriages as
flow from Inadvertency are more than repaid by it; for Reason,
though not concerned in the Injury, employs all its Force in the
Atonement. He that says, He did not design to disoblige you in such
an Action, does as much as if he should tell you, That though the
Circumstance which displeased was never in his Thoughts, he has
that Respect for you, that he is unsatisfied till it is wholly out of
yours. It must be confessed, that when an Acknowledgment of an
Offence is made out of Poorness of Spirit, and not Conviction of
Heart, the Circumstance is quite different: But in the Case of my
Correspondent, where both the Notice is taken and the Return
made in private, the Affair begins and ends with the highest Grace
on each Side. To make the Acknowledgment of a Fault in the highest
Manner graceful, it is lucky when the Circumstances of the Offender
place him above any ill Consequences from the Resentment of the
Person offended. A Dauphin of *France*, upon a Review of the Army,
and a Command of the King to alter the Posture of it by a March of
one of the Wings, gave an improper Order to an Officer at the Head
of a Brigade, who told his Highness, He presumed he had not
received the last Orders; which were to move a contrary Way. The
Prince, instead of taking the Admonition which was delivered in
a Manner that accounted for his Errour with Safety to his Understanding, shaked a Cane at the Officer; and with the Return of

[1] *Motto.* Cicero, *Pro Q. Ligario Oratio,* 2: The criminal confesses his guilt.

opprobrious Language persisted in his own Orders. The whole Matter came necessarily before the King, who commanded his Son, on Foot, to lay his right Hand on the Gentleman's Stirrup as he sate on Horseback in Sight of the whole Army, and ask his Pardon. When the Prince touched his Stirrup and was going to speak, the Officer, with an incredible Agility, threw himself on the Earth and kissed his Feet.[1]

The Body is very little concerned in the Pleasures or Sufferings of Souls truly great; and the Reparation, when an Honour was designed this Soldier, appeared as much too great to be born by his Gratitude, as the Injury was intolerable to his Resentment.

When we turn our Thoughts from these extraordinary Occurrences into common Life, we see an ingenuous Kind of Behaviour not only make up for Faults committed, but in a Manner expiate them in the very Commission. Thus many things wherein a Man has pressed too far, he implicitly excuses by owning, *This is a Trespass; You'll pardon my Confidence; I am sensible I have no Pretention to this Favour*, and the like. But commend me to those gay Fellows about Town who are directly impudent, and make up for it no otherwise than by calling themselves such, and exulting in it. But this sort of Carriage, which prompts a Man against Rules to urge what he has a Mind to, is pardonable only when you sue for another. When you are confident in Preference of your self to others of equal Merit, every Man that loves Virtue and Modesty ought, in Defence of those Qualities, to oppose you: But without considering the Morality of the thing, let us at this Time behold only the natural Consequence of Candour when we speak of our selves.

The SPECTATOR writes often in an Elegant, often in an Argumentative, and often in a Sublime Stile, with equal Success; but how would it hurt the reputed Author of that Paper, to own that of the most beautiful Pieces under his Title, he is barely the Publisher?[2] There is nothing but what a Man really performs can be an Honour to him; what he takes more than he ought in the Eye of the World, he loses in the Conviction of his own Heart; and a Man must lose his Consciousness, that is, his very self, before he can rejoice in any Falshood without inward Mortification.

Who has not seen a very Criminal at the Bar, when his Council

---

[1] Steele tells this story again in *The Theatre*, No. 19 (ed. Nichols, i. 153–4). I have not been able to identify it further.

[2] One of Steele's frequent acknowledgements of Addison's share in the *Spectator*.

and Friends have done all that they could for him in vain, prevail upon the whole Assembly to pity him, and his Judge to recommend his Case to the Mercy of the Throne, without offering any thing new in his Defence, but that he whom before we wished Convicted became so out of his own Mouth, and took upon himself all the Shame and Sorrow we were just before preparing for him? The great Opposition to this Kind of Candour, arises from the unjust Idea People ordinarily have of what we call an high Spirit. It is far from Greatness of Spirit to persist in the Wrong in any Thing, nor is it a Diminution of Greatness of Spirit to have been in the Wrong: Perfection is not the Attribute of Man, therefore he is not degraded by the Acknowledgment of an Imperfection: But it is the Work of little Minds to imitate the Fortitude of great Spirits, on worthy Occasions, by Obstinacy in the Wrong. This Obstinacy prevails so far upon them, that they make it extend to the defence of Faults in their very Servants. It would swell this Paper to too great a length, should I insert all the Quarrels and Debates which are now on Foot in this Town;[1] where one Party, and in some Cases both, is sensible of being on the faulty Side, and have not Spirit enough to Acknowledge it. Among the Ladies the Case is very common, for there are very few of them who know that it is to maintain a true and high Spirit, to throw away from it all which it self disapproves, and to scorn so pitiful a shame as that which disables the Heart from acquiring a liberality of Affections and Sentiments. The candid Mind, by acknowledging and discarding its Faults, has Reason and Truth for the Foundation of all its Passions and Desires, and consequently is happy and simple; the disingenuous Spirit by Indulgence of one unacknowledged Errour, is intangled with an After-Life of Guilt, Sorrow and Perplexity.   T

[1] Steele was aware of the political tension at this moment over the prospective peace treaty and was of course preparing for the publication two days later, in No. 384, of the Preface to Bishop Fleetwood's Sermons.

No. 383
[ADDISON]

Tuesday, May 20, 1712[1]

Criminibus debent Hortos . . .

Juv.

AS I was sitting in my Chamber, and thinking on a Subject for my next *Spectator*, I heard two or three irregular Bounces at my Landlady's Door, and upon the opening of it a loud chearful Voice enquiring whether the Philosopher was at Home. The Child who went to the Door answered very Innocently that he did not Lodge there. I immediately recollected that it was my good Friend Sir ROGER's Voice; and that I had promised to[a] go with him on the Water to *Spring-Garden*,[2] in case it proved a good Evening. The Knight put me in mind of my Promise from the bottom of the Stair-Case, but told me that if I was Speculating he wou'd stay below till I had done. Upon my coming down I found all the Children of the Family got about my old Friend, and my Landlady her self, who is a notable prating Gossip, engaged in a Conference with him, being mightily pleased with his stroaking her little Boy upon the Head, and bidding him be a good Child and mind his Book.

We were no sooner come to the *Temple* Stairs, but we were surrounded with a Crowd of Watermen offering us their respective Services. Sir ROGER, after having looked about him very attentively, spied one with a Wooden Leg, and immediately gave him Orders to get his Boat ready. As we were walking towards it, *You must know*, says Sir ROGER, *I never make use of any Body to Row me that has not either lost a Leg or an Arm. I wou'd rather bate him a few Strokes of his Oar, than not Employ an honest Man that has been wounded in the Queen's Service. If I was a Lord, or a Bishop, and kept a Barge, I wou'd not put a Fellow in my Livery that had not a Wooden Leg.*

---

[a] promised to] promised him to Fol.

[1] *Motto.* Juvenal, *Satires*, I. 75: To crimes they owe their gardens.

[2] The Spring Gardens at Vauxhall, or Fox-hall, lying across the river south-east of Westminster Abbey, are frequently mentioned, by Pepys and others, as a famous pleasure resort. Uffenbach (*London in 1710*, p. 131) paid a visit on 19 July 1710 to

Foxhall, where there is a large garden of matchless elegance called the Spring Garden, because it is most agreeable in spring, when vast quantities of birds nest and sing there. It consists entirely of avenues and covered walks where people stroll up and down, and green huts, in which one can get a glass of wine, snuff and other things, although everything is very dear and bad. Generally vast crowds are to be seen here, especially females of doubtful morals, who are dressed as finely as ladies of quality, most of them having a gold watch hung round their neck.

My old Friend, after having seated himself, and trimmed the Boat with his Coachman, who, being a very sober Man, always serves for Ballast on these Occasions, we made the best of our way for *Fox-hall*. Sir ROGER obliged the Waterman to give us the History of his Right Leg, and hearing that he had left it at *La Hogue*,ᵃ¹ with many Particulars which passed in that glorious Action, the Knight in the Triumph of his Heart made several Reflections on the Greatness of the *British* Nation; as, that one *Englishman* cou'd beat three *Frenchmen*; that we cou'd never be in Danger of Popery so long as we took care of our Fleet; that the *Thames* was the noblest River in *Europe*; that *London-bridge* was a greater Piece of Work than any of the Seven Wonders of the World; with many other honest Prejudices whichᵇ naturally cleave to the Heart of a true *Englishman*.

After some short Pause, the old Knight turning about his Head twice or thrice, to take a Survey of this great Metropolis, bid me observe how thick the City was set with Churches, and that there was scarce a single Steeple on this side *Temple-bar*. *A most Heathenish Sight!* says Sir ROGER: *There is no Religion at this End of the Town. The Fifty new Churches*² *will very much mend the Prospect; but Church-work is slow, Church-work is slow!*

I do not remember I haveᶜ any where mentioned, in Sir ROGER's Character, his Custom of Saluting every Body that passes by him, with a Good-morrow, or a Good-night. This the Old-Man does out of the Overflowings of his Humanity, tho' at the same time it renders him so popular among all his Country Neighbours, that it is thought to have gone a good way in making him once or twice Knight of the Shire.³ He cannot forbear this Exercise of Benevolence even in Town, when he meets with any one in his Morning or Evening Walk. It broke from him to several Boats that passed by us upon the Water; but to the Knight's great Surprise, as he gave the

---

ᵃ at *La Hogue*.] in *Bantry Bay*, Fol.   ᵇ which] that *Fol.*   ᶜ remember
I have] remember that I have *Fol.*

---

¹ In the Battle of La Hogue (19 May 1692) the English had destroyed a number of the enemy's ships and prevented a threatened invasion by the French. In the Folio issue the reference was to Bantry Bay (1 May 1689), where the English had been forced by the French to retire.

² The House of Commons had passed resolutions in 1711 for the building of fifty new churches, with the help of £350,000 of public money. At this time there were only 28 parish churches and 18 chapels of ease, within the bills of mortality, as against 88 dissenting chapels. Actually not half the proposed fifty new churches were built, but much of the allotted money was used in restoring and repairing the old.

³ M.P. for the county: see No. 109 (vol. i).

Good-night to two or three young Fellows a little before our Landing, one of them, instead of returning the Civility, asked us what Queer old Putt we had in the Boat; and whether he was not ashamed to go a Wenching at his Years? with a great deal of the like *Thames*-Ribaldry. Sir ROGER seemed a little shocked at first, but at length assuming a Face of Magistracy, told us, *that if he were a* Middlesex *Justice, he would make such Vagrants know that Her Majesty's Subjects were no more to be abused by Water than by Land.*

We were now Arrived at *Spring-Garden*, which is exquisitely pleasant at this time of Year. When I considered the Fragrancy of the Walks and Bowers with the Choirs of Birds that sung upon the Trees, and the loose Tribe of People that walked under their Shades, I could not but look upon the place as a kind of *Mahometan* Paradise. Sir ROGER told me, it put him in mind of a little Coppice by his House in the Country, which his Chaplain used to call an Aviary of Nightingales. *You must understand*, says the Knight, *there is nothing in the World that pleases a Man in Love so much as your Nightingale. Ah, Mr.* SPECTATOR! *The many Moonlight Nights that I have walked by my self, and thought on the Widow by the Musick of the Nightingale!*[a] He here fetched a deep Sigh, and was falling into a fit of musing, when a Masque, who came behind him, gave him a gentle Tap upon the Shoulder, and asked him if he would drink a Bottle of Mead with her? But the Knight being startled at so unexpected a Familiarity, and displeased to be interrupted in his Thoughts of the Widow, told her *She was a wanton Baggage*, and bid her go about her Business.

We concluded our Walk with a Glass of *Burton*-Ale,[1] and a slice of Hung Beef. When we had done eating our selves, the Knight called a Waiter to him, and bid him carry the Remainder to a Waterman that had but one Leg. I perceived the Fellow stared upon him at the Oddness of the Message, and was going to be saucy; upon which I ratified the Knight's Commands with a Peremptory Look.

As we were going out of the Garden, my old Friend thinking himself obliged, as a Member of the *Quorum*,[2] to animadvert upon the Morals of the Place, told the Mistress of the House, who sat at

[a] *Nightingale!*] *Nightingales!* Fol.

[1] 'A Song in Praise of Burton Ale set by Mr. John Barrett' is included in *The Bottle Companions, or Bacchanalian Club* (1709), p. 15; it begins: 'Give us noble Ale, of the right Burton pale.' Among the household goods of the late Duke of Hamilton to be sold at auction (*Post Boy*, 18 Dec. 1712) are 'Four Hogsheads of fine Burton-Ale'.
[2] See No. 2 (vol i).

the Bar, That he should be a better Customer to her Garden, if
there were more Nightingales,[1] and fewer Strumpets.   I

No. 384   *Wednesday, May 21, 1712*[2]

[STEELE; FLEETWOOD]

Hague, May 24. N. S. The same Republican Hands, who
have so often since the Chevalier *de S. George*'s Recovery, killed
him in our publick Prints, have now reduced the young Dauphin
of *France* to that desperate Condition of Weakness, and Death
it self, that it is hard to conjecture what Method they will take
to bring him to Life again. Mean time, we are assur'd, by a very
good Hand from *Paris*, That on the 20th Instant, this young
Prince was as well as ever he was known to be since the Day
of his Birth. As for the other, they are now sending his Ghost
we suppose, (for they never had the Modesty to contradict

---

[1] On 17 May 1711 Swift paid a visit to Vauxhall with Lady Kerry and Mrs. Pratt
'to hear the nightingals; but they are almost past singing' (*Journal to Stella*, ed.
Williams, p. 272).

[2] *Motto*. The passage from the Tory *Post Boy* of the preceding day comes from
a column beginning: 'On Saturday last arriv'd Tuesday's Mail from Holland; as did
yesterday that of Friday; with the following Advices.' Steele omits three sentences
relating to the 'voyage of the Earl of Strafford into England', just before the final
sentence.

The young Dauphin, the future Louis XV, was an infant of two at this time, having
been born 15 Feb. 1710, a great-grandson of Louis XIV. His parents (the Duke and
Duchess of Burgundy) and his elder brother had recently died. The Chevalier de
St. George was, of course, the Pretender, son of James II. Reports that both the
Dauphin and the Chevalier were seriously ill were current in the public prints.
According to the *Daily Courant* (15 May) and the *Post Boy* (22 May) the Pope had
ordered prayers for the recovery of the Chevalier de St. George from smallpox. The
Daily Courant of 19 May printed two dispatches from Holland reporting that the
young Dauphin was near death; the same paper on the following day reported that
he was 'a little better', but still dangerously ill.

The Baron de Bothmar, the envoy from Hanover to Great Britain, had recently
gone to Utrecht as the Elector's representative to the peace conference there. *The
Elector of Hanover's Memorial to the Queen of Great Britain, relating to the Peace with France*,
published on 28 Nov. 1711 by Lintott, had stirred up a political tempest and made
Bothmar unpopular with the Tory leaders. A second edition was published on
11 December (advertised in *Post-Man*).

The *Observator* of 21 May also attacks this issue of the *Post Boy*, and the passage
quoted by Steele is also singled out for notice in The *Medley* (No. 24 of the J. Baker
series) for 23 May, as 'a very unfortunate Passage'. The *British Mercury* of the same
date announces a report 'that Abel Roper [the writer of the *Post Boy*] is taken up by
the Government, on Account of his Post-Boy of the 20th'.

their Assertions of his Death) to *Commerci* in *Lorain,* attended only by four Gentlemen, and a few Domesticks of little Consideration. *The Baron* de Bothmar *having delivered in his Credentials, to qualify him as an Ambassador to this State,* (an Office *to which his greatest Enemies will acknowledge him to be* equal*!) is* gone to Utrecht, *whence he will proceed to* Hanover, *but not stay long at that Court, for Fear the Peace should be made during his* lamented *Absence! Post-Boy, May* 20.

I SHOULD *be thought not able to read, should I overlook some excellent Pieces lately come out. My Lord Bishop of St.* Asaph[1] *has just now published some Sermons,*[2] *the Preface to which seems to me to determine a great*

---

[1] William Fleetwood (1656–1723), the prominent and popular Whig preacher, who nevertheless won the favour of Queen Anne and was appointed by her in 1708 Bishop of St. Asaph. On the general Fast Day, 16 Jan. 1711/12, he was chosen to preach before the House of Lords and selecting as his subject 'the people that delight in war' (Ps. lxviii. 30) strongly defended the necessity of the war. The Tory ministry adjourned the House beyond the day fixed for the sermon, so that it was not delivered; but it was printed almost at once (19 Jan.) and widely advertised. The advertisement in No. 279 (vol. ii) announces that it is 'Printed for Sam. Buckley' and 'Published by A. Baldwin in Warwick-Lane'—both persons, of course, connected with the publication of the *Spectator.* After the accession of George I Fleetwood was translated, on 19 Nov. 1714, to Ely.

[2] Bishop Fleetwood's book is advertised in the *Daily Courant* (14 May):

Four Sermons. I. On the Death of Queen Mary, 1694. II. On the Death of the Duke of Gloucester, 1700. III. On the Death of King William, 1701. IV. On the Queen's Accession to the Throne, in 1703. With a large Preface. By William Lord Bishop of St. Asaph. Printed for Charles Harper, at the Flower-de-luce over-against St. Dunstan's Church in Fleetstreet.

A second edition was published on 26 May (advertisement in No. 388). The Preface, which Steele here reprints in full, is a vigorous defence of the Whigs' support of the Act of Settlement in favour of the Hanoverian claim to the throne, and a warning against the Tories' attempt to weaken this claim. (In line 2 of the Preface [p. 441] Fleetwood's text reads: 'above eight Years'.)

The Tory leaders were quick to take action upon the publication of the *Sermons.* On 10 June (the birthday of the Chevalier de St. George, as the *Medley* [J. Baker issue] of 13 June pointed out) a complaint was brought in to the House of Commons regarding the Preface. The Commons then resolved that the said Preface was 'malicious and factious', and ordered it to be 'burnt by the Hands of the common Hangman, upon Thursday next at Twelve of the Clock, in the Palace-Yard, Westminster' (*Political State,* June 1712, iii. 458–9).

Three days after the publication of No. 384 William Wagstaffe devoted the entire issue of the *Plain Dealer* (No. 7) to a denunciation of Mr. Spectator, accusing him of writing 'out of a Mercenary Consideration', and warning the Bishop of St. Asaph that if 'he flatters himself with the Thoughts of an Ar——ck, or any such Preferment, upon a Turn of the Ministry as may not happen in his Days, 'tis a Thousand to One but he will be baulked in his Endeavours . . .'. As for Mr. Spectator, the *Plain Dealer* laments 'that any one who is capable of Composing with all the Delicacy of Wit and Humour, as you are, who will be deservedly admired, as long as Arts and Sciences shall flourish, or our Language be intelligible, should be oblig'd to write in haste, *Recommend* or *Censure,* according as he is paid, and prostitute his Pen for a tolerable Subsistence'. A mock advertisement concludes this issue of the *Plain Dealer:*

A Gentleman having Yesterday, bought the 4 Sermons and Preface, lately

Point. He has, like a good Man and a good Christian, in Opposition to all the Flattery and base Submission of false Friends to Princes, asserted, That Christianity left us where it found us as to our civil Rights. The present Entertainment shall consist only of a Sentence out of the Post-Boy, *and the said Preface of my Lord of St.* Asaph. *I should think it a little odd if the Author of the* Post-Boy *should with Impunity call Men Republicans for a Gladness on Report of the Death of the Pretender; and treat Baron* Both-mar, *the Minister of* Hanover, *in such a Manner as you see in my Motto. I must own, I think, every Man in* England *concerned to support the Succession of that Family.*

'THE Publishing a few Sermons, whilst I live, the latest of which was preach'd about eight Years since, and the first above seventeen, will make it very natural for People to inquire into the Occasion of doing so: And to such I do very willingly assign these following Reasons.

printed, is willing to dispose of them at the Prices following, viz. The Sermons at One Shilling, the Preface at Three Half Pence, making together, the Sum of Thirteen Pence Half Penny, and the Binding into the Bargain. Enquire at the Corner of Beauford Buildings [Charles Lillie's address].

This number of the *Plain Dealer* is reprinted in William Wagstaffe's *Miscellaneous Works* (1726), pp. 249–58.

A number of pamphlets, pro and con, ensued. See *Political State*, June 1712, iii. 452–9, and John C. Stephens, Jr., 'Steele and the Bishop of St. Asaph's Preface', *PMLA*, lxvii (1952), 1011–23. Fleetwood himself wrote, in a letter to Bishop Burnet, 17 June 1712: 'If their Design was to intimidate me, they have lost it utterly; or, if to suppress the Book, it happens much otherwise, for every Body's Curiosity is awakened by this Usage, and the Bookseller finds his Account in it, above any one else. The *Spectator* has conveyed above 14,000 of them into other People's Hands, that would otherwise have never seen or heard of it' (*A Compleat Collection of the Sermons, Tracts, and Pieces . . . by the Right Reverend Dr. William Fleetwood* [1737], p. vi). Although the Bishop's estimate of the number of *Spectators* printed on this date seems optimistic, there can be no question of the aid given to Fleetwood's Preface by this journalistic *coup*. It was Mr. Spectator's most daring venture into the political battle. According to Nichols this number 'was not published till 12 o'clock, that it might come out precisely at the hour of her Majesty's breakfast, and that no time might be left for deliberating about serving it up with that meal, as usual'.

Even the *Examiner* (29 May 1712), in an attack on Fleetwood's Preface, admitted that the *Spectator* had done much to advertise the work. It would have lain in obscurity 'if, to make it circulate through all *England*, at the Price of one Peny, which it would never have done for Half a Crown, the *Spectator* had not thought fit to revive it as an extraordinary Piece, which I freely own it to be'. Swift's *Letter of Thanks from my Lord W*[harto]*n to the Lord B*[p] *of S. Asaph, in the Name of the Kit-Cat-Club*, printed anonymously in July, attempts to show that the Preface will please all the atheists in the kingdom, and indulges in ironic praise of the Bishop's style, particularly his repetition of the word *such*. 'O! the irresistible Charm of the Word *Such*! . . . I am resolved to employ the *Spectator*, or some of his Fraternity, (Dealers in Words) to write an Encomium upon SUCH' (*Prose Works*, ed. Davis, vi. 153). The Tories' irritation over the Preface and the *Spectator*'s share in circulating it is further evidenced in the *Examiner* for 24 July, in which Swift again attacks the Bishop (ibid. vi. 159).

'First, From the Observations I have been able to make, for these many Years last past, upon our publick Affairs; and from the natural Tendency of several Principles and Practices, that have, of late, been studiously revived, and from what has followed thereupon, I could not help both fearing and presaging, that these Nations would, some Time or other, if ever we should have an enterprizing Prince upon the Throne, of more Ambition than Virtue, Justice, and true Honour, fall into the Way of all other Nations, and lose their *Liberty*.

'Nor could I help foreseeing, to whose Charge, a great deal of this dreadful Mischief, whenever it should happen, would be laid, whether justly or unjustly was not my Business to determine; but I resolv'd, for my own particular Part, to deliver my self, as well as I could, from the Reproaches and the Curses of Posterity, by publickly declaring to all the World, that altho' in the constant Course of my Ministry, I have never failed, on proper Occasions, to recommend, urge, and insist upon, the loving, honouring, and the reverencing the Prince's Person, and holding it, according to the Laws, inviolable and sacred, and paying all Obedience and Submission to the Laws, tho' never so hard and inconvenient to private People: Yet did I never think my self at Liberty, or authoriz'd to tell the People, that either *Christ*, St. *Peter*, or St. *Paul*, or any other holy Writer, had, by any Doctrine delivered by them, subverted the *Laws* and *Constitutions* of the Country, in which they lived; or put them in a worse Condition, with Respect to their Civil Liberties, than they would have been, had they not been Christians. I ever thought it a most impious Blasphemy against that Holy Religion, to father any thing upon it, that might encourage Tyranny, Oppression, or Injustice, in a Prince; or that easily tended to make a free, and happy People, *Slaves*, and *miserable*. No: People may make themselves as wretched as they will; but let not God be called into that wicked Party. When Force, and Violence, and hard Necessity, have brought the Yoak of Servitude upon a Peoples Neck, Religion will supply them with a patient and submissive Spirit under it, 'till they can innocently shake it off: But certainly Religion never puts it on. This always was, and this at present is, my Judgment of these Matters: And I would be transmitted to Posterity (for the little share of Time such Names as mine can live) under the Character of one who loved his Country, and would be thought a *good Englishman*, as well as a *good Clergyman*.

'This Character I thought would be transmitted, by the following Sermons, which were made for, and preached in a private Audience, when I could think of nothing else but doing my Duty on the Occasions that were then offer'd by God's Providence, without any manner of Design of making them publick: And, for that Reason, I give them now, as they were then delivered. By which I hope to satisfie those People who have objected a Change of Principles to Me, as if I were not now the same Man I formerly was. I never had but one Opinion of these Matters; and that I think is so reasonable and well grounded, that I believe I never can have any other.

'Another Reason of my publishing these Sermons, at this time, is, that I have a Mind to do my self some Honour, by doing what Honour I could to the Memory of Two most excellent Princes, and who have very highly deserved at the Hands of all the People of these Dominions, who have any true Value for the *Protestant Religion*, and the *Constitution* of the *English Government*, of which they were the great *Deliverers*, and *Defenders*. I have lived to see their illustrious Names very rudely handled, and the great Benefits they did this Nation, treated slightly, and contemptuously. I have lived to see our Deliverance from *Arbitrary Power*, and *Popery*, traduced and vilified by some who formerly thought it was their greatest Merit, and made it Part of their Boast and Glory, to have had a little Hand and Share in bringing it about: And others who, without it, must have lived in Exile, Poverty, and Misery, meanly disclaiming it, and using ill *the Glorious Instrument* thereof. Who could expect such a Requital of such Merit? I have, I own it, an Ambition of exempting my self from the Number of *unthankful* People. And as I loved and honoured those Great Princes living, and lamented over them when dead, so I would gladly raise them up a Monument of Praise, as lasting as any Thing of mine can be; and I choose to do it at this Time, when it is so unfashionable a Thing to speak honourably of them.

'The Sermon that was preached upon the Duke of *Gloucester*'s Death, was printed quickly after, and is now, because the Subject was so suitable, joyn'd to the others. The Loss of that most promising and hopeful Prince was, at that Time, I saw, unspeakably great; and many Accidents since have convinced us, that it could not have been over-valued. That precious Life, had it pleased God to have prolonged it to the usual Space, had saved us many Fears, and Jealousies, and dark Distrusts, and prevented many Alarms, that have long kept us, and will keep us still, waking and uneasy. Nothing remained to comfort and support us, under this heavy Stroke, but the Necessity it brought the King and Nation under, of settling the *Succession* in the House of HANOVER, and giving it an *Hereditary Right*, by *Act* of *Parliament*, as long as it continues *Protestant*. So much Good did God, in his merciful Providence, produce from a Misfortune, which we could never otherwise have sufficiently deplored.

'The fourth Sermon was preached upon the Queen's *Accession* to the Throne, and in the first Year in which that Day was solemnly observed (for by some Accident or other, it had been over-looked the Year before) and every one will see, without the Date of it, that it was preached very early in this Reign, since I was able only to *promise* and *presage* its future Glories and Successes, from the good Appearances of Things, and the happy Turn our Affairs began to take; and could not then count up the Victories and Triumphs that, for seven Years after, made it, in the Prophets Language, *a Name, and a Praise among all the People of the Earth*.[1] Never did seven such Years together pass over the Head of any *English Monarch*, nor cover it with so much Honour: The Crown and Sceptre seemed to be the *Queen*'s least Ornaments. Those, other Princes wore in common with Her: And Her great personal Virtues were the same before, and since. But such was the Fame of Her Administration of Affairs at home; such was the Reputation of Her Wisdom and Felicity in choosing Ministers; and such was then esteemed their Faithfulness and Zeal, their Diligence and great Abilities in executing Her Commands: To such a Height of military Glory did Her Great *General* and Her *Armies* carry the *British* Name abroad: Such was the Harmony and Concord betwixt Her and Her *Allies*: And such was the Blessing of God upon all Her Councels and Undertakings, that I am as sure as History can make me, no Prince of Ours was ever yet so prosperous and successful, so loved, esteemed, and honoured, by their Subjects and their Friends, nor near so formidable to their Enemies. We were, as all the World imagined then, just entring on the Ways that promised to lead to such a Peace, as would have answered all the Prayers of our religious Queen, the Care and Vigilance of a most able Ministry, the Payments of a willing and obedient People, as well as all the glorious Toils and Hazards of the Soldiery; when God, for our Sins, permitted *the Spirit of Discord* to go

[1] Zeph. iii. 20.

forth, and, by troubling sore the Camp, the City, and the Country, (and oh that it had altogether spared the Places sacred to his Worship!) to spoil, for a Time, this beautiful and pleasing Prospect; and give us, in its Stead, I know not what —— Our Enemies will tell the rest with Pleasure. It will become me better to pray to God to restore us to the Power of obtaining such a Peace, as will be to his Glory, the Safety, Honour, and the Welfare of the Queen and her Dominions, and the general Satisfaction of all Her High and Mighty Allies.

'May 2, 1712.'   T[1]

No. 385   *Thursday, May 22, 1712*[2]
[BUDGELL]

> . . . *Theseâ pectora juncta fide.*
> Ovid.

I INTEND the Paper for this Day as a loose Essay upon *Friendship*, in which I shall throw my Observations together without any set form, that I may avoid repeating what has been often said on this Subject.

Friendship is *a strong and habitual Inclination in two Persons, to promote the Good and Happiness of one another.* Tho' the Pleasures and Advantages of Friendship have been largely celebrated by the best Moral Writers, and are considered by all as great Ingredients of Human Happiness, we very rarely meet with the Practice of this Virtue in the World.

Every Man is ready to give in a long Catalogue of those Virtues and good Qualities he expects to find in the Person of a Friend, but very few of us are careful to cultivate them in our selves.

Love and Esteem are the first Principles of Friendship, which always is imperfect where either of these two is wanting.

As on the one hand, we are soon ashamed of loving a Man whom

---

[1] A letter signed A. B. (Lillie. ii. 357–60) deplores the political tone of this number—'such bad symptoms as threaten you with a more speedy dissolution than the Post-boy seems to apprehend for his beloved Dauphin or Pretender: for, if I am informed right, it was an unfortunate touch of politicks that slew you when a tatler' (p. 357).

[2] *Motto.* Ovid, *Tristia*, 1. 3. 66: 'Hearts joined with love as strong as Theseus'.

we cannot Esteem: So, on the other, tho' we are truly sensible of a Man's Abilities, we can never raise our selves to the warmths of Friendship, without an affectionate Good-will towards his Person.

Friendship immediately banishes Envy under all its Disguises. A Man who can once doubt whether he should rejoice in his Friend's being happier than himself, may depend upon it, that he is an utter Stranger to this Virtue.

There is something in Friendship so very great and noble, that in those fictitious Stories which are invented to the Honour of any particular Person, the Authors have thought it as necessary to make their Hero a Friend as a Lover. *Achilles* has his *Patroclus*, and *Æneas* his *Achates*. In the first of these Instances we may observe, for the Reputation of the Subject I am treating of, that *Greece* was almost ruin'd by the Hero's Love, but was preserved by his Friendship.

The Character of *Achates* suggests to us an Observation we may often make on the Intimacies of great Men, who frequently chuse their Companions rather for the Qualities of the Heart than those of the Head, and prefer Fidelity in an easie inoffensive complying Temper to those Endowments which make a much greater Figure among Mankind. I do not remember that *Achates*, who is represented as the first Favourite, either gives his Advice, or strikes a Blow, thro' the whole *Aeneid*.[1]

A Friendship which makes the least Noise is very often most useful, for which Reason I should prefer a prudent Friend to a zealous one.

Atticus,[2] one of the best Men of ancient *Rome*, was a very remark-

[1] Addison had made a similar comment in No. 273 (vol. ii): though Achates 'is stiled the Hero's Friend, he does nothing in the whole Poem which may deserve that Title'. Cf. also Addison's remark concerning Virgil in the *Discourse on Ancient and Modern Learning*: 'His *Æneas* is a Compound of Valour and Piety, *Achates* calls himself his Friend, but takes no occasion of showing himself so . . .' (Guthkelch, ii. 451).

[2] The material in this and the following paragraph is taken from Bayle. In the article 'Atticus' Bayle writes that he 'passes for one of the best Men of ancient *Rome*. He carried himself so uprightly that without deviating from the Rules of an exact Neutrality he preserv'd the Esteem and Affection of Two contrary Parties.' Then follows Bayle's Remark A:

He sent Money to the Son of *Marius* who was declared an Enemy to the Republick, and insinuated himself so far into *Sylla*'s Favour that that General would always have him near him. . . . He kept quiet in *Rome* during the War between *Caesar* and *Pompey*; this did not displease *Pompey*, and it pleas'd *Caesar* exceedingly. After the Death of the latter, he sent Money to *Brutus* when the Party for Liberty began to decline, and did a thousand good Offices to *Mark Anthony*'s Wife and Friends, when that Party seem'd to be ruin'd past all Recovery. . . . Lastly, notwithstanding the bloody Dissentions that were rais'd between *Mark Anthony* and *Augustus*, our *Atticus* maintain'd himself in both their Friendships. One of them [marginal note: 'To wit, Augustus, Cornel. Nepos, in vita Attici, c. 20'] whenever he was upon

able Instance of what I am here speaking. This extraordinary Person, amidst the Civil Wars of his Country, when he saw the Designs of all Parties equally tended to the Subversion of Liberty, by constantly preserving the Esteem and Affection of both the Competitors, found means to serve his Friends on either side; and while he sent Mony to young *Marius*, whose Father was declared an Enemy of the Common-wealth, he was himself one of *Sylla*'s chief Favourites, and always near that General.

During the War between *Cæsar* and *Pompey* he still maintained the same Conduct; after the Death of *Cæsar* he sent Mony to *Brutus* in his Troubles, and did a thousand good Offices to *Anthony*'s Wife and Friends when that Party seemed ruined. Lastly, even in that Bloody War between *Anthony* and *Augustus*, *Atticus* still kept his place in both their Friendships; insomuch that the first, says *Cornelius Nepos*,[a] whenever he was absent from *Rome* in any part of the Empire writ punctually to him what he was doing, what he read, and whither he intended to go; and the latter gave him constantly an exact Account of all his Affairs.

A Likeness of Inclinations in every Particular is so far from being requisite to form a Benevolence in two Minds towards each other, as it is generally imagined, that I believe we shall find some of the firmest Friendships to have been contracted between Persons of different Humours; the Mind being often pleased with those Perfections which are new to it, and which it does not find among its own Accomplishments. Besides that a Man in some measure supplies his own Defects, and fancies himself at second hand possessed of those good Qualities and Endowments which are in the Possession of him who in the Eye of the World is looked on as his *other self*.

The most difficult Province in Friendship is the letting a Man see his Faults and Errors; which should, if possible, be so contrived that he may perceive our Advice is given him not so much to please our selves as for his own Advantage. The Reproaches therefore of a Friend should always be strictly just, and not too frequent.

The violent Desire of pleasing in the Person reproved, may other-

[a] first, says *Cornelius Nepos*,] first says, *Cornelius Nepos* Fol.

a Progress, writ punctually to him what he was doing, what he read, and whither he was to go; and when he was at *Rome*, he writ almost every Day to him for his Advice on some Question; the other [marginal note: 'To wit, Mark Anthony, ibid.'] gave him constantly an exact Account of his Affairs.

It will be noted that Budgell has inadvertently reversed the two citations from Cornelius Nepos.

wise change into a Despair of doing it, while he finds himself cen-sur'd for Faults he is not Conscious of. A Mind that is softened and humanised by Friendship cannot bear frequent Reproaches; either it must quite sink under the Oppression, or abate considerably of the Value and Esteem it had for him who bestows them.

The proper Business of Friendship is to inspire Life and Courage, and a Soul thus supported outdoes it self; whereas if it be unex-pectedly deprived of these Succours it droops and languishes.

We are in some measure more inexcusable if we violate our Duties to a Friend, than to a Relation, since the former arise from a volun-tary Choice, the latter from a Necessity to which we could not give our own Consent.

As it has been said on one side that a Man ought not to break with a faulty Friend, that he may not expose the Weakness of his Choice; it will doubtless hold much stronger with respect to a worthy one, that he may never be upbraided for having lost so valuable a Treasure which was once in his Possession.   X

No. 386   *Friday, May 23, 1712*[1]
[STEELE]

Cum Tristibus severe, cum Remissis jucunde, cum Senibus graviter, cum Juventute comiter Vivere.

Tull.

THE Piece of *Latin* on the Head of this Paper is Part of a Character extremely vitious, but I have set down no more than may fall in with the Rules of Justice and Honour. *Cicero* spoke it of *Catiline*, who, he said, lived with the Sad severely, with the Chearful agreeably, with the Old gravely, with the Young pleas-antly;[2] he added, with the Wicked boldly, with the Wanton lasciviously. The two last Instances of his Complaisance I forbear to consider, having it in my Thoughts at present only to speak of obsequious Behaviour as it sits upon a Companion in Pleasure, not a Man of Design and Intreague. To vary with every Humour in this

[1] *Motto. Cicero, Oratio pro M. Caelio, 6. 13. (Translated in the second sentence below.)*
[2] *Cowley uses this illustration from Cicero in his essay 'Of Liberty' (Essays, ed. Waller, p. 379).*

Manner cannot be agreeable, except it comes from a Man's own Temper and natural Complection; to do it out of an Ambition to excel that Way, is the most fruitless and unbecoming Prostitution imaginable. To put on an artful Part to obtain no other End[a] but an unjust Praise from the Undiscerning, is of all Endeavours the most despicable. A Man must be sincerely pleased to become Pleasure, or not to interrupt that of others: For this Reason it is a most calamitous Circumstance, that many People who want to be alone, or should be so, will come into Conversation. It is certain, that all Men who are the least given to Reflection, are seized with an Inclination that Way; when, perhaps, they had rather be inclined to Company; but indeed they had better go home, and be tired with themselves, than force themselves upon others to recover their good Humour. In all this the Cases of communicating to a Friend a sad Thought or Difficulty, in order to relieve an heavy Heart, stands excepted; but what is here meant, is, that a Man should always go with Inclination to the Turn of the Company he is going into, or not pretend to be of the Party. It is certainly a very happy Temper to be able to live with all Kinds of Dispositions, because it argues a Mind that lies open to receive what is pleasing to others, and not obstinately bent on any Particularity of its own.

This is it that makes me pleased with the Character of my good Acquaintance *Acasto*. You meet him at the Tables and Conversations of the Wise, the Impertinent, the Grave, the Frolick, and the Witty; and yet his own Character has nothing in it that can make him particularly agreeable to any one Sect of Men; but *Acasto* has natural good Sense, good Nature, and Discretion, so that every Man enjoys himself in his Company; and tho' *Acasto* contributes nothing to the Entertainment, he never was at a Place where he was not welcome a second Time. Without these subordinate good Qualities of *Acasto*, a Man of Wit and Learning would be painful to the Generality of Mankind instead of being pleasing. Witty Men are apt to imagine they are agreeable as such, and by that Means grow the worst Companions imaginable; they deride the Absent or rally the Present in a wrong Manner, not knowing that if you pinch or tickle a Man till he is uneasy in his Seat, or ungracefully distinguished from the rest of the Company, you equally hurt him.

I was going to say, the true Art of being agreeable in Company, (but there can be no such thing as Art in it,) is to appear well

<hr>

[a] no other End] no End *Fol.*

pleased with those you are engaged with, and rather to seem well entertained, than to bring Entertainment to others. A Man thus disposed is not indeed what we ordinarily call a good Companion, but essentially is such, and in all the Parts of his Conversation has something friendly in his Behaviour, which conciliates Men's Minds more than the highest Sallies of Wit or Starts of Humour can possibly do. The Feebleness of Age in a Man of this Turn, has something which should be treated with Respect even in a Man no otherwise Venerable. The Forwardness of Youth, when it proceeds from Alacrity and not Insolence, has also its Allowances. The Companion who is formed for such by Nature, gives to every Character of Life its due Regards, and is ready to account for their Imperfections, and receive their Accomplishments as if they were his own. It must appear that you receive Law from, and not give it to your Company, to make you agreeable.

I remember *Tully* speaking, I think of *Antony*, says, That *in eo facetiæ erant quæ nulla arte tradi possunt*.[1] *He had a witty Mirth which could be acquired by no Art*. This Quality must be of the Kind of which I am now speaking; for all Sorts of Behaviour which depend upon Observation and Knowledge of Life is to be acquired; but that which no one can describe, and is apparently the Act of Nature, must be every where prevalent, because every thing it meets is a fit Occasion to exert it; for he who follows Nature, can never be improper or unseasonable.

How unaccountable then must their Behaviour be, who, without any Manner of Consideration of what the Company they have just now entered are upon, give themselves the Air of a Messenger, and make as distinct Relations of the Occurrences they last met with, as if they had been dispatched from those they talk to, to be punctually exact in a Report of those Circumstances? It is unpardonable to those who are met to enjoy one another, that a fresh Man shall pop in, and give us only the last Part of his own Life, and put a Stop to ours during the History. If such a Man comes from *Change*, whether you will or not, you must hear how the Stocks go; and tho' you are never so intently employed on a graver Subject, a young Fellow of the other End of the Town will take his Place, and tell you, Mrs. such a one is charmingly handsome, because he just now saw her. But I think I need not dwell on this Subject, since I have acknowledged there can be no Rules made for excelling this Way; and

[1] Cicero, *De Oratore*, 2. 56. 227.

Precepts of this Kind fare like Rules for writing Poetry, which, 'tis said, may have prevented ill Poets, but never made good ones.[1]

T

No. 387

[ADDISON]

Saturday, May 24, 1712[2]

Quid purè tranquillet . . .

Hor.

IN my last *Saturday's* Paper I spoke of Chearfulness as it is a *Moral* Habit of the Mind, and accordingly mentioned such Moral Motives as are apt to cherish and keep alive this happy Temper in the Soul of Man: I shall now consider Chearfulness in its *natural* State, and reflect on those Motives to it, which are indifferent either as to Virtue or Vice.

Chearfulness is, in the first place, the best Promoter of Health. Repinings, and secret Murmurs of Heart, give imperceptible Strokes to those delicate Fibres of which the Vital Parts are composed, and wear out the Machine insensibly; not to mention those violent Ferments which they stir up in the Blood, and those irregular disturbed Motions which they raise in the animal Spirits. I scarce remember, in my own Observation, to have met with many old Men, or with such, who (to use our *English* Phrase) *wear well*, that had not at least a certain Indolence in their Humour, if not a more than ordinary Gaiety and Chearfulness of Heart. The truth of it is, Health and Chearfulness mutually beget each other, with this difference, that we seldom meet with a great degree of Health which is not attended with a certain Chearfulness, but very often see Chearfulness where there is no great degree of Health.

Chearfulness bears the same friendly Regard to the Mind as to the Body; it banishes all anxious Care and Discontent, sooths and composes the Passions, and keeps the Soul in a perpetual Calm.

---

[1] Sir William Temple, 'Of Poetry' (1690): 'After all, the utmost that can be atchieved or, I think, pretended by any Rules in this Art is but to hinder some men from being very ill Poets, but not to make any man a very good one' (Spingarn, iii. 84–85).

[2] *Motto*. Horace, *Epistles*, i. 18. 102: What calms the mind.

But having already touched on this last Consideration, I shall here take notice that the World, in which we are placed, is filled with innumerable Objects that are proper to raise and keep alive this happy Temper of Mind.

If we consider the World in its Subserviency to Man, one would think it was made for our Use;[1] but if we consider it in its natural Beauty and Harmony, one would be apt to conclude it was made for our Pleasure. The Sun, which is as the great Soul of the Universe, and produces all the Necessaries of Life, has a particular Influence in chearing the Mind of Man, and making the Heart glad.

Those several living Creatures which are made for our Service or Sustenance, at the same time either fill the Woods with their Musick, furnish us with Game, or raise pleasing Ideas in us by the delightfulness of their Appearance. Fountains, Lakes and Rivers, are as refreshing to the Imagination, as to the Soil through which they pass.

There are Writers of great Distinction, who have made it an Argument for Providence, that the whole Earth is covered with Green, rather than with any other Colour, as being such a right Mixture of Light and Shade, that it comforts and strengthens the Eye instead of weakning or grieving it.[2] For this Reason several Painters have a green Cloth hanging near them, to ease the Eye upon, after too great an Application to their Colouring. A Famous modern Philosopher accounts for it in the following manner: All Colours that are more luminous over-power and dissipate the animal Spirits which are employ'd in Sight; on the contrary, those that are more obscure do not give the animal Spirits a sufficient Exercise: whereas the Rays that produce in us the Idea of Green fall upon the Eye in such a due proportion that they give the animal Spirits their proper Play, and by keeping up the Struggle in a just Balance excite a very pleasing and agreeable Sensation. Let the Cause be what it will, the Effect is certain, for which Reason the Poets ascribe to this particular Colour the Epithet of *Chearful*.

To consider further this double End in the Works of Nature, and how they are at the same time both useful and entertaining, we find that the most important Parts in the Vegetable World are those

[1] Cicero, *De natura deorum*, 2. 14. 37; 2. 53. 133; 2. 62. 154; &c. Cf. also Pope's *Essay on Man*, i. 131–40.
[2] Seneca, *De ira*, 3. 9. 2; Plutarch, *Life of Demosthenes*, 22. 5. According to John Scott (*The Christian Life*, part ii, chap. iv) no colour is so grateful to the eye as green, 'the great colour of nature' (ed. 1700, part ii, p. 222).

which are the most beautiful. These are the Seeds by which the several Races of Plants are propagated and continued, and which are always lodged in Flowers or Blossoms. Nature seems to hide her principal Design, and to be industrious in making the Earth gay and delightful, while she is carrying on her great Work, and intent upon her own Preservation. The Husband-man after the same manner is employed in laying out the whole Country into a kind of Garden or Landskip, and making every thing smile about him, whilst in reality he thinks of nothing but of the Harvest, and Encrease which is to arise from it.

We may further observe how Providence has taken care to keep up this Chearfulness in the Mind of Man, by having formed it after such a manner, as to make it capable of conceiving Delight from several Objects, which seem to have very little use in them, as from the Wildness of Rocks and Desarts, and the like grotesque Parts of Nature. Those who are versed in Philosophy may still carry this Consideration higher, by observing that if Matter had appeared to us endow'd only with those real Qualities which it actually possesses, it would have made but a very joyless and uncomfortable Figure; and why has Providence given it a Power of producing in us such imaginary Qualities as Tastes and Colours, Sounds and Smells, Heat and Cold; but that Man, while he is conversant in the lower Stations of Nature, might have his Mind cheared and delighted with agreeable Sensations? In short, the whole Universe is a kind of Theatre filled with Objects that either raise in us Pleasure, Amusement or Admiration.

The Reader's own Thoughts will suggest to him the Vicissitude of Day and Night, the Change of Seasons, with all that variety of Scenes which diversifie the Face of Nature, and fill the Mind with a perpetual Succession of beautiful and pleasing Images.

I shall not here mention the several Entertainments of Art, with the Pleasures of Friendship, Books, Conversation, and other accidental Diversions of Life, because I would only take Notice of such Incitements to a Chearful Temper, as offer themselves to Persons of all Ranks and Conditions, and which may sufficiently shew us that Providence did not design this World should be filled with Murmurs and Repinings, or that the Heart of Man should be involved in Gloom and Melancholy.

I the more inculcate this Chearfulness of Temper, as it is a Virtue in which our Countrymen are observed to be more deficient than any other Nation. Melancholy is a kind of Demon that haunts our Island, and often conveys her self to us in an Easterly Wind.[1] A celebrated *French* Novelist,[2] in Opposition to those who begin their Romances with the Flowry Season of the Year, enters on his Story thus, *In the gloomy Month of* November, *when the People of* England *hang and drown themselves, a disconsolate Lover walked out into the Fields*, &c.

Every one ought to fence against the Temper of his Climate or Constitution, and frequently to indulge in himself those Considerations which may give him a Serenity of Mind, and enable him to bear up chearfully against those little Evils and Misfortunes which are common to Human Nature, and which by a right Improvement of them will produce a Satiety of Joy, and an uninterrupted Happiness.

At the same time that I would engage my Reader to consider the World in its most agreeable Lights, I must own there are many Evils which naturally spring up amidst the Entertainments that are provided for us; but these, if rightly consider'd, should be far from over-casting the Mind with Sorrow, or destroying that Chearfulness of Temper which I have been recommending. This Interspersion of Evil with Good, and Pain with Pleasure, in the Works of Nature, is very truly ascrib'd by Mr. *Lock* in his Essay on Human Understanding to a Moral Reason, in the following Words:

Beyond all this, we may find another reason why *God hath scattered up and down* several degrees of Pleasure and Pain, in all the things that environ and affect us; *and blended them together, in almost all that our Thoughts and Senses have to do with; that we finding Imperfection, Dissatisfaction, and want of compleat Happiness, in all the Enjoyments which the Creatures can afford us, might be led to seek it in the enjoyment of him,* with whom there is fulness of Joy, and at whose Right Hand are Pleasures for evermore. [a][3]

L

---

[a] *The Person who wrote a Letter to the Spectator, May the* 11th, *about an Original Picture, is desired to leave Word at Mr. Charles Lillie's, at the Corner of Beauford Buildings in the Strand, where it may be seen.* Fol.

---

[1] Cf. Sir William Temple, 'Of Poetry' (Spingarn, iii. 105–6). 'There is no Nation in *Europe*', writes Dennis, in *The Usefulness of the Stage* (1698), part i, chap. ii, 'as has been observ'd above a thousand times, that is so generally addicted to the Spleen, as the *English*', and among the causes he includes 'the reigning Distemper of the Clime' (*Works*, ed. Hooker, i. 151).

[2] He remains unidentified. Gustave Lanson quoted this sentence from the *Spectator* to illustrate a passage in Voltaire's *Lettres philosophiques* (Paris, 1909, ii. 272) without identifying the novelist. [3] Locke, *Essay*, II. vii. 5.

No. 388   *Monday, May 26, 1712*[1]

[STEELE]

> *. . . Tibi res antiquæ laudis & Artis*
> *Ingredior; Sanctos ausus recludere Fontes.*
>   Virg.

Mr. SPECTATOR,

'IT is my Custom when I read your Papers, to read over the Quotations in the Authors from whence you take them: As you mentioned a Passage lately[2] out of the second Chapter of *Solomon's Song*, it occasioned my looking into it; and upon reading it I thought the Ideas so exquisitely soft and tender, that I could not help making this Paraphrase of it, which, now it is done, I can as little forbear sending to you.[3] Some Marks of your Approbation which I have already received, have given me so sensible a Taste of them, that I cannot forbear endeavouring after them as often as I can with any Appearance of Success.

> *I am,*
>   SIR,
>   *Your most obedient*[a] *humble Servant.'*

   [a] *obedient*] *obliged* Fol.

---

   [1] *Motto.* Virgil, *Georgics*, 2. 174–5:

> For thee my tuneful Accents will I raise,
> And treat of Arts disclos'd in Ancient Days:
> Once more unlock for thee the sacred Spring. DRYDEN.

   [2] No. 327.

   [3] The author of this paraphrase is unknown. Nichols's two notes to No. 388 provide the only clues: 'See Dr. Croxall's first attempt at a version of this fine Song in the Select Collection of Miscellany Poems, 1780, Vol. IV. p. 120.' 'It has been said, that a poetical translation of a chapter in the Proverbs, and another poetical translation from the Old Testament, were the productions of a Mr. Parr, a Dissenting Minister at Morton-Hampstead in Devonshire.'

     Samuel Croxall (d. 1752), who contributed several things to Steele's *Poetical Miscellanies* of 1714, including a paraphrase of chapter iv of *Solomon's Song*, is best known for a longer adaptation of the same Biblical source, *The Fair Circassian* (1720), which 'too closely copies the oriental warmth of the original' (*DNB*). Aitken in consequence thought it 'not improbable that he was also the author of this paper'. Croxall's paraphrase, however, is not that printed in No. 388 and there is no real evidence for thinking him the author.

     As to Mr. Parr, the dissenting minister of Devonshire, no information has been turned up to verify the vague tradition reported in Nichols's edition. There was a Rev. John Parr (1633?–1716?), a dissenting minister of some note (cf. *DNB*), but he lived in Lancashire, and there is no reason to connect him with this paraphrase. A search among the scores of versions of *Solomon's Song* published has not disclosed this paraphrase.

The second Chapter of *Solomon's Song*.

I.

AS when in Sharon's *Field the blushing Rose*
Does its chaste Bosom to the Morn disclose,
Whilst all around the Zephyrs *bear*
The fragrant Odours thro' the Air.
Or as the Lillie in the shady Vale,
Does o'er each Flow'r with beauteous Pride prevail,
And stands with Dews, and kindest Sunshine blest,
In[a] *fair Pre-eminence superior to the rest;*
So if my Love with happy Influence shed,
His Eyes bright Sunshine on his Lover's Head,
Then shall the Rose of Sharon's *Field,*
And whitest Lillies, to my Beauties yield.
Then fairest Flow'rs with studious Art combine,
The Roses with the Lillies join,
And their united Charms are less than mine.[b]

II.

As much as fairest Lillies can surpass
A Thorn in Beauty, or in Height the Grass;
So does my Love among the Virgins shine,
Adorn'd with Graces more than half divine.
Or as a Tree, that, glorious to behold,
Is hung with Apples all of ruddy Gold,
Hesperian *Fruit! and beautifully high*
Extends its Branches to the Sky;
So does my Love the Virgins Eyes invite:
'Tis he alone can fix their wand'ring Sight,
Among ten thousand eminently bright.[c]

III.

Beneath his pleasing Shade
My wearied Limbs at Ease I laid,
And on his fragrant Boughs reclined my Head.
I pull'd the golden Fruit with eager Haste,
Sweet was the Fruit, and pleasing to the Taste.

[a] *In*] *With* Fol.   [b] *And their united Charms are less than mine.*] *And their united Beauties shall be less than mine.* Fol.   [c] *Among ten thousand eminently bright.*] *And stands among ten thousand eminently bright.* Fol.

With sparkling Wine he crown'd the Bowl,
With gentle Extasies he fill'd my Soul;
Joyous we sate beneath the shady Grove,
And o'er my Head he hung the Banners of his Love.

IV.

I faint, I dye! my labouring Breast
Is with the mighty Weight of Love opprest.
I feel the Fire possess my Heart,
And Pain convey'd to every Part.
ᵃThro' all my Veins the Passion flies,
My feeble Soul forsakes its Place,
A trembling Faintness seals my Eyes,
And Paleness dwells upon my Face;ᵃ
Oh! let my Love with pow'rful Odours stay
My fainting, love-sick Soul, that dyes away.
One Hand beneath me let him place,
With t'other press me in a chaste Embrace.

V.

I charge you, Nymphs of Sion, as you go
Arm'd with the sounding Quiver and the Bow,
Whilst thro' the lonesome Woods you rove,
You ne'er disturb my sleeping Love.
Be only gentle Zephyrs there,
With downy Wings to fan the Air;
Let sacred Silence dwell around,
To keep off each intruding Sound.
Andᵇ when the balmy Slumber leaves his Eyes,
May he to Joys, unknown till then, arise.

VI.

But see! he comes; with what Majestick Gate,
He onward bears his lovely State.
Now thro' the Lattice he appears,
With softest Words dispels my Fears;
Arise my Fair one, and receive
All the Pleasures Love can give.

ᵃ⁻ᵃ *These four lines bracketed in Folio.*   ᵇ *And] Then Fol.*

For now the sullen Winter's past,
No more we fear the Northern Blast:
No Storms nor threat'ning Clouds appear,
No falling Rain deforms the Year.
My[a] *Love admits of no Delay,*
Arise my Fair and come away.

VII.

Already, see! the teeming Earth
Brings forth the Flow'rs, her beauteous Birth.
The Dews, and soft descending Show'rs,
Nurse the new-born tender Flow'rs.
Hark! the Birds melodious sing,
And sweetly usher in the Spring.
Close by his Fellow sits the Dove,
And billing whispers her his Love.
The spreading Vines with Blossoms swell,
Diffusing round a grateful Smell.
Arise my fair one, and receive
All the Blessings Love can give:
For Love admits of no Delay,
Arise my Fair and come away.

VIII.

As to its Mate the constant Dove
Flies thro' the Covert of the Spicy Grove,
So let us hasten to some lonesome Shade;
There let me safe in thy lov'd Arms be laid,
Where no intruding hateful Noise
Shall damp the Sound of thy melodious Voice;
Where I may gaze, and mark each beauteous Grace,
For sweet thy Voice, and lovely is thy Face.

IX.

As all of Me, my Love is Thine,
Let all of Thee, be ever Mine.
Among the Lillies we will play,
Fairer my Love thou art than they;

[a] *My*] *Now* Fol.

Till^a *the purple Morn arise,*
And balmy Sleep forsake thine Eyes;
Till^b *the gladsome Beams of Day*
Remove the Shades of Night away:
Then when soft Sleep shall from thy Eyes depart,
Rise like the bounding Roe, or lusty Hart,
Glad to behold the Light again
From Bether's *Mountains darting o'er the Plain.*

T

No. 389
[BUDGELL]

Tuesday, May 27, 1712[1]

. . . Meliora pii docuere parentes.
Hor.

NOTHING has more surprised the Learned in *England*, than the Price which a small Book, Entitled *Spaccio della Bestia triomfante*, bore in a late Auction.[2] This Book was Sold for thirty^c Pound. As it was written by one *Jordanus Brunus*, a professed Atheist,

---

^a *Till*] *Untill* Fol.   ^b *Till*] *Untill* Fol.   ^c thirty] Fifty *Fol*.

---

[1] *Motto*. The Latin ('Our pious forefathers taught us better things') is not from Horace, but from a serio-comic poem in dialogue form entitled 'Auctio Davisiana', printed in the first volume of Addison's collection, *Musarum Anglicanarum Analecta*, in 1692 (4th ed., 1721, p. 207). The author is Addison's friend George Smalridge, later Bishop of Bristol. For the poem, which concerns the auction sale of the stock of Davis, a bankrupt Oxford bookseller, see Leicester Bradner, *Musae anglicanae* (New York, 1940), pp. 215–16. Smithers (pp. 37–40) also discusses the publication of the *Analecta* and Addison's friendship with Smalridge.

[2] Giordano Bruno, *Spaccio de la Bestia trionfante* (Paris, 1584), is Item 1005 in *Bibliotheca Bernardiana: Or, a Catalogue of the Library of the late Charles Bernard, Esq; Serjeant Surgeon to her Majesty*. The sale of this library, which began on 22 Mar. 1711, at the Black-Boy Coffee-house in Ave-Maria Lane, near Ludgate Street, and continued throughout April, is announced in the *Daily Courant* of 15 Mar. and subsequent issues. Swift purchased some books at this sale (*Journal to Stella*, 11, 13, 16 Apr. 1711). Hearne, writing on 19 Aug. (*Remarks*, iii. 209), says that this book and another of Bruno's together brought £28. Earlier, on 7 Aug. (*Remarks*, iii. 201–2), he writes that 'Jordanus Bruno's Roma Triumphante' was sold for £27, 'being bought by one Mr. Clavell of the Middle-Temple, a great Crony (unless I am misinform'd) of Toland, Stevens, Tyndale & other Atheistical & ill Men'. The volume was apparently much talked of at the time. William Wagstaffe, in *A Comment upon the History of Tom Thumb* (1711), p. 13, mentions it, adding, 'which Book, tho' very scarce, yet a *certain Gentleman*, who has it in his Possession, has been so obliging as to let every Body know where to meet with it'. Giordano Bruno was condemned by the Church and burnt alive in the Campo dei Fiori in 1600.

with a design to depreciate Religion, every one was apt to fancy, from the extravagant Price it bore, that there must be something in it very formidable.

I must confess, that happening to get a sight of one of them my self, I could not forbear perusing it with this Apprehension, but found there was so very little Danger in it, that I shall venture to give my Readers a fair Account of the whole Plan upon which this wonderful Treatise is built.

The Author pretends that *Jupiter* once upon a time resolved on a Reformation of the Constellations, for which purpose having summoned the Stars together, he complains to them of the great Decay of the Worship of the Gods, which he thought so much the harder, having called several of those Celestial Bodies by the Names of the Heathen Deities, and by that means made the Heavens as it were a Book of the Pagan Theology. *Momus* tells him that this is not to be wondred at, since there were so many scandalous Stories of the Deities; upon which the Author takes occasion to cast Reflections upon all other Religions, concluding, that *Jupiter* after a full Hearing discarded the Deities out of Heaven, and called the Stars by the Names of the Moral Virtues.

This short Fable, which has no Pretence in it to Reason or Argument, and but a very small share of Wit, has however recommended it self wholly by its Impiety to those weak Men who would distinguish themselves by the Singularity of their Opinions.

There are two Considerations which have been often urged against Atheists, and which they never yet could get over. The first is, that the greatest and most eminent Persons of all Ages have been against them, and always complied with the Publick Forms of Worship established in their respective Countries, when there was nothing in them either derogatory to the Honour of the Supream Being, or prejudicial to the Good of Mankind.[1]

The *Plato*'s and *Cicero*'s among the Ancients, the *Bacon*'s, the *Boyle*'s[2] and the *Lock*'s among our own Countrymen, are all Instances of what I have been saying, not to mention any of the Divines however celebrated, since our Adversaries challenge all those as Men who have too much Interest in this Case to be Impartial Evidences.

[1] A rephrasing of Addison's statement in No. 186 (vol. ii): 'I would therefore have them [i.e. infidels] consider that the wisest and the best of Men in all Ages of the World, have been those who lived up to the Religion of their Country, when they saw nothing in it opposite to Morality, and the best Lights they had of the divine Nature.'

[2] For Boyle's reverence see No. 531 (vol. iv).

But what has been often urged as a Consideration of much more weight, is not only the Opinion of the better sort, but the general Consent of Mankind to this great Truth, which I think could not possibly have come to pass but from one of the three following Reasons; either that the Idea of a God is innate and co-existent with the Mind it self, or that this Truth is so very obvious that it is discovered by the first Exertion of Reason in Persons of the most ordinary Capacities, or lastly that it has been delivered down to us thro' all Ages by a Tradition from the first Man.[1]

The Atheists are equally confounded, to which ever of these three Causes we assign it; they have been so pressed by this last Argument from the general Consent of Mankind, that after great Search and Pains they pretend to have found out a Nation of Atheists, I mean that Polite People the *Hottentots*.[2]

I dare not shock my Readers with a Description of the Customs and Manners of these Barbarians, who are in every respect scarce one degree above Brutes, having no Language among them, but a confused *Gabble*,[a] which is neither well understood by themselves or others.

It is not however to be imagined how much the Atheists have gloried in these their good Friends and Allies.

If we boast of a *Socrates* or a *Seneca*, they may now confront them with these great Philosophers the *Hottentots*.

Tho' even this Point has, not without Reason, been several times controverted, I see no manner of harm it could do Religion, if we should entirely give them up this Elegant Part of Mankind.

Methinks nothing more shews the Weakness of their Cause, than that no division of their Fellow-Creatures joyn with them, but those among whom they themselves own Reason is almost defaced,

---

[a] *Gabble*,] Gabling *Fol.*

---

[1] Budgell here repeats (in reverse) the three points made by Addison in No. 201 (vol. ii): that Devotion or 'Religious Worship must be the effect of a Tradition from some first Founder of Mankind, or that it is conformable to the Natural Light of Reason, or that it proceeds from an Instinct implanted in the Soul it self'.

[2] John Maxwell ('An Account of the Cape of Good Hope', *Philosophical Transactions*, No. 310, 1707) comments on the fact that the Hottentots have 'no notion of God'. They are also discussed in Dampier's *Voyages* (1703) and by various writers in the *Collection of Voyages* (1704) of A. and J. Churchill (both of these books were in Addison's library). Cf. Sir R. Blackmore, *The Nature of Man* (1711), book i:

> So void of Sense the *Hotentot* is found,
> Whose Speech is scarce articulated Sound,
> That 'tis disputed, if his doubtful Soul
> Augment the Humane or the Brutal Roll.

and who have little else but their Shape, which can entitle them to any place in the Species.

Besides these poor Creatures, there have now and then been Instances of a few crazed People in several Nations, who have denied the Existence of a Deity.

The Catalogue of these is, however, very short; even *Vanini*, the most celebrated Champion for the Cause, professed before his Judges that he believed the Existence of a God, and taking up a Straw which lay before him on the Ground, assured them, that alone was sufficient to convince him of it; alledging several Arguments to prove that 'twas impossible Nature alone could Create any thing.[1]

I was the other Day reading an Account of *Casimir Liszynski*, a Gentleman of *Poland*, who was convicted and executed for this Crime. The manner of his Punishment was very particular. As soon as his Body was burnt his Ashes were put into a Cannon and shot into the Air towards *Tartary*.[2]

I am apt to believe, that if something like this Method of Punishment should prevail in *England*, such is the natural good Sense of the *British* Nation, that whether we ramm'd an Atheist whole into[a] a great Gun, or Pulverised our Infidels as they do in *Poland*, we should not have many Charges.

I should, however, propose, while our Ammunition lasted, that instead of *Tartary*, we should always keep two or three Cannons ready pointed towards the Cape of *Good-hope*, in order to shoot our Unbelievers into the Country of the *Hottentots*.

In my Opinion, a Solemn judicial Death is too great an Honour for an Atheist, tho' I must allow the Method of exploding him, as it is practised in this ludicrous kind of Martyrdom, has something in it proper enough to[b] the nature of his Offence.

There is indeed a great Objection against this manner of treating

---

[a] an Atheist whole into] an Atheist into *Fol*.　　　[b] proper enough to] proper to *Fol*.

---

[1] Lucilio Vanini was an Italian priest whose writings caused him to be arrested on a charge of atheism. He was tortured and burnt at the stake in 1619.

[2] Casimir Liszynski was cruelly put to death on a trumped-up charge of blasphemy in 1689. The story is told in various histories of Poland and of the Counter-Reformation, but Budgell's source may well be (as for the story of Vanini) the *Entretiens sur divers sujets d'histoire* of Maturin Veyresse de la Croze (1711). The fourth and longest *entretien* consists largely of a 'Dissertation sur l'Athéisme, et sur les Athées modernes' (pp. 245–547 in the edition published at Cologne in 1733). Liszynski is dealt with at pp. 417–29. 'Le corps du prétendu Athée fut brûlé, après l'exécution, & ses cendres furent mises dans un canon qu'on tira en l'air du côté de la Tartarie' (p. 424).

them. Zeal for Religion is of so active a Nature that it seldom knows where to rest;[1] for which reason I am afraid, after having discharged our Atheists, we might possibly think of shooting off our Sectaries;[2] and as one does not foresee the Vicissitude of Human Affairs, it might one time or other come to a Man's own turn to fly out of the Mouth of a Demi-Culverin.[3]

If any of my Readers imagine that I have treated these Gentlemen in too Ludicrous a Manner, I must confess, for my own part, I think reasoning against such Unbelievers upon a Point that shocks the Common Sense of Mankind, is doing them too great an Honour, giving them a Figure in the Eye of the World, and making People fancy that they have more in them than they really have.

As for those Persons who have any Scheme of Religious Worship, I am for treating such with the utmost Tenderness, and should endeavour to shew them their Errors with the greatest Temper and Humanity; but as these Miscreants are for throwing down Religion in general, for stripping Mankind of what themselves own is of excellent Use in all great Societies, without once offering to establish any thing in the Room of it, I think the best way of dealing with them, is to retort their own Weapons upon them, which are those of Scorn and Mockery.   X

No. 390

[STEELE]

Wednesday, May 28, 1712[4]

Non pudendo sed non faciendo id quod non decet impudentiæ nomen effugere debemus.   Tull.

MANY are the Epistles I receive from Ladies extremely afflicted that they lye under the Observation of scandalous People,

[1] Addison had stated (No. 185, vol. ii) that 'most of the Massacres and Devastations that have been in the World, have taken their Rise from a furious pretended Zeal'.

[2] The High Church Tories were accustomed to linking atheists and dissenters together as dangers to the Church. In *Examiner* 29 (22 Feb. 1710/11) Swift recalled asking 'some considerable Whigs, whether it did not bring a Disreputation upon their Body, to have the whole Herd of Presbyterians, Independants, Atheists, Anabaptists, Deists, Quakers and Socinians, openly and universally Listed under their Banners?' (*Prose Works*, ed. Davis, iii. 92).

[3] A kind of cannon, formerly in use, of about 4½ inches bore.

[4] *Motto.* Cicero, *De Oratore*, i. 26. 120: We ought to fly the reproach of shamelessness, not by being ashamed at what is unbecoming, but by avoiding doing it.

who love to defame their Neighbours and make the unjustest Interpretation of innocent and indifferent Actions. They describe their own Behaviour so unhappily, that there indeed lies some Cause of Suspicion upon them. It is certain, that there is no Authority for Persons who have nothing else to do, to pass away Hours of Conversation upon the Miscarriages of other People; but since they will do so, they who value their Reputation should be cautious of Appearances to their Disadvantage. But very often our young Women, as well as the middle-aged, and the gay Part of those growing old, without entring into a formal League for that Purpose, to a Woman, agree upon a short Way to preserve their Characters, and go on in a Way that at best is only not vicious. The Method is, when an ill-natured or talkative Girl has said any thing that bears hard upon some Part of another's Carriage, this Creature, if not in any of their little Cabals, is run down for the most censorious dangerous Body in the World. Thus they guard their Reputation rather than their Modesty; as if Guilt lay in being under the Imputation of a Fault, and not in a Commission of it. *Orbicilla* is the kindest poor thing in the Town, but the most blushing Creature living: It is true she has not lost the Sense of Shame, but she has lost the Sense of Innocence. If she had more Confidence, and never did any thing which ought to stain her Cheeks, would she not be much more modest without that ambiguous Suffusion which is the Livery both of Guilt and Innocence? Modesty consists in being conscious of no Ill, and not in being ashamed of having done it. When People go upon any other Foundation than the Truth of their own Hearts for the Conduct of their Actions, it lies in the Power of scandalous Tongues to carry the World before them, and make the rest of Mankind fall in with the Ill for Fear of Reproach. On the other Hand, to do what you ought, is the ready Way to make Calumny either silent, or ineffectually malicious. *Spencer*, in his *Fairy Queen*, says admirably to young Ladies under the Distress of being defamed.

The best, said he, that I can you advise,
Is to avoid th' Occasion of the Ill;
For when the Cause, whence Evil doth arise,
Removed is, th' Effect surceaseth still.
Abstain from Pleasure, and restrain your Will;
Subdue Desire, and bridle loose Delight;

Use scanted Diet, and forbear your Fill;
Shun Secresy, and talk in open Sight;
So shall you soon repair your present evil Plight.[1]

Instead of this Care over their Words and Actions, recommended
by a Poet in old Queen *Bess's* Days, the modern Way is to do and
say what you please, and yet be the *prettiest sort of Woman in the*
World. If Fathers and Brothers will defend a Lady's Honour, she is
quite as safe as in her own Innocence. Many of the Distressed, who
suffer under the Malice of evil Tongues, are so harmless that they
are every Day they live asleep till twelve at Noon; concern themselves with nothing but their own Persons till two; take their
necessary Food between that Time and four; visit, go to the Play,
and sit up at Cards till towards the ensuing Morn; and the malicious World shall draw Conclusions from innocent Glances, short
Whispers, or pretty familiar Railleries with fashionable Men, that
these fair ones are not as rigid as Vestals. It is certain, say these
goodest Creatures very well, that Virtue does not consist in constrained Behaviour and wry[a] Faces, that must be allowed; but there
is a Decency in the Aspect and Manner of Ladies contracted from
an Habit of Virtue, and from general Reflections that regard a
modest Conduct, all which may be understood though they cannot
be described. A young Woman of this sort claims an Esteem mixed
with Affection and Honour, and meets with no Defamation; or if
she does, the wild Malice is overcome with an undisturbed Perseverance in her Innocence. To speak freely, there are such Coveys of
Coquets about this Town, that if the Peace were not kept by some
impertinent Tongues of their own Sex, which keep them under
some Restraint, we should have no Manner of Engagement upon
them to keep them in any tolerable Order.

As I am a SPECTATOR, and behold how plainly one part of Woman-
kind ballance the Behaviour of the other, whatever I may think of
Talebearers or Slanderers, I cannot wholly suppress them no more
than a General would discourage Spies. The Enemy would easily
surprise him whom they knew had no Intelligence of their Motions.
It is so far otherwise with me, that I acknowledge I permit a she
Slanderer or two in every Quarter of the Town, to live in the
Characters of Coquets, and take all the innocent Freedoms of the

---

[a] wry] awry *Fol.*

[1] Spenser, *Faerie Queene,* VI. vi. 14.

Rest, in order to send me Information of the Behaviour of their respective Sister-hoods.

But as the matter of respect to the World, which looks on, is carried on, methinks it is so very easy to be what is in the general called Virtuous, that it need not cost one Hour's Reflection in a Month to preserve that Appellation. It is pleasant to hear the pretty Rogues talk of Virtue and Vice among each other: She is the lazyest Creature in the World, but I must confess, strictly Virtuous: The Peevishest Hussy breathing, but as to her Virtue she is without blemish: She has not the least Charity for any of her Acquaintance, but I must allow rigidly Virtuous. As the unthinking Part of the Male World call every Man, a Man of Honour, who is not a Coward; so the Crowd of the other Sex, terms every Woman who will not be a Wench, Virtuous.   T

No. 391

[ADDISON]

Thursday, May 29, 1712[1]

> *. . . Non tu prece poscis emaci,*
> *Quæ nisi seductis nequeas committere Divis.*
> *At bona pars procerum tacitâ libabit acerrâ.*
> *Haud cuivis promptum est, murmurque humilesque susurros*
> *Tollere de Templis; & aperto vivere voto.*
> *Mens bona, fama, fides, hæc clarè, & ut audiat hospes.*
> *Illa sibi introrsùm, & sub lingua immurmurat: ô si*
> *Ebulliat patruus præclarum funus! Et, o si*
> *Sub rastro crepet argenti mihi seria dextro*
> *Hercule! pupillumve utinam, quem proximus hæres*
> *Impello, expungam! . . .*

Pers.

WHERE *Homer* represents *Phœnix*, the Tutor of *Achilles*, as persuading his Pupil[a] to lay aside his Resentments, and give

a his Pupil] him *Fol.*

---

[1] For notes see opposite page.

himself up to the Entreaties of his Countrymen, the Poet, in order to make him speak in Character, ascribes to him a Speech full of those Fables and Allegories which old Men take delight in relating, and which are very proper for Instruction. *The Gods, says he, suffer themselves to be prevailed upon by Entreaties. When Mortals have offended them by their Transgressions, they appease them by Vows and Sacrifices. You must know, Achilles, that PRAYERS are the Daughters of Jupiter. They are crippled by frequent Kneeling, have their Faces full of Cares and Wrinkles, and their Eyes always cast towards*[a] *Heaven. They are constant Attendants on the Goddess ATE, and march behind her. This Goddess walks forward with a bold and haughty Air, and being very light of Foot, runs thro' the whole Earth, grieving and afflicting the Sons of Men. She gets the start of PRAYERS, who always follow her, in order to heal those Persons whom she wounds. He who Honours these Daughters of Jupiter, when they draw near to him, receives great Benefit from them; but as for him who rejects them, they intreat their Father to give his Orders to the Goddess ATE to punish him for his Hardness of Heart.*[2] This noble Allegory needs but little Explanation; for whether the Goddess *ATE* signifies Injury as some have explained it, or Guilt in general as others, or Divine Justice, as I am the more apt to think, the Interpretation is obvious enough.

I shall produce another Heathen Fable relating to Prayers, which is of a more diverting kind. One would think, by some Passages in it, that it was composed by *Lucian*, or at least by some Author who

---

[a] *towards] toward* Fol.

---

[1] *Motto.* Persius, *Satires*, 2. 3–13.

> Pray; for thy Pray'rs the Test of Heav'n will bear;
> Nor need'st thou take the Gods aside to hear:
> While others, ev'n the Mighty Men of *Rome*,
> Big swell'd with Mischief, to the Temples come;
> And in low Murmurs, and with costly Smoak,
> Heav'n's Help, to prosper their black Vows, invoke.
> So boldly to the Gods Mankind reveal,
> What from each other they, for shame, conceal.
> Give me Good Fame, ye Pow'rs, and make me just:
> Thus much the Rogue to Publick Ears will trust:
> In private then:—When wilt thou, mighty *Jove*,
> My wealthy Uncle from this World remove?
> Or — O thou Thund'rer's Son, great *Hercules*,
> That once thy bounteous Deity wou'd please
> To guide my Rake, upon the chinking sound
> Of some vast Treasure, hidden under-ground!
> O were my Pupil fairly knock'd o'th'head;
> I shou'd possess th'Estate, if he were dead! DRYDEN.

Homer, *Iliad*, 9. 499–512.

has endeavoured to imitate[1] his way of Writing; but as Dissertations of this Nature are more curious than useful, I shall give my Reader the Fable, without any further Enquiries after the Author.[a]

Menippus[2] *the Philosopher was a second time taken up into Heaven by* Jupiter, *when for his Entertainment he lifted up a Trap-door that was placed by his Foot-stool. At its rising there issued through it such a Dinn of Cries as astonished the Philosopher; Upon his asking what they meant,* Jupiter *told him they were the Prayers that were sent up to him from the Earth.* Menippus, *amidst the Confusion of Voices, which was so great that nothing less than the Ear of* Jove *could distinguish them, heard the Words,* Riches, Honour, *and* Long Life *repeated in several different Tones and Languages. When the first Hubbub of Sounds was over, the Trap-door being left open, the Voices came up more separate and distinct. The first Prayer was a very odd one, it came from* Athens, *and desired* Jupiter *to encrease the Wisdom and the Beard of his humble Supplicant.* Menippus *knew it, by the Voice, to be the Prayer of his Friend* Licander *the Philosopher. This was succeeded by the Petition of one who had just laden a Ship, and promised* Jupiter, *if he took Care of it, and returned it home again full of Riches, he would make him an Offering of a Silver Cup.* Jupiter *thanked him for nothing; and bending down his Ear more attentively than ordinary heard a Voice complaining to him of the Cruelty of an* Ephesian *Widow, and begging him to breed Compassion in her Heart. This, says* Jupiter, *is a very honest Fellow, I have received a great deal of Incense from him; I will not be so cruel to him as not to hear his Prayers.[b] He was then interrupted[c] with a whole volly of Vows which were made for the Health of a Tyrannical Prince by his Subjects who prayed for him in his Presence.* Menippus *was surprised, after having listned to Prayers offered up with so much Ardour and Devotion, to hear low Whispers from the same Assembly expostulating with* Jove *for suffering such a Tyrant to live, and asking him how his Thunder could lie idle.* Jupiter *was so offended at these prevaricating Rascals that he took down the first Vows, and puffed away the last. The Philosopher*

---

[a] *The next paragraph in italics in* 18vo, 2mo; *in roman in Folio*   [b] *as not to hear his Prayers.*] 8vo; *as to hear his Prayer.* Fol.; *as to hear his Prayers.* 12mo   [c] *was then interrupted*] was interrupted Fol.

---

[1] 'Mr. Addison had too good a mind to be a successful imitator of Lucian's free manner. He is seen to more advantage when he is copying Plato' (Hurd).

[2] Menippus, the cynic philosopher of the third century B.C., was noted for his satirical writings. Although these are lost, they were imitated by Varro (*Saturae Menippeae*) and Lucian. The Fable reproduced here is an expansion of an episode in Lucian's *Icaromenippus: or, a voyage to Heaven* (translated by Thomas Brown), in which Menippus sees Jupiter listening to the prayers sent up from earth (*Works of Lucian, translated from the Greek, by several eminent hands*, 1711, i. 320–3).

seeing a great Cloud mounting upwards, and making its way directly to the Trap-door, enquired of Jupiter *what it meant. This, says* Jupiter, *is the Smoak of a whole Hecatomb that is offered me by the General of an Army, who is very importunate with me to let him cut off an hundred thousand Men that are drawn up in Array against him; What does the impudent Wretch think I see in him to believe that I will make a Sacrifice of so many Mortals as good as himself, and all this to his Glory forsooth? But hark, says* Jupiter, *there is a Voice I*[a] *never heard but in time of danger; 'tis a Rogue that is shipwrecked in the* Ionian *Sea: I saved him on a Plank but three days ago, upon his promise to mend his Manners; the Scoundrel is not worth a Groat, and yet has the Impudence to offer me a Temple if I will keep him from sinking. —But yonder, says he, is a special Youth for you, he desires me to take his Father, who keeps a great Estate from him, out of the Miseries of human Life. The old Fellow shall live till he makes his Heart ake, I can tell him that for his pains. This was followed by the soft Voice of a Pious Lady, desiring* Jupiter *that she might appear amiable and charming in the sight of her Emperor. As the Philosopher was reflecting on this extraordinary Petition, there blew a gentle Wind through the Trap-door which he at first mistook for a Gale of* Zephirs, *but afterwards found it to be a Breeze of Sighs: they smelt strong of Flowers and Incense, and were succeeded by most passionate Complaints of Wounds and Torments, Fires and Arrows, Cruelty, Despair and Death.* Menippus *fancied that such lamentable Cries arose from some general Execution, or from Wretches lying under the Torture, but* Jupiter *told him that they came up to him from the Isle of* Paphos, *and that he every Day received Complaints of the same nature from that whimsical Tribe of Mortals who are called Lovers. I am so trifled with, says he, by this Generation of both Sexes, and find it so impossible to please them, whether I grant or refuse their Petitions, that I shall order a Western Wind for the future to intercept them in their Passage, and blow them at Random upon the Earth. The last Petition I heard*[1] *was from a very aged Man of near an Hundred Years old, begging but for one Year more of Life, and then promising to die contented. This is the rarest old Fellow! says* Jupiter: *He has made this Prayer to me for above twenty Years together. When he was but Fifty Years*[b] *old, he desired only that he might live to see his Son settled in the World, I granted it. He then begged the same Favour for his Daughter, and afterwards that he might see the Education of a Grandson; when all this was brought about, he puts up a Petition that he might live to finish a House he*

---

   [a] *Voice I*] Voice that I *Fol.*   [b] *Fifty Years*] Fifty Year *Fol.*

---

   [1] 'I' can be construed as Jupiter but is probably an oversight for 'Menippus'.

was Building: In short, he is an unreasonable old Cur, and never wants an Excuse; I will hear no more of him. Upon which he flung down the Trap-Door in a Passion, and was resolved to give no more Audiences that Day.

Notwithstanding the Levity of this Fable, the Moral of it very well deserves our Attention, and is the same with that which has been inculcated by *Socrates* and *Plato*, not to mention *Juvenal* and *Persius*, who have each of them made the finest Satyr in their whole Works upon this Subject.[1] The Vanity of Mens Wishes, which are the natural Prayers of the Mind, as well as many of those[a] Secret Devotions which they offer to the Supreme Being are sufficiently exposed by it. Among other[b] Reasons for Sett Forms of Prayer, I have often thought it a very good one, that by this means the Folly and Extravagance of Mens Desires may be kept within due Bounds, and not break out in absurd and ridiculous Petitions on so great and solemn an Occasion.   I

No. 392   *Friday, May* 30, 1712[2]
[STEELE]

Per Ambages & Ministeria Deorum
Præcipitandus est liber Spiritus.

                                                            Pet.

To *the* SPECTATOR.

The Transformation of Fidelio *into a Looking-Glass.*

'I WAS lately at a Tea-Table, where some young Ladies entertained the Company with a Relation of a Coquet in the Neigh-
bourhood, who had been discovered practising before her Glass. To turn the Discourse, which, from being witty grew to be malicious, the Matron of the Family took Occasion, from the Subject, to wish that there were to be found amongst Men such faithful Monitors to dress the Mind by, as we consult to adorn the Body. She added,

---

[a] as many of those] as those *Fol.*   [b] Among other] Among many other *Fol.*

---

[1] Juvenal, *Satire* 10; Persius, *Satire* 2.
[2] *Motto.* Petronius, *Satyricon*, 118 (altered):
    A free and daring spirit mounts the starry pole,
    Tries ev'ry path, and mingles with the gods his soul.

that if a sincere Friend were miraculously changed into a Looking-Glass, she should not be ashamed to ask its Advice very often. This whimsical Thought worked so much upon my Fancy the whole Evening, that it produced a very odd Dream.[a]

'Methought, that as I stood before my Glass, the Image of a Youth, of an open ingenuous Aspect, appeared in it; who with a shrill Voice spoke in the following Manner.

'The Looking-Glass you see, was heretofore a Man, even I, the unfortunate *Fidelio*. I had two Brothers, whose Deformity in Shape was made out[1] by the Clearness of their Understanding: It must be owned however, that (as it generally happens) they had each a Perversness of Humour suitable to their Distortion of Body. The eldest, whose Belly sunk in monstrously, was a great Coward; and though his splenetick contracted Temper made him take Fire immediately, he made Objects that beset him appear greater than they were. The second, whose Breast swelled into a bold Relievo, on the contrary, took great Pleasure in lessening every thing, and was perfectly the Reverse of his Brother. These Oddnesses pleased Company once or twice, but disgusted when often seen: For which Reason the young Gentlemen were sent from Court, to study Mathematicks at the University.

'I need not acquaint you, that I was very well made, and reckoned a bright, polite Gentleman. I was the Confident and Darling of all the Fair; and if the Old and Ugly spoke ill of me, all the World knew it was because I scorned to flatter them. No Ball, no Assembly was attended till I had been consulted. *Flavia* coloured her Hair before me, *Celia* shewed me her Teeth, *Panthea* heaved her Bosom, *Cleora* brandished her Diamond; I have seen *Chloe*'s Foot, and tied artificially[2] the Garters of *Rhodope*.

''Tis a general Maxim, that those who doat upon themselves, can have no violent Affection for another: But on the contrary, I found that the Womens Passion for me rose in Proportion to the Love they bore[b] to themselves. This was verified in my Amour with *Narcissa*, who was so constant to me, that it was pleasantly said, Had[c] I been

---

[a] produced a very odd Dream.] produced so odd a Dream, that no one but the SPECTATOR could believe that the Brain, clogged in Sleep, could furnish out such a regular Wildness of Imagination. *Fol.*   [b] bore] bare *Fol.*   [c] said, Had] said that had *Fol.*

---

[1] I.e. compensated for. *Obs.* (cf. *OED*).
[2] Here, as frequently, used in the archaic sense of 'artistically, ingeniously'.

little enough, she would have hung me at her Girdle. The most dangerous Rival I had, was a gay empty Fellow, who by the Strength of a long Intercourse with *Narcissa*, joined to his natural Endowments, had formed himself into a perfect Resemblance with her. I had been discarded, had she not observed that he frequently asked my Opinion about Matters of the last Consequence: This made me still more considerable in her Eye.

'Though I was eternally caressed by the Ladies, such was their Opinion of my Honour, that I was never envyed by the Men. A jealous Lover of *Narcissa* one Day thought he had caught her in an amorous Conversation; for though he was at such a Distance that he could hear nothing, he imagined strange things from her Airs and Gestures. Sometimes with a serene Look she step'd back in a listening Posture, and brightened into an innocent Smile. Quickly after she swelled into an Air of Majesty and Disdain, then let her Eyes half shut after a languishing Manner, cover'd her Blushes with her Hand; breath'd a Sigh, and seemed ready to sink down. In rushed the furious Lover, but how great was his surprise to see no one there but the innocent *Fidelio*, with his back against the Wall betwixt two Windows.

'It were endless to recount all my Adventures. Let me hasten to that which cost me my Life, and *Narcissa* her Happiness.

'She had the Misfortune to have the Small-Pox, upon which I was expressly forbid her sight; it being apprehended that it would increase her Distemper, and that I should infallibly catch it at the first Look. Assoon as she was suffer'd to leave her Bed, she stole out of her Chamber, and found me all alone in an adjoyning Apartment. She ran with transport to her Darling, and without Mixture of Fear, least I should dislike her. But, oh me! What was her Fury when she heard me say, I was afraid and shock'd at so loathsome a Spectacle. She step'd back, swollen with Rage, to see if I had the Insolence to repeat it. I did with this Addition, that her ill-timed Passion had increased her Ugliness. Enraged, Inflamed, Distracted, she snatch'd a Bodkin, and with all her force stab'd me to the Heart. Dying I preserved my Sincerity, and express'd the Truth, though in broken Words; and by reproachful Grimaces to the last I mimick'd the Deformity of my Murderess.

'*Cupid*, who always attends the Fair, and pity'd the Fate of so useful a Servant as I was, obtained of the *Destinies*, that my Body should remain Incorruptible, and retain the Qualities my Mind had possess'd. I immediately lost the Figure of Man, and became smooth, polish'd, and bright, and to this Day am the first Favourite of the Ladies.'   T¹

No. 393   *Saturday, May 31, 1712*²
[ADDISON]

Nescio quâ præter solitum dulcedine læti.
Virg.

LOOKING over the Letters that have been sent me, I chanced to find the following one, which I received about two Years ago from an Ingenious Friend who was then in *Denmark*.³

Dear Sir,   *Copenhagen, May 1, 1710.*

THE Spring with you has already taken Possession of the Fields and Woods: Now is the Season of Solitude, and of moving Complaints upon trivial Sufferings: Now the Griefs of Lovers begin to flow, and their Wounds to bleed afresh. I too, at this distance from the softer Climates, am not without my Discontents at present. You, perhaps, may laugh at me for a most Romantick Wretch, when I have disclosed to you the Occasion of my Uneasiness; and yet I cannot help thinking my Unhappiness real, in being confin'd to a Region which is the very Reverse of *Paradise*. The Seasons here are all of them unpleasant, and the Country quite destitute of Rural Charms. I have not heard a Bird sing, nor a Brook murmur, nor a Breeze whisper, neither have I been blest with the sight of a Flowry Meadow, these two Years. Every Wind here is a Tempest, and every Water a turbulent Ocean. I hope, when you reflect a little, you will not think the Grounds of my Complaint in the least frivolous and unbecoming a Man of serious Thought; since the Love of Woods, of Fields and Flowers, of Rivers

---

¹ This paper, signed T, is usually attributed to Steele but seems obviously a contribution. No author has been suggested.

² *Motto.* Virgil, *Georgics*, 1. 412: Seized with some secret, unwonted joy.

³ Nichols thought this was probably Ambrose Philips, or perhaps 'Mr. Molesworth, author of the History of Denmark'. Philips was in Copenhagen in 1710; his 'Winterpiece' had been printed in *Tatler* 12. Miss M. G. Segar (*Poems of Ambrose Philips*, Oxford, 1937) does not mention this letter. Robert, Viscount Molesworth's *Account of Denmark* was published in 1694. Of the two, Philips seems more likely to be the author of the letter.

and Fountains, seems to be a Passion implanted in our Natures the most early of any, even before the fair Sex had a Being.

I am, SIR, &c.'

Could I transport my self with a Wish from one Country to another, I should chuse to pass my Winter in *Spain*, my Spring in *Italy*, my Summer in *England*, and my Autumn in *France*. Of all these Seasons there is none that can vie with the Spring for Beauty and Delightfulness. It bears the same figure among the Seasons of the Year, that the Morning does among the divisions of the Day, or Youth among the Stages of Life. The *English* Summer is pleasanter than that of any other Country in *Europe*, on no other account but because it has a greater mixture of Spring in it. The Mildness of our Climate, with those frequent Refreshments of Dews and Rains that fall among us, keep up a perpetual Chearfulness in our Fields, and fill the hottest Months of the Year with a lively Verdure.

In the opening of the Spring, when all Nature begins to recover her self, the same Animal Pleasure which makes the Birds sing, and the whole Brute Creation rejoice, rises very sensibly in the Heart of Man. I know none of the Poets who have observed so well as *Milton* these secret Overflowings of Gladness which[a] diffuse themselves through the Mind of the Beholder, upon surveying the gay Scenes of Nature; he has touch'd upon it twice or thrice in his *Paradise Lost*, and describes it very beautifully under the Name of Vernal Delight in that Passage where he represents the Devil himself as almost sensible of it.

> *Blossoms and Fruits at once of golden hue*
> *Appear'd, with gay enamel'd colours mixt:*
> *On which the Sun more glad impress'd his beams*
> *Than in fair evening Cloud, or humid bow,*
> *When God hath showred the earth, so lovely seem'd*
> *That Lantskip: And of pure now purer air*
> *Meets his approach, and to the heart inspires*
> *Vernal delight and joy able to drive*
> *All sadness but despair, &c.*[1]

Many Authors have written on the Vanity of the Creature, and represented the Barrenness of every thing in this World, and its

---

[a] which] that *Fol.*

[1] *Paradise Lost*, iv. 148–56.

Incapacity of producing any solid or substantial Happiness. As Discourses of this nature are very useful to the Sensual and Voluptuous, those Speculations which shew the bright side of things, and lay forth those innocent Entertainments which are to be met with among the several Objects that encompass us, are no less beneficial to Men of dark and melancholy Tempers. It was for this Reason that I endeavoured to recommend a Chearfulness of Mind in my two last *Saturdays* Papers, and which I would still inculcate, not only from the Consideration of our selves, and of that Being on whom we depend, nor from the general Survey of that Universe in which we are placed at present, but from Reflections on the particular Season in which this Paper is written. The Creation is a perpetual Feast to the Mind of a good Man, every thing he sees chears and delights him; Providence has imprinted so many Smiles on Nature that it is impossible for a Mind which is not sunk in more gross and sensual Delights to take a Survey of them without several secret Sensations of Pleasure. The Psalmist has in several of his divine Poems celebrated those beautiful and agreeable Scenes which make the Heart glad, and produce in it that Vernal Delight which I have before taken Notice of.

Natural Philosophy quickens this Taste of the Creation, and renders it not only pleasing to the Imagination, but to the Understanding. It does not rest in the Murmur of Brooks, and the Melody of Birds, in the Shade of Groves and Woods, or in the Embroidery of Fields and Meadows, but considers the several Ends of Providence which are served by them, and the wonders of Divine Wisdom which appear in them. It heightens the Pleasures of the Eye, and raises such a rational Admiration in the Soul as is little inferiour to Devotion.

It is not in the Power of every one to offer up this kind of Worship to the great Author of Nature, and to indulge these more refined Meditations of Heart, which are doubtless highly acceptable in his sight; I shall therefore conclude this short Essay on that Pleasure which the Mind naturally conceives from the present Season of the Year, by the recommending of a Practice for which every one has sufficient Abilities.

I would have my Readers endeavour to moralize this natural Pleasure of the Soul, and to improve this vernal Delight, as *Milton* calls it, into a Christian Virtue. When we find our selves inspired with this pleasing Instinct, this secret Satisfaction and Complacency, arising from the Beauties of the Creation, let us consider to whom we stand indebted for all these Entertainments of Sense, and who it is that thus opens his Hand and fills the World with Good. The Apostle instructs us to take Advantage of our present Temper of Mind, to graft upon it such a religious Exercise as is particularly conformable to it, by that Precept which advises those who are Sad to pray, and those who are Merry to sing Psalms.[1] The Chearfulness of Heart which springs up in us from the Survey of Nature's Works is an admirable Preparation for Gratitude. The Mind has gone a great way towards Praise and Thanksgiving that is filled with such a secret Gladness: A grateful Reflection on the Supreme Cause who produces it, sanctifies it in the Soul, and gives it its proper Value. Such an habitual Disposition of Mind consecrates every Field and Wood, turns an ordinary Walk into a Morning or Evening Sacrifice, and will improve those transient Gleams of Joy, which naturally brighten up and refresh the Soul on such Occasions, into an inviolable and perpetual State of Bliss and Happiness.

I

No. 394   *Monday, June 2, 1712*[2]
[STEELE]

Bene colligitur hæc Pueris & Mulierculis & Servis &
Servorum simillimis Liberis esse grata. Gravi vero
homini & ea quæ fiunt Judicio certo ponderanti probari
posse nullo modo.

Tull.

I HAVE been considering the little and frivolous things which give Men Accesses to one another, and Power with each other, not only in the common and indifferent Accidents of Life, but also in Matters of greater Importance. You see in Elections for Members to sit in Parliament, how far saluting Rows of old Women, drinking with Clowns, and being upon a Level with the lowest Part of Man-

---

[1] James v. 13.
[2] *Motto.* Cicero, *De Officiis*, 2. 16. 57 (altered): It is well observed that these things are very acceptable to children, young women, and slaves, and to such freeborn men as most resemble slaves, but that they can by no means meet with the approbation of people of thought and consideration.

kind in that wherein they themselves are lowest, their Diversions, will carry a Candidate. A Capacity for prostituting a Man's self in his Behaviour, and descending to the present Humour of the Vulgar, is perhaps as good an Ingredient as any other for making a considerable Figure in the World; and if a Man has nothing else, or better, to think of, he could not make his Way to Wealth and Distinction by properer Methods than studying the particular Bent or Inclination of People with whom he converses, and working from the Observation of such their Biass in all Matters wherein he has any Intercourse with them: For his Ease and Comfort he may assure himself, he need not be at the Expence of any great Talent or Virtue to please even those who are possessed of the highest Qualifications. Pride in some particular Disguise or other, (often a Secret to the proud Man himself) is the most ordinary Spring of Action among Men. You need no more than to discover what a Man values himself for; then of all things admire that Quality, but be sure to be failing in it your self in Comparison of the Man whom you court. I have heard, or read, of a Secretary of State in *Spain*, who served a Prince who was happy in an elegant Use of the *Latin* Tongue, and often writ Dispatches in it with his own Hand. The King shewed his Secretary a Letter he had written to a foreign Prince; and under the Colour of asking his Advice, laid a Trap for his Applause. The honest Man read it as a faithful Counsellor, and not only excepted against his tying himself down too much by some Expressions, but mended the Phrase in others. You may guess the Dispatches that Evening did not take much longer time; Mr. Secretary, assoon as he came to his own House, sent for his eldest Son, and communicated to him that the Family must retire out of *Spain* assoon as possible; for, said he, the King knows I understand *Latin* better than he does.[1]

[1] A story with a similar moral is told in *The Art of Prudence: or, a Companion for a Man of Sense* (a translation of Gracián's *Discreto*, with notes by Amelot de la Houssaie), Maxim VII, 'To have a care not to out-do ones Master' (London, 1702, p. 7):

A *Spanish* Lord having plaid a long while at Chess with *Philip* IId. and always won; when he left off he perceiv'd the King exceeding Melancholly, whereupon returning home he call'd his Children together, and thus spoke to them: *Children* (says he) we must not think to have any more to do at Court; we shall never advance our selves there, since I've observ'd the King was exceedingly Offended that he could not beat me at Chess; A Game which depends more on good Cunning, than good Fortune.

The anecdote also appears in *Menagiana* (3rd ed., 1715, i. 164), where it is pointed out that the story comes from La Houssaie's notes.

This egregious Fault, in a Man of the World, should be a Lesson to all who would make their Fortunes: But a Regard must be carefully had to the Person with whom you have to do; for it is not to be doubted but a great Man of common Sense must look with secret Indignation, or bridled Laughter, on all the Slaves who stand round him with ready Faces to approve and smile at all he says in the Gross.[1] It is good Comedy enough to observe a Superior talking half Sentences, and playing an humble Admirer's Countenance from one thing to another, with such Perplexity that he knows not what to sneer in Approbation of: But this kind of Complaisance is peculiarly the Manner of Courts; in all other Places you must constantly go farther in Complyance with the Persons you have to do with, than a meer Conformity of Looks and Gestures. If you are in a Country-Life, and would be a leading Man, a good Stomach, a loud Voice, and a rustick Chearfulness, will go a great Way, provided you are able to drink, and drink any thing. But I was just now going[a] to draw the Manner of Behaviour I would advise People to practise under some Maxim; and intimated, that every[b] one almost was governed by his Pride. There was an old Fellow about forty Years ago so peevish and fretful, though a Man of Business, that no one could come at him: But he frequented a particular little Coffeehouse, where he triumphed over every Body at Trick-track and Baggammon.[2] The Way to pass his Office well, was, first to be insulted by him at one of those Games in his leisure Hours: For his Vanity was to shew, that he was a Man of Pleasure as well as Business. Next to this sort of Insinuation, which is called in all Places (from its taking its Birth in the Housholds of Princes) making one's Court, the most prevailing Way is, by what better bred People call a Present, the Vulgar a Bribe. I humbly conceive that such a thing is conveyed with more Gallantry in a *Billet-doux* that should be understood at the *Bank*, than in gross Money; but as to stubborn

[a] just now going] going just now *Fol.*   [b] intimated, that every] intimated, every *Fol.*

[1] Pope may have taken a hint for the Atticus portrait from this passage.

[2] Trick-track, or tick-tack, an old variety of backgammon, played on a board with holes along the edge, in which pegs were placed for scoring. So called from the clicking sound made by the pieces in playing the game (*OED*). Theophilus Lucas (*Memoirs . . . of the most famous Gamesters*, 1714) describes the game and derives the title 'from Touch and Take; for if you touch a Man you must play him, though to your Loss' (p. 127). Richard Seymour (*The Compleat Gamester*, 5th ed., 1734, part iii) gives rules for playing both 'Grand Trick-Track' (pp. 45–58) and 'Tick-Tack' (pp. 62–64). For baggamon (backgammon) see Nos. 77, 106 (vol. i), 264 (vol. ii).

People, who are so surly as to accept of neither Note or Cash, having formerly dabbled in Chymistry,[1] I can only say that one Part of Matter asks one thing, and another another, to make it fluent; but there is nothing but may be dissolved by a proper Mean: Thus the Virtue which is too obdurate for Gold or Paper, shall melt away very kindly in a Liquid. The Island of *Barbadoes* (a shrewd People) manage all their Appeals to *Great Britain* by a skillful Distribution of Citron-Water among the Whisperers about Men in Power.[2] Generous Wines do every Day prevail, and that in great Points where ten thousand times their Value would have been rejected with Indignation.

But to wave the Enumeration of the sundry Ways of applying by Presents, Bribes, Management of Peoples Passions and Affections, in such a Manner as it shall appear that the Virtue of the best Man is by one Method or other corruptible; let us look out for some Expedient to turn those Passions and Affections on the Side of Truth and Honour. When a Man has laid it down for a Position, that parting with his Integrity, in the minutest Circumstance, is losing so much of his very Self; Self-love will become a Virtue. By this Means Good and Evil will be the only Objects of Dislike and Approbation; and he that injures any Man, has effectually wounded the Man of this Turn, as much as if the Harm had been to himself. This seems to be the only Expedient to arrive at an Impartiality; and a Man who follows the Dictates of Truth and right Reason, may by Artifice be led into Errour, but never can into Guilt.

T

[1] For Steele's experiments in alchemy see Aitken, i. 141–5.

[2] Citron water was 'a favourite liqueur, which was called *Barbados Waters*, by some, and *eau de Barbade*, by others who would be "French and fashionable"'. This Barbadian cordial was made by extracting the essential oil from the rind of the fruit of the citron tree, this being done by means of that French brandy which Mr. Ligon describes as "extream strong, but accounted very wholesome"' (N. Darnell Davis, *The 'Spectator's' Essays relating to the West Indies* (Demerara, British Guiana, 1885, p. 12)). It is advertised in No. 242:

> Extraordinary rich Citron-Water and Spirit of Orange-Flowers, lately imported from Barbadoes, are to be sold at Mr. Slans over against the Sugar-Loaf in Lime-street.

No. 395
[BUDGELL]

Tuesday, June 3, 1712[1]

. . . Quod nunc ratio est, Impetus ante fuit.
Ovid.

*B*EWARE *of the Ides of* March, said the *Roman* Augur to *Julius Cæsar*: *Beware of the Month of* May, says the *British Spectator* to his fair Country-women. The Caution of the first was unhappily neglected, and *Cæsar*'s Confidence cost him his Life. I am apt to flatter my self that my pretty Readers had much more Regard to the Advice I gave them,[2] since I have yet received very few Accounts of any notorious Trips made in the last Month.

But tho' I hope for the best, I shall not pronounce too positively on this point, 'till I have seen forty Weeks well over, at which Period of time, as my good Friend Sir ROGER has often told me, he has more Business as a Justice of Peace, among the dissolute young People in the Country, than at any other Season of the Year.

Neither must I forget a Letter which I received near a Fortnight since from a Lady, who, it seems, could hold out no longer, telling me she looked upon the Month as then out, for that she had all along reckoned by the New Stile.[3]

On the other hand, I have great reason to believe, from several angry Letters which have been sent to me by disappointed Lovers, that my Advice has been of very signal Service to the fair Sex, who, according to the old Proverb, were *Forewarn'd forearm'd.*

One of these Gentlemen tells me, that he would have given me an hundred Pounds, rather than I should have publish'd that Paper; for that his Mistress, who had promised to explain her self to him about the beginning of *May*, upon reading that Discourse told him that *she would give him her Answer in* June.

Thyrsis acquaints me, that when he desired *Silvia* to take a Walk in the Fields, she told him *the Spectator had forbidden her.*

Another of my Correspondents, who writes himself *Mat. Meager*, complains, that whereas he constantly used to Breakfast with his Mistress upon Chocolate,[4] going to wait upon her the first of *May*,

---

[1] *Motto.* Ovid, *Remedia amoris,* 10: What is reason now was appetite before.
[2] See No. 365 (also by Budgell).
[3] At this time England was still using the Julian calendar, eleven days behind the 'New Style' in use on the Continent.
[4] 'Romances, Chocolate, Novels, and the like Inflamers' are mentioned in No. 365.

he found his usual Treat very much changed for the worse, and has been forced to feed ever since upon Green Tea.

As I begun this Critical Season with a Caveat to the Ladies, I shall conclude it with a Congratulation, and do most heartily wish them Joy of their Happy Deliverance.

They may now reflect with Pleasure on the Dangers they have escaped, and look back with as much Satisfaction on their Perils that threatned them, as their Great-Grandmothers did formerly on the burning Plough Shares, after having passed through the Ordeal Tryal.[1] The Instigations of the Spring are now abated. The Nightingal gives over her *Love-labour'd Song*,[2] as *Milton* phrases it, the Blossoms are fallen, and the Beds of Flowers swept away by the Scythe of the Mower.

I shall now allow my Fair Readers to return to their Romances and Chocolate, provided they make use of them with Moderation, 'till about the middle of the Month, when the Sun shall have made some Progress in the *Crabb*. Nothing is more dangerous, than too much Confidence and Security. The *Trojans*, who stood upon their Guard all the while the *Grecians* lay before their City, when they fancied the Siege was raised, and the Danger past, were the very next Night burnt in their Beds. I must also observe, that as in some Climates there is a perpetual *Spring*, so in some Female Constitutions there is a perpetual *May*: These are a kind of *Valetudinarians* in Chastity,[3] whom I would continue in a constant Diet. I cannot think these wholly out of Danger, till they have looked upon the other Sex at least Five Years, through a Pair of Spectacles. WILL. HONEYCOMB has often assured me, that 'tis much easier to steal one of this Species, when she is pass'd her grand Climacterick,[4] than to carry off an *icy* Girl on this side Five and Twenty; and that a Rake of his Acquaintance, who had in vain endeavour'd to gain the Affections of a young Lady of Fifteen, had at last made his Fortune by running away with her Grandmother.

But as I do not design this Speculation for the *Ever-greens*[5] of the Sex, I shall again apply my self to those who would willingly listen to the Dictates of Reason and Virtue, and can now hear me in cold

---

[1] Cf. the account of Queen Emma in No. 198 (vol. ii).
[2] *Paradise Lost*, v. 41.
[3] This example is the earliest in *OED* to illustrate the figurative use of *valetudinarian*. The word itself had recently come into the language.
[4] See No. 295.
[5] The earliest example of this figurative use in *OED* is dated 1878.

Blood. If there are any who have forfeited their Innocence, they must now consider themselves under that Melancholy View, in which *Chamont* regards his Sister, in those beautiful Lines.

> *. . . Long she Flourish'd,*
> *Grew sweet to Sense, and lovely to the Eye,*
> *Till at the last a cruel Spoiler came,*
> *Cropt this fair Rose, and rifled all its Sweetness,*
> *Then cast it like a loathsome Weed away.*[1]

On the contrary, she who has observed the timely Cautions I gave her, and lived up to the Rules of Modesty, will now Flourish like *a Rose in* June, with all her Virgin Blushes and Sweetness about her: I must, however, desire these last to consider, how shameful it would be for a General, who has made a Successful Campaign, to be surprised in his Winter-Quarters: It would be no less dishonourable for a Lady to lose, in any other Month of the Year, what she has been at the pains to preserve in *May.*

There is no Charm in the Female Sex, that can supply the place of Virtue. Without Innocence Beauty is unlovely, and Quality contemptible, Good-breeding degenerates into Wantonness, and Wit into Impudence. It is observed, that all the Virtues are represented by both Painters and Statuaries, under Female Shapes;[2] but if any one of them has a more particular Title to that Sex, it is Modesty. I shall leave it to the Divines to guard them against the opposite Vice, as they may be overpowered by Temptations; It is sufficient for me to have warned them against it, as they may be led astray by Instinct.

I desire this Paper may be read with more than ordinary Attention, at all Tea-tables within the Cities of London *and* Westminster.   X

---

[1] Otway, *The Orphan,* iv. 294–302.
[2] 'It is a great compliment methinks to the sex', says Cynthio in Addison's *Dialogues upon Ancient Medals,* 'that your Virtues are generally shown in petticoats. I can give no other reason for it, says *Philander,* but because they chanced to be of the feminine gender in the learned languages' (Guthkelch, ii. 300).

Barbara, Celarent, Darii, Ferio, Baralipton.

HAVING a great deal of Business upon my Hands at present, I shall beg the Reader's Leave to present him with a Letter that I received about half a Year ago from a Gentleman of *Cambridge*, who stiles himself *Peter de Quir*.[2] I have kept it by me some Months, and though I did not know at first what to make of it, upon my reading it over very frequently I have at last discovered several Conceits in it: I would not therefore have my Reader discouraged if he does not take them at the first Perusal.

To Mr. SPECTATOR.

From *St.* John's *College*
Cambridge, Feb. 3. 1712.

SIR,

'THE Monopoly of Punns in this University has been an immemorial Privilege of the *Johnians*; and we can't help resenting the late Invasion of our ancient Right as to that Particular, by a little Pretender to Clenching in a neighbouring College, who in an Application to you by way of Letter, a while ago stiled himself *Philobrune*.[3] Dear Sir, as you are by Character a profest Well-wisher to Speculation, you will excuse a Remark which this Gentleman's Passion for the *Brunette* has suggested to a Brother Theorist; 'tis an Offer towards a mechanical Account of his Lapse to Punning, for he belongs to a Set of Mortals, who value themselves upon an uncommon Mastery in the more humane and polite Part of Letters.

---

[1] *Motto.* The old mnemonic verses designed to recall the moods of the syllogism begin with these words. See, e.g., John Newton, *The English Academy*, part vii, chap. iv (ed. 1677, p. 188).

[2] According to Nichols, No. 396 'was the communication of *Orator* HENLEY, who was the author of this silly letter, and another signed *Tom Tweer*; and who was a person of a character as odious, as that of a buffoon so contemptible could be'. At this time John Henley was twenty years old. Born in 1692, he entered St. John's College, Cambridge, in 1709, and graduated A.B. in 1712. He later edited the *Hyp Doctor* and gave lectures, religious on Sundays and political on Wednesdays. There seems to be no real proof that this letter is from Henley, though he had a reputation for punning. He is named as the author in the *Gentleman's Magazine*, May 1779, p. 256 (apparently by Nichols) and also by J. D. in the same journal, Apr. 1780. The biographical account of Henley in *Oratory Transactions* No. 1 (1728) makes no reference to any contributions to the *Spectator*. The *DNB* entry on Henley makes the unaccountable statement that he wrote Nos. 94 (vol. i) and 578 (vol. iv) (both by Addison).

[3] See No. 286.

A Conquest by one of this Species of Females gives a very odd Turn to the Intellectuals of the captivated Person, and very different from that Way of Thinking which a Triumph from the Eyes of another more emphatically of the fair Sex, does generally occasion. It fills the Imagination with an Assemblage of such Ideas and Pictures as are hardly any thing but Shade, such as Night, the Devil, &c. These Portraitures very near over-power the Light of the Understanding, almost benight the Faculties, and give that melancholy Tincture to the most sanguine Complexion, which this Gentleman calls an Inclination to be in a Brown-study, and is usually attended with worse Consequences in Case of a Repulse. During this Twilight of Intellects, the Patient is extremely apt, as Love is the most witty Passion in Nature, to offer at some pert Sallies now and then, by Way of Flourish, upon the amiable Enchantress, and unfortunately stumbles upon that mongrel miscreated[1] (to speak in *Miltonic*) Kind of Wit, vulgarly term'd, the Punn. It would not be much amiss to consult Dr. T——— W———[2] (who is certainly a very able Projector, and whose System of Divinity and spiritual Mechanicks obtains very much among the better Part of our Under-Graduates) whether a general Inter-marriage, enjoyn'd by Parliament, between this Sisterhood of the Olive Beauties, and the Fraternity of the People call'd Quakers, would not be a very serviceable Expedient, and abate that Overflow of Light which shines within 'em so powerfully, that it dazzles their Eyes, and dances 'em into a thousand Vagaries of Error and Enthusiasm. These Reflections may impart some Light towards a Discovery of the Origin of Punning among us, and the Foundation of its prevailing so long in this famous Body. 'Tis notorious from the Instance under Consideration, that it must be owing chiefly to the use of brown Juggs, muddy Belch,[3] and the Fumes of a certain memorable Place of Rendezvous with us at Meals, known by the Name of *Staincoat*

---

[1] *Paradise Lost*, ii. 683. See No. 285, where this word is cited.

[2] 'Perhaps Mr. Thomas Woolston, whom Orator Henley here stiles Doctor' (Nichols). Woolston (1670–1733) was a fellow of Sidney Sussex College, Cambridge, who, in Whiston's words, 'most unfortunately fell into *Origen's* Allegorical Works; and poring hard upon them, . . . he became so fanciful in that Matter, that he thought the Allegorical Way of Interpretation of the Scriptures of the *Old Testament* had been unjustly neglected by the Moderns; and that it might be useful for an additional Proof of the Truth of Christianity' (*Memoirs of the Life and Writings of Mr. William Whiston*, 1749, p. 231). It was reported later that his mind was disordered, and he lost his fellowship. There is no certainty that Woolston is the person referred to here; no other candidate has been suggested.

[3] A slang name for poor beer. The earliest example in *OED* is dated 1706.

Hole: For the Atmosphere of the Kitchen, like the Tail of a Comet, predominates least about the Fire, but resides behind, and fills the fragrant Receptacle above-mention'd. Besides, 'tis farther observable, that the delicate Spirits among us, who declare against these nauseous Proceedings, sip Tea, and put up for Critic and Amour, profess likewise an equal Abhorrency for Punning, the ancient innocent Diversion of this Society. After all, Sir, tho' it may appear something absurd, that I seem to approach you with the Air of an Advocate for Punning, (you who have justified your Censures of the Practice in a set Dissertation[1] upon that Subject;) yet, I'm confident, you'll think it abundantly atton'd for by observing, that this humbler Exercise may be as instrumental in diverting us from any innovating Schemes and Hypothesis in Wit, as dwelling upon honest Orthodox Logic would be in securing us from Heresy in Religion. Had Mr. *W——n*'s Researches[2] been confin'd within the Bounds of *Ramus* or *Crackanthorp*,[3] that learned News-monger might have acquiesc'd in what the holy Oracles pronounce upon the Deluge like other Christians; and had the surprizing Mr. *L——y*[4] been content with the Employment of refining upon *Shakespear*'s Points and Quibbles, (for which he must be allow'd to have a superlative Genius) and now and then penning a Catch or a Ditty, instead of inditing Odes, and Sonnets, the Gentlemen of the *Bon Goust* in the Pit would never have been put to all that Grimace in damning the Frippery of State, the Poverty and Languor of Thought, the unnatural Wit, and inartificial Structure of his Dramas.

I am,

SIR,

Your very humble Servant,

Peter de Quir.'

[1] No. 61 (vol. i).

[2] Identified by Nichols as William Whiston (1667-1752), an attribution accepted by subsequent editors. His *New Theory of the Earth* (1696) was praised by both Newton and Locke, and in 1703 he succeeded Newton as Lucasian professor of mathematics at Cambridge, whence he was expelled in 1710 for heterodoxy. His *Primitive Christianity Revived*, published in five volumes in 1711-12, was an attempt to revive Arian doctrines. In his *Memoirs* (1749) Whiston pays tribute to Addison as his particular friend, 'who, with his Friend Sir *Richard Steel*, brought me, upon my Banishment from *Cambridge*, to have many Astronomical Lectures at Mr. *Button*'s Coffee-house, near *Covent-Garden*, to the agreeable Entertainment of a good Number of curious Persons, and the procuring me and my Family some comfortable Support under my Banishment' (p. 302).

[3] Peter Ramus, author of the *Institutiones Dialecticae*, was killed in the massacre of St. Bartholomew's Day, 1572. Richard Crakanthorp (1567-1624) was author of *Logicae Libri quinque* (1622), which reached a fourth edition in 1677.

[4] No satisfactory identification has been offered for this name. Nichols mentions

No. 397
[ADDISON]

Thursday, June 5, 1712[1]

> . . . Dolor ipse disertum
> Fecerat . . .
>
> Ovid.

AS the *Stoick* Philosophers discard all Passions in general, they
will not allow a Wise Man so much as to pity the Afflictions
of another. If thou seest thy Friend in trouble, says *Epictetus*, thou
may'st put on a Look of Sorrow, and condole with him, but take
care that thy Sorrow be not real.[2] The more rigid of this Sect would
not comply so far as to shew even such an outward Appearance of
Grief; but when one told them of any Calamity that had befallen
even the nearest of their Acquaintance, would immediately reply
What is that to me? If you aggravated the Circumstances of the
Affliction, and shew'd how one Misfortune was followed by another,
the Answer was still, All this may be true, but what is it to me?

For my own part, I am of Opinion Compassion does not only
refine and civilize Human Nature, but has something in it more
pleasing and agreeable than what can be met with in such an
indolent Happiness, such an Indifference to Mankind as that in
which the *Stoicks* placed their Wisdom. As Love is the most delightful Passion, Pity is nothing else but Love softned by a degree of
Sorrow: In short, it is a kind of pleasing Anguish, as well as generous
Sympathy, that knits Mankind together, and blends them in the
same common Lot.

Those who have laid down Rules for Rhetorick or Poetry, advise
the Writer to work himself up, if possible, to the pitch of Sorrow
which he endeavours to produce in others.[3] There are none therefore who stir up Pity so much as those who indite their own Sufferings. Grief has a natural Eloquence belonging to it, and breaks out
in more moving Sentiments than can be supplied by the finest

'John Lacy, who altered one of Shakespeare's Plays' and was actor and playwright.
'But he had been dead more than 30 years before the date of this Paper, in Sept. 1681.'
There is also a poem published under the name of John Lacy, entitled *The Steeleids, or,
The Tryal of Wit*, mentioned by Nichols. Printed and sold (1714) by the Tory book-
seller, John Morphew, it praises the *Examiner* and contains (p. 16) a sneer at Steele
as the wren soaring up to heaven on the wings of the eagle.

[1] *Motto.* Ovid, *Metamorphoses*, 13. 228–9: Grief with eloquence the tongue inspired.
[2] Epictetus, *Enchiridion*, 16.
[3] E.g., Horace, *Ars poetica*, 102.

Imagination. Nature on this occasion dictates a thousand Passionate things which[a] cannot be supplied by Art.

It is for this Reason that the short Speeches or Sentences which we often meet with in Histories, make a deeper Impression on[b] the Mind of the Reader, than the most labour'd Strokes in a well written Tragedy. Truth and Matter of Fact sets the Person actually before us in the one, whom Fiction places at a greater distance from us in the other. I do not remember to have seen any Ancient or Modern Story more affecting than a Letter of *Ann* of *Bologne*, Wife to King *Henry* the Eighth, and Mother to Queen *Elizabeth*, which is still extant in the *Cotton* Library, as written by her own Hand.[1]

Shakespear himself could not have made her talk in a Strain so suitable to her Condition and Character. One sees in it the Expostulations of a slighted Lover, the Resentments of an injured Woman, and the Sorrows of an imprisoned Queen. I need not acquaint my Reader that this Princess was then under Prosecution for Disloyalty to the King's Bed, and that she was afterwards publickly beheaded upon the same Account, though this Prosecution was believed by many to proceed, as she her self intimates, rather from the King's Love to *Jane Seymour*, than from any actual Crime in *Ann* of *Bologne*.

Queen Ann Boleyn's *last Letter to King* Henry.

SIR,

'YOUR Grace's Displeasure, and my Imprison-   *Cotton Libr.*
ment, are things so strange unto me, as what   *Otho C.* 10.
to write, or what to excuse, I am altogether ignorant. Whereas you send unto me (willing me to confess a Truth, and so obtain your Favour) by such an one, whom you know to be mine ancient professed Enemy, I no sooner receiv'd this Message by him, than I rightly conceiv'd your Meaning; and if, as you say, confessing a Truth indeed may procure my Safety, I shall with all Willingness and Duty perform your Command.

'But let not your Grace ever imagine, that your poor Wife will ever be brought to acknowledge a Fault, where not so much as a Thought thereof preceded. And to speak a Truth, never Prince had Wife more Loyal in all Duty, and in all true Affection, than you

---

[a] which] that *Fol.*   [b] on] in *Fol.*

---

[1] The letter is printed in Peter Heylyn, *Ecclesia Restaurata; or, the History of the Reformation of the Church of England* (1661), part ii, p. 95.

have ever found in *Ann Boleyn*; with which Name and Place I could willingly have contented my self, if God, and your Grace's Pleasure had been so pleased. Neither did I at any time so far forget my self in my Exaltation, or received Queenship, but that I always looked for such an Alteration as now I find; for the Ground of my Preferment being on no surer Foundation than your Grace's Fancy, the least Alteration I knew was fit and sufficient to draw that Fancy to some other Subject. You have chosen me, from a low Estate, to be your Queen and Companion, far beyond my Desert or Desire. If then you found me worthy of such Honour, good your Grace let not any light Fancy, or bad Counsel of mine Enemies, withdraw your Princely Favour from me; neither let that Stain, that unworthy Stain, of a Disloyal Heart towards your good Grace, ever cast so foul a Blot on your most Dutiful Wife, and the Infant-Princess your Daughter. Try me, good King, but let me have a lawful Tryal, and let not my Sworn Enemies sit as my Accusers and Judges; Yea let me receive an open Tryal, for my Truth shall fear no open Shame; then shall you see either mine Innocency cleared, your Suspicion and Conscience satisfied, the Ignominy and Slander of the World stopped, or my Guilt openly declared. So that whatsoever God or you may determine of me, your Grace may be freed from an open Censure, and mine Offence being so lawfully proved, your Grace is at liberty both before God and Man, not only to Execute worthy Punishment on me as an unlawful Wife, but to follow your Affection, already setled on that Party, for whose sake I am now as I am, whose Name I could some good while since have pointed unto, your Grace being not ignorant of my Suspicion therein.

'But if you have already determined of me, and that not only my Death, but an Infamous Slander must bring you the enjoying of your desired Happiness; then I desire of God, that he will pardon your great Sin therein, and likewise mine Enemies, the Instruments thereof; and that he will not call you to a strict Account for your unprincely and cruel Usage of me, at his general Judgment Seat, where both you and my self must shortly appear, and in whose Judgment I doubt not (whatsoever the World may think of me) mine Innocence shall be openly known, and sufficiently cleared.

'My last and only Request shall be, that my self may only bear the Burthen of your Grace's Displeasure, and that it may not touch the innocent Souls of those poor Gentlemen, who (as I understand) are likewise in strait Imprisonment for my sake. If ever I have found

Favour in your sight, if ever the Name of *Ann Boleyn* hath been pleasing in your Ears, then let me obtain this Request, and I will so leave to trouble your Grace any further, with mine earnest Prayers to the Trinity to have your Grace in his good keeping, and to direct you in all your Actions. From my doleful Prison in the *Tower*, this 6th of *May*;

Your most Loyal
and ever Faithful Wife,
Ann Boleyn.'[1]

L

No. 398

[STEELE]

Friday, June 6, 1712[2]

Insanire paret certa ratione modoque.
Hor.

*C*YNTHIO and *Flavia* are Persons of Distinction in this Town, who have been Lovers these ten Months last past, and writ to each other, for Gallantry Sake, under those feigned Names; Mr. Such a one and Mrs. such a one not being capable of raising the Soul out of the ordinary Tracts and Passages of Life, up to that Elevation which makes the Life of the Enamoured so much superiour to that of the rest of the World. But ever since the beauteous *Cecilia* has made such a Figure as she now does in the Circle of charming Women, *Cynthio* has been secretly one of her Adorers. *Lætitia* has been the finest Woman in Town these three Months, and so long *Cynthio* has acted the Part of a Lover very aukwardly in the Presence of *Flavia*. *Flavia* has been too blind towards him, and has too sincere an Heart of her own to observe a thousand things which would have discovered this Change of Mind to any one less engaged than

---

[1] A letter from E. G. dated 24 June 1712 (Lillie, ii. 259–64) acknowledges the pleasure derived from 'the moving letter of Queen Anne of Boleyn', and submits a version in rhymed couplets.

[2] *Motto.* Horace, *Satires*, 2. 3. 271:

To be a Fool
By Art and Wisdom, and be mad by Rule. CREECH.

she was. *Cynthio* was musing Yesterday in the Piazza[1] in *Covent Garden*, and was saying to himself that he was a very ill Man to go on in visiting and professing Love to *Flavia*, when his Heart was enthraled to another. It is an Infirmity that I am not constant to *Flavia*; but it would be still a greater Crime, since I cannot continue to love her, to profess that I do. To marry a Woman with the Coldness that usually indeed comes on after Marriage, is ruining ones self with ones Eyes open; besides, it is really doing her an Injury. This last Consideration, forsooth, of injuring her in persisting, made him resolve to break off upon the first favourable Opportunity of making her angry. When he was in this Thought, he saw *Robin* the Porter, who waits at *Will's* Coffee-house, passing by. *Robin*, you must know, is the best Man in Town for carrying a Billet; the Fellow has a thin Body, swift Step, demure Look, sufficient Sense, and knows the Town. This Man carried *Cynthio's* first Letter to *Flavia*, and by frequent Errands ever since, is well known to her. The Fellow covers his Knowledge of the Nature of his Messages with the most exquisite low Humour imaginable: The first he obliged *Flavia* to take, was by complaining to her that he had a Wife and three Children, and if she did not take that Letter, which, he was sure, there was no Harm in, but rather Love, his Family must go supperless to Bed, for the Gentleman would pay him according as he did his Business. *Robin* therefore *Cynthio* now thought fit to make use of, and gave him Orders to wait before *Flavia's* Door, and if she called him to her, and asked whether it was *Cynthio* who passed by, he should at first be loath to own it was, but upon Importunity confess it. There needed not much Search in that Part of the Town to find a well dressed Hussey fit for the Purpose *Cynthio* designed her. Assoon as he believed *Robin* was posted, he drove by *Flavia's* Lodgings in an Hackney-Coach and a Woman in it. *Robin* was at the Door talking with *Flavia's* Maid, and *Cynthio* pull'd up the Glass as surprized, and hid his Associate. The Report of this Circumstance soon flew up Stairs, and *Robin* could not deny but the Gentleman favoured[2] his Master; yet if it was he, he was sure the Lady was but his Cousin whom he had seen ask for him; adding, that he believed she was a poor Relation, because they made her wait one Morning till he was awake. *Flavia* immediately writ the following Epistle, which *Robin* brought to *Will's*.

[1] See No. 14 (vol. i).
[2] Resembled in face or features. Now colloquial (*OED*).

SIR, *June*[a] 4, 1712.
'I T is in vain to deny it, basest, falsest of Mankind, my Maid, as well as the Bearer, saw you.

The injured Flavia.'

After *Cynthio* had read the Letter, he asked *Robin* how she looked, and what she said at the Delivery of it. *Robin* said she spoke short to him, and called him back again, and had nothing to say to him, and bid him and all the Men in the World go out of her Sight; but the Maid followed, and bid him bring an Answer.

Cynthio returned as follows.

Madam, *June 4, Three Afternoon*, 1712.
'T HAT your Maid and the Bearer has seen me very often is very certain; but I desire to know, being engaged at Picket,[1] what your Letter means by *'tis in vain to deny it*. I shall stay here all the Evening.

Your amazed Cynthio.'

As soon as *Robin* arrived with this, *Flavia* answered;

Dear Cynthio,
'I Have walked a Turn or two in my Antichamber since I writ to you, and have recovered my self from an impertinent Fit which you ought to forgive me; and desire you would come to me immediately, to laugh off a Jealousy that you and a Creature of the Town went by in an Hackney-Coach an Hour ago.

I am your most humble Servant,

Flavia.

'I will not open the Letter which my *Cynthio* writ, upon the Misapprehension you must have been under when you writ for want of hearing the whole Circumstance.'

Robin came back in an Instant, and *Cynthio* answered;

Half an Hour,[b] *six Minutes after Three*,
Madam, June 4, Will's *Coffee-house*.
'I T is certain I went by your Lodgings with a Gentlewoman to whom I have the Honour to be known, she is indeed my Relation, and a pretty sort of Woman. But your starting Manner of

---

[a] *June*] *March Fol.*   [b] *Half an Hour*,] *Half Hour, Fol.*

[1] See No. 198 (vol. ii).

Writing, and owning you have not done me the Honour so much as to open my Letter, has in it something very unaccountable, and alarms one that has had Thoughts of passing his Days with you. But I am born to admire you with all your little Imperfections.

Cynthio.'

Robin run back, and brought for Answer;

'EXACT Sir, that are at *Will*'s Coffee-house six Minutes after Three, *June* 4; one that has had Thoughts, and all my little Imperfections. Sir, come to me immediately, or I shall determine what may perhaps not be very pleasing to you.

Flavia.'

Robin gave an Account that she looked excessive angry when she gave him the Letter; and that he told her, for she asked, that *Cynthio* only looked at the Clock, taking Snuff, and writ two or three Words to the Top of the Letter when he gave him his.

Now the Plot thickened so well, as that *Cynthio* saw he had not much more to do to accomplish being irreconciliably banished, he writ,

Madam,

'I Have that Prejudice in Favour of all you do, that it is not possible for you to determine upon what will not be very pleasing to,

Your obedient Servant,

Cynthio.'

This was delivered, and the Answer returned, in a little more than two Seconds.

SIR,

'IS it come to this? You never loved me; and the Creature you were with is the properest Person for your Associate. I despise you, and hope I shall soon hate you as a Villain to

The Credulous Flavia.'

Robin ran back, with,

Madam,

'YOUR Credulity when you are to gain your Point, and Suspicion when you fear to lose it, make it a very hard Part to behave as becomes

Your humble Slave,

Cynthio.'

Robin whipt away, and returned with,

Mr. *Wellford,*

'*FLAVIA* and *Cynthio* are no more. I relieve you from the hard Part of which you complain, and banish you from my Sight for ever.

Ann Heart.'

Robin had a Crown for his Afternoon's Work; and this is published to admonish *Cecilia* to avenge the Injury done to *Flavia*.　　T

No. 399

[ADDISON]

Ut nemo in sese tentat descendere! . . .

Pers.

HYPOCRISIE, at the fashionable End of the Town, is very different from Hypocrisie in the City. The modish Hypocrite endeavours to appear more Vicious than he really is, the other kind of Hypocrite more Virtuous. The former is afraid of every thing that has the shew of Religion in it, and would be thought engaged in many Criminal Gallantries and Amours, which he is not guilty of. The latter assumes a Face of Sanctity, and covers a Multitude of Vices under a seeming Religious Deportment.

But there is another kind of Hypocrisie, which differs from both these, and which I intend to make the Subject of this Paper: I mean that Hypocrisie, by which a Man does not only deceive the World, but very often imposes on himself; That Hypocrisie, which conceals his own Heart from him, and makes him believe he is more virtuous than he really is, and either not attend to his Vices or mistake even his Vices for Virtues. It is this fatal Hypocrisie and Self-deceit, which is taken notice of in those Words, *Who can understand his Errours? cleanse thou me from secret Faults.*[2]

If the open Professors of Impiety deserve the utmost Application, and Endeavours of Moral Writers to recover them from Vice and Folly, how much more may those lay a Claim to their Care and

[1] *Motto.* Persius, *Satires,* 4. 23:
　　　　None, none descends into himself, to find
　　　　The secret Imperfections of his Mind. DRYDEN.

[2] Ps. xix. 12.

Compassion, who are walking in the Paths of Death, while they fancy themselves engaged in a Course of Virtue! I shall endeavour, therefore, to lay down some Rules for the Discovery of those Vices that lurk in the secret Corners of the Soul, and to shew my Reader those Methods by which he may arrive at a true and impartial Knowledge of himself. The usual Means prescribed for this Purpose, are to examine our selves by the Rules which are laid down for our Direction in Sacred Writ, and to compare our Lives with the Life of that Person who acted up to the Perfection of Human Nature, and is the standing Example, as well as the Great Guide and Instructor, of those who receive his Doctrines. Though these two Heads cannot be too much insisted upon, I shall but just mention them, since they have been handled by many Great and Eminent Writers.

I would therefore propose the following Methods to the Consideration of such as would find out their secret Faults, and make a true Estimate of themselves.

In the first place, let them consider well what are the Characters which they bear among their Enemies. Our Friends very often flatter us, as much as our own Hearts. They either do not see our Faults, or conceal them from us, or soften them by their Representations, after such a manner, that we think them too trivial to be taken notice of. An Adversary, on the contrary, makes a stricter[a] Search into us, discovers every Flaw and Imperfection in our Tempers, and though his Malice may set them in too strong a Light, it has generally some Ground for what it advances. A Friend exaggerates a Man's Virtues, an Enemy inflames[1] his Crimes. A Wise Man should give a just Attention to both of them, so far as they may tend to the Improvement of the one, and diminution of the other. *Plutarch* has written an Essay on the Benefits which a Man may receive from his Enemies, and, among the good Fruits of Enmity, mentions this in particular, that by the Reproaches which it casts upon us we see the worst side of our selves, and open our Eyes to several Blemishes and Defects in our Lives and Conversations, which we should not have observed, without the help of such ill-natured Monitors.[2]

In order likewise to come at a true Knowledge of our selves, we

a stricter] narrower *Fol.*

1 I.e. augments. Examples in *OED* 1672–1773.
2 'How to profit by one's enemies', *Moralia*, 89–90.

should consider on the other hand how far we may deserve the Praises and Approbations which the World bestow upon us; whether the Actions they celebrate proceed from laudable and worthy Motives, and how far we are really possessed of the Virtues which gain us Applause among those with whom we converse. Such a Reflection is absolutely necessary, if we consider how apt we are either to Value or Condemn our selves by the Opinions of others, and to Sacrifice the Report of our own Hearts to the Judgment of the World.

In the next place, that we may not deceive our selves in a point of so much Importance, we should not lay too great a stress on any supposed Virtues we possess that are of a doubtful Nature: and such we may esteem all those in which Multitudes of Men dissent from us, who are as good and wise as our selves. We should always act with great Cautiousness and Circumspection, in Points where it is not impossible that we may be deceived. Intemperate Zeal, Bigotry and Persecution for any Party or Opinion, how praiseworthy soever they may appear to weak Men of our own Principles, produce infinite Calamities among Mankind, and are highly Criminal in their own Nature; and yet how many Persons eminent for Piety suffer such monstrous and absurd Principles of Action to take Root in their Minds under the Colour of Virtues? For my own part I must own I never yet knew any Party so just and reasonable, that a Man could follow it in its height and violence, and at the same time be innocent.

We should likewise be very apprehensive of those Actions which proceed from natural Constitution, favourite Passions, particular Education, or whatever promotes our worldly Interest or Advantage. In these and the like cases, a Man's Judgment is easily perverted, and a wrong Biass hung upon his Mind. These are the Inlets of Prejudice, the unguarded Avenues of the Mind, by which a thousand Errors and secret Faults find Admission, without being observed or taken Notice of. A wise Man will suspect those Actions to which he is directed by something besides[a] Reason, and always apprehend some concealed Evil in every Resolution that is of a disputable Nature, when it is conformable to his particular Temper, his Age, or way of Life, or when it favours his Pleasure or his Profit.

There is nothing of greater Importance to us, than thus diligently to sift our Thoughts, and examine all these dark Recesses of the

[a] besides] more than *Fol.*

Mind, if we would establish our Souls in such a solid and substantial Virtue, as will turn to account in that great Day, when it must stand the Test of infinite Wisdom and Justice.

I shall conclude this Essay with observing that the two kinds of Hypocrisie I have here spoken of, namely, that of deceiving the World, and that of imposing on our selves, are touched with wonderful Beauty in the hundred thirty ninth[a] Psalm. The Folly of the first kind of Hypocrisie is there set forth by Reflections on God's Omniscience and Omnipresence, which are celebrated in as noble strains of Poetry as any other I ever met with, either Sacred or Prophane. The other kind of Hypocrisie, whereby a Man deceives himself, is intimated in the two last Verses, where the Psalmist addresses himself to the great Searcher of Hearts in that emphatical Petition; *Try me, O God, and seek the ground of my heart: prove me, and examine my Thoughts. Look well if there be any way of wickedness in me, and lead me in the way everlasting.*[1]   L

No. 400   *Monday, June 9, 1712*[2]
[STEELE]

. . . *Latet Anguis in Herba.*
Virg.

IT should methinks preserve Modesty and its Interests in the World, that the Transgression of it always creates Offence; and the very Purposes of Wantonness are defeated by a Carriage which has in it so much Boldness, as to intimate that Fear and Reluctance are quite extinguished in an Object which would be otherwise desirable. It was said of a Wit of the last Age,

> Sidley *has that prevailing gentle Art,* ⎫
> *Which can with a resistless Charm impart* ⎬
> *The loosest Wishes to the chastest Heart;* ⎭
> *Raise such a Conflict, kindle such a Fire,*
> *Between declining Virtue and Desire,*
> *That the poor vanquish'd Maid dissolves away*
> *In Dreams all Night, in Sighs and Tears all Day.*[3]

[a] hundred thirty ninth] hundred and thirty ninth *Fol.*

[1] Ps. cxxxix. 23–24 (Prayer Book version).
[2] *Motto.* Virgil, *Eclogues,* 3. 93: A snake lurks in the grass.
[3] Steele had quoted this passage earlier in No. 91 (vol. i). A few days before the

This prevailing gentle Art was made up of Complaisance, Court-ship, and artful Conformity to the Modesty of a Woman's Man-ners. Rusticity, broad Expression, and forward Obtrusion, offend those of Education, and make the Transgressors odious to all who have Merit enough to attract Regard. It is in this Taste that the Scenary is so beautifully ordered in the Description which *Antony* makes, in the Dialogue between him and *Dolabella*, of *Cleopatra* in her Barge.

> *Her Galley down the Silver* Cydnos *row'd;*
> *The Tackling Silk, the Streamers wav'd with Gold;*
> *The gentle Winds were lodg'd in purple Sails:*
> *Her Nymphs, like Nereids, round her Couch were plac'd,*
> *Where she, another Sea-born* Venus, *lay.*
> *She lay, and lean'd her Cheek upon her Hand,*
> *And cast a Look so languishingly sweet,*
> *As if, secure of all Beholders Hearts,*
> *Neglecting she could take 'em. Boys like* Cupids
> *Stood fanning with their painted Wings the Winds*
> *That play'd about her Face; but if she smil'd,*
> *A darting Glory seem'd to blaze abroad,*
> *That Men's desiring Eyes were never weary'd,*
> *But hung upon the Object. To soft Flutes*
> *The Silver Oars kept Time; and while they play'd,*
> *The Hearing gave new Pleasure to the Sight,*
> *And both to Thought . . .*[1]

Here the Imagination is warmed with all the Objects presented, and yet is there nothing that is luscious,[2] or what raises any Idea more loose than that of a beautiful Woman set off to Advantage. The like, or a more delicate and careful Spirit of Modesty, appears in the following Passage in one of Mr. *Philips*'s Pastorals.

> *Breathe soft ye Winds, ye Waters gently flow,*
> *Shield her ye Trees, ye Flowers around her grow;*
> *Ye Swains, I beg you, pass in Silence by,*
> *My Love in yonder Vale asleep does lie.*[3]

publication of this number (1 June) he had also quoted it in a letter to Pope (*Corre-spondence*, ed. Blanchard, p. 54). Sir Charles Sedley had died in 1701. The quotation is from Rochester's *Imitations of Horace: Satire* 1. 10.

[1] Dryden's *All for Love*, III. i. 162–6, 168–79.
[2] Voluptuous, wanton. The last example in *OED* is dated 1815.
[3] Ambrose Philips, *Pastorals*, vi. 61–64.

Desire is corrected when there is a Tenderness or Admiration expressed which partakes the Passion. Licentious Language has something brutal in it, which disgraces Humanity, and leaves us in the Condition of the Savages in the Field. But it may be asked to what good Use can tend a Discourse of this Kind at all? It is to alarm chaste Ears against such as have what is above called the prevailing gentle Art. Masters of that Talent are capable of cloathing their Thoughts in so soft a Dress, and something so Distant from the secret Purpose of their Heart, that the Imagination of the Unguarded is touched with a Fondness which grows too insensibly to be resisted. Much Care and Concern for the Lady's Welfare, to seem afraid least she should be annoyed by the very Air which surrounds her, and this uttered rather with kind Looks, and expressed by an Interjection, an Ah, or Oh at some little Hazard in moving or making a Step, than in any direct Profession of Love, are the Methods of skilful Admirers: They are honest Arts when their Purpose is such, but infamous when misapplied. It is certain that many a young Woman in this Town has had her Heart irrecoverably won, by Men who have not made one Advance which ties their Admirers, tho' the Females languish with the utmost Anxiety. I have often, by way of Admonition to my female Readers, given them Warning against agreeable Company of the other Sex, except they are well acquainted with their Characters. Women may disguise it if they think fit, and the more to do it, they may be angry at me for saying it; but I say it is natural to them, that they have no Manner of Approbation of Men, without some Degree of Love: For this Reason he is dangerous to be entertained as a Friend or a Visitant, who is capable of gaining any eminent Esteem, or Observation, though it be never so remote from Pretentions as a Lover. If a Man's Heart has not the Abhorrence of any treacherous Design, he may easily improve Approbation into Kindness, and Kindness into Passion. There may possibly be no Manner of Love between 'em in the Eyes of all their Acquaintance, no it is all Friendship; and yet they may be as fond as Shepherd and Shepherdess in a Pastoral, but still the Nymph and the Swain may be to each other no other, I warrant you, than *Pylades* and *Orestes*.[1]

> *When* Lucy *decks with Flowers her swelling Breast,*
> *And on her Elbow leans, dissembling Rest;*

[1] Orestes' friend Pylades assisted him in the murder of Clytemnestra. See Sophocles' *Electra*.

Unable to refrain my madding Mind,
Nor Sleep nor Pasture worth my Care I find.

Once Delia *slept, on easy Moss reclin'd,*
Her lovely Limbs half bare, and rude the Wind;
I smooth'd her Coats, and stole a silent Kiss:
Condemn me, Shepherds, if I did amiss.[1]

Such good Offices as these, and such friendly Thoughts and Concerns for one another, are what make up the Amity, as they call it, between Man and Woman.

It is the Permission of such Intercourse, that makes a young Woman come to the Arms of her Husband, after the Disappointment of four or five Passions which she has successively[a2] had for different Men, before she is prudentially given to him for whom she has neither Love nor Friendship: For what should a poor Creature do that has lost all her Friends? There's *Marinet* the Agreeable, has, to my Knowledge, had a Friendship for Lord *Welford,* which had like to break her Heart; then she had so great a Friendship for Collonel *Hardy,* that she could not endure any Woman else should do any thing but rail at him. Many and fatal have been Disasters between Friends who have fallen out, and their Resentments are more keen than ever those of other Men can possibly be: But in this it happens unfortunately, that as there ought to be nothing concealed from one Friend to another, the Friends of different Sexes very often find fatal Effects[b] from their Unanimity.

For my Part, who study to pass Life in as much Innocence and Tranquility as I can, I shun the Company of agreeable Women as much as possible; and must confess that I have, though a tolerable good Philosopher, but a low Opinion of Platonick Love:[3] For which

---

[a] successively] *1724*; successfully, *Fol., 8vo, 12mo*   [b] Sexes . . . Effects] Sexes, for want of other Amusement, often study Anatomy together; and what is worse than happens in any other Friendship, they find fatal Effects *Fol.*

---

[1] Philips, *Pastorals*, vi. 81–84, 65–68. In line 84 'Sleep' is a misprint in the *Spectator* for 'Sheep'.

[2] *Successfully,* the reading in all the early editions, appears to be a misprint for *successively.* It is true that *successfully* is given with this meaning in *OED*, marked *Obs.,* with only one example cited, from the Preface to Davenant's *Gondibert* (1651). This is an error, however. The reading *successfully* is a misprint in the 1672 edition of *Gondibert*; in the first edition of 1651, both 4to and 8vo, the reading is *successively.*

[3] The phrase *Platonic love* occurs in English from 1636 (*OED*), but the earliest example of a *Platonist* in the sense of Platonic lover is dated 1756. Mrs. Centlivre's

Reason I thought it necessary to give my fair Readers a Caution against it, having, to my great Concern, observed the Waste of a Platonist lately swell to a Roundness which is inconsistent with that Philosophy. T[1]

No. 401   *Tuesday, June 10, 1712*[2]
[BUDGELL]

> *In amore hæc omnia insunt vitia: Injuriæ,*
> *Suspiciones, Inimicitiæ, Induciæ,*
> *Bellum, pax rursum: . . .*
>
>   Ter.

I SHALL publish, for the Entertainment of this Day, an odd sort of a Packet, which I have just received from one of my Female Correspondents.

Mr. SPECTATOR,

'SINCE you have often confess'd that you are not displeased your Paper should sometimes convey the Complaints of distressed Lovers to each other, I am in Hopes you will favour one who gives you an undoubted Instance of her Reformation, and at the same time a Convincing Proof of the happy Influence your Labours have had over the most Incorrigible Part of the most Incorrigible Sex. You must know, Sir, I am one of that Species of Women whom you have often Characteriz'd under the Name of *Jilts*,[3] and that

comedy *The Platonick Lady* had been produced in 1706, but apparently was not played in 1711–12, during the run of the *Spectator*. *Tatler* 32 contained a letter from Charles Sturdy, who had fallen in love 'with a profess'd *Platonne*, the most unaccountable Creature of her Sex', and Isaac Bickerstaff followed this with an essay on the 'Order of *Platonick* Ladies'.

[1] Two letters in Lillie comment on this number. The first (i. 214–15), signed M. W., gives 'a faithful account of my friendly progress . . . with a pretty fellow. . . . I am no Platonick, neither can I agree to his gross proceedings with me; therefore, good Sir, assist me with your best advice how to withstand this friendly assailant.' The other (ii. 273–4) is from 'Adamantis', protesting against the severity of this essay: 'I think you too severe, and believe most of the judicious part of your sex would rather be distinguished by us for being agreable. . . I own my self a Platonist (but not swell'd in the wast) and think a man like a fine prospect, yet confess I admire you, and all men of sense, and could sit and listen to you in particular, whole days, without the thought of love. . . .'

[2] *Motto.* Terence, *Eunuchus*, 59–61: In love are all these plagues—affronts, jealousies, jars, parleys, wars, then peace again.

[3] No. 187 (vol. ii).

I send you these Lines, as well to do publick Penance for having so long continued in a known Error, as to beg Pardon of the Party offended. I the rather chuse this way, because it in some measure answers the Terms on which he intimated the Breach between us might possibly be made up, as you will see by the Letter he sent me the next Day after I had discarded him; which I thought fit to send you a Copy of, that you might the better know the whole Case.

'I must further acquaint you, that before I Jilted him, there had been the greatest Intimacy between us for an Year and half together, during all which time I cherished his Hopes, and indulged his Flame. I leave you to guess after this what must be his Surprise, when, upon his pressing for my full Consent one Day, I told him I wondered what could make him fancy he had ever any Place in my Affections. His own Sex allow him Sense, and all ours Good-breeding. His Person is such as might, without Vanity, make him believe himself not incapable to be beloved. Our Fortunes indeed, weighed in the nice Scale of Interest, are not exactly equal, which by the way was the true Cause of my Jilting him, and I had the Assurance to acquaint him with the following Maxim, That I should always believe that Man's Passion to be the most Violent, who could offer me the largest Settlement. I have since changed my Opinion, and have endeavoured to let him know so much by several Letters, but the barbarous Man has refused them all; so that I have no way left of writing to him, but by your Assistance. If we can bring him about once more, I promise to send you all Gloves and Favours, and shall desire the Favour of Sir ROGER and your self to stand as God-Fathers to my first Boy.

I am, SIR,
Your most Obedient
most Humble Servant,
Amoret.

Philander *to* Amoret.

Madam,

"I Am so surpris'd at the Question you were pleased to ask me yesterday, that I am still at a loss what to say to it. At least my Answer would be too long to trouble you with, as it would come from a Person, who, it seems, is so very indifferent to you. Instead of it, I shall only recommend to your Consideration the Opinion of one whose Sentiments on these matters I have often heard you say are extreamly just. *A generous and constant Passion*, says your favourite Author,[1] *in an agreeable Lover, where there is not too great a Disparity in their Circumstances, is the greatest Blessing that can befal a Person beloved; and if overlook'd in one, may perhaps never be found in another.*

"I do not, however, at all despair of being very shortly much better beloved by you than *Antenor* is at present; since whenever my Fortune shall exceed his, you were pleased to intimate your Passion would encrease accordingly.

"The World has seen me shamefully lose that Time to please a fickle Woman, which might have been employed much more to my Credit and Advantage in other Pursuits. I shall therefore take the Liberty to acquaint you, however harsh it may sound in a Lady's Ears, that tho' your Love Fit should happen to return, unless you could contrive a way to make your Recantation as well known to the Publick, as they are already apprised of the manner with which you have treated me, you shall never more see

Philander."

Amoret *to* Philander.

SIR,

"UPON Reflection I find the Injury I have done both to you and my self to be so great, that though the part I now act may appear contrary to that Decorum usually observ'd by our Sex, yet I purposely break through all Rules, that my Repentance may in some measure equal my Crime. I assure you, that in my present Hopes of recovering you, I look upon *Antenor*'s Estate with Contempt. The Fop was here yesterday in a gilt Chariot and new Liveries, but I refused to see him. Tho' I dread to meet your Eyes after what has pass'd, I flatter my self, that amidst all their Confusion you will discover such a Tenderness in mine, as none can imitate but those who Love. I shall be all this Month at Lady D——'s in the Country; but the Woods, the Fields and Gardens, without *Philander*, afford no Pleasures to the unhappy

Amoret."

'I must desire you, dear Mr. *Spectator*, to publish this my Letter to *Philander* as soon as possible, and to assure him that I know nothing at all of the Death of his rich Uncle in *Gloucestershire*.'

X

---

[1] The author is Steele, and the quotation is from *Tatler* 185.

. . . *quae*
Spectator tradit sibi . . .[a]
Hor.

WERE I to publish all the Advertisements I receive from different Hands, and Persons of different Circumstances and Quality, the very Mention of them, without Reflexions on the several Subjects, would raise all the Passions which can be felt by humane Mind. As Instances of this, I shall give you two or three Letters; the Writers of which can have no Recourse to any legal Power for Redress, and seem to have written rather to vent their Sorrow than to receive Consolation.

Mr. SPECTATOR,

'I Am a young Woman of Beauty and Quality, and suitably married to a Gentleman who doats on me: But this Person of mine is the Object of an unjust Passion in a Nobleman who is very intimate with my Husband. This Friendship gives him very easy Access, and frequent Opportunities of entertaining me apart. My Heart is in the utmost Anguish, and my Face is covered over with Confusion, when I impart to you another Circumstance, which is, that my Mother, the most mercenary of all Women, is gained by this false Friend of my Husband to sollicit me for him. I am frequently chid by the poor believing Man my Husband, for shewing an Impatience of his Friend's Company; and I am never alone with my Mother, but she tells me Stories of the discretionary[2] Part of the World, and such a one, and such a one who are guilty of as much as she advises me to. She laughs at my Astonishment; and seems to hint to me, that as virtuous as she has always appeared, I am not the Daughter of her Husband. It is possible that printing this Letter may relieve me from the unnatural Importunity of my Mother, and the perfidious Courtship of my Husband's Friend. I have an

---

[a] *Motto added in 8vo and 12mo*

---

[1] *Motto.* Horace, *Ars poetica*, 181–2 (altered): Which the Spectator to himself doth yield.
[2] An obsolete form of *discreet*. This quotation is the first in *OED* for the word in this sense.

unfeigned Love of Virtue, and am resolved to preserve my Innocence. The only Way I can think of to avoid the fatal Consequences of the Discovery of this Matter, is to fly away for ever; which I must do to avoid my Husband's fatal Resentment against the Man who attempts to abuse him, and the Shame of exposing a Parent to Infamy. The Persons concerned will know these Circumstances relate to 'em; and though the Regard to Virtue is dead in them, I have some Hopes from their Fear of Shame upon reading this in your Paper; which I conjure you to do if you have any Compassion for Injured Virtue.

Sylvia.'

Mr. SPECTATOR,

'I Am the Husband of a Woman of Merit, but am fallen in Love, as they call it, with a Lady of her Acquaintance, who is going to be married to a Gentleman who deserves her. I am in a Trust relating to this Lady's Fortune, which makes my Concurrence in this Matter necessary; but I have so irresistible a Rage and Envy rise in me when I consider his future Happiness, that against all Reason, Equity, and common Justice, I am ever playing mean Tricks to suspend the Nuptials. I have no manner of Hopes for my self; *Emilia*, for so I'll call her, is a Woman of the most strict Virtue; her Lover is a Gentleman who of all others I could wish my Friend; but Envy and Jealousy, though placed so unjustly, waste my very Being, and with the Torment and Sense of a Dæmon, I am ever cursing what I cannot but approve. I wish it were the Beginning of Repentance, that I sit down and describe my present Disposition with so hellish an Aspect; but at present the Destruction of these two excellent Persons would be more welcome to me than their Happiness. Mr. SPECTATOR, pray let me have a Paper on these terrible groundless Sufferings, and do all you can to exorcise Crowds who are in some Degree possessed as I am.

Canniball.'

Mr. SPECTATOR,

'I Have no other Means but this to express my Thanks to one Man and my Resentment against another. My Circumstances are as follows. I have been for five Years last past courted by a Gentleman of greater Fortune than I ought to expect, as the Market for Women goes. You must to be sure have observed People who live in that sort of Way, as all their Friends reckon it will be a Match, and are marked out by all the World for each other. In this View we have been regarded for some Time, and I have above these three Years loved him tenderly. As he is very careful of his Fortune, I always thought he lived in a near Manner to lay up what he thought was wanting in my Fortune to make up what he might expect in another. Within few Months I have observed his Carriage very much altered, and he has affected a certain Art of getting me alone, and talking with a mighty Profusion of passionate Words, How I am not to be resisted longer, how irresistible his Wishes are, and the like. As long as I have been acquainted with him, I could not on such Occasions say downright to him, you know you may make me yours when you please. But the other Night he with great Frankness and Impudence explained to me, that he thought of me only as a Mistress. I answered this Declaration as it deserved; upon which he only doubled the Terms on which he proposed my Yielding. When my Anger heightened upon him, he told me he was sorry he had made so little Use of the unguarded Hours we had been together so remote from Company, as indeed, continued he, so we are at present. I flew from him to a neighbouring Gentlewoman's House, and tho' her Husband was in the Room, threw my self on a Couch, and burst into a Passion of Tears. My Friend desired her Husband to leave the Room, but, said he, there is something so extraordinary in this, that I will partake in the Affliction; and be it what it will, she is so much your Friend, that she knows she may command what Services I can do her. The Man sate down by me, and spoke so like a Brother, that I told him my[a] whole Affliction. He spoke of the Injury done me with so much Indignation, and animated me against the Love he said he saw I had for the Wretch who would have betrayed me with so much Reason and Humanity to my Weakness, that I doubt not of my Perseverance. His Wife and he are my Comforters, and I am under no more Restraint in their Company than if I were alone; and I doubt not but in a small Time Contempt and Hatred will take Place of the Remains of Affection to a Rascal.

> *I am,*
> SIR,
> *Your affectionate Reader*,
> Dorinda.'[1]

---

[a] told him my] told my *Fol.*

---

[1] The original letter, dated 12 May 1712, is preserved among the manuscripts

Mr. SPECTATOR,

'I Had the Misfortune to be an Uncle before I knew my Nephews from my Nieces, and now we are grown up to better Acquaintance they deny me the Respect they owe. One upbraids me with being their Familiar, another will hardly be perswaded that I am an Uncle, a third calls me little Uncle, and a fourth tells me there is no Duty at all due to an Uncle. I have a Brother-in-law whose Son will win all my Affection, unless you shall think this worthy of your Cognizance, and will be pleased to prescribe some Rules for our future reciprocal Behaviour. It will be worthy the Particularity of your Genius to lay down Rules for his Conduct who was as it were born an old Man, in which you will much oblige,

SIR,

Your most obedient Servant,

Cornelius Nepos.'

T

No. 403   *Thursday, June* 12, 1712[1]
[ADDISON]

Qui mores hominum multorum vidit . . .

Hor.

WHEN I consider this great City in its several Quarters and Divisions, I look upon it as an Aggregate of various Nations distinguished from each other by their respective Customs, Manners and Interests. The Courts of two Countries do not so much differ from one another, as the Court and City in their peculiar ways of Life and Conversation. In short, the Inhabitants of St. *James's*, notwithstanding they live under the same Laws, and speak the same Language, are a distinct People from those of *Cheapside*, who are likewise removed from those of the *Temple* on the one side, and those of *Smithfield* on the other, by several Climates and Degrees in their ways of Thinking and Conversing together.

For this Reason, when any Publick Affair is upon the Anvil, I love

in Blenheim Palace, and the present version represents Steele's considerable revision. For the text of the original letter see Appendix.

[1] *Motto.* Horace, *Ars poetica*, 142: Who saw the various customs of mankind.

to hear the Reflections that arise upon it in the several Districts and Parishes of *London* and *Westminster*, and to ramble up and down a whole Day together, in order to make my self acquainted with the Opinions of my Ingenious Countrymen. By this means I know the Faces of all the principal Politicians within the Bills of Mortality; and as every Coffee-house has some particular Statesman belonging to it, who is the Mouth of the Street where he lives, I always take care to place my self near him, in order to know his Judgment on the present Posture of Affairs. The last Progress that I made with this Intention, was about three Months ago, when we had a Current Report of the King of *France*'s Death. As I foresaw this would produce a new Face of things in *Europe*, and many curious Speculations in our *British* Coffee-houses, I was very desirous to learn the Thoughts of our most eminent Politicians on that Occasion.

That I might begin as near the Fountain-head as possible, I first of all called in at St. *James's*,[1] where I found the whole outward Room in a Buzz of Politics. The Speculations were but very indifferent towards the Door, but grew finer as you advanced to the upper end of the Room, and were so very much improved by a Knot of Theorists, who sat in the inner Room within the Steams of the Coffee Pot, that I there heard the whole *Spanish* Monarchy disposed of, and all the Line of *Bourbon* provided for in less than a Quarter of an Hour.

I afterwards called in at *Giles's*,[2] where I saw a Board of *French* Gentlemen sitting upon the Life and Death of their *Grand Monarque*. Those among them who had espoused the Whig Interest, very positively affirm'd, that he departed this Life about a Week since, and therefore proceeded without any further delay to the Release of their Friends on the Gallies, and to their own Re-establishment; but finding they cou'd not agree among themselves, I proceeded on my intended Progress.

Upon my Arrival at *Jenny Man's*,[3] I saw an *alerte*[a][4] young Fellow

---

[a] *alerte*] alerte *Fol.*

[1] St. James's Coffee-house. See No. 16 (vol i).
[2] Giles's Coffee-house was also in St. James's Street.
[3] The Tiltyard Coffee-house, near the old Tilt-Yard, just north of the Banqueting Hall of Whitehall, popular as a meeting-place for soldiers. See Nos. 109 (vol. i), 283. For a description of a visit to this, 'the most Eminent *Coffee-House* at this end of the Town', see Ned Ward's *London Spy*, part ix (Casanova Society ed., pp. 203–8).
[4] This is the earliest quotation in *OED* for this word, defined as 'lively, brisk, active, nimble'.

that cocked his Hat[1] upon a Friend of his, who entered just at the same time with my self, and accosted him after the following manner. Well *Jack*, the old Prig[2] is dead at last. Sharp's the Word. Now or never Boy. Up to the Walls of *Paris* directly. With several other deep Reflections of the same Nature.

I met with very little variation in the Politics between *Charing-Cross* and *Covent-Garden*. And upon my going into *Will's*[3] I found their Discourse was gone off from the Death of the *French* King to that of Monsieur *Boileau*, *Racine*, *Corneille*, and several other Poets, whom they regretted on this Occasion, as Persons who would have obliged the World with very noble[a] Elegies on the Death of so great a Prince, and so eminent a Patron of Learning.[4]

At a Coffee-house near the *Temple*, I found a couple of young Gentlemen engaged very smartly in a Dispute on the Succession to the *Spanish* Monarchy.[5] One of them seemed to have been retained as Advocate for the Duke of *Anjou*, the other for his Imperial Majesty. They were both for regulating the Title to that Kingdom by the Statute Laws of *England*; but finding them going out of my depth I passed forward to *Paul*'s Church-Yard, where I listned with great Attention to a learned Man, who gave the Company an Account of the deplorable State of *France* during the Minority of the *deceased* King.

I then turned on my right Hand into *Fish-street*,[6] where the chief Politician of that Quarter, upon hearing the News, (after having taken a Pipe of Tobacco, and ruminated for some time) If, says he, the King of *France* is certainly dead we shall have plenty of Mackerell this Season; our Fishery will not be disturbed by Privateers, as it has been for these ten Years past. He afterwards considered how

---

[a] noble] beautiful *Fol.*

---

[1] See No. 38 (vol. i).

[2] Defined in *OED* as 'a vague term of dislike or disrespect' and marked *Obs.*, the last quotation being dated 1749.

[3] See No. 1 (vol. i).

[4] Boileau died on 13 Mar. (N.S.) 1711; his death is announced in the *Daily Courant* of 17 Mar. 1711, in a dispatch from Paris dated 21 Mar. (N.S.). Racine had died in 1699, Corneille in 1684.

[5] The two persons named here, the Duke of Anjou (grandson of Louis XIV) and 'his Imperial Majesty', were the rival claimants for the Spanish throne after the death of Charles II of Spain in 1700. By the Treaty of Utrecht the Duke of Anjou was allowed to ascend the throne as Philip V. The other candidate, Charles, younger son of the Emperor Leopold, was known as Charles III of Spain by his supporters, and after the death of his brother Joseph in 1711 had become Emperor Charles VI.

[6] Fish Street extended east and west between Bread Street and Old Change.

the Death of this great Man would affect our Pilchards, and by several other Remarks infused a general Joy into his whole Audience.

I afterwards entered a By-Coffee-house that stood at the upper End of a narrow Lane, where I met with a Nonjuror, engaged very warmly with a Laceman who was the great Support of a neighbouring Conventicle. The Matter in Debate was, whether the late *French* King was most like *Augustus Cæsar*, or *Nero*. The Controversie was carried on with great Heat on both sides, and as each of them looked upon me very frequently during the course of their Debate, I was under some Apprehension that they would appeal to me, and therefore laid down my Penny at the Barr, and made the best of my way to *Cheapside*.

I here gazed upon the Signs for some time before I found one to my Purpose. The first Object I met in the Coffee-room was a Person who expressed a great Grief for the Death of the *French* King; but upon his explaining himself, I found his Sorrow did not arise from the Loss of the Monarch, but for his having sold out of the Bank about three Days before he heard the News of it: Upon which a Haberdasher,[1] who was the Oracle of the Coffee-house, and had his Circle of Admirers about him, called several to witness that he had declared his Opinion above a Week before, that the *French* King was certainly dead; to which he added, that considering the late Advices we had received from *France*, it was impossible that it could be otherwise. As he was laying these together, and dictating to his Hearers with great Authority, there came in a Gentleman from *Garraway*'s,[2] who told us that there were several Letters from *France* just come in, with Advice that the King was in good Health, and was gone out a hunting the very Morning the Post came away: Upon which the Haberdasher stole off his Hat that hung upon a Wooden Pegg by him, and retired to his Shop with great Confusion. This Intelligence put a Stop to my Travels, which I had prosecuted with much[a] Satisfaction; not being a little pleased to hear so many different Opinions upon so great an Event, and to observe how naturally upon such a Piece of News every one is apt to consider it with a regard to his own particular Interest and Advantage.[3]   L

[a] much] great *Fol.*

---

[1] This figure recalls Addison's Political Upholsterer of the *Tatler* (Nos. 155, 160).
[2] See No. 138 (vol. ii).
[3] The *Plain Dealer* No. 13 (5 July 1712) has a similar paper, probably inspired by

No. 404   *Friday, June* 13, 1712[1]

. . . *Non omnia possumus omnes.*
                                                        Virg.

NATURE does nothing in vain;[2] the Creator of the Universe
has appointed every thing to a certain Use and Purpose, and
determined it to a settled Course and Sphere of Action, from which,
if it in the least deviates, it becomes unfit to answer those Ends for
which it was designed. In like Manner is it in the Dispositions of
Society, the civil Oeconomy is formed in a Chain as well as the
natural; and in either Case the Breach but of one Link puts the
Whole into some Disorder. It is, I think, pretty plain, that most of
the Absurdity and Ridicule we meet with in the World, is generally
owing to the impertinent Affectation of excelling in Characters
Men are not fit for, and for which Nature never designed them.

Every Man has one or more Qualities which may make him useful
both to himself and others: Nature never fails of pointing them out,
and while the Infant continues under her Guardianship, she brings
him on in his Way, and then offers herself for a Guide in what
remains of the Journey; if he proceeds in that Course, he can hardly
miscarry: Nature makes good her Engagements; for as she never
promises what she is not able to perform, so she never fails of performing what she promises. But the Misfortune is, Men despise
what they may be Masters of, and affect what they are not fit for;
they reckon themselves already possess'd of what their Genius
inclined them to, and so bend all their Ambition to excell in what
is out of their Reach: Thus they destroy the Use of their natural
Talents, in the same Manner as covetous Men do their Quiet and
Repose; they can enjoy no Satisfaction in what they have, because

this essay, which shows how the report 'that the D—— had fitted out a Fleet, and
were coming to besiege Portsmouth', was received at Garraway's, Robin's, Batson's,
and other coffee-houses in London. It is reprinted in the *Miscellaneous Works* of
William Wagstaffe (1726), pp. 305–14.

[1] *Motto.* Virgil, *Eclogue*, 8. 63: Not all things can we all do. Also the motto of
No. 318. In the Folio sheets the motto was Virgil, *Georgics*, i. 60–61: *Continuo has leges
aeternaque foedera certis/Imposuit natura locis* (From the first, Nature laid these laws and
eternal covenants).

The authorship of this number is unknown. Budgell has been suggested (by
Morley and Aitken); Norman Ault thought it was by Pope and included it in the
Prose Works of Pope (Oxford, 1936), vol. i. The manuscript is among the papers at
Blenheim Palace: see Appendix.

[2] For this Aristotelian statement see No. 210 (vol. ii).

of the absurd Inclination they are possessed with for what they have not.

Cleanthes had good Sense, a great Memory, and a Constitution capable of the closest Application: In a Word, there was no Profession in which *Cleanthes* might not have made a very good Figure; but this wont satisfy him, he takes up an unaccountable Fondness for the Character of a fine Gentleman; all his Thoughts are bent upon this, instead of attending a Dissection, frequenting the Courts of Justice, or studying the Fathers,[a] *Cleanthes* reads Plays, dances, dresses, and spends his Time in Drawing-rooms, instead of being a good Lawyer, Divine, or Physician,[b] *Cleanthes* is a downright Coxcomb, and will remain to all that knew him a contemptible Example of Talents misapplied. It is to this Affectation the World owes its whole Race of Coxcombs: Nature in her whole Drama never drew such a Part; she has sometimes made a Fool, but a Coxcomb is always of a Man's own making,[1] by applying his Talents otherwise than Nature designed, who ever bears an high Resentment for being put out of her Course, and never fails of taking her Revenge on those that do so. Opposing her Tendency in the Application of a Man's Parts, has the same Success as declining from her Course in the Production of Vegetables; by the Assistance of Art and an hot Bed, we may possibly extort an unwilling Plant, or an untimely Sallad; but how weak, how tasteless and insipid? Just as insipid as the Poetry of *Valerio*: *Valerio* had an universal Character, was genteel, had Learning, thought justly, spoke correctly; 'twas believed there was nothing in which *Valerio* did not excell; and 'twas so far true, that there was but one; *Valerio* had no Genius for Poetry, yet he's resolved to be a Poet; he writes Verses, and takes great Pains to convince the Town, that *Valerio* is not that extraordinary Person he was taken for.

If Men would be content to graft upon Nature, and assist her Operations, what mighty Effects might we expect? *Tully* would not

---

[a] Fathers,] Fathers. *all edd.*   [b] Physician,] Physician; *all edd.* I have restored the punctuation of the MS. here (see Appendix), since the reading of all the early editions ruins the meaning. Modern practice would punctuate further by placing a semicolon after 'Drawing-rooms'.

---

[1] Cf. Pope, *Essay on Criticism*, 26–27:

> Some are bewildered in the maze of schools,
> And some made coxcombs nature meant but fools.

Norman Ault cited this (*Prose Works of Pope*, i, p. xliv) as evidence for Pope's authorship.

stand so much alone in Oratory, *Virgil* in Poetry, or *Cæsar* in War. To build upon Nature, is laying the Foundation upon a Rock; every thing disposes its self into Order as it were of Course, and the whole Work is half done as soon as undertaken. *Cicero's* Genius inclined him to Oratory, *Virgil's* to follow the Train of the Muses; they piously obeyed the Admonition, and were rewarded. Had *Virgil* attended the Bar, his modest and ingenuous Virtue would surely have made but a very indifferent Figure; and *Tully's* declamatory Inclination would have been as useless in Poetry. Nature, if left to her self, leads us on in the best Course, but will do nothing by Compulsion and Constraint; and if we are not satisfied to go her Way, we are always the greatest Sufferers by it.

Wherever Nature designs a Production, she always disposes Seeds proper for it, which are as absolutely necessary to the Formation of any moral or intellectual Excellence, as they are to the Being and Growth of Plants; and I know not by what Fate and Folly it is, that Men are taught not to reckon him equally absurd that will write Verses in Spite of Nature, with that Gardiner that should undertake to raise a Junquil or Tulip without the Help of their respective Seeds.

As there is no good or bad Quality that does not affect both Sexes, so it is not to be imagined but the fair Sex must have suffered by an Affectation of this Nature, at least as much as the other: The ill Effect of it is in none so conspicuous as in the two opposite Characters of *Cælia* and *Iras*; *Cælia* has all the Charms of Person, together with an abundant Sweetness of Nature, but wants Wit, and has a very ill Voice; *Iras* is ugly and ungenteel, but has Wit and good Sense: If *Cælia* would be silent, her Beholders would adore her; if *Iras* would talk, her Hearers would admire her; but *Cælia's* Tongue runs incessantly, while *Iras* gives herself silent Airs and soft Languors; so that 'tis difficult to perswade ones self that *Cælia* has Beauty and *Iras* Wit: Each neglects her own Excellence, and is ambitious of the other's Character; *Iras* would be thought to have as much Beauty as *Cælia*, and *Cælia* as much Wit as *Iras*.

The great Misfortune of this Affectation is, that Men not only lose a good Quality, but also contract a bad one: They not only are unfit for what they were designed, but they assign themselves to what they are not fit for; and instead of making a very good Figure one Way, make a very ridiculous one another. If *Semanthe* would have been satisfied with her natural Complexion, she might still have been celebrated by the Name of the Olive Beauty;[1] but *Semanthe* has taken up an Affectation to White and Red, and is now distinguish'd by the Character of the Lady that paints so well. In a Word, could the World be reform'd to the Obedience of that fam'd Dictate, *Follow Nature*, which the Oracle of *Delphos* pronounc'd to *Cicero* when he consulted what Course of Studies he should pursue,[2] we should see almost every Man as eminent in his proper Sphere as *Tully* was in his, and should in a very short Time find Impertinence and Affectation banish'd from among the Women, and Coxcombs and false Characters from among the Men. For my Part, I could never consider this preposterous Repugnancy to Nature any otherwise, than not only as the greatest Folly, but also one of the most heinous Crimes, since it is a direct Opposition to the Disposition of Providence, and, (as *Tully* expresses it) like the Sin of the Giants, an actual Rebellion against Heaven.[3]　　　Z

No. 405　　　　　　　　*Saturday, June* 14, 1712[4]
[ADDISON]

Οἱ δὲ πανημέριοι μολπῇ θεὸν ἱλάσκοντο,
Καλὸν ἀείδοντες παιήονα κοῦροι Ἀχαιῶν,
Μέλποντες Ἑκάεργον. ὁ δὲ φρένα τέρπετ' ἀκούων.
　　　　　　　　　　　　　　　　　　　　　Hom.

I AM very sorry to find, by the Opera Bills for this Day, that we are likely to lose the greatest Performer in Dramatick Musick that is now living, or that perhaps ever appeared upon a Stage. I need not acquaint my Reader, that I am speaking of *Signior Nicolini*.[5] The Town is highly obliged to that Excellent Artist, for

---

[1] See No. 396.
[2] Plutarch, *Life of Cicero*, 5. 1.
[3] *De Senectute*, 2. 5 (cf. the motto in the original manuscript version).
[4] *Motto*. Homer, *Iliad*, 1. 472–4.

With Hymns Divine the joyous Banquet ends,
The Paeans lengthen'd 'till the Sun descends:
The *Greeks* restor'd, the grateful Notes prolong;
Apollo listens, and approves the Song. POPE.

[5] Cf. Nos. 5, 18 (vol. i). An advertisement in this number announces: 'At the Queen's Theatre in the Hay-Market, this present Saturday being the 14th Day of June, Signor Cavaliero Nicolino Grimaldi will take his leave of England, in the Opera of Antiochus. And by reason of the Hot Weather, the Water Fall will Play all the time.' Farewell final performances had previously been advertised for 4 and 11 June

having shewn us the *Italian* Musick in its Perfection, as well as for that generous Approbation he lately gave to an Opera of our own Country, in which the Composer endeavoured to do Justice to the Beauty of the Words, by following that Noble Example, which has been set him by the greatest Foreign Masters in that Art.[1]

I could heartily wish there was the same Application and Endeavours to cultivate and improve our Church-Musick, as have been lately bestowed on that of the Stage. Our Composers have one very great Incitement to it: they are sure to meet with Excellent Words, and, at the same time, a wonderful Variety of them. There is no Passion that is not finely expressed in those parts of the Inspired Writing, which are proper for Divine Songs and Anthems.

There is a certain Coldness and Indifference in the Phrases of our *European* Languages, when they are compared with the Oriental Forms of Speech; and it happens very luckily, that the *Hebrew* Idioms run into the *English* Tongue with a particular Grace and Beauty. Our Language has received innumerable Elegancies and Improvements, from that Infusion of *Hebraisms*, which are derived to it out of the Poetical Passages in Holy Writ. They give a Force and Energy to our Expressions, warm and animate our Language, and convey our Thoughts in more ardent and intense Phrases, than any that are to be met with in our own Tongue. There is something so pathetick in this kind of Diction, that it often sets the Mind in a Flame, and makes our Hearts burn within us.[2] How cold and dead does a Prayer appear, that is composed in the most Elegant and Polite Forms of Speech, which are natural to our Tongue, when it is not heightened by that Solemnity of Phrase, which may be drawn

---

in the opera *Hercules*. Steele's *Poetical Miscellanies* of 1714 includes a short poem, 'On Nicolini's leaving the Stage' (*Occasional Verse*, ed. Blanchard, pp. 65–66), which Miss Blanchard thinks is by Steele himself. But the tone is unfriendly and quite different from the usual manner in which Steele and Addison speak of Nicolini, however much they may have disliked Italian opera. Hughes writing to Nicolini 4 Feb. 1709/10 says he had told Steele of the obliging manner in which the singer had spoken of Mr. Bickerstaff, 'en disant que vous aviez beaucoup d'inclination à étudier l'Anglois pour avoir seulement le plaisir de lire le *Tatler*' (*Correspondence*, Dublin, 1773, i. 33–34). Nicolini later returned to the London stage. He played the part of Hydaspes in the opera of that name at the Haymarket on Saturday, 7 May 1715, and several times later; he took the name-part of Rinaldo in this opera three times in June; and he also played Hydaspes at the Haymarket on 27 Aug. 1715, with Signora Margarita de l'Épine as Bernice.

[1] William Duncombe (Preface to *Poems* of Hughes, 1735, i, p. xix) identifies this as *Calypso and Telemachus*, the libretto by Hughes and the music by Galliard. *Calypso and Telemachus* is advertised in the *Spectator* as 'an English Opera', to be given at the Haymarket on 17 May 1712, and also on the 21st and 24th.

[2] Luke xxiv. 32.

from the Sacred Writings. It has been said by some of the Ancients, that if the Gods were to talk with Men, they would certainly speak in *Plato*'s Stile;[1] but I think we may say, with Justice, that when Mortals converse with their Creator, they cannot do it in so proper a Stile as in that of the Holy Scriptures.

If any one would judge of the Beauties of Poetry that are to be met with in the Divine Writings, and examine how kindly the *Hebrew* Manners of Speech mix and incorporate with the *English* Language; after having perused the Book of Psalms, let him read a literal Translation of *Horace* or *Pindar*. He will find in these two last such an Absurdity and Confusion of Stile with such a Comparative Poverty of Imagination, as will make him very sensible of what I have been here advancing.[2]

Since we have therefore such a Treasury of Words, so beautiful in themselves, and so proper for the Airs of Musick, I cannot but wonder that Persons of Distinction should give so little Attention and Encouragement to that kind of Musick, which would have its Foundation[a] in Reason, and which would improve our Virtue in proportion as it raised our Delight. The Passions that are excited by ordinary Compositions, generally flow from such silly and absurd Occasions, that a Man is ashamed to reflect upon them seriously; but the Fear, the Love, the Sorrow, the Indignation that are awakened in the Mind by Hymns and Anthems, make the Heart better, and proceed from such Causes as are altogether reasonable and praise-worthy. Pleasure and Duty go hand in hand, and the greater our Satisfaction is, the greater is our Religion.

Musick among those who were stiled the chosen People was a Religious Art. The Songs of *Sion*, which we have reason to believe were in high repute among the Courts of the Eastern Monarchs, were nothing else but Psalms and Pieces of Poetry that adored or celebrated the Supreme Being. The greatest Conqueror in this Holy Nation, after the manner of the old *Grecian* Lyricks, did not only compose the Words of his Divine Odes, but generally set them to Musick himself: After which, his Works, tho' they were consecrated to the Tabernacle, became the National Entertainment, as well as the Devotion of his People.

a Foundation] Foundations *Fol.*

[1] Plutarch, *Life of Cicero*, 24. 3.
[2] These are also the sentiments of Hughes, who defends paraphrase: in Horace 'his Sense is close-wrought, and wou'd appear stiff and obscure in a literal Translation . . .' (*Poems*, 1735, i, pp. xi–xii).

The first Original of the Drama was a Religious Worship consisting only of a Chorus, which was nothing else but an Hymn to a Deity. As Luxury and Voluptuousness prevailed over Innocence and Religion, this form of Worship degenerated into Tragedies; in which however the Chorus so far remembered its first Office, as to brand every thing that was vicious, and recommend every thing that was laudable, to intercede with Heaven for the Innocent, and to implore its Vengeance on the Criminal.

Homer and *Hesiod* intimate to us how this Art should be applied, when they represent the Muses as surrounding *Jupiter*, and warbling their Hymns about his Throne.[1] I might shew, from innumerable Passages in Ancient Writers, not only that Vocal and Instrumental Musick were made use of in their Religious Worship, but that their most favourite Diversions were filled with Songs and Hymns to their respective Deities. Had we frequent Entertainments of this Nature among us, they wou'd not a little purifie and exalt our Passions, give our Thoughts a proper Turn, and cherish those Divine Impulses in the Soul, which every one feels that has not stifled them by sensual and immoderate Pleasures.

Musick, when thus applied, raises noble Hints in the Mind of the Hearer, and fills it with great Conceptions. It strengthens Devotion, and advances Praise into Rapture. It lengthens out every act of Worship, and produces more lasting and permanent Impressions in the Mind, than those which accompany any transient Form of Words that are uttered in the ordinary Method of Religious Worship.[2]

O

[1] *Iliad*, 1. 601–4, &c.

[2] A letter in Lillie (ii. 274–8) signed Trueman English, dated 16 June 1712, objects to the praise of Nicolini in this essay, praises the English opera [*Calypso and Telemachus*], and thinks that English church music should be given the same encouragement which is given church music abroad. On *Calypso and Telemachus* he writes (p. 277):

I hope this opera, notwithstanding all the opposition it has met with, will at length have the approbation of a great majority of our nobility and gentry, and succeed so well, as to give the author and composer of it, and others, encouragement to provide more entertainments for us of the same kind.

If some persons, who are extreme on the other hand (and think no foreigners ought to have any encouragement from us) shall object, that the composer and two of the singers in this opera are foreigners, it may be answered, these persons having lived many years in this kingdom, daily conversant with the English, settled, and spending what they get amongst us, (never remitting money into foreign parts, as some others have done) may well be looked upon as English: and certainly the ingenious gentleman who composed this opera, and Mrs. Margaretta and her sister, very much deserve encouragement from the English nation, and much more than some foreigners who have had the greatest; their excellence in their several ways of performance, (particularly the two former of them) being not only to as great a degree as any that have been here, if not greater, but their

[STEELE]

Hæc studia Adolescentiam alunt, Senectutem oblectant,
secundas res ornant, adversis solatium & perfugium
præbent, delectant domi, non impediunt foris; Pernoctant
nobiscum, peregrinantur, rusticantur.

Tull.

THE following Letters bear a pleasing Image of the Joys and Satisfactions of private Life. The first is from a Gentleman to a Friend, for whom he has a very great Respect, and to whom he communicates the Satisfaction he takes in Retirement;[2] the other is a Letter to me, occasioned by an Ode written by my *Lapland* Lover; this Correspondent is so kind as to translate another of *Scheffer's* Songs in a very agreeable Manner. I publish them together, that the Young and Old may find something in the same Paper which may be suitable to their respective Taste in Solitude; for I know no Fault in the Description of ardent Desires, provided they are honourable.

Dear Sir,

'YOU have obliged me with a very kind Letter; by which I find you shift the Scene of your Life from the Town to the Country, and enjoy that mixt State which wise Men both delight in, and are qualified for. Methinks most of the Philosophers and Moralists have run too much into Extremes in praising entirely either Solitude or publick Life; in the former Men generally grow useless by too much Rest, and in the latter are destroy'd by too much Precipitation: As Waters lying still, putrify and are good for nothing; and running violently on, do but the more Mischief in their Passage to others, and are swallow'd up and lost the sooner themselves. Those who,

endeavours to please the nation much more, particularly in learning the English language, and by conforming to the genius of the English nation in all respects as much as possibly they can.

[1] *Motto.* Cicero, *Pro Archia*, 7. 16 (altered): These studies nourish youth; delight old age; are the ornament of prosperity; the solace and comfort of adversity; they delight us at home and are not burdensome abroad; they gladden us at nights, and on our journeys, and in country solitudes.

[2] This letter, by Pope, was reprinted in *Letters of Mr. Pope and several eminent persons* (1735), where it is dated '*June* 18', 1712. See Pope's *Correspondence*, ed. Sherburn, i. 146–7.

like you, can make themselves useful to all States, should be like gentle Streams, that not only glide through lonely Vales and Forests amidst the Flocks and Shepherds, but visit populous Towns in their Course, and are at once of Ornament and Service to them. But there is another sort of People who seem design'd for Solitude, those I mean who have more to hide than to shew: As for my own Part, I am one of those of whom *Seneca* says, *Tam Umbratiles sunt, ut putent in turbido esse quicquid in luce est.*[1] Some Men, like Pictures, are fitter for a Corner than a full Light; and I believe such as have a natural Bent to Solitude, are like Waters which may be forc'd into Fountains, and exalted to a great Height, may make a much nobler Figure and a much louder Noise, but after all run more smoothly, equally, and plentifully, in their own natural Course upon the Ground. The Consideration of this would make me very well contented with the Possession only of that Quiet which *Cowley* calls the Companion of Obscurity;[2] but whoever has the Muses too for his Companions, can never be idle enough to be uneasy. Thus, Sir, you see I would flatter my self into a good Opinion of my own Way of living: *Plutarch* just now told me, that 'tis in humane Life as in a Game at Tables, one may wish he had the highest Cast, but if his Chance be otherwise, he is e'en to play it as well as he can, and make the best of it.[3]

> *I am,*
>
> SIR,
>
> *Your most obliged,*
> *and most humble Servant.*'

Mr. SPECTATOR,

'THE Town being so well pleased with the fine Picture of artless Love, which Nature inspired the *Laplander* to paint in the Ode[4] you lately printed; we were in Hopes that the ingenious[a] Translator would have obliged it with the other also which *Scheffer* has given us; but since he has not, a much inferiour Hand has ventur'd to send you this.

[a] ingenious] ingenuous *Fol.*

[1] *Epistulae morales*, I. 3. 6. (*Quidam adeo in latebras refugerunt, ut putent in turbido esse quicquid in luce est.* Some men shrink into dark corners, to such a degree that they see darkly by day.)
[2] From the poem concluding the essay 'Of Obscurity' (ed. Waller, p. 400).
[3] Plutarch, 'On Tranquillity of Mind', *Moralia* 467 A–B, quoting Plato (*Republic*, 604C); the passage is also quoted in Plutarch's 'Consolation to Apollonius' (*Moralia*, 112 E–F).   [4] See No. 366.

'It is a Custom with the Northern Lovers to divert themselves with a Song, whilst they journey through the fenny Moors to pay a Visit to their Mistresses. This is address'd by the Lover to his Rain-Deer, which is the Creature that in that Country supplies the Want of Horses. The Circumstances which successively present themselves to him in his Way, are, I believe you will think, naturally interwoven. The Anxiety of Absence, the Gloominess of the Roads, and his Resolution of frequenting only those, since those only can carry him to the Object of his Desires; the Dissatisfaction he expresses even at the greatest Swiftness with which he is carry'd, and his joyful Surprize at an unexpected Sight of his Mistress as she is bathing, seem beautifully described in the Original.

'If all those pretty Images of Rural Nature are lost in the Imitation, yet possibly you may think fit to let this supply the Place of a long Letter, when Want of Leisure or Indisposition for Writing will not permit our being entertained by your own Hand. I propose such a Time, because tho' it is natural to have a Fondness for what one does one's self, yet I assure you I would not have any thing of mine displace a single Line of yours.'[1]

I.

Haste my Rain-Deer, and let us nimbly go
Our am'rous Journey through this dreery Waste:
Haste, my Rain-Deer, still still thou art too slow,
Impetuous Love demands the Lightning's Haste.

II.

Around us far the Rushy Moors are spread:
Soon will the Sun withdraw his chearful Ray;
Darkling and tir'd we shall the Marshes tread
No Lay unsung to cheat the tedious Way.

III.

The wat'ry Length of these unjoyous Moors
Does all the flow'ry Meadows Pride excel;
Through these I fly to her my Soul adores;
Ye flow'ry Meadows, empty Pride, Farewel.

---

[1] Another verse translation is given in the English version of Scheffer (Oxford, 1674, pp. 112–13; ed. 1704, pp. 286–7). The version in the *Spectator* may be by Ambrose Philips; cf. No. 366.

IV.

Each Moment from the Charmer I'm confin'd,
My Breast is tortur'd with impatient Fires;
Fly, my Rain-Deer, fly swifter than the Wind,
Thy tardy Feet wing with my fierce Desires.

V.

Our pleasing Toil will then be soon o'erpaid,
And thou, in Wonder lost, shalt view my Fair,
Admire each Feature of the lovely Maid,
Her artless Charms, her Bloom, her sprightly Air.

VI.

But lo! with graceful Motion there she swims,
Gently removing each ambitious Wave;
The crowding Waves transported clasp her Limbs:
When, when, oh when, shall I such Freedoms have!

VII.

In vain, you envious Streams, so fast you flow,
To hide her from a Lover's ardent Gaze:
From ev'ry Touch you more transparent grow,
And all reveal'd the beauteous Wanton plays.

T

No. 407
[ADDISON]

Tuesday, June 17, 1712[1]

. . . abest facundis Gratia dictis.
Ov.

MOST Foreign Writers who have given any Character of the *English* Nation, whatever Vices they ascribe to it, allow in general, that the People are naturally Modest.[2] It proceeds perhaps

[1] *Motto.* Ovid, *Metamorphoses,* 13. 127: No Charm does his Eloquence adorn.
[2] Individualism is perhaps the chief trait of the English in the eyes of foreign observers; this could result in a 'sturdy good sense' or—as noted in No. 432—'pride'. See Ascoli, i. 423–46.

from this our National Virtue, that our Orators are observed to make use of less Gesture or Action than those of other Countries. Our Preachers stand stock-still in the Pulpit, and will not so much as move a Finger to set off the best Sermons in the World.[1] We meet with the same speaking Statues at our Bars, and in all Publick Places of Debate. Our Words flow from us in a smooth continued Stream, without those Strainings of the Voice, Motions of the Body, and Majesty of the Hand, which are so much celebrated in the Orators of *Greece* and *Rome*. We can talk of Life and Death in cold Blood, and keep our Temper in a Discourse which turns upon every thing that is dear to us. Though our Zeal breaks out in the finest Tropes and Figures, it is not able to stir a Limb about us. I have heard it observed more than once by those who have seen *Italy*, that an untravelled *Englishman* cannot relish all the Beauties of *Italian* Pictures, because the Postures which are expressed in them are often such as are peculiar to that Country. One who has not seen an *Italian* in the Pulpit, will not know what to make of that noble Gesture in *Raphael*'s Picture of St. *Paul* preaching at *Athens*,[2] where the Apostle is represented[a] as lifting up both his Arms, and pouring out the Thunder of his Rhetorick amidst an Audience of Pagan Philosophers.

It is certain, that proper Gestures and vehement Exertions of the Voice cannot be too much studied by a Publick Orator. They are a kind of Comment to what he utters, and enforce every thing he says, with weak Hearers, better than the strongest Argument he can make use of. They keep the Audience awake, and fix their Attention to what is delivered to them, at the same time that they shew the Speaker is in earnest, and affected himself with what he so passionately recommends to others. Violent Gesture and Vocifera-tion naturally shake the Hearts of the Ignorant, and fill them with a kind of Religious Horror. Nothing is more frequent than to see Women weep and tremble at the sight of a moving Preacher, though

---

[a] Picture . . . represented] School of *Athens*, where St. *Paul* is represented *Fol.*

---

[1] Action 'is a Thing quite lost in the World; . . . the better Preachers give it over as a thing to be despaired of, and instead of taking the Eye and Ear, they seize on the Mind' (E. Chamberlayne, *Magnae Britanniae Notitia*, ed. 1708, p. 249). J. C. Scaliger (*Poetices*, lib. iii, cap. 16) called the English *stolidi, amentes, inertes, inhospitales, immanes* (quoted in Robert Plot, *Natural History of Oxfordshire*, Oxford, 1677, p. 224). *Tatlers* 66 and 70 comment on English preachers' neglect of the art of speaking, with the proper ornaments of voice and gesture. For testimonies of French visitors to the restraint of English preachers see Ascoli, i. 404–5.

[2] One of the cartoons at Hampton Court (see No. 226, vol. ii).

he is placed quite out of their Hearing; as in *England* we very frequently see People lulled asleep with solid and elaborate Discourses of Piety, who[a] would be warmed and transported out of themselves by the Bellowings and Distortions of Enthusiasm.

If Nonsense, when accompanied with such an Emotion of Voice and Body, has such an Influence on Mens Minds, what might we not expect from many of those admirable Discourses which are Printed in our Tongue, were they delivered with a becoming Fervour, and with the most agreeable Graces of Voice and Gesture?

We are told, that the great *Latin* Orator very much impaired his Health by this *laterum contentio*,[1] this Vehemence of Action, with which he used to deliver himself. The *Greek* Orator was likewise so very Famous for this Particular in Rhetorick, that one of his Antagonists, whom he had banished from *Athens*, reading over the Oration which had procured his Banishment, and seeing his Friends admire it, could not forbear asking them, if they were so much affected by the bare reading of it, how much more they would have been alarmed, had they heard him actually throwing out such a Storm of Eloquence?[2]

How cold and dead a Figure, in Comparison of these two Great Men, does an Orator often make at the *British* Bar, holding up his Head with the most insipid Serenity, and stroaking the sides of a long Wigg that reaches down to his Middle? The truth of it is, there is often nothing more ridiculous than the Gestures of an *English* Speaker; you see some of them running their Hands into their Pockets as far as ever they can thrust them, and others looking with great Attention on a piece of Paper that has nothing written in it; you may see many a smart Rhetorician turning his Hat in his Hands, moulding it into several different Cocks, examining sometimes the Lining of it, and sometimes the Button, during the whole course of his Harangue. A Deaf Man would think he was cheapning a Beaver,[3] when perhaps he is talking of the Fate of the *British* Nation. I remember, when I was a young Man, and used to frequent *Westminster Hall*, there was a Councellor who never pleaded without a Piece of Pack-thread in his Hand, which he used to twist about

[a] who] that *Fol.*

---

[1] Cicero, *Brutus*, 91. 313.
[2] Aeschines was the antagonist mentioned here, who paid this tribute to Demosthenes (Cicero, *De Oratore*, 3. 56. 213). The incident is related at some length in *Tatler* 66.
[3] I.e. bargaining for a hat (cf. No. 323).

a Thumb, or a Finger, all the while he was speaking: The Waggs of those Days used to call it the Thread of his Discourse, for he was not able to utter a Word without it. One of his Clients, who was more merry than wise, stole it from him one Day in the midst of his Pleading, but he had better have let it alone, for he lost his Cause by his Jest.

I have all along acknowledged my self to be a Dumb Man, and therefore may be thought a very improper Person to give Rules for Oratory; but I believe every one will agree with me in this, that we ought either to lay aside all kinds of Gesture, (which seems to be very suitable to the Genius of our Nation,) or at least to make use of such only as are graceful and expressive.   O

No. 408   *Wednesday, June 18, 1712*[1]

Decet affectus animi neque se nimium erigere, nec subjacere serviliter.

Tull. de Finibus.

Mr. SPECTATOR,

'I HAVE always been a very great Lover of your Speculations, as well in Regard to the Subject, as to your Manner of treating it. Humane Nature I always thought the most useful Object of humane Reason, and to make the Consideration of it pleasant and entertaining, I always thought the best Employment of humane Wit: Other Parts of Philosophy may perhaps make us wiser, but this not only answers that End, but makes us better too. Hence it was that the Oracle pronounced *Socrates* the wisest of all Men living, because he judiciously made Choice of humane Nature for the Object of his Thoughts; an Enquiry into which as much exceeds all other Learning, as it is of more Consequence to adjust the true Nature and Measures of Right and Wrong, than to settle the Distance of the Planets, and compute the Times of their Circumvolutions.

[1] *Motto.* (The proper state of mind is neither too forward nor humbly servile.) The quotation is not from *De Finibus.* It seems to be a reminiscence of *De Officiis*, I. 34. 124: *Privatum autem oportet aequo et pari cum civibus jure vivere neque summissum et abjectum neque se efferentem* .... (The private individual ought first, in private relations, to live on fair and equal terms with his fellow citizens, with a spirit neither servile and grovelling nor yet domineering.)

'One good Effect that will immediately arise from a near Observation of humane Nature, is, that we shall cease to wonder at those Actions which Men are used to reckon wholly unaccountable; for as nothing is produced without a Cause, so by observing the Nature and Course of the Passions, we shall be able to trace every Action from its first Conception to its Death: We shall no more admire at the Proceedings of *Cataline*[1] or *Tiberius*, when we know the one was actuated by a cruel Jealousy, the other by a furious Ambition; for the Actions of Men follow their Passions as naturally as Light does Heat, or as any other Effect flows from its Cause; Reason must be employed in adjusting the Passions, but they must ever remain the Principles of Action.

'The strange and absurd Variety that is so apparent in Mens Actions, shews plainly they can never proceed immediately from Reason; so pure a Fountain emits no such troubled Waters: They must necessarily arise from the Passions, which are to the Mind as the Winds to a Ship,[2] they only can move it, and they too often destroy it; if fair and gentle they guide it into the Harbour, if contrary and furious they overset it in the Waves: In the same Manner is the Mind assisted or endangered by the Passions; Reason must then take the Place of Pilot, and can never fail of securing her Charge if she be not wanting to her self: The Strength of the Passions will never be accepted as an Excuse for complying with them; they were designed for Subjection, and if a Man suffers them to get the upper Hand, he then betrays the Liberty of his own Soul.

'As Nature has framed the several Species of Beings as it were in a Chain,[3] so Man seems to be placed as the middle Link between Angels and Brutes: Hence he participates both of Flesh and Spirit by an admirable Tie, which in him occasions perpetual War of Passions; and as a Man inclines to the angelick or brute Part of his Constitution, he is then denominated good or bad, virtuous or wicked; if Love, Mercy, and good Nature prevail, they speak[4] him of the Angel; if Hatred, Cruelty, and Envy predominate, they declare his Kindred to the Brute. Hence it was that some of the Ancients imagined, that as Men in this Life inclined more to the

---

[1] Sallust, *Bellum Catilinae*, II. I.

[2] Hughes had used this familiar figure in No. 224 (vol. ii). 'The gentle Gales of the Passions' (below, in paragraph six) repeats the language of No. 224.

[3] For the position of man in the chain of being, midway between angels and brutes, see A. O. Lovejoy, *The Great Chain of Being* (Cambridge, Mass., 1936).

[4] *Speak* in this sense (to show a person as possessing a certain character) is marked *Arch.* in *OED*, with quotations ranging from 1605 to 1796-7.

Angel or the Brute, so after their Death they should transmigrate into the one or the other; and it would be no unpleasant Notion to consider the several Species of Brutes, into which we may imagine that Tyrants, Misers, the Proud, Malicious, and Ill-natured might be changed.[1]

'As a Consequence of this Original, all Passions are in all Men, but all appear not in all; Constitution, Education, Custom of the Country, Reason, and the like Causes, may improve or abate the Strength of them, but still the Seeds remain, which are ever ready to sprout forth upon the least Encouragement. I have heard a Story of a good religious Man, who, having been bred with the Milk of a Goat, was very modest in Publick by a careful Reflection he made on his Actions, but he frequently had an Hour in Secret, wherein he had his Frisks and Capers; and if we had an Opportunity of examining the Retirement of the strictest Philosophers, no Doubt but we should find perpetual Returns of those Passions they so artfully conceal from the Publick. I remember *Matchiavel*[2] observes, that every State should entertain a perpetual Jealousy of its Neighbours, that so it should never be unprovided when an Emergency happens; in like Manner should the Reason be perpetually on its Guard against the Passions, and never suffer them to carry on any Design that may be destructive of its Security; yet at the same Time it must be careful, that it don't so far break their Strength as to render them contemptible, and consequently it self unguarded.

'The Understanding being of its self too slow and lazy to exert it self into Action, it's necessary it should be put in Motion by the gentle Gales of the Passions, which may preserve it from stagnating and Corruption; for they are as necessary to the Health of the Mind, as the Circulation of the animal Spirits is to the Health of the Body; they keep it in Life, and Strength, and Vigour; nor is it possible for the Mind to perform its Offices without their Assistance: These Motions are given us with our Being, they are little Spirits that are born and dye with us; to some they are mild, easy, and gentle, to others wayward and unruly, yet never too strong for the Reins of Reason and the Guidance of Judgment.

'We may generally observe a pretty nice Proportion between the Strength of Reason and Passion; the greatest Genius's have commonly the strongest Affections, as on the other Hand, the weaker

---

[1] See Nos. 211 (vol. ii), 343.
[2] Machiavelli, *The Prince*, chap. xiv (*Works*, 1694, pp. 218-19).

Understandings have generally the weaker Passions; and 'tis fit the Fury of the Coursers should not be too great for the Strength of the Charioteer. Young Men whose Passions are not a little unruly, give small Hopes of their ever being considerable; the Fire of Youth will of Course abate, and is a Fault, if it be a Fault, that mends every Day; but surely unless a Man has Fire in Youth, he can hardly have Warmth in Old-age. We must therefore be very cautious, least while we think to regulate the Passions, we should quite extinguish them, which is putting out the Light of the Soul; for to be without Passion, or to be hurried away with it, makes a Man equally blind.[1] The extraordinary Severity used in most of our Schools has this fatal Effect, it breaks the Spring of the Mind, and most certainly destroys more good Genius's than it can possibly improve. And surely 'tis a mighty Mistake that the Passions should be so intirely subdued; for little Irregularities are sometimes not only to be born with, but to be cultivated too, since they are frequently attended with the greatest Perfections. All great Genius's have Faults mixed with their Virtues, and resemble the flaming Bush which has Thorns among Lights.

'Since therefore the Passions are the Principles of humane Actions, we must endeavour to manage them so as to retain their Vigour, yet keep them under strict Command; we must govern them rather like free Subjects than Slaves, least while we intend to make them obedient, they become abject, and unfit for those great Purposes to which they were designed. For my Part I must confess, I could never have any Regard to that Sect of Philosophers, who so much insisted upon an absolute Indifference and Vacancy from all Passion; for it seems to me a thing very inconsistent for a Man to divest himself of Humanity, in order to acquire Tranquility of Mind, and to eradicate the very Principles of Action, because it's possible they may produce ill Effects.

I am,

SIR,

Your affectionate Admirer,

T. B.' Z[2]

---

[1] Cf. Antoine Le Grand, *Man without Passion; or, the Wise Stoick according to the sentiments of Seneca* (1675).

[2] 'As the same train of thought that runs through this Paper occurs not unfrequently in Pope's Works, and is illustrated very happily in his "Essay on Man," it is not unreasonable to suppose that Pope might be the writer of the Papers marked with the signature Z . . .' (Nichols). This number has been frequently claimed in

> ... *Musæo contingere cuncta lepore.*
> Lucr.

GRATIAN very often recommends *the fine Taste*,[a] as the utmost Perfection of an accomplished Man.[2] As this Word arises very often in Conversation, I shall endeavour to give some Account of it, and to lay down Rules how we may know whether we are possessed of it, and how we may acquire that fine Taste of Writing, which is so much talked of among the Polite World.

Most Languages make use of this Metaphor, to express that Faculty of the Mind, which distinguishes all the most concealed Faults and nicest Perfections in Writing. We may be sure this Metaphor would not have been so general in all Tongues, had there not been a very great Conformity between that Mental Taste, which is the Subject of this Paper, and that Sensitive Taste which gives us a Relish of every different Flavour that affects the Palate. Accordingly we find, there[b] are as many Degrees of Refinement in the intellectual Faculty, as in the Sense, which is marked out by this common Denomination.

I knew a Person who possessed the one in so great a Perfection, that after having tasted ten different Kinds of Tea, he would distinguish, without seeing the Colour of it, the particular Sort which was offered him; and not only so, but any two sorts of them that were mixt together in an equal Proportion; nay, he has carried the

---

[a] *the fine Taste*,] the fine Taste, *Fol.*   [b] find, there] find, that there *Fol.*

---

fact for Pope, and is printed by Norman Ault in volume i of the *Prose Works* of Pope (Oxford, 1936). The ideas expressed and many of the particular examples will be found in the *Essay on Man.* They are commonplaces of philosophy, however, and parallels can be found for most of them (as for Pope's poem), so that there is no real evidence for Pope's authorship. The third sentence, for example, expresses exactly Pope's point of view, yet, as Mark Pattison observed of the opening lines of Epistle II of the *Essay on Man,* 'This is the oldest dictum of logic or philosophy on record'.

[1] *Motto.* Lucretius, *De rerum natura,* i. 934 (altered): To grace each subject with wit.
[2] For Gratian see No. 293. The reference here is to his *Arte de ingenio* (1642), in which he praises the taste for conceits. Addison's analysis of the term *taste* and his observations on its proper use in criticism lay the foundations for most eighteenth-century speculation on the subject in England. The French form of the word is used in No. 277, and the Italian (*gusto*) in Nos. 229, 244 (vol. ii), and 592 (vol. iv).

Experiment so far, as upon tasting the Composition of three different sorts, to name the Parcels from whence the three several Ingredients were taken. A Man of a fine Taste in Writing will discern, after the same manner, not only the general Beauties and Imperfections of an Author, but discover the several Ways of thinking and expressing himself, which diversify him from all other Authors, with the several Foreign Infusions of Thought and Language, and the particular Authors from whom they were borrowed.

After having thus far explained what is generally meant by a fine Taste in Writing, and shown the Propriety of the Metaphor which is used on this Occasion, I think I may define it to be *that Faculty of the Soul, which discerns the Beauties of an Author with Pleasure, and the Imperfections with Dislike.* If a Man would know whether he is possessed of this Faculty, I would have him read over the celebrated Works of Antiquity, which have stood the Test of so many different Ages and Countries; or those Works among the Moderns, which have the Sanction of the Politer Part of our Contemporaries. If upon the Perusal of such Writings he does not find himself delighted in an extraordinary manner, or, if upon reading the admired Passages in such Authors, he finds a Coldness and Indifference in his Thoughts, he ought to conclude, not (as is too usual among tasteless Readers) that the Author wants[a] those Perfections which have been admired in him, but that he himself wants the Faculty of discovering them.

He should, in the second place, be very careful to observe, whether he tastes the distinguishing Perfections, or, if I may be allowed to call them so, the Specifick Qualities of the Author whom he peruses; whether he is particularly pleased with *Livy* for his manner of telling a Story, with *Sallust* for his entering into those internal Principles of Action which arise from the Characters and Manners of the Persons he describes, or with *Tacitus* for his displaying those outward Motives of Safety and Interest, which give birth to the whole Series of Transactions which he relates.

He may likewise consider, how differently he is affected by the same Thought, which presents it self in a great Writer, from what he is when he finds it delivered by a Person of an ordinary Genius. For there is as much difference in apprehending a Thought cloathed in *Cicero*'s Language, and that of a common Author, as in seeing an Object by the Light of a Taper, or by the Light of the Sun.

[a] wants] has not *Fol.*

It is very difficult to lay down Rules for the acquirement of such a Taste as that I am here speaking of. The Faculty must in some degree be born with us, and it very often happens, that those who have other Qualities in Perfection are wholly void of this. One of the most eminent Mathematicians of the Age has assured me, that the greatest Pleasure he took in reading *Virgil*, was in examining *Æneas* his Voyage by the Map;[1] as I question not but many a Modern Compiler of History would be delighted with little more in that Divine Author, than in the bare matters of Fact.

But notwithstanding this Faculty must in some measure be born with us, there are several Methods for Cultivating and Improving it, and without which it will be very uncertain, and of little use to the Person that possesses it. The most natural Method for this Purpose is to be conversant among the Writings of the most Polite Authors. A Man who has any Relish for fine Writing, either discovers new Beauties, or receives stronger Impressions from the Masterly Stroaks of a great Author every time he peruses him: Besides that he naturally wears himself into the same manner of Speaking and Thinking.

Conversation with Men of a Polite Genius is another Method for improving our Natural Taste. It is impossible for a Man of the greatest Parts to consider any thing in its whole Extent, and in all its variety of Lights. Every Man, besides those general Observations which are to be made upon an Author, forms several Reflections that are peculiar to his own manner of Thinking; so that Conversation will naturally furnish us with Hints which we did not attend to, and make us enjoy other Mens Parts and Reflections as well as our own. This is the best Reason I can give for the Observation which several have made, that Men of great Genius in the same way of Writing seldom rise up singly, but at certain Periods of Time appear together, and in a Body; as they did at *Rome* in the Reign of *Augustus*, and in *Greece* about the Age of *Socrates*. I cannot think that *Corneille*,[a] *Racine*, *Moliere*, *Boileau*, *la Fontaine*, *Bruyere*, *Bossu*, or the *Daciers*, would have written so well as they have done, had they not been Friends and Contemporaries.

[a] that *Corneille*,] that either *Corneille*, Fol.

---

[1] Newton has been guessed at here, but I know of no evidence for this supposition.

It is likewise necessary for a Man who would form to himself a finished Taste of good Writing, to be well versed in the Works of the best *Criticks* both Ancient and Modern. I must confess that I could wish there were Authors of this kind, who, beside the Mechanical Rules which a Man of very little Taste may discourse upon, would enter into the very Spirit and Soul of fine Writing, and shew us the several Sources of that Pleasure which rises in the Mind upon the Perusal of a noble Work. Thus altho' in Poetry it be absolutely necessary that the Unities of Time, Place and Action, with other Points of the same Nature should be thoroughly explained and understood; there is still something more essential, to the Art, something that elevates and astonishes the Fancy, and gives a Greatness of Mind to the Reader, which few of the Criticks besides *Longinus* have consider'd.

Our general Taste in *England* is for Epigram, turns of Wit, and forced Conceits, which have no manner of Influence, either for the bettering or enlarging the Mind of him who reads them, and have been carefully avoided by the greatest Writers, both among the Ancients and Moderns. I have endeavoured in several of my Speculations to banish this *Gothic* Taste which has taken Possession among us.[1] I entertained the Town for a Week together with an Essay upon Wit, in which I endeavoured to detect several of those false kinds which have been admir'd in the different Ages of the World; and at the same time to shew wherein the nature of true Wit consists. I afterwards gave an Instance of the great force which lies in a natural Simplicity of Thought to affect the Mind of the Reader, from such Vulgar Pieces as have little else besides this single Qualification to recommend them. I have likewise examined the Works of the greatest Poet which our Nation or perhaps any other has produced, and particularized most of those rational and manly Beauties[2] which give a value to that Divine Work. I shall next *Saturday* enter upon an Essay *on the Pleasures of the Imagination*, which though it shall consider that Subject at large, will perhaps suggest to the Reader what it is that gives a Beauty to many Passages of the finest Writers both in Prose and Verse. As an Undertaking of this

[1] In this and the following three sentences Addison reminds his readers of his papers on wit (Nos. 58–63, vol. i), on the ballads (Nos. 70, 74, 85, vol. i), and on Milton (Nos. 267, &c., vols. ii–iii).

[2] Johnson may be echoing this phrase in his comment on Addison's *Campaign*: 'The rejection and contempt of fiction is rational and manly' (World's Classics ed., i. 446).

nature is entirely new, I question not but it will be receiv'd with
Candour.[1]   O

No. 410   *Friday, June 20, 1712*[2]

[STEELE]

> ... *Dum foris sunt, nihil videtur Mundius,*
> *Nec Magis compositum quidquam, nec magis elegans:*
> *Quæ, cum amatore suo cum cœnant, Liguriunt,*
> *Harum videre ingluviem, sordes, inopiam:*
> *Quam inhonestæ solæ sint domi, atque avidæ cibi,*
> *Quo pacto ex Jure Hesterno panem atrum vorent.*
> *Nosse omnia hæc, salus est adolescentulis.*
>
>   Ter.

WILL HONEYCOMB who disguises his present Decay, by visiting the Wenches of the Town only by Way of Humour, told
us, that the last rainy Night he with Sir ROGER DE COVERLY was
driven into the *Temple* Cloister, whither had escaped also a Lady
most exactly[3] dressed from Head to Foot. WILL made no Scruple to
acquaint us, that she saluted him very familiarly by his Name, and
turning immediately to the Knight, she said, she supposed that was
his good Friend Sir ROGER DE COVERLY: Upon which nothing less

---

[1] For this word see No. 253 (ii. 482).

[2] *Motto*. Terence, *Eunuchus*, 934–40 (altered): When they're abroad forsooth, none
so cleanly, none so modish, and genteel, none so delicately neat as they: when their
Ladyships feast with their Gallants, they feed as nicely as possible: But to see the
insatiable Gluttony, the vile Nastiness, the griping Penury of these filthy Jades at
home, how greedy of a Crust, how eagerly they slabber and soss upon Brown-George
out of stinking Pottage, to know all this beforehand, may be the saving of a young
Man.

According to Nichols the first part of this number was 'most probably' written by
Tickell, since it is signed T. The signature T, however, had been used by Steele as
early as No. 95 (vol. i), and from No. 136 (vol. ii) this had been his regular signature. The statements made in Nichols's edition, in the notes to Nos. 328*, 334,
and elsewhere, that T at times stood for Tickell and at times represented Steele's
'transcribed' numbers, will not bear examination. Budgell has recorded (*The Bee*,
No. 1, Feb. 1733) that Addison 'was so heartily vexed when he read this Paper, that
he immediately called a Coach, went to his Friend Sir *Richard*, and never left him, till
he had made him promise that he would meddle no more with Sir *Roger*'s Character'.
In No. 544 (vol. iv) Steele attempts to defend this incident as only an example 'of the
Simplicity and Innocence' of Sir Roger's mind.

[3] I.e. to perfection. The last quotation in *OED* in this sense is dated 1726.

could follow than Sir ROGER's Approach to Salutation, with Madam the same at your Service. She was dressed in a black Tabby[1] Mantua and Petticoat, without Ribbands; her Linnen striped Muslin, and in the whole in an agreeable Second-Mourning;[2] decent Dresses being often affected by the Creatures of the Town, at once consulting Cheapness and the Pretention to Modesty. She went on with a familiar easy Air, your Friend, Mr. HONEYCOMB, is a little surprised to see a Woman here alone and unattended; but I dismissed my Coach at the Gate, and tripped it down to my Council's Chambers, for Lawyers Fees take up too much of a small disputed Joynture to admit any other Expences[a] but meer Necessaries. Mr. HONEYCOMB begged they might have the Honour of setting her down, for Sir ROGER's Servant was gone to call a Coach. In the Interim the Footman returned, with no Coach to be had; and there appeared nothing to be done but trusting her self with Mr. HONEYCOMB and his Friend to wait at the Tavern at the Gate for a Coach, or be subjected to all the Impertinence she must meet with in that publick Place. Mr. HONEYCOMB being a Man of Honour determined the Choice of the first, and Sir ROGER, as the better Man, took the Lady by the Hand, leading through all the Shower covering her with his Hat, and gallanting a familiar Acquaintance through Rows of young Fellows, who winked at *Sukey* in the State she marched off, WILL HONEYCOMB bringing up the Rear.

Much Importunity prevailed upon the Fair one to admit of a Collation, where, after declaring she had no Stomach, and eaten a Couple of Chickens, devoured a Trusse[3] of Sallet, and drunk a full Bottle to her Share, she sung the Old Man's Wish[4] to Sir ROGER. The Knight left the Room for some Time after Supper, and writ the following Billet, which he conveyed to *Sukey*, and *Sukey* to her Friend WILL HONEYCOMB. WILL has given it to Sir ANDREW FREEPORT, who read it last Night to the Club.

---

^a Expences] Expence *Fol*.

---

[1] Waved or watered silk.
[2] 'A style of dress allowed by etiquette to be worn when strict mourning is discarded' (*OED*).
[3] 'A collection of things bound together, a bundle, pack' (*OED*).
[4] 'The Old Man's Wish', the poem by Walter Pope. 'Doctor Pope's Wish: a Ballad' first appeared in H. Playford's *Theater of Musick* (1685); it was printed separately in 1693, and frequently thereafter.

Madam,

'I Am not so meer a Country-Gentleman, but I can guess at the Law-Business you had at the *Temple*. If you would go down to the Country and leave off all your Vanities but your Singing, let me know at my Lodgings in *Bow-street Covent-Garden*,[1] and you shall be encouraged by,

Your humble Servant,

ROGER DE COVERLY.'

My good Friend could not well stand the Raillery which was rising upon him; but to put a Stop to it I delivered WILL HONEYCOMB the following Letter, and desired him to read it to the Board.

Mr. SPECTATOR,

'H AVING seen a Translation of one of the Chapters in the *Canticles* into *English* Verse inserted among your late Papers,[2] I have ventured to send you the 7th Chapter of the *Proverbs* in a poetical Dress.[3] If you think it worthy appearing among your Speculations, it will be a sufficient Reward for the Trouble of

Your constant Reader,

A. B.'

> *MY Son, th' Instruction that my Words impart,*
> *Grave on the living Tablet of thy Heart;*
> *And all the wholesome Precepts that I give,*
> *Observe with strictest Reverence, and live.*
>   *Let all thy Homage be to Wisdom paid,*
> *Seek her Protection, and implore her Aid;*
> *That she may keep thy Soul from Harm secure,*
> *And turn thy Footsteps from the Harlot's Door.*

[1] The first street east of Covent Garden, leading north from Russell Street to Hart Street.

[2] No. 388.

[3] The author is James Ward; the paraphrase is reprinted under his name in Matthew Concanen's collection, *Miscellaneous Poems, Original and Translated, by several Hands* (1724), pp. 337–40. The text is virtually the same as that in the *Spectator*: line 18 reads 'And pass'd the Corner of the *Harlot*'s Gate'; line 26: 'Now she 's within, now in the Streets does stray'; and line 47: 'Upon her Tongue did such soft Mischief dwell.' Ward entered Trinity College, Dublin, 24 Jan. 1706/7, at sixteen; he graduated B.A. 1711; M.A. 1714; was later chaplain to Lord Carteret, the Lord Lieutenant of Ireland; and in 1726 became Dean of Cloyne. He died in 1736. See Burtchaell and Sadleir, *Alumni Dublinenses* (1935); Henry Cotton, *Fasti Ecclesiae Hibernicae*, i (1848), 283; and W. Maziere Brady, *Clerical and Parochial Records of Cork, Cloyne, and Ross* (1864), ii. 203. Ward also contributed a poem to the second series of the *Spectator* (No. 632, vol. v).

Who with curs'd Charms lures the Unwary in,
And sooths with Flattery their Souls to Sin.
  Once from my Window as I cast mine Eye
On those that pass'd in giddy Numbers by,
A Youth among the foolish Youths I spy'd,
Who took not sacred Wisdom for his Guide.
  Just as the Sun withdrew his cooler Light,
And Evening soft led on the Shades of Night,
He stole in covert Twilight to his Fate,
And pass'd the Corner near the Harlot's Gate;
When, lo, a Woman comes! . . .
Loose her Attire, and such her glaring Dress,
As aptly did the Harlot's Mind express:
Subtle she is, and practis'd in the Arts,
By which the Wanton conquer heedless Hearts:
Stubborn and loud she is; she hates her Home,
Varying her Place and Form, she loves to roam;
Now she's within, now in the Street do's stray,
Now at each Corner stands, and waits her Prey.
The Youth she seiz'd and laying now aside
All Modesty, the Female's Justest Pride,
She said, with an Embrace, here at my House
Peace-offrings are, this Day I paid my Vows.
I therefore came abroad to meet my Dear,
And, Lo, in Happy Hour I find thee here.
  My Chamber I've adorn'd, and o'er my Bed
Are Cov'rings of the richest Tap'stry spread,
With Linnen it is[a] *deck'd from Egypt brought,*
And Carvings by the Curious Artist wrought;
It wants no Glad Perfume Arabia yields
In all her Citron Groves, and spicy Fields;
Here all her store of richest Odours meets,
I'le lay thee in a Wilderness of Sweets.
Whatever to the Sense[b] *can grateful be*
I have collected there . . . I want but Thee.
My Husband's gone a Journey far away, ⎫
Much Gold he took abroad, and long will stay, ⎬
He nam'd for his return a distant Day. ⎭
  Upon her Tongue did such smooth mischeif dwell,

<hr>

[a] *it is*] *is it* Fol.   [b] *Whatever to the Sense*] *Whate'er unto the sence* Fol.

And from her lips such welcome Flatt'ry fell,
Th' unguarded Youth, in Silken Fetters ty'd
Resign'd his Reason, and with Ease comply'd.
Thus does the Ox to his own Slaughter^a go,
And thus is senseless of th' impending Blow.
Thus flies the simple Bird into the snare,
That skilful Fowlers for his Life prepare.
But let my Sons attend, Attend may they
Whom Youthful Vigour may to Sin betray:
Let them false Charmers fly, and guard their Hearts
Against the wily Wanton's pleasing Arts.
With Care direct their steps, nor turn astray
To tread the Paths of her deceitful Way;
Least they too late of Her fell Power complain,
And fall, where many mightier have been Slain.

T

No. 411

[ADDISON]

Saturday, June 21, 1712[1]

Avia Pieridum peragro loca, nullius ante
Trita solo; juvat integros accedere fonteis;
Atque haurire: . . .

Lucr.

OUR Sight is the most perfect and most delightful of all our Senses.[2] It fills the Mind with the largest Variety of Ideas

---

^a *to his own Slaughter*] *unto the slaughter* Fol.

---

[1] *Motto.* Lucretius, *De rerum natura*, 1. 926–8:
> The Muses close Retreat I wander o'er,
> Their unacquainted Solitudes explore,
> At the Spring-head it charms me to be first,
> And in th' untainted Stream to quench my Thirst.

Nos. 411–421, the series of eleven papers on 'the pleasures of the imagination', are a revision of a single long essay on this subject, portions of which survive in the manuscript notebook first published by J. Dykes Campbell in 1864 (cf. Nos. 170–1 and 255–7, vol. ii) and now in the library of Harvard University. The first pages are missing, and of No. 411 only parts of paragraphs 4 and 7 are represented in the notebook.

[2] Cf. Cicero, *De Oratore*, 2. 87. 357.

converses with its Objects at the greatest Distance, and continues the longest in Action without being tired or satiated with its proper Enjoyments. The Sense of Feeling can indeed give us a Notion of Extention, Shape, and all other Ideas that enter at the Eye, except Colours; but at the same time it is very much streightned and confined in its Operations, to the number, bulk, and distance of its particular Objects. Our Sight seems[a] designed to supply all these Defects, and may be considered as a more delicate and diffusive kind of Touch, that spreads it self over an infinite Multitude of Bodies, comprehends the largest Figures, and brings into our reach some of the most remote Parts of the Universe.

It is this Sense which furnishes the Imagination with its Ideas; so that by the Pleasures of the Imagination[1] or Fancy[2] (which I shall use promiscuously) I here mean such as arise from visible Objects,[3]

---

[a] Sight seems] Sight therefore seems *Fol.*

---

[1] While Addison cannot be credited with originating this phrase, this series of papers unquestionably helped to make it popular among eighteenth-century critics and aestheticians. It had been used by Sir William Temple (see note below); and Lady Mary Pierrepont in a letter of 21 July 1709 had written: 'How happy must I think myself when I fancy your friendship to me even great enough to overpower your judgment! I am afraid this is one of the pleasures of the Imagination . . .' (*Letters of Lady Mary Wortley Montagu*, ed. W. Moy Thomas, i. 38). The editor notes that Lady Mary had written a poem with this title. Akenside's poem in 1744 gave the phrase further currency.

[2] Throughout the greater part of the century the two terms were used interchangeably. Occasionally, as in William Duff's *Essay on Original Genius* (1767), an effort is made to distinguish between them, but up to the time of Wordsworth the terms are practically synonymous, as in William Gerard's popular *Essay on Genius* (1774). James Beattie writes in 1783:

According to the common use of words, Imagination and Fancy are not perfectly synonymous. They are, indeed, names for the same faculty; but the former seems to be applied to the more solemn, and the latter to the more trivial, exertions of it. A witty author is a man of lively Fancy; but a sublime poet is said to possess a vast Imagination. However, as these words are often, and by the best writers, used indiscriminately, I shall not further distinguish them (*Dissertations moral and critical*, ed. Dublin, 1783, i. 87).

The more transient, brilliant, unstable qualities of fancy (as opposed to the comprehensive, plastic nature of the imagination) are emphasized in the innumerable odes to 'Fancy' in the latter half of the century. See further John Bullitt and W. J. Bate, 'Distinctions between Fancy and Imagination in Eighteenth-century English Criticism', *Modern Language Notes*, lx (1945), 8–15; and Wilma L. Kennedy, *The English Heritage of Coleridge of Bristol, 1798* (New Haven, Conn., 1947).

[3] Addison is following here the dominant empirical tradition of seventeenth-century philosophy, in which imagination is regarded as a means of simple apprehension, the collection of 'phantasms' or sense-impressions, stored up for the scrutiny of reason and the making of abstract conceptions. 'Now our *simple* apprehension of corporal objects, if *present*, we call *Sense*; if absent, we properly name it *Imagination*.' These words of Joseph Glanvill (*Scepsis scientifica*, 1665, p. 71) may be found duplicated in the writings of many of Addison's predecessors. Hobbes was only stating the point with characteristic vigour in calling imagination 'decaying sense' (*Leviathan*,

either when we have them actually in our view, or when we call up their Ideas into our Minds by Paintings, Statues, Descriptions, or any the like Occasion. We cannot indeed have a single Image in the Fancy that did not make its first Entrance through the Sight; but we have the Power of retaining, altering and compounding[1] those Images, which we have once received, into all the varieties of Picture and Vision that are most agreeable to the Imagination; for by this Faculty a Man in a Dungeon is capable of entertaining himself with Scenes and Landskips more beautiful than any that can be found in the whole Compass of Nature.

There are few Words in the *English* Language which are employed in a more loose and uncircumscribed Sense than those of the *Fancy* and the *Imagination*. I therefore thought it necessary to fix and determine the Notion of these two Words, as I intend to make use of them in the Thread of my following Speculations, that the Reader may conceive rightly what is the Subject which I proceed upon. I must therefore desire him to remember, that by the Pleasures of the Imagination, I mean only such Pleasures as arise originally from Sight, and that I divide these Pleasures into two kinds: My Design being first of all to Discourse of those Primary Pleasures of the Imagination, which entirely proceed from such Objects as are before our Eyes;[a] and in the next place to speak of those Secondary Pleasures of the Imagination which flow from the Ideas of visible Objects, when the Objects are not actually before the Eye, but are called up into our Memories, or form'd into agreeable Visions of Things that are either Absent or Fictitious.[2]

The Pleasures of the Imagination, taken in their full Extent, are not so gross as those of Sense, nor so refined as those of the Understanding.[3] The last are, indeed, more preferable, because they are founded on some new Knowledge or Improvement in the Mind of

---

[a] before our Eyes;] present to the Eye; *Fol.*

1651, chap. ii). A few years after the *Spectator* we find this effort at formal definition: 'That Faculty which presents to the Mind's view the Images or Ideas of external sensible Objects, or by which the Mind perceives them, is what we call the *Imagination*' (Zachary Mayne, *Two Dissertations concerning Sense, and the Imagination*, 1728, pp. 69–70).

[1] These activities of the imagination had long been recognized; as the century progresses, critics come to be increasingly impressed by the liveliness with which the imagination performs these functions.

[2] In adopting the terms 'primary' and 'secondary' pleasures Addison probably has in mind Locke's distinction between the primary and secondary qualities.

[3] In placing imagination midway between the sense and the understanding Addison follows an old tradition. See M. W. Bundy, *The Theory of Imagination in*

Man; yet it must be confest, that those of the Imagination are as great
and as transporting as the other. A beautiful Prospect delights
the Soul, as much as a Demonstration; and a Description in *Homer*
has charmed more Readers than a Chapter in *Aristotle*.[1] Besides, the
Pleasures of the Imagination have this Advantage, above those of
the Understanding, that they are more obvious, and more easie to
be acquired. It is but opening the Eye, and the Scene enters. The
Colours paint themselves on the Fancy, with very little Attention
of Thought or Application of Mind in the Beholder. We are struck,
we know not how, with the Symmetry of any thing we see, and
immediately assent to the Beauty of an Object, without enquiring
into the particular Causes and Occasions of it.[2]

A Man of a Polite Imagination, is let into a great many Pleasures
that the Vulgar are not capable of receiving.[3] He can converse with
a Picture, and find an agreeable Companion in a Statue. He meets
with a secret Refreshment in a Description, and often feels a greater
Satisfaction in the Prospect of Fields and Meadows, than another
does in the Possession. It gives him, indeed, a kind of Property in
every thing he sees, and makes the most rude uncultivated Parts of
Nature administer to his Pleasures: So that he looks upon the
World, as it were, in another Light, and discovers in it a Multitude
of Charms, that conceal themselves from the generality of Mankind.[4]

There are, indeed, but very few who know how to be idle and
innocent, or have a Relish of any Pleasures that are not Criminal;
every Diversion they take is at the Expence of some one Virtue or

Classical and Mediaeval Thought (University of Illinois Studies in Language and Literature, vol. xii, nos. 2–3), Urbana, Illinois, 1927.
  [1] Addison originally wrote 'a description in Virgil has perhaps charm'd more
readers . . .'
  [2] Sir William Temple, in the Preface to his *Observations upon the United Provinces of
the Netherlands*, had written in a similar vein (*Works*, 1720, vol. i, sig. B3):

> For all the Pleasures of Sense, that any Man can enjoy, are within the reach of
> a private Fortune, and ordinary Contrivance; Grow fainter with Age, and duller
> with Use; Must be revived with Intermissions, and wait upon the returns of
> Appetite, which are no more at Call of the Rich, than the Poor. The Flashes of Wit
> and good Humour, that rise from the Vapours of Wine, are little different from
> those that proceed from the heats of Blood in the first Approaches of Fevers, or
> Frenzies; and are to be valued, but as (indeed) they are, the Effects of Distemper.
> But the Pleasures of Imagination, as they heighten and refine the very Pleasures of
> Sense, so they are of larger Extent, and longer Duration.

Guardian 49 (by Berkeley) repeats many of the ideas expressed here by Addison.
  [3] A point of view frequently expressed by neo-classical critics: although taste
might be dependent in theory on the appeal to universality, in practice it was likely
to be found among the most 'polite' in the most polite ages.
  [4] Apparently this paragraph and the one following were interpolated in the MS.
An asterisk indicates an addition at this point, but the pages are missing.

another, and their very first Step out of Business is into Vice or Folly. A Man should endeavour, therefore, to make the Sphere of his innocent Pleasures as wide as possible, that he may retire into them with Safety, and find in them such a Satisfaction as a wise Man would not blush to take. Of this Nature are those of the Imagination, which do not require such a Bent of Thought as is necessary to our more serious Employments, nor, at the same time, suffer the Mind to sink into that Negligence and Remissness, which are apt to accompany our more sensual Delights, but, like a gentle Exercise to the Faculties, awaken them from Sloth and Idleness, without putting them upon any Labour or Difficulty.

We might here add, that the Pleasures of the Fancy are more conducive to Health, than those of the Understanding, which are worked out by Dint of Thinking, and attended with too violent a Labour of the Brain. Delightful Scenes, whether in Nature, Painting, or Poetry, have a kindly Influence on the Body, as well as the Mind, and not only serve to clear and brighten the Imagination, but are able to disperse Grief and Melancholly, and to set the Animal Spirits in pleasing and agreeable Motions. For this reason Sir *Francis Bacon*, in his Essay upon Health, has not thought it improper to prescribe to his Reader a Poem or a Prospect,[1] where he particularly dissuades him from knotty and subtile Disquisitions, and advises him to pursue Studies, that fill the Mind with splendid and illustrious Objects, as Histories, Fables, and Contemplations of Nature.[2]

I have in this Paper, by way of Introduction, settled the Notion of those Pleasures of the Imagination, which are the Subject of my present Undertaking, and endeavoured, by several Considerations, to recommend to my Reader the Pursuit of those Pleasures. I shall, in my next Paper, examine the several Sources from whence these Pleasures are derived.   O[3]

[1] The MS. reads: 'a prospect or a description'.
[2] Bacon, Essay 30, 'Of Regiment of Health' (*Essays*, ed. W. A. Wright, 1892, p. 132).
[3] Nichols conjectures that these papers signed O were written by Addison at his office, 'or perhaps composed from sketches in his *Common-Place-Book* written when at *Oxford*'. Hurd comments: 'This essay on the pleasures of the imagination [i.e. Nos. 411–21] is by far the most masterly of all Mr. Addison's critical works. The scheme of it, as the motto to this introductory paper intimates, is original; and the style is finished with so much ease, as to merit the best attention of the reader. . . .'

No. 412   *Monday, June 23, 1712*[1]
[ADDISON]

. . . *Divisum sic breve fiet Opus.*
Mart.

I SHALL first consider those Pleasures of the Imagination, which[a] arise from the actual View and Survey of outward Objects: And these, I think, all proceed from the Sight of what is *Great, Uncommon,* or *Beautiful.*[2] There may, indeed, be something so terrible or offensive, that the Horrour or Loathsomness of an Object may over-bear[3] the Pleasure which results from its *Greatness, Novelty,* or *Beauty*; but still there will be such a Mixture of Delight in the very Disgust it gives us, as any of these three Qualifications are most conspicuous and prevailing.

By *Greatness,* I do not only mean the Bulk of any single Object, but the Largeness of a whole View, considered as one entire Piece. Such are the Prospects of an open Champian[4] Country, a vast uncultivated Desart, of huge Heaps of Mountains, high Rocks and Precipices, or a wide Expanse of Waters, where we are not struck with the Novelty or Beauty of the Sight, but with that rude kind of Magnificence which appears in many of these stupendous Works of Nature. Our Imagination loves to be filled with an Object, or to graspe at any thing that is too big for its Capacity. We are flung into a pleasing Astonishment at such unbounded Views, and feel a delightful Stillness and Amazement in the Soul at the Apprehension of them. The Mind of Man naturally hates every thing that looks like a Restraint upon it, and is apt to fancy it self under a sort

---

      [a] which] that *Fol.*

---

[1] *Motto.* Martial, *Epigrams,* 4. 82. 8: The work thus divided will become brief.

[2] Aristotle had insisted that beauty depends on 'magnitude and order' (*Poetics,* 7. 4), and the 'uncommon' had long been recognized as a principal factor in aesthetic appreciation. The combination of magnitude and novelty had been made in a sermon by Robert South (on Prov. iii. 17), in which the 'pleasure in speculation of divine things' is based on the twofold ground of 'greatness' and 'the newness of the object' (*Twelve Sermons,* 6th ed., 1727, i. 18–23). No precise source for Addison's triad, the great, the uncommon, and the beautiful, quoted so frequently in the eighteenth century, has been noted. See, among the vast amount that has been written on the subject, two articles by Clarence D. Thorpe, 'Addison's Theory of the Imagination as "Perceptive Response"', *Papers of the Michigan Academy of Science, Arts and Letters,* xxi (1935), 509–30, and 'Addison and Some of his Predecessors on "Novelty"', *PMLA,* lii (1937), 1114–29.

[3] I.e. outweigh. This is the earliest example in *OED* of the word in this sense.

[4] For the spelling cf. No. 5 (vol. i).

of Confinement, when the Sight is pent up in a narrow Compass, and shortned on every side by the Neighbourhood of Walls or Mountains.[1] On the contrary, a spacious Horison is an Image of Liberty, where the Eye has Room to range abroad, to expatiate at large on the Immensity of its Views, and to lose it self amidst the Variety of Objects that offer themselves to its Observation. Such wide and undetermined Prospects are as pleasing to the Fancy, as the Speculations of Eternity or Infinitude are to the Understanding. But if there be a Beauty or Uncommonness joyned with this Grandeur, as in a troubled Ocean, a Heaven adorned with Stars and Meteors, or a spacious Landskip cut out into Rivers, Woods, Rocks, and Meadows, the Pleasure still grows upon us, as it arises from more than a single Principle.

Every thing that is *new* or *uncommon* raises a Pleasure in the Imagination, because it fills the Soul with an agreeable Surprise, gratifies its Curiosity, and gives it an Idea of which it was not before possest. We are, indeed, so often conversant with one Sett of Objects, and tired out with so many repeated Shows of the same Things, that whatever is *new* or *uncommon* contributes a little to vary Human Life, and to divert our Minds, for a while, with the Strangeness of its Appearance: It serves us for a kind of Refreshment, and takes off from that Satiety we are apt to complain of in our usual and ordinary Entertainments.[2] It is this that bestows Charms on a Monster, and makes even the Imperfections of Nature please[a] us. It is this that recommends Variety, where the Mind is every Instant called off to something new, and the Attention not suffered to dwell too long, and waste it self on any particular Object.[3] It is this, likewise, that improves what is great or beautiful, and makes

[a] please] to please *Fol.*

---

[1] This sentence and the two following are added in Addison's hand in the MS.
[2] In chap. vi of his *Remarks on Prince Arthur* (1696) Dennis had commented unfavourably on the 'wearisome Uniformity' of Blackmore's poem, in language similar to Addison's.

For the Mind does not care for dwelling too long upon an Object, but loves to pass from one thing to another; because such a Transition keeps it from languishing, and gives it more Agitation. Now Agitation only can give it Delight. For Agitation not only keeps it from mortifying Reflections, which it naturally has when it is not shaken, but gives it a Force which it had not before, and the Consciousness of its own Force delights it (*Critical Works*, ed. Hooker, i. 109).

In *The Advancement and Reformation of Modern Poetry* (1701), chap. vi, Dennis again speaks of the advantages in having the imagination fired with the motion and 'violent Agitation' of images (ibid. i. 218).

[3] This sentence is added in Addison's hand in the MS.

it afford the Mind a double Entertainment. Groves, Fields, and Meadows, are at any Season of the Year pleasant to look upon, but never so much as in the opening of the Spring, when they are all new and fresh, with their first Gloss upon them, and not yet too much accustomed and familiar to the Eye. For this reason there is nothing that more enlivens a Prospect than Rivers, Jetteaus,[1] or Falls of Water, where the Scene is perpetually shifting, and entertaining the Sight every Moment with something that is new. We are quickly tired with looking upon Hills and Valleys, where every thing continues fixt and settled in the same Place and Posture, but find our Thoughts a little agitated and relieved at the sight of such Objects as are ever in Motion, and sliding away from beneath the Eye of the Beholder.[2]

But there is nothing that makes its way more directly to the Soul than *Beauty*,[3] which immediately diffuses a secret Satisfaction and Complacency thro' the Imagination, and gives a Finishing to any thing that is Great or Uncommon. The very first Discovery of it strikes the Mind with an inward Joy, and spreads a Chearfulness and Delight through all its Faculties.[4] There is not perhaps any real Beauty or Deformity more in one piece of Matter than another, because we might have been so made, that whatsoever now appears loathsom to us, might have shewn it self agreeable; but we find by Experience, that there are several Modifications of Matter which the Mind, without any previous Consideration, pronounces at first sight Beautiful or Deformed. Thus we see that every different Species of sensible Creatures has its different Notions of Beauty, and that each of them is most affected with the Beauties of its own kind.[5] This is no where more remarkable than in Birds of the same Shape and Proportion, where we often see the Male determined in

---

[1] On this spelling (earlier *jetto*) see *OED*.

[2] These two sentences are not in the MS.

[3] Addison does not define this word, beyond saying that there are 'several Modifications of Matter' which the mind instantly recognizes as beautiful or deformed, although he distinguishes between beauty as raising sexual desire and beauty deriving from colours, symmetry, and arrangement.

[4] This sentence is also added in Addison's hand in the MS.

[5] This sentence and the following passage, down to 'together' (p. 544, l. 4), represent an addition made by Addison in the MS. The Latin verses are, as Nichols suspected, by Addison, and appear in the MS. in his own hand with his corrections. In the 1744 12mo edition of the *Spectator* they are translated:

> The feather'd Husband, to his Partner true,
> Preserves connubial Rites inviolate.
> With cold Indifference every Charm he sees,
> The milky Whiteness of the stately Neck,

his Courtship by the single Grain or Tincture of a Feather, and never discovering any Charms but in the Colour of its Species.[a]

> *Scit thalamo servare fidem, sanctasque veretur*
> *Connubii leges, non illum in pectore candor*
> *Sollicitat niveus; neque pravum accendit amorem*
> *Splendida Lanugo, vel honesta in vertice crista,*
> *Purpureusve nitor pennarum; ast agmina latè*
> *Fœminea explorat cautus, maculasque requirit*
> *Cognatas, paribusque interlita corpora guttis:*
> *Ni faceret, pictis sylvam circum undique monstris*
> *Confusam aspiceres vulgò, partusque biformes,*
> *Et genus ambiguum, & Veneris monumenta nefandæ.*
>   *Hinc merula in nigro se oblectat nigra marito,*
> *Hinc socium lasciva petit Philomela canorum,*
> *Agnoscitque pares sonitus, hinc Noctua tetram*
> *Canitiem alarum, & Glaucos miratur ocellos.*
> *Nempe sibi semper constat, crescitque quotannis*
> *Lucida progenies, castos confessa parentes;*
> *Dum virides inter saltus lucosque sonoros*
> *Vere novo exultat, plumasque decora Juventus*
> *Explicat ad solem, patriisque coloribus ardet.*

There is a second kind of *Beauty* that we find in the several Products of Art and Nature, which does not work in the Imagination with that Warmth and Violence as the Beauty that appears in our proper Species, but is apt however to raise in us a secret Delight, and a kind of Fondness for the Places or Objects in which we

---

[a] its Species.] its own Species. *Fol.*

The shining Down, proud Crest, and purple Wings:
But cautious with a searching Eye explores
The female Tribes, his proper Mate to find,
With kindred Colours mark'd: Did he not so,
The Grove with painted Monsters wou'd abound,
Th' ambiguous Product of unnatural Love.
The Black-bird hence selects her sooty Spouse;
The Nightingale her musical Compeer,
Lur'd by the well-known Voice: the Bird of Night,
Smit with his dusky Wings, and greenish Eyes,
Wo[o]s his dun Paramour. The beauteous Race
Speak the chaste Loves of their Progenitors;
When, by the Spring invited, they exult
In Woods and Fields, and to the Sun unfold
Their Plumes, that with paternal Colours glow.

discover it. This consists either in the Gaiety or Variety of Colours, in the Symmetry and Proportion of Parts, in the Arrangement and Disposition of Bodies, or in a just Mixture and Concurrence of all together. Among these several kinds of Beauty the Eye takes most Delight in Colours. We no where meet with a more glorious or pleasing Show in Nature, than what appears in the Heavens at the rising and setting of the Sun, which is wholly made up of those different Stains of Light that shew themselves in Clouds of a different Situation. For this Reason we find the Poets, who are always addressing themselves to the Imagination, borrowing more of their Epithets from Colours than from any other Topic.

As the Fancy delights in every thing that is Great, Strange, or Beautiful, and is still more pleased the more it finds of these Perfections in the same Object, so is it capable of receiving a new Satisfaction by the Assistance of another Sense.[1] Thus any continued Sound, as the Musick of Birds, or a Fall of Water,[2] awakens every moment the Mind of the Beholder, and makes him more attentive to the several Beauties of the Place that lie before him. Thus if there arises a Fragrancy of Smells or Perfumes, they heighten the Pleasures of the Imagination, and make even the Colours and Verdure of the Landskip appear more agreeable; for the Ideas of both Senses recommend each other, and are pleasanter together than when they enter the Mind separately: As the different Colours of a Picture, when they are well disposed, set off one another, and receive an additional Beauty from the Advantage of their Situation.

O

No. 413   *Tuesday, June 24, 1712*[3]
[ADDISON]

. . . Causa latet, vis est notissima . . .
Ovid.

THOUGH in Yesterday's Paper we considered how every thing that is *Great*, *New*, or *Beautiful*, is apt to affect the Imagination with Pleasure, we must own that it is impossible for us to assign the

[1] This sentence is also added in the MS. in Addison's hand.

[2] In the MS. Addison had written: 'as that of Bells or of Water at a convenient distance.'

[3] *Motto.* Ovid, *Metamorphoses*, 4. 287: The cause is secret, but the effect is known.

necessary Cause of this Pleasure, because we know neither the Nature of an Idea, nor the Substance of a Human Soul, which might help us to discover the Conformity or Disagreeableness of the one to the other; and therefore, for want of such a Light, all that we can do in Speculations of this kind, is to reflect on those Operations of the Soul that are most agreeable, and to range, under their proper Heads, what is pleasing or displeasing to the Mind, without being able to trace out the several necessary and efficient Causes[a] from whence the Pleasure or Displeasure arises.[1]

Final Causes lye more bare and open to our Observation, as there are often a great Variety that belong to the same Effect; and these, tho' they are not altogether so satisfactory, are generally more useful than the other, as they give us greater Occasion of admiring the Goodness and Wisdom of the first Contriver.

One of the Final Causes of our Delight, in any thing that is *great*, may be this. The Supreme Author of our Being has so formed the Soul of Man, that nothing but himself can be its last, adequate, and proper Happiness. Because, therefore, a great Part of our Happiness must arise from the Contemplation of his Being, that he might give our Souls a just Relish of such a Contemplation, he has made them naturally delight in the Apprehension of what is Great or Unlimited. Our Admiration, which is a very pleasing Motion of the Mind, immediately rises at the Consideration of any Object that takes up a great deal of room in the Fancy, and, by consequence, will improve into the highest pitch of Astonishment and Devotion when we contemplate his Nature, that is neither circumscribed by Time nor Place, nor to be comprehended by the largest Capacity of a Created Being.

He has annexed a secret Pleasure to the Idea of any thing that is *new* or *uncommon*, that he might encourage us in the Pursuit after Knowledge,[2] and engage us to search into the Wonders of his Creation; for every new Idea brings such a Pleasure along with it, as rewards any Pains we have taken in its Acquisition, and consequently serves as a Motive to put us upon fresh Discoveries.

---

[a] necessary and efficient Causes] necessary Causes *Fol.*

---

[1] The 'efficient cause' in Aristotelian philosophy is the impetus or instrument by which a thing is produced. Since we cannot understand what causes the imagination to be affected pleasurably by the great, the new, or the beautiful (the 'efficient' cause), Addison turns to consider why we are so affected (the 'final' cause).

[2] Cf. Seneca, *Dialogues*, 8. 5. 3.

He has made every thing that is *beautiful in our own Species* pleasant, that all Creatures might be tempted to multiply their Kind, and fill the World, with Inhabitants; for 'tis very remarkable that where-ever Nature is crost in the Production of a Monster (the Result of any unnatural Mixture) the Breed is incapable of propagating its Likeness, and of founding a new Order of Creatures;[1] so that unless all Animals were allured by the Beauty of their own Species, Generation would be at an end, and the Earth unpeopled.

In the last place, he has made every thing that is beautiful in all other Objects pleasant, or rather has made so many Objects appear beautiful, that he might render the whole Creation more gay and delightful. He has given almost every thing about us the Power of raising an agreeable Idea in the Imagination: So that it is impossible for us to behold his Works with Coldness or Indifference, and to survey so many Beauties without a secret Satisfaction and Complacency. Things would make but a poor Appearance to the Eye, if we saw them only in their proper Figures and Motions: And what Reason can we assign for their exciting in us many of those Ideas which are different from any thing that exists in the Objects themselves, (for such are Light and Colours)[2] were it not to add Supernumerary[a] Ornaments to the Universe, and make it more agreeable to the Imagination? We are every where entertained with pleasing Shows and Apparitions, we discover imaginary Glories in the Heavens, and in the Earth, and see some of this Visionary Beauty poured out upon the whole Creation; but what a rough unsightly Sketch of Nature should we be entertained with, did all her Colouring disappear, and the several Distinctions of Light and Shade vanish?[3] In short, our Souls are at present delightfully lost and bewildered in a pleasing Delusion, and we walk about like the Enchanted Hero of a Romance, who[b] sees beautiful Castles, Woods and Meadows; and at the same time hears the warbling of Birds, and the purling of Streams; but upon the finishing of some secret

---

[a] Supernumerary] *12mo*; Supernumary *Fol.*, *8vo*   [b] who] that *Fol.*

---

[1] This sentence up to this point originally formed (with some changes) a part of the passage which Addison interpolated in No. 412, where it followed (p. 542, line 28) the sentence ending 'Beauties of its own kind'.

[2] The MS. reads here 'Symmetry & colours'.

[3] This portion of the sentence is an addition to the MS. in Addison's hand: 'but what a rough unsightly Sketch of Nature shall we hereafter be entertain'd wth when all that Colouring disappears and the several distinctions of Light and Shade vanish?'

Spell, the fantastick Scene breaks up, and the disconsolate Knight finds himself on a barren Heath, or in a solitary Desart. It is not improbable that something like this may be the State of the Soul after its first Separation, in respect of the Images it will receive from Matter; tho' indeed the Ideas of Colours are so pleasing and beautiful in the Imagination, that it is possible the Soul will not be deprived of them, but perhaps find them excited by some other Occasional Cause, as they are at present by the different Impressions of the subtle Matter on the Organ of Sight.

[1]I have here supposed that my Reader is acquainted with that great Modern Discovery, which is at present universally acknowledged by all the Enquirers into Natural Philosophy: Namely, that Light and Colours, as apprehended by the Imagination, are only Ideas in the Mind, and not Qualities that have any Existence in Matter.[2] As this is a Truth which[a] has been proved incontestably by many Modern Philosophers, and is indeed one of the finest Speculations in that Science, if the *English* Reader would see the Notion explained at large, he may find it in the Eighth Chapter of the Second Book of Mr. *Lock*'s Essay on Human Understanding.[b]

O

[a] which] that *Fol.*
[b] *No. 413 ends at this point in 8vo and 12mo; in Fol. it concludes with the following letter:*
Mr. SPECTATOR,   *June* 24. 1712.
'I Would not divert the Course of your Discourses, when you seem bent upon obliging the World with a train of Thinking, which, rightly attended, may render the Life of every Man, who reads it, more easy and happy for the future. The Pleasures of the Imagination are what bewilder Life, when Reason and Judgment do not interpose; It is therefore a worthy Action in you, to look carefully into the Powers of Fancy, that other Men, from the Knowledge of them, may improve their Joys, and allay their Griefs, by a just use of that Faculty: I say, Sir, I would not interrupt you in the Progress of this Discourse; after that, but, if you will do me the Favour of inserting this Letter in your next Paper, you will do some Service to the Publick, tho' not in so noble a way of Obliging, as that of improving their Minds. Allow me, Sir, to acquaint you with a Design (of which I am partly Author) tho' it tends to no greater a Good than that of getting Mony. I should not hope for the Favour of a Philosopher in this Matter, if it were not attempted under all the Restrictions which you Sages put upon private Acquisitions.

'The first Purpose which every good Man is to propose to himself, is the Service of his Prince and Country; after that is done, he cannot add to himself but he must also be beneficial to them. This Scheme of Gain is not only consistent with that End, but has its very Being in Subordination to it, for no Man can be a Gainer here, but at the same time he himself, or some other, must succeed in their Dealings with the

---

[1] This final paragraph of No. 413 is not found in the MS.
[2] See Locke, *Essay concerning Human Understanding*, book ii, chap. viii: 'Some farther considerations concerning our simple ideas.'

No. 414   *Wednesday, June 25, 1712*[1]
[ADDISON]

> . . . *Alterius sic*
> *Altera poscit opem res & conjurat amicè.*
>   Hor.[a]

IF we consider the Works of *Nature* and *Art*,[b] as they are qualified
to entertain the Imagination, we shall find the last very defective,
in Comparison of the former; for though they may sometimes appear
as Beautiful or Strange, they can have nothing in them of that Vast-

Government. It is called the *Multiplication Table*,[2] and is so far calculated for the
immediate Service of Her Majesty, that the same Person who is fortunate in the
Lottery of the State, may receive yet further Advantage in this Table. And I am
sure nothing can be more pleasing to Her gracious Temper, than to find out additional Methods of encreasing their good Fortune who adventure any thing in Her
Service, or laying Occasions for others to become capable of serving their Country,
who are at present in too low Circumstances to exert themselves. The manner of
executing the Design is by giving out Receipts for half Guineas received, which shall
entitule the fortunate Bearer to certain Sums in the Table, as is set forth at large in
the Proposals Printed the 23d Instant. There is another Circumstance in this Design
which gives me hopes of your Favour to it, and that is what *Tully* advises, to wit,
that the Benefit is made as diffusive as possible.[3] Every one that has half a Guinea is
put into a possibility from that small Sum to raise to himself an easie Fortune.
When these little parcels of Wealth are, as it were, thus thrown back again into the
Redonation of Providence, we are to expect that some who live under Hardship or
Obscurity, may be produced to the World in the Figure they deserve by this means.
I doubt not but this last Argument will have Force with you, and I cannot add
another to it, but what your Severity will, I fear, very little regard, which is, that

> I am, SIR,
> *Your greatest Admirer,*
> Richard Steele.'

[a] *Motto.* Hor.] om. *Fol.*   [b] *Italics added in 8vo and 12mo*

---

[1] *Motto.* Horace, *Ars poetica*, 410–11:
   Each by it self is vain, I'm sure, but join'd,
   Their Force is strong, each proves the others Friend. CREECH.

[2] On 1 July Swift wrote to Stella: 'Steel was arrested tother day for making a
Lottery, directly agst an Act of Parlmt. He is now under Prosecution, but they
think it will be droppt out of Pity. I believe he will very soon lose his Employmt,
for he has been mighty impertinent of late in his Spectators, and I will never offer
a Word in his behalf' (*Journal to Stella*, ed. H. Williams, p. 546). Swift is here only
repeating an inaccurate rumour: Steele had not been arrested, although his scheme
for raising money (see Aitken, *Steele*, i. 346–8) had certainly placed him in a
dangerous position; on the same day in which his advertisement appeared an Act
against illicit lotteries came into force. An advertisement in No. 417 (and in the *Daily
Courant* of the same date) announces that the proposal has been withdrawn because
of 'an Information from the Attorney-General' and that money will be repaid to subscribers who call 'at the last House on the Left Hand in Ship-Yard in Bartholomew-
Lane'. A further advertisement in the *Daily Courant* of 2 July urges persons to call
'who have not yet demanded their Money in the Multiplication-Table'.

[3] Cicero, *De Finibus*, 3. 20. 65.

ness and Immensity, which afford so great an Entertainment to the Mind of the Beholder. [1]The one may be as Polite and Delicate as the other, but can never shew her self so August and Magnificent in the Design. There is something more bold and masterly in the rough careless Strokes of Nature,[2] than in the nice Touches and Embellishments of Art. The Beauties of the most stately Garden or Palace lie in a narrow Compass, the Imagination immediately runs them over, and requires something else to gratifie her; but, in the wide Fields of Nature, the Sight wanders up and down without Confinement, and is fed with an infinite variety of Images, without any certain Stint or Number. [3]For this Reason we always find the Poet in love with a Country-Life, where Nature appears in the greatest Perfection, and furnishes out all those Scenes that are most apt to delight the Imagination.

> *Scriptorum chorus omnis amat nemus & fugit Urbes.* Hor.[4]

> *Hic Secura quies, & nescia fallere vita,*
> *Dives opum variarum; hic latis otia fundis,*
> *Speluncæ, vivique lacus, hic frigida Tempe,*
> *Mugitusque boum, mollesque sub arbore somni.* Vir.[5]

But tho' there are several of these wild Scenes, that are more delightful than any artificial Shows; yet we find the Works of Nature still more pleasant, the more they resemble those of Art:

[1] This sentence and the one following are added in the MS. in Addison's hand.

[2] On the antithesis of nature and art, and the shifting concepts of nature at this period, see A. O. Lovejoy, ' "Nature" as aesthetic norm', *Modern Language Notes*, xlii (1927), 444–50.

[3] This passage, much worked over, is added to the MS. in Addison's hand. At first he wrote: 'For this reason we find the poets always crying up a Country Life, where Nature is left to her-self, and appears to y[e] best advantage.' He then changed it to read:

For this reason we find all Fanciful men and y[e] poets in particular still in Love wth a Country Life, where Nature is left to her-self, and furnishes out all y[e] Variety of Scenes y[t] are most delightfull to y[e] Imagination.
. . . hic latis otia campis,
Speluncae, vivique lacus; hic frigida Tempe,
Mugitusque Boum, mollesque sub arbore somni.

[4] Horace, *Epistles*, 2. 2. 77.
Each Writer hates the Town and Woods approves. CREECH.

[5] Virgil, *Georgics*, 2. 467–70.
Unvex'd with Quarrels, undisturb'd with Noise,
The Country King his peaceful Realm enjoys:
Cool Grots, and living Lakes, the Flow'ry Pride
Of Meads, and Streams that thro' the Valley glide;
And shady Groves that easie Sleep invite,
And after toilsome Days, a soft repose at Night. DRYDEN.

For in this case our Pleasure arises from a double Principle; from the Agreeableness of the Objects to the Eye, and from their Similitude to other Objects: We are pleased as well with comparing their Beauties, as with surveying them, and can represent them to our Minds, either as Copies or Originals. Hence it is that we take Delight in a Prospect which is well laid out, and diversified with Fields and Meadows, Woods and Rivers, in those accidental Land-skips of Trees, Clouds and Cities, that are sometimes found in the Veins of Marble, in the curious Fret-work of Rocks and Grottos, and, in a Word, in any thing that hath such a Variety or Regularity as may seem the Effect of Design, in what we call the Works of Chance.

If the Products of Nature rise in Value, according as they more or less resemble those of Art, we may be sure that artificial Works receive a greater Advantage from their Resemblance of such as are natural; because here the Similitude is not only pleasant, but the Pattern more perfect.[1] The prettiest Landskip[2] I ever saw, was one

---

[1] The MS. contains at this point the following passage, later deleted:

I believe, most readers are pleas'd with the Eastern King's device, y^t made his Garden ye Map of his Empire; where ye great Roads were represented by ye Spacious walks & allies, ye woods & forests by little thickets & tufts of Bushes. A crooked rill discover'd ye windings of a mighty River, & a Summer-house or Turret ye Situation of a huge City or Metropolis. This natural draught of his Dominions was doubtless pleasanter y^n a more accurate one of another kind made by ye strokes of a pen or pencil; because ye materials of ye Map had more of nature in 'em, and were liker ye things, they represented.

[2] Addison probably has in mind the scene obtained by a camera obscura, or possibly that produced by the projection of two on opposite walls. There was such a camera obscura at Greenwich Park. (In the first draft Addison wrote 'Sea', then 'River Thames', and finally altered it to 'a navigable River'.) Hugh Blair, in his lectures at Edinburgh in the 1760's, recalled the experiment:

The scene, which I am inclined to think Mr. Addison here refers to, is Greenwich Park, with the prospect of the Thames, as seen by a Camera Obscura, which is placed in a small room in the upper story of the Observatory; where I remember to have seen, many years ago, the whole scene here described, corresponding so much to Mr. Addison's account of it in this passage, that, at the time, it recalled it to my memory. As the Observatory stands in the middle of the Park, it over-looks, from one side, both the river and the park; and the objects afterwards mentioned, the ships, the trees, and the deer, are presented in one view, without needing any assistance from opposite walls (*Lectures on Rhetoric and Belles Lettres*, 1783, i. 469).

For the 'moving pictures' which were being exhibited at the time the *Spectator* was being published see notes to No. 31 (vol. i). One of these, exhibited at the Duke of Marlborough's Head in Fleet Street in 1710 and 1711, is advertised in *Tatler* 127. In the *Daily Courant* of 20 Feb. 1709/10 it is described as follows:

It is a most noble Landskip finely Painted by the best Hand, it contains the prospect of a City with a Harbour; a large Extent of Land with a River winding and running into the Sea; a Bridge leading to the City; and near 70 Figures in lively Motion:

drawn on the Walls of a dark Room, which[a] stood opposite on one side to a navigable River, and on the other to a Park. The Experiment is very common in Opticks. Here you might discover the Waves and Fluctuations of the Water in strong and proper Colours, with the Picture of a Ship entering at one end, and sailing by Degrees through the whole Piece. On another there appeared the Green Shadows of Trees, waving to and fro with the Wind, and Herds of Deer among them in Miniature, leaping about upon the Wall. I must confess, the Novelty of such a sight may be one occasion of its Pleasantness to the Imagination, but certainly the chief Reason is its near Resemblance to Nature, as it does not only, like other Pictures, give the Colour and Figure, but the Motion of the Things it represents.

[1]We have before observed, that there is generally in Nature something more Grand and August, than what we meet with in the Curiosities of Art. When, therefore, we see this imitated in any measure, it gives us a nobler and more exalted kind of Pleasure than what we receive from the nicer and more accurate Productions of Art. On this Account our *English* Gardens are not so entertaining to the Fancy as those in *France* and *Italy*,[2] where we see a large Extent of Ground covered over with an agreeable mixture of Garden and Forest, which represent every where an artificial Rudeness, much more charming than that Neatness and Elegancy which we meet with in those of our own Country. It might, indeed, be of ill Consequence to the Publick, as well as unprofitable to private Persons, to alienate so much Ground from Pasturage, and the Plow, in many Parts of a Country that is so well peopled, and cultivated to a far greater Advantage. But why may not a whole Estate be thrown

[a] which] that *Fol.*

---

viz. Several stately Ships and Vessels sailing; a Coach and 4 Horses; a Gentleman in a Chair saluting the Company. . . .

This seems to be similar to one which Swift describes to Stella on 27 Mar. 1713: 'You see a Sea ten miles wide, a Town on tothr end, & Ships sailing in the Sea, & discharging their Canon. You see a great Sky with Moon & Stars &c.' (ed. H. Williams, p. 647). Addison's account, however, must have been written much earlier, and more likely refers to the scene produced by the camera obscura, probably at Greenwich.

[1] The remainder of the essay is not in the original MS.

[2] Addison here contrasts the formal gardens of England, owing something to the Dutch influence introduced at the time of William III, with the private gardens of France and Italy—not, of course, the great gardens of Le Nôtre at Versailles. Later in the century it is the *jardin à l'anglaise* which is to become popular on the Continent.

into a kind of Garden by frequent Plantations, that may turn as much to the Profit, as the Pleasure of the Owner? A Marsh overgrown with Willows, or a Mountain shaded with Oaks, are not only more beautiful, but more beneficial, than when they lie bare and unadorned. Fields of Corn make a pleasant Prospect, and if the Walks were a little taken care of that lie between them, if the natural Embroidery of the Meadows were helpt and improved by some small Additions of Art, and the several Rows of Hedges set off by Trees and Flowers, that the Soil was capable of receiving, a Man might make a pretty Landskip of his own Possessions.[1]

Writers, who have given us an Account of *China*, tell us, the Inhabitants of that Country laugh at the Plantations of our *Europeans*, which are laid out by the Rule and Line; because, they say, any one may place Trees in equal Rows and uniform Figures.[2] They chuse rather to shew a Genius in Works of this Nature, and therefore always conceal the Art by which they direct themselves. They have a Word, it seems, in their Language, by which they express the particular Beauty of a Plantation that thus strikes the Imagination at first Sight, without discovering what it is that has so agreeable an Effect. Our *British* Gardeners, on the contrary, instead of humouring Nature, love to deviate from it as much as possible. Our Trees rise in Cones, Globes, and Pyramids. We see the Marks of the Scissars upon every Plant and Bush. I do not know whether I am singular in my Opinion, but, for my own part, I would rather look upon a Tree in all its Luxuriancy and Diffusion of Boughs and Branches, than when it is thus cut and trimmed into a Mathematical Figure; and cannot but fancy that an Orchard in Flower looks infinitely more delightful, than all the little Labyrinths of

[1] The English garden at this time was a combination of orchard and vegetable garden with flower gardens. See Sir William Temple's 'Upon the Gardens of Epicurus; or, of Gardening, In the Year 1685', in *Miscellanea*, part ii (*Works*, 1720), i. 181–3.

[2] Sir William Temple's essay just referred to (*Works*, i. 186) is clearly the source of Addison's statements here:

Among us, the Beauty of Building and Planting is placed chiefly in some certain Proportions, Symmetries, or Uniformities; our Walks and our Trees ranged so, as to answer one another, and at exact Distances. The *Chineses* scorn this way of Planting, and say a Boy that can tell an Hundred, may plant Walks of Trees in strait Lines, and over-against one another, and to what Length and Extent he pleases. But their greatest Reach of Imagination, is employed in contriving Figures, where the Beauty shall be great, and strike the Eye, but without any Order or Disposition of Parts, that shall be commonly or easily observ'd. And though we have hardly any Notion of this sort of Beauty, yet they have a particular word to express it; and where they find it hit their Eye at first Sight, they say the *Sharawadgi* is fine or is admirable, or any such Expression of Esteem.

the most finished Parterre. But as our great Modellers of Gardens have their Magazines of Plants to dispose of, it is very natural for them to tear up all the Beautiful Plantations of Fruit Trees, and contrive a Plan that may most turn to their own Profit, in taking off their Evergreens, and the like Moveable Plants, with which their Shops are plentifully stocked.   O

No. 415   *Thursday, June 26, 1712*[1]
[ADDISON]

Adde tot egregias urbes, operumque laborem:
                                                    Virg.

HAVING already shewn how the Fancy is affected by the Works of Nature, and afterwards considered in general both the Works of Nature and of Art, how they mutually assist and compleat each other, in forming such Scenes and Prospects as are most apt to delight the Mind of the Beholder, I shall in this Paper throw together some Reflections on that Particular Art, which has a more immediate Tendency, than any other, to produce those primary Pleasures of the Imagination, which have hitherto been the Subject of this Discourse. The Art I mean is that of Architecture, which I shall consider only with regard to the Light in which the foregoing Speculations have placed it, without entring into those Rules and Maxims which the great Masters of Architecture have laid down, and explained at large in numberless Treatises upon that Subject.

Greatness, in the Works of Architecture, may be considered as relating to the Bulk and Body of the Structure, or to the *Manner* in which it is built. As for the first, we find the Antients, especially among the Eastern Nations of the World, infinitely superior to the Moderns.

Not to mention the Tower of *Babel*, of which an old Author says, there were the Foundations to be seen in his time, which looked like a Spacious Mountain;[2] what could be more noble than the Walls

---

[1] *Motto.* Virgil, *Georgics*, 2. 155:
    Next add our Cities of Illustrious Name,
    Their costly Labour and stupendous Frame.   DRYDEN

[2] Much of the material in this number comes from Herodotus and Diodorus Siculus, but this passage has not been identified.

of *Babylon*,[1] its hanging Gardens, and its Temple to *Jupiter Belus*,[2] that rose a Mile high by Eight several Stories, each Story a Furlong in Height, and on the Top of which was the *Babylonian* Observatory? I might here, likewise, take Notice of the huge Rock that was cut into the Figure of *Semiramis*,[3] with the smaller Rocks that lay by it in the Shape of Tributary Kings; the Prodigious Basin, or artificial Lake, which took in the whole *Euphrates*, till such time as a new Canal was formed for its Reception, with the several Trenches through which that River was conveyed.[4] I know there are Persons who look upon some of these Wonders of Art as Fabulous, but I cannot find any Grounds for such a Suspicion, unless it be that we have no such Works among us at present. There were indeed many greater Advantages for Building in those Times, and in that Part of the World, than have been met with ever since. The Earth was extreamly fruitful, Men lived generally on Pasturage, which requires a much smaller number of Hands than Agriculture: There were few Trades to employ the busie Part of Mankind, and fewer Arts and Sciences to give Work to Men of Speculative Tempers; and what is more than all the rest, the Prince was absolute; so that when he went to War, he put himself at the Head of a whole People: As we find *Semiramis* leading her three[a] Millions[5] to the Field, and yet overpower'd by the Number of her Enemies. 'Tis no wonder, therefore, when she was at Peace, and turned her Thoughts on Building, that she could accomplish so great Works, with such a prodigious Multitude of Labourers: Besides that, in her Climate, there was small Interruption of Frosts and Winters, which make the Northern Workmen lie half the Year Idle. I might mention too, among the Benefits of the Climate, what Historians say of the Earth, that it sweated out a Bitumen[6] or natural kind of Mortar, which is doubt-

---

[a] three] two *Fol.*

[1] Herodotus (*History*, 1. 178) describes the wall of Babylon as of 50 royal cubits thickness and 200 cubits height. The Hanging Gardens, according to Diodorus Siculus (*Library of History*, 2. 10. 1), was built not by Semiramis but by a later Syrian king (actually Nebuchadrezzar, 605–562 B.C.).

[2] Semiramus built in the centre of the city a temple of Zeus, whom the Babylonians call Belus (Diodorus Siculus, 2. 9. 4). Cf. also Herodotus, 1. 181.

[3] Diodorus Siculus, 2. 13. 2.

[4] Semiramis built dikes on the plain, but it was the second queen, Nitocris, who changed the course of the Euphrates (Herodotus, 1. 184–5).

[5] According to Diodorus Siculus (2. 17. 1) the army consisted of 3,000,000 foot-soldiers, 200,000 cavalry, and 100,000 chariots.

[6] According to Herodotus (1. 179) they made bricks from the earth and used hot bitumen for cement, the bitumen derived from the river Is, a tributary of the Euphrates. See also Quintus Curtius, 5. 1. 12.

less the same with that mentioned in Holy Writ, as contributing to the Structure of *Babel*. *Slime they used instead of Mortar*.[1]

In *Egypt* we still see their Pyramids, which answer to the Descriptions that have been made of them; and I question not but a Traveller might find out some Remains of the Labyrinth that covered a whole Province, and had a hundred Temples disposed among its several Quarters and Divisions.[2]

The Wall of *China* is one of these Eastern Pieces of Magnificence, which makes a Figure even in the Map of the World, altho' an Account of it would have been thought Fabulous, were not the Wall it self still extant.[3]

We are obliged to Devotion for the noblest Buildings, that have adorned the several Countries of the World. It is this which[a] has set Men at work on Temples and Publick Places of Worship, not only that they might, by the Magnificence of the Building, invite the Deity to reside within it, but that such stupendous Works might, at the same time, open the Mind to vast Conceptions, and fit it to converse with the Divinity of the Place. For every thing that is Majestick, imprints an Awfullness and Reverence on the Mind of the Beholder, and strikes in with[4] the Natural Greatness of the Soul.

In the Second place we are to consider *Greatness of Manner* in Architecture, which has such force upon the Imagination, that a small Building, where *it* appears, shall give the Mind nobler Ideas than one of twenty times the Bulk, where the Manner is ordinary or little. Thus, perhaps, a Man would have been more astonished with the Majestick Air that appeared in one of *Lysippus's*[b] Statues of *Alexander*,[5] tho' no bigger than the Life, than he might have been with Mount *Athos*, had it been cut into the Figure of the Heroe, according to the Proposal of *Phidias*,[6] with a River in one Hand, and a City in the other.

---

[a] which] that *Fol.*   [b] *Lysippus's*] *Protogenes's Fol.*

---

[1] Gen. xi. 3.

[2] Diodorus Siculus, I. 61. 2; I. 66. 3–6.

[3] Sir William Temple, 'Of Heroick Virtue', *Miscellanea*, part ii (*Works*, 1720, i. 198); Louis Le Comte, *Memoirs and Observations* . . . (1697), pp. 75–76.

[4] Strike in with, i.e. fit in with, agree with. *OED* gives quotations from 1704 to 1714.

[5] According to Plutarch (*Life of Alexander*, 4. 1) these gave the best representation of Alexander's person.

[6] An error for Stasicrates (Plutarch, *Life of Alexander*, 72. 4). See also Plutarch, 'On the Fortune of Alexander' (*Moralia*, 335C).

Let any one reflect on the Disposition of Mind he finds in himself, at his first Entrance into the *Pantheon*[1] at *Rome*, and how his Imagination is filled with something Great and Amazing; and, at the same time, consider how little, in proportion, he is affected with the Inside of a *Gothick* Cathedral, tho' it be five times larger than the other; which can arise from nothing else, but the Greatness of the Manner in the one, and the Meanness in the other.[2]

I have seen an Observation upon this Subject in a *French* Author, which very much pleased me. It is in Monsieur *Freart*'s Parallel of the Ancient and Modern Architecture.[3] I shall give it the Reader with the same Terms of Art which he has made use of. *I am observing (says he) a thing which, in my Opinion, is very curious, whence it proceeds, that in the same quantity of Superficies, the one* Manner *seems great and magnificent, and the other poor and trifling; the Reason is fine and uncommon. I say then, that to introduce into Architecture this Grandeur of Manner, we ought so to proceed, that the Division of the Principal Members of the Order may consist but of few Parts, that they be all great and of a bold and ample Relievo, and Swelling; and that the Eye, beholding nothing little and mean, the Imagination may be more vigorously touched and affected with the Work that stands before it. For Example; In a Cornice, if the Gola or Cymatium*[4] *of the Corona, the Coping, the Modillions or Dentelli, make a noble Show by their graceful Projections, if we see none of that ordinary Confusion which is the Result of those little Cavities, Quarter Rounds of the Astragal,*[5] *and*

---

[1] The Pantheon, or Rotunda, and St. Peter's were the two buildings which Addison especially sought out on his first visit to Rome. 'I must confess the Eye is better fill'd at first entering the *Rotund*, and takes in the whole Beauty and Magnificence of the Temple at one view. But such as are built in the Form of a Cross, give us a greater Variety of Noble Prospects. Nor is it easie to conceive a more glorious Show in Architecture, than what a Man meets with in St. *Peters*, when he stands under the Dome' (*Remarks on Italy*, 1705, p. 177).

[2] In the *Remarks on Italy* Addison praises St. Peter's in contrast to the Gothic churches:

The Proportions are so very well observ'd, that nothing appears to an Advantage, or distinguishes it self above the rest. It seems neither extreamly high, nor long, nor broad, because it is all of 'em in a just Equality. As on the contrary in our *Gothic* Cathedrals, the Narrowness of the Arch makes it rise in Height, or run out in Length; the Lowness often opens it in Breadth, or the Defectiveness of some other Particular makes any single Part appear in greater Perfection (pp. 174-5).

[3] The *Parallele de l'architecture antique et de la moderne* (1650) by Roland Fréart, Sieur de Chambray, was translated by John Evelyn in 1664. The second edition, 'with large Additions', of Evelyn's translation, printed for D. Midwinter, is advertised in No. 20. The passage quoted is from chap. ii ('Of the Dorique Order'), pp. 10-11.

[4] Gola (gula) or cymatium (cyma) is defined in *OED* as 'a moulding of the cornice; the outline of which consists of a concave and a convex line'.

[5] A small moulding placed round the top or bottom of columns and used to separate the different parts of the architrave in ornamental entablatures (*OED*).

I know not how many other intermingled Particulars, which produce no effect in great and massy Works, and which very unprofitably take up Place to the prejudice of the Principal Member, it is most certain that this Manner will appear Solemn and Great; as on the contrary, that will have but a poor and mean Effect, where there is a Redundancy of those smaller Ornaments, which divide and scatter the Angles of the Sight into such a Multitude of Rays, so pressed together that the whole will appear but a Confusion.

Among all the Figures in Architecture, there are none that have a greater Air than the Concave and the Convex; and we find in all the Ancient and Modern Architecture, as well in the remote Parts of *China*, as in Countries nearer home, that round Pillars and Vaulted Roofs make a great part of those Buildings which are designed for Pomp and Magnificence. The Reason I take to be, because in these Figures we generally see more of the Body, than in those of other Kinds. There are, indeed, Figures of Bodies, where the Eye may take in two Thirds of the Surface; but as in such Bodies the Sight must split upon several Angles, it does not take in one uniform Idea, but several Ideas of the same kind. Look upon the Outside of a Dome, your Eye half surrounds it; look up into the Inside,[1] and at one Glance you have all the Prospect of it; the entire Concavity falls into your Eye at once, the Sight being as the Center that collects and gathers into it the Lines of the whole Circumference: In a Square Pillar, the Sight often takes in but a Fourth part of the Surface, and, in a Square Concave, must move up and down to the different Sides, before it is Master of all the inward Surface. For this Reason, the Fancy is infinitely more struck with the view of the open Air, and Skies, that passes through an Arch, than what comes through a Square, or any other Figure. The Figure of the Rainbow does not contribute less to its Magnificence, than the Colours to its Beauty,[a] as it is very Poetically described by the Son of *Sirach*: *Look upon the Rainbow, and praise him that made it; very beautiful it is in its Brightness; it encompasses the Heavens with a Glorious Circle, and the Hands of the most High[b] have bended it.*[2]

[a] contribute . . . Beauty,] contribute less to its Beauty, than the Colours, *Fol.*
[b] *the most High*] *the Almighty* Fol.

---

[1] Of the dome of St. Peter's Addison wrote: 'If he looks upward he is astonish'd at the spacious Hollow of the Cupola, and has a Vault on every side of him, that makes one of the beautifullest *Vistas* that the Eye can possibly pass thro'" (*Remarks on Italy*, p. 177).
[2] Ecclus. 43. 11.

Having thus spoken of that Greatness which affects the Mind in Architecture, I might next shew the Pleasure that arises in the Imagination from what appears new and beautiful in this Art; but as every Beholder has naturally a greater Taste of these two Perfections in every Building which offers it self to his View, than of that which I have hitherto considered, I shall not trouble my Reader with any Reflections upon it. It is sufficient for my present purpose, to observe, that there is nothing in this whole Art which pleases the Imagination, but as it is Great, Uncommon, or Beautiful.

O[1]

No. 416   *Friday, June 27,* 1712[2]
[ADDISON]

Quatenûs hoc simile est oculis, quod mente videmus.
                                                                    Lucr.

I AT first divided the Pleasures of the Imagination, into such as arise from Objects that are actually before our Eyes, or that once entered in at our Eyes, and are afterwards called up into the Mind, either barely by its own Operations, or on occasion of something without us, as Statues or Descriptions. We have already considered the first Division, and shall therefore enter on the other, which, for Distinction sake, I have call'd the Secondary Pleasures of the Imagination. When I say the Ideas we receive from Statues, Descriptions, or such like Occasions, are the same that were once actually in our View, it must not be understood that we had once seen the very Place, Action, or Person which are carved or described. It is sufficient, that we have seen Places, Persons, or Actions, in general, which bear a Resemblance, or at least some remote Analogy with what we find represented. Since it is in the Power of the

---

[1] No. 415 is not represented in the original draft of the essay on the 'pleasures of the imagination'.

[2] *Motto.* Lucretius, *De rerum natura*, 4. 750: Because the objects which we fancy in our mind represent what we see with the eye.

Nos. 416 and 417 are combined somewhat differently in the original draft. After the first two sentences of No. 416 Addison continued with the bulk of No. 417. The remaining part of No. 416 represented in the MS. consists of a portion of paragraph 3, and paragraphs 4 and 5.

Imagination, when it is once Stocked with particular Ideas, to en-large, compound, and vary them at her own Pleasure.[1]

Among the different Kinds of Representation, *Statuary* is the most natural, and shews us something *likest* the Object that is represented.[2] To make use of a common Instance, let one who is born Blind take an Image in his Hands, and trace out with his Fingers the different Furrows and Impressions of the Chissel, and he will easily conceive how the Shape of a Man, or Beast, may be represented by it; but should he draw his Hand over a *Picture*, where all is smooth and uniform, he would never be able to imagine how the several Prominencies and Depressions of a Human Body could be shewn on a plain Piece of Canvas, that has in it no Unevenness or Irregularity. *Description* runs yet further from the things it represents than Paint-ing; for a Picture bears a real Resemblance to its Original, which Letters and Syllables are wholly void of. Colours speak all Languages, but Words are understood only by such a People or Nation. For this reason, tho Mens Necessities quickly put them on finding out Speech, Writing is probably of a later Invention than Painting; particularly we are told, that in *America* when the *Spaniards* first arrived there, Expresses were sent to the Emperor of *Mexico* in Paint, and the News of his Country delineated by the Strokes of a Pencil, which was a more natural way than that of Writing, tho' at the same time much more imperfect, because it is impossible to draw the little Connexions of Speech, or to give the Picture of a Conjunction or an Adverb. It would be yet more strange, to repre-sent visible Objects by Sounds that have no Ideas annexed to them, and to make something like Description in *Musick*. Yet it is certain, there may be confused, imperfect Notions of this Nature raised in the Imagination by an Artificial Composition of Notes; and we find that great Masters in the Art are able, sometimes, to set their Hearers in the heat and hurry of a Battel, to overcast their Minds with melancholy Scenes and Apprehensions of Deaths and Funerals, or to lull them into pleasing Dreams of Groves and Elisiums.

In all these Instances, this Secondary Pleasure of the Imagination proceeds from that Action of the Mind, which compares the Ideas

---

[1] The combinatory powers of the imagination had long been recognized, without any suggestion of a creative faculty in the 'romantic' sense of the phrase. M. W. Bundy (*Theory of Imagination*, p. 85 n.) quotes an example from Philoponus, a sixth-century commentator on Aristotle.

[2] One must recall that dimension is a primary quality, whereas colour is a secondary quality, which does not exist in reality. See Mario M. Rossi, *L'estetica dell' empirismo inglese* (Florence, 1944), i. 279.

arising from the Original Objects, with the Ideas we receive from the Statue, Picture, Description, or Sound that represents them. It is impossible for us to give the necessary Reason, why this Operation of the Mind is attended with so much Pleasure, as I have before observed[1] on the same Occasion; but we find a great variety of Entertainments derived from this single Principle: For it is this that not only gives us a relish of Statuary, Painting and Description, but makes us delight in all the Actions and Arts of Mimickry. It is this that makes the several kinds of Wit pleasant, which consists, as I have formerly shown,[2] in the Affinity of Ideas: And we may add, it is this also that raises the little Satisfaction we sometimes find in the different sorts of false Wit; whether it consist in the Affinity of Letters, as in Anagram, Acrostick; or of Syllables, as in Doggerel Rhimes, Ecchos; or of Words, as in Puns, Quibbles; or of a whole Sentence or Poem, to Wings, and Altars. The *final Cause*, probably, of annexing Pleasure to this Operation of the Mind, was to quicken and encourage us in our Searches after Truth, since the distinguishing one thing from another, and the right discerning betwixt our Ideas, depends wholly upon our comparing them together, and observing the Congruity or Disagreement that appears among the several Works of Nature.

But I shall here confine my self to those Pleasures of the Imagination, which[a] proceed from Ideas raised by *Words*, because most of the Observations that agree with Descriptions, are equally Applicable to Painting and Statuary.

Words, when well chosen, have so great a Force in them, that a Description often gives us more lively Ideas than the Sight of Things themselves. The Reader finds a Scene drawn in stronger Colours, and painted more to the Life in his Imagination, by the help of Words, than by an actual Survey of the Scene which they describe.[3] In this Case the Poet seems to get the better of Nature; he takes, indeed, the Landskip after her, but gives it more vigorous Touches, heightens its Beauty, and so enlivens the whole Piece, that the Images, which flow from the Objects themselves, appear

---

[a] which] that *Fol.*

[1] No. 413.   [2] No. 62 (vol. i).
[3] In his early essay on Virgil's *Georgics* (1697) Addison had praised this as Virgil's masterpiece, 'where we receive more strong and lively *Ideas* of things from his words, than we could have done from the objects themselves: And find our imaginations more affected by his descriptions, than they would have been by the very sight of what he describes' (Guthkelch, ii. 8).

weak and faint, in Comparison of those that come from the Expressions. The Reason, probably, may be, because in the Survey of any Object we have only so much of it painted on the Imagination, as comes in at the Eye; but in its Description, the Poet gives us as free a View of it as he pleases, and discovers to us several Parts, that either we did not attend to, or that lay out of our Sight when we first beheld it. As we look on any Object, our Idea of it is, perhaps, made up of two or three simple Ideas; but when the Poet represents it, he may either give us a more complex Idea of it, or only raise in us such Ideas as are most apt to affect the Imagination.

It may be here worth our while to Examine, how it comes to pass that several Readers, who are all acquainted with the same Language, and know the Meaning of the Words they read, should nevertheless have a different Relish of the same Descriptions. We find one transported with a Passage, which another runs over with Coldness and Indifference, or finding the Representation extremely natural, where another can perceive nothing of Likeness and Conformity. This different Taste must proceed, either from the *Perfection of Imagination* in one more than in another,[a] or from the *different Ideas* that several Readers affix to the same Words. For, to have a true Relish, and form a right Judgment of a Description, a Man should be born with a good Imagination, and must have well weighed the Force and Energy that lie in the several Words of a Language, so as to be able to distinguish which are most significant and expressive of their proper Ideas, and what additional Strength and Beauty they are capable of receiving from Conjunction with others. The Fancy must be warm, to retain the Print of those Images it hath received from outward Objects; and the Judgment discerning, to know what Expressions are most proper to cloath and adorn them to the best Advantage. A Man who is deficient in either of these Respects, tho' he may receive the general Notion of a Description, can never see distinctly all its particular Beauties: As a Person, with a weak Sight, may have the confused Prospect of a Place that lies before him, without entering into its several Parts, or discerning the variety of its Colours in their full Glory and Perfection.   O

---

[a] than in another,] *8vo*; than another, *Fol., 12mo*

No. 417
[ADDISON]

Saturday, June 28, 1712[1]

Quem tu Melpomene semel
Nascentem placido lumine videris,
Illum non labor Istmius
Clarabit pugilem, non equus impiger, &c.
Sed quæ Tibur aquæ fertile perfluunt,
Et Spissæ nemorum comæ
Fingent Æolio carmine nobilem.

Hor.

WE may observe, that any single Circumstance of what we have formerly seen often raises up a whole Scene of Imagery, and awakens numberless[a] Ideas that before slept in the Imagination; such a particular Smell or Colour is able to fill the Mind, on a sudden, with the Picture of the Fields or Gardens where we first met with it, and to bring up into View all the Variety of Images that once attended it. Our Imagination takes the Hint, and leads us unexpectedly into Cities or Theatres, Plains or Meadows. We may further observe, when the Fancy thus reflects on the Scenes that have past in it formerly, those, which were at first pleasant to behold, appear more so upon Reflection, and that the Memory heightens the Delightfulness of the Original. A *Cartesian*[2] would account for both these Instances in the following Manner.

---

[a] numberless] a Thousand *Fol.*

---

[1] *Motto.* Horace, *Odes*, 4. 3. 1–4, 10–12:

> The Youth, whose Birth the kindly Muse
> With an indulgent Aspect views,
> Shall neither at the Barrier shine,
> Nor the Olympic Garland win.
> But Tibur's Streams, and verdant Glades,
> The limpid Spring and gloomy Shades,
> Shall fill his nev'r dying Lays,
> And crown him with immortal Praise.

In the original draft No. 417, lacking the two final paragraphs, followed the opening two sentences of No. 416.

[2] Descartes, in *Les Passions de l'âme* (1649), art. xxi (Eng. trans., 1650, pp. 18–19), states that imaginations

> proceed from nothing but this, that the spirits being agitated severall wayes, and meeting the traces of divers impressions preceding them in the brain, they take their course at haphazzard through some certaine pores, rather than others. Such are the illusions of our dreames, and those dotages we often are troubled with

The Sett of Ideas, which we received from such a Prospect or Garden, having entered the Mind at the same time, have a Sett of Traces belonging to them in the Brain, bordering very near upon one another; when, therefore, any one of these Ideas arises in the Imagination, and consequently dispatches a flow of Animal Spirits to its proper Trace, these Spirits, in the violence of their Motion, run not only into the Trace, to which they were more particularly directed, but into several of those that lie about it: By this means they awaken other Ideas of the same Sett, which immediately determine a new Dispatch of Spirits, that in the same manner open other Neighbouring Traces, till at last the whole Sett of them is blown up, and the whole Prospect or Garden flourishes in the Imagination. But because the Pleasure we received from these Places far surmounted, and overcame the little Disagreeableness we found in them, for this Reason there was at first a wider Passage worn in the Pleasure Traces, and, on the contrary, so narrow a one in those which[a] belonged to the disagreeable Ideas, that they were quickly stopt up, and rendered incapable of receiving any Animal Spirits, and consequently of exciting any unpleasant Ideas in the Memory.

[1]It would be in vain to enquire, whether the Power of Imagining Things strongly proceeds from any greater Perfection in the Soul, or from any nicer Texture in the Brain of one Man than of another. But this is certain, that a noble Writer should be born with this Faculty in its full Strength and Vigour, so as to be able to receive lively Ideas from outward Objects, to retain them long, and to range them together, upon occasion, in such Figures and Representations as are most likely to hit the Fancy of the Reader. A Poet should take as much Pains in forming his Imagination, as a Philosopher in cultivating his Understanding. He must gain a due Relish of the Works of Nature, and be throughly conversant in the various Scenary of a Country Life.[2]

[a] which] that Fol.

---

waking, when our thought carelessely roames without applying it selfe to any thing of its own.

In the original MS. the sentence reads: 'In both these instances y[e] reasons possibly may be, as follows.'

[1] This paragraph and the three which follow (down to 'pleasing Scenes', p. 565, l.18) are added in Addison's hand in the MS.

[2] Between this sentence and the next the MS. contains the following passage:

He must love to hide himself in Woods and to Haunt the Springs and Meadows. [Then follow the six lines from Horace used as the Motto for this number.] His

When he is stored with Country Images, if he would go beyond Pastoral, and the lower kinds of Poetry, he ought to acquaint himself with the Pomp and Magnificence of Courts. He should be very well versed in every thing that is noble and stately in the Productions of Art, whether it appear in Painting or Statuary, in the great Works of Architecture which[a] are in their present Glory, or in the Ruins of those which[b] flourished in former Ages.[1]

Such Advantages as these help to open a Man's Thoughts, and to enlarge his Imagination, and will therefore have their Influence on all Kinds of Writing, if the Author knows how to make right use of them. And among those of the learned Languages who[c] excell in this Talent, the most perfect in their several Kinds, are perhaps *Homer*, *Virgil*, and *Ovid*. The first strikes the Imagination wonderfully with what is Great, the second with what is Beautiful, and the last with what is Strange. Reading the *Iliad* is like travelling through a Country uninhabited, where the Fancy is entertained with a thousand Savage Prospects of vast Desarts, wide uncultivated Marshes, huge Forests, mis-shapen Rocks and Precipices. On the contrary, the *Æneid* is like a well-ordered Garden, where it is impossible to find out any Part unadorned, or to cast our Eyes upon a single Spot, that does not produce some beautiful Plant or Flower. But when we are in the *Metamorphosis*, we are walking on enchanted Ground, and see nothing but Scenes of Magick lying round us.

Homer is in his Province, when he is describing a Battel or a Multitude, a Heroe or a God. *Virgil* is never better pleas'd, than when he is in his *Elysium*, or copying out an entertaining Picture. *Homer*'s Epithets generally mark out what is Great, *Virgil*'s what is Agreeable. Nothing can be more Magnificent than the Figure *Jupiter*[d] makes in the First *Iliad*, nor more Charming than that of *Venus* in the First *Æneid*.

---

[a] which] that *Fol*.   [b] which] that *Fol*.   [c] who] that *Fol*.   [d] Figure *Jupiter*] Figure that *Jupiter* Fol.

---

head must be full of the Humming of Bees, the Bleating of flocks and the melody of Birds. The verdure of the Grass, the Embroidery of the Flowrs, and the Glistring of the Dew must be painted strong on his Imagination.

[1] Between this sentence and the next the MS. contains the following sentence:

Milton w[d] never have bin Able to have built his Pandemonium or to have Laid out his Paradise had not he seen y[e] Palaces & Gardens of Italy: & it w[d] be easy to shew several descriptions out of y[e] old poets y[t] probably owd their original to pictures and Statues y[t] were Then in Vogue.

'Η, καὶ κυανέῃσιν ἐπ' ὀφρύσι νεῦσε Κρονίων·
'Αμβρόσιαι δ' ἄρα χαῖται ἐπερρώσαντο ἄνακτος,
Κρατὸς ἀπ' 'Αθανάτοιο· μέγαν δ' ἐλέλιξεν ῎Ολυμπον.[1]

Dixit, & avertens roseâ cervice refulsit:
Ambrosiæque comæ divinum vertice odorem
Spiravere: Pedes vestis defluxit ad imos:
Et vera incessu patuit Dea . . .[2]

Homer's Persons are most of them God-like and Terrible: *Virgil* has scarce admitted any into his Poem, who are not beautiful, and has taken particular Care to make his Heroe so.

. . . *lumenque juventæ*
Purpureum, & lætos oculis afflavit honores.[3]

In a Word, *Homer* fills his Readers with Sublime *Ideas,*[a] and, I believe, has raised the Imagination of all the good Poets that have come after him. I shall only instance *Horace,* who immediately takes Fire at the first Hint of any Passage in the *Iliad* or *Odyssee,* and always rises above himself, when he has *Homer* in his View. *Virgil* has drawn together, into his *Æneid,* all the pleasing Scenes his[b] Subject is capable of admitting, and in his *Georgics* has given us a Collection of the most delightful Landskips that can be made out of Fields and Woods, Herds of Cattle, and Swarms of Bees.

Ovid, in his *Metamorphosis,* has shewn us how the Imagination may be affected by what is Strange. He describes a Miracle in every Story, and always gives us the Sight of some new Creature at the end of it. His Art consists chiefly in well-timing his Description, before the first Shape is quite worn off, and the new one perfectly finish'd;

[a] Ideas,] 8vo; Ideas, Fol., *12mo*   [b] Scenes his] Scenes that his Fol.

----

[1] *Iliad,* 1. 528–30:
This said, his kingly Brow the Sire inclin'd;
The large black Curls fell awful from behind,
Thick-shadowing the stern Forehead of the God:
Olympus trembled at th' Almighty Nod. TICKELL.

[2] *Aeneid,* 1. 402–5:
Thus having said, she turn'd, and made appear
Her Neck refulgent, and dishevel'd Hair;
Which flowing from her Shoulders, reach'd the Ground,
And widely spread Ambrosial Scents around:
In length of Train descends her sweeping Gown,
And by her graceful Walk, the Queen of Love is known. DRYDEN.

[3] *Aeneid,* 1. 590–1:
And gave his rolling Eyes a sparkling Grace,
And breath'd a youthful Vigour on his Face. DRYDEN.

so that he every where entertains us with something we never saw before, and shews Monster after Monster, to the end of the *Metamorphosis*.

If I were to name a Poet that is a perfect Master in all these Arts of working on the Imagination, I think *Milton* may pass for one: And if his *Paradise Lost* falls short of the *Æneid* or *Iliad* in this respect, it proceeds rather from the Fault of the Language in which it is written, than from any Defect of Genius in the Author. So Divine a Poem in *English*, is like a stately Palace built of Brick, where one may see Architecture in as great a Perfection as in one of Marble, tho' the Materials are of a coarser Nature. But to consider it only as it regards our present Subject: What can be conceiv'd greater than the Battel of Angels, the Majesty of Messiah, the Stature and Behaviour of Satan and his Peers? What more beautiful than *Pandæmonium*, Paradise, Heaven, Angels, *Adam* and *Eve*? What more strange, than the Creation of the World, the several Metamorphoses of the fallen Angels, and the surprising Adventures their[a] Leader meets with in his Search after Paradise? No other Subject could have furnished a Poet with Scenes so proper to strike the Imagination, as no other Poet could have painted those Scenes in more strong and lively Colours.   O

No. 418   *Monday, June* 30, 1712[1]
[ADDISON]

. . . *ferat & rubus asper amomum.*
                                                        Virg.

THE Pleasures of these Secondary Views of the Imagination, are of a wider and more universal Nature than those it has, when joined with Sight; for not only what is Great, Strange or Beautiful, but any Thing that is Disagreeable when look'd upon, pleases us in an apt Description. Here, therefore, we must enquire after a new Principle of Pleasure, which is nothing else but the Action of the Mind, which *compares* the Ideas that arise from Words,

---

a Adventures their] Adventures that their *Fol.*

---

[1] *Motto.* Virgil, *Eclogues*, 3. 89: And myrrh instead of thorns shall grow.
The opening paragraph of No. 418 was originally combined with a part of paragraph 3 of No. 416.

with the Ideas that arise from the Objects themselves; and why this Operation of the Mind is attended with so much Pleasure, we have before considered. For this Reason therefore, the Description of a Dung-hill is pleasing to the Imagination, if the Image be represented[a] to our Minds by suitable Expressions; tho', perhaps, this may be more properly called the Pleasure of the Understanding than of the Fancy, because we are not so much delighted with the Image that is contained in the Description, as with the Aptness of the Description to excite the Image.

But if the Description of what is Little, Common or Deformed, be acceptable to the Imagination, the Description of what is Great, Surprising or Beautiful, is much more so; because here we are not only delighted with *comparing* the Representation with the Original, but are highly pleased with the Original it self. Most Readers, I believe, are more charmed with *Milton*'s Description of Paradise, than of Hell; they are both, perhaps, equally perfect in their Kind, but in the one the Brimstone and Sulphur are not so refreshing to the Imagination, as the Beds of Flowers, and the Wilderness of Sweets in the other.

[1]There is yet another Circumstance which recommends a Description more than all the rest, and that is, if it represents to us such Objects as are apt to raise a secret Ferment in the Mind of the Reader, and to work, with Violence, upon his Passions. For, in this Case, we are at once warmed and enlightned, so that the Pleasure becomes more Universal, and is several ways qualified to entertain us. Thus, in[b] Painting, it is pleasant to look on the Picture of any Face, where the Resemblance is hit, but the Pleasure encreases, if it be the Picture of a Face that is beautiful, and is still greater, if the Beauty be softned with an Air of Melancholly or Sorrow. The two leading Passions which[c] the more serious Parts of Poetry endeavour to stir up in us, are Terror and Pity. And here, by the way, one would wonder how it comes to pass, that such Passions as are very unpleasant at all other times, are very agreeable when excited by proper Descriptions. It is not strange, that we should take Delight in such Passages as are apt to produce Hope, Joy, Admiration, Love, or the like Emotions in us, because they never rise in the Mind

---

[a] represented] *8vo*; presented *Fol.*, *12mo*   [b] in] as in *Fol.*   [c] which] that *Fol.*

---

[1] This paragraph and the two following are not represented in the MS.

without an inward Pleasure which[a] attends them. But how comes it to pass, that we should take delight in being terrified or dejected by a Description, when we find so much Uneasiness in the Fear or Grief which[b] we receive from any other Occasion?

If we consider, therefore, the Nature of this Pleasure, we shall find that it does not arise so properly from the Description of what is Terrible, as from the Reflection we make on our selves at the time of reading it. When we look on such hideous Objects, we are not a little pleased to think we are in no Danger of them. We consider them at the same time, as Dreadful and Harmless; so that the more frightful Appearance they make, the greater is the Pleasure we receive from the Sense of our own Safety. In short, we look upon the Terrors of a Description, with the same Curiosity and Satisfaction that we survey a dead Monster.

> . . . *Informe cadaver*
> *Protrahitur, nequeunt expleri corda tuendo*
> *Terribiles oculos: vultum, villosaque setis*
> *Pectora semiferi, atque extinctos faucibus ignes.* Virg.[1]

It is for the same Reason that we are delighted with the reflecting upon Dangers that are past, or in looking on a Precipice at a distance, which would fill us with a different kind of Horrour, if we saw it hanging over our Heads.

In the like manner, when we read of Torments, Wounds, Deaths, and the like dismal Accidents, our Pleasure does not flow so properly from the Grief which[c] such melancholly Descriptions give us, as from the secret Comparison which we make between our selves and the Person who[d] suffers. Such Representations teach us to set a just Value upon our own Condition, and make us prize our good Fortune which exempts us from the like Calamities.[2] This is, however, such a kind of Pleasure as we are not capable of receiving, when we

---

[a] which] that *Fol.*   [b] which] that *Fol.*   [c] which] that *Fol.*   [d] who] that *Fol.*

---

[1] Virgil, *Aeneid*, 8. 264-7:

The wond'ring Neighbourhood, with glad surprize,
Behold his shagged Breast, his Gyant Size,
His Mouth that flames no more, and his extinguish'd Eyes. DRYDEN.

[2] In his remarks on chap. vi of Aristotle's *Poetics* Dacier comments: tragedy 'disposes the most miserable, to think themselves happy, when they Compare their own Misfortunes, with those, which Tragedy has represented to them. In whatever Condition a Man may be, yet when he shall see, an *Oedipus*, a *Philoctetes*[,] an *Orestes*, he can but think his own Afflictions light in Comparison with theirs' (p. 79).

see a Person actually lying under the Tortures that we meet with
in a Description; because, in this Case, the Object presses too close
upon our Senses, and bears so hard upon us, that it does not give
us time or leisure to reflect on our selves. Our Thoughts are so
intent upon the Miseries of the Sufferer, that we cannot turn them
upon our own Happiness. Whereas, on the contrary, we consider
the Misfortunes we read in History or Poetry, either as past, or as
fictitious, so that the Reflection upon our selves rises in us insensibly,
and over-bears the Sorrow we conceive for the Sufferings of the
Afflicted.

But because the Mind of Man requires something more perfect in
Matter, than what it finds there, and can never meet with any
Sight in Nature which sufficiently answers its highest Ideas of
Pleasantness; or, in other Words, because the Imagination can fancy
to it self Things more Great, Strange, or Beautiful, than the Eye
ever saw, and is still sensible of some Defect in what it has seen;
on this account it is the part of a Poet to humour the Imagination
in its own Notions, by mending and perfecting Nature where he
describes a Reality, and by adding greater Beauties than are put
together in Nature, where he describes a Fiction.

He is not obliged to attend her in the slow Advances which she
makes from one Season to another, or to observe her Conduct, in
the successive Production of Plants and Flowers. He may draw into
his Description all the Beauties of the Spring and Autumn, and
make the whole Year contribute something to render it the more
agreeable. His Rose-trees, Wood-bines, and Jessamines, may flower
together, and his Beds be covered at the same time with Lillies,
Violets, and Amaranths. His Soil is not restrained to any particular
Sett of Plants, but is proper either for Oaks or Mirtles, and adapts it
self to the Products of every Climate. Oranges may grow wild in it;
Myrrh may be met with in every Hedge, and if he thinks it proper
to have a Grove of Spices, he can quickly command Sun enough to
raise it. If all this will not furnish out an agreeable Scene, he can
make several new Species of Flowers, with richer Scents and higher
Colours, than any that grow in the Gardens of Nature. His Con-
sorts of Birds may be as full and harmonious, and his Woods as thick
and gloomy as he pleases. He is at no more Expence in a long Vista,
than a short one, and can as easily throw his Cascades from a Precipice of half a Mile high, as from one of twenty Yards. He has his
choice of the Winds, and can turn the Course of his Rivers in all the

variety of *Meanders*, that are most delightful to the Reader's Imagination. In a word, he has the modelling of Nature in his own Hands, and may give her what Charms he pleases, provided he does not reform her too much, and run into Absurdities, by endeavouring to excell.[1]

No. 419
[ADDISON]

Tuesday, July 1, 1712[2]

> . . . *mentis gratissimus Error.*
>
> Hor.

THERE is a kind of Writing, wherein the Poet quite loses sight of Nature, and entertains his Reader's Imagination with the Characters and Actions of such Persons as have many of them no Existence, but what he bestows on them.[3] Such are Fairies, Witches, Magicians, Demons, and departed Spirits. This Mr. *Dryden* calls *the Fairie way of Writing*,[4] which is, indeed, more difficult than any other that depends on the Poet's Fancy, because he has no Pattern to follow in it, and must work altogether out of his own Invention.

There is a very odd turn of Thought required for this sort of Writing, and it is impossible for a Poet to succeed in it, who has not a particular Cast of Fancy, and an Imagination naturally fruitful and superstitious. Besides this, he ought to be very well versed in Legends and Fables, antiquated Romances, and the Traditions of Nurses and old Women, that he may fall in with our natural Prejudices, and humour those Notions which we have imbibed in our Infancy. For, otherwise, he will be apt to make his Fairies talk like People of his own Species, and not like other Setts of Beings, who converse with different Objects, and think in a different manner from that of Mankind;

---

[1] This final paragraph is apparently an addition to the original draft. The only portion, however, in the MS. is a fragment of the last three sentences.

[2] *Motto.* Horace, *Epistles* 2. 2. 140. A most pleasant delusion.

[3] In No. 279 (vol. ii) Addison had praised Milton for depicting characters which 'lie out of nature, and were to be formed purely by his own invention'.

[4] In his Dedication (to the Marquis of Halifax) of *King Arthur* (1691) Dryden speaks of 'that Fairy kind of writing, which depends only upon the Force of Imagination'.

Sylvis deducti caveant, me Judice, Fauni
Ne velut innati triviis ac pæne forenses
Aut nimium teneris juvenentur versibus . . . Hor.[a1]

I do not say with Mr. *Bays* in the *Rehearsal*, that Spirits must not be confined to speak Sense,[2] but it is certain their Sense ought to be a little discoloured, that it may seem particular, and proper to the Person and the Condition of the Speaker.

These Descriptions raise a pleasing kind of Horrour in the Mind of the Reader, and amuse[3] his Imagination with the Strangeness and Novelty of the Persons who are represented in them. They bring up into our Memory the Stories we have heard in our Child-hood, and favour those secret Terrours and Apprehensions to which the Mind of Man is naturally subject.[4] We are pleased with surveying the different Habits and Behaviours of Foreign Countries, how much more must we be delighted and surprised when we are led, as it were, into a new Creation, and see the Persons and Manners of another Species? Men of cold Fancies, and Philosophical Dispositions, object to this kind of Poetry, that it has not Probability enough to affect the Imagination. But to this it may be answered, that we are sure, in general, there are many Intellectual Beings in the World besides our selves, and several Species of Spirits, who[b] are subject to different Laws and Oeconomies from those of Mankind;[5] when we see, therefore, any of these represented naturally, we cannot look upon the Representation as altogether impossible; nay, many are prepossest with such false Opinions, as dispose them to believe these particular Delusions; at least, we have all heard so many

---

a Hor.] *Added in 8vo, 12mo*   b who] that *Fol.*

---

[1] Horace, *Ars poetica*, 244–6:
A Satyr that comes staring from the Woods,
Must not at first speak like an Orator:
But, tho' his Language should not be refin'd,
It must not be Obscene, and Impudent. ROSCOMMON.

[2] *The Rehearsal*, v. i: 'Did you ever hear any people in clouds speak plain? They must be all for flight of fancy, at its full range, without the least check or control upon it. When once you tie up spirits and people in clouds to speak plain, you spoil all.'
[3] Here used almost in the obsolete sense 'to bewilder, puzzle' (*OED*), but with 'a pleasing kind of Horrour'. In the next paragraph ('to amuse mankind') the word is used in the ordinary eighteenth-century meaning, 'to beguile, delude, cheat'. The last quotation in *OED* in this sense is dated 1817.
[4] Cf. No. 7 (vol. i).
[5] In No. 12 (vol. i) Addison had written: 'I am apt to join in Opinion with those who believe that all the Regions of Nature swarm with Spirits. . . .'

pleasing Relations in favour of them, that we do not care for seeing through the Falshood, and willingly give our selves up to so agreeable an Imposture.

The Ancients have not much of this Poetry among them, for, indeed, almost the whole Substance of it owes its Original to the Darkness and Superstition of later Ages, when pious Frauds were made use of to amuse Mankind, and frighten them into a Sense of their Duty. Our Forefathers looked upon Nature with more Reverence and Horrour, before the World was enlightened by Learning and Philosophy, and loved to astonish themselves with the Apprehensions of Witchcraft, Prodigies, Charms and Enchantments. There was not[a] a Village in *England* that had not a Ghost in it, the Church-yards were all haunted, every large Common had a Circle of Fairies[1] belonging to it, and there was scarce a Shepherd to be met with who had not seen a Spirit.

Among all the Poets of this Kind our *English* are much the best, by what I have yet seen, whether it be that we abound with more Stories of this Nature, or that the Genius of our Country is fitter for this sort of Poetry. For the *English* are naturally Fanciful, and very often disposed by that Gloominess and Melancholly of Temper, which is so frequent in our Nation,[2] to many wild Notions and Visions, to which others are not so liable.

Among the *English*, *Shakespear* has incomparably excelled all others.[3] That noble Extravagance of Fancy, which he had in so great Perfection, throughly qualified him to touch this weak superstitious

---

[a] not] scarce *Fol.*

---

[1] On these and other supernatural evidences see Robert Plot, *Natural History of Stafford-shire* (Oxford, 1686), pp. 9–19. Addison refers to the fairy circles in his early poem, *Machinae Gesticulantes* (trans. Thomas Fitzgerald):

> At Noon of Night, by *Phœbe's* lightsom Ray,
> Thus the brisk Tribe of slender Fairies play,
> Still round and round their circling Dance pursue,
> And leave their Footsteps in the Morning Dew.
> The fruitful Earth hence draws a quick Produce,
> And teems luxuriant with a mystic Juice,
> Pours forth full Crops, where they have led the Round,
> And verdant Circles mark the sacred Ground.
>
> (*Poems on Several Occasions*, 1733, p. 21.)

[2] See No. 387.

[3] In the Account of Shakespeare prefixed to the edition of the plays brought out by Tonson in 1709 Rowe comments that 'the greatness of this Author's Genius do's no where so much appear, as where he gives his Imagination an entire Loose, and raises his Fancy to a flight above Mankind and the Limits of the visible World' (i, p. xxiii). 'His Magick has something in it very Solemn and very Poetical . . .' (p. xxiv).

Part of his Reader's Imagination; and made him capable of succeeding, where he had nothing to support him besides the Strength of his own Genius. There is something so wild and yet so solemn in the Speeches of his Ghosts, Fairies, Witches, and the like Imaginary Persons, that we cannot forbear thinking them natural, tho' we have no Rule by which to judge of them, and must confess, if there are such Beings in the World, it looks highly probable they should talk and act as he has represented them.

There is another sort of Imaginary Beings, that we sometimes meet with among the Poets, when the Author represents any Passion, Appetite, Virtue or Vice, under a visible Shape, and makes it a Person or an Actor in his Poem. Of this Nature are the Descriptions of Hunger and Envy in *Ovid*,[1] of Fame in *Virgil*,[2] and of Sin and Death in *Milton*.[3] We find a whole Creation of the like shadowy Persons in *Spencer*,[4] who had an admirable Talent in Representations of this kind. I have discoursed of these Emblematical Persons in former Papers, and shall therefore only mention them in this Place. Thus we see how many ways Poetry addresses it self to the Imagination, as it has not only the whole Circle of Nature for its Province, but makes new Worlds of its own, shews us Persons who[a] are not to be found in Being, and represents even the Faculties of the Soul, with her several Virtues and Vices, in a sensible Shape and Character.

I shall, in my two following Papers, consider in general, how other kinds of Writing are qualified to please the Imagination, with which I intend to conclude this Essay.   O[5]

ᵃ who] that *Fol.*

---

[1] *Metamorphoses*, 2. 768–82.   [2] *Aeneid*, 4. 173–88.
[3] Cf. No. 357, where Addison criticizes particularly these 'extended Allegories'.
[4] In No. 297 Addison had coupled Spenser with Ariosto as a writer of allegories, contrasting them with Homer and Virgil.
[5] No. 419 is not represented in the original draft of the essay on 'the pleasures of the imagination'.

No. 420   *Wednesday, July 2, 1712*[1]
[ADDISON]

. . . *Quocunque volunt mentem Auditoris agunto.*
                                                            Hor.

AS the Writers in Poetry and Fiction borrow their several
Materials from outward Objects, and join them together at
their own Pleasure, there are others who are obliged to follow
Nature more closely, and to take entire Scenes out of her. Such are
Historians, natural Philosophers, Travellers, Geographers, and, in
a Word, all who describe visible Objects of a real Existence.

It is the most agreeable Talent of an Historian, to be able to draw
up his Armies and fight his Battels in proper Expressions, to set
before our Eyes the Divisions, Cabals, and Jealousies of Great Men,
and to lead us Step by Step into the several Actions and Events of
his History. We love to see the Subject unfolding it self by just
Degrees, and breaking upon us insensibly, that so we may be kept
in a pleasing Suspence, and have Time given us to raise our Expectations, and to side with one of the Parties concerned in the
Relation. I confess this shews more the Art than the Veracity of the
Historian, but I am only to speak of him as he is qualified to please
the Imagination. And in this respect *Livy* has, perhaps, excelled all
who ever went before him, or have written since his Time.[2] He
describes every thing in so lively a manner, that his whole History
is an admirable Picture, and touches on such proper Circumstances
in every Story, that his Reader becomes a kind of Spectator, and
feels in himself all the variety of Passions, which are correspondent
to the several Parts of the Relation.

But among this Sett of Writers, there are none who more gratifie
and enlarge the Imagination, than the Authors of the new Philosophy, whether we consider their Theories of the Earth or Heavens,
the Discoveries they have made by Glasses, or any other of their

---

[1] *Motto.* Horace, *Ars poetica,* 100 (altered):
And raise men's passions to what height they will. ROSCOMMON.

[2] Cf. Rapin, *Reflections upon History,* chap. x: 'It is now about Two thousand Years,
that the Majesty of this Historian has commanded the Respect and Admiration of
all the World. Nothing so fills my Soul, as that excellent Choice of Words, which are
always proportion'd to his Thoughts, and that genuine Expression of his Thoughts,
which are always conformable to his Subject' (*Whole Critical Works,* 1706, ii. 273).
Cf. No. 409, where Livy's 'manner of telling a story' is contrasted with the special
excellences of Sallust and Tacitus.

Contemplations on Nature. We are not a little pleased to find every green Leaf swarm with Millions of Animals, that at their largest Growth are not visible to the naked Eye.[a] There is something very engaging to the Fancy, as well as to our Reason, in the Treatises of Metals, Minerals, Plants and Meteors. But when we survey the whole Earth at once, and the several Planets that lie within its Neighbourhood, we are filled with a pleasing Astonishment, to see so many Worlds hanging one above another, and sliding round their Axles in such an amazing Pomp and Solemnity. If, after this, we contemplate those wide Fields of *Ether*, that reach in height as far as from *Saturn* to the fixt Stars, and run abroad almost to an Infinitude, our Imagination finds its Capacity filled with so immense a Prospect, and puts it self upon the Stretch to comprehend it. But if we yet rise higher, and consider the fixt Stars as so many vast Oceans of Flame, that are each of them attended with a different Sett of Planets, and still discover new Firmaments and new Lights, that are sunk farther in those unfathomable Depths of *Ether*, so as not to be seen by the strongest of our Telescopes,[b] we are lost in such a Labyrinth of Suns and Worlds, and confounded with the Immensity and Magnificence of Nature.

Nothing is more pleasant to the Fancy, than to enlarge it self, by Degrees, in its Contemplation of the various Proportions which[c] its several Objects bear to each other, when it compares the Body of Man to the Bulk of the whole Earth, the Earth to the Circle it describes round the Sun, that Circle to the Sphere of the fixt Stars, the Sphere of the fixt Stars to the Circuit of the whole Creation, the whole Creation it self to the Infinite Space that is every where diffused about it; or when the Imagination works downward, and considers the Bulk of a Human Body, in respect of an Animal, a hundred times less than a Mite, the particular Limbs of such an Animal, the different Springs which[d] actuate the Limbs, the Spirits which[e] set these Springs a going, and the proportionable Minuteness of these several Parts, before they have arrived at their full Growth and Perfection. But if, after all this, we take the least Particle of these Animal Spirits, and consider its Capacity of being wrought into a World, that shall contain within those narrow Dimensions a Heaven and Earth, Stars and Planets, and every different Species

[a] not visible to the naked Eye.] not big enough to be Visible. *Fol.*   [b] seen by the strongest of our Telescopes,] visible to the naked Eye. *Fol.*   [c] which] that *Fol.*   [d] which] that *Fol.*   [e] which] that *Fol*

575

of living Creatures, in the same Analogy and Proportion they bear to each other in our own Universe; such a Speculation, by reason of its Nicety, appears ridiculous to those who have not turned their Thoughts that way, tho', at the same time, it is founded on no less than the Evidence of a Demonstration. Nay, we might yet carry it farther, and discover in the smallest Particle of this little World, a new inexhausted Fund of Matter, capable of being spun out into another Universe.

I have dwelt the longer on this Subject, because I think it may shew us the proper Limits, as well as the Defectiveness, of our Imagination; how it is confined to a very small Quantity of Space, and immediately stopt in its Operations, when it endeavours to take in any thing that is very great, or very little. Let a Man try to conceive the different Bulk of an Animal, which is twenty, from another which is a hundred times less than a Mite, or to compare, in his Thoughts, a length of a thousand Diameters of the Earth, with that of a Million, and he will quickly find that he has no different Measures in his Mind, adjusted to such extraordinary Degrees of Grandeur or Minuteness. The Understanding, indeed, opens an infinite Space on every side of us, but the Imagination, after a few faint Efforts, is immediately at a stand,[1] and finds her self swallowed up in the Immensity of the Void that surrounds it: Our Reason can pursue a Particle of Matter through an infinite variety of Divisions, but the Fancy soon loses sight of it, and feels in it self a kind of Chasm, that wants to be filled with Matter of a more sensible Bulk.[2] We can neither widen nor contract the Faculty to the Dimensions of either Extreme: The Object is too big for our Capacity, when we would comprehend the Circumference of a

---

[1] The traditional view was that, since the imagination is closely tied to sense-representations, we can only imagine what we are capable of picturing to ourselves. Descartes (*Six Metaphysical Meditations*, 1680, p. 84) illustrates this by the thousand-angled figure, or chiliogon, which can be understood to be a figure of a thousand sides as easily as a triangle can be understood to be a figure of three sides; 'but I do not in the same manner Imagine, or behold as present those thousand sides, as I do the three sides of a Triangle'. Many English writers had adopted the same position, e.g. Hobbes (*Leviathan*, chap. iii).

[2] Cf. Fontenelle, *Entretiens sur la pluralité des mondes* (Londres, 1707), pp. 52–53:

Ma raison est assez bien convaincuë, dit la Marquise, mais mon imagination est accablée de la multitude infinie des Habitans de toutes ces Planetes, & embarassée de la diversité qu'il faut établir entr'eux; car je voy bien que la Nature, selon qu'elle est ennemie des repetitions, les aura tous faits différens, mais comment se representer cela? Ce n'est pas à l'imagination à pretendre le representer, répondis-je, elle n'est pas propre à aller plus loin que les yeux.

This book was in Addison's library.

World, and dwindles into nothing, when we endeavour after the Idea of an Atome.

It is possible this Defect of Imagination may not be in the Soul it self, but as it acts in Conjunction with the Body. Perhaps there may not be room in the Brain for such a variety of Impressions, or the Animal Spirits may be incapable of figuring them in such a manner, as is necessary to excite so very large or very minute Ideas. However it be, we may well suppose that Beings of a higher Nature very much excell us in this respect, as it is probable the Soul of Man will be infinitely more perfect hereafter in this Faculty, as well as in all the rest; insomuch that, perhaps, the Imagination will be able to keep Pace with the Understanding, and to form in it self distinct Ideas of all the different Modes and Quantities of Space.   O[1]

No. 421

[ADDISON]

Thursday, July 3, 1712[2]

> *Ignotis errare locis, ignota videre*
> *Flumina gaudebat; studio minuente laborem.*
>   Ov.

THE Pleasures of the Imagination are not wholly confined to such particular Authors as are conversant in material Objects, but are often to be met with among the Polite Masters of Morality, Criticism, and other Speculations abstracted from Matter; who, though they do not directly treat of the visible Parts of Nature, often draw from them their Similitudes, Metaphors, and Allegories. By these Allusions a Truth in the Understanding is as it were reflected by the Imagination; we are able to see something like Colour and Shape in a Notion, and to discover a Scheme of Thoughts traced out upon Matter. And here the Mind receives a great deal of Satisfaction, and has two of its Faculties gratified at the same time, while the Fancy is busy in copying after the Understanding, and transcribing Ideas out of the Intellectual World into the Material.

---

[1] Only a small portion of No. 420 is extant in the original draft—the first paragraph and the opening sentence of the third.

[2] *Motto.* Ovid, *Metamorphoses*, 4. 294–5:

> He sought fresh Fountains in a foreign Soil;
> The Pleasure lessen'd the attending Toil.

The Great Art of a Writer shews it self in the Choice of pleasing Allusions, which are generally to be taken from the *great* or *beautiful* Works of Art or Nature; for though whatever is New or Uncommon is apt to delight the Imagination, the chief Design of an Allusion being to illustrate and explain the Passages of an Author, it should be always borrowed from what is more known and common, than the Passages which are to be explained.

[1]Allegories, when well chosen, are like so many Tracks of Light in a Discourse, that make every thing about them clear and beautiful. A noble Metaphor, when it is placed to an Advantage, casts a kind of Glory round it, and darts a Lustre through a whole Sentence: These different Kinds of Allusion are but so many different Manners of Similitude, and, that they may please the Imagination, the Likeness ought to be very exact, or very agreeable,[2] as we love to see a Picture where the Resemblance is just, or the Posture and Air graceful. But we often find eminent Writers very faulty in this respect; great Scholars are apt to fetch their Comparisons and Allusions from the Sciences in which they are most conversant, so that a Man may see the Compass of their Learning in a Treatise on the most indifferent Subject. I have read a Discourse upon Love, which none but a profound Chymist could understand, and have heard many a Sermon that should only have been preached before a Congregation of *Cartesians*. On the contrary, your Men of Business usually have recourse to such Instances as are too mean and familiar. They are for drawing the Reader into a Game of Chess or Tennis, or for leading him from Shop to Shop, in the Cant of particular Trades and Employments. It is certain, there may be found an infinite Variety of very agreeable Allusions in both these kinds, but, for the generality, the most entertaining ones lie in the Works of Nature, which are Obvious to all Capacities, and more delightful than what is to be found in Arts and Sciences.

It is this Talent of affecting the Imagination, that gives an Embellishment to good Sense, and makes one Man's Compositions more agreeable than another's. It setts off all Writings in general, but is the very Life and highest Perfection of Poetry. Where it shines in an Eminent Degree, it has preserved several Poems for many Ages, that have nothing else to recommend them; and where all the other Beauties are present, the Work appears dry and insipid, if

---

[1] This paragraph forms an addition to the MS. in Addison's hand.
[2] Addison first wrote 'very Surprising or very Beautiful'.

this single one be wanting. It has something in it like Creation; It bestows a kind of Existence, and draws up to the Reader's View, several Objects which are not to be found in Being. It makes Additions to Nature, and gives a greater variety to God's Works. In a word, it is able to beautifie and adorn the most illustrious Scenes in the Universe, or to fill the Mind with more glorious Shows and Apparitions, than can be found in any Part of it.

We have now discovered the several Originals of those Pleasures that gratifie the Fancy; and here, perhaps, it would not be very difficult to cast under their proper Heads those contrary Objects, which[a] are apt to fill it with Distaste and Terrour; [1]for the Imagination is as liable to Pain as Pleasure. When the Brain is hurt by any Accident, or the Mind disordered by Dreams or Sickness, the Fancy is over-run with wild dismal Ideas, and terrified with a thousand hideous Monsters of its own framing.

> *Eumenidum veluti demens videt Agmina Pentheus,*
> *Et solem geminum, & duplices se ostendere Thebas.*
> *Aut Agamemnonius scenis agitatus Orestes,*
> *Armatam facibus matrem & serpentibus atris*
> *Cum videt, ultricesque sedent in limine Diræ.* Vir.[2]

There is not a Sight in Nature so mortifying as that of a Distracted Person, when his Imagination is troubled, and his whole Soul disordered and confused. *Babylon* in Ruins is not so melancholly a Spectacle. But to quit so disagreeable a Subject, I shall only consider, by way of Conclusion, what an infinite Advantage this Faculty gives an Almighty Being over the Soul of Man, and how great a measure of Happiness or Misery we are capable of receiving from the Imagination only.

We have already seen the Influence that one Man has over the

---

[a] which] that *Fol.*

---

[1] This portion of the essay, down to 'a Spectacle' in the next paragraph, is not represented in the MS.
[2] Virgil, *Aeneid*, 4. 469–73 (in Virgil line 473 begins *Cum fugit*):

> Like *Pentheus*, when distracted with his Fear,
> He saw two Suns, and double *Thebes* appear:
> Or mad *Orestes*, when his Mother's Ghost
> Full in his Face, infernal Torches tost;
> And shook her snaky locks: he shuns the sight, ⎱
> Flies o're the Stage, surpris'd with mortal fright; ⎰
> The Furies guard the Door; and intercept his flight. ⎰ DRYDEN.

Fancy of another, and with what Ease he conveys into it a Variety of Imagery; how great a Power then may we suppose lodged in him, who knows all the ways of affecting the Imagination, who can infuse what Ideas he pleases, and fill those Ideas with Terrour and Delight to what Degree he thinks fit? He can excite Images in the Mind, without the help of Words, and make Scenes rise up before us and seem present to the Eye, without the Assistance of Bodies or Exterior Objects. He can transport the Imagination with such beautiful and glorious Visions, as cannot possibly enter into our present Conceptions, or haunt it with such ghastly Spectres and Apparitions, as would make us hope for Annihilation, and think Existence no better than a Curse. In short, he can so exquisitely ravish or torture the Soul through this single Faculty, as might suffice to make up the whole Heaven or Hell of any finite Being.

This Essay on the Pleasures of the Imagination having been published in separate Papers, I shall conclude it with a Table of the principal Contents in each Paper.

The CONTENTS.

PAPER I.

THE Perfection of our Sight *above our other Senses. The* Pleasures of the Imagination *arise originally from Sight. The Pleasures of the Imagination divided under* two Heads. *The Pleasures of the* Imagination *in some respects equal to those of the Understanding. The* Extent *of the Pleasures of the Imagination. The Advantages a Man receives from a* Relish of these Pleasures. *In what respect they are* preferable *to those of the Understanding.*

PAPER II.

Three Sources *of all the Pleasures of the Imagination, in our Survey of outward Objects. How what is* Great *pleases the Imagination. How what is* New *pleases the Imagination. How what is* Beautiful, *in our own Species, pleases the Imagination. How what is* Beautiful *in general pleases the Imagination. What other Accidental Causes may contribute to the* heightening *of these Pleasures.*

PAPER III.

Why the Necessary Cause *of our being pleased with what is Great, New or Beautiful, unknown. Why the* Final Cause *more known and more useful. The Final Cause of our being pleased with what is* Great. *The Final Cause of our being pleased with what is* New. *The Final Cause of our being pleased with what is* Beautiful in our own Species. *The Final Cause of our being pleased with what is* Beautiful in general.

PAPER IV.

The Works of Nature *more pleasant to the Imagination than those of* Art. *The Works of Nature still more pleasant, the more they* resemble *those of Art. The Works of Art more pleasant, the more they* resemble *those of Nature. Our* English Plantations *and* Gardens *considered in the foregoing Light.*

PAPER V.

Of Architecture *as it affects the Imagination.* Greatness *in Architecture relates either to the* Bulk *or to the* Manner. *Greatness of Bulk in the* Ancient Oriental Buildings. *The ancient Accounts of these Buildings confirmed,* 1. *From the Advantages, for raising such Works, in the first Ages of the World and in the Eastern Climates:* 2. *From several of them which are still Extant. Instances how* Greatness of Manner *affects the Imagination. A* French *Author's Observation on this Subject. Why Concave and Convex Figures give a Greatness of Manner to Works of Architecture. Every thing that pleases the Imagination in Architecture is either Great, Beautiful or New.*

PAPER VI.

The Secondary *Pleasures of the Imagination. The several Sources of these Pleasures* (Statuary, Painting, Description and Musick) *compared together. The* Final Cause *of our receiving Pleasure from these several Sources. Of Descriptions in Particular. The Power of Words over the Imagination. Why one Reader* more pleased *with Descriptions than another.*

PAPER VII.

How a whole Sett of Ideas Hang together, *&c. A Natural Cause assigned for it. How to* perfect *the Imagination of a Writer. Who among the* Ancient Poets *had this Faculty in its greatest Perfection.* Homer *excelled in Imagining what is Great;* Virgil *in Imagining what is Beautiful;* Ovid *in Imagining what is New. Our own Country-man* Milton, *very perfect in all three respects.*

PAPER VIII.

Why any thing that is unpleasant *to behold, pleases the Imagination when well Described. Why the Imagination receives a more Exquisite*

Pleasure from the Description of what is Great, New, or Beautiful. This Pleasure still heightened, if what is described raises Passion in the Mind. Disagreeable Passions pleasing when raised by apt Descriptions. Why Terrour and Grief are pleasing to the Mind, when excited by Descriptions. A particular Advantage the Writers in Poetry and Fiction have to please the Imagination. What Liberties are allowed them.

PAPER IX.

Of that kind of Poetry which Mr. Dryden calls the Fairy-way of Writing. How a Poet should be Qualified for it. The Pleasures of the Imagination that arise from it. In this respect, why the Moderns excell the Ancients. Why the English excell the Moderns. Who the Best among the English. Of Emblematical Persons.

PAPER X.

What Authors please the Imagination who have nothing to do with Fiction. How History pleases the Imagination. How the Authors of the New Philosophy please the Imagination. The Bounds and Defects of the Imagination. Whether these Defects are Essential to the Imagination.

PAPER XI.

How those please the Imagination who treat of Subjects abstracted from Matter, by Allusions taken from it. What Allusions most pleasing to the Imagination. Great Writers how Faulty in this respect. Of the Art of Imagining in General. The Imagination capable of Pain as well as Pleasure. In what Degree the Imagination is capable either of Pain or Pleasure.

O

No. 422   *Friday, July 4, 1712*[1]
[STEELE]

Hæc scripsi non otii abundantia sed amoris erga te.
Tull. Epis.

I DO not know any thing which gives greater disturbance to Conversation, than the false Notion some People have of Raillery. It

[1] *Motto. Cicero, Epistulae ad Familiares, 7. 1. 6: I have writ this not thro' abundance of leisure, but of love towards thee.*

ought certainly to be the first point to be aimed at in Society, to gain the good Will of those with whom you converse. The way to that, is to shew you are well inclined towards them: What then can be more absurd, than to set up for being extremely sharp and biting, as the Term is, in your Expressions to your Familiars? A Man who has no good Quality but Courage, is in a very ill way towards making an agreeable figure in the World, because that which he has superiour to other People cannot be exerted, without raising himself an *Enemy*. Your Gentleman of a Satyrical Vein is in the like Condition. To say a thing which perplexes the Heart of him you speak to, or brings blushes into his Face, is a degree of Murder; and it is, I think, an unpardonable Offence to shew a Man you do not care, whether he is pleased or displeased. But won't you then take a Jest? Yes, but pray let it be a Jest. It is no Jest to put me, who am so unhappy as to have an utter Aversion to speaking to more than one Man at a Time, under a necessity to explain my self in much Company, and reducing me to shame and derision, except I perform what my infirmity of Silence disables me to do.

Callisthenes[1] has great Wit accompanied with that Quality (without which a Man can have no Wit at all) a sound Judgment. This Gentleman rallies the best of any Man I know, for he forms his ridicule upon a Circumstance which you are in your Heart not unwilling to grant him, to wit, that you are Guilty of an Excess in something which is in it self laudable. He very well understands what you would be, and needs not fear your Anger for declaring you are a little too much that thing. The Generous will bear being reproached as Lavish, and the valiant rash, without being provoked to resentment against their Monitor. What has been said to be a mark of a good Writer, will fall in with the Character of a good Companion. The good Writer makes his Reader better pleased with himself, and the agreeable Man makes his Friends enjoy themselves,

---

[1] The philosopher and friend of Alexander, noted for his freedom of language in criticizing Alexander. He was put to death c. 328 B.C. The wit of Callisthenes described here has sometimes been taken as Steele's indirect way of criticizing Addison. 'If the testimony of Swift can be relied upon, Addison delighted and excelled in this species of *Raillery*' (Nichols). The allusion is to Swift's remark on Stella ('On the Death of Mrs. Johnson', *Works*, Dublin, 1772, xii. 405):

Whether this proceeded from her easiness in general, or from her indifference to certain persons, or from her despair of mending them, or from the same practice which she much liked in Mr. Addison, I cannot determine; but when she saw any of the company very warm in a wrong opinion, she was more inclined to confirm them in it, than oppose them. The excuse she commonly gave when her friends asked the reason, was, that it prevented noise, and saved time.

rather than him, while he is in their Company. *Callisthenes* does this with inimitable Pleasantry. He whispered a Friend the other Day, so as to be overheard by a young Officer, who gave Symptoms of Cocking[1] upon the Company, that Gentleman has very much of the Air of a General Officer. The Youth immediately put on a Composed behaviour, and behaved himself suitably to the Conceptions he believed the Company had of him. It is to be allowed that *Callisthenes* will make a Man run into impertinent Relations to his own Advantage, and Express the Satisfaction he has in his own dear self till he is very ridiculous, but in this case the Man is made a Fool by his own consent, and not exposed as such whether he will or no. I take it therefore that to make raillery agreeable, a Man must either not know[a] he is rallied, or think never the worse of himself if he sees he is.

Acetus[2] is of a quite contrary Genius, and is more generally admired than *Callisthenes*, but not with Justice. *Acetus* has no regard to the Modesty or Weakness of the Person he Rallies; but if his Quality or Humility gives him any Superiority to the Man he would fall upon, he has no Mercy in making the Onset. He can be pleased to see his best Friend out of Countenance, while the Laugh is loud in his own Applause: His Raillery always puts the Company into little Divisions and separate Interests, while that of *Callisthenes* cements it, and makes every Man not only better pleased with himself, but also with all the rest in the Conversation.

To rally well, it is absolutely necessary that Kindness must run thro' all you say, and you must ever preserve the Character of a Friend to support your Pretentions to be free with a Man. *Acetus*[b] ought to be banished humane Society, because he raises his Mirth upon giving Pain to the Person upon whom he is pleasant. Nothing but the Malevolence, which is too general towards those who excell, could make his Company tollerated; but they with whom he converses, are sure to see some Man sacrificed wherever he is admitted, and all the Credit he has for Wit is owing to the Gratification it gives to other Mens ill Nature.

Minutius has a Wit that conciliates a Man's Love, at the same

---

[a] know] shew *Fol. Corrected in Errata* (*No. 423*)   [b] *Acetus*] *Actius* Fol.

---

[1] To swagger, strut; to brag (*OED*).
[2] The name seems to be derived from *acetum* (Latin, vinegar). *Acetum Italicum* is the proverbial phrase for the rude humour of the old Italian.

time that it is exerted against his Faults. He has an Art of keeping the Person he rallies in Countenance, by insinuating that he himself is guilty of the same Imperfection. This he does with so much Address, that he seems rather to bewail himself, than fall upon his Friend.

It is really monstrous to see how unaccountably it prevails among Men, to take the Liberty of displeasing each other. One would think sometimes that the Contention is, who shall be most disagreeable. Allusions to past Follies, Hints which revive what a Man has a Mind to forget for ever, and deserves that all the rest of the World should, are commonly brought forth even in Company of Men of Distinction. They do not thrust with the Skill of Fencers, but cut up with the Barbarity of Butchers. It is, methinks, below the Character of Men of Humanity and Good-manners, to be capable of Mirth while there is any one of the Company in Pain and Disorder. They who have the true Taste of Conversation, enjoy themselves in a Communication of each others Excellencies, and not in a Triumph over their Imperfections. *Fortius* would have been reckoned a Wit, if there had never been a Fool in the World: He wants not Foils to be a Beauty, but has that natural Pleasure in observing Perfection in others, that his own Faults are overlooked out of Gratitude by all his Acquaintance.

After these several Characters of Men who succeed or fail in Raillery, it may not be amiss to reflect a little further what one takes to be the most agreeable Kind of it; and that to me appears when the Satyr is directed against Vice, with an Air of Contempt of the Fault, but no ill Will to the Criminal. Mr. *Congreve's Doris* is a Master-piece in this Kind. It is the Character of a Woman utterly abandoned, but her Impudence by the finest Piece of Raillery is made only Generosity.[1]

> *Peculiar therefore is her Way,*
> *Whether by Nature taught,*
> *I shall not undertake to say,*
> *Or by Experience bought.*

[1] In the dedication to Congreve, prefixed to the *Poetical Miscellanies* of 1714, Steele praises 'Your inimitable DORIS, which excels, for Politeness, fine Raillery, and courtly Satyr, any Thing we can meet with in any Language. . . . DORIS is the Character of a Libertine Woman of Condition, and the Satyr is work'd up accordingly: For People of Quality are seldom touched with any Representation of their Vices, but in a Light which makes them Ridiculous' (*Correspondence*, ed. Blanchard, p. 473).

For who o'er Night obtain'd her Grace,
She can next Day disown,
And stare upon the strange Man's Face,
As one she ne'er had known.

So well she can the Truth disguise,
Such artful Wonder frame,
The Lover or distrusts his Eyes,
Or thinks 'twas all a Dream.

Some censure this as lewd or low,
Who are to Bounty blind;
But to forget what we bestow,
Bespeaks a noble Mind.

T

No. 423

[STEELE]

Saturday, July 5, 1712[1]

. . . Nuper Idoneus.
Hor.

I LOOK upon my self as a Kind of Guardian to the Fair, and am always watchful to observe any thing which concerns their Interest. The present Paper shall be employed in the Service of a very fine young Woman; and the Admonitions I give her, may not be unuseful to the rest of the Sex. *Gloriana* shall be the Name of the Heroine in to Day's Entertainment; and when I have told you that she is rich, witty, young, and beautiful, you will believe she does not want Admirers. She has had since she came to Town about twenty five of those Lovers, who make their Addresses by Way of Jointure and Settlement. These come and go, with great Indifference on both Sides; and as beauteous as she is, a Line in a Deed has had Exception enough against it, to outweigh the Lustre of her Eyes, the Readiness of her Understanding, and the Merit of her general Character. But among the Crowd of such cool Adorers, she has two who are very assiduous in their Attendance. There is something so extraordinary and artful in their Manner of Application,

[1] *Motto.* Horace, *Odes*, 3. 26. 1: Till lately fit [for girls].

that I think it but common Justice to alarm her in it. I have done it in the following Letter.

Madam,

'I Have for some Time taken Notice of two Gentlemen who attend you in all publick Places, both of whom have also easy Access to you at your own House: But the Matter is adjusted between them, and *Damon*, who so passionately addresses you, has no Design upon you; but *Strephon*,[1] who seems to be indifferent to you, is the Man who is, as they have settled it, to have you. The Plot was laid over a Bottle of Wine; and *Strephon*, when he first thought of you, proposed to *Damon* to be his Rival. The Manner of his breaking of it to him, I was so placed at a Tavern, that I could not avoid hearing. *Damon*, said he, with a deep Sigh, I have long languished for that Miracle of Beauty *Gloriana*; and if you will be very stedfastly my Rival, I shall certainly obtain her. Do not, continued he, be offended at this Overture; for I go upon the Knowledge of the Temper of the Woman, rather than any Vanity that I should profit by an Opposition of your Pretensions to those of your humble Servant. *Gloriana* has very good Sense, a quick Relish of the Satisfactions of Life, and will not give her self, as the Crowd of Women do, to the Arms of a Man to whom she is indifferent. As she is a sensible Woman, Expressions of Rapture and Adoration will not move her neither; but he that has her must be the Object of her Desire, not her Pity. The Way to this End I take to be, that a Man's general Conduct should be agreeable, without addressing in particular to the Woman he loves. Now, Sir, if you will be so kind as to sigh and die for *Gloriana*, I will carry it with great Respect towards her, but seem void of any Thoughts as a Lover. By this Means I shall be in the most amiable Light of which I am capable; I shall be received with Freedom, you with Reserve. *Damon*, who has himself no Designs of Marriage at all, easily fell into the Scheme; and you may observe, that where-ever you are *Damon* appears also. You see he carries on an unaffecting Exactness in his Dress and Manner, and strives always to be the very Contrary of *Strephon*. They have already succeeded so far, that your Eyes are ever in Search of *Strephon*, and turn themselves of Course from *Damon*. They meet and compare Notes upon your Carriage; and the Letter which was brought to you the other Day, was a Contrivance to remark your Resentment.

---

[1] These conventional names of lovers are used also in *Tatlers* 37, 60, 247.

When you saw the Billet subscribed *Damon*,[a] and turned away with a scornful Air, and cried Impertinence! you gave Hopes to him that shuns you, without mortifying him that languishes for you.

'What I am concerned for, Madam, is, that in the disposal of your Heart, you should know what you are doing, and examine it before it is lost. *Strephon* contradicts you in Discourse with the Civility of one who has a value for you, but gives up nothing like one that loves you. This seeming Unconcern gives this behaviour the advantage of Sincerity, and insensibly obtains your good Opinion, by appearing disinterested in the purchase of it. If you watch these Correspondents hereafter, you will find that *Strephon* makes his Visit of Civility immediately after *Damon* has tired you with one of Love. Tho' you are very discreet, you will find it no easy matter to escape the Toils so well laid, as when one studies to be disagreeable in Passion, the other to be pleasing without it. All the Turns of your Temper are carefully watched, and their quick and faithful Intelligence gives your Lovers irresistible advantage. You will please, Madam, to be upon your guard, and take all the necessary precautions against one who is amiable to you before you know he is enamoured.

> *I am,*
> *Madam,*
> *Your most obedient Servant.*'

Strephon makes great Progress in this Lady's good Graces; for most Women being actuated by some little Spirit of Pride and contradiction, he has the good effects of both those Motives by this Covert-Way[1] of Courtship. He received a Message Yesterday from *Damon* in the following Words, superscribed *With speed.*[b]

'ALL goes well; she is very angry at me, and I dare say hates me in earnest. It is a good time to Visit.

> *Yours.*'

The Comparison of *Strephon*'s gayety to *Damon*'s Languishment, strikes her Imagination with a prospect of very agreeable Hours with such a Man as the former, and abhorrence of the insipid prospect with one like the latter. To know when a Lady is displeased

---

[a] *Damon,*] *1724; Strephon, Fol., 8vo, 12mo*   [b] *With speed.*] with speed. *Fol.*

---

[1] I.e. a covered way in fortification. This quotation is the earliest cited in *OED* in a figurative sense.

with another, is to know the best time of advancing your self. This method of two Persons playing into each other's Hand is so dangerous, that I cannot tell how a Woman could be able to withstand such a Siege. The condition of *Gloriana*, I am afraid, is irretreivable, for *Strephon* has had so many Opportunities of pleasing without suspicion, that all which is left for her to do is to bring him, now she is advised, to an explanation of his Passion, and beginning again, if she can conquer the kind Sentiments she has already conceived for him. When one shews himself a Creature to be avoided, the other proper to be fled to for succour, they have the whole Woman between them, and can occasionally rebound[1] her Love and Hatred from one to the other, in such a manner as to keep her at a distance from all the rest of the World, and cast Lots for the Conquest.

N. B. *I have many other Secrets which concern the Empire of Love, but I consider that while I alarm my Women, I instruct my Men.*　　　T

No. 424

Monday, July 7, 1712[2]

[STEELE]

Est Ulubris, animus si te non deficit . . .
Hor.

Mr. SPECTATOR,　　　　　　　　　　　　　*London, June 24.*

'A MAN who has it in his Power to chuse his own Company, would certainly be much to blame should he not, to the best of his Judgment, take such as are of a Temper most suitable to his own; and where that Choice is wanting, or where a Man is mistaken in his Choice, and yet under a Necessity of continuing in the same Company, it will certainly be his Interest to carry himself as easily as possible.

'In this I am sensible I do but repeat what has been said a thousand times, at which however I think no Body has any Title

---

[1] Here used in the rare transitive meaning, 'To cause to bound back; to cast or throw back, to return' (*OED*).

[2] *Motto.* Horace, *Epistles*, I. 11. 30:
. . . Ev'n at Ulubra you'll find,
If you can have but a contented Mind.

This had been used as motto for No. 196 and for *Tatler* 202 (both by Steele).

to take Exception, but they who never failed to put this in Practice ——Not to use any longer Preface, this being the Season of the Year in which great Numbers of all sorts of People retire from this Place of Business and Pleasure to Country Solitude, I think it not improper to advise them to take with them as great a Stock of Good-humour as they can; for though a Country-Life is described as the most pleasant of all others, and though it may in Truth be so, yet it is so only to those who know how to enjoy Leisure and Retirement.

'As for those who can't live without the constant Helps of Business or Company, let them consider, that in the Country there is no *Exchange*, there are no Play-houses, no Variety of Coffee-houses, nor many of those other Amusements which serve here as so many Reliefs from the repeated Occurrences in their own Families; but that there the greatest Part of their Time must be spent within themselves, and consequently it behoves them to consider how agreeable it will be to them before they leave this dear Town.

'I remember, Mr. SPECTATOR, we were very well entertained last Year, with the Advices you gave us from Sir ROGER's Country-Seat; which I the rather mention because 'tis almost impossible not to live pleasantly, where the Master of a Family is such a one as you there describe your Friend, who cannot therefore (I mean as to his domestick Character) be too often recommended to the Imitation of others. How amiable is that Affability and Benevolence with which he treats his Neighbours, and every one, even the meanest of his own Family! And yet how seldom imitated? instead of which we commonly meet with ill natured Expostulations, Noise, and Chidings——And this I hinted, because the Humour and Disposition of the Head, is what chiefly influences all the other Parts of a Family.

'An Agreement and kind Correspondence between Friends and Acquaintance, is the greatest Pleasure of Life. This is an undoubted Truth, and yet any Man who judges from the Practice of the World, will be almost perswaded to believe the contrary; for how can we suppose People should be so industrious to make themselves uneasy? what can engage them to entertain and foment Jealousies of one another upon every the least Occasion? Yet so it is, there are People who (as it should seem) delight in being troublesome and vexatious, who (as *Tully* speaks) *Mira sunt alacritate ad litigandum, Have a certain Chearfulness in wrangling.*[1] And thus it

---

[1] Cicero, *Epistula ad Atticum*, 2. 7.

happens, that there are very few Families in which there are not Feuds and Animosities, tho' 'tis every one's Interest, there more particularly, to avoid 'em, because there (as I would willingly hope) no one gives another Uneasiness, without feeling some Share of it ——But I am gone beyond what I designed, and had almost forgot what I chiefly proposed; which was, barely to tell you, how hardly we who pass most of our Time in Town dispence with a long Vacation in the Country, how uneasy we grow to our selves and to one another when our Conversation is confin'd, insomuch that by *Michaelmas* 'tis odds but we come to downright squabbling, and make as free with one another to our Faces, as we do with the rest of the World behind their Backs. After I have told you this, I am to desire that you would now and then give us a Lesson of Good-humour, a Family-Piece;[1] which, since we are all very fond of you, I hope may have some Influence upon us——

'After these plain Observations give me leave to give you an Hint of what a Set of Company of my Acquaintance, who are now gone into the Country, and have the Use of an absent Nobleman's Seat, have settled among themselves, to avoid the Inconveniences above-mentioned. They are a Collection of ten or twelve, of the same good Inclination towards each other, but of very different Talents and Inclinations: From hence they hope, that the Variety of their Tempers will only create Variety of Pleasures. But as there always will arise, among the same People, either for want of Diversity of Objects, or the like Causes, a certain Satiety, which may grow into ill Humour or Discontent, there is a large Wing of the House which they design to employ in the Nature of an Infirmary. Whoever says a peevish thing, or acts any thing which betrays a Sowerness or Indisposition to Company, is immediately to be conveyed to his Chambers in the Infirmary; from whence he is not to be relieved, till by his Manner of Submission, and the Sentiments expressed in his Petition for that Purpose, he appears to the Majority of the Company to be again fit for Society. You are to understand, that all ill natured Words or uneasy Gestures are sufficient Cause for Banishment; speaking impatiently to Servants, making a Man repeat what he says, or any thing that betrays Inattention or Dis-humour,[2] are also criminal without Reprieve: But it is provided,

[1] Here, as in No. 525 (vol. iv), used not in the sense of a family picture but of a literary composition depicting the doings of a family.

[2] I.e. ill-humour. This is the earliest example given in *OED*. Steele uses the word again in No. 479 (vol. iv).

that whoever observes the ill natured Fit coming upon himself, and voluntarily retires, shall be received at his Return from the Infirmary with the highest Marks of Esteem. By these and other wholesome Methods it is expected, that if they cannot cure one another, yet at least they have taken Care that the ill Humour of one shall not be troublesome to the rest of the Company. There are many other Rules which the Society have established for the Preservation of their Ease and Tranquility, the Effects of which, with the Incidents that arise among them, shall be communicated to you from Time to Time for the publick Good, by,

SIR,

Your most humble Servant,

R. O.'

T

No. 425   *Tuesday, July 8, 1712*[1]

Frigora mitescunt Zephyris, Ver proterit Aestas
   Interitura, simul
Pomifer Autumnus fruges effuderit, & mox
   Bruma recurrit iners.

Hor.

Mr. SPECTATOR,

'THERE is hardly any thing gives me a more sensible Delight, than the Enjoyment of a cool still Evening after the Uneasiness of a hot sultry Day. Such a one I pass'd not long ago, which made me rejoyce when the Hour was come for the Sun to set, that I might enjoy the Freshness of the Evening in my Garden, which then affords me the pleasantest Hours I pass in the whole Four and twenty. I immediately rose from my Couch, and went down into it. You descend at first by twelve Stone Steps into a large Square divided into four Grass-plots, in each of which is a Statue of white

---

[1] *Motto.* Horace, *Odes,* 4. 7. 9–12:

The Spring the Winter, Summer wastes the Spring,
  And Summer's beauty's quickly lost,
When drunken Autumn spreads her drooping Wing
  And next cold Winter creeps in Frost. CREECH.

Marble. This is separated from a large Parterre by a low Wall, and from thence, thro' a Pair of Iron Gates, you are led into a long broad Walk of the finest Turf, set on each Side with tall Yews, and on either Hand border'd by a Canal, which on the Right divides the Walk from a Wilderness parted into Variety of Allies and Arbours, and on the Left from a kind of Amphitheatre, which is the Receptacle of a great Number of Oranges and Myrtles. The Moon shone bright, and seem'd then most agreeably to supply the Place of the Sun, obliging me with as much Light as was necessary to discover a thousand pleasing Objects, and at the same Time divested of all Power of Heat. The Reflection of it in the Water, the Fanning of the Wind rustling on the Leaves, the Singing of the Thrush and Nightingale, and the Coolness of the Walks, all conspired to make me lay aside all displeasing Thoughts, and brought me into such a Tranquility of Mind, as is I believe the next Happiness to that of hereafter. In this sweet Retirement, I naturally fell into the Repetition of some Lines out of a Poem of *Milton's*, which he entitles *Il Penseroso*, the Ideas of which were exquisitely suited to my present Wandrings of Thought.[1]

> *Sweet Bird! that shun'st the Noise of Folly,*
> *Most musical! most melancholly!*
> *Thee Chauntress, oft the Woods among,*
> *I wooe to hear thy Evening Song;*
> *And missing thee, I walk unseen*
> *On the dry, smooth-shaven Green,*
> *To behold the wandring Moon,*
> *Riding near her highest Noon,*
> *Like one that hath been led astray,*
> *Thro' the Heav'ns wide pathless Way,*
> *And oft, as if her Head she bow'd,*
> *Stooping thro' a fleecy Cloud.*
>
> *Then let some strange mysterious Dream,*
> *Wave with his Wings in airy Stream,*
> *Of lively Portraiture display'd,*
> *Softly on my Eyelids laid;*
> *And as I wake, sweet Musick breathe*
> *Above, about, or underneath;*

---

[1] *Il Penseroso*, 61–72, 147–54. (Line 64, even-song; line 69, that had bin; line 147, And let; line 148, Wave at his Wings; line 153, Sent by som spirit.)

Sent by Spirits to Mortals Good,
Or th' unseen Genius of the Wood.

'I reflected then upon the sweet Vicissitudes of Night and Day, on the charming Disposition of the Seasons, and their Return again in a perpetual Circle; and oh! said I, that I could from these my declining Years, return again to my first Spring of Youth and Vigour; but that alass! is impossible: All that remains within my Power, is to soften the Inconveniencies I feel, with an easy contented Mind, and the Enjoyment of such Delights as this Solitude affords me. In this Thought I sate me down on a Bank of Flowers and dropt into a Slumber, which whether it were the Effect of Fumes and Vapours, or my present Thoughts, I know not; but methought the Genius of the Garden stood before me, and introduc'd into the Walk where I lay this Drama and different Scenes of the Revolution of the Year, which whilst I then saw, even in my Dream, I resolv'd to write down, and send to the SPECTATOR.

'The first Person whom I saw advancing towards me, was a Youth of a most beautiful Air and Shape, tho' he seem'd not yet arriv'd at that exact Proportion and Symmetry of Parts which a little more Time wou'd have given him; but however, there was such a Bloom in his Countenance, such Satisfaction and Joy, that I thought it the most desirable Form that I had ever seen. He was cloath'd in a flowing Mantle of green Silk, interwoven with Flowers: He had a Chaplet of Roses on his Head, and a *Narcissus* in his Hand; Primroses and Violets sprang up under his Feet, and all Nature was cheer'd at his Approach. *Flora* was on one Hand and *Vertumnus*[1] on the other in a Robe of changeable Silk. After this I was surpriz'd to see the Moon-beams reflected with a sudden Glare from Armour, and to see a Man compleatly arm'd advancing with his Sword drawn. I was soon inform'd by the Genius it was *Mars*, who had long usurp'd a Place among the Attendants of the *Spring*. He made Way for a softer Appearance, it was *Venus*, without any Ornament but her own Beauties, not so much as her own Cestus, with which she had incompass'd a Globe, which she held in her right Hand, and in her left she had a Sceptre of Gold. After her followed the Graces with their Arms intwined within one another, their Girdles were loosed, and they moved on to the Sound of soft Musick, striking the Ground alternately with their Feet: Then came up the three

[1] For Vertumnus, the Italian god of the changing seasons, see Ovid, *Metamorphoses*, 14. 642 ff.

Months which belong to this Season. As *March* advanced towards me, there was methought in his Look a louring Roughness, which ill befitted a Month which was rank'd in so soft a Season; but as he came forwards his Features became insensibly more mild and gentle: He smooth'd his Brow and look'd with so sweet a Countenance that I could not but lament his Departure, though he made way for *April*. He appear'd in the greatest Gayety imaginable, and had a thousand Pleasures to attend him: His Look was frequently clouded, but immediately return'd to its first Composure, and remain'd fix'd in a Smile. Then came *May* attended by *Cupid*, with his Bow strung, and in a Posture to let fly an Arrow: As he pass'd by methought I heard a confused Noise of soft Complaints, gentle Extasies, and tender Sighs of Lovers; Vows of Constancy, and as many Complainings of Perfidiousness; all which the Winds wafted away assoon as they had reached my Hearing. After these I saw a Man advance in the full Prime and Vigor of his Age, his Complexion was sanguine and ruddy, his Hair black, and fell down in beautiful Ringlets not beneath his Shoulders, a Mantle of hair-colour'd Silk hung loosely upon him: He advanc'd with a hasty Step after the *Spring*, and sought out the Shade and cool Fountains which plaid in the Garden. He was particularly well pleas'd when a Troop of *Zephyrs* fann'd him with their Wings: He had two Companions who walk'd on each Side, that made him appear the most agreeable, the one was *Aurora* with Fingers of Roses, and her Feet dewy, attir'd in grey: The other was *Vesper* in a Robe of Azure beset with Drops of Gold, whose Breath he caught whilst it pass'd over a Bundle of Honey-Suckles and Tuberoses which he held in his Hand. *Pan* and *Ceres* followed them with four Reapers, who danced a Morrice to the Sound of Oaten Pipes and Cymbals. Then came the attendant Months, *June* retain'd still some small Likeness of the *Spring*; but the other two seem'd to step with a less vigorous Tread, especially *August*, who seem'd almost to faint whilst for half the Steps he took the Dog-Star levell'd his Rays full at his Head: They pass'd on and made Way for a Person that seemed to bend a little under the Weight of Years; his Beard and Hair, which were full grown, were compos'd of an equal Number of black and grey; he wore a Robe which he had girt round him of a yellowish Cast, not unlike the Colour of fallen Leaves, which he walk'd upon. I thought he hardly made Amends for expelling the foregoing Scene by the large Quantity of Fruits which he bore in his Hands. *Plenty* walk'd by his Side with an healthy fresh Countenance, pouring out from an Horn all the various Product of the Year. *Pomona* followed with a Glass of Cyder in her Hand, with *Bacchus* in a Chariot drawn by Tygres, accompanied by a whole Troop of Satyrs, Fauns, and Sylvans. *September*, who came next, seemed in his Looks to promise a new *Spring*, and wore the Livery of those Months. The succeeding Month was all soil'd with the Juice of Grapes, as if he had just come from the Wine-Press. *November*, though he was in this Division, yet by the many Stops he made seem'd rather inclin'd to the *Winter*, which follow'd close at his Heels: He advanced in the Shape of an old Man in the Extremity of Age: The Hair he had was so very white it seem'd a real Snow; his Eyes were red and piercing, and his Beard hung with a great Quantity of Icicles: He was wrap'd up in Furrs, but yet so pinch'd with excess of Cold, that his Limbs were all contracted and his Body bent to the Ground, so that he could not have supported himself had it not been for *Comus* the God of Revels, and *Necessity* the Mother of Fate,[1] who sustain'd him on each Side. The Shape and Mantle of *Comus* was one of the things that most surpriz'd me; as he advanc'd towards me his Countenance seem'd the most desirable I had ever seen: On the fore Part of his Mantle was pictur'd Joy, Delight, and Satisfaction, with a thousand Emblems of Merriment, and Jests with Faces looking two Ways at once; but as he pass'd from me I was amaz'd at a Shape so little correspondent to his Face: His Head was bald, and all the rest of his Limbs appear'd old and deformed. On the hinder Part of his Mantle was represented Murder, with dishevel'd Hair and a Dagger all bloody, Anger in a Robe of Scarlet, and Suspicion squinting with both Eyes; but above all the most conspicuous was the Battle of the *Lapithæ* and the *Centaurs*.[2] I detested so hideous a Shape and turned my Eyes upon *Saturn*, who was stealing away behind him with a Scythe in one Hand and an Hour-Glass in t'other unobserv'd. Behind *Necessity* was *Vesta* the Goddess of Fire, with a Lamp which was perpetually supply'd with Oyl, and whose Flame was eternal. She cheer'd the rugged Brow of *Necessity*, and warm'd her so far as almost to make her assume the Features and Likeness of *Choice*. *December*, *January* and *February*, pass'd on after the rest all in Furrs; there was little Distinction to be made amongst them, and they

[1] Perhaps suggested by Plato, *Republic*, 617D: 'the words of the maiden Lachesis [one of the Fates], daughter of Necessity.'
[2] The battle of the Lapithae and the Centaurs is described in Ovid, *Metamorphoses* 12. 210 ff.

were only more or less displeasing as they discover'd more or less
Haste towards the grateful Return of *Spring*.   Z¹

No. 426   *Wednesday, July 9, 1712*²

[STEELE]

> *. . . Quid non mortalia Pectora cogis*
> *Auri sacra fames . . .*
>   Virg.

A VERY agreeable Friend of mine the other Day carrying me in
his Coach into the Country to Dinner, fell into Discourse concerning the Care of Parents due to their Children, and the Piety of
Children towards their Parents. He was reflecting upon the Succession of particular Virtues and Qualities there might be preserved
from one Generation to another, if these Regards were reciprocally
held in Veneration: But as he never fails to mix an Air of Mirth and
good Humour with his good Sense and Reasoning, he entered into
the following Relation.

I WILL not be confident in what Century, or under what Reign it
happened, that this Want of mutual Confidence and right Understanding between Father and Son was fatal to the Family of the
Valentines in *Germany*.³ *Basilius Valentinus* was a Person who had

¹ The authorship of this number, like that of the other papers signed Z, is
uncertain. In the edition of 1789 this number is said to be 'probably by Pope, or
Dr. Parnell'. Morley attributes it to Budgell, Aitken to Budgell or Pope. Ault includes it in the *Prose Works* of Pope (vol. i, Oxford, 1936).

² *Motto.* Virgil, *Æneid*, 3. 56-57:
             O sacred Hunger of pernicious Gold,
             What bands of Faith can impious Lucre hold! DRYDEN

³ Valentinus Basilius was a noted German alchemist, who lived in the early
fifteenth century and who made important discoveries in chemistry. The story told
here may derive from the legend associated with the famous Arabian physician
Lokman, in *The Voyages & Travels of the Ambassadors from the Duke of Holstein, to the
Great Duke of Muscovy and the King of Persia*, by Adam Olearius (1637), book v (trans.
by John Davies of Kidwelly, 1662, p. 255). Lokman leaves three glasses filled with
miraculous waters to his son, who, like Alexandrinus in the *Spectator* story, fails to
apply them to his father's body. When it came his turn to die,
    he commanded a man that waited on him, to make use of those Glasses, as his
    Father had taught him. The man having caus'd his Master's body to be brought
    into the Bath . . ., poured upon it the two first Glasses, which wrought the effect,
    which *Lokman* had promised they should; insomuch that the Master sitting up,
    and impatient to return to Life, cries out *bris, bris*, that is to say, *pour, pour*; at
    which words the Fellow was so frightned, that he let the third Glasse fall down to
    the ground. . . .

arrived at the utmost Perfection in the Hermetick Art, and initiated his Son *Alexandrinus* into the same Mysteries: But as you know they are not to be attained but by the Painful, the Pious, the Chaste, and Pure of Heart. *Basilius* did not open to him, because of his Youth, and the Deviations too natural to it, the greatest Secrets of which he was Master, as well knowing that the Operation would fail in the Hands of a Man so liable to Errors in Life as *Alexandrinus*. But believing, from a certain Indisposition of Mind as well as Body, his Dissolution was drawing nigh, he called *Alexandrinus* to him, and as he lay on a Couch, over-against which his Son was seated, and pre-pared by sending out Servants one after another, and Admonition to examine that no one over-heard them, he revealed the most important of his Secrets with the Solemnity and Language of an Adept.[1] My Son, said he, many have been the Watchings, long the Lucubrations, constant the Labours of thy Father, not only to gain a great and plentiful Estate to his Posterity, but also to take Care that he should have no Posterity. Be not amazed, my Child: I do not mean that thou shalt be taken from me, but that I will never leave thee, and consequently cannot be said to have Posterity. Behold, my dearest *Alexandrinus*, the Effect of what was propagated in nine Months: We are not to contradict Nature, but to follow and to help her; just as long as an Infant is in the Womb of its Parent, so long are these Medicines of Revification in preparing. Observe this small Phial and this little Gallipot, in this an Unguent, in the other a Liquor. In these, my Child, are collected such Powers, as shall revive the Springs of Life when they are yet but just ceased, and give new Strength, new Spirits, and, in a Word, wholly restore all the Organs and Senses of the humane Body to as great a Dura-tion, as it had before enjoyed from its Birth, to the Day of the Application of these my Medicines. But, my beloved Son, Care must be taken to apply them within ten Hours after the Breath is out of the Body, while yet the Clay is warm with its late Life, and yet capable of Resuscitation. I find my Frame grown crasy with perpetual Toil and Meditation; and I conjure you, assoon as I am dead, to anoint me with this Unguent; and when you see me begin to move, pour into my Lips this inestimable Liquor, else the Force of the Ointment will be ineffectual. By this Means you will give me

---

[1] Used originally by the alchemists to signify one who has attained the great secret. Johnson defines it as 'He that is completely skilled in all the secrets of his art'. Examples in *OED* range from 1663 to 1785.

Life as I have you, and we will from that Hour mutually lay aside the Authority of having bestowed Life on each other, but live as Brethren, and prepare new Medicines against such another Period of Time as will demand another Application of the same Restoratives. In a few Days after these wonderful Ingredients were deliver'd to *Alexandrinus*, *Basilius* departed this Life. But such was the pious Sorrow of the Son at the Loss of so excellent a Father, and the first Transports of Grief had so wholly disabled him from all manner of Business, that he never thought of the Medicines till the Time to which his Father had limited their Efficacy was expired. To tell the Truth, *Alexandrinus* was a Man of Wit and Pleasure, and considered his Father had lived out his natural Time, his Life was long and uniform, suitable to the Regularity of it; but that he himself, poor Sinner, wanted a new Life, to repent of a very bad one hitherto; and in the Examination of his Heart, resolved to go on as he did with this natural Being of his, but repent very faithfully, and spend very piously the Life to which he should be restored by Application of these Rarities, when Time should come, to his own Person.

It has been observed, that Providence frequently punishes the Self-love of Men who would do immoderately for their own Offspring, with Children very much below their Characters and Qualifications, insomuch that they only transmit their Names to be born by those who give daily Proofs of the Vanity of the Labour and Ambition of their Progenitors.

It happened thus in the Family of *Basilius*; for *Alexandrinus* began to enjoy his ample Fortune in all the Extremities of Houshold Expence, Furniture, and insolent Equipage; and this he pursued till the Day of his own Departure began, as he grew sensible, to approach. As *Basilius* was punished with a Son very unlike him, *Alexandrinus* was visited with one of his own Disposition. It is natural that ill Men should be suspicious, and *Alexandrinus*, besides that Jealousy, had Proofs of the vitious Disposition of his Son *Renatus*, for that was his Name.

Alexandrinus, as I observ'd, having very good Reasons for thinking it unsafe to trust the real Secret of his Phial and Gally-pot to any Man living, projected to make sure Work, and Hope for his Success depend from the Avarice, not the Bounty of his Benefactor.

With this Thought he call'd *Renatus* to his Bed-side, and bespoke him in the most pathetick Gesture and Accent. As much, my Son, as you have been addicted to Vanity and Pleasure, as I also have been before you, you nor I could escape the Fame, or the good Effects of the profound Knowledge of our Progenitor the Renown'd *Basilius*. His Symbol is very well known in the Philosophick World, and I shall never forget the venerable Air of his Countenance, when he let me into the profound Mysteries of the *Smaragdine Table of Hermes*.[1] *It is true*, said he, *and far removed from all Colour of Deceit, That which is Inferiour is like that which is Superiour, by which are acquired and perfected all the Miracles of a certain Work. The Father is the Sun, the Mother the Moon, the Wind is in the Womb, the Earth is the Nurse of it, and Mother of all Perfection. All this must be received with Modesty and Wisdom.* The Chymical People carry in all their Jargon a whimsical Sort of Piety, which is ordinary with great Lovers of Money, and is no more but deceiving themselves, that their Regularity and Strictness of Manners for the Ends of this World, has some Affinity to the Innocence of Heart which must recommend them to the next. *Renatus* wondered to hear his Father talk so like an Adept, and with such a Mixture of Piety; while *Alexandrinus* observing his Attention fixed, proceeded: This Phial, Child, and this little Earthen-Pot will add to thy Estate so much, as to make thee the richest Man in the *German* Empire. I am going to my Long Home, but shall not return to common Dust. Then he resumed a Countenance of Alacrity, and told him, That if within an Hour after his Death he anointed his whole Body, and pour'd down his Throat that Liquor which he had from old *Basilius*, the Corps would be converted into pure Gold. I will not pretend to express to you the unfeigned Tendernesses that passed between these two extraordinary Persons; but if the Father recommended the Care of his Remains with Vehemence and Affection, the Son was not behind-hand in professing that he would not cut the least Bit off him, but upon the utmost Extremity, or to provide for his younger Brothers and Sisters.

Well, *Alexandrinus* died, and the Heir of his body (as our Term is) could not forbear, in the Wantonnesses of his Heart, to measure the Length and Breadth of his beloved Father, and cast up the ensuing Value of him before he proceeded to Operation. When he knew the immense Reward of his Pains, he began the Work: But lo! when he had anointed the Corps all over, and began to apply the Liquor, the Body stirr'd, and *Renatus*, in a Fright, broke the Phial.   T

---

[1] The *Tabula Smaragdina* (1541) was a medieval Latin work on alchemy, attributed to the Egyptian Hermes Trismegistus. The Greek word *smaragdine* means 'emerald green'.

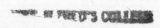